Coping with the Nazi Past

Studies in German History

Published in Association with the German Historical Institute, Washington, DC

General Editor: Christof Mauch, Director of the German Historical Institute, Washington, DC, and Professor of Modern History at the University of Cologne

Coping with the Nazi Past

West German Debates on Nazism and
Generational Conflict, 1955–1975

❧

Edited by

Philipp Gassert

and

Alan E. Steinweis

Berghahn Books
NEW YORK • OXFORD

Published in 2006 by
Berghahn Books

www.berghahnbooks.com

© 2006, 2007 Philipp Gassert and Alan E. Steinweis
First paperback edition published in 2007

Library of Congress Cataloging-in-Publication Data

Coping with the Nazi past : West German debates on Nazism and generational conflict,
1955–1975 / edited by Philipp Gassert and Alan E. Steinweis.
    p. cm. — (Studies in German history ; 2)
Includes bibliographical references and index.
ISBN 978-1-84545-505-7
    1. Germany (West)—Historiography. 2. Holocaust, Jewish (1939–1945)—
Psychological aspects. 3. Conflict of generations—Germany (West). 4. National
socialism—Psychological aspects. 5. Germany (West)—Ethnic relations. 6. New
Left—Germany (West). I. Gassert, Philipp. II. Steinweis, Alan E. III. Series.

DD258.7.C66 2006
943.086072—dc22

                                                                      2006014196

British Library Cataloguing in Publication Data

A catalogue record for this book is available from
the British Library.

Printed in the United States on acid-free paper

ISBN: 978-1-84545-217-9 (hbk.) 978-1-84545-506-4 (pbk.)

CONTENTS

PREFACE

This volume grew out of a German Historical Institute conference that took place at the University of Nebraska-Lincoln in April 2001. Both the conference and the volume underscore the transatlantic character of scholarship about the legacy of the Nazi past. Like German history more generally, the study of this subject has developed into an international endeavor with deep roots on the American side of the Atlantic. The Nebraska conference was the first international meeting devoted specifically to the issue of the Nazi past during the "long 1960s." It proved to be a highly stimulating event, at which more questions were raised than could possibly be answered. We therefore hope that this volume will convey some of the original excitement of our proceedings in Lincoln and contribute to further scholarly exploration of the politics of the past during a defining period of postwar West German history.

The Lincoln conference would not have been possible without the generous financial support of the Fritz Thyssen Stiftung of Cologne, the German Historical Institute-Washington, and the University of Nebraska-Lincoln. At Nebraska, indispensable assistance was provided by Kim Weide, Doreen Wagenaar, and David Snyder. We would also like to express our gratitude for support provided by Jean Cahan, Director of the Harris Center for Judaic Studies. At the University of Heidelberg, Claudia Müller and Chris Roesch provided crucial support during the months preceding the conference. We would like to recognize a number of scholars who made important contributions at the conference but are not represented in this volume: Pertti Ahonen (Sheffield), Lloyd Ambrosius (Lincoln, NE), David Cahan (Lincoln, NE), Detlev Claussen (Hanover), Geoff Eley (Ann Arbor), Norbert Frei (Jena), Elizabeth Heinemann (Iowa City), Jeffrey Herf (College Park, MD), Detlef Junker (Heidelberg), Harold Marcuse (Santa Barbara), Daniel Mattern (Washington), Dirk Moses (Sydney), Axel Schildt (Hamburg), Jeremy Varon (Madison, NJ), and Lora Wildenthal (Houston).

For almost twenty years the German Historical Institute in Washington, DC, has been an important facilitator of transatlantic dialogue in the historical sciences. Its director, Christof Mauch, has been highly supportive from the beginning of this project and never lost faith during the long process of publication. Christa

Brown, Dieter H. Schneider, and Bärbel Thomas were involved in the organization of the conference. David Lazar, the German Historical Institute's senior editor, and Shawn Kendrick of Berghahn Books deserve our special thanks for taking on the formidable task of editing a large and complicated manuscript that was the product of two academic cultures. Lastly, Marion Berghahn of Berghahn Books has given much appreciated support throughout the publication process.

Philipp Gassert and Alan E. Steinweis
Heidelberg, Germany, and Lincoln, Nebraska
June 2006

INTRODUCTION

Philipp Gassert and Alan E. Steinweis

Every generation of Germans since the end of World War II has been confronted by the challenge of working through the moral and historical implications of Nazism and the Holocaust. Germany's problematic history of dictatorship and genocide has had profound consequences not only for the political system and the international relations of the two postwar German republics, but also for national identity, religious faith, education, legal practice, social policy, gender roles, and other dimensions of daily life.[1] As West and East Germans created new polities and set out to transform their societies, and as they sought domestic and international legitimacy, their common recent past always informed, and often dominated, debates on the present. Serious scholarly attention to the post-1945 legacy of Nazism has focused primarily on the 1950s, the decade in which the two newly established German states were consolidated. But a new frontier in this area of research has recently opened, that of the 1960s, a period usually considered a crucial turning point in postwar history.[2] During the "tumultuous sixties," West German youth, much like young people elsewhere, rebelled against a culture that many believed had become excessively materialistic. They criticized the politics of West German realignment toward the West, and they looked critically at their own nation's past and present, pointing to alleged continuities that persisted from the Nazi era. These included authoritarianism (not least in the institutions of higher education, in the police forces, and in the legal system), xenophobia, technocracy, and patriarchy. Purging society of these legacies became an urgent priority of the West German New Left.[3]

In recent years, the once widespread consensus that the leftist impetus of the late 1960s instigated a sea change in how Germans dealt with the Nazi past has come under scrutiny. Many historians now argue that the public debate really

Notes for this section begin on page 9.

took off during the late 1950s and accelerated during the first half of the 1960s.[4] The pivotal events are already well known: the anti-Semitic graffiti that appeared on synagogue walls in Cologne and other West German cities at the end of 1959 and the beginning of 1960; the Eichmann trial in Jerusalem; the Fischer and Jaspers controversies; the Auschwitz trial in Frankfurt; the parliamentary debates about the extension of the statute of limitations; the emergency laws; scandals involving disclosures of Nazi-era activities of high-ranking politicians; the rise of a large-scale extraparliamentary opposition; the resurgence of a neo-Nazi party; and the Six Day War of 1967.

Picking up on some of the contemporary debates of the 1960s, historians are now assessing the ambiguities of the transformation that took place during that tumultuous decade. The "68ers" radicalized the discourse about the Nazi past, but in the process their emphasis on a generic "fascism" also tended to universalize and dehistoricize that past. They may have raised public consciousness about continuities from the Nazi era to the Federal Republic, but their often strident rhetoric and drastic methods may well have been counterproductive inasmuch as they alienated significant segments of the West German population. Moreover, quite apart from the activism of the 68ers, there were other factors at work that forced West Germans to confront the past. The rise of the ultra-right-wing National Democratic Party (NPD), for example, deeply affected the outcome of the debates inside and outside the Bundestag.

As several of the contributions in this volume clearly demonstrate, the changing atmosphere of the 1960s and the evolving discourse on the Nazi past did not automatically prompt a radical transformation with regard to what Norbert Frei has called *Vergangenheitspolitik* (politics of the past)—the bundle of political and legal measures designed to integrate the majority of the former Nazi perpetrators into West German society by shielding them from criminal prosecution.[5] To be sure, the 1960s may have witnessed a remarkable change in how the legacies of National Socialism were publicly addressed. But despite the changing nature of the West German culture of memory, the "crucial decade" was still marked by a remarkable degree of continuity in many areas of *Vergangenheitspolitik*. Compensation to Jews for their "Aryanized property" remained inadequate, for example, and some of the worst Nazi perpetrators continued to escape prosecution.

Now that the 1960s are on the agenda of historians, this volume intends to provide an overview of research on the collective memory of the Nazi past and the evolving *Vergangenheitspolitik* in West Germany during that era. The contributions aim to achieve a better understanding of the political, social, and cultural forces that shaped the politics of, as well as the discourse about, the Nazi past. As Konrad Jarausch observes in "Critical Memory and Civil Society," his essay in this collection, such an understanding requires us to set the "critical decade" of the 1960s within the long-term context of postwar German history. The recent political skirmishes over the "youthful radicalism" of German politicians of the '68 or post-'68 generation, most notably Foreign Minister Joschka Fischer, have added a third contested layer of history to an already complex discussion.[6]

Because of the overwhelming presence of the Nazi era in recent German debates about the past, it is no accident that the question of how 68ers confronted Nazism has become one of the central issues in controversies about "1968." Nevertheless, just how important the confrontation with the Nazi past was for the self-conception of the protest movement of the late 1960s remains an open question. Ulrich Herbert has recently argued that references to National Socialism served mainly as a kind of code for a critical examination of the deficiencies of West German society in general.[7] In this context, one must also consider the possible detrimental effects of the manner in which the Nazi past was addressed in the late 1960s. Did the 68ers contribute to the liberalization and democratization of the Federal Republic by initiating "a freer discussion of the Nazi past," as the protagonists themselves have claimed? Or did they introduce "new myths through a shallow combination of neo-Marxism and pop-psychology," as their critics argue? Did their instrumentalization of the past, which summarily accused West German elites of fascist connections and which was at times aided by the East German regime, actually hinder a freer discussion? Answering these questions requires a thorough understanding of the general character of the "controversial 1960s," and, as Jarausch observes in his contribution here, it also requires an assessment of what exactly was remembered and what was forgotten during the immediate postwar years.[8]

Four contributions to this volume examine how West Germany confronted, or failed to confront, the crimes of National Socialism during the 1960s. Habbo Knoch's study of photographs presents an innovative way of understanding how the subject of Nazi crimes was injected into the public sphere.[9] Knoch addresses a central question of the politics of memory during the 1960s: how did Germans deal with the contradiction between their self-perception as victims of World War II and Germany's apparent departure from the norms of Western civilization? According to Knoch, the increasingly frequent display of images of Nazi crimes during that decade created visual impressions that did not conform to the prevalent individual and collective memory of Germans as a "community of victims." This "crisis of interpretation" intersected with the breakdown of intergenerational consensus, given that the younger generation did not share painful personal experiences of wartime. The extraparliamentary opposition of the 1960s responded to this cleavage by explaining "Auschwitz" in terms of a fascist, imperialist, and capitalist power structure. Student protesters of the 1960s often counted themselves among the victims of this oppressive structure. This interpretation of the past created a "second silence" because it focused on iconic sites such as Auschwitz and on industrialized mass murder rather than on the more typical experiences of the older generation under Nazism. As Knoch argues, the universalization of Nazi crimes may well have undercut the self-stylization of Germans as victims, yet it also absolved the older generation of direct, personal responsibility for Nazism.

Bernhard Brunner's contribution, "The 'Comprehensive Investigative Proceedings—France,'" looks at a large-scale criminal investigation by West German authorities into Nazi crimes committed in France during World War II.

Of the 199 high-ranking perpetrators Brunner has identified, 119 theoretically could have been prosecuted after the war (the rest had died or disappeared). Yet after twenty years of investigations, only nine were brought to trial, three of whom were convicted in 1980. This result, Brunner argues, cannot be attributed exclusively to a lack of interest on the part of the West German justice system. A fuller explanation also requires us to consider the legal and political contexts of the prosecution. One major obstacle was posed by the treaties between the three Western Allies and the Federal Republic, the intention of which had been to insulate immediate postwar Allied war crimes prosecutions from the German justice system. Until the 1970s, legal interpretations of these treaties impeded investigation of perpetrators who had already been convicted in absentia in France. Brunner observes that the 1960s witnessed a more intensive legal prosecution of Nazi crimes, on the one hand, but also a more restrictive development with regard to the legal and political framework, on the other.

This last point is reinforced by Marc von Miquel's essay on West German debates over the prosecution of Nazi crimes. In Miquel's view, conflict was the central characteristic of West German discussions of this issue in the 1960s. The initiation of large-scale court cases brought the annihilation of European Jewry to the forefront of public debates. This led to a decreasing willingness to permit former perpetrators to remain integrated within West German society without bringing them to trial. At the same time, however, the 1960s witnessed the high point of the so-called *Schlußstrich* mentality: public opinion polls showed that a majority of the West German population was in favor of letting bygones be bygones and of closing the door on further prosecutions. According to Miquel, many Germans were simply unwilling to accept the conclusion that could and should have been drawn from the trials—that the genocidal politics of the Third Reich had not been the actions of a few outsiders but instead had come from the mainstream of German society. Although a larger amnesty scheme did fail in the Bundestag, the clandestine (and often forgotten) exploitation of a minor article in the penal code intended to decriminalize traffic violations led to the termination of pretrial proceedings against former members of the Reich Security Main Office. In many ways, the "normal" legal framework was not suited to the requirements of prosecuting crimes against humanity.

A similar argument is advanced by Jürgen Lillteicher in his essay on the restitution of Jewish property. Any effort to compensate for the loss of property during the Nazi regime was destined to raise highly complicated legal and political issues. The central paradox was that although after 1945 West Germany became a society that adhered to the rule of law, many of its members had benefited from illegal acts, including the plundering of Jewish and other properties before 1945. External (and to a certain degree internal) political pressure led to gradual improvements in the laws governing the return and compensation of lost property, but the process was hampered nonetheless by the extremely legalistic approach taken by bureaucrats and judges. Furthermore, an observable lack of goodwill on the part of the institutions involved in compensation amplified the shortcomings of the civil law code for dealing with the consequences of the war. Lillteicher illustrates his findings with the vivid example of several Holocaust survivors who were required by the courts to demonstrate that their belongings, which had been taken from them at the ramp in Auschwitz, had been brought into the part of Germany that later became the territory of the Federal Republic. In the absence of such evidence, the West German courts refused jurisdiction over the cases. Thus, an overstretched legal system met with the unwillingness of the courts to handle the issues of restitution in a generous way.

A central question in the history of West Germany is how members of German professional and occupational groups addressed, or failed to address, their own complicity in the crimes of the regime. Three essays here focus on this question. Klaus Weinhauer's essay deals with one such group, the German police. Weinhauer's analysis of West German police addresses the long-standing debate over the extent and significance of continuity of personnel between the Third Reich and the Federal Republic, especially in the civil service.[10] As Weinhauer shows, investigations of policemen who had committed crimes during National Socialism were often blocked or impeded by the culture of camaraderie among police officers. Although in the early 1960s politicians and police union functionaries began to question the role of the police during the Third Reich, many policemen saw themselves as victims, having been exploited by an overwhelmingly coercive regime. Efforts to address their complicity were countered by the heroification and mythologization of the Weimar police. Furthermore, Weinhauer argues, authoritarian leadership ideas among police were only gradually abandoned during the late 1950s and early 1960s, when technical innovations forced police officers to act more independently. Only the delayed generational change of the mid-1970s resulted in a deep caesura in the personnel structure of the police.

Karen Schönwälder's contribution, "West German Society and Foreigners in the 1960s," focuses on the role of the West German Federation of Employer's Associations. Schönwälder argues that the presence of the past was an important factor in the response to foreigners in Germany and asserts that the recruitment of foreign labor during the 1960s was consciously placed in a historical perspective. Employers urged their German employees to develop positive attitudes toward foreign workers and to convey a tolerant image of Germany. Potential negative perceptions abroad, therefore, were a major determining factor in West German policy toward foreigners. In contrast, efforts to exclude "Afro-Asians" from recruitment as "guest workers" highlighted the continuity of racist thinking among officials and demonstrated the limits of the shift toward a more self-critical reflection of Germany's past.

In her essay on debates over health care policy, Sigrid Stöckel argues that the primary confrontation with the past in the health care system did not occur in the 1960s but earlier, in the late 1940s and the 1950s. Stöckel emphasizes the existence of several pasts, not merely the Nazi one, that had to be confronted. Because of the experiences of Weimar and the Third Reich, public health officers in the Federal Republic came under pressure from general practitioners. Since social medicine was associated, fairly or unfairly, with the "state" medicine of the Third Reich, Stöckel argues, West German developments in this sphere were less advanced in comparison to those in other countries.

Generational transition is, of course, a factor of profound importance in explaining the shift toward a more confrontational attitude toward the past in West Germany.[11] Detlef Siegfried's essay considers the influence of 1960s pop culture media on the formation of collective historical memory of Nazism among German youths. Siegfried concentrates primarily on the magazine *Twen* and the television music program *Beat Club*, but looks also at other examples, including the magazine *Konkret*. According to Siegfried, such media encouraged their young readers to disassociate themselves from the nationalistic political views and aesthetic tastes of their parents' generation. While this message was often communicated implicitly—for example, through the championing of Anglo-American pop music—it also took the form of explicit repudiation of the elder generation's connection to attitudes associated with the Nazi era, such as anti-Semitism and authoritarianism. Siegfried's analysis of how young people in West Germany responded to such messages yields a complex picture. Many, Siegfried argues, disassociated themselves from the German past as a matter of cultural preference, but without necessarily confronting that past intellectually. Siegfried suggests that this outlook may well have fueled the utopian political sensibility that was to become a hallmark of student radicalism by the end of the decade.

Defining exactly what it was that the 68ers were rebelling against is the central question in Dagmar Herzog's contribution, "The Sexual Revolution and the Legacies of the Nazi Past." Herzog challenges the generally accepted notion that in the realm of sexual mores, 68ers rebelled against traditions associated with Nazism. In actuality, she argues, they rebelled against the "postfascist settlement" in the sphere of sexuality, that is, the sexually repressive, family-oriented culture of the 1950s, which the 68ers regarded—in Herzog's opinion, mistakenly—as a continuation of the sexual policies of the Third Reich. In their attempts to posit a clear continuity between Nazism and sexual conservatism, sex reformers of the 1960s selectively appropriated Frankfurt School writings about fascism and sex. As a consequence, they misrepresented not only the opinions of scholars such as Max Horkheimer and Theodor Adorno but also the sexual policies of Nazism, which, Herzog maintains, had not been repressive with regard to "regime-loyal or regime-indifferent heterosexual 'Aryans.'"

In recent years, historians and political commentators have strongly disagreed about the impact of the student movement on West German discourse on the Nazi past.[12] Whereas some have seen "1968" as a symbolic new founding of an antifascist Federal Republic, others have criticized the protest movement for instrumentalizing and dehistoricizing the Nazi past through fascism theory.[13] Three contributions to this volume deal with this question. Michael Schmidtke addresses the issue by analyzing the contemporary discourse about fascism and by looking at the use of the past in political education and during the protests against the so-called emergency laws. Schmidtke argues that the original contribution of the student movement lay not so much in initiating public debate over the Nazi past as in promoting political and social change through acts of civil courage, as well as in pedagogical experiments such as the *Kinderladen* movement. "Coming to terms with the past" was thus primarily aimed at the overthrow of the "authoritarian character."

Elizabeth Peifer subtitles her essay on public demonstrations "Participatory Democracy or Leftist Fascism?" The debates about public demonstrations, Peifer argues, can be used to help understand how the Nazi past was addressed during the 1960s because many critics saw street demonstrations as reminiscent of the mass rallies of a totalitarian past. Emphasizing the ambiguous legacy of the 1960s, Peifer maintains that the public demonstrations contributed to a broadening of democratic practices in Germany.

Belinda Davis devotes her essay to an examination of how the rhetoric surrounding violent encounters between radicals and police during the 1960s resonated with references to the legacy of Nazism. Davis observes that between 1965 and 1977 West Germans from all political camps regularly "instrumentalized" the past. For New Leftists, state-authorized violence in reaction to demonstrations was interpreted as proof of the continuation of "fascism" in the Federal Republic. From their point of view, the silencing of the New Leftist critique of West German society, and the alleged failure to address the issue of fascism, resulted in a large-scale corruption of the public sphere.

The student movement and the West German New Left inspired an intellectual response on the right that has largely been ignored by scholars. Two essays here attempt to fill this void in the historiography. Joachim Scholtyseck's essay on conservative intellectuals addresses alleged similarities between left-wing radicalism in the 1960s and right-wing radicalism of an earlier era. According to Scholtyseck, conservative thinkers of the 1960s were much more deeply involved in discussions about the meaning of Nazism for Germany's past and present than has been assumed by their critics. The leitmotifs of the conservative view included the "demonism" of Hitler, the dynamics of "mass and power," and the role of secularization and de-Christianization. Many conservatives, Scholtyseck argues, had become convinced that the Federal Republic was immune to the dangers of extreme nationalism and Nazism, and therefore felt helpless when they were confronted with a changing discourse about the Nazi past during the 1960s.

Michael Hochgeschwender's essay examines a segment of German society that was deeply affected by "1968" but that is often left out of the story: Catholic student fraternities. While the social and cultural forces that manifested themselves during the 1960s transformed the Catholic milieu in a very profound manner over the long term, the immediate impact of the 68ers was rather limited. Catholic fraternities distanced themselves from the protest movement for several reasons: their organizational culture, their revulsion at revolutionary rhetoric and neo-Marxist language, and their objections to wholesale condemnations of the role of the Catholic Church during the Third Reich. Its own powerful mythology—above all, its resistance to Hitler—provided the Catholic milieu with a response to the radical critique of the 68ers. Furthermore, Catholics, for decades a minority in the German Reich, did not show any inclination to respond to the New Left critique of what they finally considered to be "their" state.

West German debates over the Nazi past were never an exclusively West German affair. The relations of the Federal Republic not only to its eastern neighbors, but also to its western allies, were in several respects determined by the culture of memory and the politics of the past. The simple fact that Germany had been responsible for two world wars confronted allies like France and the United States with the security problem of containing potential German power in Europe while harnessing it in the global confrontation with the Soviet Union.[14] In her essay, Carole Fink analyzes the complicated relationship between the two states most closely connected with the legacies of the Holocaust: Israel and West Germany. Placing the "special relationship" between Israel and the Federal Republic in international context, Fink interprets the Six Day War as a major turning point in German-Israeli relations. Out of necessity, West Germany and Israel had formed a reluctant "special relationship" before 1967. In 1965, the two states had established formal diplomatic relations, and the advent of the Christian Democratic–Social Democratic "grand coalition" government in the autumn of 1966 had signaled a "more self-assured, less penitent West Germany." Despite the West German public's overwhelming support for Israel during the Six Day War, relations between the two states were transformed by Bonn's gradual opening to the East and the eventual breakdown of the Cold War consensus. Automatic support was no longer given to Israel's policy as West German governments tried to "normalize" the country's relationship to the survivor state, despite the often expressed "special moral obligation emanating from our past" (Willy Brandt).

In his essay on the American public relations executive Julius Klein, Jonathan Wiesen analyzes the strategies of government and business circles in responding to accusations of corporate criminality during the National Socialist era. Because West German identity had come to depend so heavily on the economic prowess that had produced the *Wirtschaftswunder* (economic miracle) of the 1950s, the German economy, once a locus of Nazi crimes, became a means for securing a new, democratic Germany. During the 1960s, as discussions shifted from abstract totalitarianism to a focus on specific crimes, including those of German industry, memory started to play a more complex role. For one thing, it became increasingly difficult to fend off memories of the Holocaust, and the role of German big business in it, by mobilizing the anticommunist fears of American politicians.

Susanna Schrafstetter's essay, "Auschwitz and the Nuclear *Sonderweg*," focuses on the key security issue of the Cold War: the possession and control of nuclear weapons. The renunciation of nuclear weapons by Adenauer in 1954 had been a precondition of West Germany's entry into NATO. This step, however, could also be seen as the last Allied wartime restriction on a defeated Germany. Therefore, questions of nuclear policy were always inextricably linked to the German past. This became clear during the heated debate over the Non-Proliferation Treaty in 1967–68. German supporters of the treaty pointed out that Germany had to accept the legacy of defeat, whereas its foes, including many high-ranking Christian Democratic politicians, saw the treaty as yet another attempt to impose unfair, vindictive terms upon Germany.

Although these essays encompass a broad range of themes and reflect an impressive amount of archival research on the part of the contributors, this volume makes no claim to comprehensiveness or definitiveness. Numerous questions remain on the agenda of historians seeking to elucidate the relationship between the collective memory of Nazism and the impulses for change in German society in the 1960s. These questions include the role of relations with the German Democratic Republic, the impact of gender on everyday life and religion, the reconfiguration of class and capital, and, more generally, the progressive "westernization" of the Federal Republic. We need further detailed investigation of the media, education, and a host of related fields. Even in relatively well-researched areas, such as the reintegration of ex-Nazis into West German society or the politics and diplomacy of compensation to the victims of Nazism, much work remains to be done. Hopefully, this volume will not only serve its purpose as a synopsis of important work accomplished to date, but will also serve as a point of departure for future research.

Notes

1. Recent syntheses of the role of the Nazi past include Jeffrey Herf, *Divided Memory: The Nazi Past in the Two Germanys* (Cambridge, MA, 1997); Edgar Wolfrum, *Geschichtspolitik in der Bundesrepublik Deutschland: Der Weg zur bundesrepublikanischen Erinnerung 1948–1990* (Darmstadt, 1999); Aleida Assmann and Ute Frevert, *Geschichtsvergessenheit, Geschichtsversessenheit: Vom Umgang mit deutschen Vergangenheiten nach 1945* (Stuttgart, 1999); Peter Reichel, *Vergangenheitsbewältigung in Deutschland: Die politisch-justitielle Auseinandersetzung mit der NS-Diktatur nach 1945* (Bonn, 2003).

2. This standard "whig interpretation" (Andreas Rödder) of postwar West German history is prevalent in recent surveys of the Federal Republic. See, for example, Manfred Görtemaker, *Geschichte der Bundesrepublik Deutschland: Von der Gründung bis zur Gegenwart* (Munich, 2000), and Heinrich August Winkler, *Der lange Weg nach Westen*, 2 vols. (Munich, 2000). For a critique, see the inaugural lecture by Andreas Rödder, "'Umgründung der Republik'? Zur Bedeutung des 'Machtwechsels' von 1969 für die Geschichte der Bundesrepublik" (ms., Stuttgart, 2001).

3. Hans-Ulrich Thamer, "Die NS-Vergangenheit im politischen Diskurs der 68er-Bewegung," *Westfälische Forschungen* 48 (1998): 39–53. For a survey of contemporary texts, see Philipp Gassert and Pavel A. Richter, eds., *1968 in West Germany: A Guide to Sources and Literature of the Extra-Parliamentarian Opposition*, German Historical Institute (GHI), Reference Guide, no. 9 (Washington, DC, 1998), also available through the GHI Web site (http://www.ghi-dc.org).

4. Axel Schildt, *Ankunft im Westen: Ein Essay zur Erfolgsgeschichte der Bundesrepublik* (Frankfurt am Main, 1999), 133–39; Detlef Siegfried, "Zwischen Aufarbeitung und Schlußstrich: Der Umgang mit der NS-Vergangenheit in den beiden deutschen Staaten," in *Dynamische Zeiten: Die 60er Jahre in den beiden deutschen Gesellschaften*, ed. Axel Schildt, Detlef Siegfried, and Karl Christian Lammers (Hamburg, 2000), 77–113; Ulrich Herbert, *Wandlungsprozesse in*

Westdeutschland: Belastung, Integration, Liberalisierung 1945–1980 (Göttingen, 2002), 47–48.

5. Norbert Frei, *Vergangenheitspolitik: Die Anfänge der Bundesrepublik Deutschland und die NS-Vergangenheit* (Munich, 1996), 13–14.

6. On the controversies surrounding Fischer, see Wolfgang Kraushaar, *1968 als Mythos, Chiffre und Zäsur* (Hamburg, 2000), 41–42, and Kraushaar, *Fischer in Frankfurt* (Hamburg, 2001). See also the recent extended essay by Paul Berman, *Power and the Idealists: The Passion of Joschka Fischer, and Its Aftermath* (New York, 2005).

7. Herbert, *Wandlungsprozesse*, 47.

8. Reinterpretations of the 1950s include Frei, *Vergangenheitspolitik*; Robert G. Moeller, *Protecting Motherhood: Women and the Family in the Politics of Postwar West Germany* (Berkeley, 1993), and Moeller, *War Stories: The Search for a Usable Past in the Federal Republic of Germany* (Berkeley, 2001); and Elisabeth D. Heineman, *What Difference Does a Husband Make? Women and Marital Status in Nazi and Postwar Germany* (Berkeley, 1999).

9. For details on Knoch's findings, which are part of a larger project on the role of photographs in German memory after World War II, see Habbo Knoch, *Die Tat als Bild: Fotografien und Erinnerung der NS-Verbrechen in Deutschland nach 1945* (Hamburg, 2001).

10. See, for example, Wilfried Loth and Bernd A. Rusinek, eds., *Verwandlungspolitik: NS-Eliten in der westdeutschen Nachkriegsgesellschaft* (Frankfurt am Main, 1998).

11. On the 1945 generation, see Dirk Moses, "The Forty-Fivers: A Generation Between Fascism and Democracy," *German Politics and Society* 17, no. 1 (1999): 95–127.

12. For a survey of some of the recent German literature on the student movement in Germany, see Kraushaar, *1968 als Mythos*, 253–347.

13. See Harold Marcuse, "The Revival of Holocaust Awareness in West Germany, Israel, and the United States," in *1968: The World Transformed*, ed. Carole Fink, Philipp Gassert, and Detlef Junker (Cambridge, 1998), 421–38.

14. See Detlef Junker, "Politics, Security, Economics, Culture, and Society: Dimensions of Transatlantic Relations," introduction to *The United States and Germany in the Era of the Cold War: A Handbook*, vol. 1, *1945–1968*, ed. Detlef Junker (Cambridge, 2004), 1–28.

Chapter 1

CRITICAL MEMORY AND CIVIL SOCIETY
The Impact of the 1960s on German Debates about the Past

Konrad H. Jarausch

❦

The intensifying insistence on the need to remember is beginning to produce a backlash that suggests it might be more constructive to forget. During the Viennese congress, "The Memory of the Century," the British commentator Timothy Garton Ash and the French scholar Pierre Nora criticized the "flourishing global memory industry" as counterproductive to historical understanding and counseled merciful oblivion instead. One point of dispute was the asymmetry between the media's attention to Nazi crimes and the general amnesia about Stalinist excesses, while another area of contention concerned the doubtful consequences of opening communist secret service files.[1] Along somewhat similar lines, Peter Novick's scholarly examination of the Americanization of the Holocaust and Norman Finkelstein's scurrilous attack on the "Holocaust industry" reveal a growing impatience with the intellectual rituals of contrition.[2] These increasingly emotional disputes about the current compulsion to remember raise the more general question: how much memory is essential for political democracy?

The politics of the past are particularly complicated in the case of Germany due to the troubled legacy of its two dictatorships. For decades, the "hot memories" of Nazi crimes were the "central reference point" for discussions about the past, as illustrated by the surprisingly positive reception of the German translation of Daniel Goldhagen's *Hitler's Willing Executioners*, the storm over the *Wehrmachtausstellung* documenting the complicity of the armed forces, and the pressure to compensate slave laborers.[3] During the 1990s, the "cold memories" of communist repression, articulated in the public hearings of the Bundestag and the growing nostalgia of many East Germans for the imagined security of the SED regime, began to complicate these debates by introducing the debris of a

Notes for this chapter begin on page 27.

second dictatorship.[4] More recently, the attacks of Christian Democratic politicians in the media against the youthful radicalism of Foreign Minister Joschka Fischer, Minister of the Environment Jürgen Trittin, and even SPD Chancellor Gerhard Schröder have added the history of the old Federal Republic as a third (lukewarm?) contentious area, thereby calling the self-evident success story of capitalist democracy into question. The result of this tripling of the burden of history has been an even greater ambivalence about confronting the past.

As a side effect, the assault on the so-called 68ers (most of whom first became politically active in the 1970s) has also raised the collateral issue of the role of the 1960s in dealing with the Third Reich. Were the sixties a long overdue step toward social democratization that broke up the authoritarian patterns of the Adenauer era? Or was the youth revolt the beginning of later disorientation, cultural decadence, and terrorist violence? Did the rebellious students initiate a freer discussion of the Nazi past by accusing prominent elders like Chancellor Kurt-Georg Kiesinger of complicity or did they introduce new kinds of myths based on a shallow combination of neo-Marxism and pop psychology, as evident in the writings of Herbert Marcuse? The media has had a field day with charges and counter-charges that reflect the distance between former activists like Daniel Cohn-Bendit who were involved in the melee and CDU careerists like Friedrich Merz who stayed at home. Though former President Johannes Rau tried to calm the waves by praising the liberating impulse of 1968 and bemoaning some of its nefarious consequences, the argument is likely to go on, since it is about personal identity, political partisanship, and control of public memory.[5]

The scholarly literature on the politics of memory is unfortunately only moderately helpful because it is topically segmented and overly emotional. One central problem is the conflation of memory and the Holocaust trauma, which has displaced all other recollections as culturally less significant no matter how strongly they are felt.[6] Another issue is the ideological effort to prove communist crimes to be of the same magnitude as the Nazi genocide, which is making it difficult to discuss the peculiar character of Marxist repression.[7] Moreover, the negative fixation on the effort to cope with the terrible legacies of dictatorships has largely prevented a critical look at the creation, character, and role of memory culture in maintaining democratic societies.[8] In spite of some laudable efforts to capture the elusive phenomenon of 1968 on its thirtieth anniversary, there is no comprehensive account of the generational revolt in the German context.[9] While the issue of *Vergangenheitsbewältigung* during that turbulent decade tends to come up in surveys of the Federal Republic as well as in overviews of memory politics, few authors have focused specifically on it so far.[10]

To distinguish the particular role of that decade in German memory debates more clearly, several key questions have to be answered. First, what was the general character of the controversial 1960s? That decade still evokes contradictory images, ranging from the building of the Berlin Wall or the purchase of the first television set to Willy Brandt's call for "daring more democracy" or the assassination attempt on Rudi Dutschke. Second, what was remembered and what was forgotten in the aftermath of the war and the prosperous fifties? While leftist authors like Ralph Giordano raise the accusation of a willful forgetting of Nazi crimes, conservative commentators tend to point out the degree to which public leaders distanced themselves from the Hitler regime.[11] Third, which impulses eventually overcame the reluctance of large parts of the public to confront their own prior complicity and initiated a lengthy process of developing more self-critical views? In comparative perspective, the replacement of living memories of a domestic majority by synthetic recollections of an externalized minority was an astounding development that still begs a fuller explanation.[12]

The Dynamic Decade

Long after the event, the 1960s still serve as an irritant that can stop party conversation and produce fierce arguments at the very mention of that decade. Even normally detached commentators grow agitated, feeling compelled to add their own experiences and begin their sentences with "As a 68er, I can tell you that...." Conservatives like the neonationalist journalist Rainer Zitelmann have long blamed 1968 for "the fall from grace which expelled the Germans from the Adenauer paradise and brought them foreigners, feminism and other horrors." In contrast, leftists like the Green Bundestag deputy Antje Vollmer have praised the spirit of rebellion for "civilizing the Germans," and considered the late 1960s "a social refoundation of the republic" that turned an authoritarian postfascist state into a Western democracy. The current polemics, joined by some renegades like Thomas Schmidt and Götz Aly, are breaking with the latter consensus, holding "the new barbarians" responsible for leftist terrorism.[13] As is typical of such debates, this controversy is not so much about an accurate reading of the past as about an ideological positioning in the present.

Part of the reason for the public confusion is the slowness of contemporary history, or *Zeitgeschichte*, to engage the problems of the 1960s in a systematic fashion. After this subdiscipline was created in the late 1940s as an effort to confront the horrors of World War II and the crimes of the Nazi era, the Institut für Zeitgeschichte spent most of its energies on explaining the failure of the Weimar Republic and the rise of the Third Reich.[14] Only during the 1960s did contemporary historians breach the 1945 barrier and begin to examine the nature of Allied occupation policies and the reasons for the establishment of two competing German states. It took until the 1980s for historical research to move into the Adenauer and Ulbricht period of the 1950s and to contrast the "conservative modernization" of the West with the more radical communist restructuring of the East.[15] Once social scientists abandoned their analysis of the youth revolt,[16] the 1960s remained at the mercy of contending memories, serving as an autobiographical marker for individual life-stories and as a reference point for literary debates in the feuilletons.

The resulting mythologization of 1968 has only recently begun to give way to serious historical research on the sixties as a decade. The anniversary syndrome that produced newspaper articles, radio talk shows, and TV documentaries inspired more serious efforts in 1998 to put the youth revolt into international perspective.[17] Since the actual events of the generational rebellion were minor in comparison with other confrontations, it took until the advent of the new cultural history for scholars to be able to address what seemed to be an opaque and elusive subject. Gradually, the inexorable march of the 30-year rule started to open up access to government documents covering the 1960s while the neoconservative backlash against some of its cultural consequences renewed intellectual interest in the problem. To break out of the ritual of condemnation and apology for the changes symbolized by 1968, it is necessary to broaden the focus to the somewhat perplexing character of the entire period. In many ways, this was "a hinge decade" in which the hostilities of the Cold War abated, the spread of prosperity fundamentally changed lifestyles, and democracy became more deeply rooted.[18]

Among the many issues to be resolved about the sixties is the question of their precise beginning and endpoint. Since a decade is merely a calendrical artifact without inherent significance, more meaningful markers need to be established. Did the sixties already begin with the Sputnik shock and Adenauer's third term in 1957, the SPD's adoption of the Godesberg Program in 1959, or only with the building of the Wall in 1961, with the *Spiegel* affair a year later, or with Adenauer's fall in 1963? Did the decade end with the culmination of the generational revolt in 1968, the ascendancy of the first social-liberal (SPD-FDP) government in 1969, or the *Ostpolitik* of the early seventies—not to mention the impact of the oil price shocks and Brandt's resignation in 1973–74?[19] Some studies of "the miracle years" operate with the construct of "the long fifties" by emphasizing developments such as the power and policies of the CDU, the effects of which reached well into the mid-sixties. Taking an early starting date to emphasize the continuity from antirearmament protests to the youth revolt and picking a late conclusion of the upheaval would ironically reverse that conceptualization and suggest a concept of the "long sixties" instead.[20]

A related problem, evident in the conflicting labels suggested by historians, is the significance of 1968 as a kind of "soft caesura" in the longer narrative of West and (due to the invasion of Czechoslovakia) also East German postwar history. Only one such designation, namely, the "inner refounding of the Republic," deals with the change of governments and ideological directions.[21] Some descriptions like "the decisive decade of Americanization" or the broader tag "westernization" try to combine the political and the cultural realms.[22] Other attempts to catch the essence of the sixties, such as the notions of a "postmaterial shift" or a "cultural revolution," relate to individual values and collective behaviors.[23] While Axel Schildt argues that "with enormous speed, the Federal Republic left the postwar period completely behind and assumed features of cultural modernity," Hanna Schissler claims precisely the contrary: "1968 marks the transition from 'modernity' to 'postmodernity' with all its benefits, but also with all its liabilities."[24] The difficulty with the modernization perspective is the vagueness of the central concept and its normative connotation in the German context, which ignores the negative consequences of the process. In the East, the debate revolves around the popular disillusionment with Marxist ideology as a consequence of Soviet suppression of the Prague Spring.[25]

Connected with the problem of labeling is the question of which developments are to be considered typical of the sixties. While there is agreement that this was a period of "fermentation" in which many changes were coming to a head, identifying them is much more difficult, since they did not begin or end there, but only received a new intensity.[26] Although the building of the Wall, the fall of Adenauer, the grand coalition, the change of government, the initiation of reforms, and the reconciliation with the East were important political developments, none equals the significance of 1918, 1933, 1945, or 1989.[27] It is, rather, the social changes that made possible an unprecedented level of mass consumption—such as the spread of prosperity to the lower classes, the arrival of the foreign "guest workers," and the shortening of the workweek—that mark a new quality of life. The sixties are the decade of motorization (the number of cars multiplied from four to twelve million) and the proliferation of consumer durables (record players, washing machines, televisions), which made possible new forms of mass tourism and leisure. The result was a novel popular culture of Hollywood films, rock music, and television sitcoms that shifted emphasis from work to entertainment; with some delay, it even reached the GDR.[28]

In spite of some attendant excesses, this catch-up modernization contributed to what may be called the breakthrough of "civil society" in West Germany. Because many of these trends first appeared in the United States or Western Europe, they are often mistaken as Americanization or westernization, and little distinction made between local styles and broader dynamics. More useful might be an overarching concept like civil society,[29] which would be drawn from the positive features of Western countries without also including the historical ballast of slavery or imperialism. If defined as relating to market competition, social self-organization, political participation, and more humane interpersonal relations, such a standard would suggest a drastic transformation. The explosion of mass consumption in the West conclusively proved the superiority of the so-called social-market economy over communist planning; the spread of grass roots protest in the student movement and the "extra-parliamentary opposition" (APO) that fed the new social movements of pacifism, feminism, and environmentalism opened up new realms of voluntary association; the many national reforms of the social-liberal coalition and similar changes in local institutions like the university widened the scope of participation on all levels; and finally, the tone of contacts between people as well as sexual mores grew less authoritarian and more tolerant of other styles or preferences.[30]

Transcending the current polemics about the impact of 1968 therefore requires a conscious questioning of personal memories as well as a shift to different analytical strategies. Instead of falling back upon reminiscences, scholars should interrogate their own feelings about these changes, turning them from a self-evident standard into an intellectual problem.[31] Moreover, they ought to analyze the importance of 1968 as an ideological reference point that an entire generation has used to position itself vis-à-vis others. Historians also need to probe the cultural character of the changes through unconventional sources such as photographs and television news footage, since much of the protest was about values and styles that are rarely visible in government documents. Finally, they also ought to decide how to fit the decade of the sixties into the long-term process of "liberalization" of German society that already began around the turn of the century and only came to fruition in that decade.[32] Though only a half-truth, Daniel Cohn-Bendit's often-cited quip that the East Germans were different because they did not experience 1968 correctly suggests a fundamental reshaping of West Germany that was essential for the development of a more critical view of the past.

Conflicted Memories

Because the record itself is so contradictory, evaluations of the German relationship to the recent past have varied widely among commentators. Conservative observers tend to emphasize that a critical engagement with the Nazi regime began immediately after the end of World War II as a result of Allied reeducation efforts and the attempt of democratic Germans to understand the multiple reasons for the catastrophe of National Socialism. More liberal intellectuals, in contrast, often stress that popular recollections of a peaceful and prosperous *Volksgemeinschaft* were bound to linger, that most perpetrators and collaborators engaged in a conspiracy of silence, and that a critical self-understanding is a goal that has yet to be reached.[33] As the playwright Rolf Hochhuth has pointed out, judgments about the honesty of confronting the past depend largely upon one's analytical perspective: viewed from the twenty-first century, the continuity of Nazi views into the postwar world seems overwhelming, but seen from the Third Reich, the distancing appears to have been equally drastic. This clash of evaluations raises the central question: how far did the dispirited Germans rethink their past actions and future political loyalties?[34]

Even if 1945 was in no way a "zero hour," the depth of the psychological rupture in individual lives as well as in German politics must be acknowledged.[35] After the loss of the battle of Stalingrad and the beginning of saturation bombing, large sections of the German public had begun to distance themselves from the Nazi regime. The failed assassination plot of the bourgeois resistance indicates that previously repressed doubts about the criminal nature of Hitler's policies resurfaced with increasing vigor among members of the old elites. The Klemperer diaries graphically describe how many Germans quickly disassociated themselves from a losing cause and opportunists repositioned themselves as longstanding opponents of the regime, instantly forgetting their prior collaboration.[36] Only a few bitter-enders clung to their nationalist or racist beliefs in the hope of the Führer's promised miracle. Even if many elements of Nazi language and prejudices were to linger on, the transformation of attitudes that would reshape memories had already begun before the final defeat.

The Allied resolution to "eradicate German militarism and Nazism" accelerated this difficult process of rethinking the past, even if it also produced fresh resentment. The cumbersome denazification questionnaires required a thorough reexamination of individual lives that turned prior Nazi honors into liabilities. The insistent efforts at reeducation in the media and the schools also demanded a questioning of previous traditions that had seemed to be untarnished. The mandated visits to liberated concentration camps compelled shocked civilians to witness the terrible consequences of Nazi policies in the piles of corpses or walking ghosts. The widespread coverage of the Nuremberg trials in licensed newspapers, in weekly newsreels, and on the radio made many Germans aware of the enormity of the crimes committed in their name.[37] No doubt these efforts often grated upon the feelings of the defeated, generated resentment against "victors' justice," and prompted countless efforts at evasion, as evident in Ernst von Salomon's popular novel *Der Fragebogen*.[38] But with the exception of the futile campaign for decartelization, they were not nearly as ineffective as has often been claimed, since they signaled the need for outward conformity with a more critical understanding of the recent German past.

It should also not be forgotten that a minority of dedicated German opponents of National Socialism insisted upon a negative evaluation of the Third Reich. Political leaders like Konrad Adenauer, Kurt Schumacher, and Theodor Heuss in the West or Otto Grotewohl and Walter Ulbricht in the East had no love for the Nazi regime, since they had been harassed, imprisoned, or forced to emigrate.[39] Even if the Allies had no interest in allowing the "antifascist committees" that sprang up in the interregnum to assume real power, these generally leftist groups demonstrated the existence of internal opponents bent on rejecting the Nazi past. Among intellectuals, the surviving or returning proponents of Weimar culture could be counted upon to advocate a break with Third Reich kitsch, while the extent of the suffering inflicted by the collapsing regime turned many former collaborators in the middle class against such an inhumane system. Even if they sought to salvage the national tradition, the attempts of leading historians like Friedrich Meinecke and Gerhard Ritter to come to terms with the "German catastrophe" indicate a profound self-questioning of nationalist assumptions during the immediate postwar years.[40]

Within this "society in collapse," apologetic views nonetheless persisted. The preoccupation with survival among the ruins, the perilous flight from the East, the struggle for food and shelter prohibited a deeper reflection on the causes of the misfortune.[41] The normalization impulse to gather lost family members, to rebuild houses or apartments, and to find gainful employment also militated against potentially upsetting inquiries. Since every application for a job or public assistance required a clean résumé and convincing recommendations, an entire cottage industry sprang up to provide so-called *Persilscheine*, certificates named after a detergent that would whitewash stained careers.[42] Psychologically, it was apparently also necessary to come up with an innocuous version of one's own life story, carefully expurgated of anything that might cause offense, which could be told in social situations. Hence, public narratives created the image of a harmless citizenry that somehow seemed to have been absent during the atrocities of the Third Reich, while more private stories communicated late at night under the influence of alcohol revealed more horrifying experiences.

By the early 1950s, the public mood therefore shifted toward reintegrating Nazi collaborators into the two political systems. In the East, the mechanism was a convincing "conversion story" that would, like Hans Modrow's account, tell of an encounter with a staunch antifascist who opened the eyes of a deluded member of the Hitler Youth and turned him toward a progressive direction. A public recanting of prior errors sufficed for acceptance into the SED, especially if a convert volunteered as instructor to entice other comrades into similar commitments to the Socialist cause.[43] In the West, the process involved the pardoning of the entire group of collaborators. Calling for an end to the humiliation of denazification, rightist parties like the Block der Heimatvertriebenen und Entrechteten (BHE) and the Freie Demokratische Partei (FDP) pushed for the reintegration of refugees into the bureaucracy at their prior levels, including the reinstatement of many *NS-Mitläufer* (Nazi fellow travelers) who had been temporarily dismissed. This goal was accomplished by the infamous "131 law" that ostensibly alleviated the suffering due to the wholesale expulsion, but also rehabilitated numerous former Nazis in the civil service and the universities. Though claiming symbolic distance from the Third Reich, the "politics of the past" in effect turned a blind eye on many of its former supporters.[44]

More problematic still was the effect of the campaign for the return of POWs and an amnesty for convicted war criminals. Wanting the several million prisoners back was understandable, since families hoped to be reunited and a recovering economy also needed additional labor. While trying to find soldiers who had committed atrocities, the Soviets used the captured as cheap manpower to help rebuild some of their damaged facilities. Until it was resolved by the return of a pitiful remnant from Russia in the mid-1950s, the POW issue required separating the clean Wehrmacht from the criminal SS, thereby distorting military memories.[45] Even less comprehensible was the public clamor, orchestrated once again by rightwing parties, to free convicted war criminals, mostly former generals still held in Allied prisons. Sentiments of national solidarity in defeat may have played a role, and Adenauer yielded to such demands in order to expand the electoral base of his own CDU further to the right. The unfortunate effect of this agitation was a sanitized picture of the recent past that largely absolved the military of responsibility for its own actions.

During the 1950s, the East-West confrontation compelled both German states to adopt public rhetoric that was critical of the Nazi past. The GDR could establish antifascism as its founding myth as its leaders claimed credit for the communist resistance, whether they had survived Stalin's purges in Moscow or Hitler's persecution in Berlin. Moreover, the Comintern definition of fascism as the highest stage of monopoly capitalism provided a clear structural explanation for the catastrophe that could be translated into political action by expropriating the supporters of the Third Reich. The FRG could also point to the anti-Nazi record of most of its leaders, to the democratic character of the Basic Law, and to the policy of restitution toward Israel, which tried to alleviate some of the suffering of the Holocaust victims through material restitution. But it had a higher number of former Nazis in visible positions, and its historical explanations for the disaster were more complex.[46] Though speeding the reintegration of former Nazis, the Cold War forced political rhetoric to continue denouncing the Hitler regime as both German states competed for international recognition as the better Germany that had truly learned the lessons of the past.

Personal memories of the Nazi regime were considerably more benign since they tended to fasten onto the years of full employment and peace before the outbreak of World War II. Well into the 1960s, many West German respondents to opinion polls were of the opinion that National Socialism was basically a good idea that had been badly implemented. Despite public condemnations, a strong minority continued to consider Hitler an important leader, and an increasing proportion of respondents also favored a moratorium on looking into the unsavory past, preferring instead to move ahead to a more promising future. Though similar polling data do not exist for East Germany, there is little reason to think that currents of popular opinion differed noticeably.[47] Publicly, both successor states proscribed expressions of neo-Nazi sentiment, thereby continuing Allied prohibitions with laws against *Volksverhetzung* (incitement) that criminalized any open avowal of National Socialist sentiment. The West legally banned the Sozialistische Reichspartei, a rightist splinter party that appealed to former Nazis, while the East set up a special party in the National-Demokratische Partei Deutschlands (NDPD) to channel such feelings. As a result of not being engaged, positive memories of National Socialism were pushed below the surface—only to erupt time and again in scandals at the most inopportune moments.

This conflicted memory regime of the 1950s was reconciled, if at all, by the trope of victimization that evaded the issue of responsibility. Even liberal members of the German establishment were rather allergic to the presumed accusation of "collective guilt" until Karl Jaspers suggested distinguishing it from "collective shame." Memories of suffering, recounted in countless personal or literary "war stories," were real enough; almost everyone had lost someone at the front or had experienced loss of home or possessions. But most actual victims, having been killed by Hitler's willing helpers or having emigrated after the war, were no longer present to bear witness to the Nazis' crimes.[48] At the same time, leading intellectuals as well as most historians tended to talk about the Third Reich in abstract categories of fate or modern mass society. They treated the Nazi years as an aberration from German history, not as its logical outcome because that smacked too much of the Luther-to-Hitler treatises of Allied war propaganda. If one did not look too carefully at the question of agency, everyone could somehow seem a victim of war and repression, in the very words later enshrined by Helmut Kohl in the Neue Wache memorial in Berlin.[49]

The Critical Turn

Surprisingly, this compromise between distancing and forgetting was repudiated in the following decade by a turn toward more critical perspectives. No doubt, much elite reluctance to probe into the brown past, administrative and judicial foot-dragging in restitution cases, and legal evasiveness in persecuting Nazi crimes continued. But increasing temporal distance to the events and the gradual retirement of those chiefly implicated made it easier for a succeeding, less compromised age-cohort to condemn the prior system. The return of prosperity also created enough stability in daily life to allow a return to the unfinished business of troubling memories. Moreover, the easing of the Cold War confrontation between East and West, the loosening of social hierarchies, and the gradual pluralization of the media rendered it possible to question prior taboos. Finally, the continuing pressure of international opinion and the increase in foreign travel on the part of West Germans allowed a gradual softening of narrowly national views.[50]

What were some of the impulses that ultimately broke through the "collective silence" regarding the participation of "ordinary Germans" in Nazi crimes?[51] Chief among the sources of a more critical attitude was a series of spectacular court cases like the so-called Einsatzgruppen trial in Ulm initiated in the late 1950s by individual suits against former SS members. Victims' groups and the East German government called attention to the continued employment of "blood judges," thereby revealing the scandalous reluctance of a previously Nazified judiciary to prosecute Nazi criminals in the West. As a result of a controversial exhibition mounted by the SDS (Sozialistischer Deutscher Studentbund), critical columnists and legislators compelled the creation of a new federal prosecutor's office in Ludwigsburg to prepare the prosecution of suits against Nazi perpetrators; despite its strictly limited powers, the Ludwigsburg office and the commitment of courageous prosecutors like Fritz Bauer helped galvanize judicial activity. The international repercussions of the Eichmann trial in Jerusalem also spurred similar West German efforts in the Auschwitz, Treblinka, and Sobibor trials. While the sentences were often unsatisfactory, the intensive press coverage of the trials confronted normal German citizens with irrefutable proof of widespread complicity in genocide.[52]

These shocking revelations were reinforced by the "return of the images" in literary representations and media broadcasts that helped create a critical public opinion. During the late 1950s, talented younger authors such as Günter Grass, Heinrich Böll, and Martin Walser published novels that candidly revealed the seamy underside of the Nazi system. A few years later, the playwright Rolf Hochhuth produced a searing indictment of papal complicity with genocide, while the author Peter Weiss presented an equally compelling stage version of the revelations of the Auschwitz trial.[53] In 1963, the broadcast of a fifteen-episode television series on the Third Reich, viewed by approximately one-quarter of the entire population of the Federal Republic, signaled a shift of media attitudes in a more critical direction. Though conservative spokesmen like Rainer Barzel still sought to evade the issue of German responsibility, in the 1965 debate about the extension of the statute of limitations on Nazi crimes the Social Democratic Bundestag representative Adolf Arndt delivered a moving confession of personal inadequacy in opposing such atrocities. His distinction between criminal guilt to be established in the courts, and historical-moral responsibility carried the day and made the Bundestag agree to an extension of the statute of limitations to 1969. Although many people preferred amnesia, these and other interventions helped establish a memory culture that made forgetting impossible.[54]

The writings of a new group of contemporary historians were also essential in providing scholarly authority for the critical views of the National Socialist regime. Both the Allies and democratic parliamentarians wanted to establish an institute for research on the Nazi era, but their conceptions diverged on the relative importance of public education and academic scholarship. After some unedifying quarrels, both the funding for an institute of contemporary history and its scholarly character were settled. The guiding spirit of the newly established Institut für Zeitgeschichte (IfZ) was Hans Rothfels, a conservative reémigré who had sought refuge abroad during the Nazi era on account of his partially Jewish family background. Rothfels also edited the institute's new journal, which became known for its high scholarly standards and systematic efforts to separate hard facts from the myths surrounding the Third Reich. The IfZ made an especially important contribution to the prosecution of Nazi perpetrators by providing briefs and expert opinions establishing the criminal nature of the Third Reich. While the monographs published by IfZ scholars were slow to engage the issue of genocide and not always free of apologetic undertones, their solid research nonetheless provided an unassailable documentary foundation for recognizing the full extent of Nazi atrocities.[55]

The generational revolt of the 1960s therefore did not initiate the confrontation with the Nazi past, but rather dramatized and popularized an ongoing process, at the risk of creating new misunderstandings. Though most activists hailed from liberal backgrounds, many rebellious youths began their crusade at home by pointedly asking their fathers or uncles about their roles in the Third Reich. In public, students also loved to create scandals about the backgrounds of political leaders, charging that Adenauer's assistant Hans Globke had written a legal commentary on the Nuremberg laws, that Prime Minister Hans Filbinger of Baden-Württemberg had freely handed out death sentences as a military judge, that Chancellor Kurt-Georg Kiesinger had been an important Nazi official in the Foreign Office, and, finally, that President Heinrich Lübke had drawn up plans for concentration camps.[56] Critical spirits also sought to confront their own institutions, such as the universities, with their unsavory pasts. They demanded *Ringvorlesungen* (lecture series) on the complicity of entire disciplines such *Germanistik*, and singled individual professors with a tarnished record. Student activists also disrupted lectures with "go-ins," prompting Jewish survivors and some liberals to warn that such violations of the freedom of speech might signal the resurgence of totalitarian tendencies from the other end of the spectrum.[57]

Though the insistence on a critical view did raise new questions about the German past, the public rhetoric of protest indiscriminately indicted all presumed enemies under the label of "fascism." The impulse to find a collective explanation of the Nazi dictatorship that linked it to structural continuities in society was no doubt laudable and helped turn historians toward *Gesellschaftsgeschichte* (social history). Similarly, the insistence on the economic roots of collective behavior also rehabilitated Marxist voices in the West that had been silenced as a result of the Cold War. The effort to plumb the psychological depths of the "authoritarian personality" and to probe the repressive features of capitalist consumption and popular culture along the lines of the Frankfurt School added weight to the critical indictment. But stretching the term "fascism" to impugn all and sundry forms of authority and to reject "bourgeois secondary virtues" like honesty or cleanliness deprived the concept of analytical utility.[58] Once the difference between democracy and dictatorship was obliterated in the heat of ideological battle, the impulse to confront the unsavory past could easily turn into a justification for sloth, indolence, and irresponsibility in the present.

As a result, a significant segment of the student movement disavowed its humanistic values by turning to terrorist violence, which in turn produced counterterrorist repression by the state. Hardly aware of their own antecedents, most activists lacked the interest and persistence to find out what had really transpired in the Third Reich—instead, they were preoccupied with protesting the present in order to change the future. Content with a stylized understanding of the Nazi dictatorship, they saw analogues everywhere, even in the democratic United States, and used their imaginative rhetoric to justify "resistance" against what they considered neofascist dangers. When the provoked authorities hit back clumsily, their excessive response appeared to validate the Marxisant analysis and provoked increasingly serious forms of illegal protest: violence against things eventually escalated toward a sort of urban guerilla warfare against people, who were dehumanized as representatives of a corrupt system. There is no need to retell the sorry story of the RAF or its offshoots in order to note their frequent references to antifascism as a justification for their actions and their equally drastic disregard for human life—a contradiction that eventually cost them the support of their intellectual sympathizers.[59]

A more positive consequence of the generational rebellion was the spread of critical attitudes throughout the cultural institutions of the Federal Republic. The restructuring of school curricula to pay more attention to the history of the Third Reich had already begun in the early 1960s, when, in response to the pressure of progressive parents and inquisitive youngsters, the Conference of State Ministers of Education issued new guidelines on teaching the history of the recent past.[60] In the media, too, the spirit of contradiction had sharpened an antiestablishment bent among journalists, who took pleasure in exposing scandals and broadcasting the attacks of youthful rebels. Participation in the public confrontations, Marxist study circles, antiauthoritarian workshops, and the like pushed an active minority of the age cohort in a critical direction. As they gradually completed their "long march through the institutions" and became teachers, judges (particularly in the social courts), and television journalists, the former radicals broadcast their antifascist views from the inside with the help of public funds. In spite of the fierce resistance of their elders or conservative opponents who tried to ban leftists from public service, critical views, albeit in somewhat attenuated form, won out with time as a result of a general transformation of values.[61]

In response to the challenge from the New Left, conservative thinkers, too, had to distance themselves from Nazi atrocities and to come up with their own explanations of how National Socialism had been possible. Nationalist historians liked to point to the culpability of a small clique of rabid Nazis and Hitler's somehow "demonic" appeal, which decent people could not resist. Religious thinkers in particular denounced National Socialism as a form of "secular religion" that had appropriated the cult trappings of the churches but perverted their humane intent. Yet another favorite argument held that modern mass societies, lacking intermediary authorities, were susceptible to the magnetism of charismatic leaders. Another form of relativizing the enormity of German crimes was to point to the international nature of racism, anti-Semitism, and other inhumane ideological currents.[62] Though these partial truths could serve as correctives to neo-Marxist oversimplifications, their thrust was to confine the blame to a small circle, exculpate the majority of decent burghers, and explain the Third Reich as the result of overwhelming forces that a single individual could not control.

Gradually, these controversies shifted attention from German war experiences and the debate about the Nazi system to the suffering of the victims of the Nazis' racial ideology, the Jews and, to a lesser degree, the Slavs. In East Germany, the stress on the antifascist resistance and the economic focus of Marxism largely effaced the genocidal aspect of the Third Reich.[63] In West Germany, intellectual critics instead constructed a "negative memory" that stressed racist persecution but stopped short of confronting the final act of annihilation. This reticence slowly began to break down as a result of testimony, presented in various court cases, that broadcast the real purpose of the death camps; it was overcome by the moving survivor narratives of Primo Levi and Eli Wiesel that were avidly read by the literary public; and it was undermined by a stream of "brown books" produced in East Germany exposing the complicity of the Bonn establishment. According to the sociologist Michael Bodemann, the crucial development was the Six Day War in 1967 because it helped turn the heroic fighting Israelis into a something like honorary German cousins—sympathy for the Israelis in the present also created a new kind of empathy for the suffering of the Jews in the past.[64]

The result of the increasing chorus of critical voices, no matter how divided, was the emergence of a symbolic politics of contrition that broke the relative silence of the previous decade. For instance, on the local level victims' groups finally succeeded in convincing some communities where concentration camps had been located to accept their responsibility and establish memorials on their former sites.[65] On the person-to-person level, programs like Aktion Sühnezeichen sprang up that sought to link youths from different countries by having them work together at sites of suffering and in cemeteries across borders in a spirit of cooperation.[66] On the national level, the critical attitude proved strong enough to withstand the backlash against accusations of German guilt and the accompanying rise of the neo-Nazi Nationaldemokratische Partei Deutschlands (NPD).[67] On the international level, the new spirit of contrition allowed the inauguration of an *Ostpolitik* designed to reconcile Germans with their former victims in Eastern Europe who had been ignored by Adenauer's westernization policy. The most moving expression of such symbolic expiation was Chancellor Willy Brandt's spontaneous but photogenic gesture of kneeling at the Warsaw Ghetto Memorial.[68]

Memory and Democracy

The sixties were a decisive decade in the establishment of a critical memory culture in West Germany. Despite the reluctance of jurists to break ranks with their compromised comrades, victims' groups succeeded in forcing a resumption of legal proceedings against prominent Nazi perpetrators. One consequence of these spectacular trials was the emergence of a self-critical outlook willing to acknowledge German responsibility and determined to prevent evasion of that responsibility. Initially developed by writings and intellectuals, this mind-set gradually came to be espoused by the West German print and electronic media. With the arrival of the SPD-FDP coalition, the political class also began to understand that something more than lip-service condemnation of the Nazi regime was required and that apologetic statements were to be considered scandalous. It was also during this decade that school curricula were revised to give more time to recent history and to provide a fuller and more compassionate portrayal of the anti-Semitic and anti-Slavic genocide. Finally, the new subdiscipline of contemporary history matured sufficiently so as to give unchallengeable academic support to critical views of the recent German past.[69]

As a result of these developments in the West, the difference in the memory cultures of the GDR and FRG grew more pronounced during this period. The antifascism of East German leaders and intellectuals, which initially had been at least in part genuine, had gradually narrowed and become a ritual for state observances. The memorial and permanent exhibition set up at the Buchenwald concentration camp reflected the growing privileging of communist resisters over Jewish victims of racial violence. The ideological focus on capitalists and Junkers as the prime culprits also absolved many lesser collaborators from admitting their own guilt.[70] In the West, spectacular trials, literary portrayals, political speeches, and academic monographs spread blame more widely and forced a much larger group of individuals to confront their personal pasts. The resulting public controversy kept the issue alive and made it difficult to treat the Third Reich as something remote, of no concern to the present. While in East Germany professions of antifascism were more unequivocal, in West Germany the past became a major irritant that forced even those who were reluctant to engage the subject to develop negative opinions about the Nazi era, lest they seem insensitive.[71]

The process of reversing the direction of memories from exculpation to criticism was necessarily messy and contested, since it proceeded largely via public controversy. In effect, it was a minority consisting of Nazism's opponents and victims who sought to make their remembrance of suffering prevail against the more positive recollections of a majority comprising perpetrators and collaborators. With the help of the Allied occupation forces, the proponents of critical memory captured public space, outlawed expressions of neo-Nazi sentiment, and thereby confined such feelings to private or at best semipublic communication. With many perpetrators and collaborators preferring embarrassed silence, the oral transmission of their unofficial counter-memories created some important disjunctions with the politically approved versions of the past, but was never strong enough to shake their hegemony. Moreover, many "war stories" or "survival tales" contained enough suffering to make even onetime supporters of the regime question the consequences of National Socialism.[72] Though apologetic accounts sought to further a particular agenda, group representations like those of veterans or expellees could only articulate themselves publicly if they respected the need to distance themselves from the Third Reich. Hence, it took several decades for the reversal to work itself out.

One indicator of the transformation of memories is the change of the pictorial representations of the Nazi era in the German media. The initial images of defeat focused upon the damage from bombing and fighting, on the horrific scenes of flight and expulsion, as well as military debris and ruinous cityscapes that fascinated American photographers.[73] Soon thereafter began the critical efforts to decenter the Nazi propaganda in newsreels as well as the heroic portrayal of German troops in the popular *Landserheftchen* (military pulp fiction) by attempting to portray in movie form the full savagery of the war. Both sets of images, however, reinforced conceptions of German victimhood. Because of Allied prohibitions of Nazi materials, it took much longer for the media to present images of the Nazi dictatorship. The press often drew upon the regime's self-representations but juxtaposed them with images of the terrible consequences of repression and provided critical commentary. In the late 1950s, images of concentration camps finally began to present the real targets of Nazism and created a new kind of symbolic iconography of evocative images that contradicted the exculpatory tales. Auschwitz thereby became a negative reference of transcendent power. The haunting pictures eventually made it possible for younger Germans to identify with the suffering of others.[74]

The halting recognition of the victims of German aggression and genocide was a result of an unusual combination of circumstances that did not affect Japan or Italy to the same degree.[75] First, international public opinion, shocked by the revelations that had only begun with the Nuremberg trials, kept demanding apologies from the defeated enemy as precondition for readmission to the community of civilized nations, which was essential for a revival of the economy. Second, the internal minority of regime opponents and victims that insisted on contrition was strong enough to prevent the rise of exculpatory myths like that of the French Resistance, which would overshadow the reality of widespread collaboration in representations of Vichy France. Third, generational succession created enough distance so that those born at a later time and not implicated directly could rebelliously begin to question their parents in particular and the previous political regimes in general. Fourth, the relative public silence maintained by perpetrators and collaborators shifted the transmission of images of the past into the hands of mediating institutions like the media and the schools, making it possible for critical pictures to be handed down to the young, many of whom accepted them as a kind of second-hand memory. Finally, the establishment of a veritable memory industry in memorials at the actual sites, a memory calendar of problematic dates, and a new group of historical journalists created a powerful lobby that insisted on a negative perception of the German past.[76] Even if the process slowed again during the 1970s, it had been launched on a critical trajectory.

What, finally, of the relationship between critical memory and political democracy? Citing the examples of Spain and Portugal or Poland and other East European countries, commentators like Adam Michnik have taken up the argument, advanced by Hermann Lübbe in the German context, that the healing effect of oblivion expedites the transition to democracy.[77] Other members of the anticommunist resistance like Johannes Gauck insist on opening all secret archives, investigating the atrocities of the dictatorial regime, and informing the public as the precondition for the reestablishment of freedom.[78] While forgetting no doubt facilitates the many compromises necessary for former oppressors to relinquish their power peacefully, exposure creates painful controversy that may have a cathartic effect on public life. To this observer, the tortuous process of *Vergangenheitsbewältigung* in postwar Germany suggests that establishing a stable democracy requires a confrontation with the ghosts of the past in order to lay them to rest. If the crimes of the past are not openly discussed, perpetrators, bystanders, and victims ultimately cannot come to terms with them; their ugly memories will reappear to poison the future.[79] Though it is never easy to admit to misdeeds, forgetting continues to breed resentment, while remembering can inspire forgiveness. Critical memory is therefore an essential prerequisite for a healthy civil society.

Notes

1. Ulrich Speck, "Wenn Dracula flattert: Geschichte, Erinnerung und Wahrheit," *Frankfurter Rundschau*, 14 March 2001; cf. Claudia Keller, "Kalte Erinnerung, heiße Erinnerung ... zu viel Erinnerung?" *Der Tagesspiegel*, 14 March 2001.

2. Peter Novick, *The Holocaust in American Life* (Boston, 1999); Norman G. Finkelstein, *The Holocaust Industry: Reflections on the Exploitation of Jewish Suffering* (London, 2000).

3. Manfred Hettling, "Die Historisierung der Erinnerung—Westdeutsche Rezeptionen der nationalsozialistischen Vergangenheit," *Tel Aviver Jahrbuch für deutsche Geschichte* 29 (2000): 357–78.

4. Dietrich Mühlberg, "Die Verwandlung der Erinnerung an die DDR," in *Verletztes Gedächtnis. Zeitgeschichte und Erinnerung im Konflikt*, ed. Konrad H. Jarausch and Martin Sabrow (Frankfurt am Main, 2002), 217ff.

5. Axel Schildt, "Die Erfindung der Geschichte," *Der Tagesspiegel*, 27 January 2001; cf. Timothy Garton Ash, "Rauschhafter Drang. Mit der 'Fischer-Affäre' und der 68-er Retrospektive steht Deutschland vor einer letzten Vergangenheitsbewältigung," *Frankfurter Rundschau*, 28 February 2001. See also the recent extended essay by Paul Berman, *Power and the Idealists: The Passion of Joschka Fischer, and Its Aftermath* (New York, 2005).

6. Luisa Passerini, ed., *Memory and Totalitarianism* (Oxford, 1992), vol. 1 of the *International Yearbook of Oral History and Life Stories*, 1–19. Cf. Alon Confino and Peter Fritzsche, eds., *The Work of Memory: New Directions in the Study of German Society and Culture* (Urbana, 2002).

7. Stephane Courtois et al., eds., *Das Schwarzbuch des Kommunismus: Unterdrückung, Verbrechen und Terror* (Munich, 1998). Cf. Eric D. Weitz, *A Century of Genocide: Utopias of Race and Nation* (Princeton, 2003).

8. Peter Reichel, *Politik mit der Erinnerung: Gedächtnisorte im Streit um die nationalsozialistische Vergangenheit* (Munich, 1995); Edgar Wolfrum, *Geschichtspolitik in der Bundesrepublik Deutschland: Der Weg zur bundesrepublikanischen Erinnerung 1948–1990* (Darmstadt, 1999).

9. Ingrid Gilcher-Holtey, ed., *1968: Vom Ereignis zum Gegenstand der Geschichtswissenschaft* (Göttingen, 1998); Arthur Marwick, *The Sixties: Cultural Revolution in Britain, France, Italy and the US, c. 1958–c. 1974* (Oxford, 1998).

10. Peter Graf Kielmansegg, *Nach der Katastrophe: Eine Geschichte des geteilten Deutschland* (Berlin, 2000); cf. Axel Schildt, Detlef Siegfried, and Karl Christian Lammers, eds., *Dynamische Zeiten: Die 60er Jahre in den beiden deutschen Gesellschaften* (Hamburg, 2000).

11. Ralph Giordano, *Die zweite Schuld oder von der Last Deutscher zu sein* (Cologne, 2000); cf. Manfred Kittel, *Die Legende von der "zweiten Schuld": Vergangenheitsbewältigung in der Ära Adenauer* (Berlin, 1993).

12. Ian Buruma, *The Wages of Guilt: Memories of War in Germany and Japan* (New York, 1994); Sebastian Conrad, *Auf der Suche nach der verlorenen Nation: Geschichtsschreibung in Westdeutschland und Japan 1945–1960* (Göttingen, 1999).

13. Stefan Reinecke, "Die Wiederholer," *Der Tagesspiegel*, 13 January 2001. See also Jochen Bölsche, "Die verlorene Ehre der APO," *Der Spiegel* 55, no. 5 (2001): 68–85.

14. Horst Möller and Udo Wengst, eds., *50 Jahre Institut für Zeitgeschichte: Eine Bilanz* (Munich, 1999); Wolfgang Benz, "Wissenschaft oder Alibi? Die Etablierung der Zeitgeschichte," in *Wissenschaft im geteilten Deutschland. Restauration oder Neubeginn nach 1945?* ed. Walter H. Pehle and Peter Sillem (Frankfurt am Main, 1992), 11–25.

15. Anselm Doering-Manteuffel, "Deutsche Zeitgeschichte nach 1945: Entwicklung und Problemlagen der historischen Forschung zur Nachkriegszeit," *Vierteljahrshefte für Zeitgeschichte* 41 (1993): 1–29; Christoph Klessmann, *Zeitgeschichte in Deutschland nach dem Ende des Ost-West-Konflikts* (Essen, 1998).

16. Klaus Allerbeck, *Soziologie radikaler Studentenbewegungen: Eine vergleichende Untersuchung in der Bundesrepublik Deuschland und den Vereinigten Staaten* (Munich, 1973).

17. Carole Fink, Philipp Gassert, and Detlef Junker, eds., *1968: The World Transformed* (Cambridge, 1998). See also Elizabeth Peifer, "1968 in German Political Culture, 1967–1993: From Experience to Myth" (PhD diss., University of North Carolina, 1997).

18. Axel Schildt, "Die Erfindung der Geschichte," *Der Tagesspiegel*, 27 January 2001.

19. Axel Schildt, *Ankunft im Westen: Ein Essay zur Erfolgsgeschichte der Bundesrepublik* (Frankfurt am Main, 1999), 34–48.

20. Hanna Schissler, ed., *The Miracle Years: A Cultural History of West Germany, 1949–1968* (Princeton, 2001), 3–15, 459–67.

21. Manfred Görtemaker, *Geschichte der Bundesrepublik Deutschland: Von der Gründung bis zur Gegenwart* (Munich, 1999).

22. Anselm Doering-Manteuffel, *Wie westlich sind die Deutschen? Amerikanisierung und Westernisierung im 20. Jahrhundert* (Göttingen, 1999). See also Axel Schildt, "Sind die Westdeutschen amerikanisiert worden? Zur zeitgeschichtlichen Erforschung kulturellen Transfers und seiner gesellschaftlichen Folgen nach dem Zweiten Weltkrieg," *Aus Politik und Zeitgeschichte* (2000), B 50: 3–19.

23. Heinz Bude, *Das Altern einer Generation: Die Jahrgänge 1938 bis 1948* (Frankfurt am Main, 1997); Ronald Inglehart, *The Silent Revolution: Changing Values and Political Styles among Western Publics* (Princeton, 1977).

24. Schildt, Siegfried, and Lammers, *Dynamische Zeiten*, 13; cf. Schissler, *Miracle Years*, 465.

25. Armin Mitter and Stefan Wolle, *Untergang auf Raten: Unbekannte Kapitel der DDR-Geschichte* (Munich, 1993).

26. Klaus Schönhoven, "Aufbruch in die sozialliberale Ära: Zur Bedeutung der 60er Jahre in der Geschichte der Bundesrepublik," *Geschichte und Gesellschaft* 25 (1999): 123–45.

27. Wolfgang Schieder, for example, does not include 1968 in his list of twentieth-century "upheavals" in Germany in his essay "Die Umbrüche von 1918, 1933, 1945 und 1989 als Wendepunkte deutscher Geschichte," in *Deutsche Umbrüche im 20. Jahrhundert*, ed. Dietrich Papenfuß and W. Schneider (Cologne, 2000), 3–18.

28. Axel Schildt und Arnold Sywottek, eds., *Modernisierung im Wiederaufbau: Die westdeutsche Gesellschaft der 50er Jahre* (Bonn, 1993).

29. Michael Walzer, ed., *Toward a Global Civil Society* (Providence, 1995); Jürgen Kocka, "Zivilgesellschaft als historisches Problem und Versprechen," in *Europäische Zivilgesellschaft in Ost und West: Begriff, Geschichte, Chancen*, ed. Manfred Hildermeier et al. (Frankfurt am Main, 2000), 13–39.

30. Konrad H. Jarausch, "Die Zivilisierung der Deutschen" (ms., Berlin, 2001).

31. Konrad H. Jarausch, "Zeitgeschichte und Erinnerung: Deutungskonkurrenz oder Interdependenz?" in Jarausch and Sabrow, *Verletztes Gedächtnis*, 9–37.

32. Wolfgang Kraushaar, "Der Zeitzeuge als Feind des Historikers? Neuerscheinungen zur 68er Bewegung," *Mittelweg 36* 8, no. 6 (1999): 49–72. Cf. Ulrich Herbert, ed., *Wandlungsprozesse in Westdeutschland: Belastung, Integration, Liberalisierung 1945–1980* (Göttingen, 2002).

33. Compare Kittel, *Die Legende von der "zweiten Schuld"* and Norbert Frei, *Vergangenheitspolitik: Die Anfänge der Bundesrepublik und die NS-Vergangenheit* (Munich, 1996).

34. Rolf Hochhuth, "Was wisst ihr von uns? Notizen zur Geschichtsschreibung," *Der Tagesspiegel*, 1 April 2001.

35. Alexander von Plato and Almuth Leh, eds., *"Ein unglaublicher Frühling": Erfahrene Geschichte im Nachkriegsdeutschland, 1945–1948* (Bonn, 1997).

36. Victor Klemperer, *Ich will Zeugnis ablegen bis zum letzten. Tagebücher 1933–1945*, vol. 2 (Berlin, 1995).

37. Lutz Niethammer, *Die Mitläuferfabrik: Die Entnazifizierung am Beispiel Bayerns* (Berlin, 1982).

38. Ernst von Salomon, *Der Fragebogen* (Reinbek, 1946).

39. Jeffrey Herf, *Divided Memory: The Nazi Past in the Two Germanies* (Cambridge, MA, 1997).

40. Friedrich Meinecke, *Die deutsche Katastrophe* (Wiesbaden, 1946); Gerhard Ritter, *Geschichte als Bildungsmacht: Ein Beitrag zur historisch-politischen Neubesinnung* (Stuttgart, 1946).

41. Wolfgang Malanowski, ed., *1945: Deutschland in der Stunde Null* (Reinbek, 1985).

42. Lutz Niethammer, "Biografie und Biokratie: Nachgedanken zu einem westdeutschen Oral History-Projekt in der DDR fünf Jahre nach der deutschen Vereinigung," *Mitteilungen aus der kulturwissenschaftlichen Forschung* 19 (1996): 370–87.

43. Hans Modrow, *Ich wollte ein neues Deutschland* (Berlin, 1998).

44. Frei, *Vergangenheitspolitik*, passim, and Norbert Frei, ed., *Karrieren im Zwielicht: Hitlers Eliten nach 1945* (Frankfurt am Main, 2001). See also Bernd Weisbrod, ed., *Akademische Vergangenheitspolitik: Beiträge zur Wissenschaftskultur der Nachkriegszeit* (Göttingen, 2002).

45. Robert Moeller, "War Stories: The Search for a Usable Past in the Federal Republic of Germany," *American Historical Review* 101 (1996): 1008–48; Frank Biess, "The Protracted War: Returning POWs and the Making of East and West German Citizens, 1945–1955" (PhD diss., Brown University, 1999).

46. Jürgen Danyel, ed., *Die geteilte Vergangenheit: Zum Umgang mit Nationalsozialismus und Widerstand in beiden deutschen Staaten* (Berlin, 1995); Annette Weinke, *Die Verfolgung von NS-Tätern im geteilten Deutschland: Vergangenheitsbewältigung 1949–1969* (Paderborn, 2002). Cf. Herf, *Divided Memory*, passim.

47. See the literature cited in Gerhard A. Ritter, *Über Deutschland: Die Bundesrepublik in der Deutschen Geschichte* (Munich, 1998), 122ff.

48. Elizabeth Heineman, "The Hour of the Woman: Memories of West Germany's 'Crisis Years' and West German National Identity," *American Historical Review* 101 (1996): 354–95.

49. Christoph Stölzl, ed., *Die Neue Wache unter den Linden: Ein deutsches Denkmal im Wandel der Geschichte* (Berlin, 1993); Sabine Moller, *Die Entkonkretisierung der NS-Herrschaft in der Ära Kohl* (Hanover, 1998).

50. For the general context, see Konrad H. Jarausch, *Die Umkehr: Deutsche Wandlungen 1945–1990* (Munich, 2004), 133ff.

51. Hermann Lübbe, "Der Nationalsozialismus im politischen Bewußtsein der Gegenwart," in Martin Broszat et al., eds., *Deutschlands Weg in die Diktatur* (Berlin, 1983), 329–49.

52. Marc von Miquel, *Ahnden oder amnestieren? Westdeutsche Justiz und Vergangenheitspolitik in den sechziger Jahren* (Göttingen, 2004).

53. Phrase from Habbo Knoch, *Die Tat als Bild: Fotografien des Holocaust in der deutschen Erinnerungskultur* (Hamburg, 2001). The literary dimension of public opinion is often neglected. See also Hermann Glaser, *Deutsche Kultur 1945–2000* (Munich, 1997).

54. Miquel, *Ahnden oder amnestieren?*; Norbert Frei, Dirk van Laak, and Michael Stolleis, eds., *Geschichte vor Gericht: Historiker, Richter und die Suche nach Gerechtigkeit* (Munich, 2000).

55. Conrad, *Auf der Suche nach der verlorenen Nation*, 219–81, in contrast to the more critical Nikolas Berg, *Der Holocaust und die westdeutschen Historiker: Erforschung und Erinnerung* (Göttingen, 2003).

56. On East German attempts to discredit the Federal Republic, see Annette Weinke, *Die Verfolgung von NS-Tätern im geteilten Deutschland: Vergangenheitsbewältigungen 1949–1969, oder: Eine deutsch-deutsche Beziehungsgeschichte im Kalten Krieg* (Paderborn, 2002).

57. Karl Christian Lammers, "Die Auseinandersetzung mit der "braunen" Universität: Ringvorlesungen zur NS-Vergangenheit an westdeutschen Hochschulen," in Schildt, Siegfried, and Lammers, *Dynamische Zeiten*, 148–65.

58. Michael Schmidtke, *Der Aufbruch der jungen Intelligenz: Die 68er Jahre in der Bundesrepublik und den USA* (Frankfurt am Main, 2003).

59. Jillian Becker, *Hitler's Children: The Story of the Baader-Meinhof Terrorist Gang* (Philadelphia, 1977), and Jeremy Varon, *Bringing the War Home: The Weather Underground, the Red Army Faction, and Revolutionary Violence in the Sixties and Seventies* (Berkeley, 2005).

60. Literature in Schmidtke, *Aufbruch*.

61. This process is still underresearched. See Martin and Sylvia Greiffenhagen, *Ein schwieriges Vaterland: Zur politischen Kultur im vereinigten Deutschland* (Munich, 1993).

62. See the contribution by Joachim Scholtysek in this volume. Cf. on the left Hans-Ulrich Wehler, *Deutsche Gesellschaftsgeschichte*, vol. 4: *Vom Beginn des Ersten Weltkriegs bis zur Gründung der beiden deutschen Staaten* (Munich, 2003).

63. Mario Keßler, *Die SED und die Juden—Zwischen Repression und Toleranz* (Berlin, 1995). Cf. Simone Barck, *Antifa-Geschichte(n): Eine literarische Spurensuche in der DDR der 1950er und 1960er Jahre* (Cologne, 2003).

64. Y. Michal Bodemann, "Vom Prozeß in Jerusalem zum Kniefall in Warschau und darüber hinaus: Proben im Gedächtnistheater in Deutschland 1960–1975," in Jarausch and Sabrow, *Verletztes Gedächtnis*, 177ff.

65. Harold Marcuse, *Legacies of Dachau: The Uses and Abuses of a Concentration Camp, 1933–2001* (Cambridge, 2001).

66. Karl-Klaus Rabe, *Umkehr in die Zukunft: Die Arbeit der Aktion Sühnezeichen/Friedensdienste* (Bornheim-Merten, 1983).

67. Uwe Hoffmann, *Die NPD: Entwicklung, Ideologie und Struktur* (Frankfurt am Main, 1999).

68. For a classic description of the scene, see Günter Grass, *Mein Jahrhundert* (Göttingen, 1999).

69. Detlef Siegfried, "Zwischen Aufarbeitung und Schlußstrich: Der Umgang mit der NS-Vergangenheit in den beiden deutschen Staaten 1958 bis 1969," in Schildt, Siegfried, and Lammers, *Dynamische Zeiten*, 77–113. Cf. Norbert Frei, *1945 und wir: Das Dritte Reich im Bewußtsein der Deutschen* (Munich, 2005).

70. Thomas Heimann, *Bilder von Buchenwald: Die Visualisierung des Antifaschismus in der DDR (1945–1990)* (Cologne, 2005).

71. Herf, *Divided Memory*, passim.

72. Peter Fritzsche, "Volkstümliche Erinnerung und deutsche Identität nach dem Zweiten Weltkrieg," in Jarausch and Sabrow, *Verletztes Gedächtnis*, 75ff. Cf. Konrad Jarausch and Michael Geyer, *Shattered Past: Reconstructing German Histories* (Princeton, 2003), 317ff.

73. For instance, Margaret Bourke-White, *Deutschland April 1945* (Munich, 1979).

74. Knoch, *Die Tat als Bild*, passim.

75. R. J. B. Bosworth, *Explaining Auschwitz and Hiroshima: History Writing and the Second World War, 1945–1990* (London, 1993).

76. Mary Fulbrook, *German National Identity after the Holocaust* (Cambridge, 1999). For a comparative view, see the essays by Henry Rousso and others in Konrad H. Jarausch and Thomas Lindenberger, eds., *Thinking Europe: Towards a Europeanization of Contemporary Histories* (New York, 2006).

77. Hermann Lübbe, "Der Nationalsozialismus im deutschen Geschichtsbewußtsein," *Historische Zeitschrift* 236 (1983): 579–99; and Burkhard Bischof, "Zwischen Hypererinnerung und Amnesie: Vergangenheitsbewältigung als Industrie," *Die Presse*, 14 March 2001.

78. Ibid., and Andreas Breitenstein, "Die Präsenz der Absenz: Vergangenheitspolitik zwischen heißer und kalter Erinnerung," *Neue Züricher Zeitung*, 13 March 2001.

79. Alexander Mitscherlich, *The Inability to Mourn: Processes of Collective Behavior* (New York, 1975). The extension of the mandate of the Institute of National Memory (IPN) suggests that Polish opinion is also gradually coming around to a more self-critical approach.

Chapter 2

THE RETURN OF THE IMAGES
Photographs of Nazi Crimes and the West German
Public in the "Long 1960s"

Habbo Knoch

❧

Images of Shame: Atrocity Photographs and Visual Amnesia

Photographs of the Nazis' crimes reentered the German public sphere between 1955 and 1965, bringing to an end a ten-year period in which those crimes were visually absent.[1] The German public had earlier had an intensive but short experience of the shocking photographs Allied photographers had taken in the liberated concentration camps.[2] They were confronted with this evidence of atrocity as part of an improvised information campaign that was halted in June 1945, and by early 1946 the photos had effectively disappeared from public view.[3] These images of shame did not develop into symbols of liberation, as in the United States, or of an acceptance of collective guilt. Instead, they became the absent reminders of German memory, pernicious fetishes representing the trauma of decivilization.

Nevertheless, the end of the visual amnesia and the return of the images a decade later were not simply the starting point of Germany's "coming to terms with the past." The return of the images in the mid-1950s after a decade's absence suggests West Germany's *Vergangenheitsbewältigung*, its attempt to come to terms with the Nazi past, did not first begin with the student revolt of 1968. The visual program of Holocaust remembrance that emerged between 1955 and 1965 must be seen as both a response to and a product of previous attempts to create a usable public history of the catastrophes of the recent past.

To understand the development and limitations of Germany's engagement with its past, photographs and visual remembrance need to be given more attention than they have received so far.[4] In an age of photographic imagery, their

---

importance in shaping historical imagination cannot be underestimated.[5] Modern violence and modern media have developed in complex interaction with each other. Although the era of television documentaries had just begun as the images of the Nazi crimes returned in the mid-1950s, it was in this period of media transformation that a cluster of images of Nazi atrocities was established that remained the representative Holocaust imagery in West Germany until the 1980s. The symbolic value of this handful of photographs has to be analyzed from a historical perspective, not only with regard to their intrinsic pictorial code, but as essential means for the production of images of the recent past.[6] The use of photographs in different media over a period of time reveals the palimpsestic structure of public memory.

This symbolic importance of established visual programs has been demonstrated in the recent debates on the "limits of representation" of the Holocaust and, particularly in Germany, on the representational value of monuments and exhibitions.[7] One of the most disturbing aspects of the so-called *Wehrmachtausstellung* for many visitors was the presentation of private, unofficial photos of German soldiers enacting or about to enact war crimes.[8] This part of the German war in the East had been left out of the public memory since 1945. These photos had been well-known in Poland and the Soviet Union, but in West Germany images of the Nazis' crimes were dominated by photographs of the concentration camps, helpless victims, and destroyed cultural artifacts. They coexisted in a visual repository of remembrance that must be analyzed from both a comparative and a transnational perspective.

The "limits of representation" cannot be discussed only theoretically. The rules of showing and hiding specific aspects of the crimes have to be discovered through a close reading of the cultural practices of remembrance, which include the various methods of producing and representing historical information. Here, photographs, because of their manifold meanings and their documentary character, play a different role than words. Photographs leave their traces more quickly than words; they produce long-lived imprints as elements of virtual symbolic memory collages. Photographs are subject to close and political observation because of the revelatory nature of documentary images. More intensively than words, they represent the political and cultural boundary lines between remembering, repression, and forgetting.

Given this relationship, German reactions to the atrocity photographs in 1945 were of crucial importance—not the pictures themselves, which were publicly displayed for only a few weeks—but the specific perception of atrocity, guilt, and occupation ascribed to them. Soon perceived as embodying an accusation of "collective guilt," the pictures were immediately seen as political symbols: the visualization of Nazi crimes was initially regarded as propagandistic and untrustworthy.[9] For most Germans, aside from those who had been inside the camps before 1945 and a minority of others, the atrocity images did not correspond to the public image of the concentration camps and ghettos that the Nazis themselves had promoted.[10] Many Germans interpreted the photographs of dead bodies as being similar to the scenes they had experienced during the air raids in German towns, thus denying their specific character.[11] Others dismissed the pictures as fakes or claimed they had been taken in India during a recent famine. Only a minority was willing to accept them as symbols of German guilt. Regardless of individual reception, the crimes took on a translocal character as a result of the style of the photographs, which only rarely gave an indication of the exact topography or location of the camps. Seen as political symbols of defeat and shame, the photographs became a first layer of visual memory that had to be covered over in order to establish a collective self-consciousness. The return of the images of atrocity ten years later was closely connected to attempts to redefine the purpose of the public sphere and the foundations of West German political culture.

Fields of Remembrance: Holocaust Imagery and the Politics of Morality

The debates over German war guilt and similar issues in the immediate postwar period were an important link between National Socialist rhetoric and the politics of moral rehabilitation after the founding of the Federal Republic. The language of victimization, the subordination of the fate of the Nazis' victims to the fate of the Germans in general, the attribution of responsibility first and foremost to Nazi Party leaders and SS members, and the search for the "other Germany" became established in this period within the broader intellectual discourse. These arguments were put forward in a pluralist public sphere that became distinctly less pluralist as it adapted to the principles of market economics. Likewise, the political founding of the Federal Republic and the establishment of its autonomy in most of its domestic affairs brought certain interest groups to the forefront who claimed rehabilitation and material restitution. The demands of refugees, expellees, and war victims were mainly material, thus contributing to the financial burdens the young state had to shoulder during its foundation crisis. With regard to the politics of memory, the claims of former professional soldiers and of Germans who had been convicted as Nazi criminals were even more relevant.[12] The former demanded rehabilitation, with little success, and the latter, more successfully, a general amnesty; these demands were to become the main issues in the integration of former National Socialists and their collaborators within West German social and political life after 1949. One of the main consequences of this process of integration was a clear-cut line between a very small group of perpetrators and the rest of the German society. At once, however, former Nazis and Nazi collaborators contributed to the repression of Nazi crimes and to the skewing of the broad public discussion of the character of the Nazi regime.

That discussion was dominated by a shameless willingness to ignore the millions of victims and, in particular, the circumstances of their persecution. Only vaguely mentioned in this politics of self-rehabilitation, the Nazis' victims were displaced by a German community of victims consisting of defeated soldiers, prisoners of war, expellees, and war widows. It provided an integrative narrative for Germany's splintered society and as a basis for the moral legitimation of Germany generally. It also functioned as a political antidote that rendered harmless the discontent of groups whose expectations were not fulfilled. The government and most of the media did not play upon the genuine potential for a new militarism or for a glorification of National Socialism. They contributed to the establishment of a rather tragic, "feminine," unheroic, and private image of Germany's victimhood instead of—and in opposition to—a victorious, "masculine," heroic, nationalistic, and militaristic image. The tragic, unheroic image of victimhood was embodied in photographs of returning prisoners of war and of defeated soldiers, as well as in war monuments. The nationalistic, heroic image, with its deep roots in the commemorative practices of the late Weimar Republic and the Nazi era, loomed as a menacing alternative.[13]

It was Theodor Heuss, the first president of the Federal Republic, who advocated the integration of all German victims, including soldiers, expellees and war widows, into a single remembrance culture. Something like what Heuss conceived was realized with the reestablishment of *Volkstrauertag*, the national day of mourning for the war dead, in 1952. Even the Volksbund deutsche Kriegsgräberfürsorge, the organization that tended to military cemeteries, pursued a more balanced, though of course still nationalized, approach to war remembrance. Victims of persecution and concentration camp prisoners were mentioned at the end of a hierarchy of victims with Germans at the top. The former could thus be left out, which was most often the case. At the same time, however, Germany had to reintegrate itself into an international moral and political community. In pursuing that goal, restitution was a crucial issue. By the time the Federal Republic and Israel came to agreement on restitution to Jewish victims, Germans had begun to develop more of a sensitivity to issues of persecution and destruction, albeit very selective and episodic. In 1953, *Reichskristallnacht* was remembered officially for the first time in many West German towns. No images could be found, however, aside from a few of burning synagogues, which, like commemoration speeches and some early novels, reduced the Holocaust to the years up until 1938. Somehow the Jews had had to "leave" Germany. Some politicians even interpreted *Reichskristallnacht* as the beginning of the devastating defeat of 1945.[14]

This elliptic, incomplete commemorative discourse was overwhelmed by the popularization of World War II that began in the early 1950s. Movies, illustrated magazine features, and the first *Landserhefte* (pulp war story magazines produced in a strong tradition with similar Nazi publications and under the strong influence of American commercialization) began to flood Germany and coexisted in German popular culture with, for instance, the notorious *Heimatfilme*.[15] The German soldier was revived: not as a Nazi, but as a heroic and tragic figure, not as a Prussian militarist, but as a brave, unpolitical warrior who was at once the innocent tool and victim of a terror regime. In connection with the public commemoration of "Stalingrad" beginning in 1952, the memory of war in Germany took on a new quality. It stressed the remarkable personal traits of the German soldier, the *Landser*, that could be integrated and serve the rebuilding of Germany and the reconstruction of civil society. In thousands of photographs, the *Landser* became the incarnation not only of the *saubere Wehrmacht*; he was also obviously intended to be seen as a victim, but, on account of his inner and physical strengths, he also represented the ultimate victory of "true" German values such as independence and morality.

It fits well into this picture that, despite various forms of obstruction and protest, images of German resistance fighters began to be produced and circulated at this time.[16] The term "fighter" (*Kämpfer*) was intentionally misleading because none of them fought in the strict sense of the word. But calling people like Stauffenberg or Leber "resistance fighters" brought them, even though most of them were officers, into the same realm of comradeship, trustworthiness, and decency where the common soldier had found his place.

The 1950s were not, as has long been argued, a time of only silence and repression in West Germany. *Vergangenheitsbewältigung* took the form, however, of interwoven attempts to produce images of the recent past that coincided with the goals of rehabilitating Germany morally and rebuilding the country physically.[17] The German people were represented as double victims—victims of both the National Socialist regime and the war. A core element of visual representations, this "usable past"[18] was staged against the confrontation with Nazi crimes in 1945, dominated the discourse of commemoration, and was a precondition for the return of the images of atrocity. Visualizing the recent past in this way provided reusable iconic elements for the public discourse and led, finally, to the awareness that photographs of Nazi crimes could and should be used as a political means to bring visual amnesia to an end.

Visual Archives of Commemoration: Holocaust Images in West German Public Life, 1955–1965

The stages of the return of Nazi crimes to the German public sphere coincided with those of the historical development of the Nazi era. In the years immediately following 1945, the concentration camps, which had been created in 1933, served as a symbol of Germany under National Socialist rule. In the early 1950s, the persecution of the German Jews prior to 1938 became a topic of public concern. A few years later, after 1955, a broader picture of Nazi crimes began to develop that included the next stages of the persecution of the Jews—deportation and annihilation. Not until the 1960s did Auschwitz become the main symbol of the mass annihilation of the Jews, which itself became the central element of public memory, although historically it was only one, albeit crucial, aspect of the Nazis' crimes.

Publications about and representations of Nazi crimes began to appear in growing numbers in West Germany from 1955 on, and the flow increased in the first half of the 1960s. Leon Poliakov and Josef Wulf published a documentary anthology in 1955 that included a photographic narrative of the different stages of the persecution of the Jews.[19] Gerhard Schoenberner's *Der gelbe Stern* (1960), based on his work in Polish and other archives, gave a more detailed version of that narrative.[20] A few years earlier, Raimund Schnabel had published a collection of images that condemned the SS and its crimes from a communist and anti-imperialistic perspective.[21] Alain Resnais' documentary *Nuit et brouillard* (*Night and Fog*, 1955) was immediately put to use by schools, churches, and political groups as a source of basic information. On account of its high aesthetic quality, this film is still regarded as one of the best ever made on this subject. Its content has, however, been received and remembered in a variety of ways: as a film about a European system of concentration camps and collaboration, for example, or, particularly in Germany, as a documentation of the Holocaust (which Resnais had not intended the film to be). Almost as successful as *Nuit et brouillard* was Erwin Leiser's *Mein Kampf*, which connected the crimes of the Nazis to a general narrative of German history in the twentieth century.[22] Illustrated and news magazines were among the first media to make use of Holocaust photos when they reported on the trials of former Nazi officials, most notably the 1960–61 trial of Adolf Eichmann in Jerusalem. Although magazines published historical photographs only to illustrate personal stories, and although they did not aim to write the history of Nazi crimes, they made some of the hidden photographs available to the public for the first time, and, in so doing, they opened the way for them to be used by other media as well. The photographs appeared, in turn, in print, including in school books, and in exhibitions. Thus, starting in 1955 a broad range of Holocaust images was gradually disseminated in the German public realm and became a part of German political culture, continuously challenging the consensus of the 1950s, despite being a relatively minor presence.

The various media used photographs of Nazi crimes for different purposes and at different points during the period 1955–65. The illustrated magazines played a leading role in reinventing the visualization of Nazi crimes beginning in 1956. Schoolbooks began using the photographs two years later. A series of small exhibitions took place between 1958 and 1962, and larger exhibitions followed in the mid-1960s. Newspapers and political magazines intensified their use of these images between 1960 and 1965. The relevance of these photographs as documentation shifted from one medium to another. They were subject to different modes of perception and interpretation. Moreover, the different media did not use the same photographs. Although some photographs can be found more often than others, the field of visual memory was too heterogeneous, too complex, and too unstructured to be reduced to "icons of annihilation."[23] Only later did certain images become canonical.

The return of these images was inextricably linked to the democratization and pluralization of the West German public sphere. The reasons behind this new stage in West Germany's *Vergangenheitsbewältigung* cannot be reduced to specific events such as the trials of Nazi criminals or the wave of anti-Semitic incidents in the late 1950s. Two developments cleared the way for removing the limits of representation set in the first postwar decade: the pressure for prosecution of

Nazi-era offenses decreased and the atmosphere of secrecy relaxed. The coverage of the Hungarian uprising in 1956 brought vivid images of violence into a media domain that had previously excluded pictures of this sort for the most part. Criticizing the growing popular interest in World War II, some German intellectuals demanded limits for this kind of representation and insisted that information about Nazi crimes be made available so as to prevent a glorification of the Nazi era. The West German campaigns against the country's rearmament and acquisition of nuclear weapons often referred to Nazi crimes and made many people more sensitive to the subject. Finally, new representations of persecution under the Nazis—the story of Anne Frank, for example—created a deeper awareness and influenced the ways the photos were used. But most important for the visual representation of Nazi crimes in West Germany was the image of German society in opposition to the Nazi regime and the perpetrators of atrocities.

Images of Perpetrators and the Dynamics of Visual Politics

Because the Holocaust was represented in vague, distorting, and often religious terms until the late 1950s, it was present only as a mysterious event. This was compounded by the frequent assertion that most Germans were not aware of the crimes. As a result, perpetrators who had been reintegrated after 1945 remained more or less invisible in the shadow of the new Federal Republic. But the problem of the former perpetrators was eventually brought back into the public domain. As the overview of the new representations has shown, at least three modes of dealing with the past have to be differentiated and seen as interwoven activities: the private and public search for a "usable past," minor but growing attempts to bring the crimes back to the public conscience, and an official political discourse which produced vague and elliptical images of the recent past. Between 1956 and 1961, West Germany's politics of integration came under challenge. The German Democratic Republic's campaign against the Federal Republic was only one factor.[24] There was also extensive media coverage of and comment on the trials of perpetrators (some of whom had been among the last prisoners of war to return), the proliferation of anti-Semitic incidents and criminal prosecution of such acts,[25] and the revelation that some former Nazi officials and supporters had been living in the Federal Republic under fake identities. A teacher prosecuted for his anti-Semitic speeches, one journalist wrote, represented the "phenomenon of mental splitting" within German society. Behind the civil facade a hidden personality was lurking "full of aggressions and fanatical hatred."[26]

   With the revelation of the presence of Nazi criminals in the Federal Republic and the so-called *antisemitische Schmierwelle* (anti-Semitic graffiti wave) of 1959–60, the civic order established after 1945 was revealed to be very fragile. Supported by studies pointing to the appalling state of knowledge about the recent past among the German youth, government officials and educators made plans to intensify history teaching in schools and to improve textbooks. As a result of those efforts and the pressure of the recent media visualization of Nazi crimes, textbooks began to include a few Holocaust photographs. Those photos were, however, outnumbered by war images, including pictures of Landser, and iconographically paralleled by images of German "resistance fighters."

Individuals prosecuted in the postwar period for Nazi-era offenses or anti-Semitic actions were portrayed as demonic, misguided, or mentally broken—even if they were otherwise participants in West German civil society. Portraying these offenders as somehow deviant was in large part a political measure directed primarily against criticism from the GDR. But it was also a response to those West German communists and Social Democrats who tried to hold the social and political system of the Federal Republic responsible for shielding former Nazis. From its founding in 1949, the antifascist weekly *Die Tat*, edited by the association of those formerly persecuted by the Nazi government (*Vereinigung der Verfolgten des Naziregimes*), published photographs of German crimes committed in the years from 1933 onward.[27] They were used to illustrate the major themes of *Die Tat*: remilitarization, limitations on democracy, the restoration of fascism, and the return of capitalism and big business. While continuing to address these topics, *Die Tat* concentrated more and more on the identification and prosecution of Nazi criminals over the course of the 1950s. It was the first and—aside from some smaller communist publications—the only magazine that published not only images from the concentration camps but also of the terror during the German occupation in the East. These photographs showed German soldiers carrying out executions. The use of these often unclear photographs was condemned as politically inspired and tendentious above all because it broke the taboo on the visualization of the Holocaust and the murderous activities of German troops in the field. The ties between *Die Tat*, the Communist Party, and the GDR were obvious and invoked as a political argument to discredit use of the photos by the West German left. Publishing photographs showing Germans taking active part in atrocities was reason enough for many West Germans to voice skepticism or to engage in charges of defamation. Not making use of these types of photographs had been one of the ground rules for maintaining a consensual visual pattern of the Holocaust.

The illustrated magazines were much more interested in Nazi perpetrators than in the Nazi political system itself. Their images of the recently prosecuted individuals fit well with the general sensationalist press attitude toward criminality and the astonishment that people who presumed to be "normal" were responsible for mass murder. One of the articles on Martin Sommer, the "Buchenwald Executioner" (*der Henker von Buchenwald*), opened with the observation that he had been living among "us" previously "as if he was a human being like us."[28] Obviously, his participation in the Nazi regime's crimes made him different. To reinforce this wall of difference, the illustrated magazines used photographs and comments to reveal his civic identity as a façade. Nevertheless, the image remained ambiguous. Because Sommer was portrayed as old and in need of help from a young nurse, his self-presentation in court could be interpreted in two ways. He could be seen, on the one hand, as a dangerously adaptable monster who deliberately kept an innocent young woman beside him in the courtroom in order to show his civil face. Or, on the other hand, he could also be considered a victim of the prosecution whose appearance in court invited the widely discussed question of whether the exposure of Nazi crimes was necessary at all.

Pointing to ambiguities was more a response to that question than an attempt to describe and explain Nazi crimes. At least in the illustrated magazines, persecution and murder were subordinated to the criminals' life stories. Nevertheless, some historical photographs were published that allowed readers to gain an impression of the events in which the accused had been involved. These pictures caused a twofold sensation—by appearing after a decade of visual amnesia and by functioning as illustrations for a sensational issue. Some editors and journalists justified the use of these images by describing them as indispensable tools for learning about the Nazi past. Sensationalism was not limited to the press. Historian Martin Broszat, for example, took issue in his edition of Rudolf Höß's memoirs with how the illustrated magazines portrayed the Nazi genocide of the Jews, but he could not entirely avoid sensational elements in his own portrayal of the onetime commander of Auschwitz.[29]

This question provoked even more debate in West Germany following the Israeli capture of Adolf Eichmann in Argentina in 1960. He was not one of the concentration camp butchers, but one of the main bureaucrats of mass murder. Against the background of Eichmann's trial in Jerusalem, Nazi crimes were finally discussed in Germany as an attempt at systematic annihilation of the Jews. Again, some commentators saw him as "terribly and terrifyingly normal [*schrecklich und erschreckend normal*]"[30] or as "mentally not very different from us (and with 'us' I do not mean Germans only)."[31] The press coverage of the trial led the journalist Gerhard Schoenberner to the verdict that Eichmann was not an "exceptional case of evil" but only an example of a bureaucracy that, "thanks to its maniacal sense of duty [*Pflichtbesessenheit*]," served as the executive of a terror regime.[32] Schoenberner objected to the many accounts that, as a result of misunderstandings of the organization of the mass murder, represented Eichmann as some sort of demon. The tabloid *Bild* called Eichmann "a devil incarnate," for instance, and *Revue* described him as the "omnipotent master of death" and "evil's supplier."[33]

The photographs that appeared in the press underscored this interpretation. In an article in *Quick*, for example, an image of Eichmann's face with eyes gazing downward was placed above a large photo of naked Jewish women taken shortly before they were executed. The accompanying caption stated incorrectly that the photo had been taken in Treblinka.[34] *Der Spiegel* arranged a large photograph of Eichmann's head and a similar sized image of a crematorium oven parallel to each other, so that the forms of both corresponded graphically.[35] By making the Holocaust visual again and as a result of the way images were used, the Eichmann trial seemed to confirm that only a few individuals had been responsible. They seemed to be "normal," but closer examination revealed that they were unnatural, abnormal personalities. That was the case when, in a government press release, Eichmann was declared "one of the leading technicians who gave the horror a system by means of his perverted organizational talent."[36] Eichmann was often seen as representing the anonymity of a bureaucratic machine in which human beings were turned into "robots of terror."[37] But even these interpretations did not see Eichmann or other perpetrators as individuals in control of their lives. So long as they were considered not entirely "normal"—and the visual evidence helped reinforce that impression—the perpetrators could be like "us" while still remaining distinct from "us."

The Eichmann trial thus offered an ideal opportunity to refocus the debate over the Federal Republic's policy toward former Nazi officials. The return of the images made the systematic mass murder conducted in the concentration camps the central issue in the discussion of Nazi crimes and depoliticized the issue of the rehabilitation and reintegration of Nazi officials. This divisive issue was put to rest with the new image of the perpetrators that incorporated multiple perspectives on them and the Holocaust. With the Eichmann trial, the Holocaust became the focus of a pessimistic cultural critique of modernity's technological threats and of a general debate on individual responsibility in modernity. The multiplicity of interpretations Eichmann inspired is an indication of the growing pluralism of West German society around 1960, which itself was one of the main preconditions for the return of the images.

Narrative Structures and the Closure of Remembrance

With the Eichmann trial, details of the monstrous crime were publicly discussed in West Germany for the first time. The stages from persecution to destruction were visualized by series of a few pictures each. Reduced to photographs that were taken as representative, the stages of the process—discrimination, deportation, ghettoization, and annihilation—were consistent with a teleological view of the Nazi mass murder, focusing on anti-Semitic motivation as well as on the pessimistic view of modernity highlighted during the Eichmann trial.

But the Eichmann trial was neither the first nor the only chance to give the Holocaust a visual narrative. Nazi crimes had already been represented in visual narratives a few years earlier. While written representations avoided concrete descriptions, the photographs made a more vivid impression. The relation between images and text was very ambiguous during this period. Photographs were used to illustrate, to create a sensation, or to teach. Sometimes they were presented on their own as autonomous arguments. In most cases, they were not interpreted or woven into the fabric of an accompanying text. Photographs thus complemented one another even if they were not printed on the same page. Often, however, they were deliberately presented together to produce a visual story of the Holocaust or some aspect of it.

Visual narratives were a proven means to convey information about the Holocaust. Several large, successful exhibitions—in particular one on the Warsaw Ghetto (1963) and another on Auschwitz (1963–65)—underscored the new importance of the image.[38] Books also presented photographs in narrative sequences. Gerhard Schoenberner's *Der gelbe Stern* was the most prominent. He divided the Holocaust into several acts and illustrated each with a number of pictures arranged in theater-like sequences. Film was clearly an influence in the manner of visual presentation in *Der gelbe Stern*. Montage was frequently used to heighten the visual impression. But it was the use of narrative—closer to theater than film as a result of the division of the story into acts—that brought this representation of the Holocaust from amnesia into the realm of modern visual mass media. Schoenberner and the others responsible for this narrativization used photographs of a specific graphic density to structure their presentations. The images' graphic elements were more important than the historical information they conveyed.

Even single images became a part of these virtual narratives in the 1960s when accompanied by captions that referred to overarching interpretations. Photographs became a structuring element of the overall image of Nazi crimes. They channeled public awareness of the Holocaust, designating certain elements as significant and setting them within overarching narratives. There were three fundamental narratives: explaining National Socialism as rule by terror, presenting the persecution of the Jews as the defining Nazi crime, and demonstrating the criminal structure of National Socialism and certain parts of German society.

Photographs taken early in the concentration camp period were published widely in combination with images showing how Nazi Party organizations, such as the Hitlerjugend, reorganized German society. Common to both types of images were the scenes of people passively arranged in rows by someone in uniform. Sometimes the images were juxtaposed so that the rows were set in contrast. This juxtaposition, following the double-victim-model, represented "the Germans" collectively as victims of the Nazi regime and supported the then new interpretation of Nazism as a form of totalitarianism. As a result of this narrative, even images that had provoked fascination at least into the early 1950s—photos, for example, of the Nazi Party rallies in Nuremberg—were now classified as representations of a criminal regime. But among the hundreds of images used to illustrate the twelve years of Nazi rule and the war, photographs of Nazi crimes played a minor role in terms of quantity. It was clear that they could not be left out anymore, however, precisely because they were needed to illustrate the totalitarianism argument, with its clear distinction between Nazism and German society.

Another category of scenes involved the persecution and destruction of the European Jews. Before the term "the Holocaust" became current in the 1970s, a visual narrative had evolved of the manifold events and processes encompassed by that term. Certain types of photographs representing key events—*Reichskristallnacht*, for example, or a transport arriving at the Birkenau concentration camp—were singled out. They were disconnected from the moment and place where they were taken and integrated into a symbolism of simplification. Less important as information, these images were imbued with a symbolic function and used as a stimulus for commemoration. Each of these scenes marked another step toward death and destruction. The impression they conveyed of a completely different world stemmed in part from the fact that most showed only Jews as helpless victims and also showed none of the perpetrators.

A third integrating narrative was based on a provocative, sometimes political use of photographs found in opposition newspapers and publications. Images of perpetrators, either portraits or pictures of them "at work," were deliberately juxtaposed with images of victims. In many cases, the victims were not only Jews. The juxtaposition was intended to argue against the main restrictions of both the totalitarianism narrative and the destruction narrative. Most challenging was that these images added industry, the army, and the bureaucracy to representations of the Third Reich, thereby extending the circle of people and institutions implicated in the Nazi system. Illustrating their involvement was, of course, not easy. These narratives were, therefore, dominated by the visual construction of the relationship between perpetrators and victims. Portraits were arranged with photographs showing camps or victims, and the relationship between the subjects depicted in the portraits and their victims was explained in a caption or accompanying text. The use of images that were not part of the other integrating narratives was different in another respect: one could see executions or dead bodies. This confrontation took up the repressed imagery from 1945 with the political intent to criticize not only the involvement of those depicted in the Nazi past but also the fragmentary memory and political restoration that accompanied the other integrating narratives.

Photographic Emotionality and the Symbolic Texture of Memory

The range of Holocaust photographs that were published was broader than a term like "icons of annihilation" might suggest. Although a few images were used more often than others, none stood out. The only one that came close to being an exception was the image of a young boy with his arms raised in the air that was taken during the liquidation of the Warsaw ghetto. There are two more reasons why it would be misleading to use the term "icon" in connection with Holocaust imagery. First, its religious connotation cannot be transferred to these photographs and the ways they have been used. Only in a few cases were these images thought to be of commemorative value; more often, they were used primarily as sources of information or as illustrations. Secondly, icons are normally associated with faces and individuals. Only a minor part of the Holocaust imagery in Germany showed individuals. The visual discourse was dominated, rather, by images of groups, of masses of people, or scenes without any people at all. The visualization of the Holocaust generally did not present the victims as either individuals or as stylized, representative figures to be admired.

The imagery of the Holocaust in Germany was nonetheless iconographically structured through certain recurrent scenes, motifs, and visual elements. Hands, bodies, faces, and postures made individuals and groups recognizable as victims.

One of these motifs was the poignant facial expressions of the victims. Images of this sort came closest to functioning as icons, although this motif could be found in a broad range of photographs. But they served as a certain kind of emotionalization, since the terrified victims were used as a *punctum*, as Roland Barthes defines the term,[39] that attracted the viewer. They embodied an exceptional symbolic intensity compared with the many deserted camp images.[40] They corresponded to the leading style in photo journalism in the 1950s, "Life"-photography. Challenged by the growing technical possibilities of the television, press photographers elaborated a style which had already been invented by war coverage in the 1930s. It stressed dramatic moments and human emotions which needed to be represented as straight as possible without covering the brutality as such. Images of people looking at dead bodies or crying in front of the camera were an innovation of this period. Thus, the principles according to which Holocaust photographs were chosen were influenced by more general trends of photo journalism.

Holocaust photos of this sort were used in particular in textbooks to bring students close to the recent past on an emotional level. The use of "exemplary images" as a pedagogic method was developed in the 1950s and had served as an important tool in the teaching of history in German schools.[41] Whereas icons create identification through distance, the use of these exemplary images in schools was meant to overcome the distance between present and past and to foster the return to a human view of the victims. At the same time, these images made the cruelty of Nazi crimes a taboo; for pedagogic reasons, it was a rule until the 1990s not to use any of the atrocity images in schools.

Rather than showing dead bodies, Holocaust imagery in Germany was generally limited to passive but still living victims. Their body language presented them exactly as the opposite to the German *Landser*. As the *Landser* was part of a general attempt to overcome the "crisis of masculinity" in the 1950s, the Jewish victims were not presented as fighters or even as strong individuals. Even when the Warsaw Ghetto uprising was visualized, publishers and authors selected pictures from the "Stroop Report" that showed Jews as cowering families or groups guarded by victorious German soldiers. Obviously, there was a need to bring the pain and the horror of the Jews back to the German people. But in addressing that need, visual stereotypes that had long been used by anti-Semites to stigmatize Jews were reproduced. To be sure, some photographs of defeated German soldiers were part of the public visual memory. But these images dovetailed with the attempt to integrate the German army within the category of victims, and they were offset by a multitude of photographs portraying soldiers as courageous and noble.

A third element of the symbolic structure of visual memory was topographic.[42] Photographic images of sites where Nazi crimes had taken place created an extraterritorial perspective. Most of these pictures were of concentration camps. Because these photographs were often denounced as fabrications and seen as attempts to undermine German political culture, they were kept out of sight as far as possible. This practice continued a tradition that had developed before 1945, when the Nazis countered accusatory visual materials from Eastern Europe

did refer to the war when they mentioned Auschwitz. But what mattered was the war experience of helpless children, the victims of an anonymous system of destruction that could be associated with a more general structure of economic exploitation and capitalist interests. Nazi crimes per se seem to have held much less relevance for the students and activists than their projection of their own experience of war and violence onto those crimes. By stressing this, they imbued the visual representation of Nazi crimes with a new political interpretation, but they did not overcome the shortcomings of its visual symbolism, which still left out the intimate relationship between Nazi crimes and German society.

Conclusion

The political adaptation of the Auschwitz photographic imagery of Nazi crimes by intellectuals, students, and political activists makes clear that the set of images that was established between 1955 and 1965 was open to manifold interpretations. West German memory culture was multipartite and contested, even if the dominant narratives of the destruction of the Jews and of Auschwitz as a death factory had such a determining quality that they were not really challenged by opposing interpretations. To understand this phenomenon, one has to take into account its roots in the 1950s and, especially, German reactions in 1945. The brief upheaval in the late 1960s was only a variation on this general narrative. It added certain perspectives on the recent past but did not produce a new perspective that overcame the inherent repression of memory. Thus, the "modernization" of memory took place between 1955 and 1965 when Nazi crimes attracted public attention and when they were reinvented as a visual, emotional, but virtual and limited experience. In the "long" 1960s that began in the second half of the 1950s, West German society continued its long process of "coming to terms with the past." It produced its images of Nazi crimes to serve not as a mirror but as a movie of something that took place far away and remote from everyday life. Central elements of the crimes remained repressed in the imagery into the 1990s, even among the onetime student activists. The visual archive of Nazi crimes in Germany reveals the inherent limitations of the commemorative pattern and of the power of cultures to determine the meaning of polysemic photographs.

Notes

1. See my study *Die Tat als Bild: Fotografien des Holocaust in der deutschen Erinnerungskultur* (Hamburg, 2001), covering the use of photographs of Nazi atrocities between 1933 and 1970 in a wide range of public media such as daily newspapers, illustrated magazines, schoolbooks, exhibitions, films and book publications. More detailed references will be found there. See also, with a detailed discussion of several important examples, but somewhat neglectful of the socio-cultural context, Cornelia Brink, *Ikonen der Vernichtung: Öffentlicher Gebrauch von Fotografien aus nationalsozialistischen Konzentrationslagern nach 1945* (Berlin, 1998).
2. For the iconographical context, see Dagmar Barnouw, *Germany 1945: Views of War and Violence* (Bloomington, 1996). Their use in the US is discussed at length in Barbie Zelizer, *Remembering to Forget: Holocaust Memory Through the Camera's Eyes* (Chicago, 1998).
3. Cf. Knoch, *Tat als Bild*, 123–236; Brink, *Ikonen der Vernichtung*, 23–99.
4. For early overviews concentrating on the political-legal dimension, see Peter Steinbach, "Zur Auseinandersetzung mit nationalsozialistischen Gewaltverbrechen in der Bundesrepublik Deutschland: Ein Beitrag zur politischen Kultur nach 1945," *Geschichte in Wissenschaft und Unterricht* 35 (1984): 65–85; Peter Reichel, "Vergangenheitsbewältigung als Problem unserer politischen Kultur: Einstellungen zum Dritten Reich und seine Folgen," in *Vergangenheitsbewältigung durch Strafverfahren? NS-Prozesse in der Bundesrepublik Deutschland*, ed. Jürgen Weber and Peter Steinbach (Munich, 1984), 145–63; Detlef Garbe, "Äußerliche Abkehr, Erinnerungsverweigerung und 'Vergangenheitsbewältigung': Der Umgang mit dem Nationalsozialismus in der frühen Bundesrepublik," in *Modernisierung im Wiederaufbau: Die westdeutsche Gesellschaft der 50er Jahre*, ed. Axel Schildt and Arnold Sywottek (Bonn, 1993), 693–716.
5. Unfortunately, the topic of photography and memory has been left out almost completely by the protagonists of a German "Gedächtniswissenschaft," Jan and Aleida Assmann. See, for example, Jan Assmann, *Das kulturelle Gedächtnis: Schrift, Erinnerung und politische Identität in frühen Hochkulturen* (Munich, 1992), or Aleida Assmann, *Erinnerungsräume: Formen und Wandlungen des kulturellen Gedächtnisses* (Munich, 1999). Although the topic deserves more systematic attention, an important starting point is Roland Barthes, *Die helle Kammer: Bemerkung zur Photographie* (Frankfurt am Main, 1985). Still important is Eric L. Santner, *Stranded Objects: Mourning, Memory, and Film in Postwar Germany* (Ithaca, 1990).
6. Conceptual observations with regard to images of the recent past were first made by Jürgen Hanig, "Bilder, die Geschichte machen: Anmerkungen zum Umgang mit 'Dokumentarfotos' in Geschichtslehrbüchern," *Geschichte in Wissenschaft und Unterricht* 40 (1989): 10–32, and Harald Welzer, "Die Bilder der Macht und die Ohnmacht der Bilder: Über Besetzung und Auslöschung von Erinnerung," in *Das Gedächtnis der Bilder: Ästhetik und Nationalsozialismus*, ed. Harald Welzer (Tübingen, 1995), 165–94. On photographs of the Holocaust as sources, see the early studies by Sybil Milton, e.g., "The Camera as Weapon: Documentary Photography and the Holocaust," *Simon Wiesenthal Center Annual* 1 (1984): 45–68; Milton, "Images of the Holocaust," *Holocaust and Genocide Studies* 1 (1986): 27–61, 193–216.
7. Cf. Saul Friedländer, ed., *Probing the Limits of Representation* (Cambridge, MA, 1992).
8. Cf. Helmut Lethen, "Der Text der Historiografie und der Wunsch nach einer physikalischen Spur. Das Problem der Fotografie in den beiden Wehrmachtsausstellungen," *Zeitgeschichte* 29 (2002): 76–86.
9. Cf. Norbert Frei, "Von deutscher Erfindungskraft oder: Die Kollektivschuldthese in der Nachkriegszeit," *Rechtshistorisches Journal* 16 (1997): 621–34; Bernd Weisbrod, "Der 8. Mai in der deutschen Erinnerung," *Werkstatt Geschichte* 13 (1996): 72–81.
10. Cf. Robert Gellately, *Backing Hitler: Consent and Coercion in Nazi Germany* (Oxford, 2001); Knoch, *Tat als Bild*, 65–122.
11. Cf. Knoch, *Tat als Bild*, 123–236; Brink, *Ikonen der Vernichtung*, 23–99.
12. Cf. Norbert Frei, *Vergangenheitspolitik. Die Anfänge der Bundesrepublik und die NS-Vergangenheit* (Munich, 1996).

13. Cf. Edgar Wolfrum, "Der Kult um den verlorenen Nationalstaat in der Bundesrepublik Deutschland bis Mitte der 60er Jahre," *Historische Anthropologie* 5 (1997): 83–114, and *Geschichtspolitik in der Bundesrepublik Deutschland. Der Weg zur bundesrepublikanischen Erinnerung 1948–1990* (Darmstadt, 1999).

14. One example is Ernst Reuter's speech in 1953, "'Kristallnacht' 1938. Erinnerungsansprache," *Bulletin des Bundespresseamtes*, 15 November 1951, 56.

15. Cf. Knoch, *Tat als Bild*, 429–67. For illustrated magazines, see especially Michael Schornstheimer, *Bombenstimmung und Katzenjammer. Vergangenheitsbewältigung: Quick und Stern in den 50er Jahren* (Cologne, 1989).

16. Cf. Bundeszentrale für Heimatdienst, ed, *20. Juli 1944* (Bonn, 1953); *Bekenntnis und Verpflichtung. Reden und Aufsätze zur zehnjährigen Wiederkehr des 20. Juli 1944* (Stuttgart, 1955).

17. For further indications, see Clemens Vollnhals, "Zwischen Verdrängung und Aufklärung. Die Auseinandersetzung mit dem Holocaust in der frühen Bundesrepublik," in Ursula Büttner, ed., *Die Deutschen und die Judenverfolgung im Dritten Reich* (Hamburg, 1992), 357–92; Hartmut Berghoff, "Zwischen Verdrängung und Aufarbeitung. Die bundesdeutsche Gesellschaft und ihre nationalsozialistische Vergangenheit in den fünfziger Jahren," *Geschichte in Wissenschaft und Unterricht* 49 (1998): 96–114; Axel Schildt, "Der Umgang mit der NS-Vergangenheit in der Öffentlichkeit der Nachkriegszeit," in Wilfried Loth, Bernd A. Rusinek, eds., *Verwandlungspolitik. NS-Eliten in der westdeutschen Nachkriegsgesellschaft* (Frankfurt am Main, 1998), 19–54.

18. Moeller, *War Stories*.

19. Léon Poliakov and Joseph Wulf, *Das Dritte Reich und die Juden* (Berlin, 1955).

20. Gerhard Schoenberner, *Der gelbe Stern. Die Judenvernichtung in Europa 1933–1945* (Hamburg, 1960).

21. Reimund Schnabel, *Macht ohne Moral. Dokumentation über die SS* (Frankfurt am Main 1957).

22. Cf. Erwin Leiser, *Mein Kampf: Eine Bilddokumentation* (Frankfurt am Main 1961).

23. Contrary to what is suggested by the title, Cornelia Brink has discussed this problematic concept only in an annex to her book, *Ikonen der Vernichtung*.

24. Cf. Klaus Bästlein, "'Nazi-Blutrichter als Stützen des Adenauer-Regimes'. Die DDR-Kampagnen gegen NS-Richter und -Staatsanwälte, die Reaktionen der bundesdeutschen Justiz und ihre gescheiterte Selbstreinigung 1957–1968," in Helge Grabitz, Klaus Bästlein, Johannes Tuchel, eds., *Die Normalität des Verbrechens. Bilanz und Perspektiven der Forschung zu den nationalsozialistischen Gewaltverbrechen* (Berlin, 1994), 408–43; Michael Lemke, "Kampagnen gegen Bonn. Die Systemkrise der DDR und die West-Propaganda 1960–1963," *Vierteljahrshefte für Zeitgeschichte* 41 (1993): 153–174.

25. Cf. Werner Bergmann, *Antisemitismus in öffentlichen Konflikten: Kollektives Lernen in der politischen Kultur der Bundesrepublik 1949–1989* (Frankfurt am Main. 1997).

26. Horst Krüger, "Die Schatten von gestern. Ist der Antisemitismus in Deutschland noch lebendig?" *Die Welt*, 20 April 1956.

27. Cf. Knoch, *Tat als Bild*, 266, 495, 533, 559, and 647.

28. "Der Satan heißt Sommer," *Stern*, 1956, no 42.

29. Martin Broszat, "Einleitung [1958]," in Martin Broszat, ed., *Kommandant in Auschwitz. Autobiographische Aufzeichnungen des Rudolf Höß* (Munich, 1985), 7–21.

30. Hans Egon Holthusen, "Hannah Arendt, Eichmann und die Kritiker," *Vierteljahrshefte für Zeitgeschichte* 13 (1965): 178–90, 183.

31. Klaus Mehnert, "Was haben wir mit Eichmann zu tun?" *Christ und Welt*, 21 April 1961.

32. Gerhard Schoenberner, "Der Prozeß Eichmann—und die Folgen," *Frankfurter Hefte* 16 (1961): 433–34, 434.

33. *Bild*, 16 June 1961; *Revue* 1961, no. 17, 8.

34. "Jetzt steht die Vergangenheit auf," *Quick* 1961, no. 14, 19.

35. "Der Endlöser," *Spiegel* 1960 no. 25, 20–21.

36. "Bulletin des Bundespresseamtes," quoted in Hans Lamm, ed., *Der Eichmann-Prozeß in der deutschen öffentlichen Meinung* (Frankfurt am Main, 1961), 1.

37. Robert Penderl, "Weil ich Treue geschworen hatte …," *Die Zeit*, 21 July 1961.

38. Cf. Cornelia Brink, *Auschwitz in der Paulskirche: Erinnerungspolitik in Fotoausstellungen der 60erJahre* (Frankfurt am Main, 2001).

39. Roland Barthes, *Die helle Kammer. Bemerkung zur Photographie* (Frankfurt am Main, 1985), 36.

40. This emptiness of the camps has been commented photographically by Reinhard Matz, *Die unsichtbaren Lager. Das Verschwinden der Vergangenheit im Gedenken* (Reinbek, 1993); Dirk Reinartz, *Totenstill. Bilder aus ehemaligen deutschen Konzentrationslagern* (Göttingen, 1994); Erich Hartmann, *Stumme Zeugen. Photographien aus Konzentrationslagern* (Gerlingen, 1995).

41. For this concept, see, for example, Konrad Barthel, "Das Exemplarische im Geschichtsunterricht," *Geschichte in Wissenschaft und Unterricht* 8 (1958): 216–30.

42. Cf. Detlef Hoffmann, "Fotografierte Lager. Überlegungen zu einer Fotogeschichte deutscher Konzentrationslager," *Fotogeschichte* 14 (1994) no. 54: 3–20; Habbo Knoch, "Die Erinnerung der Ruinen. Fotografische Landschaften des Holocaust," *Jahrbuch für Volkskunde* N.F. 23 (2000): 135–56.

43. Cf. Alf Lüdtke, "Der Bann der Wörter: 'Todesfabriken'. Vom Reden über den NS-Völkermord—das auch ein Verschweigen ist," *Werkstatt Geschichte* 13 (1996): 5–18.

44. Cf. Yasmin Doosry, "Vom Dokument zur Ikone: Zur Rezeption des Auschwitz-Albums," in Yasmin Doosry, ed., *Representations of Auschwitz. 50 Years of Photographs, Paintings, and Graphics* (Oswiecim, 1995), 95–102.

45. See, for example, *Weltbild*, 2 and 9 December 1960; *Spiegel* 1963, no. 51; *Spiegel* 1964, no. 12; *Vorwärts*, 31 August 1966, as well as in Schoenberner, *Der gelbe Stern*; Heinz Huber, Artur Müller, *Das Dritte Reich. Seine Geschichte in Texten, Bildern und Dokumenten*, vol. 2 (Munich, 1964), 531; Internationale Föderation der Widerstandskämpfer, ed., *Die SS-Henker und ihre Opfer. Auschwitz 1940–1945* (Vienna, 1965), 11–12; H. G. Adler, Hermann Langbein, and Ella Lingens-Reiner, eds., *Auschwitz. Zeugnisse und Berichte* (Frankfurt am Main, 1962).

46. Cf. Detlef Hoffmann, "Auschwitz im visuellen Gedächtnis. Das Chaos des Verbrechens und die symbolische Ordnung der Bilder," Fritz-Bauer-Institut, ed., *Auschwitz: Geschichte, Wirkung und Rezeption* (Frankfurt am Main, 1996), 223–58; and the valuable studies in Detlef Hoffmann, ed., *Das Gedächtnis der Dinge. KZ-Relikte und KZ-Denkmäler 1945–1995* (Frankfurt am Main, 1998).

47. Cf. Hans-Ulrich Thamer, "Die NS-Vergangenheit im politischen Diskurs der 68er-Bewegung," *Westfälische Forschungen* 48 (1998): 39–53; Detlef Siegfried, "Zwischen Aufarbeitung und Schlußstrich. Der Umgang mit der NS-Vergangenheit in den beiden deutschen Staaten 1958 bis 1969," in Axel Schildt, Detlef Siegfried, and Karl Christian Lammers, eds., *Dynamische Zeiten. Die 60er Jahre in den beiden deutschen Gesellschaften* (Hamburg, 2000), 77–113; Bernd-A. Rusinek, "Von der Entdeckung der NS-Vergangenheit zum generellen Faschismusverdacht—akademische Diskurse in der Bundesrepublik der 60er Jahre," in Schildt, et al., *Dynamische Zeiten*, 114–47.

Chapter 3

EXPLANATION, DISSOCIATION, APOLOGIA

The Debate over the Criminal Prosecution of
Nazi Crimes in the 1960s

Marc von Miquel

❧

The major Nazi trials of the 1960s inspired more than a few intellectuals to reflect on how the past was being dealt with in the Federal Republic of Germany. Tübingen sociologist Ralf Dahrendorf was one such figure. He noticed a relaxing of the historical memory—or, perhaps more accurately, the historical forgetting—of the Adenauer era: "The long, stifling silence is breaking, and serious coping [will be] possible."[1] In Dahrendorf's opinion, the trials were having a widespread impact that should not be underestimated. That was true above all of the Auschwitz trial, which received significant coverage in all the major daily newspapers from its opening before a Frankfurt court in December 1963. "In fact," he wrote in a commentary for the Basel *National-Zeitung*, "these trials have found such wide publicity that even those [West Germans] who would dearly like to shield themselves are unable to totally avoid [the trial's] terrible disclosures." The sociologist not only called for the punishment of Nazi perpetrators, but he also addressed the then hotly debated question of whether the statute of limitations on murders committed by the Nazis should be extended beyond 8 May 1965.

In contrast to Chancellor Ludwig Erhard, who tried to maneuver through the politically charged debate, Dahrendorf held that the legal obligation to punish the Nazis' mass crimes outweighed the formal juridical arguments. He called for the statute to be extended so that even perpetrators who had yet to be identified could eventually be brought to court. What makes Dahrendorf's statement interesting is his effort, in which he was not alone during the debate over the statute of limitations, to take account of how the Nazi past was being dealt with in the 1960s. Looking beyond the positions taken in the debate, Dahrendorf

---

Notes for this chapter begin on page 61.

asked why West Germans were now ready "to openly and clearly name the crimes by name"—why at that particular moment in history and not previously.[2] The search for the reasons behind this "[serious] coping" also motivates the reflections that follow. It took fifteen years for the West German justice system to begin prosecuting Nazi crimes in earnest. The reasons for the delay are anything but self-evident. The delay requires an explanation.

From a historical perspective, the most important outcome of these trials was the way they thematized the central crimes of National Socialism and the destruction of European Jewry. The manner in which they did this requires careful exploration. Which legal, political, and media typologies were employed to represent National Socialist crimes, above all the Holocaust? How was the murderous violence judged? Explanation, dissociation, and apologia, I contend, were all themes evident in the debate over the Nazi past in the 1960s. At times, these themes conflicted with each other; at other moments, they overlapped. The 1960s were a decade characterized by conflict. In the case of Nazi crimes, this meant that the previous consensus favoring the integration of Nazi perpetrators into postwar society began to erode. In retrospect, one can see in the 1960s a pronounced normative break from National Socialism.

An interdisciplinary discourse on the reasons for this break and its consequences is now underway. Recent years have seen a welcome increase in historical, legal, literary, pedagogic, and psychoanalytic studies. This essay aims to contribute to this discussion from a historical perspective by outlining some important stages in the course of the public debate over Nazi crimes. These include: an increase in prosecutions beginning in 1957–58; the public discourse on the Eichmann and Auschwitz trials; and the debate over the statute of limitations (1965). In closing, I will take up Dahrendorf's ideas again in a speculative summary of the origins and effects of these debates.

The Increase in Prosecutions

In the early postwar years, the reestablished German courts in the Western zones of occupation tried a considerable number of criminal murder cases connected with the National Socialist "euthanasia" program, actions in concentration camps, and atrocities during the final phases of the war.[3] There were very few prosecutions during the 1950s. Preliminary investigations, too, all but dried up in a society that sought to integrate even the most serious Nazi perpetrators.[4] Criminal charges were filed only in isolated cases and without the support of justice officials. It is surprising, then, that the number of prosecutions began to increase in 1957–58 and that these trials sparked remarkable public interest.

The first of this new wave of court cases was the Schörner trial in the fall of 1957. It presented the alarming argument that individual Wehrmacht units were responsible for mass executions.[5] Next came the Bayreuth criminal case against former SS member Martin Sommer in 1958. This trial of Buchenwald's *Arrestverwalter* found great resonance in the media. The witnesses against Sommer left a tormenting impression of the excessive force used in the camp, triggering deep emotional responses. Sensitized by this trial, journalists then turned to the ongoing trial in Ulm of one-time Einsatzgruppen members accused of the mass murder of Lithuanian Jews. For the first time since the Nuremberg trials of leading war criminals, the public was confronted with detailed information about the destruction of European Jewry. The Ulm trial revealed that hundreds of those who had participated in murderous actions had not yet been brought before the courts. Consequently, the justice system was accused of a massive failure.[6] This public outcry would not have occurred were it not for Erwin Schüle, the lead prosecutor in the Ulm trial. Schüle, supported by Stuttgart public prosecutor Erich Nellmann, expanded his investigation to look into the actions of others in addition to the individual originally accused, former police commander Bernhard Fischer-Schweder. Schüle conducted intensive archival research and brought charges against nine additional members of the task force (*Einsatzcommando*) to which Fischer-Schweder belonged.

Startled both by the extent of the crimes and the lack of interest in them, particularly among justice officials, Schüle and Nellmann pushed to systematically strengthen prosecutorial efforts. Fast action was required, however, as the statute of limitations on the vast majority of Nazi crimes was set to expire on 8 May 1960.[7] Following accepted precedent, acts of manslaughter and abetment would soon be out of the reach of the law.[8] In 1958, justice officials did not consider extending the statute of limitations.

Shortly after the verdict in the Ulm trial, Nellmann gave the decisive stimulus for a public discussion about establishing a central authority for prosecuting Nazi crimes. He had proposed the ideas to the justice minister of Baden-Württemberg and published an article in the *Stuttgarter Zeitung*. As its title made clear, the article was an appeal: "Central Committee of Inquiry Must Bring Clarity to [National Socialist] Crimes."[9] Nellmann suggested, first, that the officials of the new central office be given unlimited prosecutorial authority, and second, that they should be responsible for investigation as well as prosecution. In October 1958, the state justice ministers adopted a plan to create such an office, which was to be based in Ludwigsburg, but they restricted its competence. Under the agreement of the states, the central office would be responsible only for preliminary investigations; it would have to turn cases over to the states for prosecution. Moreover, it had to restrict its investigations to criminal acts committed outside of the territory of the Federal Republic of Germany. Above all, the central office was intended to address the extermination of European Jews and the crimes committed in concentration camps. Investigation of military war crimes, including the murder of Soviet prisoners of war, military participation in the Holocaust, and the massacre of civilian populations carried out under the guise of "antipartisan actions," was explicitly excluded from its purview. In the minds of its founders, the central office would be a temporary agency. To prevent it from "getting out of hand," it was allowed no more than eleven public attorneys and an equal number of administrative assistants.[10]

Considering the serious restrictions placed upon the central office, why were policy makers willing to establish it in the first place? At the time, they maintained that the Ulm trial alone had been the impetus. They did not anticipate how the justice system, suffering from a lack of legitimacy involving more than public criticism of prosecutorial shortcomings, would react. The general charges against the West German justice system were expressed most clearly by the noted jurist Ernst Müller-Meiningen, Jr., in the *Süddeutsche Zeitung*. In an article on the outcome of the Ulm trial, Müller-Meiningen went beyond calling for investigation of suspected Nazi perpetrators. He lashed out, calling it a scandal that former Nazi judges (*Sonderrichter*) continued to practice their profession despite their incriminating pasts. "Would it have been possible to avoid this entire dunghill cleaning?" He asked. "Only if one had fundamentally reorganized the courts at war's end—by replacing personnel—and had handed the administration of justice over to a new generation. Because this was not possible at the time, the undeniable and inextricable film of past injustice still clings to us. As before, this places the German rule of law in question."[11]

These fundamental reservations about the West German judicial system were reinforced by an East German propaganda campaign against so-called blood judges (*Blutrichter*). The steady stream of "revelations" coming out of East Berlin caused such a sensation, first in England and then in the Federal Republic, that policymakers felt compelled to take action. While the accusation of insufficient prosecutions could be refuted with help from the central office in Ludwigsburg, the "cleansing" of individual judges remained an issue, to say nothing of the prosecution of past juridically sanctioned murders. The response was the enactment of the "judges law" (*Richtergesetz*) in 1961, which led to the early retirement of 135 judges. This law reflected, however, the general strategy of appeasement on the part of the government and parliamentary opposition alike.[12] Their most important objective was to avoid public debate. But despite such steps, the West German government found itself increasingly on the defensive toward the end of the Adenauer era. Bonn's policy was also driven by further revelations out of East Germany concerning Chief Federal Prosecutor Wolfgang Fränkel. He had previously served in the Reich Solicitor's office and in that capacity had sought the death penalty in numerous cases of petty offences.[13]

The Public Discourse on the Eichmann and Auschwitz Trials

Even Konrad Adenauer, who spoke of Nazi crimes only with great reluctance, could not avoid commenting on the Eichmann trial. The start of the trial in 1961 prompted the chancellor to hold a series of press conferences and even a television address. He predicted that the trial would "once again dig up all the heinousness of the Hitler regime" and said it would be "very human if unbiased persons recoiled from these horrors."[14] The West German public was, however, anything but unbiased. Inge Deutschkron, then a journalist in Bonn, reported that the

Germans were shocked and virtually paralyzed by feelings of guilt when first confronted with news of the testimony and accusations by Holocaust survivors.[15]

Far from ignoring the proceedings in Jerusalem as Adenauer speculated they might, up to 85 percent of the population followed them in detail through both newspaper and television reports.[16] The attitude of Germans toward the trial in Israel, which was seen as the "land of the victims," oscillated between fascination and dismissal. A public opinion poll at the end of the trial found that 85 percent approved of the death penalty for Eichmann, 53 percent wished to forget the Nazis' crimes, and only 8 percent felt "somehow implicated."[17] Opinion polls at the time of the Auschwitz trial produced no less contradictory findings. On the one hand, 60 percent of those surveyed expressed a more or less constant interest in the case against twenty-four former members of the Auschwitz camp staff. On the other hand, between 52 and 69 percent surveyed in 1964–65 wanted to see an end to the prosecution of Nazi crimes. Only 34 percent had expressed that view in 1958. One year after the Auschwitz trial, the figure had sunk back to 44 percent.[18]

In all likelihood, it was the intensive media coverage of the Auschwitz trial that turned the public against the prosecution of Nazi crimes. National daily newspapers covered almost all of the proceedings for a year and a half, from December 1963 until a verdict was pronounced on 19 August 1965. The most impressive accounts were the sober, unembellished reports by Bernd Naumann of the *Frankfurter Allgemeine Zeitung*, which later served as the basis for Peter Weiss's play *The Investigation (Die Ermittlung)*.[19] Other media outlets—radio, television, and the tabloid press—also came to report regularly on the Auschwitz trial. One result of this coverage was that a nearly empty courtroom eventually filled. Altogether, some twenty thousand spectators came to the court seeking an immediate impression of the proceedings.[20] Together with the extensive media coverage, these numbers attest to the exceptional attention paid to the Auschwitz trial compared with other Nazi trials in West Germany. The concurrent trial in Düsseldorf against former SS men from the Treblinka concentration camp was hardly noticed by the national press. A year later, the Sobibor trial before the state court in Hagen received almost no attention.[21] The topic of National Socialist mass crimes seemed to have run its course as a media event with the Auschwitz trial. But this did not reflect the views of the population, which had undergone fundamental change.

How were Nazi trials represented in the West German press? What picture of the National Socialist regime and its monstrous crimes was presented? The national daily and weekly newspapers as well as television commentators saw the two major Nazi crime trials as opportunities to retell the history of the era, presenting a new account that clearly abandoned interpretations of the recent past publicly cultivated during the 1950s. The myths that had grown out of totalitarian theory, in which a small clique led by Hitler alone carried the responsibility for the mass crimes, gave way to a more nuanced account. The Eichmann trial in particular turned into a lesson in contemporary history. The prosecution attempted to reconstruct the genocide in its entirety from its genesis, making clear the connections between institutions and relying on both documentation and eyewitness accounts. Unavoidably, the trial's findings, in keeping with the rules of journalistic brevity, were presented by the press in cursory fashion. Nevertheless, the educational function of the reporting—to explain the history of Nazi rule and the regime's crimes—stands out. This was the case, first and foremost, with the television documentary *The Third Reich*. This fourteen-part series, a joint production of the Süd- and Westdeutschen Rundfunk, was broadcast during the Eichmann trial and rebroadcast in 1963 before the opening of the Auschwitz trial. It was seen by at least fifteen million West Germans. Although the television series offered a comprehensive interpretation of the period between 1933 and 1945, it confined itself to the history of political events and left out the question of the shared responsibility of segments of society such as the conservative bourgeoisie.[22]

The enormous media interest in the Eichmann and Auschwitz trials reinforced prevailing historical distortions. Many press accounts demonized the accused. This tendency was already apparent in the prosecution's argument in Jerusalem, and the press, especially the tabloids, eagerly took it up. More than a few West German journalists saw Eichmann as a sadistic murderer simply playing the role of an upright, dispassionate administrator, as someone whose inconspicuous appearance camouflaged a capacity for unusual cruelty. News stories about the Auschwitz trial tended to treat the division of labor involved in the genocide—the central structural characteristic of the Holocaust—only in brief. They emphasized instead so-called excessive acts. "The Coup de Grâce during the Breakfast Break" and "Women Driven into Fire Alive" were among the sensational headlines that appeared in the tabloid press's coverage of the trial.[23]

Over the course of the trial, the names of the torturer Wilhelm Boger and the killer Oswald Kaduk became synonyms for Nazi crimes. By constructing this image of tantalizingly abhorrent individual perpetrators, the media was able to bring its coverage in line with the judgments of the West German courts. Those were based on the definition of murder dating back to the criminal code of 1871, not on the doctrine of crimes against humanity established in Nuremberg. But according to legal scholar Claus Roxin, one of the first jurists to attempt to reassess Nazi injustices according to appropriate legal criteria, the murder statute was geared toward "conventional" offenses committed by individuals against social norms and was thus not adequate for addressing "criminal acts in the realm of [an] organized power apparatus."[24] Even more decisive than the inadequacy of the murder statute was the frequently strained interpretation of it by West German judges, who often contradicted their own findings. Judges ascribed a subordinate role to the majority of defendants and found them guilty of the less serious offense of accessory to murder. Moreover, the courts developed the practice of terminating proceedings in cases where the details of every defendant's participation in acts of murder could not be determined.

This judicial practice reflected the dominant attitude toward Nazi criminals in West German society. Many judges and members of the press insisted on viewing the accused as individual perpetrators who had acted outside the social norms of the Nazi era. This position reflected a widespread need to create distance and to defend German society against feelings of guilt. If Eichmann, Boger, and Kaduk fit the conventional conception of the perverse criminal, contemporaries could ignore the insight that struck every attentive observer of the trials—namely, that the accused were *ordinary men* of their time, as the historian Christopher R. Browning later made clear in his study of Reserve Police Battalion 101.[25] In his summation at the Auschwitz trial, Henry Ormond, an attorney appearing as a joint plaintiff, stressed that the accused almost all came from "solid middle-class families"; eight of them had completed university degrees, two had passed their preliminary examinations, and the rest had apprenticed as salesmen or craftsmen. In addition, they were all raised as Christians, "something that did not hinder their unscrupulous sinning against all of God's commandments."[26]

If the accused were not outsiders but typical representatives of German society during the Nazi era, then perhaps, in contrast to the view implicit in the court rulings and press accounts, most adults had the potential, in the radical political and moral atmosphere of the time, to commit such murders. This conclusion, however strongly supported by evidence presented during the trials, was resisted by the public.[27] A debate on the different forms of complicity—be it the involvement of elite functionaries in the politics of genocide or the profit a sizeable portion of the population derived from the dispossession of Jews—could be voided by this focus on individual perpetrators.

The Debate on the Statute of Limitations

However varied opinions and forms of representation may have been, the West German discourse on the Nazi trials consistently revolved around the question of guilt. Karl Jaspers had addressed the issue in a brief study published in 1946, and for the next decade the question seemed to have been settled.[28] With the proliferation of trials beginning in the late 1950s, questions of guilt and responsibility were taken up with a new sense of urgency. In the political sphere, this was clearly evident in the controversy surrounding the statute of limitations on the prosecution of Nazi murders. The contrasting opinions on who should be assigned guilt and how responsibility ought to be judged were presented in a now famous Bundestag debate on 10 March 1965. Representing one side was Rainer Barzel, leader of the joint Christian Democratic Union-Christian Social Union (CDU/CSU) caucus; the other side was led by Adolf Arndt, the legal expert of the Social Democratic Party (SPD).

Barzel, true to the prevailing attitude of the 1950s, echoed the central tenets of an apologetic politics of memory in the opening of his speech. Because he misused their patriotism, Hitler bore "enormous guilt before the German people," but the Germans bore no collective responsibility.[29] Barzel repeated an established interpretation of the past in which the Germans were represented as the helpless victims of the dictator. With regard to criminal prosecution, Barzel argued that only the courts had the right to judge individual guilt. All forms of complicity that did not lead to legal convictions, he insisted, fell under the "right of political error," a concept put forward by Eugen Kogon in 1947. Barzel's argument implicitly posited the individual's right to disavow responsibility for one's own actions during the Nazi dictatorship.[30]

Arndt took the opposite standpoint in the debate. His spontaneous and unscripted performance is considered a shining moment in German parliamentary history. Following Jaspers, Arndt reflected on the various forms of responsibility. In addition to criminal responsibility, which Barzel had acknowledged, there was, he noted, also historical and moral responsibility. In the spirit of a Protestant examination of conscience (*Gewissensbefragung*), Arndt confessed his personal responsibility. He said that he had known during the war that the disabled were being systematically murdered, and he maintained that many Wehrmacht soldiers stationed in the occupied East had known of the extermination of Jews. "The essentials were known," he concluded, contradicting prevailing excuses.

The SPD representative went beyond this provocative claim and declared: "I know of my own responsibility, because you see, I did not go onto the streets and cry out as I saw that the Jews were being transported by truck out of our midst. I did not don the yellow star and say: Me too! I cannot say that I did enough. I do not know who wants to say this. But it obliges us—it is an inheritance."[31] This statement is surprising, especially considering that Arndt, whose father had converted from Judaism to Protestantism, himself had experienced repression under the Nazis.[32] Perhaps his statements represent the feelings of guilt many survivors felt toward murdered relatives and friends. In any event, the most extraordinary aspect of the speech lay in Arndt's sincere attempt at personal accountability. Compared to the parliamentary speeches of his older colleagues, such as Thomas Dehler of the Free Democratic Party (FDP), Arndt—by recalling his personal experience, by his uncomfortable candor and his moral claims—decisively broke out of the behavioral pattern of his generation.

Arndt's stance in the parliamentary debate marked a change in public opinion in 1965. So, too, did the closely following remarks of the young CDU representative Ernst Benda, who had initiated the bill to extend the statute of limitations. That a change in the culture of remembrance was underway is most clearly evident in Benda's closing remarks before the Bundestag: "The desire to forget extends the exile, and the secret of deliverance is called remembrance."[33] This quote, taken from the Hall of Remembrance in Yad Vashem, Israel's national memorial to the murdered Jews of Europe, is widely understood to have first entered the canon of West German thinking about the Holocaust twenty years later, in a speech by Richard von Weizsäcker on 8 May 1985. The difficulties inherent in transferring this concept from an Israeli memorial into the decidedly Christian context of West Germany could already be recognized in Benda's 1965 parliamentary address. Apart from scattered allusions, Benda did not discuss Nazi crimes during his speech. For him, the quotation from Yad Vashem fulfilled the function of a religiously appropriate, quiet mourning that rested on the certainty of purification and redemption.[34]

Nonetheless, Benda's address and the tone it set reflected an attempt to integrate the perspective of the victim—a remarkable change in the discourse about the Nazi period. A change of course also took place in the political sphere in 1965. A majority in the Bundestag passed a resolution to extend the statute of limitations until 1969. And in April 1965, the number of attorneys in the central office for the prosecution of Nazi crimes was increased from fifteen to fifty, and fifty-seven additional staff members were added.[35]

As the political negotiations over the statute of limitations make clear, however, it was not the intensive debate in the West German media over changing opinions that brought about the revision, but rather massive international pressure on the Federal Republic's political leaders. Domestic protests by victims' associations and Jewish organizations followed on the heels of demonstrations outside the West German embassies in Israel, Western Europe, and the United States. These proved far more effective than agitation from the German Democratic Republic. In early 1965, most Western governments and parliaments issued resolutions strongly supporting an extension of the statute of limitations.[36] The integration of the Federal Republic into the so-called Western community of values had progressed to such an extent that legal policy on Nazi crimes, previously upheld as the touchstone of national self-determination, could no longer reflect the denial evident in West German public opinion. In this respect, the decision to extend the statute of limitations represents the supplanting of the 1950s perspective, which was still marked in large measure by the values of the Nazi-era *Volksgemeinschaft*. It points to a new trend—to the westernization of the politics of memory in the Federal Republic.

Yet West Germany's "arrival in the West," already apparent in many aspects of society in the 1960s,[37] can be asserted in this connection only with certain reservations. In the debates over the statute of limitations in 1965 and again in 1969, CDU and FDP policy-makers pressed for an amnesty as compensation for extending the statute. They claimed to want to protect "only" ordinary SS men from criminal prosecution.[38] In fact, the amnesty proposal was aimed at all perpetrators within the National Socialist administrative machinery. Their efforts foundered on the resistance of the SPD, which, represented in the "grand coalition" (CDU-CSU/SPD) by Justice Minister Gustav Heinemann, vetoed their proposals.

The amnesty, however, could be realized through other means, specifically by way of an obscure amendment to Article 50/2 of the criminal code in 1968. In a new law on administrative offences (*Ordnungswidrigkeitengesetz*), which primarily concerned the decriminalization of traffic violations, a change was inserted that imposed lesser sentences on accessories to murder than those for principal offenders. The decisive element in the amendment was its interpretation of the statute of limitations, which claimed that the statute covering accessories to murder should have expired in 1960. It remains unclear whether the amendment represented a general attempt to fill a legislative gap (*Gesetzgebungspanne*) or whether officials at the Federal Ministry of Justice wrote it in the interest of Nazi perpetrators.

The facts, however, are clear. In May 1969, the Fifth Criminal Division of the Federal Court announced the judicially controversial but politically desirable ruling that the statute of limitations had already expired even for those who had filled positions of major responsibility within the Nazi murder apparatus. The court effectively satisfied the calls from the CDU and FDP for an amnesty. The responsible judges were the court clerk (*Berichterstatter*) Rudolf Börker, former counsel to the military tribunal in the Wehrmacht prison at Torgau, and the presiding judge Werner Sarstedt, an intellectual and rather liberal jurist, who, however, also supported immunity (*Straffreiheit*) for Nazi jurists. Only after this ruling was announced were the Christian Democrats prepared to go ahead with the Social Democrats to extend the statute of limitations for murder a further ten years beyond its impending expiration in May 1969. The most significant consequence of this amnesty was, without question, the stay of proceedings against personnel of the Reichssicherheitshauptamt (Reich Security Main Office). This trial, which was just about to open, would have brought the central decision-making authority behind the Nazis' policy of extermination to public attention and served as a counterpart to the Frankfurt trial of hands-on perpetrators at Auschwitz.[39]

Conclusion

What conclusions can be drawn from these findings? First and foremost, the politics of memory of the 1950s, which sought immunity for the elites of the Nazi regime, came to an end in the late 1960s despite resistance and certain countervailing developments. A new pattern of addressing the Nazi past emerged that was closely tied to legal decisions and trials. The issue of prosecution became a normative question that went to the core of West German self-perception. The results were ambiguous: Auschwitz was discussed, but alongside new forms of silence. The "crimes in the East," which had previously been left quite nebulous, found concrete form primarily through individual accounts of murder before the courts. At the same time, though, the "big picture" was left out of focus. With its monopoly on rendering verdicts, the justice system shaped an interpretation of Nazi crimes that in many ways took an apologetic course. An ever smaller number of perpetrators, mostly from the subordinate ranks of the Nazi regime's hierarchy, were convicted. Mid- and high-ranking officials were considered accessories and thus could count on either lesser punishments or stays of the proceedings brought against them. As a result, the image of the individual, abnormal perpetrator solidified alongside the corresponding view of top-level Nazi bureaucrats as helpless victims unjustly delivered for judgment before the courts.[40]

At no point were such interpretations left unchallenged. First, East German propaganda produced considerable irritation. The GDR's campaign against compromised judges, civil servants, and politicians presented a caricature of the "fascist

Federal Republic." However, the campaign did prompt a critical debate over the past in the West. Liberal newspaper and radio editors increasingly took on the topic of Nazi crimes. Students loudly protested over the continuities of personnel in the judicial system, and they later turned their attention to these continuities at institutions of higher education. By the mid-1960s, many West Germans were surprised by the critical response to both the Auschwitz trial and the debate over the statute of limitations had developed to an extent that surprised many.

Even Ralph Dahrendorf was amazed. As one of the sharpest contemporary observers of West German society, he sought to understand why the Nazi past attained such immense significance at that particular time. He did not attribute particular significance to the trials themselves. Rather, he focused on the public debates. For Dahrendorf, the decisive impetus came from generational change and the growing temporal distance from the crimes. He argued that the period since the war saw a generation come of age that was "able to ask the [right] questions without having to fear that they themselves [would] be hurt by the answers."[41] This conclusion was focused principally on the cohort born after 1945, which, as Dahrendorf noted, already made up a third of West German society in 1965.

To understand the generational change fully, we must also consider the cohort that came between the supporters of the Nazi regime and the postwar children—the cohort of which Dahrendorf himself was a member. Born in 1929, he belonged to the so-called *Flakhelfer* generation, that is, those who had experienced the war as rear-guard auxiliaries rather than as frontline soldiers and who had taken over leadership positions in the Federal Republic beginning in the early 1960s.[42] The formative experience of Dahrendorf's youth was not deployment as an antiaircraft auxiliary, however; it was the arrest of his father, a Social Democratic activist who had been in contact with the resistance movement of 20 July, as well as his own imprisonment in an SS reeducation work camp at war's end.[43] The young sociology professor sought to establish a new, independent view of the prehistory of West German society through his research.[44] In his analysis, he placed greater stress on temporal distance than generational change. "It could be that the monstrousness of the crimes, whose perpetration by National Socialist Germany has stained the German name, also created a daily, palpable feeling for every individual that, for a long time, was simply too overwhelming to be articulated by the persons affected," he wrote. "Only the distance of twenty years places the past in a perspective that makes its horrors humanly bearable; in other words, the passing of time opens the human conscience. Time is here more merciful than the matter deserves."[45]

Dahrendorf directed most of his attention to the mental stabilization of West Germans that accompanied the improvement of economic and social circumstances in the second postwar decade. Nazi crimes began to lose their threatening character under these conditions, just as Adolf Arndt demonstrated as a representative of the elder generation in the debate over the statute of limitations in 1965. An open and above all more public reflection on Auschwitz could only begin in the first half of the 1960s. Yet while numerous court proceedings were launched after the Auschwitz trial, public interest in them waned surprisingly quickly. The critical recollection of the facts and circumstances of the Nazis' murderous acts set out in the Frankfurt court proceedings thus remained a short-term phenomenon. Without a secure anchoring in the collective memory, such historical details quickly disappeared.

— *Translated from the German by Andrew Oppenheimer*

Notes

1. Ralf Dahrendorf, "Zur Frage der Verjährungsfrist für Naziverbrechen," *National-Zeitung* (Basel), 8 January 1965.
2. Ibid.
3. For statistics on prosecutions and convictions for Nazi crimes in West German courts, see Adalbert Rückerl, *NS-Verbrechen vor Gericht* (Heidelberg, 1982).
4. For an account of how Allied purges (*Säuberungspolitik*) fell into disrepute and of the integration of perpetrators into West German society, see Norbert Frei, *Vergangenheitspolitik: Die Anfänge der Bundesrepublik Deutschland und die NS-Vergangenheit* (Munich, 1996).
5. For an account of the Schörner trial, see "Wer half Schörner," *Der Spiegel*, 16 October 1957, 23ff.
6. For an account of the Ulm trial and its reception, see Marc von Miquel, *Ahnden oder amnestieren? Westdeutsche Justiz und Vergangsheitpolitik in den sechziger Jahren* (Göttingen, 2004).
7. Justizministerium Baden-Württemberg, 411E "Ermittlungsverfahren gegen Fischer-Schweder und andere," Schüle to Nellmann on "Strafverfolgung weiterer 17 Beschuldigten" and "Weitere bekanntgewordene Exekutionen," 19 August 1958.
8. Until the early 1960s, the prosecutor's office had to presume that accessories to murder committed before May 1943 would fall under that statute of limitations. According to the Federal Constitutional Court, the period in which charges could be filed was to be 15 years, the same as for manslaughter. The statutes of limitations on accessory to murder and manslaughter were first decoupled in a revision of the criminal code enacted on 29 May 1943. See Jürgen Baumann, "Die strafrechtliche Problematik der nationalsozialistischen Gewaltverbrechen," in *Die nationalsozialistischen Gewaltverbrechen: Geschichte und Gericht*, ed. Reinhard Henkys (Stuttgart, 1964), 279f. The verdict in the Ulm trial is documented in Adelheid L. Rüter-Ehlermann and C. F. Rüter, eds., *Justiz und NS-Verbrechen: Sammlung deutscher Strafurteile wegen nationalsozialistischer Tötungsverbrechen 1945–1966*, 22 vols. (Amsterdam, 1968–81), here vol. 15, 232ff.
9. *Stuttgarter Zeitung*, 3 September 1958.
10. Bundesarchiv Koblenz, Bundesjustizministerium, B 141/33770, Protokoll der 27. Justizministerkonferenz in Bad Harzburg, 1–3 October 1958 and "Verwaltungsvereinbarung über die Errichtung einer zentralen Stelle der Landesjustizverwaltungen zur Aufklärung nationalsozialistischer Verbrechen," 13 November 1958. See also Adalbert Rückerl, *NS-Verbrechen vor Gericht* (Heidelberg, 1982), 142ff.
11. *Süddeutsche Zeitung*, 30 August 1958.
12. On the origins of the *Richtergesetz*, see Dieter Gosewinkel, "Politische Ahndung an den Grenzen des Justizstaats: Die Geschichte der nationalsozialistischen Justiz im Deutschen Richtergesetz von 1961," in *Geschichte vor Gericht. Historiker, Richter und die Suche nach Gerechtigkeit*, ed. Norbert Frei, Dirk van Laak, and Michael Stolleis (Munich, 2000), 60–71.

13. On the Fränkel affair, see *Der Spiegel*, 11 July 1962, 22f., as well as *Süddeutsche Zeitung*, 11 July 1962.

14. Press conference of 10 March 1961, quoted from Inge Deutschkron, *Israel und die Deutschen* (Cologne, 1970), 146f.

15. Ibid., 157ff.

16. This figure comes from an Infratest survey; for details, see ibid., 157.

17. Elisabeth Noelle-Neumann and Ernst-Peter Neumann, eds., *Jahrbuch der Öffentlichen Meinung, 1965–1968* (Allensbach, 1969), 227ff.

18. According to surveys conducted by the Wickert-Institut Tübingen in November 1961, 69 percent spoke out for the cessation of prosecutions. Details in *Welt der Arbeit*, 13 November 1965, 5. A parallel survey by the Allensbach Institut in early 1965 found that 52 percent wished for an end (*Schlußstrich*) to the Nazi trials; Noelle-Neumann and Neumann, *Jahrbuch der Öffentlichen Meinung*, 166.

19. Peter Weiss, *Die Ermittlung*, in Weiss, *Stücke I* (Frankfurt am Main, 1976), 257–449. Naumann's reports on the trial were subsequently published as a book: Bernd Naumann, *Auschwitz: Bericht über die Strafsache gegen Mulka und andere vor dem Schwurgericht Frankfurt* (Frankfurt am Main, 1965).

20. On the course and reception of the Auschwitz trial, see two excellent recent books: Rebecca Wittmann, *Beyond Justice: The Auschwitz Trial* (Cambridge, MA, 2005), and Devin O. Pendas, *The Frankfurt Auschwitz Trial 1963–1965: Genocide, History, and the Limits of the Law* (Cambridge, 2006). See also Pendas, "'I didn't know what Auschwitz was': The Frankfurt Auschwitz Trial and the German Press, 1963–1965," *Yale Journal of Law and the Humanities* 12 (Summer 2000): 397–446.

21. On the Eichmann and Auschwitz trials, see the reports by journalist Heiner Lichtenstein in his *Im Namen des Volkes? Eine persönliche Bilanz der NS-Prozesse* (Cologne, 1984), 196ff.

22. Christoph Classen, *Bilder der Vergangenheit: Die Zeit des Nationalsozialismus im Fernsehen der Bundesrepublik Deutschland 1955–1965* (Cologne, 1999), 157ff.

23. Headlines quoted in Martin Walser, "Unser Auschwitz," in *Kursbuch* 1 (1965): 189–200, here 200.

24. Claus Roxin, "Straftaten im Rahmen organisatorischer Machtapparate," *Goltdamer Archiv* (1963): 193–207.

25. Christopher R. Browning, *Ordinary Men: Reserve Police Batallion 101 and the Final Solution in Poland* (New York, 1992).

26. Naumann, *Auschwitz*, 253.

27. On this point, see Gesine Schwan's reflections in her *Politik und Schuld: Die zerstörerische Macht des Schweigens* (Frankfurt am Main, 1997).

28. Karl Jaspers, *Die Schuldfrage* (Basel, 1949).

29. Quoted from the transcript of the Bundestag debate of 10 March 1965, reprinted in Deutscher Bundestag, ed., *Zur Verjährung nationalsozialistischer Verbrechen: Dokumentation der parlamentarischen Bewältigung des Problems 1960–1979* (Bonn, 1980), 172.

30. Eugon Kogon, "Das Recht auf den politischen Irrtum," *Frankfurter Hefte* 1 (1947): 641–55.

31. Deutscher Bundestag, *Zur Verjährung*, 213.

32. On Arndt's life during the Nazi era, see Dieter Gosewinkel, *Adolf Arndt: Die Wiederbegründung des Rechtsstaats aus dem Geist der Sozialdemokratie (1945–1961)* (Bonn, 1991), 60ff.

33. Deutscher Bundestag, *Zur Verjährung*, 166. Benda rephrased a statement attributed to Baal Shem Tov, the founder of Chassidic Judaism. The exact translation reads: "Forgetting extends the exile! The secret of deliverance lies in remembrance." See Detlef Claussen, *Grenzen der Aufklärung: Die gesellschaftliche Genese des modernen Antisemitismus* (Frankfurt am Main, 1994), 14f.

34. See Micha Brumlik, "Trauerrituale und politische Kultur nach der Shoah in der Bundesrepublik," in *Holocaust: Die Grenzen des Verstehens: Eine Debatte über die Besetzung der Geschichte*, ed. Hanno Loewy (Hamburg, 1992), 209f.

35. On the reorganization of the central office, see Adalbert Rückerl, *NS-Verbrechen vor Gericht* (Heidelberg, 1982), 178ff.

36. For press documentation, see Rolf Vogel, *Ein Weg aus der Vergangenheit: Eine Dokumentation zur Verjährungsfrage und zu den NS-Prozessen* (Berlin, 1969).

37. See Axel Schildt, *Ankunft im Westen* (Frankfurt am Main, 1999).

38. The proposal to exempt from punishment Nazi perpetrators accused of murder was inserted as Article 3 in the draft law on calculating the statute of limitations for criminal offenses; text reprinted in Deutscher Bundestag, *Zur Verjährung*, 255.

39. For a detailed analysis of the amnesty introduced by the changes in the penal code, see Miquel, *Ahnden oder amnestieren?* 327ff.

40. Pendas, "'I didn't know what Auschwitz was.'"

41. Dahrendorf, "Zur Frage der Verjährungsfrist."

42. On the "auxiliary" generation and how its members dealt with the Nazi past, see Clemens Albrecht, *Die intellektuelle Gründung der Bundesrepublik: Eine Wirkungsgeschichte der Frankfurter Schule* (Frankfurt am Main, 1999), 497ff.

43. Dahrendorf discusses his imprisonment in a jail in Frankfurt/Oder and later in the labor camp Schwetig in his autobiography, Ralf Dahrendorf, *Reise nach innen und außen: Aspekte der Zeit* (Stuttgart, 1984), 13, 200f.

44. This attempt is most evident in Dahrendorf's major study, *Gesellschaft und Demokratie in Deutschland* (Munich, 1965), in which he broaches the question, "how was Auschwitz possible?" (17ff.).

45. Dahrendorf, "Zur Frage der Verjährungsfrist."

Chapter 4

THE "COMPREHENSIVE INVESTIGATIVE PROCEEDINGS—FRANCE"

West German Judicial Inquiries into Nazi Crimes

Bernhard Brunner

∽

The intensification of efforts to investigate and prosecute National Socialist crimes of violence is rightfully considered one of the hallmarks of the 1960s in the Federal Republic of Germany. But the decade was also marked by continuing and effective attempts to put an end to such trials. A conspicuous example is provided by one of the longest and most extensive judicial investigations of Nazi crimes undertaken by the West German justice system, the investigation of violent crimes committed by Germans in occupied France, the so-called *Frankreich-Komplex*[1] or "Comprehensive Investigative Proceedings—France" (CIP—France).

During the Nazi occupation of France, some 75,000 Jews were deported to Poland—primarily to Auschwitz—and only 2,570 of them survived.[2] In addition, approximately 29,000 persons were executed as "expiatory hostages"[3] or killed in "antipartisan operations" or "cleanup measures" during the German military evacuation of the occupied area.[4] West German judicial inquiries into these crimes were initiated in 1961. That same year, a list of more than a hundred suspects was drawn up. The investigation expanded into a comprehensive "wide-scale inquiry"[5] attempting to cover all Nazi crimes committed in France. It was established that culpability for both the "shooting of hostages" and the deportations lay primarily with members of a relatively delimited functionary elite made up of officers of the Security Police (Sicherheitspolizei, or Sipo) and Security Service (Sicherheitsdienst, or SD). Even though other German offices in occupied France, in particular the military administration and the German embassy in Paris, were complicit in these crimes, the commanders of the Sipo and SD (*Kommandeure der Sipo und des SD*, KdS) and their leading staff played the chief role.

All of these individuals had been identified by 1974: some 200 men, the most notorious of whom today is probably Klaus Barbie, the "butcher of Lyon." West German authorities were able to establish the whereabouts of 119 of these men who were living in the Federal Republic. Beginning in 1979, nine were brought to trial. The spectacular "Lischka trial" in Cologne ended in 1980 with three convictions; one defendant was acquitted in a subsequent trial. Another defendant avoided trial by committing suicide, and the proceedings against the remaining four men were terminated on grounds of their inability to stand trial. The overwhelming majority of the men linked to the shootings and deportations in France were never brought to justice. Most had been able to build new careers after the war, and some rose to positions of influence and power in the highest echelons of government and business.[6]

The balance: after nearly twenty years of judicial inquiry, a grand total of three individuals were convicted in 1980 of responsibility for the deportation of Jews from occupied France. Not a single perpetrator responsible for the mass hostage executions and killing of partisans was ever brought to trial. Indeed, not a single indictment had been issued.[7]

How can we account for this miserable record? One may accuse the justice system of a lack of resolve in pursuing suspected offenders, but that is not enough. The juridical and political context of the proceedings must also be taken into account. One salient fact is that there was strong resistance in West Germany during the 1950s to the prosecution of any kind by the victorious Allies. Many members of the political class and the public rejected the numerous trials in France as illegitimate, as a form of "victors' justice," and took up the struggle against them. This categorical rejection impeded a cool and sober examination of the charges, and the individuals indicted by the French authorities were uniformly seen as "victims" in West Germany regardless of their alleged crimes. That attitude proved resilient. It persisted into the 1960s and helped to impede newly initiated judicial procedures. The growing conviction that the Nazis' crimes had to be investigated and the perpetrators brought to justice ran up against powerful social forces whose aim was precisely the opposite, namely, to prevent a judicial reckoning. What was the upshot? Until the mid-1960s, the opponents of prosecution were so successful in having such severe restrictions imposed that public prosecutors saw little prospect for success in trying suspected Nazi perpetrators and thus largely abandoned their efforts to do so.

Criminal Prosecution in France and West German Reactions

French military tribunals began prosecuting Nazi perpetrators in the immediate aftermath of the liberation in 1944. Of the three Western Allies, France was the only one that had suffered Nazi occupation. That is why France pressed ahead with the indictment and prosecution of war criminals on its own territory rather than leaving such proceedings to courts in Germany, as Great Britain and the

United States did. The French practice was in accordance with the guidelines adopted by the Allies for criminal prosecution: defendants were to be tried in the countries where they had allegedly committed crimes.[8]

The juridical foundation for prosecution was the general French penal code and the military penal code, supplemented by decrees issued on 28 August 1944 and 25 September 1948.[9] The first decree stipulated that the proceedings should take place before military tribunals, the majority of whose members were to be former Resistance fighters. The second empowered military courts to convict members of those organizations declared "criminal" at the International Military Tribunal in Nuremberg unless they could establish their innocence. French courts convicted at least 1,918 Germans for crimes committed in France during the occupation on this judicial basis.[10]

A distinctive feature of French criminal prosecution was the practice of trial and conviction in absentia. If the military courts had information on crimes attributed to a defendant who was not in their custody, they conducted purely formal proceedings. The accused had no proper opportunity for defense, and such trials often ended with the courts handing down the most severe sentence possible.[11] But under French law, a sentence issued to a defendant in absentia could not be carried out; if French authorities gained custody of a defendant so convicted, they had to conduct a new conventional trial. These verdicts in absentia, a peculiar feature of French justice, were thus closer to arrest warrants than to final judgments. At least 914 Germans were convicted and sentenced in absentia.[12]

In West Germany, there was virulent criticism of these verdicts and the French trials in general. The Adenauer government put heavy pressure on Paris to terminate such proceedings[13] and also actively opposed them through non-diplomatic channels. In 1949, the Central Office for Legal Protection (Zentrale Rechtschutzstelle, ZRS) was established. According to the legislation creating the ZRS, its purpose was "to ensure the legal protection of those Germans ... being held in custody in several Allied countries and suspected of or charged with complicity in war crimes."[14] That France was the main country the Bundestag had in mind is evident from the debate preceding the vote on the legislation. Federal Minister of Justice Thomas Dehler told the parliament he had serious misgivings about the legal basis for the French prosecution of German war criminals. In the same speech, Dehler also stated that it was not the intention of the Bonn government to protect war criminals.[15] Yet the course pursued by the ZRS suggested otherwise. Initially part of the Justice Ministry and later a subsection of the Foreign Ministry, the ZRS worked diligently on behalf of all Germans in custody abroad, regardless of the accusations against them. ZRS director Hans Gawlik had been senior prosecutor with the Breslau District Court during the Nazi period; after the war, he was appointed defense lawyer for the SD at the Nuremberg Tribunal.[16]

The first concern of the ZRS was the Germans held in Allied custody who were awaiting trial or had already been sentenced. Because East European authorities did not countenance any interference in trials, the ZRS concentrated its efforts on the

Western democracies. The main focus was France, which had initiated or conducted far more criminal cases against German defendants than any other Western country.

To aid individuals threatened by French proceedings, the ZRS collected evidence for the defense, provided lawyers, had legal expert opinions prepared, and took care of the needs of imprisoned defendants. One distinctive service it provided was to furnish all German defendants, bar none, with sworn testimony in their defense by high-ranking German officials. These officials were clearly briefed beforehand by Gawlik on what they had to say. They even gave written testimony on behalf of the accused, which made it difficult for them to alter the line of their testimony later. To bolster the line of defense it developed, the ZRS had Hans Luther, a former Sipo and SD staffer who had himself been assisted by the ZRS, assemble documentation on German occupation polices after his release from French custody. The materials Luther prepared were to have a tremendous impact on the way courts treated the hostage question. Luther's apologia was also to percolate into historical writing on the Nazi era; using the same documentation he provided the ZRS, the former Nazi functionary wrote a doctoral dissertation that is still cited by historians today as a standard work on German hostage policy.[17]

In this way, the ZRS was able to propagate a skewed picture of the German occupation. The policy of hostage executions was presented as a measure that was harsh but nonetheless fully in accord with international law. Cases where such policies exceeded the bounds of international law, according to the ZRS, could be attributed to Hitler's direct influence. The persecution of the Jews was largely excluded from consideration.

Working with the German embassy in Paris, the ZRS was able to forestall and prevent the enactment of virtually all death sentences against German war criminals. By 1962 it had managed to secure the pardon and release of the last of the convicted Germans in French custody. The Vatican and nongovernmental organizations such as the Red Cross and several veteran associations also championed the cause of the Germans behind French bars.

Gawlik and his associates not only saw to the needs of the Germans in French custody, but they also tried to prevent Germans who had been sentenced in absentia from falling into the hands of the French justice system. Although those individuals were protected against extradition by West Germany's Basic Law, some of them had traveled to France unaware that they had been tried and convicted there in absentia. They were arrested and arraigned once more, now in person. These cases caused political friction between Bonn and Paris. The ZRS had from its founding occasionally warned individuals convicted in absentia not to venture across the border into France, and it began systematically issuing such warnings in 1954.[18] To locate these men, the ZRS worked with the Red Cross and the veterans' association Verband der Heimkehrer, both of which had extensive address files. It is difficult to determine precisely how many such warning the ZRS issued; according to an internal memo, the ZRS had collected the names of 340 Germans sentenced in absentia by 1959 and had forewarned 102 of them.[19] When this practice became public knowledge several years later, Gawlik justified it by claiming that such warnings had been issued only "if, on the basis of documentation available to the ZRS, there was reason to believe that the sentence was unjust."[20] Lists of names that later surfaced indicate that this statement was inaccurate. On one list, for example, Klaus Barbie's name appears with the comment "has been notified" and a reference number indicating the year 1956. The abbreviation *erl.* (*erledigt*, "taken care of") appeared alongside many names, including that of Alois Brunner, the second most wanted mass murderer after Adolf Eichmann.[21] This practice was in line with the widespread tendency among members of the West German political community and general public during the 1950s to consider everyone pursued as a war criminal to be innocent, no matter what the charge.

The situation began to change in the early 1960s. The Central Office of State Authorities for the Investigation of National Socialist Crimes of Violence (Zentralstelle der Landesjustizverwaltungen zur Aufklärung nationalsozialistischer Gewaltverbrechen, ZStL) in Ludwigsburg, established at the end of the 1950s, began to prosecute suspected perpetrators of Nazi crimes. But as the example of the CIP-France illustrates, the defensive strategies developed in the 1950s proved to be tenacious and lingered on to hinder the work of the Ludwigsburg prosecutors.

The Beginning of Judicial Investigations

Proceedings in the CIP-France commenced with a complaint by a private citizen. In June 1960, writer Thomas Harlan, son of the famous Nazi film director Veit Harlan, filed a suit with Frankfurt public prosecutor Fritz Bauer against five persons, among them Klaus Barbie.[22] Bauer suggested Harlan get in touch with the ZStL; Harlan later filed suit against 96 individuals with the Ludwigsburg prosecutors.[23]

Harlan's awareness of the issue of unpunished Nazi criminals had been sharpened over the years by confrontation with his father. In the late 1950s, he had watched as a number of former Nazi functionaries regained respected and powerful positions in the Federal Republic while the West German justice system did nothing.[24] Harlan was incensed, and published an appeal to the Bundestag, accusing several former top Nazi officials, such as former SS General Franz Alfred Six, of serious crimes and demanding they be brought to justice.[25] Six and his attorney Ernst Achenbach responded by threatening Harlan with a libel suit.[26]

Who was Ernst Achenbach? From 1940 to 1944, he had served as director of the political department in the German embassy in Paris and was regarded as the most important decision-maker in occupied France. Even though Achenbach had been directly implicated in the deportations of Jews from France, he was appointed counsel at Nuremberg to defend his former Foreign Ministry colleagues. He went on to become a leading figure in the Free Democratic Party in the state of North Rhine-Westphalia and in 1957 was elected to the Bundestag. There, he became a key figure in the concerted struggle against the prosecution of Nazi crimes.

As a consequence of Achenbach's threat of a libel suit, Harlan was forced to produce evidence for his charges that could stand up in court. He made use of contacts to Poland to gain access to the archives there in order to search for documentation of Nazi crimes. Harlan's inquiries developed into a systematic research project that extended over a number of years. He amassed documentation that led to numerous suits against Nazi criminals. Harlan buttressed his charges against Nazi perpetrators in France with photocopies of materials in Polish archives and later with evidence from French archives as well. These materials proved extremely valuable to the Ludwigsburg prosecutors because next to nothing was known in 1960 about the crimes committed in occupied France. There were no German historical accounts of the occupation aside from several self-exculpatory memoirs and Hans Luther's doctoral dissertation.[27]

The Convention of 1954

The Federal Republic of Germany achieved sovereignty in war-related judicial matters with the promulgation of the 1954 Convention on the Settlement of Matters Arising out of the War and Occupation.[28] In the difficult and extended negotiations on the terms of the convention, the Bonn government had worked toward a popularly desired end: a halt to all Allied court proceedings against Germans accused of war crimes and atrocities. Adoption of the convention resulted in the accelerated release of war criminals in Allied custody in West Germany.[29] But the convention proved inadequate when it came to halting criminal proceedings in France. All attempts to convince the French to put an end to criminal prosecutions came to naught. Consequently, West German authorities, the ZRS in particular, sought to make greater use of the existing options under French law. It was possible to intervene in individual cases through, for example, requests for grants of reprieve and applications for conditional release. As a result of this approach, all German war criminals imprisoned on French soil had been released by 1962.

Bonn was nonetheless unable to have the verdicts handed down in absentia rescinded, and they continued to burden German-French relations. The pardoned and released war criminals were also a source of recurring friction. Under existing juridical agreements, West German courts had to institute their own proceedings against many who had been granted amnesty in France. That was bound to provoke further ill will and resentment, given the extent of German efforts to secure reprieves for defendants convicted in absentia.

To escape this predicament, West German judicial authorities interpreted the stipulations of the 1954 convention in a way aimed at avoiding friction. The foundation for their actions was Article 3 of the convention. Concerned that the sentences handed down by Allied tribunals might be overturned en masse, the Allies insisted that the convention stipulate that "criminal proceedings against natural persons" could not be challenged in the German justice system if the "investigation of the alleged offence was finally completed by the prosecuting authorities of the power or powers concerned." The formulation of these paragraphs was vague, leaving the West German courts room to interpret the meaning of the phrase "finally completed."[30]

The German judicial system seized on this built-in latitude to construct a restrictive interpretation of the treaty that can be viewed as the logical continuation of the 1950s policy of trying to close the book on the past. This interpretation emerged in three stages. First, the convention was cited as grounds for excluding a retrial of defendants already convicted before Allied courts. Disregarding a ruling by the Federal Supreme Court (*Bundesgerichtshof*), the Federal Prosecutor's Office and Ministry of Justice believed that the exclusionary clause in Article 3, which had originally pertained to Allied judicial "investigations" that had been "finally completed," applied to cases in which a verdict had been handed down.[31] This was a major difference in interpretation. In the ministry and federal prosecutor's reading of the convention, West German authorities were enjoined from prosecuting *any and all* suspected war criminals who had already stood trial in an Allied court. A defendant who had been acquitted could not be brought to trial again even if incriminating new evidence relevant to former charges surfaced.

This position relieved German justice authorities of the obligation to reprosecute a large number of Nazi criminals who, thanks to West German diplomatic pressure, had previously been granted reprieves.[32] Because broad sections of the West German public repudiated Allied prosecution of Germans and also actively sought the release of condemned war criminals since the early 1950s, any attempt at reprosecution would have run up against a storm of popular opposition.[33] Moreover, retrying those who had received reprieves would have compromised the decisions of the Allied occupation authorities more broadly. That had to be avoided, since it would have rendered further remissions impossible, seriously complicating future cooperation.

West German prosecutors began to bring such proceedings to an end, citing the 1954 convention. But because there was no final decision from the highest court that might serve to unify this practice, one question was now often raised: when were West German courts obliged under the terms of the convention to proceed with criminal prosecution of individuals who had been tried for wartime offenses in other countries? The convention had envisioned a simple rule for such conflicts. In cases of doubt, the courts could request the embassy of the country that had tried the person for a go-ahead to initiate criminal proceedings. The West German Justice Ministry viewed this, however, as a restriction on German judicial jurisdiction, and, after consulting with the Foreign Ministry, it rejected the idea of requesting "ambassador certificates." That was the second step toward a restrictive reading of the convention.[34]

The third came when the Federal Supreme Court (Bundesgerichtshof) found a uniform but radical solution. In the so-called Hempen verdict of 1966, it ruled that German courts generally could not conduct inquiries into any case that had already been heard before an Allied court, *irrespective of the form of the proceedings and their outcome.* Not only were all judicial inquiries and trials that had ended in a verdict to be regarded as "finally completed," but so, too, were the verdicts French courts handed down on defendants tried in absentia.[35] This meant that it was forbidden for German prosecutors to prosecute Nazi criminals who had already been condemned before an Allied tribunal or judged in absentia. This blockade was not, as some later maintained, an unintended secondary effect. Rather, it was the consistent next step in the process of "liquidating" the criminal prosecution of Nazi German defendants by French courts.

The judges of the Federal Supreme Court who handed down the Hempen verdict were well aware that they were imposing heavy restrictions on the West German criminal prosecution system. They fully realized that thereafter many Nazi perpetrators could not be brought to justice. One must wonder why they arrived at such a consequential decision—one that from today's vantage point must be regarded as obviously ill-conceived. Although Ernst Achenbach lobbied vigorously in the run-up to the Hempen verdict, it would be mistaken to attribute it solely to the politicking of such former Nazi functionaries and their representatives.[36] The effort to reestablish German jurisdiction over prosecuting suspected Nazi criminals played a central role, as the negative reaction to the "ambassador certificates" indicates. The West German justice system would no longer be under pressure from verdicts handed down by Allied courts and tribunals, especially French in absentia convictions, because it regarded itself as the sole competent authority to prosecute Nazi criminals. The outright rejection of Allied claims to jurisdiction made it quite easy for the opponents of criminal prosecution to prevail. The desire for sovereignty far outweighed the resolve to punish the perpetrators.

The worst fears of the French judiciary thus came true. It was precisely the German Nazi criminals whom they had put on their "most wanted list" by convicting them in absentia who, on account of those convictions, would no longer be pursued. The hands of the French courts were also tied because these men lived in the Federal Republic and the Basic Law prohibited their extradition to France.

The CIP—France after the Hempen Verdict

In practical terms, this decision brought the *Frankreich-Komplex* to a virtual standstill. The only Nazi functionaries liable to judicial inquiry were suspects who had not been convicted by the French courts. To determine who might still be subject to prosecution, the French records had to be consulted, but, in a new twist, the previously cooperative French authorities now refused to place their files at the disposal of German investigators.[37]

French noncooperation added to the problems faced by the public prosecutor's office in Cologne, which had been entrusted with the CIP-France by the ZStL. The Cologne prosecutors first had to reconstruct the crimes, determine who was culpable, and locate evidence that would stand up in court. They then had to establish the whereabouts of the suspected perpetrators. The prosecutors were assisted in this by a special commission of the State Criminal Investigation Office (Landeskriminalamt, LKA), which did not conclude its work until 1974. The LKA was able to trace a total of 64 suspected former Nazi functionaries who were still alive in 1974.

The prosecutors had to prove in each individual case that the accused was not only *implicated* in the deportation of Jews from France but also *aware* of the mass murder of Jews taking place in the East. If prosecutors could not demonstrate such awareness, the accused could be seen only as an accessory to murder, and that offense fell under the statute of limitations.[38] Of course, the former Nazi functionaries, some of them lawyers themselves, were well aware of this point and denied they had had any prior knowledge of the mass slaughter in the concentration camps.

The general legal situation thus made the task confronting the prosecutors in Cologne very difficult. After the Federal Supreme Court's ruling in the Hempen case, they were also burdened by the new responsibility of ascertaining who among the suspects had already been tried and convicted in France. Unable to check the French files, the Cologne prosecutors were certain of only nine men who had not been found guilty in French courts; those nine were, however, minor functionaries implicated in less serious offenses.[39] To proceed against them alone would have meant sparing the main culprits while pursuing their subordinates. So the Cologne prosecutors followed a different strategy. On 4 September 1966, they suggested to the Justice Ministry that a special agreement be signed with France rescinding the exclusionary clause on convictions in absentia in the 1954 convention.[40] In view of the fact the Federal Supreme Court's reading of Article 3 contradicted the original intent of the French in joining the convention, this move was somewhat paradoxical. But such an accord based on the treaty's language might provide a way out of the impasse that the Federal Supreme Court had created for the German justice system. The Cologne prosecutors were seriously considering calling a halt to the proceedings against suspects in the CIP-France if such an agreement could not be arranged.[41]

The Loosening of the Blockade: The Supplementary Agreement to the Convention of 1954

Officials in the Ministry of Justice were well aware of the injustices arising from the widened reading of the 1954 convention. In working for the Hempen verdict, their goal had been prophylactic; they wanted to limit the impact of Allied verdicts on the West German justice system. They realized that if they succeeded, major offenders like Klaus Barbie could no longer be pursued, and they accepted that as part of the cost of assuring the judicial sovereignty of the Federal Republic. Once that sovereignty had been secured with the Hempen verdict, the ministry believed there was sufficient latitude to take action against serious offenders.

The government therefore decided to act on the Cologne prosecutors' suggestion and broached the proposal in Paris. The Supplementary Agreement to the Convention of 1954 was designed to enable West German agencies to press ahead with prosecuting those convicted in France in absentia. The other regulations established by the Hempen verdict were to remain unaffected. After difficult negotiations, the agreement was concluded in 1969. It took another six years, however, for the Bundestag to ratify it.[42]

The proposed agreement divided the West German political parties and the public down the middle. Leading the opposition to the agreement was, once again, the veteran crusader Ernst Achenbach. Until 1966, his espousal of amnesty for all Nazi criminals had meshed with the Justice Ministry's goal of augmenting West German judicial sovereignty, but this silent alliance had come to an end. Achenbach had in the meantime risen to become chairperson of the Bundestag's influential foreign relations committee. He held a key position in the parliamentary machinery because the committee's stamp of approval was a prerequisite to a vote on the agreement by the full Bundestag. Achenbach proved an adept partisan tactician, effectively blocking discussion of the 1969 agreement for years and impeding its way to a vote. Other vocal opponents were active in veterans' associations such as the Verband der Heimkehrer and the Mutual Relief Association (Hilfsgemeinschaft auf Gegenseitigkeit, HIAG), an organization of former members of the Waffen-SS that championed the interests of *Kriegsverurteilte* (persons convicted for war crimes). Others, such as former Bundeswehr general and SPD Bundestag member Friedrich Beermann, were driven by one overriding concern, that of avoiding any new discussion of the wartime role of the Wehrmacht in connection with consideration of the deportation of Jews from France and, in particular, the shooting of hostages.[43]

Despite massive and prolonged opposition, the Supplementary Agreement was finally passed in 1975, in large measure as a result of the efforts of Serge and Beate Klarsfeld. They had launched a political campaign against amnesty for Nazi criminals and conceived a bold venture: they attempted to abduct Kurt Lischka, the best-known former functionary of the Security Police and SD who had been a major beneficiary of the exclusionary paragraph. The abduction of Lischka, then living inconspicuously as an office worker in Cologne, miscarried. Beate Klarsfeld was subsequently taken to court, and Lischka was called as a witness to testify against her. The trial became a scandal and soon developed into a global media event.[44] In the process, the blockade erected against the CIP–France became widely known to the public, and a spotlight was also cast on the dubious role Achenbach had played in the affair. He was ultimately forced to resign from his position in the foreign relations committee. Under his successor, the committee approved the agreement and sent it to the Bundestag floor for ratification.

At that point, investigative proceedings against those convicted in absentia could at last be initiated. The French government agreed to reopen the files of the French military courts. Initially, the Cologne prosecutors extended their inquiries to twenty-two highly incriminated functionaries.[45] It was not until 1979, however, that the prosecutor's office was ready to bring the most serious offenders within this group—Herbert Hagen, Kurt Lischka, and Ernst Heinrichsohn—to trial. The Cologne prosecutors can justifiably be criticized for this undue delay. Notwithstanding the substantial difficulties under which they had to work, they should have been faster in indicting these three men, whose role in the mass murder of Jews had been known as early as 1965. Their indictment was due in part to the special efforts and commitment of one prosecutor in particular, Rolf Holtfort, whose transfer to another position after the Lischka trial prevented him from further work on the *Frankreich-Komplex* cases. The difficulties were compounded by the Cologne chief prosecutor's decision to handle the CIP-France as a large number of individual cases, which were then turned over to prosecutors across West Germany.[46] Unfortunately, most prosecutors' offices had no experience with Nazi cases and, given the division of labor in the Nazis' crimes, little prospect of success in their proceedings against individual perpetrators. That was one of the principal reasons why there was a total of only three convictions after the Supplementary Agreement was ratified.

One complicating factor was the advancing age of the Nazi perpetrators. Of 119 suspects who had survived the war and whose whereabouts were known, only 64 were still alive in 1974, among them 15 heavily incriminated former regional commanders of the Security Police and SD (KdS). By 1986, the number of these commanders had diminished to six. Arguing cases became more and more difficult as both defendants and witnesses claimed their memories were growing weaker. Defendants were also generally successful in bringing investigations to a halt on the grounds of failing health. Inability to stand trial or interrogation thus became the greatest obstacle of efforts to bring these perpetrators to justice.

The meager results of the thirty-year-long Frankreich-Komplex are to be explained above all by the restrictive West German interpretation of the 1954 convention. More than any of the juridical difficulties, the Hempen verdict limited the prosecutors' scope of action. The year 1966, consequently, was both a terminus and turning point. The Federal Supreme Court's Hempen verdict brought a close to the West German justice system's efforts to nullify the results of Allied criminal prosecutions. The initiative to amend the Convention, on the other hand, signaled the resolve of prosecutors to limit the damage that had been done.

— Translated from the German by William Templer

Notes

1. The German legal term *Komplex* is best understood as "comprehensive investigative proceedings" on a number of related cases. For further information on the topic, see my publications: *Der Frankreich-Komplex: Die nationalsozialistischen Verbrechen in Frankreich und die Justiz der Bundesrepublik Deutschland* (Göttingen, 2004); "Lebenswege der deutschen Sipo-Chefs in Frankreich nach 1945," in *Wandlungsprozesse in Westdeutschland: Belastung, Integration, Liberalisierung 1945–1980*, ed. Ulrich Herbert (Göttingen, 2002), 214–42; "Der 'Frankreich-Komplex': Die juristische Aufarbeitung der in Frankreich verübten NS-Gewaltverbrechen," in *NS-Unrecht vor Kölner Gerichten nach 1945*, ed. Anne Klein and Jürgen Wilhelm (Cologne 2003), 183–200. See also Claudia Moisel, *Frankreich und die deutschen Kriegsverbrecher: Politik und Praxis der Strafverfolgung nach dem Zweiten Weltkrieg* (Göttingen, 2004), and Marc von Miquel, *Ahnden oder Amnestieren? Westdeutsche Justiz und Vergangenheitspolitik in den sechziger Jahren* (Göttingen, 2004).

2. On the various statistics, see Juliane Wetzel, "Frankreich und Belgien" in *Dimension des Völkermordes: Die Zahl der jüdischen Opfer des Nationalsozialismus*, ed. Wolfgang Benz (Munich, 1996), 105–37. Wetzel takes into account the figures in various publications, which sometimes deviate considerably, arriving at this result after checking the detailed presentation by Serge Klarsfeld. See also Serge Klarsfeld, *Vichy-Auschwitz: Die Zusammenarbeit der deutschen und französischen Behörden bei der "Endlösung der Judenfrage" in Frankreich* (Nördlingen, 1998).

3. *Sühnepersonen* were individuals seized and executed in retaliation for attacks against German soldiers.

4. According to official French data presented at the International Military Tribunal, Nuremberg, a total of 29,660 persons were shot in France, 28,068 of these within the area under the control of the Military Commander/France. See the statistics presented on 21 December 1945 at the Trial of the Major War Criminals, IMT Nuremberg (RF 266 = IMT 37-212). According to information in the French literature, the numbers were significantly higher (ranging up to 100,000). See Hans Luther, *Der französische Widerstand gegen die deutsche Besatzungsmacht und seine Bekämpfung* (Tübingen, 1957) (Studien des Instituts für Besatzungsfragen in Tübingen zu den deutschen Besetzungen im 2. Weltkrieg, no. 11), 269.

5. *Ermittlungskomplex*, in the legal terminology of the time.

6. If one takes, for example, just the commanding officers, i.e., the supreme commander (BdS) and regional commanders (KdS) of the Security Police and SD, there were twenty-eight men whose whereabouts and activities were known to authorities. Fourteen of them died soon after the end of the war, one died in a French prison, and another committed suicide while in German investigative custody. Two of those remaining were indicted and convicted in the 1960s of crimes against German citizens—thus not in response to charges of complicity in Nazi crimes in France. Four former regional commanders rose to high positions in private business in the postwar period; one was active as an attorney and notary public. Five other regional commanders held high-ranking posts in the civil service and in politics: one as a senior official with the administrative court in Baden-Württemberg, two as ranking officials with district courts, one as head of an office for investigating suspected tax evasion, and one as ministerial head in the Federal Economics Ministry.

7. The CIP-France (*Frankreich-Komplex*, File no. 114 AR-Z 1670/61) was introduced in 1961 by the Central Office of State Authorities for the Investigation of National Socialist Crimes of Violence in Ludwigsburg (ZStL). After conducting initial investigations of both the deportation of Jews and the "execution of hostages," the ZStL concentrated first on the deportations. In 1965, it passed the case on to the Cologne Public Prosecutor's Office (StA Cologne), where the investigation was given the file number 24 JS 1/66 (z). After the Lischka trial in 1980, the Cologne chief state prosecutor ordered the proceedings broken up into numerous individual cases, and these were passed on to the local competent public prosecutor for further action. In 1965, the ZStL intensified its investigation of the "execution of hostages," and the inquiry was given the file number 104 AR-Z 40/67. When the ZStL decided to pass on this case as well,

there was a dispute over competency. That was resolved when the StA Dortmund took over the case to the extent that it involved members of Security Police and SD units (45 JS 29/75). The section involving charges against former Wehrmacht members was taken over by the StA Munich, while that dealing with members of the military administration was handled by the StA Stuttgart. None of the proceedings came to a trial.

8. The "Moscow Declaration on Atrocities," 30 October 1943, stated that Nazi criminals should be arraigned and tried in the countries where their crimes were committed. Reprinted in Gerd. A. Ueberschär, ed., *Der Nationalsozialismus vor Gericht: Die alliierten Prozesse gegen Kriegsverbrecher und Soldaten 1943–1952* (Frankfurt am Main, 1999), 33.

9. See Ulrich Brochhagen, *Nach Nürnberg: Vergangenheitsbewältigung und Westintegration in der Ära Adenauer* (Berlin, 1999), 147.

10. Data according to notes for a speech by the director of the ZStL, Adalbert Rückerl, September/October 1980, in ZStL, General Files 98-30, fol. 150.

11. The corresponding paragraph of the French penal code is actually taken from an ordinance dated 1670. See René Garraud, *Traité d'Instruction Criminelle et de Procédure Pénale*, vol. 4 (Paris, 1926), 498. Quoted in ZStL, 104 AR-Z 1670/61, Final Report, 26 November 1965, 190.

12. Data according to an overview signed by Rückerl, in ZStL, 114 AR-Z 578/74. In other documents, the figure indicated is 1,026 (Note, JM B.-W., 18 June 1971, in JM B.-W. 9361 F 2–IV/5).

13. For more details, see Brochhagen, *Nach Nürnberg*, 147.

14. "Antrag der CDU/CSU Fraktion vom 29.09.1949," *Drucksachen des Deutschen Bundestages*, No. 60.

15. "Protokolle des Deutschen Bundestages, Sitzung vom 1.12.1949," 545.

16. See Ulrich Herbert, *Best: Biographische Studien über Radikalismus, Weltanschauung und Vernunft 1903–1989* (Bonn, 1996), 442.

17. Hans Luther, "Zu den gegenwärtigen Kriegsverbrecherprozessen in Frankreich," *Neue Juristische Wochenschau* (NJW), October 1954; Luther, *Widerstand*. While Luther is largely silent in his book regarding the deportations, he deals in detail with the shooting of hostages and even quotes from the trial documents, though he never mentions his own involvement. Luther's dissertation has been used, for example, by Eberhard Jäckel and Hans Umbreit in their studies. For the juridical assessment, see in particular the studies by Erich Schwinge, professor of criminal law at the University of Marburg, who as a defense attorney in French trials worked closely with the ZRS and Luther. The documentation is housed in the Federal Archive Koblenz (BAK) under the file number ALL Proz 20/6.

18. Inter alia, this is noted in a memo by Gawlik, 24 September 1956, in BAK B 305/317.

19. List of the ZRS, 17 July 1959, in BAK B 305/317.

20. Letter from ZRS to Head, Federal Chancellery, n.d. in BAK B 141/30542.

21. This is documented in two letters from the ZStL: ZStL to Higher State Prosecutor's Office Bonn, 18 June 1968, and ZStL to Federal Justice Ministry, 27 August 1968, both in ZStL: 115 AR 504/68.

22. This is noted in Thomas Harlan to ZStL, 5 October 1960, in ZStL, General Files, 1-36/45.

23. Personal communication from Thomas Harlan to the author, 21 November 1999. The suit was filed on 5 October 1960 and can be found in ZStL, General Files, 1-36/45.

24. Personal communication from Thomas Harlan to the author, 21 November 1999.

25. See *Frankfurter Allgemeine Zeitung*, 28 November 1959.

26. Achenbach to Harlan, 10 February 1959 and other correspondence, in JM B.-W. 4111 b–IV/106ff. Harlan recalls he was visited in Berlin by three young men, sent by Achenbach, who invited him on a hunting trip. Harlan felt it was dangerous and declined the offer. Achenbach then filed a libel suit against him. Personal communication from Thomas Harlan to the author, 21 November 1999.

27. One example is Otto Abetz, *Das offene Problem: Ein Rückblick auf zwei Jahrzehnte deutscher Frankreichpolitik* (Cologne, 1951).

28. The "Convention on the Settlement of Matters Arising out of the War and Occupation" (*Überleitungsvertrag*, hereafter, Convention of 1954) was agreed in its final version in October

1954 and went into effect on 5 May 1955 (*Bundesgesetzblatt,* 30 April 1955, part 1, 405ff.). It derived from Article 8 on regulating the general treaty of 26 May 1952, which provided for the possibility of such a supplementary treaty.

29. See Norbert Frei, *Vergangenheitspolitik: Die Anfänge der Bundesrepublik und die NS-Vergangenheit* (Munich, 1996), 234–64.

30. See Helmut Rumpf, "Deutsche Gerichtsbarkeit über Tatbestände mit Besatzungsberühung," *Juristenzeitschrift* (JZ) 1957: 654ff.

31. Originally it was argued that a new trial of Nazi criminals who had already been prosecuted and convicted was illegal, based on the principle that no one could be tried twice for the same crime. Yet that argument was rendered void by a further ruling of the Federal Supreme Court (BGH 5 STR 64/57, printed in NJW 59, 1690 and BGHSt 12, 326). The decision was further modified by another Supreme Court ruling ("Urteil des 2. Strafsenates des BGH vom 9.1.1959," AR s 59/58, NJW 1959, 779). The dissenting view of the federal justice minister can be found in the lecture manuscript of an unnamed senior state prosecutor from Hesse, 16 November 1959, in ZStL, General Files 40-3, fols. 15ff. See also Federal Justice Ministry to State Justice Administrations, 4 October 1959, in Justizministerium Baden-Württemberg (JM B-W) 9160a, vol. 22, 50. It was favorably received by most of the judges and state prosecutors dealing with Nazi crimes.

32. Prior to this, a large number of proceedings had been instituted across the Federal Republic against former Nazi functionaries who had already been tried before Allied courts, including a number of incriminated former leaders of mobile killing units (*Einsatzgruppen*) and their constituent subunits (*Einsatzkommandos*). See Report, ZStL to JM. B.-W., 3 September 1959, in ZStL, General Files 40-3.

33. See Brochhagen, *Nach Nürnberg,* 34.

34. As noted by Mefert, in NJW 56, 1468; see also Rumpf, JZ 1957, 654. This opinion was confirmed by the BGH. In its verdict, the Supreme Court stated that the courts had no right to demand such a certificate (NJW 60/1116); Foreign Ministry to Federal Justice Ministry, 11 January 1963, in BAK B 141/25629, vol. 4, 66.

35. "Beschluss des Grossen Senats für Strafsachen vom 14.2.1955" GSSt 1/65.

36. Achenbach was the first to argue that a verdict in absentia was an obstacle to German criminal prosecution. He had presented such arguments to the Federal Justice Ministry (Memo, Federal Justice Ministry, 8 December 1961, in BAK B 141/25629, vol. 4, 17; see also interview with Hans-Georg Schätzler by the author, 5 December 1999). In addition, he had been able to force a termination of proceedings against a former Nazi functionary he had represented as an attorney, "Einstellungsbeschluss 2. Strafkammer des LG Essen am 18. Mai 1962," 29 KS 1/60 (BAK B 141/25629, vol. 2, 130).

37. A state prosecutor with the ZStL, while on a research trip to Paris from 23 to 27 October 1966, was prevented by French authorities from consulting the files and was forced to return to Germany empty-handed. See Report, ZStL, 28 October 1966, in ZStL, General Files 9-30/19 S. 6-13.

38. On legal decisions pertaining to acting as an accessory, see Herbert, *Best,* 495ff.; Michael Greve, "Amnestierung von NS-Gehilfen—eine Panne? Die Novellierung des § 50 Abs. StGB und dessen Auswirkungen auf die Strafverfolgung," *Kritische Justiz* 2000/3: 412–424; Ingo Müller, *Furchtbare Juristen: Die unbewältigte Vergangenheit unserer Justiz* (Munich, 1987), 250ff.; Jörg Friedrich, *Die kalte Amnestie: NS-Täter in der Bundesrepublik* (Munich, 1994), 353ff.; Jürgen Baumann, "Die strafrechtliche Problematik der nationalsozialistischen Gewaltverbrechen," in Reinhard Henkys, *Nationalsozialistische Gewaltverbrechen: Geschichte und Gericht* (Stuttgart, 1965), 267–322.

39. Report, StA Cologne, 19 April 1967, in ZStL, 114 AR-Z 1670/61, 1121ff.

40. This is evident from a report of the ZStL: ZStL, General Files, 114 AR-Z 578/74.

41. Six-Month Report, StA Cologne, 1 January 1967, in Main State Archive Düsseldorf (HStA), D I a 30.

42. "Beschluss des Deutschen Bundestages vom 3.1 1975," *Bundestag-Drucksachen,* 7/130.

43. See letter from Verband der Heimkehrer (VdH) to Chief Minister Filbinger, Baden-Württemberg, 30 October 1974 (JM B.-W., 9361 F 2 IV/50), and Verband der Heimkehrer, ed., *Mahnung in letzter Stunde. Gefahr für Europa: Der Verband der Heimkehrer Deutschlands warnt vor der Ratifizierung des deutsch-französischen Zusatzabkommens zum Überleitungsvertrag* (Bonn, n.d. [1974]). The brochure contains an essay by Erich Heimeshoff entitled "Klarsfeld, Lischka und die deutsch-französische Freundschaft," which had been the centerpiece of the previous campaign waged by the VdH periodical *Der Heimkehrer*. The campaign was also given legal help by Pierre Boissier, member of the International Committee of the Red Cross, who from 1946 on had been director of the I.C.R.C. commission for providing care for German POWs in France. Boissier was a staunch opponent of French criminal prosecution. The former federal magistrate Günther Willms, who had been involved in the Hempen judgment, published an article in the *Frankfurter Allgemeine Zeitung* against the Supplementary Agreement ("Späte Aufregung in Paris," *FAZ,* 2 August 1974). SPD parliamentarian Friedrich Beermann asked the ZStL for a list of former Wehrmacht officers who might be affected before approving the agreement in the Committee on Foreign Relations (see ZStL 114 AR-Z 578/74, 36ff.).

44. See Beate Klarsfeld, *Wherever They May Be!* (New York, 1975); Heiner Lichtenstein, *Im Namen des Volkes? Eine persönliche Bilanz der NS-Prozesse* (Cologne, 1984); Rudolf Hirsch, *Um die Endlösung: Prozessberichte über den Lischka-Prozess in Köln und den Auschwitz-Prozess in Frankfurt/M* (Rudolstadt, 1983). The author is now preparing a comprehensive study.

45. Memo, StA Cologne, 20 September 1974, in Main State Archive Düsseldorf, Branch Kalkum, Rep. 158/vol. 1606, 832.

46. Order, StA Cologne, 7 February 1983, in Main State Archive Düsseldorf, Branch Kalkum, Rep. 158/vol. 1612, 2024.

Chapter 5

WEST GERMANY AND COMPENSATION FOR NATIONAL SOCIALIST EXPROPRIATION

The Restitution of Jewish Property, 1947–1964

Jürgen Lillteicher

❧

The "Aryanization" of property owned by Jews during the years of National Socialist rule was doubtless one of the most massive transfers of property in modern German history.[1] A large number of people and institutions had participated in the almost anarchic dispossession of the German Jews, and the process of confiscation later spread beyond Germany to the areas it occupied. Attempts after 1945 to reverse the material consequences of this gigantic spree of plunder faced a multitude of complex challenges and problems. For one, any program of restitution would be limited by the restricted legal means available. Further, restitution was to take place in a society whose members were heavily implicated in National Socialist crimes of violence and the policy of "Aryanization." It was thus likely that German officials involved in restitution would have a very different understanding of the immediate past than the victims. Postwar lawmakers and officials had to confront a number of questions: How was restitution to be implemented? How large should the program be? Who was entitled to compensation? Should there be indemnification to individual victims or to collective bodies that represented them? Should money paid in compensation remain in Germany or could these sums be transferred abroad? Who was to be responsible for oversight and who was to pay administrative expenses?

Thanks in large part to the Western Allies, particularly the Americans, a program of restitution designed to take account of the unusual character of the injustices committed was enacted.[2] It entailed radical solutions that were not popular in Germany. The first law on restitution of property in the American Zone of Occupation had to be pushed through as a military law against the will of the

Stuttgart State Council (Stuttgarter Länderrat), the representative body of the German states in the zone. The law was thus imposed from above on the German population by the military occupation.[3] Acting on its own authority, the American Military Government issued a law on restitution, Military Law No. 59, on 10 November 1947.[4] The purpose of the law was to return identifiable items of property to their rightful owners who had been dispossessed of the same in the period from 30 January 1933 to 8 May 1945, for reasons of race, religion, nationality, or political opposition to National Socialism. This was to be done in a speedy and comprehensive manner.[5] Additional laws in the other occupation zones soon followed. The French, mindful of the American example, passed a law on restitution in their zone that very same day.[6] The British bided their time, waiting another 18 months. In May 1949, the British military authorities finally passed a law on restitution that differed from the American law only in some minor details.[7]

German officials had earlier been involved in the effort to draft a restitution law, and they saw the attempts by the Americans and French to go it alone as an act of victors' justice or, as moderates put it, an "act of military impatience."[8] Given the general German support for restitution of possessions confiscated by the Nazi state, it may be surprising that restitution of possessions ran into prolonged delays; not until the end of the 1960s, after a series of obstacles had been overcome, was the process brought to completion.

This essay focuses on the process and results of restitution by the West German state. It is useful to restrict the scope of analysis in order to sketch the history of restitution from the 1950s to the late 1960s. Two major phases can be distinguished. The first saw the preparation and implementation of Allied legislation from 1947 to 1957; the second, the preparation and implementation of the Federal Restitution Law (*Bundsrückerstattungsgesetz*, hereafter, FRL) of 1957–64, which was handled almost exclusively by the West German authorities. The focus here is on how the various restitution laws were dealt with in practice by German authorities and courts. In particular, I ask whether there was a basic difference in how cases involving plunder under the Nazis were handled under the Allied and West German laws. Did attitudes toward the Nazi past play a role in the implementation of restitution laws? Did the change in West German perceptions and sentiments during the 1960s have an impact on restitution policy? Or was restitution unaffected by the changes West German society was then experiencing?

Background and Procedural Prerequisites

One consequence of Allied restitution legislation was that *all* legal transactions involving Jews in Germany after 30 January 1933 were suspected of having been carried out under duress. Moreover, this legislation viewed all measures by the state and Nazi Party that targeted the economic situation of the Jews, ranging from discriminatory taxes and obligatory levies to forced surrender of precious metals and other valuables, as unjustified "dispossession."[9]

Initially, restitution decisions were the prerogative of restitution agencies. If two parties could not reach an "amicable settlement," the matter could be decided by the restitution chambers in the district courts (*Landgerichte*) and courts of higher instance, namely, the Superior Regional Courts (*Oberlandesgerichte*) and the boards of review (*oberste Rückerstattungsgerichte*).[10] The boards of review were the supreme instance in each zone of occupation, and until 1955 the judges sitting on them were Allied judges appointed by the occupying powers.[11] After the Federal Republic regained most of its sovereignty with the 1954 Paris Treaties, Allied judges sat together with German judges on the bench in deciding restitution cases—a novelty in legal history.[12] By 1971, courts in the Federal Republic and West Berlin decided some 1.2 million individual claims and oversaw restitution totaling DM 7.5 billion.[13]

The character of the court proceedings hinged in large measure on the parties involved. If a case involved property transfer between private individuals, the "partners to the transaction" confronted one another, in person or through their attorneys. These confrontations could, depending on circumstances, become quite heated or emotional encounters.[14]

Restitution proceedings had a quite different character in cases where victims sought to regain property from the former German Reich. Those deliberations were far more impersonal, since the beneficiary, the National Socialist state, did not exist as such as a person. Claims against the former Reich had to be filed against the German federal government. Its financial interests were represented by the Federal Finance Ministry or the Regional Finance Offices (*Oberfinanzdirektionen*) in the individual states. Officials from the Regional Finance Offices appeared in court to respond to victims' claims. As a result of the high degree of continuity in administrative personnel, the officials responsible for restitution claims were very often the very same individuals who had earlier meticulously carried out the liquidation and seizure of Jewish property.[15]

Almost all cases revolved around monetary payments because assets confiscated by the Nazi state had immediately been converted to cash. The funds the treasury and other agencies realized through the dispossession of the Jews either disappeared into the pockets of Nazi Party members or, more often, had gone straight toward the Reich budget.

Courts in the early 1950s decided in favor of claimants in restitution suits against the German Reich even though it was not yet clear whether the Federal Republic would become the legal successor to the Third Reich or to what extent it would have to assume responsibility for the numerous robberies committed by the Nazi state on its territory. The restitution courts in the American and British zones[16] had handed down so-called declaratory judgments (*Feststellungsbeschlüsse*), while clarification as to whether the recognized sum would actually be paid was left to future discussions between the West German government and the Allies.

These questions were subsequently addressed in the Convention on the Settlement of Matters Arising out of the War and Occupation, signed on 26 May 1952.[17] The Federal Republic accepted the obligation to meet restitution claims against the Reich up to a total of DM 1.5 billion. A ministerial assessment, by contrast, had put the Reich's obligations at DM 5 billion marks.[18] With the convention, an agreement was reached on an institutional, legal, and financial framework. Negotiations with the state of Israel and the Jewish Claims Conference[19] dealt with more precise revisions and changes in legislation on compensation and restitution. Protocol No. 1 of the Convention with the Claims Conference (10 September 1952) contained certain enhancements to restitution that had been agreed upon in the negotiations.[20]

Restitution by the Treasury within the Framework of Allied Legislation

The restitution of goods and assets confiscated by the National Socialist state turned out to be the most difficult and protracted chapter in the story of restitution.[21] Most claims against private individuals had been settled by the mid-1950s, but a final settlement of claims against the state was not in sight at that time. This was due to unresolved questions regarding the extent of the state's liability as well as to the Treasury's inflexibility when it came to acceding to victims' demands. Every second case in Hamburg that involved the Treasury, for example, ended up in the restitution chambers of the regional courts (*Wiedergutmachungskammern*).[22] Officials in the regional finance offices effectively utilized the instruments at their disposal to reduce the liability of the Federal Republic to the lowest tenable minimum.[23] The reconstruction of facts in many cases had little to do with the actual events of the expropriation. In the investigations and discussions of both the courts and the Federal authorities, victims' stories of persecution were often distorted beyond recognition, fragmented, and stripped of concrete details; one British military official aptly described the results as "surreal."[24] The events surrounding the Aryanization of Jewish property had to be adapted to the abstract schemata of contract and property law. This was done, however, with an excessive zeal that reflected the bias against restitution prevalent among finance officials. The decisions by the highest Allied restitution courts demonstrate how different judicial assessment could be if events were evaluated from a different historical and legal perspective. The actual context of persecution and expropriation stood, with astonishing clarity, at the center of attention in the Allied proceedings. By contrast, the German courts, taking an overly formalistic interpretation, could adjudicate the past without even mentioning the actual events and thereby stripped the stories of any authentic sense of the actual persecution of real people.[25] I will present several examples in order to illustrate the structural problems associated with restitution by the state.

The dispute over whether collection of the Reich Flight Tax (*Reichsfluchtsteuer*) ought to be viewed as a measure of persecution illustrates the excessively legalistic approach West German officials took to Nazi injustices. The state financial departments had doubted whether the flight tax, which had been introduced by Chancellor Heinrich Brüning in 1931 in connection with his reparations policy to prevent capital flight, had been applied discriminatorily.[26] The tax, they argued, had been levied on all "emigrants" from the Reich, not just Jews. German courts concurred with this view, so complainants had to carry their legal action to the highest level of appeal. Commenting on the attitude of the German justice system toward the Reich Flight Tax, the Board of Review observed: "A hammer is not an instrument of persecution—unless and until it is used to hit somebody on the head."[27] Claims for the restitution of other discriminatory and exorbitant taxes and special levies, such as the Jewish Property Tax[28] and the so-called Dego Tax[29] were rejected by the regional finance offices. The reason most commonly given was that the revenue from special taxes and levies had been channeled by the treasury departments into the Reich Treasury and utilized there to help finance the national budget. Consequently, these special levies could no longer be considered identifiable (*feststellbare*) items of property, as the law demanded; in legal terms, the funds did not "exist." This positivistic interpretation of what was "identifiable" allowed the regional finance offices, using preprinted forms, to request a rejection of the restitution claim in all other similar cases. Officials in the regional finance offices were also aided by the law's ambiguity. Experts were extremely divided over what goods could still be regarded as "identifiable" property.[30] Someone who had paid forced taxes with stock shares that quite probably still existed after 1945 could hope for restitution, while those who had paid in cash or by bank draft came away empty-handed.[31]

Even in seemingly clear-cut cases, the regional finance offices often attempted to block restitution. Finance officials might, for example, dispute the liability of the German Reich for property confiscated by individual Reich agencies. They rejected the view that the Reich—and, as its legal successor, the Federal Republic—could be held liable for the auctioning of furniture and household effects by the Gestapo on the ground that, strictly speaking, the Gestapo had not been an agency of the German Reich.[32] This argument was also applicable in the case of auctions by so-called trustees in the absence of the owners. Disregarding their responsibility to safeguard the property in their care, trustees had often obtained permission from regional state courts to dispose of the household goods of emigrants at auction.[33] Had the Hamburg finance office succeeded with its argument, the city-state's treasury would not have had to pay restitution on property claims amounting to at least 7.2 million Reichsmarks.[34]

Following the finance offices' line of reasoning, the German Reich bore no responsibility or liability for the actions of the Reich Association of Jews in Germany even though that organization had been set up on instructions from the state. Its assigned duties came under the jurisdiction of the Reich, and it had to obey instructions from Reich agencies. For example, Jews were required to pay a special separate emigration levy to the Reich Association. German Jews deported to Theresienstadt had been forced to offset the costs of their "accommodations" there by concluding so-called home purchase contracts.[35] In most cases, the deportees, acting under duress, were obliged to transfer all of their assets to the Reich Association.

The Treasury attempted to exert a "corrective" effect on restitution decisions against private individuals by the simple measure of including the former victims in the post-1949 obligation to pay taxes. Allied restitution laws forbade the Treasury from collecting taxes retroactively from persons entitled to restitution for the period during which the individual had been deprived of any right of disposal over his or her property.[36] That did not prevent the tax offices from demanding that the old owners be required to pay property, corporation, and inheritance taxes for the entire period of confiscation until the date of the court-ordered restitution. In 1952 the Federal Supreme Finance Court (Bundesfinanzhof, BFH) halted this practice, but it also established the new legal principle that victims would be required to pay back taxes for a far more circumscribed period, namely, from the issuance of the restitution laws until the final restitution judgment in their case. The BFH believed it had satisfied the terms of the restitution laws with this ruling while, at the same time, defending the Treasury's claim to back taxes from victims of expropriation.[37] The former owners were thereupon required to pay taxes for the entire period during which they could in theory have filed a claim for restitution or during which they were waiting for a judgment on a claim. In practice, they could find themselves liable for a decade's worth of back taxes or even more. The Allies believed that this practice seriously undermined the restitution laws and felt forced to intervene. On instruction from the Allied High Commission, the BFH's ruling was rescinded and the case passed on to the United States Court of Restitution Appeals for a judgment.[38] The West German government feared that the country's highest court for financial matters might be publicly compromised, which would harm Germany's image abroad, so it asked to have the matter resolved out of court.[39] The High Commission acceded after it had been given assurance that all German tax offices would be instructed to refrain from implementing the BFH's ruling.[40] As one British official commented, "At first sight, the [BFH's] decision appears to be an example, in purest form, of German judicial surrealism. Whatever may be thought of its conclusions, its reasoning is, to say the least, breath-taking."[41]

Nazi Persecution and the Federal Restitution Law

Only in 1957 did the Federal Republic take the long overdue step of introducing procedures for payment of restitution claims against the Reich. Regulations for those procedures were finally set down in the Federal Restitution Law of 19 July 1957.[42] By limiting the total amount of restitution to DM 1.5 billion, the Federal Republic held restitution awards to a maximum of 50 percent of the value of lost property and made payment in installments over the course of many years.[43]

With the enactment of the Federal Restitution Law, all declaratory judgments handed down during the 1950s on the basis of the Allied restitution laws had to be reexamined by the regional finance offices.[44] The regional finance offices thereupon served a double function. Previously, they had appeared in restitution proceedings as one of two litigants. As a consequence of the new regulations, they became both a party to restitution disputes as well as a court for adjudicating such disputes; their decisions could, however, still be reviewed by a court.[45] By 1 July 1971, regional finance offices had issued orders for some 128,000 restitution payments.[46]

The Federal Restitution Law was not only intended to provide overdue clarification of long-standing legal uncertainties. It was the express will of West German lawmakers that more extensive restitution claims should be heard and settled. Dispossessions that had taken place outside the territory of the Federal Republic were to be dealt with in a more liberal fashion. According to Allied restitution laws, the return of property confiscated in territories occupied by Germany was not possible unless proof could be presented as to the exact location the goods had been shipped to within the territory of the Federal Republic and West Berlin.[47] Only in rare cases, however, were victims able to demonstrate precisely where their possessions had been shipped by the Nazi authorities for *Verwertung* (utilization). Officials had to reject such claims on the grounds that it was impossible to clarify which authority was now competent to deal with the matter, as the last known location of the stolen goods was automatically the venue of the trial. This deplorable state of affairs had to be remedied.

The new law permitted restitution of property in cases in which the final destination in West Germany or West Berlin could not be established. The law did, however, require proof that the goods had been brought to the territory of the Federal Republic or West Berlin, or that the removal of the goods to those areas was at least plausible and could not be ruled out.[48] A fiction was created for such cases: it was decided that the stolen goods had been shipped to Greater Berlin. Those cases would then come under the jurisdiction of the Berlin courts.[49]

The effective scope of restitution law was thus significantly expanded to encompass the seizure of property of persecuted minorities throughout Europe. Payment of restitution awards could, however, be made only to claimants living in countries with which the Federal Republic maintained diplomatic relations.[50] This political proviso substantially restricted the circle of claimants who might potentially receive restitution. All the states of the Eastern bloc except the Soviet Union fell under this exclusionary clause. Consequently, payments in accordance with the Federal Restitution Law initially could only be made to victims resident in Western European countries.[51] The law nonetheless brought a major expansion in the investigative activities of the restitution agencies and courts.

The Federal Restitution Law provided a new framework for dealing with several types of confiscated property, including:

1. the spoils of large-scale "furniture operations" in which occupation authorities in France, the Netherlands, Luxembourg, and Belgium had shipped off furniture belonging to deported Jews for distribution to Germans who had lost their household possessions during air raids;[52]
2. property confiscated from Jews upon their arrival in extermination and labor camps, and which was then sent back to the Reich by the camp

Verwertung departments; this included clothing and valuables such as cash and jewelry;[53]

3. all objects confiscated in the course of Operation Reinhardt[54] as well as goods seized during all other deportation actions in German-occupied areas.

The following case involving the claims of a concentration camp survivor illustrate how the Federal Restitution Law was implemented in practice. I have selected this case because it entailed a number of conflicts that illuminate the complex interplay of legal and financial administrations, the limits of a narrow, fiscal way of thinking, and the interdependency between restitution and politics.

Together with his wife and son, Emanuel Kugler had been deported from Czechoslovakia by the German security authorities and transported to the Auschwitz extermination camp. There, the Kuglers' clothing and remaining belongings were taken from them. Emanuel Kugler survived Auschwitz and returned to Czechoslovakia. Like other Holocaust survivors in Eastern European countries, he received no compensation for his physical and mental suffering in Auschwitz.[55] After the Federal Restitution Law went into effect, he filed a claim with the restitution authorities in Berlin for compensation for the clothing seized from him and his family members. His claim was rejected on the grounds that he could not prove that his belongings had arrived at a destination in the territory of the Federal Republic or West Berlin.[56] According to the official who reviewed Kugler's claim, it was unlikely that the confiscated clothing had ended up in the territory of the Federal Republic or West Berlin because under SS regulations all articles of clothing were to be handed over to the office responsible for assisting ethnic German settlers in the East, the Volksdeutsche Mittelstelle (VOMI). Emanuel Kugler objected. As a prisoner in Auschwitz, he himself had packed large bales of clothing and helped load them onto freight trains which he believed were to be dispatched to Germany. In his complaint to the restitution agency, he wrote that it was a mockery of logic and justice to argue that it could not be "proven" that the articles had been sent to Germany. He requested that the agency recognize his human and legal rights.[57]

Civil Law Chamber 143 of the Berlin Supreme Court of Appeals ruled on this case.[58] The judges confirmed the original decision by the restitution agency, adding that even if Kugler's assertion were true, the articles of clothing could just as easily have been shipped to the territory of the Soviet Occupation Zone. Consequently, the Federal Republic had no legal obligation to make restitution.

Kugler's attempt to receive compensation from the German state for the clothing confiscated from him appeared to be hopeless. It is astonishing for the observer today that the victim was asked to offer proof for something which he could not possibly substantiate with the means available to him. But fortune smiled on Kugler in the form of professional assistance by the Comité International d'Auschwitz. The general secretary of the Committee, Hermann Langbein,[59] took over the correspondence with the Berlin authorities. Langbein stressed the claimant's destitution and pointed to documents proving what the claimant alleged. He noted that Kugler had been in negotiation with the Federal Finance Ministry for some time and requested that the decision of the Berlin Civil Division of the Supreme Court of Appeal be rescinded.[60] Only after receiving Langbein's letter did the Berlin authorities initiate more careful inquiries. There was a lively exchange of letters between Langbein and the Civil Division regarding the probative force of various documents he had submitted. The opposing party in the case, the Office for the Administration of Special Property and Buildings (Sondervermögens- und Bauverwaltung) in the Berlin finance department, did not seem to be informed about the negotiations between the Comité International d'Auschwitz and the Federal Finance Ministry. Nor had it made much of an effort to research the background and history of the case. The court proceedings continued although Kugler's case and other similar legal actions[61] were awaiting possible resolution out of court.

The civilian courts—on this occasion the Third Division of the Supreme Court of Appeals (3. Zivilkammer des Kammergerichtes [Oberlandesgericht])—dealt with this case a second time on 27 September 1961. The request was rejected once again. The ruling verdict[62] indicated that the court had taken a more careful look at the machinery for *Verwertung* of confiscated goods in the death camps. Nonetheless, the court was unable to find any evidence in the documentation submitted that clothing shipped from the Auschwitz extermination camp had gone primarily to Western Germany or Berlin. The court noted that one of the documents indicated textiles had been distributed via the VOMI to ethnic German settlers living mainly in the Eastern territories. The line adopted by the Supreme Court of Appeals was thus identical to that pursued by the official in the Berlin restitution agency at the very outset of the proceedings. The court did not appear to be persuaded by other documents attesting to how clothing and textiles, and even the hair of victims murdered in Auschwitz, were meticulously gathered for subsequent *Verwertung*. Apparently the court found no solid evidence in its examination of the lists of plunder, nor did it comment in any way on the horrendous actions that took place in Auschwitz.

A higher-level review by the Supreme Restitution Court in Berlin proved unnecessary once negotiations between the victims' organizations and the Federal Finance Ministry ended in success. The Sondervermögens- und Bauverwaltung agreed to pay DM 350 to indemnify the cost of the clothing of Emanuel Kugler, DM 300 for that of his wife Herta Kugler, and DM 350 for that of his son Andrej.[63] The settlement became effective on 4 July 1962. But Emanuel Kugler still did not receive anything. Paragraph 45 of the Federal Restitution Law prohibited payment to any person resident in countries with which the Federal Republic did not have diplomatic relations. Repeated petitions by Kugler to the restitution agencies in Berlin, in which he made reference to his advanced age—he had in the meantime turned eighty-four—could do nothing to end the legal impasse. Eleven years after the decision by the restitution division, the Berlin regional finance office wrote to Kugler promising to initiate payment proceedings as soon as diplomatic relations were established with Czechoslovakia.[64]

It is unlikely that Emanuel Kugler lived long enough to receive the DM 1,000 that he had been awarded.

A striking disparity between the reality of persecution and the reconstruction of events by the courts was evident in the proceedings initiated on the basis of suits brought by former concentration camp inmates. The interpretation of the Federal Restitution Law by the courts and finance authorities led to a reductionist and, as British military officials had correctly observed, almost surreal presentation of the history of Nazi persecution. The judiciary avoided any commentary on the monstrosity of the machinery for *Verwertung* of plundered goods in the extermination camps.[65] Although the Federal Restitution Law substantially improved the situation for claimants by making provision for acts of confiscation committed outside the territory of the Federal Republic, it nonetheless failed to help the people who experienced the worst of the Nazi system of persecution. Without professional assistance, it was impossible for survivors of the death camps to prove that their property had indeed been shipped to a location that now lay within the territory of the Federal Republic. This difficulty was compounded by the fact that the courts limited their investigations to hearing cases and verifying the statements of the two parties even though they were obliged by the Federal Restitution Law to pursue further inquiry.[66] Only after being subjected to pressure by victims' organizations did the courts gradually begin to address what had transpired in the death camps. It was unclear whether the courts and, in particular, the regional finance offices, lacked access to better historical information than the victims, or whether they chose to leave it to the victims to "prove" what was already known. At least in professional circles, the Berlin judiciary was notorious for causing unnecessary delays in restitution cases.[67]

To survivors like Kugler, this official approach, strictly oriented to the letter of procedural law, must have seemed absurd, especially when they themselves had witnessed what was done with the confiscated belongings of the murdered. The tension between the victims' direct experience of persecution and the juridical logic of bureaucratic procedure, which in most cases worked out to the clear benefit of the West German Treasury, was most clearly evident here.

Conclusion

Is there evidence of a difference in attitude between restitution proceedings based on Allied law and those based on the Federal Restitution Law? Probably not. The examples and cases presented here are not a representative sample; they were selected, rather, because they point to structural problems in restitution by the state. Cases that sparked heated conflict might have represented only a small minority of all cases, yet it is precisely these legal actions that can serve to illuminate the basic structures of the phenomenon as a whole. Only controversial cases have left their mark in the documentation, and historians are at the mercy of the surviving evidence.

In restitution cases adjudicated before West German courts on the basis of Allied legislation, as we have seen, the accused party, i.e., the German Treasury, generally interpreted the measures of the National Socialist regime legalistically and construed the liability of the former German Reich to be quite limited. Following a formalistic interpretation of Allied legislation oriented more to the principles of the civil code, financial officials chose either to reduce plaintiffs' claims substantially or reject them entirely. Years of litigation were required before higher courts rectified or repudiated the view of the law prevailing in regional finance offices. The habits of official foot-dragging, excessive litigiousness, and drawing out restitution proceedings were clearly at odds with the law, as one of the central provisions of the restitution laws stipulated that restitution should be as speedy and comprehensive as possible. The belligerency and disputatiousness of the finance authorities led to the precise opposite.

Although the Federal Restitution Law was not tainted by Allied dictate, it was nonetheless in essence the implementation of contractual agreements oriented to the guidelines and goals of the Allied legislation. The Convention of 26 May 1952, and the agreements with the Claims Conference concluded on 10 September 1952, ensured that restitution would continue. The Convention also set the financial limits of restitution and ensured that restitution would be extended to cover other aspects of Nazi persecution. At the same time, the Federal Restitution Law provided definitive answers to unresolved legal questions that had arisen with the beginning of restitution in the three Western occupation zones. The implementation of German law was not accompanied by any evident change in the basic attitudes of the judiciary and the Treasury. Despite changes in the legal framework, the practice of abstracting the history of persecution and interpreting the law in ways that favored the German finance authorities continued. Restitution was not an issue of broad public interest in the Federal Republic. The Treasury and plaintiffs both shunned the limelight. The media treated the topic cursorily, if at all, singling out cases that involved seemingly "excessive" demands or attempts by claimants to deceive the authorities.[68]

What causes underlay the abiding inflexible attitude on the part of the Treasury authorities? There were three main factors. First, although the Federal Restitution Law had been passed by the Bundestag, it was anchored in spirit in Allied military legislation. Consequently, it still struck the West German public as something alien, even repulsive. Many of the defensive mechanisms of the justice system and finance administration derived from the fact that the Germans had to act within the confines of regulations and laws that had been imposed on them from without.[69] Many Germans were reluctant to place a stamp of legitimacy on such regulations. The memory of Versailles lingered on and made politicians and officials hypersensitive to dictates by the victorious powers—to the point that any cooperation with the Allies was construed by many as collaboration.[70] Judges and restitution officials did not recognize that the restitution laws were ultimately a compromise between West Germany and the Western Allies. These laws and the oversight by Allied courts were considered a kind of tutelage for German administrators, which were seen to compromise their executive sovereignty.

Secondly, the claims of the victims of persecution were always viewed as part of the general burdens resulting from the lost war—even though the persecution and annihilation of the Jews had been not an unintended consequence of the war but an explicit war aim of the National Socialists. Few West Germans seemed aware that the economic disenfranchisement and financial plundering of the German Jews had begun in 1933. From this blinkered perspective, restitution demands were not old debts Germany had to pay; rather, they were new claims that had been granted a stamp of legality by Allied intervention. The perception of many Germans that they themselves had been victims during the war obscured qualitative differences between the groups of victims. Most West Germans either put the demands of the victims of Nazism on the same level as the claims for compensation by German expellees, former civil servants, and German citizens who had suffered wartime losses, or they regarded the victims' claims as secondary.

Thirdly, continuity in personnel in the justice system and public administration had a strong adverse impact on the adjudication of restitution claims. Especially in the first decade of restitution proceedings, the rejection of a claim—and thus the negation of Nazi injustice—served indirectly to exculpate the judiciary and the finance administration. Full recognition of a claim for restitution would have been tantamount to admission of complicity with the unjust National Socialist regime. Thus, the deficiencies in implementation of the restitution laws presented here cannot be explained solely by pointing to the incompatibility of bureaucratic procedure and historical reality. Rather, it was the reluctance of justice and finance officials that made restitution an area of conflict through the late 1960s. Although there was an evident shift in West German attitudes toward the Nazi past during the 1960s, it was barely reflected in restitution matters. On the contrary, there seems to have been a move in the opposite direction that culminated in a call on behalf of the "victims of restitution." As the occupation receded into the past, revisionists became ever more vocal in demanding rectification of purported injustices in private restitution committed under the Allied restitution laws. The ministries now turned a sympathetic ear to former "Aryanizers" who believed that *they* had been injured by restitution or the claims of Jews (*Rückerstattungs- oder Judengeschädigte*) and were therefore demanding financial indemnification.[71]

— *Translated from the German by William Templer*

Notes

1. See Frank Bajohr, *"Arisierung" in Hamburg: Die Verdrängung der jüdischen Unternehmer 1933–1945* (Hamburg, 1997), 9.
2. JCS 1067, Para. 48, in Wilhelm Cornides und Hermann Volle, eds., *Um den Frieden mit Deutschland: Dokumente zum Problem der deutschen Friedensordnung* (Oberursel, 1948), 72.
3. The genesis of the American restitution law is treated in detail in Constantin Goschler, *Wiedergutmachung: Westdeutschland und die Verfolgten des Nationalsozialismus (1945–1954)* (Munich, 1992), 106–26.
4. *Amtsblatt der Militärregierung Deutschland—Amerikanisches Kontrollgebiet*, Ausgabe G, 1.
5. Article 1 of the restitution law issued in the American Zone of Occupation. See Hans Freiherr von Godin, *Rückerstattung feststellbarer Vermögensgegenstände* (Berlin, 1950), 1.
6. Order 120 of the French Supreme Commander in Germany, 10 November 1947 on the restitution of stolen items of property, emended by orders 156, 186, and 213. See *Journal Officiel—Amtsblatt des französischen Oberkommandos in Deutschland* 1949, Nos. 279, 280, 281, 282: 2060.
7. The law went into effect on 12 May 1949, see *Amtsblatt der Militärregierung Deutschland, Britisches Kontrollgebiet*, No. 28, 1169. The British were afraid restitution payments made to Jewish organizations could indirectly reach the hands of Jewish paramilitary groups in Palestine, weakening the British mandatory power in its struggle against the Jewish underground there. O'Reagan P. to Robb, M. A., 24 April 1947, Public Record Office, Kew (PRO), FO 371/65059, and Finance Division to Foreign Office, 2 July 1947, PRO, FO 1046/184. In the British Zone, General Order No. 10 had put a legal restraint on property from an early point and permitted persons to file restitution claims. But a final legal regulation was not instituted until 1949.
8. See Otto Küster, "Das geschäftliche Unternehmen in der Rückerstattung," in *Weitere praktische Fragen der Rückerstattung* (Heidelberg, 1950), 55.
9. *Entziehung* (dispossession) was the seizure or handover of property under duress. Since victims often found it impossible to prove there had been coercion, the law provided for facilitation of proof in the form of legal suspicion. It was determined under what circumstances the court could accept that duress had been involved and under what conditions such suspicion could be refuted and rejected. See Walter Schwarz, *Rückerstattung nach den Gesetzen der alliierten Mächte* (Munich, 1974), 145–46.
10. In the British zone, the Board of Review (BOR); in the American zone, the Court of Restitution Appeals (CORA); and in the French zone the Cour Supérieur pour les Restitutions (CSR). See Schwarz, *Rückerstattung*, 275, 321.
11. In the third section of the Convention on the Settlement of Matters Arising out of the War and the Occupation, of 26 May 1952 (*Überleitungsvertrag*), West Germany agreed with the Allies on a model based on parity. But it was not until 1955, after the Convention became effective, that the Board of Review, the Court of Restitution Appeals and the Court Superieur were amalgamated into the Supreme Restitution Court, which was divided into separate divisions (*Senate*) in the three zones. The five-member commission of each division had two judges appointed by the occupational power, two German judges and a neutral chairman. "Vertrag zur Regelung aus Krieg und Besatzung entstandener Fragen," *Bundesgesetzblatt* I: 215ff.; Schwarz, *Rückerstattung*, 275–77.
12. It remains a curious fact in the legal history of the Federal Republic, for example, that in one division of the Supreme Restitution Court, a lawyer from Illinois, a former chief justice from Khartoum, and a state prosecutor from Algiers, together with German judges and chaired by a chief judge from Stockholm, adjudicated in a legal action on the restitution of a factory in Dortmund. See Walter Schwarz, "Das Recht der Wiedergutmachung und seine Geschichte," *Juristische Schulung* (1986): 433.
13. Statistical Report on Internal Restitution, 1 July 1971, Bundesarchiv Berlin (BArch B) 136/3318, 5.

14. My dissertation examines private restitution in West Germany in detail. See Lillteicher, "Die Rückerstattung jüdischen Eigentums in Westdeutschland nach dem Zweiten Weltkrieg: eine Studie über Verfolgungserfahrung, Rechtsstaatlichkeit und Vergangenheitspolitik 1945–1971" (PhD diss., University of Freiburg, 2002).

15. Alfons Kenkmann and Bernd A. Rusinek, eds. *Verfolgung und Verwaltung: Die wirtschaftliche Ausplünderung der Juden und die westfälischen Finanzbehörden* (Münster, 1999), 12; see also Gerd Blumberg, "Etappen der Ausraubung und ihre bürokratische Apparatur," in Kenkmann and Rusinek, *Verfolgung und Verwaltung*, 38–39.

16. Order No. 120, which dealt with restitution in the French zone, only envisioned return of items of property still actually in existence. Consequently, only in such cases could the former German Reich be ordered to restitute the property. See Schwarz, *Rückerstattung*, 295.

17. On 26 May 1952, Adenauer, Schumann, Acheson and Eden signed the Convention in the framework of the Treaty on Germany. Due to a lack of support in the French National Assembly for the European Defense Community, which was connected with the Treaty on Germany, the entire treaty complex did not go into effect, subsequent to new negotiations, until 1955. Regulations on restitution are contained in the third section of the treaty. See Goschler, *Wiedergutmachung*, 255.

18. Statement of Opinion on the Remarks of the Allied Experts on the German Memorandum on Article 5a Sec. I of the Convention—Restitution Obligations of the Reich, BArch B 141/9082, no pagination. For the present value in Euro, multiply by a factor of 5.

19. Memorandum regarding the status and purposes of the conference on Jewish material claims against Germany, Central Archives for the History of the Jewish People, Jerusalem (CAHJP), CC New York, 7078; see Conference on Jewish Material Claims against Germany, ed., *Twenty Years Later: Activities of the Conference on Jewish Material Claims against Germany 1952–1972* (New York, 1972); Ronald W. Zweig, *German Reparations and the Jewish World: A History of the Claims Conference* (Boulder, 1987), 15–27.

20. Planned Regulations on the Expansion of Restitution Legislation, 6 August 1952, I Point 2, CAHJP, CC, NY, 7048.

21. The findings of my investigation are based on intensive case studies in Hamburg, examination of the general judgments in the periodical *Rechtsprechung zum Wiedergutmachungsrecht* (RzW) and my reading of corresponding general files of the Restitution Agency, Hamburg.

22. "Bericht über die Tätigkeit des Wiedergutmachungsamtes im Jahre 1952," 1 January 1953, Archiv des Wiedergutmachungsamtes am Landgericht Hamburg (WgA LGHH), 11.00-20.

23. This practice was likewise disliked by officials in the restitution agencies because it caused unnecessary delays in restitution. See Monthly Report, Hamburg Restitution Agency, 31 January 1951, WgA LGHH, 11.00-20; Annual Report of the Restitution Agency for the Year 1950, WgA LGHH, 11.00-20.

24. Bathurst, M. E. to Fuchs, H.R, Office of the Legal Adviser, 15 December 1952, PRO FO 1060/698.

25. See Ulrich Herbert and Olaf Groehler, *Zweierlei Bewältigung: Vier Beiträge über den Umgang mit der NS-Vergangenheit in den beiden deutschen Staaten* (Hamburg, 1992), 13.

26. "Verordnung des Reichspräsidenten zur Sicherung von Wirtschaft und Finanzen und zum Schutze des inneren Friedens vom 8.12.1931, Siebenter Teil, Drittes Kapitel, Erster Abschnitt, §1–13," *Reichsgesetzblatt* I, 699; see Bajohr, *"Arisierung,"* 153.

27. Decision, Board of Review, 6 November 1951, BOR 51/141, 143, RzW 52, no. 1 (1949): 14–15. See Schwarz, *Rückerstattung*, 283.

28. The so-called *Judenvermögensabgabe*. Dr. Topp OFD Hamburg to WgA Hamburg, 24 November 1949, Staatsarchiv Hamburg (StAHH) 314–15, Oberfinanzpräsident, A5, fol. 3708).

29. Or *Degoabgabe*. The transfer of assets abroad was made more difficult by this so-called *disagio*, a large deduction that had to be paid in foreign currency to the Deutsche Golddiskontbank (Dego) when converting a closed emigrant account. This sum could amount to up to 90 percent of the capital. See WgA LGHH, Z 2; Bajohr, *"Arisierung,"* 153.

30. A dispute arose as to whether the items of property had to be "identifiable," i.e., whether their location had to be known at the time of confiscation or at the time a claim was filed. RzW 50, no. 12 (1949): 361; RzW 50, no. 7 (1949): 217–19.

31. RzW 50, no. 10 (1949): 320. Walter Schwarz, *In den Wind gesprochen? Glossen zur Wiedergutmachung des nationalsozialistischen Unrechts* (Munich, 1969), 52.

32. The Gestapo was a part of the Reich Security Main Office (RSHA) and thus the SS. Yet the Reich Interior Ministry had assigned it genuine governmental functions, such as internal security and protection of the citizenry, so that it was acting on orders of the Reich.

33. WgA LGHH, Z 1114.

34. This was the total proceeds from the auction of packed household goods owned by Jewish emigrants to be shipped abroad and stored in the Hamburg port. Down to 31 March 1943, the contents of some 3,000 wooden containers (with a capacity of several tons) was sold at give-away prices by auction to the Hamburg population. Handwritten memo by a finance official on the accounts of the Gestapo, 18 July 1950. StAHH, Oberfinanzpräsident, 314–15, 47 UA 13, fol. 10. On the process of dispossession, see Bajohr, *"Arisierung" in Hamburg*, 332–37.

35. Case Isac Feilchenfeld, PRO, FO 371/109798, BOR/53/627, 21 July 1954, "Ausgewählte Entscheidungen des Obersten Rückerstattungsgerichts, Zweiter Senat," 197.

36. Art. 91, USREG, see von Godin, *Rückerstattung*, 256f.

37. "Entscheidung des Bundesfinanzhofes vom 7.11.1952," in *Sammlung der Entscheidungen und Gutachten des Bundesfinanzhofes* 56 (1953): 618–22.

38. Letter, U. F. Golay, Secretary General of the Allied High Commission to Ministerial Director Blankenhorn, Office of the Chancellor of the Federal Republic of Germany, 21 February 1953. PRO, FO 1060/698.

39. Letter, Ministerial Director Blankenhorn to W. Neate, Secretary General of the Allied High Commission, Bad Godesberg, 15 April 1953, PRO, FO 1060/698.

40. Draft of a coordinating decree of the highest financial authorities in the states on the restitution laws, Appendix 1, Minutes of a Special Meeting of the Law Committee with Representatives of the Federal Government held at Mehlemer Aue on Monday, 11 May 1953 at 1500 hours, PRO, FO 1060/698.

41. Bathurst, M. E. to Fuchs, H.R, Office of the Legal Adviser, 15 December 1952, PRO FO 1060/698.

42. "Bundesgesetz zur Regelung der rückerstattungsrechtlichen Geldverbindlichkeiten des deutschen Reiches und gleichgestellter Rechtsträger (BRüG)," *Bundesgesetzblatt* I: 374 (hereafter, FRL).

43. See essays by Constantin Goschler and Jürgen Lillteicher, in Goschler and Lillteicher, *"Arisierung" und Restitution* (Göttingen, 2002).

44. Precisely how the previous decisions were to be changed is stipulated in §§ 15–16, FRL. See Friedrich Biella, "Die Entstehung des Bundesrückerstattungsgesetzes," in *Die Wiedergutmachung nationalsozialistischen Unrechts durch die Bundesrepublik Deutschland*, ed. Federal Finance Minister in cooperation with Hermann Schwarz (Munich, 1974–87), 2:91–96.

45. See Walter Schwarz, "Einige praktische Fragen zum Bundesrückerstattungsgesetz," RzW, no. 12 (1957): 380.

46. According to §38 3. Änd.-Ges. BRüG, there was a total of 128,219 decisions by regional finance offices including West Berlin, leading to payment of DM 2,502,111,622. "Statistischer Bericht über die innere Rückerstattung vom 1. Juli 1971," BArch B 136/3318, 6.

47. Friedrich Biella, "Die Entstehung des Bundesrückerstattungsgesetzes," in Federal Finance Minister and Schwarz, *Das Bundesrückerstattungsgesetz*, 2:85.

48. See para. 5, FRL.

49. Berlin within the boundaries laid down in Art. 4 of the Berlin Constitution of 1950.

50. § 45 BRüG," *Bundesgesetzblatt* 1957 I: 742.

51. Accordng to para. 45 of the FRL, those excluded were legal claimants who were resident or had their permanent address in Cambodia, the People's Republic of Korea, Laos, Nepal, Taiwan, and

all states in the Eastern bloc except for the Soviet Union. This stipulation referred to residence at the time of the proceedings, not the time of confiscation. "Bekanntmachung des Bundesministeriums der Finanzen gemäß §45 BRüG vom 26.08.1975," *Bundesanzeiger*, No. 168.

52. On the "M-Aktion," see Bajohr, *"Arisierung" in Hamburg*, 333ff.
53. On the warehouses found in Auschwitz after liberation, see the report of the Russian commission headed by Cpt. Gentovitch, 4 March 1945. The commission concluded here that the items stolen from the murdered were sorted, repaired and sent back to Germany. Archiv für Wiedergutmachung beim Landesarchiv Berlin, B 039-01 Nr. 350, fols. 506–10.
54. See Wilfried Wirth, "Entziehung von Sachvermögen außerhalb des Geltungsbereichs des Bundesrückerstattungsgesetzes," in Federal Finance Minister and Schwarz, *Das Bundesrückerstattungsgesetz*, 2:272.
55. See Ulrich Herbert, "Nicht entschädigungsfähig. Die Wiedergutmachungsansprüche der Ausländer," in Ludolf Herbst and Constantin Goschler, eds., *Wiedergutmachung in der Bundesrepublik Deutschland* (Munich, 1989), 273–303.
56. Resolution, Berlin Restitution agencies, 4 September 1959, Wiedergutmachungsämter von Berlin, 51/54 WGA 3385/57, fols. 4–5.
57. Letter, Emanuel Kugler to the Restitution agencies Berlin, 4 September 1959, Wiedergutmachungsämter von Berlin, 51/54 WGA 3385/57, fol. 8.
58. Resolution, Civil Division 143, Berlin District Court, 31 January 1961, Wiedergutmachungsämter von Berlin, 51/54 WGA 3385/57, fols. 11–12.
59. Hermann Langbein was himself an Auschwitz survivor. His investigations helped lead to the Frankfurt Auschwitz Trial. Until 1961, Langbein served as General Secretary of the International Auschwitz Committee (IAK). In 1964 he became secretary of the Comité International des Camps founded by the Union International de la Résistance et de la Déportation.
60. Letter, Hermann Langbein to Civil Division 143 of the Berlin District Court, 23 March 1961, Wiedergutmachungsämter von Berlin, 51/54 WGA 3385/57, fols. 17–18.
61. The attorney H.G. Philipp alone represented some 700 French Auschwitz survivors. Nagel, Office for the Administration of Special Property and Buildings, to Supreme Court of Appeals, Berlin-Charlottenburg, 14 August 1961, Wiedergutmachungsämter von Berlin, 51/54 WGA 3385/57, fol. 29.
62. Judgment, Berlin Supreme Court of Appeals, 27 September 1961. Wiedergutmachungsämter von Berlin, 51/54 WGA 3385/57, fols. 32–40.
63. Letter, Dr. H.G. Philipp to Berlin Supreme Court of Appeals, 11 May 1962, and letter, Office for the Administration of Special Property and Buildings, Regional Finance Office Berlin to the Berlin Supreme Court of Appeals, 16 May 1962. Wiedergutmachungsämter von Berlin, 51/54 WGA 3385/57, fols. 44–45.
64. Letter, Alpermann, competent official on the case, Regional Finance Office Berlin to Emanuel Kugler, 25 April 1973, Wiedergutmachungsämter von Berlin, 51/54 WGA 3385/57, fol. 62.
65. The lists submitted in the proceedings documented that three tons of women's hair had been sent to the Reich Economy Ministry. On 6 August 1942, an order was issued stipulating that hair shorn from prisoners was to be utilized in the manufacture of felt shoes for submarine personnel and Reichsbahn employees. Quoted in Raul Hilberg, *Die Vernichtung der europäischen Juden* (Frankfurt am Main, 1994), 2:1020.
66. The basis here was the procedural rules in matters of voluntary jurisdiction (*freiwillige Gerichtsbarkeit*) according to para. 2, FRL No. 59. Yet this did not vitiate the fundamental ideas in the Code of Civil Procedure.
67. Walter Schwarz to Ministerialrat Dr. Koppe, FMF, 12 June 1958, BArch, B 126/9965. Schwarz wrote: "es ist leider nicht das erste Mal, dass die Berliner Wiedergutmachungsämter den Ablauf der Wiedergutmachung hemmen."
68. The Deutsch case had an unusually broad echo in the press in the 1960s. He was a Hungarian attorney who represented the restitution claims of the family Hatvany. Shortly before the end of the war, the SS had confiscated and sent their large collection of art to the Reich. The restitution

demands amounted to some 50 million marks. The Federal Finance Ministry accused the attorney of having utilized false documents.

69. Thus, for example, officials in the Hamburg Restitution Agency believed that the restitution law was a product of Allied victors' justice and that restitution could be seen in some way as a kind of "second confiscation" and that the individual restitutors should themselves be compensated in the near future for the hardships *they* had endured. See Monthly Report, Hamburg Restitution Agency, 31 August 1950, WgA LGHH, 11.00-20.

70. The Axis Victims League also gave a similar analysis of the situation in Germany. Every Federal German government which gave massive support to the Allied restitution laws was considered, especially in the eyes of the opponents of restitution, as the "servant of a foreign power." Axis Victims League, Memorandum on Restitution, February 1951, PRO, FO 1008/83. See on this in detail my forthcoming book, and Constantin Goschler, "Die Politik der Rückerstattung in Westdeutschland," in Goschler and Lillteicher, *"Arisierung" und Restitution*, 99–12.

71. The Law on Compensation for Damages Due to Reparation, Restitution, and Destruction (Gesetz zur Abgeltung von Reparations-, Restitutions-, Zerstörungs- und Rückerstattungsschäden) of 12 February 1969 also made it possible for indemnification to be awarded to individual restitutors.

Chapter 6

THE MODERNIZATION OF WEST GERMAN POLICE
Between the Nazi Past and Weimar Tradition

Klaus Weinhauer

❧

In March 1964, a leading Hamburg police doctor summarized factors impeding a "mental renewal" of the police in West Germany. First, during the Third Reich the police saw itself "abused" and, following its traditional duty of obedience, embroiled in an innocent tragedy (even if the misdemeanors of some civil servants were undisputed). Among policemen it had been forgotten that the "moral balance sheet of the Bundeswehr, the judges, the educators, or the doctors is equally in deficit." Second, police were "extremely sensitive to criticism. Not all police leaders understand that police affairs are not a preserve insulated from public scrutiny."[1]

Given the important position the police occupy in modern states and societies, it is worth analyzing the reasons behind the elitist professional ethics and isolation of West German police. It is even more important to ask how this organization, which exercised a domestic monopoly of force in postwar German society, came to terms with its Nazi past. Did it partake in what Hermann Lübbe dubbed the *gewisse Stille* (certain silence) about its role in that period?

West German historians have only just started to study the social reintegration of former Nazi elites.[2] The process of reintegration, as Norbert Frei has noted, produced a "loyal civil service that was obliged to the state under the rule of law," but at the cost of "moral and political deficits."[3] This was especially true of West German police forces and the justice system. Looking at the police, it is impossible to answer the question of what "consequence National Socialism had *inside* the democracy."[4] One reason why this question cannot be answered is the absence of case studies of the police forces of the individual West German states. In addition, although valuable studies of the criminal police and the Gestapo have been published, the

---

history of the police under Nazi rule is still insufficiently researched.[5] Identifying specific police practices inherited from National Socialism is also extremely difficult because there was no radical break in police traditions after World War II. The reconstruction of police forces in the American and British zone was strongly influenced by traditions of the Prussian police forces of the Weimar Republic.[6] Moreover, there were strong personal continuities with the Nazi years.[7]

To analyze how West Germany dealt with the Nazi past(s), we should not limit our view to individuals or the nation as a whole. Focusing on organizations, as an intermediate level of analysis, also holds promise. Given the continuities in their personnel, it is useful to take a closer look at the transformations that occurred in these institutions as they were compelled to adapt to social and political change. There have only been preliminary steps so far toward analyzing the personnel structure of the civil service in the early Federal Republic, and there is almost no scholarship on the day-to-day work of civil service institutions and how it changed over the years.[8]

There are several points of departure for studying the social history of the West German police. One way to enhance our understanding of the police as one of the most important institutions of West German domestic society is to study the factors that contributed to its cohesion. This means analyzing its internal group structures as well as the narratives circulated among its members.[9] A critical look at comradeship in its mythological and practical forms is an especially promising methodology for constructing a social and cultural historical of the police.[10]

This essay focuses on the police forces of North Rhine-Westphalia. After providing some background information on the police during the Nazi era and the postwar reorganization of West German police forces, it will focus on the debate over the Nazi past and the police forces of North Rhine-Westphalia during the years 1956 to 1963. It will also consider police traditions in West Germany, which were strongly influenced by the example of the Prussian police of the Weimar Republic. The debate over the Nazi past coincided with the implementation of far-reaching changes aimed at modernizing police work in West Germany.[11] These changes, I will argue, meant a sharp break with many police traditions.

There were three career groups (*Laufbahngruppen*) open to police in West Germany. In 1961, 95.6 percent of the policemen of North Rhine-Westphalia belonged to the intermediate service (*mittlerer Dienst*), 4.0 percent to the superior service (*gehobener Dienst*), and 0.4 percent to the senior service (*höherer Dienst*).[12] One of the most important challenges in modernizing West German police forces in the 1950s and 1960s was the persistence of Weimar traditions. Theoretically, policemen who had been born as late as 1912 would have had the chance to serve in the police of the Weimar Republic. In North Rhine-Westphalia, the proportion of policemen in this age-group clearly decreased during the 1960s, falling from 23.9 percent of the whole in 1961 to 11.9 percent in 1967. In the senior service, the figure fell from over 80 percent to 30 percent.

Police service during Nazi rule covered a wide range of activities. In August 1940, for example, 134,000 out of 244,000 members of the Order Police were assigned to station duty (*Revierdienst*), 60,000 were members of police battalions, 16,000 belonged to the police division created at the beginning of World War II, and 8,000 were active as military police in the Wehrmacht.[13] Thus, in 1940 approximately 30 percent of the members of the Order Police were active at least occasionally in units engaged in "nonlocal interventions." These interventions very often went hand in hand with mass murder. Until the 1990s, these activities were played down as "antipartisan" or "antigang" actions (*Partisanen- oder Bandenbekämpfung*).[14] It is impossible to draw sharp distinctions among the various activities of the police because members of the police battalions were often temporarily transferred back to their home garrison for station duty. Even if West German policemen did not have a common Nazi past, many of them shared the experience of antipartisan warfare.

The "131ers" and the Debate over Membership in Nazi Organizations

Article 131 of the Federal Republic's Basic Law stipulated that the Bundestag pass legislation to regulate "the legal status of those persons who on May 8, 1945, were employed in the public service ... and who until now have not been employed or are not employed in a position corresponding to their former position."[15] On 11 May 1951, the Law Regulating the Legal Status of Persons Falling under Article 131 of the Basic Law was promulgated. It mandated that all government bodies and public enterprises had a "placement obligation" (*Unterbringungspflicht*). At least 20 percent of all regular positions were reserved for the "participants of the placement program" (*Unterbringungsteilnehmer*). Moreover, the public service was obliged to commit at least 20 percent of its total pay expenditures for the salaries of these employees. Until this quota was reached, government agencies or enterprises were obliged to hire placement program participants for all vacant or newly created positions.[16] The placement program extended even to many onetime members of the Gestapo and the Reich Security Main Office (*Reichssicherheitshauptamt*).[17]

For the police, the 20 percent obligation applied only to the senior service.[18] Of all positions (*Sollstellen*) in the North Rhine-Westphalia police, so-called 131ers held between 13.4 (1957) and 15.7 (1961) percent. The figures varied from region to region. In the Bielefeld police district, for example, the proportion of 131ers was especially high among members of the superior service, amounting to 68 percent in 1955 and 40 percent in 1958–59.[19] In Hamburg, some 1,600 131ers returned to the police force during the 1950s and constituted roughly a quarter of the force.[20]

The Nazi past was the subject of intense public discussion in West Germany in late 1950s.[21] One manifestation of the increased awareness of Nazi crimes was the establishment of the Central Office of State Justice Administrations for the Investigation of National Socialist Crimes (Zentrale Stelle der Landesjustizverwaltungen zur Aufklärung nationalsozialistischer Verbrechen) in Ludwigsburg in 1958. A regional central office was set up in North Rhine-Westphalia in 1961.[22] The state's Office for

Criminal Investigations (Landeskriminalamt) also created a special commission to investigate "illegal killings in former units of the Schutzpolizei before 1945."[23]

There were formidable obstacles to investigating Nazi crimes of violence committed by policemen. Even in normal times, extensive networks of comradeship within police forces cut the police off from the outside world. Those networks became all but impenetrable mazes for investigators of Nazi-era offenses. Moreover, accused policemen could usually count on *Kameradenhilfe* (comradely assistance), such as prepared statements or prearranged testimony.[24] Looking back at the 1960s, a detective who participated in the investigation of Police Battalion 322 recalled such arrangements inside the "well informed police apparatus": "Wherever we went, all were informed."[25] Moreover, investigating policemen were labeled as *Nestbeschmutzer* (troublemakers) and were "openly disgraced."[26]

Until the mid-1950s, the Nazi past of the police was not openly discussed in either Hamburg or North Rhine-Westphalia. Between the summer of 1956 and late 1959, a lively debate about the Nazi past of leading police officials took place in North Rhine-Westphalia. The debate focused on individuals' membership in organizations implicated in Nazi crimes: the SS, SD, and Gestapo. This focus reflected the prevailing understanding of the problem of Nazi crimes in the years before the Central Office in Ludwigsburg began its investigations. The debate was initiated by the public employees union ÖTV (Gewerkschaft Öffentliche Dienste, Transport und Verkehr), which included police. In the summer of 1956, the ÖTV presented a list of 27 high-ranking members of North Rhine-Westphalia's police forces to the state's Social Democratic interior minister, Hubert Biernat. Most of the men named had been officers in the SS, and all were members of the police union GdP (Gewerkschaft der Polizei).[27]

The investigations did not bring to light evidence that any of these officers had participated actively in the SS or SD. Following the testimony of Werner Best, a high-ranking SS member and official in the Reichssicherheitshauptamt, at the Nuremberg tribunal, it was determined that they had become officers of the SS through the *dienstgradmäßige Angleichung* (alignment of ranks). Best had maintained that police officers had been under "indirect pressure" to apply for membership in the SS. The GdP, too, argued that "alignment" had resulted "more or less automatically."[28] That argument was later challenged by West German historian Hans Buchheim. In the report he prepared in late 1963 for the Auschwitz trial, Buchheim explained that a policeman did not automatically receive an aligned rank if he joined the SS and that alignment was carried out only after review.[29] In October 1957, Biernat issued a press release stressing that this affair should be considered closed.[30] But the ÖTV did not let the matter rest and turned to Chancellor Konrad Adenauer. Because the union could not supply any new evidence, the official responsible at the Federal Ministry of the Interior recommended in December 1959 that the affair should be "considered settled."[31]

At the same time, the North Rhine-Westphalian state parliament became active in the matter. The state's interior minister was now the conservative Christian Democrat Josef-Hermann Dufhues. Like the Social Democrats, Dufhues wanted to close the books on this affair once and for all.[32] Union newspapers and the state parliament did not want to endanger the "confidence of foreign countries in West German democracy."[33] Even the main employee representative (*Hauptpersonalrat*) of the state police, while noting that the process of denazification had been concluded years earlier and could not be reinitiated, joined in the call for a final resolution of the matter.[34] All of the participants in the debates of 1956–59 focused on the police officers' membership in the three stigmatized organizations, the SS, SD, and Gestapo. Nobody discussed the actual actions of the officers, but, at the same time, the main issue was individual guilt, not institutional complicity. There was a widely held assumption that the police forces had been "forced and led into the abuse of power" during the Third Reich, which resulted in the serious offenses committed by some members of the police.

During this debate, doubts arose about the political reliability of the police as a whole. Nobody offered a counterargument, for example, when the chief of police in Gelsenkirchen stated in December 1959 that in "in times of distress" the state could not count on the "absolute reliability" of all members of the police.[35] In February 1960, the GdP gave a more cautious assessment. "Most" policemen, the union said, were convinced that democracy was worth defending. But there were also some who, on account of their "particularly close ties to the National Socialist state," were no longer interested in politics, and, according to the GdP, "considerable numbers" of officers so inclined held leading positions within West German police forces. They could not be expected to assert a "positive influence on the civic attitudes" of other officers.[36] Consequently, great hopes were placed on instruction in civics (*Staatsbürgerkunde*), especially as part of the training of new police officers, as a means for overcoming this problem.[37]

Internal police surveys conducted in the late 1950s suggested, however, that civics lessons had failed to achieve the desired aim.[38] The lessons concentrated almost exclusively on the formal functions of the state and the responsibilities of the police. Young officers who had received this instruction often felt disillusioned about their "real" duties after being assigned to station duty.[39] Another reason civics lessons were ineffective lay in the organization of police training in West Germany. During training, which lasted between two and three years, police cadets were quartered in barracks. The main phase of training was conducted under the supervision of the riot police (Bereitschaftspolizei), which was considered the "paternal home" (*Vaterhaus*) of all police officers. Networks of comradeship left officers little space for cultivating democratic norms and values during their training and service as patrolmen.[40]

1963: A New Concreteness in Addressing the Nazi Past

West German police had to face challenges from East Germany at the beginning of the 1960s. In late 1961, documents signed by the "Committee for Cleanliness and Order in the Police" turned up in a number of police institutions. These documents denounced various members of the police for their Nazi pasts. Simultaneously, a "Committee for German Unity" in East Berlin published a booklet entitled "Gestapo and SS Leaders Command the West German Police," which described the activities of 250 high-ranking West German policemen during Nazi rule. The booklet also denounced the murderous actions of police battalions in dramatic terms.[41]

The debate on the Nazi pasts of many West German policemen came to a head in 1963 and extended beyond members of criminal investigative forces (*Kriminalpolizei*) to include uniformed patrolmen (*Schutzpolizei*). In May 1963, Dortmund District Attorney Lothar Hentrich delivered a speech titled "The Misuse of the Police under the Third Reich" at the annual "Police Week" conference organized by the ÖTV. Shortly thereafter, Berlin political scientist Franz Kotowski presented a report on the "Reasons for Crimes Committed by Policemen during the War."[42] Kotowski stated—correctly—that no policeman would have been in mortal danger if he had refused to carry out an order. That assertion provoked a lively debate.[43] Policemen who had served during the Third Reich often insisted that anyone who had refused an order in those days would have been either reassigned to a disciplinary unit (*Bewährungsbataillon*) or shot. Kotowski, on the other hand, contended that under the prevailing Nazi ideology young police recruits were led to believe that even killing infants could be lawful.

The state election of 1962 brought a number of politicians in their forties to office in North Rhine-Westphalia. One was the Free Democrat Willy Weyer (born in 1917), who took over as minister of the interior.[44] In contrast to his predecessors, Weyer did not try to obscure the Nazi past of the police. The state parliament's working group on police matters addressed the issue of the role of the police in the Nazi state more directly than in years previous. Even if the *Schlussstrich* mentality had not vanished completely, this discussion was characterized by a new concreteness.[45] In 1963, departing from the earlier focus on membership in the SS, SD, and Gestapo, precise figures were given for the number of police officers in the state who had been prosecuted for violent crimes committed during Nazi rule. Moreover, policemen's actions were discussed in concrete detail. There was also discussion of possible punishment for Nazi era offenses. In July 1963, Weyer informed the parliamentary working group on police matters of the number of policemen in the state who were incriminated on account of membership in National Socialist organizations.[46] According to Weyer's figures, 90 North Rhine-Westphalia policemen had been involved in criminal or disciplinary proceedings relating to National Socialist crimes of violence; 38 of them were members of investigative units and 52 were patrolmen. Another 14 policemen had been imprisoned for Nazi crimes. Approximately 1 percent of the members of investigative units were incriminated by their pasts, compared to only 0.2 percent of all patrolmen.[47]

Weyer assured the parliamentary working group that he would do everything possible "to remove from active service policemen who had committed crimes of violence or who are suspected of such crimes." As a less-than-ideal solution, he recommended that policemen who had been acquitted of Nazi crimes should be employed in positions where they would not be "in the focus of public attention." Police union head Werner Kuhlmann advised the working group that officials should "not be too soft" in dealing with incriminated policemen."[48] Even if the questions posed by some members of the state parliament suggested that Weyer had promised more than he would be able to deliver, the open discussion of the Nazi past of members of the police was a departure from the soothing and obfuscating pronouncements of Weyer's predecessors, such as Dufhue's comment in 1961 that "not a few [policemen] had been abused by the National Socialist rulers in an especially disastrous way."[49]

But even with the new concreteness of the discussion about the Nazi past of West German policemen, unshakeable certainties still remained. Waldemar Reuter of the Federation of German Trade Unions (Deutscher Gewerkschaftsbund, DGB), for example, declared in September 1963 that two points were obvious: the "mass" of policemen acted "decently" during the years of Nazi rule, and it was unthinkable that policemen had participated in mass crimes (*Massenverbrechen*) except under compulsion.[50]

Heroic Weimar Police and the Patriarchal Offensive

There generally appears to have been no discussion about the Nazi past within the police like the one initiated by certain trade unionists and younger politicians. Policemen of the early 1960s referred to the Nazi era with vague euphemisms, such as the "ill-fated twelve years,"[51] and did not talk about perpetrators, victims, or specific incidents. There was, however, much discussion of the Prussian police of the Weimar Republic. There were two characteristic features of this "invention of tradition:" the political and democratic deficiencies of the Prussian police were ignored,[52] and a glorifying, sometimes even mythologizing perspective dominated. In late 1959, a senior police official in North Rhine-Westphalia made the point that during the Weimar Republic policemen had "enthusiastically" fulfilled their duties and had always proven themselves to be firm "defenders of the state."[53] In 1960, an ÖTV official said that he knew that there had been a "truly democratically minded police" in late 1932 that was later turned into "a murder weapon."[54]

This glorification of the police forces of the Weimar Republic did not stem from ignorance. Rather, I would argue, it was part of a self-exculpatory account of the past. So mighty were the Nazis that even the heroic Weimar police force, that bulwark of democracy, was brought to its knees. Ordinary policemen had little chance of resisting the almost supernatural force of National Socialism. With this interpretation of the past, individual policemen and the police as a whole received a double acquittal: it had been far beyond their power to prevent the destruction of the Weimar Republic and rise of National Socialism, just as it was later impossible to resist participation in the Nazis' crimes.

Arguing along these lines, West Berlin Police Commander Hans-Ulrich Werner called attention in 1960 to the close ties between the police and the state. Werner stressed that the "degeneration of the coercive power of the police" had always been a "consequence of the degeneration of democracy itself": thus, the degeneration of police authority was preceded by the degeneration of the state.[55] In 1960, Hamburg region GdP official Kurt Hopp (born in 1920) spoke confidently of the "astonishingly fast renewal" of the police "from the inside." According to Hopp, "real renewal (must) come out of the body of the police itself." Looking back at the recent past, he contended that "unsuitable elements" had either excluded themselves by their behavior or had been "excreted as an alien element by the healthy organism."[56] Thus, in Hopp's view, there was no need for outsiders to interfere in police matters. Policemen, he added, would see it as a sign of illness or weakness of the "body of the police" (*Polizeikörper*) if such interference were allowed to take place.

As mentioned at the beginning of this essay, this self-regulation and detachment from the outside world, which led to the "intellectual isolation of the police,"[57] was not merely wishful thinking on the part of the police. It thus comes as no surprise that almost no police officers have written about the Nazi past of the police since 1964.[58] Obviously, the police had brought the discussions about its Nazi past to a close, and the matter was left to the courts or politicians and union officials.[59]

This isolation of the police must be explained. One problem that is immediately apparent is that from roughly 1962 policemen demanded that comradeship and the cohesion of the police needed to be strengthened.[60] These appeals often were issued by policemen who had been born about 1912 or earlier. These policemen, whom I would like to call "the patriarchs," launched an offensive designed to close the ranks of the police and to cut the police off from the outside world. They wanted to establish a community whose members shared a common destiny, a *Schicksalsgemeinschaft*.[61] As Kassel Police Commander Heinz Quittnat (born in 1908) put it, police officers should strive to create a "well-integrated occupational community."[62] Here the "service community" (*dienstliche Gemeinschaft*) played an important role.[63] Differences among members "should not be deepened" but rather "reconciled step by step." It was the duty of the superior (*Vorgesetzte*) to resolve all these problems.[64] The key component of this "comradely service community" (*kameradschaftliche Dienstgemeinschaft*) was comradeship, exemplified by a willingness among the members to make sacrifices for one another and to try to understand each other.

"Genuine" or "commendable" police traditions, police officials also insisted, should be given much more prominence.[65] As a rule, these traditions were modeled on the Prussian police of the Weimar Republic. The remarks of a police commissioner in Essen serve as a good example of the narrative of tradition that circulated in station houses during the 1960s. This tradition rested on an image of a vigorous, homogenous organization that engaged in rigorous action, and, again, it presumed a close connection between the state and the police. Discussing the "dreadful fratricidal war" between supporters of the Communist and Nazi Parties, the Essen commissioner said the Weimar era police had succeeded in restoring public order thanks to their tactical training and "decisive and vigorous actions." Another reason for their success, at least according to this extremely distorted narrative, was that the "inner structure" of the police "had been in order from the highest superior down to the last patrolman."[66]

The patriarchs saw state and society as a single organism. They propagated a vision of a hierarchical, authoritarian state in which everybody had to strive for conformity. Moreover, they had an organic-biologistic view of society. In such a society, it was the duty of the police, as police officer Tonis Hunold (born in 1914) explained in 1968, to ensure that the "*Volkskörper* is not harmed." In fulfilling this duty, the police had to maintain the equilibrium of the *Volkskörper*.[67] In sum, the notions of *esprit de corps*, comradeship, and tradition espoused by the patriarchs and even some younger police officers were based on a model of manliness that gave preference to attributes such as vigor, toughness, courage, and loyalty to the state.[68]

Until about 1963 or 1964, the patriarchs wanted to (re)form the *Schutzpolizei* into a tight body by reverting to Weimar models. These efforts can be interpreted in part as countermeasures to calm the worries roused by investigations of policemen who had participated in Nazi crimes of violence. This impulse was intensified by the clear arguments about the Nazi past of the police voiced in 1963. Obviously, a police united by an esprit de corps, by comradeship, and by a "comradely service community" could maintain its composure in the face of investigations of Nazi crimes.

None of these efforts could, however, prevent the issue of the Nazi past of the police from arising again. In the late 1960s, patrolmen had to listen to students marching through city streets chanting "*Polizei, SA, SS*."[69] At the same time, "ordinary men" who had served in the *Schutzpolizei* were on trial for Nazi-era offenses. As the Central Office at Ludwigsburg intensified its investigations, prosecutors initiated proceedings against a number of former members of Nazi-era police battalions between 1965 and 1969. Members of Police Battalion 316 went on trial in Bochum in late 1966, for example, and members of Police Battalion 101 were tried in Hamburg between October 1967 and April 1968—during the peak period of student protests. At roughly the same time, members of Police Battalion 306 were on trial in Wuppertal.[70]

Technological-Organizational Modernization as a Caesura

The networks of police stations in North-Rhine Westphalia and other West German states were reorganized during the last third of the 1950s. Many smaller stations were shut as larger stations, with as many as 100 officers, were created. The number of policemen assigned to radio patrol cars was also increased. Against a background of a change in values (*Wertewandel*)[71] in West German society and the changing age structure of police forces, this organizational and technical modernization brought about a deep-reaching change in police work. Under these circumstances, it was very hard for the patriarchs to stick to traditional ideals of police work and paternalistic ideals of the qualifications for leadership.

Radio patrol car duty could not easily be integrated into traditional police work. Before the expanded use of patrol cars, patrolmen on the beat had had tightly structured duty assignments. Officers in patrol cars, by contrast, had to act more independently.[72] That meant that their superiors, too, had to change the way they thought. It became increasingly difficult for them to control their men. Because policemen in patrol cars were responsible for much wider areas than police walking beats, they had to be more flexible in their approach to police work.

The example of North Rhine-Westphalia illustrates nationwide developments.[73] The areas for which police departments in the state's cities were responsible were reorganized and, beginning in 1959, *Schutzbereiche* (protection districts) were established. There was one central station (*Hauptwache*) in each *Schutzbereich* and several smaller stations. This reorganization was intended to get as many as 600 officers out of station houses and onto the street, and it represented a radical break with the system of numerous small and medium-sized stations that had been established in the 1870s.[74]

The central stations in the *Schutzbereiche* were led by "watch and intervention leaders" (*Wach- und Einsatzführer*), many of whom had previously been in charge of medium-sized police stations as *Revierleiter*. The responsibilities of the station leaders were curtailed. They no longer held sole decision-making authority, for example, in assigning officers' shifts; that responsibility was now shared with deployment officials (*Sachbearbeiter für Einsatz und Verwendung*). This differentiation and specialization meant that the former station leaders employed as "watch and intervention leaders" had to give up their independence as well as their privileged positions.

The introduction of radio patrol car service and the reorganization of police stations placed a heavy burden on the patriarchs. They held to a model of leadership in which paternalism played an important role and superiors' behavior, on and off the job, was to serve as an example to be followed. Additionally, the superior had to know everything—he had to be literally a know-it-all.[75] As West German police forces underwent technological and organizational modernization, this leadership model became impossible to realize. The patriarchs' notions of police work were thus called into question. One former station leader, for example, understood effective policing as a form of "guerrilla warfare." He was convinced that the best chance for winning the "daily fight to secure public safety and order" lay in the deployment of "small units of policemen [led] by leaders who know their way around very well and who know every hiding place."[76] It should be mentioned that an understanding of police work as a kind of guerrilla warfare undertaken by small units commanded by all-knowing leaders was also rooted in part in police service during World War II. In a paper prepared in 1956 for a seminar at the Police Institute in Hiltrup, Wilhelm Schell emphasized that small groups led by experienced commanders played an important role in the "antipartisan war." *Jagdkommandos* (literally, hunting commandos) had had the task of "tracking down, cornering, and taking care of the [partisan] bands," Schell wrote. In this "partisan war" (*Bandenkampf*), he argued, a "well-adjusted and inspired community" led by a "determined personality" was highly important.[77]

Technological and organizational modernization also threatened the patriarchs' notion of manliness. They saw their ability to integrate their subordinates into closely tied comradely communities as a key component of manliness. This expectation had been inscribed into German police practice during the Weimar Republic. For the patriarchs, the end of an organizational system based on small and medium-sized police stations meant the curtailment of their ability to act as men; modernization, in other words, meant the erosion of their qualifications as leaders.[78]

Modernization in the late 1950s, in sum, resulted in a deep caesura in routine police work in West Germany's big cities. It was not until a decade later, however, that new tactics were adopted for large-scale police actions. In the late 1960s, younger politicians and police chiefs—individuals born in the 1920s—developed more flexible and less confrontational tactics for crowd and riot control with an eye toward protecting the reputation of West German democracy. Many members of the Schutzpolizei were initially opposed to this "soft wave" (*weiche Welle*),[79] but they were unable to prevent the failure of the old "civil war model" (*Bürgerkriegmodell*),[80] of police engagement in dealing with the demonstrations of the late 1960s.[81] Some leading members of the Schutzpolizei did, however, eventually come to support the new, more flexible tactics.

The early 1970s saw another series of police reform efforts focused on station service. Modernizers—officers born in the 1920s—played an important role in these reforms. In the course of the debate on reform, manliness was redefined. Vigor, toughness, courage, and loyalty to the state became less important with the emergence of a more flexible and dynamic model of manliness that demythologized the state and put more emphasis on individual performance (*Leistung*). Nonetheless, "order" (*Ordnung*) was still held in high esteem, and "softness" (*Weichheit*), whatever that might mean, continued to be held in disdain.[82]

Conclusion

In the early 1960s, younger activists in the police unions and liberal politicians finally succeeded in overcoming the *Schlußstrich* mentality and efforts to blur over the history of the police during the Nazi era. Those strategies had obviously lost their persuasiveness in the face of changes in West German political culture and social values. A new concreteness in addressing the past became evident, especially in the year 1963. Within the police forces, however, there was still a tendency to discuss National Socialist rule without specific mention of the actions of the police during that period.

Never amenable to outside scrutiny or criticism, the police responded to intensified discussion of the Nazi past by trying to close ranks more closely than ever.

Older officers, the so-called patriarchs born before World War I, launched an offensive to strengthen the sense of comradely community within police forces. This offensive was intended to serve a dual purpose. It was, on the one hand, directed against the consequences of technological and organizational modernization, in particular the challenges modernization posed to patriarchal ideas of qualification and to long-established tactics and structures. The patriarchal offensive also sought to protect police from investigations into Nazi crimes of violence. It became obvious in the early 1960s, however, that West Germany's police would have to abandon the mythic stories about the heroic police of the Weimar Republic if they were going to come to terms with the Nazi past. Even with regard to tactics, one of the last strongholds of Weimar police tradition, it was clear by the end of the decade that modernization was necessary.

What Ute Frevert has written about West German society of the 1960s undoubtedly holds true for the country's police as well: the soldierly man, "this icon of the Nazi years," became an anachronism.[83] Reforms enacted in the early 1970s helped to modernize police training and equipment.[84] This process was reinforced by a fundamental change in the personnel structure of the Schutzpolizei in the mid-1970s as officers born around 1914 retired. That change had begun earlier in the ranks of the senior service in North Rhine-Westphalia. There was an influx of officers born in the 1920s during the 1960s,[85] and they were less attached to Weimar police traditions, at least inasmuch as antiriot and crowd control tactics were concerned.[86]

But there were also tendencies that worked against the police becoming a more civilian organization. During the actions against the student protests of the late 1960s, an aggressive and elitist ideal of masculinity developed among younger riot policemen, the 68ers of the police.[87] The influence of this ideal has not yet been studied in detail, but one point must be mentioned: those young men had good chances of promotion. Many officers retired in the mid-1970s, as noted above, and, simultaneously, police forces were adding personnel. What these developments meant when West Germany's police were confronted with political terrorism remains an open question.[88]

Until the late 1950s, the *gewisse Stille* about some aspects of the Nazi past had undoubtedly contributed to the stabilization of West German democracy. Simultaneously, the reconstruction of West Germany's police forces as civil service organizations was strongly influenced by the model of their Weimar predecessors. In the 1960s, selective silence about the Nazi past and Weimar traditions became a burden that hindered West Germany's police forces in adapting to social change. Confrontation with the Nazi past prompted West German police to intensify their separation from the rest of society. That separation, together with the glorification of the Weimar police, in turn impeded the modernization of the police as a central institution of the state. Thus, the question arises whether this mechanism was at work in other civil service institutions. In other words, were the suppression of the Nazi past and the example of Weimar traditions indirect obstacles to the modernization of West German state and society in the 1960s?

Notes

1. (Eckbert) Zylmann, *Die psychologische Situation der Polizei: Ein Bericht über eine Studienreise* (Hamburg, 1964), 4.
2. For an overview, see Wilfried Loth and Bernd-A. Rusinek, eds., *Verwandlungspolitik: NS-Eliten in der westdeutschen Nachkriegsgesellschaft* (Frankfurt am Main, 1998); Norbert Frei, *Karrieren im Zwielicht: Hitlers Eliten nach 1945* (Frankfurt am Main, 2001).
3. Norbert Frei, *Vergangenheitspolitik: Die Anfänge der Bundesrepublik und die NS-Vergangenheit* (Munich, 1996), 99f. As a solid case study, see Frank Liebert, "'Die Dinge müssen zur Ruhe kommen, man muß einen Strich dadurch machen': Politische 'Säuberung' in der niedersächsischen Polizei," in *Nachkriegspolizei: Sicherheit und Ordnung in Ost- und Westdeutschland 1945–1969*, ed. Gerhard Fürmetz, Herbert Reinke, and Klaus Weinhauer (Hamburg, 2001), 71–103. See also Stephan Linck, *Der Ordnung verpflichtet. Deutsche Polizei 1933–1949: Der Fall Flensburg* (Paderborn, 2000), 269ff.
4. Theodor W. Adorno, "Was bedeutet Aufarbeitung der Vergangenheit," *Theodor W. Adorno, Erziehung zur Mündigkeit: Vorträge und Gespräche mit Hellmut Becker 1959–1960*, in Gerd Kadelbach (Frankfurt am Main, 1971), 10 (emphasis in original).
5. For the criminal police, see Patrick Wagner, *Volksgemeinschaft ohne Verbrecher: Konzeptionen und Praxis der Kriminalpolizei in der Zeit der Weimarer Republik und des Nationalsozialismus* (Hamburg, 1996); Gerhard Paul and Klaus-Michael Mallmann, eds., *Die Gestapo im Krieg* (Darmstadt, 2000).
6. See Fürmetz, Reinke, and Weinhauer, *Nachkriegspolizei*; Falco Werkentin, *Die Restauration der deutschen Polizei: Innere Rüstung von 1945 bis zur Notstandsgesetzgebung* (Frankfurt am Main, 1984); Erika S. Fairchild, *German Police: Ideals and Reality in the Post-War Years* (Springfield, 1988).
7. For studies that focus mainly on personnel continuities, see Norbert Steinborn and Karin Schanzenbach, *Die Hamburger Polizei nach 1945: Ein Neuanfang, der keiner war* (Hamburg, 1990); Heiner Lichtenstein, *Himmlers grüne Helfer: Die Schutz- und Ordnungspolizei im "Dritten Reich"* (Cologne, 1990).
8. As an overview, see Michael Ruck, "Beharrung im Wandel: Neue Forschungen zur deutschen Verwaltung im 20. Jahrhundert," *Neue Politische Literatur* 42 (1997): 200–256; and for details, see Curt Garner, "Public Service Personnel in West Germany in the 1950s: Controversial Policy Decisions and Their Effects on Social Composition, Gender Structure, and the Role of Former Nazis," *Journal of Social History* 29 (1995–96): 25–80; Curt Garner, "Der öffentliche Dienst in den 50er Jahren: Politische Weichenstellungen und ihre sozialgeschichtlichen Folgen," in *Modernisierung im Wiederaufbau: Die westdeutsche Gesellschaft der 50er Jahre*, uncondensed and revised student edition, ed. Axel Schildt and Arnold Sywottek (Bonn, 1998), 759–90.
9. For trends in the analysis of organizations, see Mary Jo Hatch, *Organization Theory: Modern, Symbolic and Postmodern Perspectives* (Oxford, 1997).
10. For the analysis of group pressure, see Christopher R. Browning, *Ganz normale Männer: Das Reserve-Polizeibataillon 101 und die "Endlösung" in Polen. Mit einem Nachwort (1998)* (Reinbek, 1999); Omer Bartov, *Hitlers Wehrmacht: Soldaten, Fanatismus und die Brutalisierung des Krieges* (Reinbek, 1995); Thomas Kühne, "Gruppenkohäsion und Kameradschaftsmythos in der Wehrmacht," in *Die Wehrmacht: Mythos und Realität*, ed. Rolf-Dieter Müller and Hans-Erich Volkmann (Munich, 1999), 534–49.
11. See Fairchild, *German Police*. For a discussion of the terms "modern" and "modernization," see Axel Schildt, *Moderne Zeiten: Freizeit, Massenmedien und "Zeitgeist" in der Bundesrepublik der 50er Jahre* (Hamburg, 1995).
12. All numbers are calculated according to LtNW (Landtag Nordrhein-Westfalen), Vorlage 1723, 3 July 1961, Anlage 9, ALtNW (Archiv des Landtags Nordrhein-Westfalen); LtNW, Vorlage 372, 7 November 1967, ALtNW.

13. See Hans-Joachim Neufeldt, Jürgen Huck, and Georg Tessin, *Zur Geschichte der Ordnungspolizei 1936–1945* (Koblenz, 1957), part 2, 15, 19; see also Peter Longerich, *Politik der Vernichtung: Eine Gesamtdarstellung der nationalsozialistischen Judenverfolgung* (Munich, 1998), 306.

14. See Wolfgang Kahl, "Vom Mythos der 'Bandenbekämpfung': Polizeiverbände im Zweiten Weltkrieg," *Die Polizei* 89 (1998): 47–55.

15. For quote, see Garner, "Public Service," 39. For details, see Garner, "Öffentliche Dienst," and Frei, *Vergangenheitspolitik*, 69–100.

16. Garner, "Public Service," 44.

17. Ibid. This included all persons, who had been transferred to the Gestapo "for offical reasons" (*von Amts wegen*). For further discussions of this section 67 of the "131er" Law, see Garner, "Public Service," 46.

18. Calculated according to Hauptstaatsarchiv Düsseldorf NW 652-210, Lists from 1 September 1957, 30 September 1958, 30 September 1960, 30 September 1961. For details on the participants of the replacement program in the police, see Georg Anders, *Gesetz zur Regelung der Rechtsverhältnisse der unter Artikel 131 des Grundgesetzes fallenden Personen*, 1st–4th eds. (Stuttgart, 1951–59).

19. Calculations based on Staatsarchiv Detmold D 2 A Bielefeld 196. In the Foreign Office (Auswärtiges Amt), this quota was about 40 percent, while in the Federal Ministry of the Interior, it reached even 42 percent; see Frei, *Vergangenheitspolitik*, 85.

20. For the numbers, see Steinborn and Schanzenbach, *Hamburger Polizei*, 129–31.

21. See Loth and Rusinek, *Verwandlungspolitik*; for the 1960s, see Detlef Siegfried, "Zwischen Aufarbeitung der Vergangenheit und Schlußstrich: Der Umgang mit der NS-Vergangenheit in den beiden deutschen Staaten 1958–1969," in *Dynamische Zeiten: Die 60er Jahre in den beiden deutschen Gesellschaften*, ed. Axel Schildt, Detlef Siegfried, and Karl Christian Lammers (Hamburg, 2000), 77–113.

22. See *Der Spiegel*, 19 December 1966, 56–58, here 56; Edict of the North Rhine-Westphalian Minister of the Interior, 21 October 1961, Staatsarchiv Detmold D 1-26083.

23. LtNW session of the AkPol, 9 June 1960, Anlage 2, ALtNW. For Hamburg, see Helge Grabitz, *Täter und Gehilfen des Endlösungswahns: Hamburger Verfahren wegen NS-Gewaltverbrechen* (Hamburg, 1999).

24. On the comradely aid (*Kameradenhilfe*) organized by Werner Best, see Ulrich Herbert, *Best: Biographische Studien über Radikalismus, Weltanschauung und Vernunft, 1903–1989* (Bonn, 1996), 491–510.

25. *Der Spiegel*, no. 44, 27 October 1986, 76–99, quote on 80.

26. Ibid.

27. *Der Spiegel*, no. 44, 10 October 1959, 30–32, here 31. See also Polizei-Hauptpersonalrat beim Innenminister des Landes Nordrhein-Westfalen an alle Polizeibediensteten des Landes, 5 October 1959, Staatsarchiv Detmold D 2 A Bielefeld 236; *DP/NW* (Deutsche Polizei/Landesteil Nordrhein-Westfalen) (1959): 88–90, 98. For a review, see *DP/NW* (1961): 4–5.

28. LtNW cosession of HA/AfIV (Hauptausschuss des Landtags Nordrhein-Westfalen/Ausschuss für innere Verwaltung des Landtags Nordrhein-Westfalen), 24 November 1959, 5, 9f., ALtNW; *DP/NW* (1959): 89.

29. Hans Buchheim, "Die SS—das Herrschaftsinstrument," in *Anatomie des SS-Staates* (Munich, 1967), 13–212, here 113. As Buchheim emphasized, prior to the alignment of ranks, those concerned must have written an application for membership in the SS. Thus, this alignment did not come automatically; rather, there had to be an "express promotion" (*ausdrückliche Beförderung*) made by the responsible section of the SS.

30. *Der Spiegel*, no. 44, 28 October 1959, 32.

31. ÖTV to chancellor Adenauer, 7 September 1959, Bundesarchiv Koblenz B 136-5031; Note, 23 December 1959, Bundesarchiv Koblenz B 136-5031.

32. LtNW cosession of HA/AfIV, 24 November 1959 (Minister of the Interior Dufhues, CDU and Smektala, SPD), ALtNW

33. LtNW cosession of HA/AfIV, 24 November 1959 (press declaration), ALtNW; for the position of the GdP, see *DP/NW* (1959): 88–90; Polizei-Hauptpersonalrat beim Innenminister des Landes Nordrhein-Westfalen an alle Polizeibediensteten des Landes, 5 October 1959, Staatsarchiv Detmold D 2 A Bielefeld 236; see for the position of the DGB *Welt der Arbeit* No 41, 9 October 1959.

34. Polizei-Hauptpersonalrat beim Innenminister des Landes Nordrhein-Westfalen an alle Polizeibediensteten des Landes, 5 October 1959, Staatsarchiv Detmold D 2 A Bielefeld 236.

35. Meeting, 14 December 1959, Hauptstaatsarchiv Düsseldorf NW 242-381.

36. Meeting, 23 February 1960, Hauptstaatsarchiv Düsseldorf NW 242-381.

37. See first conference symposium for teachers in civics of the police of North Rhine-Westphalia held at the state police school (Landespolizeischule) "Erich Klausener" in Düsseldorf, 4–7 November 1957, Hauptstaatsarchiv Düsseldorf NW 167–287.

38. For a summary, see Klaus Weinhauer, "Staatsbürger mit Sehnsucht nach Harmonie? Gesellschaftsbild und Staatsverständnis in der westdeutschen Polizei der sechziger Jahre," in Schildt, Siegfried, and Lammers, *Dynamische Zeiten*, 444–70.

39. See Hans-Joachim Wendler, "Der erste Tag," *Die Polizei* 62 (1971): 151–52.

40. See Friedrich Czirr, "Der jugendliche Polizeianwärter: Probleme der Beschulung und ihre Bewältigung," *Die Polizei* 57 (1966): 18–20; Werner Giese, "Stellung und Aufgaben der Polizei-Abteilung Hamburg (mot.) im Stadtstaat Hamburg," *Polizei, Technik, Verkehr* (1962): 97–99, quote on 99; Albin Moseberg, "Ein Unterführer und neun Mann …," in *10 Jahre Polizeiabteilung Hamburg (mot): 1951–1961* (Hamburg, 1961), 34–35.

41. *Gestapo- und SS-Führer kommandieren die westdeutsche Polizei: Eine Dokumentation über 250 leitende Polizeioffiziere Westdeutschlands* (Berlin/East, c. 1961/62).

42. See Hauptvorstand der Gewerkschaft ÖTV, ed., *Polizeinachrichten*, Stuttgart, 29 May 1963 (Hentrich), Staatsarchiv Hamburg Nachlass Otto Grot 13; *DP* 1963, 192–94 (Kotowski).

43. On the problem of the refusal to obey orders, see Adalbert Rückerl, "Zur Diskussion um die NS-Verbrecher-Prozesse," *Die Polizei* 63 (1972): 199–202.

44. See Gerhard Brunn and Jürgen Reulecke, *Kleine Geschichte von Nordrhein-Westfalen 1946–1996* (Cologne, 1996), 119.

45. See LtNW session of AKPol (Arbeitskreis für Polizeifragen des Ausschusses für Innere Verwaltung des Landtags Nordrhein-Westfalen), 5 July 1963 (Smektala, SPD), ALtNW.

46. See for the following LtNW session of AKPol, 5 July 1963, ALtNW.

47. In 1963 there were 22,997 Schutzpolizisten and 3,826 criminal policemen, LtNW session of AKPol, 15 October 1963, Anlage, ALtNW.

48. LtNW session of AKPol, 5 July 1963 (Weyer, FDP), ALtNW.

49. Speech of Minister of the Interior Dufhues on the delegates' conference of the GdP (region North Rhine-Westphalia), 18 May 1961, 4, Staatsarchiv Detmold D 1-24278.

50. For the following, see Polizei-Institut Hiltrup, Probleme der Inneren Führung. 12. Arbeitstagung des Polizei-Instituts Hiltrup für Leiter von Polizeibehörden und leitende Polizei-Exekutivbeamte, 24–26 September 1963 in Hamburg (Hiltrup, 1963), 5 (Waldemar Reuter).

51. Bruno Kuhnke, "Probleme der 'Inneren Führung,'" *Die Polizei* 54 (1963): 144–48.

52. On the antirepublican positions of the officers of the Prussian police, see Peter Leßmann, *Die preußische Schutzpolizei in der Weimarer Republik: Streifendienst und Straßenkampf* (Düsseldorf, 1989), 319–30.

53. Meeting, 14 December 1959, Hauptstaatsarchiv Düsseldorf NW 242-381.

54. Meeting, 23 February 1960, Hauptstaatsarchiv Düsseldorf NW 242-381.

55. Hans-Ulrich Werner, "Sitte, Moral und Recht als Grenzen des polizeilichen Einsatzes," *Die Polizei* 51 (1960): 102–6, 133–36.

56. Kurt Hopp, "Der Bürger und seine Polizei," in Gewerkschaft der Polizei, ed., *10 Jahre Landesbezirk Hamburg, 1950–1960* (Hamburg, n.d.), 197–209, quote on 199.

57. Zylmann, *Die psychologische Situation*, 4, 15 (quote).

58. An exception is Robert Weida, "NS-Gewaltverbrechen in polizeilicher Sicht," *Kriminalistik* 20 (1966): 329–35.

59. Siegfried, "Zwischen Aufarbeitung," 100, describes this shifting of the discussions on the Nazi past to the political arena that began in the mid-1960s.

60. See Ernst Werner Weiß, "Gedanken über das 'Innere Gefüge' der Polizei," *Die Polizei* 52 (1961): 257–58; Heinz Quittnat, "Menschliche Gegensätze und dienstliche Gemeinschaft," *Die Polizei* 55 (1964): 111–14; Johannes Otto, "Innere Führung und Inneres Gefüge," *Die Polizei* 53 (1962): 145–48; Heinz Quittnat, "Das 'Innere Gefüge' beim Einzeldienst," *Die Polizei* 53 (1962): 242–43.

61. On patriarchal rule and its dominating "sacredness of traditions" (*Traditionsheiligkeit*), see Max Weber, *Wirtschaft und Gesellschaft: Grundriß der verstehenden Soziologie*, 5th rev. ed. (Tübingen, 1980), 581.

62. Quittnat, "Das 'Innere Gefüge,'" 243; see also Herbert Scheffler, "Zum Problem der personellen Verstärkung der Polizei," *Die Polizei* 51 (1960): 97–102, 136–39.

63. For the following, see Quittnat, "Menschliche Gegensätze," 111f.

64. Ibid., 113.

65. Walter Gerloff, "Die Heranbildung des Oberbeamten-Nachwuchses," *Polizei, Technik, Verkehr*, 1962, 43–47, quote on 43; Otto, "Innere Führung," 146.

66. Otto, "Innere Führung," 148; see also Scheffler, "Verstärkung," 98f.

67. Tonis Hunold, *Polizei in der Reform: Was Staatsbürger und Polizei voneinander erwarten können* (Düsseldorf, 1968), 106.

68. See Klaus Weinhauer, "'Freund und Helfer' an der 'Front': Patriarchen, Modernisierer und Gruppenkohäsion in der westdeutschen Polizei," in *Demokratisierung und gesellschaftlicher Aufbruch: Die sechziger Jahre als Wendezeit der Bundesrepublik*, ed. Matthias Frese et al. (Paderborn, 2003), 549–73.

69. See Klaus Weinhauer, *Schutzpolizei in der Bundesrepublik. Zwischen Bürgerkrieg und Innerer Sicherheit: Die turbulenten sechziger Jahre* (Paderborn, 2003), chap. 5.3.

70. See Adalbert Rückerl, *NS Verbrechen vor Gericht: Versuch einer Vergangenheitsbewältigung* (Heidelberg, 1982), 193; *Der Spiegel*, no. 52, 19 December 1966, 56–58; for Hamburg, see Grabitz, *Täter und Gehilfen*; for Wuppertal, see Lichtenstein, *Himmlers grüne Helfer*. See also the contributions by Stefan Klemp and Heiner Lichtenstein in *Wessen Freund und wessen Helfer: Die Kölner Polizei im Nationalsozialismus*, ed. Harald Buhlan and Werner Jung (Cologne, 2000).

71. Helmut Klages, "Verlaufsanalyse eines Traditionsbruchs: Untersuchungen zum Einsetzen des Wertewandels in der Bundesrepublik Deutschland in den 60er Jahren," in *Staat und Parteien: Festschrift für Rudolf Morsey zum 65. Geburtstag*, ed. Karl Dietrich Bracher et al. (Berlin, 1992), 517–44.

72. Werner Giese, "Motorisierter Streifendienst in der Bewährung," *DP* (1960), 311–12, quote on 312.

73. For the following, see Hans-Wilhelm Tilgner, "Die Neugliederung der Schutzpolizei in den städtischen Kreispolizeibehörden des Landes Nordrhein-Westfalen," *Schriftenreihe für Oberbeamte: Mitteilungen aus dem Polizei-Institut*, no. 1 (1960): 12–22.

74. Albrecht Funk, *Polizei und Rechtsstaat: Die Entwicklung des staatlichen Gewaltmonopols in Preußen 1848–1914* (Frankfurt am Main, 1986), 277–87.

75. See Weinhauer, "'Freund und Helfer.'"

76. Bublies, "Gedanken zur Neuorganisation der Schutzpolizei," *DP/NW* (1960), 37–39, quote on 38.

77. Wilhelm Schell, *Der Bandenkampf als polizeiliche Aufgabe* (Hiltrup, 1956), 20f.

78. See Weinhauer, *Schutzpolizei*, chap. 2.1.

79. Klaus Weinhauer, "Innere Unruhe: Studentenproteste und die Krise der westdeutschen Schutzpolizei in den sechziger Jahren," in Fürmetz, Reinke, and Weinhauer, *Nachkriegspolizei*, 303–25, quote on 315.

80. Albrecht Goeschel, "Die Polizei als Dienstleistungsbetrieb: Neue Funktionen der Polizei in der spätindustriellen Gesellschaft," *Atomzeitalter* (1967): 700–709, and *Atomzeitalter* (1968): 46–56.

81. See Weinhauer, "Staatsbürger," and Weinhauer, "Innere Unruhe."

82. See Werner Giese, "Gedanken über Menschenführung in der Polizei," *Die Polizei* 62 (1971): 337–39, and 3 (1972): 19–22.

83. Ute Frevert, "Umbruch der Geschlechterverhältnisse: Die 60er Jahre als geschlechterpolitischer Experimentierraum," in Schildt, Siegfried, and Lammers, *Dynamische Zeiten*, 642–60, quote on 658. For the 1950s, see the contributions in *Signs* 24 (1998): 101–69.

84. Heiner Busch et al., *Die Polizei in der Bundesrepublik* (Frankfurt am Main, 1988).

85. See Weinhauer, *Schutzpolizei*, chap. 1.3.3.

86. For the age structure of German political and administrative elites, see Michael Ruck, *Korpsgeist und Staatsbewußtsein: Beamte im deutschen Südwesten 1928 bis 1972* (Munich, 1996).

87. For details, see Weinhauer, *Schutzpolizei*, chap. 5.3.7.

88. For a review of the literature, see Klaus Weinhauer, "Terrorismus in der Bundesrepublik der Siebzigerjahre: Aspekte einer Sozial- und Kulturgeschichte der Inneren Sicherheit," *Archiv für Sozialgeschichte* 44 (2004): 219–42.

Chapter 7

WEST GERMAN SOCIETY AND FOREIGNERS IN THE 1960S

Karen Schönwälder

❧

In 1966, the Bundesvereinigung der Deutschen Arbeitgeberverbände (BDA), an umbrella organization of employers' associations, held a conference on foreign labor in West Germany. In his opening remarks, BDA president Siegfried Balke proudly referred to a "similar event" the employers had organized in 1908.[1] He did not go so far as to quote from a 1908 paper arguing that as German workers were becoming more educated and better trained, it seemed desirable "to use undemanding foreign workers for the more primitive tasks."[2] But Balke's reference to the 1908 gathering does illustrate that the recruitment of foreign labor in the 1960s was placed in a historical continuum and that this continuum was generally not seen as problematic. If there was an inherited burden, the BDA president suggested, it lay in the minds of ordinary Germans. Indeed, one of the main purposes of the conference was to counter prejudice and to win support for the idea that the employment of foreigners was indispensable: "We have to encourage understanding for the foreigners among German employees. They must learn to tolerate differences because tolerance alone forms the key to an understanding of the foreigners."[3] Balke emphasized that "[t]he world's general opinion of German hospitality and the German attitude to other countries depends not least on whether and to what extent we manage to solve this problem."[4]

The 1960s was a period of major migratory movements to (and from) West Germany. The 1961 census recorded 686,000 foreign citizens and stateless persons; over the next six years, that figure almost trebled. Between summer 1960 and autumn 1964, the number of foreign workers rose from 279,000 to about 1,000,000; by June 1966, a record 1.3 million non-Germans were working in the Federal Republic.[5] Twenty-eight percent of them had already spent more than

---

Notes for this chapter begin on page 122.

three years in Germany.[6] The huge numbers of foreign workers, the continuation of foreign recruitment over several years, and the growing number of married couples, some with children, suggested that immigration was a phenomenon German society could not ignore.[7] At the same time—as Balke's speech indicated—the question of how far West Germany had indeed overcome the Nazi past gained new urgency.

How did the history of the exploitation of millions of forced laborers during the Nazi era figure—if at all—in the policy debates of the 1960s about migrant labor? This essay argues that the presence of the past was a characteristic feature of 1960s responses to the mass encounter with foreigners in West Germany. To some extent, this thesis runs counter to previous research. Scholars such as Knuth Dohse, Hartmut Esser, and Ulrich Herbert have been struck by the absence of a critical review of the wartime experience as large-scale employment of foreigners recommended and the West German government partly revived older institutional and legal instruments to regulate it.[8] While it is beyond doubt that the exploitation of forced laborers in Nazi Germany was not explored in detail or widely discussed in public in West Germany during the 1960s, I do not believe that this public silence reflected "ruptured perceptions" or an understanding of foreign recruitment as something novel.[9] The past was present, if sometimes only in the subtext of public communication.

Explanations of the Presence of Labor Migrants

To help them make sense of the influx of hundreds of thousands of foreigners into their country, West Germans were offered several different justifications. The employment of foreigners was presented first as an economic necessity. Given that the "economic miracle" was a cornerstone of German self-confidence, this was a very powerful argument. Secondly, migration was related to the European vision in which cooperation among the peoples of Europe and freedom of movement figured prominently. West Germans were thus encouraged to accept migration as a side effect of the European integration they desired and of the Federal Republic's acceptance into the Western community of nations. Thirdly, it was common to remind the public that Germany had traditionally used foreign labor. According to this line of argument, history showed that employment of foreigners was normal and nothing to fear. *Überfremdung* (overforeignization, or being overwhelmed by foreigners) was not a real threat.[10] Although it often skipped over the period between 1910 and 1955, the historical argument presented the recruitment of foreigners as a normal feature of German economic life.

It is unlikely that the presence of millions of foreign workers on more or less every farm and in every factory across Germany during the Third Reich had been forgotten twenty years after the regime's collapse. Throughout the 1950s, before the increase in foreign recruitment, about half a million foreigners were registered in the Federal Republic.[11] In 1966, the number of *Heimatlose Ausländer* (literally, homeless foreigners) was estimated at 155,000; many of them were former forced laborers. These Displaced Persons provided the most obvious link between past and present, between Nazi Germany's *Ostarbeiter* (eastern workers) and the Federal Republic's *Gastarbeiter* (guest workers).[12]

A number of scholars have noted that the term *Fremdarbeiter* (foreign workers) that had been commonly used before 1945 did not disappear until the late 1960s even though it was avoided in official usage.[13] Nazism and the history of intolerance and racism were rarely explicitly mentioned. But when a journalist pointed out that Germany still had a long way to go before the transgressions (*Verfehlungen*) of the past would be forgiven and that the treatment of guest workers would be regarded as a test case for the sincerity of the Germans' commitment to democracy,[14] or when a widely distributed magazine published by the Bundeszentrale für politische Bildung (Federal Office for Political Education) argued that the injustice done to forced laborers during the war remained a burden that "even today we help to reduce with every friendly word, every helping hand extended to the guest workers,"[15] they were only clarifying a message that was omnipresent. Vague references to a special German obligation to show tolerance typically coexisted with a lack of sensitivity displayed in the continued use of the terms *Fremdarbeiter* and *Überfremdung*.[16] As there had been no public (or internal) debate about the past, there was no clear line between democratic attitudes and the nationalism of the past.

This is also illustrated by the ways in which the presence of foreign workers was used as an opportunity to boost German confidence. A one-page feature in the *Frankfurter Allgemeine Zeitung*, for instance, emphasized the civilizing mission of the Germans. A "uniform, sober West German society" had "forced the softer southerners, if they wanted to get by, to adjust," the paper reported. "It seems that it is indeed possible to transform the more passive (*vegetativ*) Mediterranean type into a stable, focused worker type." The workers' countries of origin and Europe as a whole would thus profit from Germany's influence, the *Frankfurter Allgemeine* concluded.[17] Similarly, Hanns-Joachim Rüstow of the Munich-based ifo-Institut claimed "that through the training we give them these people become disciplined workers at home and valuable members of society."[18]

Had they not been valuable members of society before? Germans were invited to interpret the recruitment of thousands of foreign workers as evidence of their own economic superiority, of their role as a leading civic force in Europe and even as political educators. Life in "our free economic order" would, as BDA president Balke and Federal Labor Minister Theodor Blank believed, convince foreign workers of the advantages of that order.[19] Labor migration thus contributed to the fight against communism. In this guise, nationalism and feelings of superiority were allowed to survive and were even encouraged. But at the same time, German workers were reproachfully reminded of their duty to improve Germany's image abroad and thus—if often inexplicitly—of the burden and guilt of the past.

The Contained Conflict

There were hints of explosive potential in this mixture of continued nationalism and consciousness of a historic burden, a burden, notably, that was placed on the shoulders of ordinary Germans. A series on foreign labor in the mass-circulation tabloid *Bild* involved a grocer who, in a fictitious pub talk, rejected the demand that foreigners had to be treated with particular friendliness on account of "the horrible foreign-labor policy."[20] When the weekly magazine *Neue Illustrierte* published a ferocious attack on foreigners in 1965, it claimed that it was only articulating popular feelings suppressed by the fear that "the Germans would again be accused of racial prejudice."[21] Similarly, a Bundestag member who belonged to the liberal Free Democratic Party (Freie Demokratische Partei, FDP) argued that Germans should learn to discuss the question of *Überfremdung* unburdened by feelings of resentment[22]—in other words, that they should overcome an enforced silence and openly complain about alleged *Überfremdung*.

Although radical right-wing views are commonly presented under the pretext of breaking taboos, there might be some truth in the assumption that the burdens of the past and the fear of negative consequences for the country's image abroad did indeed help contain hostility to the growing presence of foreigners in West Germany during the 1960s. As far as we know, there were very few incidences of racist violence or rioting against foreigners. Unlike Britain, strikes for "color bars" (i.e., quota on the employment of immigrants) and extended protests against foreign neighbors do not seem to have occurred. There were, of course, tensions. German workers are reported to have complained, for example, about preferential treatment of foreigners who were served special food in factory cafeterias or who received housing in employer-built hostels. Many Germans seem to have disliked the transformation of train stations into meeting places and the fact that foreigners hung around in the streets after work—something well-behaved Germans did not do at the time.[23] There was housing discrimination, and some pubs put up signs barring Italians and other foreigners from entry. In 1966, thousands of workers in the engineering industry went on strike after the widely read tabloid *Bild* published a headline suggesting that foreigners might be better workers than their German counterparts.[24] This event was quite exceptional, however. The protests did not extend beyond the factory gates and were quickly contained, thanks in part to the intervention of the metalworkers' union IG Metall. Union officials were worried about "residue from the past" (*Schlacken der Vergangenheit*) that might fuel a dangerous anti-immigration campaign.[25] Opposition to immigration was not an important campaign issue for the extreme right-wing National Democratic Party (Nationaldemokratische Partei Deutschlands, NPD), but it is not clear whether the growing presence of foreigners nonetheless contributed to the party's success in a series of state elections in the late 1960s.[26] Foreign workers may have been subject to discrimination, but there was in general no open conflict over their presence in the Federal Republic.

The media generally supported a policy of appeasement. The papers were uninterested in exploring tensions and generally refrained from stirring them up. The above-mentioned criticism of *Gastarbeiter* in an issue of the *Neue Illustrierte* remained an isolated incident. There seems to have been an unspoken agreement to pass silently over issues that might adversely affect Germany's image abroad as well as to promote the image of the Federal Republic as a westernized and liberal society.

Although an open, critical debate on the exploitation of forced laborers during the Nazi era did not take place in the 1960s, the past was present in other ways. There were feelings of guilt and an awareness that no grounds should be given to doubt the democratic character of West German society. When, for example, the Christian Democratic chancellor Ludwig Erhard and FDP leader Erich Mende publicly expressed their opposition to immigration and tried to exploit nationalist sentiment, they tread very carefully.[27] The presence of the past thus helped contain hostility to foreign workers and prevent the political exploitation of the immigration issue.

The "Hitler Man" Returns

This coexistence of caution and an unreflective confidence was also typical of government policy, as an event in the early phase of organized recruitment of foreign workers illustrates. On 28 May 1960, the German ambassador to Greece informed the Foreign Ministry in Bonn that he had put a member of the German recruiting office in Athens on a plane back to Germany that day.[28] A recruitment treaty had been signed on 30 March, and a three-man delegation arrived a month later to set up a recruiting office for the Federal Labor Agency (Bundesanstalt für Arbeit). In late May, left-wing Greek newspapers revealed that the chief recruiting officer, Herrmann Westermayer, was no newcomer to Greece: headlines in Athens labeled him "The Hitler man who sends workers to Germany again."[29] Foreign Minister Heinrich von Brentano and his deputy, State Secretary Karl Carstens, were embarrassed and angry. In Carstens's view, it had been "completely unacceptable politically that [Westermayer] was sent again to Greece to recruit laborers."[30] The Ministry of Labor needed to be lectured on the need to take account of the "political imponderables." As Carstens went on to explain, "Labor recruitment during the Third Reich is nowadays generally burdened with the infamy of deportation, even if individuals may have acted in a correct and loyal manner." The German authorities had to keep this view of the past in mind as it was "of the greatest importance" for the success and public image of the recruiting operation "that the activities of the German commissions are not in any way inhibited by burdens from the period of occupation."[31]

The Westermayer case is instructive for a number of reasons. Senior officials at the Federal Labor Agency had been aware of Westermayer's wartime service in Greece and had nevertheless decided to send him there once again. As nothing untoward had been held against him and Greek witnesses had helped him in his denazification proceedings, they thought Westermayer posed no problem; rather, his knowledge of Greece and its language made him seem well-qualified for the job.[32] Obviously, they saw his wartime experience as valuable for the West German recruitment program. Labor recruitment and displacement were not regarded as part of a system of occupation and exploitation of a foreign country, or of a criminal Nazi regime. Westermayer himself defended his wartime service, arguing that recruitment had been strictly voluntary. In the years 1942–44, he insisted, he had worked above all "for the poor and hungry Greeks."[33] "Even then," he declared, "my work was devoted to a 'unified Europe.'"[34]

West German politicians and officials might perhaps have been careless because Germany's wartime exploitation of foreign labor turned out not to be a major public issue in Italy, Greece, or, later, Yugoslavia when the Federal Republic sought to recruit workers. Italian officials in 1954–55 partly used a 1937 agreement on labor recruitment as a model for the new agreement on labor migration. Because of the tradition of seasonal migration to Germany, they expected many Italians would be willing to work in the Federal Republic.[35] The Federal Ministry for Labor recorded reports of Italians willing to work in Germany on account of previous experience there.[36] Some German employers are reported to have written to Italians who had formerly worked for them (some as prisoners of war) asking them to come back.[37] Few scholars who have researched the subject have found evidence of reservations among Italians about labor migration to Germany on account of the treatment of their compatriots in Nazi Germany.[38] Italian and Greek newspapers, mainly on the left, occasionally drew parallels between past and present in criticizing the living conditions of foreign workers in Germany. For instance, an article in the communist paper *L'Unita* announced in October 1960: "The Italians in Germany have returned to the 'camps.'"[39] In Greece, the newspaper *Avghi* printed a series of articles that attacked the "racist arrogance" of the Germans and interpreted the exclusion of foreign workers from some pubs as a continuation of Nazi practices.[40]

German authorities closely watched the media response to the recruitment program. The Federal Labor Agency reported to the Labor Ministry, for example, in response to a reader's letter in *L'Unita* alleging that Italian workers were housed in the barracks of a former concentration camp where the remains of a gas chamber could still be seen.[41] And the Foreign Ministry's response to the Westermayer case illustrates that at least the politicians and diplomats who were responsible for West Germany's image abroad were aware of the political dynamite contained in links with the past. The Foreign Ministry's nervousness should be placed in this context. In May 1960, Theodor Oberländer resigned as a government minister following accusations regarding his role as an SS officer during the war. And, as Ulrich Brochhagen has emphasized, the wave of anti-Semitic graffiti in 1959–60 had attracted considerable attention abroad.[42] Although West Germany's policy toward foreigners did not become the subject of international media attention, a heightened sensitivity is clearly noticeable. Furthermore, the recruitment program was intended to help stabilize the conservative governments then in power in Italy and Greece and not to provide ammunition for communist critics. At the Foreign Ministry, Carstens was no more interested than his counterparts at the Federal Labor Agency and Ministry of Labor in what Westermayer might actually have been doing between 1942 and 1944.[43] It was West Germany's image abroad that concerned them.

"Practical evidence for our democratic commitments": The 1965 Aliens Act

Another example illustrates the heightened sensitivity to possible links between West German and Nazi policies evident from about 1960 onward. On 7 January 1960, the Berlin *Tagesspiegel* published an editorial demanding that the 1938 regulation on aliens that was still in effect, the *Ausländer-Polizeiverordnung*, be replaced. Given the "shameful 'handwriting on the wall' of our cities" [i.e., anti-Semitic graffiti], the newspaper saw an increasingly urgent need for a new law. "We have ample reason not just to stamp the federal eagle over the faded swastika on Germany's front entrance but rather to acquire a spotless new one."[44]

The Berlin senator (minister) of the interior sent a copy of this editorial to the Federal Interior Ministry, which had already started work on drafting a new aliens act. Creating a more liberal and democratic legal framework was not the prime motive; rather, officials repeatedly mentioned the need to cleanse West German law of Nazi elements.[45] And from the outset—and this can be seen as a response to contemporary debates about the Nazi legacy—the new legislation was presented as an expression of a liberal and *weltoffen* (cosmopolitan, open-minded) policy toward foreigners. As Federal Minister of the Interior Hermann Höcherl (Christian Social Union) explained in 1964, the aliens act should "demonstrate to the whole civilized world that the Federal Republic of Germany is striving to overcome the unseemly aspects of the past through positive regulations."[46] At the same time, the bill was often presented to West Germans as a measure designed to allow the state to suppress the political activities of foreigners more effectively.[47] But when the Bundestag finally passed the bill in 1965, the emphasis was on liberalism and democratic renewal. As the three speakers uniformly emphasized, West Germany was breaking with the past with the new law and making "a major contribution to the reshaping of our internal order."[48] "We have provided practical evidence for our democratic commitments," the interior minister declared.[49]

Was this pride justified? Opinions on the aliens act are, as might be expected, divided.[50] Critics have argued that the new law was in fact stricter than the 1938 ordinance.[51] While this assessment is quite harsh, the new law did give authorities wide discretionary powers but did not grant foreigners the right to stay in the Federal Republic. It was based on the view that the state's interests should be given preference over the interests of the foreign individual. At the same time, though, the right to asylum, which had been guaranteed in the Basic

Law and was now incorporated in the new law, marked major differences from the 1930s, and foreigners were also given opportunity to seek judicial review of administrative decisions.

The Bundestag had not made a serious effort to explore what a liberal and democratic policy toward foreigners might be. It did not seize the opportunity to reflect upon the treatment of foreigners in the past and in the present, upon the tolerance or intolerance of the Germans, or upon the implications of migration that was already turning into permanent immigration. Nor did the parliament ask whether it was wise to grant state and local authorities wide discretionary powers.

Criticism was raised, however, by the Social Democratic government of Hessen, which asked whether the bill did indeed represent "a progressive revision" of the law "that takes account of the modern view of the priority of human rights and that is in line with the general efforts toward a far-reaching rapprochement among states." It demanded that restrictions on individual rights be applied with great caution.[52] In contrast to their party colleagues in the Bundestag, Hessen's Social Democrats made their criticism of the proposed law public. In 1962, Hessian Minister of Labor Heinrich Hemsath argued in the Bundesrat (the chamber of states) that the bill included provisions that did not accord with the Basic Law. It failed to provide refugees with protection against deportation, he argued, and impinged upon the fundamental right of freedom of expression.[53] When the bill came up for vote in the Bundesrat, Hessen abstained.

Although the aliens law was passed unanimously in the Bundestag, there had been considerable debate behind the scenes on the choice between a more restrictive or a more liberal "westernized" policy on foreigners. It would be too simple to assume that all involved merely wanted to provide window dressing while retaining the substance of the 1938 regulations. State and federal authorities were at odds on how to balance perceived security needs and the goals of integration within the West and economic liberalization. The Federal Ministry of the Interior came under repeated criticism while drafting the new legislation from the Foreign Ministry and the Federal Economics Ministry, which feared that the law might counteract the trend toward greater freedom of movement in Europe and could therefore provoke negative reactions abroad. The Economics Ministry believed some of the provisions in the draft legislation were more restrictive than the 1938 regulations and asked whether that was necessary. More liberal tendencies were to be preferred, the ministry maintained: "Otherwise the law would be in danger of being regarded as a step backwards." "Does liberalization alone mean progress?" retorted an Interior Ministry official in a note in the margin.[54] When the draft began with the statement that foreigners could be admitted if they were worthy of German hospitality, the Foreign Ministry complained that this formulation recalled National Socialist vocabulary by which "a foreigner was assumed inferior to the German master race until the opposite be proved."[55]

The status of refugees and former displaced persons (DPs) was another source of controversy. A Foreign Ministry official remarked in 1963 that the time had come to restrict the rights of refugees.[56] Interior Minister Höcherl took a principled stance—against demands from a Bavarian government led by his own party—and insisted that the right to asylum ranked above security concerns. As Höcherl's deputy explained, "Considering the past, the Federal Republic has a lot to make up for in this area."[57]

The fact that only a few weeks later the Bundestag was to take a decision on the statute of limitations (to allow a continued prosecution of Nazi crimes) may have been one reason for the decision to make the Bundestag "debate" on the aliens act a unified demonstration for an imagined foreign audience. No member of parliament voted against the new law.[58] In the parliamentary commission, a redrafting of the first paragraph had been instigated in order to give the law a friendlier appearance, since, as one Social Democratic member of parliament argued, it would attract more attention abroad than other bills.[59] Some very cautious reservations had been expressed regarding the limited political rights of foreigners and the provisions on expulsions.[60] But altogether the work of the Bundestag demonstrates that—while immigration was being debated in public—sensitivity for human rights issues developed slowly. Neither Germany's history with regard to immigration and foreign employment and its consequences nor the contours of a democratic immigration policy were debated in the Bundestag. If this was a time of a "highly condensed debate on National Socialism," and if a "far-reaching consensus" existed on the need for a self-critical debate on the Nazi past,[61] it did not extend to immigration policy. But it should also be noted that while clearly not every member of parliament approved of the mass employment of foreigners in Germany, there was no open and concerted resistance against it.

As the controversies surrounding the aliens act demonstrate, West German politicians and governmental officials did try to draw conclusions from the experience of the past, albeit only tentatively and largely behind closed doors. In public, they did not see the need for a comprehensive reevaluation of Germany's policy on foreigners in connection with the goal of presenting the country to the world as a liberal democracy. An open public discussion about the differences between authoritarian and liberal policies toward foreigners, about the past and its consequences, was not yet desired.

Concluding Remarks

As this essay has demonstrated, West German attitudes toward foreigners and views about the relevance of the Nazi past in thinking about foreigners were multifaceted. The possibility of negative responses from abroad was a major factor in shaping policy on foreigners, as was the wish to demonstrate that democratic and liberal change had occurred in the Federal Republic. It was widely assumed that the treatment of foreigners was regarded as a test case of West Germany's commitment to democracy. But at the same time, politicians were often more concerned about appearance than substance, and they were usually content with superficial adjustments. Critical voices—among the public[62] as well as among state and federal officials—called for a more substantial liberalization and more respect for individual rights. But an open and thoroughgoing debate about past experience with foreign labor and the treatment of foreigners did not take place. As the example of migration policy illustrates, the evidence of the parliamentary debates on the statute of limitations should not lead us to assume there was a general shift toward critical reflection on the nation's past.

The debate over migration policy lost much of its urgency following the economic downturn of 1966, which resulted in the more or less voluntary departure of thousands of foreign workers. When the debate resumed in the early 1970s, it was in many ways a transformed, more broadly critical discussion. But even then, references to the exploitation of forced laborers during the war were rare.[63] It was more common to liken the situation of foreigners in contemporary Germany to American blacks than to the *Fremdarbeiter* of the war years.

Notes

1. Siegfried Balke, "Begrüssung und Eröffnung," in *Magnet Bundesrepublik. Probleme der Ausländerbeschäftigung: Informationstagung der Bundesvereinigung der Deutschen Arbeitgeberverbände am 30. und 31. März 1966 in Bad Godesberg* (Cologne, 1966), 8. In a further contribution at the conference, Balke again emphasized Germany's "long tradition in the field of foreign employment." Siegfried Balke, "Die Ausländerbeschäftigung aus der Sicht der Wirtschaft," in ibid., 168–82, here 177. Several aspects of this chapter of German history are explored in more detail in my book, Karen Schönwälder, *Einwanderung und ethnische Pluralität: Politische Entscheidungen und öffentliche Debatten in Grossbritannien und der Bundesrepublik Deutschland von den 1950er bis zu den 1970er Jahren* (Essen, 2001).

2. Quoted in Ulrich Herbert, *Geschichte der Ausländerbeschäftigung in Deutschland 1880 bis 1980: Saisonarbeiter, Zwangsarbeiter, Gastarbeiter* (Bonn, 1986), 49–50. In 1957, Julius Scheuble, president of the Bundesanstalt für Arbeitsvermittlung und Arbeitslosenversicherung, had published a study written by his predecessor Friedrich Syrup. Here, Syrup emphasized the "great national dangers" a mass influx of foreign workers posed "for the body of the German Volk" (*für den deutschen Volkskörper*). In spite of revisions, the text remained marked by an attitude of superiority over the culturally inferior, dangerous foreigners. Friedrich Syrup, *Hundert Jahre staatliche Sozialpolitik 1839–1939*, rev. Otto Neuloh, ed. Julius Scheuble (Stuttgart, 1957), 224ff.

3. Siegfried Balke, "Die Verantwortung der Betriebe," *Der Arbeitgeber* 17 (1965): 279.

4. Balke, "Begrüssung und Eröffnung," 9.

5. Figures should only be roughly compared, as the statistical basis was different. For 1961 census figures, see "Die Ausländer im Bundesgebiet," *Wirtschaft und Statistik*, no. 11 (1964): 645–50. Using the locally recorded figures for officially registered foreigners, a 1967 total of 1,807 million citizens was established. See "Ausländer im Bundesgebiet," *Wirtschaft und Statistik*, no. 7 (1969): 360–61, here 378. Embassy and consular staff as well as members of foreign armies were not included. Detailed figures on foreign workers (gainfully employed persons) can be found in the *Erfahrungsberichte* of the Bundesanstalt für Arbeitsvermittlung und Arbeitslosenversicherung.

6. Helmuth Weicken, "Die Ausländerbeschäftigung in der Bundesrepublik Deutschland—Stand und Entwicklung," *Arbeit, Beruf und Arbeitslosenhilfe* 18 (1967): 5–9, here 6.

7. According to an estimate by the Bundesanstalt für Arbeitsvermittlung und Arbeitslosenversicherung, in 1966, 341,000 foreign couples lived in the Federal Republic. See Bundesanstalt für

Arbeitsvermittlung und Arbeitslosenversicherung, ed., *Beschäftigung, Anwerbung, Vermittlung ausländischer Arbeitnehmer: Erfahrungsbericht 1967* (Nuremberg, 1968), 20–21. The figures seem to be based on couples in which the man or both partners were foreigners.

8. Knuth Dohse, *Ausländische Arbeiter und bürgerlicher Staat. Genese und Funktion von staatlicher Ausländerpolitik und Ausländerrecht: Vom Kaiserreich bis zur Bundesrepublik Deutschland* (Königstein, 1981); Hartmut Esser, "Gastarbeiter," in *Die Geschichte der Bundesrepublik Deutschland*, vol. 2: *Wirtschaft*, ed. Wolfgang Benz, updated and extended edition (Frankfurt am Main, 1989), 326–61.

9. Ulrich Herbert and Karin Hunn suggest that there was a "Wahrnehmungsbruch" and a "Fiktion der Voraussetzungslosigkeit der neuerlichen Ausländerbeschäftigung"; see Ulrich Herbert and Karin Hunn, "Gastarbeiter und Gastarbeiterpolitik in der Bundesrepublik: Vom Beginn der offiziellen Anwerbung bis zum Anwerbestopp (1955–1973)," in *Dynamische Zeiten: Die 60er Jahre in den beiden deutschen Gesellschaften*, ed. Axel Schildt, Detlef Siegfried, and Karl C. Lammers (Hamburg, 2000), 273–310, here 309–10. However, Herbert also argues that "in the formulation of policy toward foreign workers after 1955 and the crystallization of attitudes toward guest workers, experiences of a decade earlier with forced laborers were still a conscious and operative factor." See Ulrich Herbert, *A History of Foreign Labor in Germany, 1880–1990: Seasonal Workers, Forced Laborers, Guest Workers* (Ann Arbor, 1990), 4.

10. This line of argument was popularized by the Federal Employment Service. See Bundesanstalt für Arbeitsvermittlung und Arbeitslosenversicherung, ed., *Beschäftigung, Anwerbung, Vermittlung ausländischer Arbeitnehmer: Erfahrungsbericht 1964* (Nuremberg, 1965). Further examples include "1910 gab es mehr Gastarbeiter," in *Neue Ruhrzeitung*, 21 June 1964; "Gastarbeiter sind kein neues Problem für Deutschland," in *Welt der Arbeit*, 11 June 1965.

11. "Die Ausländer im Bundesgebiet," *Wirtschaft und Statistik*, no. 8 (1951): 313–15, 965–66; "Die Ausländer im Bundesgebiet" (1964). The presence of the Allied armies surely added to the perception that Germany had a sizable foreign population.

12. There are indications that the threat posed by foreign laborers released after the war had made a deep impression on the Germans. An article in the *Süddeutsche Zeitung*, for instance, described hostile attitudes toward foreign workers on the part of Wolfsburg inhabitants who had not forgotten "dass es bei Kriegsende in Wolfsburg Tausende von plötzlich freigewordenen Fremdarbeitern gab, die sich für die erlittene Unbill an den Wolfsburgern schadlos hielten." See "Die Italiener in Wolfsburg haben Heimweh," *Süddeutsche Zeitung*, 23 November 1962. See also Ulrich Herbert, "Apartheid nebenan: Erinnerungen an die Fremdarbeiter im Ruhrgebiet," in *"Die Jahre weiss man nicht, wo man die heute hinsetzen soll": Faschismuserfahrungen im Ruhrgebiet*, ed. Lutz Niethammer (Bonn, 1983), 233–66, here 233, 259.

13. See, e.g., "Die wachsende Last der Fremdarbeiter," in *Hamburger Abendblatt*, 11 March 1966; "Arbeitslosigkeit und Kurzarbeit Alarmsignale?" in *Politisch-Soziale Korrespondenz* 16 (1967): 15–16. Even in parliamentary debates the term was still used, for instance, by Hannsheinz Bauer, SPD (*Verhandlungen des Deutschen Bundestages*, 12 December 1962, 2297), and on 25 March 1965 by Schwörer, CDU (8817f.) and Opitz, FDP (8822). But see also the critical comments by the trade union official Eberhard de Haan, who insisted that the term was discredited because of the treatment of millions of forced laborers during the Nazi regime. "Integration, Assimilation oder was?" in *Bildungswerk Europäische Politik, Arbeitsplatz Europa: Langfristige Perspektiven und europäische Aspekte zum Problem ausländischer Arbeitnehmer* (Cologne, 1966), 52–55, here 53.

14. Richard Kaufmann, "Der Gastarbeiter als gesellschaftliches Problem," in ibid., 19–39, here 29.

15. "Fremde—Gäste—Freunde: Gastarbeiter in Deutschland" was published in spring 1966; 182,000 copies were printed and distributed. A historical survey entitled "Von der 'Sachsengängerei' bis zu den 'Fremdarbeitern'" (20–21) described the period of forced labor as a "dark chapter" in which foreigners had been treated as second-class humans but had also encountered sympathy.

16. In the mid-1960s, the term *Überfremdung* became widely used when debates in Switzerland seemed to suggest that the recruitment of foreigners involved such a threat. "Keine Gefahr der

Überfremdung" (*Mannheimer Morgen*, 31 March 1966) was a typical newspaper headline after the 1966 BDA conference, where several speakers had ensured the audience that such a danger did not exist in Germany.

17. "Die Völkerwanderung zum Arbeitsmarkt," by Günther von Lojewski, 9 May 1964.

18. See Rüstow's contribution to the discussion in "Probleme der ausländischen Arbeitskräfte in der Bundesrepublik: Bericht über den wissenschaftlichen Teil der 29. Mitgliederversammlung der Arbeitsgemeinschaft deutscher wirtschaftswissenschaftlicher Forschungsinstitute e. V. in Bad Godesberg am 24. und 25. Juni 1966," *Beihefte der Konjunkturpolitik*, no. 13 (1966): 158.

19. Balke, "Die Verantwortung der Betriebe." See also, with similar comments, Theodor Blank, "Ein Schritt zur Völkerverständigung," *Der Arbeitgeber* 17 (1965): 280.

20. "Nix Amore," 22 April 1966.

21. Major headlines included "Dreiste Gastarbeiter raus!" and "Noch gehört Deutschland uns," *Neue Illustrierte*, no. 18, 2 May 1965.

22. Alfred Ollesch, "Einreisende Gastarbeiter schärfer kontrollieren," fdk, 15 March 1966.

23. While repeated surveys were carried out to assess the prevalence of anti-Semitism, attitudes to foreigners or foreign workers were rarely investigated. In September 1965, according to an Emnid survey, 51 percent of the population still tended to oppose the importation of foreigners as guest workers. Only 27 percent generally supported this policy. About one-third of those opposed (that is, about 17 percent of those questioned) pointed to the behavior and alleged characteristics of the immigrants, including their racial characteristics. *Emnid-Informationen* 17, no. 49, 6 December 1965. In 1964, 32 percent had termed the "guest workers" a "difficult problem," while 36 percent thought things were going quite well. "Laut und sparsam: Wie die Deutschen die Gastarbeiter beurteilen," *Allensbacher Berichte*, no. 1 (1972): 6.

24. "Gastarbeiter fleissiger als deutsche Arbeiter," *Bild*, 31 March 1966.

25. Günter Stephan, Deutscher Gewerkschaftsbund, 7. Ordentlicher Bundeskongress Berlin, *Protokoll* [1966], 101.

26. See Hermann Bott, *Die Volksfeind-Ideologie: Zur Kritik rechtsradikaler Propaganda* (Stuttgart, 1969); Reinhard Kühnl, Rainer Rilling, and Christine Sager, *Die NPD: Struktur, Ideologie und Funktion einer neofaschistischen Partei* (Frankfurt am Main, 1969). In contemporary press reports on the NPD, its attitude toward foreigners was rarely mentioned. See, however, "Gäste im Zerrspiegel," *Frankfurter Rundschau*, 30 December 1966, which claimed that NPD attacks on foreigners had won support for it.

27. Erhard repeatedly emphasized that if only the Germans were prepared to work one hour more per week, foreign employment could be substantially reduced. See, e.g., *Verhandlungen des Deutschen Bundestages*, 133. Sitzung/4. WP, 25 June 1964, 6529; ibid., 5. WP, 10 November 1965, 17–33. FDP leader Erich Mende included hostile remarks on the employment of foreigners during the 1965 election campaign. See "DGB verteidigt Gastarbeiter," *Frankfurter Rundschau*, 16 September 1965; "Erich Mende: Was mein Bild betrifft …," *Rheinischer Merkur*, 3 September 1965.

28. Telegraph Seelos, Athen, to Auswärtiges Amt, 28 May 1960, in Politisches Archiv des Auswärtigen Amts, Bonn (PA AA) 505/791; apart from this file, see also B 2/82 (Büro Staatssekretär) in the same archive.

29. See quotations from *Avghi* in Botschaft der Bundesrepublik Deutschland in Athens to Auswärtiges Amt, 10 June 1960, in PA AA 505/791.

30. *Staatssekretär's* notes, 1 June 1960, in PA AA 505/791. Comments on several documents show that Carstens and the minister, Heinrich von Brentano, followed the case.

31. AA to BMA, 21 July 1960, in Bundesarchiv Koblenz (hereafter BA Ko) B 149/22390.

32. Note Dr. Zöllner, Bundesanstalt, 3 June 1960, in BA Ko B 119/3076.

33. Bundesanstalt, note of 3 June 1960: "Stellungnahme des V.I. Hermann Westermayer zu dem Bericht der kommunistischen Zeitung 'die Morgenröte' in Athen vom 27.5.60," in BA Ko B 119/3076.

34. Memo Westermayer of 30 May 1960, in BA Ko B 119/3076.

35. Livia Novi, "Die italienisch-deutsche Anwerbevereinbarung von 1955 im Rahmen der italienischen Wanderungspolitik der fünfziger Jahre" (MA thesis, Osnabrück University, 1994), 47, 60.

36. Here I rely on Barbara Sonnenberger, who mentioned relevant comments to me that can be found in BA Ko B 149/6230. See also Yvonne Rieker, "Südländer, Ostagenten oder Westeuropäer? Die Politik der Bundesregierung und das Bild der italienischen Gastarbeiter 1955–1970," *Archiv für Sozialgeschichte* 40 (2000): 231–58, here 244.

37. Herbert Spaich, *Fremde in Deutschland* (Weinheim, 1981), 209. According to the *Süddeutsche Zeitung*, a firm in Ramseck/Sauerland employed fifty Italian miners, two-thirds of whom had already worked in Ramseck during the war ("Italienische Arbeiter bewähren sich," 2 September 1955). Again, I owe these references to Barbara Sonnenberger.

38. Italians had initially been recruited, or sent by the Mussolini regime, but after 1943, workers had been forced to stay in Germany, and about six hundred thousand Italian prisoners of war were turned into forced laborers. See, however, Behrmann and Abate, who were told by Italian migrants from Sicily that they had initially been reluctant to apply for work in Germany because after the experience of World War II, fear of the Germans was still widespread. Meike Behrmann and Carmine Abate, *Die Germanesi: Geschichte und Leben einer süditalienischen Dorfgemeinschaft und ihrer Emigranten* (Frankfurt am Main, 1984), 41. Rieker believes that bad memories of Germany played an important part in the "collective memory" of the Italians, but seems to rely more or less on the evidence quoted here. See Rieker, "Südländer, Ostagenten oder Westeuropäer?" 245.

39. I used a translation in BA Ko B 106/47434. The article stated cynically that many German employers held the same attitudes as twenty years ago. It also claimed that recruitment was a "Menschenhandel im Stile der Deportation." The BA files also contain a translation of an article of 4 July 1956 in *L'Unita*, which claimed that the food Italian workers received recalled the memories of the concentration camps, BA Ko B 119/3040.

40. Undated translations are contained in "Wochenbericht der Deutschen Kommission in Griechenland an den Präsidenten der Bundesanstalt" of 5 May 1961, in BA Ko B 119/3075. The issue was also taken up by the GDR paper *Neues Deutschland*; see "Protest Italiens gegen Nazimethoden in Nürnberg," 2 June 1963, an article that referred to pub signs and quoted references to the "Nazism virus" and to racism from Italian papers.

41. The letter was published on 26 February 1965 under the heading "Italiani allogiati nei vecchi campi di concentramento." The BA informed the BMA (on 13 July 1965) that the allegations were false (BA Ko B 149/22380).

42. Ulrich Brochhagen, *Nach Nürnberg: Vergangenheitsbewältigung und Westintegration in der Ära Adenauer* (Hamburg, 1994), 276ff. On page 295, Brochhagen quotes from a letter from the AA to the embassies of 10 March 1960, which stated that in the West nothing had been forgotten and confidence in the Federal Republic rested on a weak foundation.

43. According to his own report, Westermayer had in 1941 been sent to Yugoslavia to work as a *Vermittler* (recruitment officer). Early in 1942, he had been sent to Salonika to set up an office, which—after a few months—he also did in Athens, where he stayed until 1944. Memo of 30 May 1960, BA Ko B 119/3076. German recruitment in Greece started in January 1942 but was generally not very successful. Initially, recruitment seems to have been "voluntary," although in many cases unemployment and hunger forced Greeks to go to the Reich. According to some sources, organized recruitment to the Reich was terminated at the end of 1942. Hadziiossif reports that from autumn 1943, violence was used to recruit workers. See Christos Hadziiossif, "Griechen in der deutschen Kriegsproduktion," in *Europa und der "Reichseinsatz": Ausländische Zivilarbeiter, Kriegsgefangene und KZ-Häftlinge in Deutschland 1938–1945*, ed. Ulrich Herbert (Essen, 1991), 210–33. Westermayer may have been involved in recruiting Greek workers for German factories in Greece. For the general context, see Mark Mazower, *Inside Hitler's Greece: The Experience of Occupation, 1941–44* (New Haven, 1993), and Rainer Eckert, "Die wirtschaftliche Ausplünderung Griechenlands durch seine deutschen Okkupanten vom Beginn

der Besetzung im April 1941 bis zur Kriegswende im Winter 1942/43," *Jahrbuch für Geschichte* 35 (1988): 235–66.

44. "Unsere Meinung: Ausländer-Polizeiverordnung," attached to Der Senator für Inneres Berlin to the Bundesminister des Innern, Gerhard Schröder, 9 January 1960, in BA Ko B 106/47380.

45. A memo by Unterabteilungsleiter Dr. Füsslein, BMI, of 26 October 1957, listed a number of reasons for a new law, including the fact that the current regulations still contained elements of National Socialist thinking, in BA Ko B 106/47379. I have analyzed the discussions about the need for a new aliens act and what form it should take in greater detail elsewhere. See Karen Schönwälder, "'Ist nur Liberalisierung Fortschritt?' Zur Entstehung des ersten Ausländergesetzes der Bundesrepublik," in *50 Jahre Bundesrepublik—50 Jahre Einwanderung*, ed. Jan Motte, Rainer Ohliger, and Anne von Oswald (Frankfurt am Main, 1999), 127–44, and chap. 3.3.2 in Schönwälder, *Einwanderung und ethnische Pluralität*.

46. Hermann Höcherl, "Ausländer in der Bundesrepublik Deutschland," *Bulletin des Presse- und Informationsamtes der Bundesregierung*, no. 126, (1964), 1189–90.

47. See the interview with Hermann Höcherl on the WDR's *Die Woche in Bonn* on 17 March 1963, verbatim report of the Bundespresseamt, in Presseausschnittsammlung des SPD-PV, DW 2-9f4, in Archiv der sozialen Demokratie, Bonn. One of the SPD's home affairs spokesmen, Hermann Schmitt-Vockenhausen, demanded that the new aliens act provide measures "um verhindern zu können, dass hier ein Eldorado rechts- oder linksradikaler Emigranten-Organisationen entsteht." "Die SPD teilt mit," 30 April 1963, in BA Ko B 106/39959.

48. Hermann Schmitt-Vockenhausen, *Verhandlungen des Deutschen Bundestages*, 163. Sitzung/4. WP, 12 February 1965, 8034; and similar words by Dietrich-Wilhelm Rollmann (CDU), ibid., 8059–60. The three speakers included a representative of the parliamentary committee for interior affairs, of the SPD and the Interior Minister.

49. Ibid., 8035–40.

50. For different views, see Ulrich Erdmann, "Das Ausländergesetz von 1965 im internationalen Vergleich," *Verwaltungsarchiv* 59 (1968): 311–44; Diemut Majer, "Entspricht unser Ausländerrecht der internationalen Rechtsauffassung? Ein Rechtsvergleich," in *Ausländergesetz '65. Alternativentwurf '70: Kritik und Reform*, ed. Forschungsinstitut der Friedrich-Ebert-Stiftung, studentische politik no. 1 (1970), 50ff.

51. Fritz Franz, "Zur Reform des Ausländer-Polizeirechts," *Deutsches Verwaltungsblatt* 78 (1963): 797–803, here 797.

52. Der Hessische Minister des Innern to the BMI, 25 January 1962, in BA Ko B 106/39961.

53. *Verhandlungen des Bundesrates*, 249. Sitzung, 26 October 1962: 189.

54. BMWi to BMI, 11 December 1961; Ministerialdirektor Walter, BMWi, to Ministerialdirektor Schäfer, BMI, 7 February 1962, in BA Ko B 106/39961.

55. AA to BMI, 24 November 1961, in ibid.

56. Notes of Abt. V of the AA of 14 January 1963 on the parliamentary debates on the aliens bill, in PA AA V 6/1849. At a meeting of regional home office representatives, the Bavarian official Dr. Mayer remarked that times had changed, since under pressure from the occupying powers the asylum decree had been passed. Protocol of a meeting of AK I "Staatsrecht, Verwaltung und Verwaltungsgerichtsbarkeit" and AK II "öffentliche Sicherheit und Ordnung" of the Arbeitsgemeinschaft der Innenministerien der Bundesländer on 9 March 1964 in Bonn, in BA Ko B 106/39960.

57. BMI Höcherl to Staatsminister Heinrich Junker (Bavaria), 4 June 1964, in BA Ko B 106/39960; protocol of the meeting of the Ständige Konferenz der Innenminister der Länder on 11 and 12 June 1964 in Husum, 19–24, in BA Ko B 106/38054.

58. The second and third readings took place on 12 February 1965; the first reading had taken place on 16 January 1963, but without debate.

59. Deutscher Bundestag, 4. Wahlperiode, Kurzprotokoll der 72. Sitzung des Ausschusses für Inneres des Deutschen Bundestages, 28 November 1963, in Bundestags-Archiv, Bonn.

60. Deutscher Bundestag, 4. Wahlperiode, Kurzprotokoll der 84. Sitzung des Ausschusses für Inneres, 12 March 1964, in Bundestags-Archiv, Bonn.

61. Detlef Siegfried, "Zwischen Aufarbeitung und Schlussstrich: Der Umgang mit der NS-Vergangenheit in den beiden deutschen Staaten 1958 bis 1969," in Schildt, Siegfried, and Lammers, *Dynamische Zeiten,* 77–113, here 95, 100.

62. See, e.g., Paul Schallück, "Der unbequeme Bruder," *Gewerkschaftliche Monatshefte* 17 (1966): 257–61.

63. See, however, in the *Schwarzbuch: Ausländische Arbeiter* of the Jungsozialisten (Frankfurt am Main, 1972) a historical chapter that covered forced labor during the Nazi regime. See also Ruth Becker, Gerhard Dörr, and Karl H. Tjaden, "Fremdarbeiterbeschäftigung im deutschen Kapitalismus," *Das Argument* 68 (1971): 741–56.

Chapter 8

THE WEST GERMAN PUBLIC HEALTH SYSTEM AND THE LEGACY OF NAZISM

Sigrid Stöckel

❧

Generally speaking, the 1960s form a crucial watershed in the evolution of attitudes toward Germany's history in the twentieth century. But such a watershed is not apparent when one looks at developments in the field of social medicine. Instead, one sees a complex pattern of continuities and discontinuities with the past, especially the Nazi past. To understand the ways in which German medicine in the 1960s came to terms with its past, it is first necessary to outline these continuities and discontinuities. The main focus of this essay is not the German medical or public health system per se, but rather the concept of *Gesundheitsfürsorge*, which refers to comprehensive, preventive, and socially oriented health care for the needy. This concept lay behind the development of municipal health services during the Weimar Republic. Not only was it perverted by the Nazis, but it was also further impaired by West German society in the 1950s and 1960s.[1]

The expression "coming to terms with the past" suggests a positive, optimistic development that put an end to the Nazi legacy. In the case of *Gesundheitsfürsorge*, addressing the past brought about a break not only with the Nazi health care system, but also with that of the Weimar Republic. Given the strong eugenic element in the concept of social hygiene underlying both Weimar and Nazi health care, this break might be seen as advantageous. But it also meant the loss of a comprehensive, socially oriented health care system, and the reduction of the concept of *Gesundheitsfürsorge* to physician-controlled responsive medicine in the 1960s. This essay thus challenges the notion that the decade under discussion necessarily brought about liberalization and change for the better.

Notes for this chapter begin on page 140.

Gesundheitsfürsorge during the Weimar Republic

The concept of *Gesundheitsfürsorge* originated in the observation that there was a connection between people's health and their living conditions. In Germany, this notion received scientific articulation at the turn of the century in the field of "social hygiene," a medical discipline that combined social science and medicine. A professorship in social hygiene was established in 1921, and three specialist academies were established soon thereafter. In 1912, Alfred Grotjahn, professor of social hygiene in Berlin, had defined his field as "not necessarily medically oriented."[2] Groups that faced specific risks should receive special care. The risks ranged from age-specific threats (e.g., to infants) to harmful living conditions and resulting diseases such as tuberculosis and venereal diseases. Care was defined primarily as medical supervision, but social support was also seen as necessary to ensure the objective of maintaining health and preventing the spread of disease. Social support consisted above all of education and advice on leading a healthy and "hygienic" life—and it contributed to "taming the working class"—but it could also include benefits such as grants to breastfeeding mothers and extra food for families afflicted by tuberculosis.[3]

Gesundheitsfürsorge had come into being as part of the social welfare movement, which, in turn, had its roots in the bourgeois women's movement and the Social Democratic women's welfare organization, the Arbeiterwohlfahrt.[4] For the women of both groups, it was essential to maintain a personal relationship between helper and client. A family's circumstances and the consequences of those circumstances on illness and recovery had to be taken into account. With follow-up home visits, practical advice was combined with social control.

Social work became firmly established as a profession at the beginning of the Weimar Republic as municipal governments set up health and welfare agencies that saw social work as one of their tasks. The Reich government passed laws on youth welfare (1922) and welfare obligations (1924) that prescribed the communities' duties to care for the financially disadvantaged and physically handicapped and their offspring. At the same time, the political focus of *Gesundheitsfürsorge* shifted from charity to the politics of the body—to strengthening the population and uplifting the race.[5] This shift challenged the notion of "positive eugenics," which concentrated on improving living conditions in order to improve biological development, and raised the question whether hygienic measures would encourage the reproduction of the "wrong stock." In short, the intention was to accomplish eugenic aims by preventing "reproduction of inferior persons." In times of economic crisis and shortages, the claim of the biologically "inferior" to *Fürsorge*—the welfare entitlement that had become a key element of social policy—would inevitably come under question.

Although historians have established that social hygiene did not exist outside the eugenic context and thus helped pave the way for Nazi population policy, they have also made clear that social hygiene was not necessarily tied to any single political position.[6] It would therefore be reasonable to investigate this concept further and give some attention to its "social" side—its concern for social conditions as a precondition for people's health—and also to assess the consequences of its later erosion.

By the mid-1920s, conflict had arisen within the medical profession between *Kassenärzte* (general practitioners), who treated members of health insurance plans, and *Fürsorgeärzte*, the municipal physicians responsible for overseeing the health of groups at special risk. While *Kassenärzte* supported a traditional concept of responsive medical care delivered to the individual, the *Fürsorgeärzte* championed the concept of social hygiene, which took social circumstances into account, and which offered more than just medical help.[7] An agreement between *Kassenärzte* and *Fürsorgeärzte* was worked out to ensure that only the former could offer therapy, while the latter were restricted to diagnosis.

Gesundheitsfürsorge was thus undermined in the last years of the Weimar Republic not only by the Great Depression, which put an enormous burden on public budgets, but also by conflict between the two professional groups. The advocates of *Gesundheitsfürsorge* cited the cost and health benefits of health promotion when they urged a reform of the Imperial Insurance Act in 1930. The *Kassenärzte*, by contrast, argued for a more focused concentration on responsive medicine rather than for an extension of health-related social initiatives. Even Fritz Rott, the head of the professional association of social hygienists, supported a circumscribed view of social hygiene when he suggested that the registration of illnesses should be the main task of social hygiene. His statement reflects continuity between the Weimar concept of social hygiene and the Nazi policy of *Erfassung* of the mentally ill and physically disabled. The trend in social hygiene at the end of the Weimar Republic was to register, rather than to assist, persons with illnesses.

The National Socialist Era

The focus of *Gesundheitsfürsorge* under the National Socialists was not the individual or groups of individuals at shared risk, but rather the fiction of the racial *Volkskörper*. Accordingly, prevention was based on identifying both the superior and the harmful elements of the *Volk*. This change in perspective was aggravated by the consolidation of municipal and state health administrations in 1934, a measure that had been under discussion during the Weimar years.[8] As a consequence of the consolidation, local and municipal health departments had to register the disabled and "those of minor value" as a preparatory step for the "hereditary registration of the German people"; in other words, they had to prepare the way for the Nazis' sterilization and "euthanasia" programs. The change from customary local health care for the needy to state registration of so-called *Minderwertige* (inferiors) and antisocial elements was, therefore, not only institutional, but also substantive.

The Nazi Party's social welfare organization, the Nationalsozialistische Volkswohlfahrt, enhanced the system of *Gesundheitsfürsorge* by providing not only medical observation but extra social support for "racially healthy" families.[9] Furthermore, health authorities put emphasis on the theory that individuals were capable of improving their own health. Special attention was given to the individual's attitude toward his or her body. Not so much the external conditions were seen as essential, but rather one's ability to maintain the body. Training programs were supposed to help individuals achieve optimal performance at work and maintain their own health. During the war, however, productivity and efficiency became far more important than health.

These changes severely undermined the culture of a socially oriented *Gesundheitsfürsorge*. The 1934 consolidation created many new communal health offices, but they were run primarily by Nazi Party members. Public health officers and social workers who were Jews, communists, or Social Democrats were forced from their jobs. Public health offices thus took on an explicitly National Socialist character.

The Postwar Denazification of the Health Service

The consolidation law of 1934 was suspended in eastern Germany after the war on the grounds that it was a Nazi law. In the West, the Allies regarded centralization as such as National Socialist and tried to avoid it, whereas German proponents of nationalization defended it as sensible and efficient. Though there was not much of a discussion about keeping the consolidation law in effect, it was understood that the health care system required reform,[10] and opinions were divided about the best organizational form for health departments. A municipal organization might have been more effective for *Gesundheitsfürsorge*[11] and, in view of postwar suspicion of overbearing central government, might well have been more acceptable to many.[12] But public health officers feared that being part of a municipal administration would weaken their position.[13] So they favored the "national solution" and tried to avoid offending the Allies by placing an emphasis on the "spirit of work" rather than on organizational issues.[14] The institutional nature of the Public Health Service, the Öffentlicher Gesundheitsdienst (ÖGD), can thus be seen as a structural outcome of National Socialism—a fact that some have argued was detrimental to the rebuilding of *Gesundheitsfürsorge* in German communities.[15]

Yet within the medical profession it was not the organizational character of *Gesundheitsfürsorge* that was attacked after the war. Rather, *Kassenärzte* accused *Fürsorgeärzte* of having acted as puppets of the fascist state. Denazification hit members of the ÖGD harder than it did "normal" physicians. As civil servants, they were more likely to be prosecuted than general practitioners, who rarely faced dismissal and who were rarely categorized as seriously complicit by denazification authorities.[16] The reputation of the ÖGD, therefore, was precarious. Its representatives tried to avert these "denunciations."[17] In 1949, the former municipal health officer Franz Redeker (1891–1962) did his best to rehabilitate the ÖGD by drawing a clear division of labor. The responsibilities of public health officials, he argued, fell under the ancient concept of *Physiké*, the care for the environment and social community; the "free" physicians, on the other hand, focused on *Iatriké*, therapeutic measures for individuals. And he suspected that the medical fraternity used public health officers as scapegoats, foisting upon them the responsibility for the medical crimes of the recent past. He emphasized that among the leaders of the German medical doctors who were accused in Nuremberg there were only representatives of the *Iatriké*, but none of the *Physiké*.[18]

Five years later Fritz Pürckhauer, a public health officer since 1931 and chairman of the medical officers' league in 1951[19] defended his colleagues by claiming that the health offices were still "young creations ... shaken by the storms of tempestuous times" and "shattered by heavy waves of de-Nazification." He declared—incorrectly—that his colleagues had "in no way" participated in concentration-camp crimes. In spite of these assertions, the ÖGD was burdened by the legacy of Nazi medicine. In the dispute about how the disastrous human medical experiments had come about, the only means against misconduct, many believed, was the independence of physicians from state control or bureaucratic pressure.

Institutional Consequences

When the German federal government started to rearrange the relationship between *Kassenärzte* and the insurance system in the 1950s, the physicians, who had only cautiously asserted their interests during the Allied occupation, could influence the framing of the new health insurance act for their own benefit.[20] These doctors were granted the monopoly on ambulatory treatment, and in 1960 the Federal Constitutional Court struck down regulations governing the ratio of physicians to insured persons as well as the ratio of general practitioners to medical specialists. The result was "freedom of residence" for the physicians and the elimination of external means for structuring the provision of medical services.[21] What was more, the "free physicians" tried to declare *Gesundheitsfürsorge* as having been their original task. The senior functionaries of the federal association of *Kassenärzte* called for annual checkups by "family doctors" and complained about the "appetite" of the ÖGD for "swallowing" clinics.[22] The ÖGD protested, arguing that the *Kassenärzte* had never before been interested in *Gesundheitsfürsorge*.[23] In a workshop on social reform in 1955 the public health officers tried to counter the fear of state-controlled medicine by conceding that precautionary health check-ups would not be compulsory, the results would not be registered, and those who refused to take part would not have to fear any disadvantage.[24] Clearly, this consideration hearkened back to experiences suffered under National Socialism. Nonetheless, the ÖGD could not prevent the physicians' take-over of annual check-ups. In the 1960s the process was taken a step further, when the insurance system began to cover costs for routine annual medical check-ups undertaken by *Kassenärzte*.[25]

The general political effort to replace public welfare by social insurance[26]—or as Abelshauser put it, to make "the welfare state the democratic substitute for the National Socialist *Volksgemeinschaft*"[27]—ironically impeded any attempt to return to *Gesundheitsfürsorge*. Hagen—a former public health officer and member of the Federal Ministry of the Interior in the early 1950s—explicitly warned against handing preventive medicine over to *Kassenärzte*, since they had to wait for their patients to come to them.[28] In the debate about the reorganization of social services,[29] Hagen suggested a division of competencies between public health officers and *Kassenärzte*, according to which insurance would pay for medical supervision and early diagnosis, which could be performed by private physicians. Furthermore, insurance would pay for all social groups so that nobody would be dependent on the public health office for treatment. But beyond this, public health departments had the special task of providing for basic social needs. These would include making certain that infants were brought to physicians (which could be guaranteed by a social worker who visited the family at home and observed the child), or that chronically sick persons complied with medical instructions.[30] Hagen's proposal, though presented to parliament, failed to gain political support.[31] The notion that everybody would have access to medical services was attractive to both politicians and private medical doctors. Public health officers hardly protested. But those who had worked in Weimar insisted that for their work the now-fashionable concept of "preventive medicine" was not sufficiently all-encompassing and needed to be replaced by the traditional term "social hygiene." Yet even proponents of social hygiene underlined the priority of medical observation and screenings.[32]

So even though in 1959 the Conference of Health Ministers had proclaimed that public health offices were responsible for the diagnoses of population groups at risk,[33] in the 1960s social insurance started taking over the cost of check-ups. The change occurred gradually. In 1960, for example, job-related check-ups for apprentices were handed over to *Kassenärzte*. Later in the decade medical checkups for pregnant women replaced the classical pregnancy counseling offered by the health department. This development culminated in the "Health Insurance Modification Law" (*Krankenversicherungsänderungsgesetz*) of 1970, which decreed that medical check-ups for children under the age of four, women under 20, and men over 45 had to be paid for by insurance and performed by physicians.[34] The crisis at the ÖGD was evident, and so was the public health disadvantage of these reforms. Preventive medicine was limited to early diagnoses, and only to people who found their way to the physician. Private physicians could not perform the role of social workers, visiting families at home in order to assess the need for medical care or social support. The comprehensive "Weimar" character of *Gesundheitsfürsorge* had thus been undermined by reforms of the West German democratic state. But to what degree had this legacy of the Weimar Republic been contaminated by 12 years of National Socialism? Were there in fact continuities between National Socialism and the ÖGD of the postwar era?

Conceptual Continuities: *Konstitution* and *Gesundheitsführung*

In the 1950s, "disposition" and "constitution" were still regarded as important factors within the medical fraternity as a whole. At the annual meeting of physicians in 1951, Carl Coerper, who had been an important health administrator since the 1920s, recommended annual check-ups for the whole family.[35] He proposed that up to three generations be examined not only physically, but also with respect to their social habits and individual behaviors. This would permit the identification of hereditary factors, and would encourage personal responsibility for one's own health. These intentions fit well into Coerper's concept of social biology, which had been part of the discussion among German racial hygienists[36] and which he had pursued since the 1920s and with increasing intensity during the Nazi era.[37] A similar approach was taken by the school medical officer Theodor Fürst, who interpreted pupils' personalities, skills, and willingness to perform as "constitutional."[38]

This approach to human beings, classifying them in categories of different social value and aiming toward a fully rationalized society, was not confined to the ÖGD. Coerper suggested that panel doctors, with the support of social workers, should perform check-ups and pass the data on to health offices. The members of the Ärztetag approved his proposal, but the insurance system refused to pay for it. Thus, while "constitution" and its implications for the social value of the individual was widely accepted within the medical community, the structure of the health system was not favorable to its institutionalization.

The concept of biological "constitution" was not the only continuity from before 1945. Health education was still influenced by the idea of *Gesundheitsführung*—strong, centralized guidance to healthy behavior—which contained elements of the National Socialist *Führermythos*. When members of the ÖGD defined their tasks, they often stressed the need for *Gesundheitsführung* as an antidote to the disorders of postwar society. However, a closer look reveals that these arguments were backed by an anthropology which had been enhanced by philosophers in the Nazi era.[39] In this view, human individuals were seen as "instinctless" and therefore completely dependant on the *Gemeinschaft* ("organic" community) of the identical stock. Both the *Gemeinschaft* and the individual were not only socially but also biologically dependent upon each other.[40] This concept provided an implicit link to the Nazi notion of weak individuals requiring decisive leadership. Since this link was not made explicit, it was neither identified nor criticized. Hence, it allowed public health officers who had been active members of the National Socialist health system to retain and pursue convictions formed before 1945.

The notion of *Gesundheitsführung* also provided a theoretical barrier against the "reckless individualism" of couples seeking divorce, or of lovers seeking to marry despite hereditary risks. It had the consequence of placing social adaptation or "finding one's way back into the *Gemeinschaft*" at the center of *Gesundheitsfürsorge*.

Eugenic Counseling and Sterilization: Debates in the 1950s and 1960s

Neither the Allies nor leading members of the ÖGD had seen any reason to change the Nazi laws for preventing offspring with hereditary disease (*erbkranken Nachwuchs*). When health legislation was reprinted in a compilation of public health laws in 1950/52, only the term *Rassenpflege* had been changed to *Erbpflege* (hereditary care), as the word "race" was now seen as objectionable. In the 1950s, however, a leading member of the ÖGD pointed out that "race" remained a valid concept, as race hygiene belonged to medical science, and its abuse by National Socialists should not be grounds for abandoning legitimate ideas regarding eugenics and population policy.[41]

In a meeting of the Health Advisory Council of Lower Saxony in 1952, Otto Buurman proposed a "mental and physical refinement of the new generation" through the "observation of hereditary factors."[42] Marriage counseling, he suggested, would provide the needed hereditary prognosis. Although marriage counseling had been "severely discredited by the recent past,"[43] an association of marriage and youth counselors was initiated by Jochen Fischer and the geneticist Lothar Loeffler (1901–83), the latter a former consultant to Nazi Erbgesundheitsgerichte (hereditary health courts).[44] In 1959 the association advised Germans to "consider future generations when you choose the father or mother of your children" and to "take heed of your partner's family."[45]

Sterilization stirred up more controversy than eugenically conscious marriage counseling. Though geneticists like Hans Nachtsheim (1890–1979), who since 1941 had been director of several national institutes of hereditary biology and pathology,[46] strongly advocated sterilization to prevent degeneration, and the Allied occupation authorities had not abolished Nazi laws for the prevention of hereditary diseases, the hereditary health courts had been closed, and the future of sterilization was unclear.[47] Nachtsheim acknowledged that a new sterilization act could hardly be publicly advocated in the immediate postwar environment, but he persisted in the belief that eugenic sterilization remained a legitimate concept.[48] In the early 1960s he declared that his advocacy of sterilization had nothing in common with National Socialism but was an essential of rational population policy.[49] Critical voices like the psychiatrist Alexander Mitscherlich and his colleague Peter Matussek pointed to the dangers of abuse, referring to the historical experience.[50] But the necessity of discussing sterilization was widely recognized, and by no means confined to the ÖGD.

During the 1950s, the ÖGD journal reported sterilization practices in other countries, thus promoting their cause indirectly through the example of others. In the 1960s this issue was hardly discussed. The few articles on reproduction were on contraception and genetic counseling.[51]

Fischer continued to advocate sterilization for eugenic reasons and proposed official registration of hereditary disabilities. Nevertheless, in the mid-1960s articles in the journal devoted to marriage counseling focused on issues such as starting a family and partnership problems. Concerning sterilization, Loeffler approved it "in certain cases"—for instance when there was a genetic abnormality that led to Down's syndrome—"if parents wanted it."[52] The change of the discourse from population policy to individual decision-making cannot be described here, but apparently it happened outside of the ÖGD.

Within the ÖGD, the issue as such was hardly discussed. But when family planning was recommended as a way to avoid high birth rates among poor and destitute families,[53] sterilization was cited as a legitimate method. Hans Harmsen (1899–1989), director of the Akademie für Staatsmedizin from 1945 and propagator of eugenics from the 1920s to the 1980s,[54] saw disadvantages not only for the families, but also for the community as a whole if genetically weak people were allowed to multiply at random. He recommended the example of English social workers, who not only provided advice but also "introduced" contraception to families and convinced them to use it.[55]

The Crises of the ÖGD

Although the generation which had experienced Weimar and National Socialism retired during the 1960s, the discourse at ÖGD meetings, which could be followed in its journal, showed substantial continuities. It comported with Abelshauser's scheme of the "long fifties" extending to 1966. In that year, 45-year-old Christian Göttsching spoke on "Health care—its value and its problems." Göttsching stressed "sound morals" as the most vital force for achieving health. Even disease had a regulating effect on regaining social order. "Adaptation" was the key issue: "The tenets of adaptation illustrate the important requirement of constant strain to which everybody must be subject in order to maintain their best form physically and mentally."[56] Perhaps the continuity of the argument that public health was the outcome of a properly ordered society was less notable than the fact that another member of the ÖGD disagreed openly with this contention. He stated that it was definitely not enough to "decide to be healthy," and that the "regulating order of disease" could not be proved in terms of social medicine.[57]

The difficult situation of the health offices at the end of the 1960s led to fundamental reconsiderations. ÖGD representatives recommended removing state-related duties from health departments and reevaluating their ethos as a "medical police," focusing instead on prevention and health promotion, especially among groups who were "not economically profitable," such as the disabled, elderly and chronically ill.[58] Furthermore the ÖGD had to inform the public about "technological progress and its detrimental consequences."[59] In addition, a State Academy should be founded in which not only epidemiology but also social pedagogy and social psychiatry would be taught. Professorships for social hygiene should be established in every medical faculty. The proposed change of profile reflected a tendency to focus on social relations.

The real task of the ÖGD was described as "the individual approach of the physician toward everybody in need."[60] This notion was underscored by articles on the duty of medical doctors to keep their patients' secrets, which emphasized that this directive also applied to physicians of the ÖGD.[61] However, facing a shortage of high-ranking positions in the local or state administration, lack of equipment, and practically no staff to replace the retiring public health officers, the only tasks remaining for the ÖGD would be the dissemination of health information and the collection of statistical data for epidemiological purposes.

The Debate over *Gesundheitsfürsorge* and Social Work

The traditional Weimar concept of family welfare was vigorously promoted by social workers and their professional associations.[62] Accordingly, there was a lingering conflict about the relationship between social workers and public health officers. Once family welfare work was subordinated to the health department, registration was carried out for medical, not social purposes. In the 1950s this had been characterized by the director of a social work school, Olga Heerdegen, as being a "result of National Socialism" as well as the result of gender conflict between domineering males misemploying or exploiting subordinate females.[63] The quarrel developed into a conflict about social work itself when Walda Rocholl, director of a school for social work in Heidelberg, alleged that social workers were treated as "errand girls." Consequently, Rocholl demanded the removal of social work from the realm of the health department and its integration into the social welfare department. This would enable social workers to pursue their real vocation of helping people.[64]

Even as public health officials strongly supported the combination of social and health welfare,[65] they attacked social work as a deviation from the well-proved traditional German *Gesundheitsfürsorge* concept. Because social workers did not have sufficient training in *Gesundheitsfürsorge*—it had been shortened dramatically from 1 year to 6 months in the 1950s and to 3 months in 1966—a separate profession, defined as a public-health nurse, was needed.[66] This proposal triggered sharp reactions. The professional association of social workers insisted on thorough knowledge of social problems as a prerequisite for any effective response. Furthermore, in France and Great Britain similar concepts of "comprehensive polyvalent family-centered service" had emerged.[67] One group of social workers repudiated the way their profession was described as "kind-hearted," with an "intuitively helping hand" and sound common sense. This description was not only old-fashioned, but "authoritarian and incompatible with the German constitution" because it violated the client's right to decide for himself. To enable the client to decide for himself "is where our job starts. To alleviate emergencies is not enough."[68] The old concept of practical assistance, or *Verhältnisprävention,* turned out to be offensive to the modern social worker.

The new paradigm for social work was explained by medical sociologist Viefhues in several articles from 1966 to 1969. In short, problems no longer appeared to be the result of social conditions, but rather of social relations. Need and deprivation were seen as independent of economic class.[69] Social work involved supporting persons who suffered from psycho-social disturbances. These disturbances were identified as the cause of every problem.[70] Ironically, this approach was associated with the authority status of the social worker, as the needy were perceived as being unable to solve their problems on their own. Female welfare workers were particularly criticized because they supposedly "infantilized" their clients.

Social workers' efforts to improve the "adaptation" of their clients were beyond suspicion. This perception was shared and advanced by the social workers themselves.[71] The dichotomy of "adaptation or emancipation" was discussed at the annual meeting in 1969. The key term "adaptation" was not seen in its connection with recent German history, but was perceived as an idiom of American social work, fluctuating between "adjustment" and "accommodation." Moreover, adaptation might include disputes and quarrels and could be a very active process.[72] Social work was characterized as dynamic, critical, open-minded, and nonbureaucratic,[73] alternating between integration into and severe criticism of society, thereby representing the whole spectrum of an emancipated, modern society. However, it was understood that this would be achieved at the expense of practical assistance.

Changes in the Practical Work of the ÖGD?

Was there a conceptual change in the customary duties of the health department? The main task of the ÖGD—aside from hygienic and epidemic concerns—had become the care for groups at the margins of society. In a 1967 article about homeless, derelict families, the director of one health department identified the main problem as that of infectious diseases.[74] The deficiency might be eliminated by improving housing conditions, i.e., providing a separate toilet for every family. Furthermore, the family should be repeatedly reminded to maintain cleanliness, since "these people didn't take care of themselves." To prevent any deterioration of the situation, family planning should be promoted. Furthermore, the community should undertake reintegration in order to prevent aggressive and dangerous behavior. Thus, if the problem was as familiar as that of infectious disease and the clients belonged to the margins of society, the old paradigm of social hygiene seemed to be still valid. Here the emphasis was on prevention through better housing conditions, education in personal hygiene, and discouragement from reproduction, for the sake of the suffering families as well as for that of society as a whole.

Political Shifts in the Late 1960s: Implications for Public Health

Clearly, the watershed metaphor cited at the beginning of this chapter derives from the fundamental critique which political scientists, philosophers, and sociologists launched against bourgeois society in the late 1960s. Did they pay any attention to the *Gesundheitsfürsorge* situation? And if so, would the ÖGD experts notice?

A valuable source for answering the first question is the journal for philosophy and social sciences *Das Argument* and its subsidiary publication *Jahrbuch für kritische Medizin*. *Das Argument* had been founded in 1959 by Wolfgang Fritz Haug, at that time a student, and from 1979 a professor of philosophy, who made it a platform for critical philosophy and social science. In its tenth volume (1969), the editors for the first time addressed the fields of psychology, psychiatry, and medicine. Medical sociologist Hans-Ulrich Deppe began his article with Virchow's famous quote, "medicine is a social science." Deppe argued that a medicine which declared itself as a purely "natural science" obscured social conditions because it accepted "facts" as natural, although they might have social roots.[75] The following year, the *Jahrbuch für kritische Medizin* was founded. In an editorial, the purpose of the new publication was defined as the application of social science to medicine. Points of special interest were the social analysis of diseases and the examination of the effects of the health system.[76] The articles focused on occupational medicine, psychiatry, and on the deplorable fact that medicine dealt with difficulties in the individual, rather than in society, and thus "stabilized the social wrong."[77] Apparently the Weimar model of social hygiene had caught on and its messages were related to contemporary problems of the 1970s.[78] In 1978, an article on "Social Work and Medicine" underscored the problems of the current situation: only very few of the insured made use of precautionary medical inspections, community-based health services did not exist, and the public health offices were in bad shape. Prevention, it was emphasized, should include remedies against material, social, and psychological deprivation.[79] The critical political perspective of the analysis ensured that social conditions were considered.

Did this development reach the ÖGD experts? In 1969 von Manger-König, state secretary at the Federal Ministry of Health, had underlined the "traditional right of the ÖGD" to be responsible for precautionary care (*Vorsorge*) and emphasized "community medicine" as a new task. Medical education should train physicians who would practice medicine in health departments, factories, or private medical offices.[80] In 1975 he proposed "community-related tasks" as the future focus of the ÖGD. These would include "environmental hygiene, social hygiene for population groups at risk, supervision of health facilities and health professions, epidemiology, and planning, coordination and evaluation of all health measures."[81] His statement may be seen as an anticipation of the so-called new public health of the 1980s, which combined care for high-risk groups with supervision of health facilities and an evaluation of health measures.

A change in practice was apparent when reformers within the ÖGD presented a blend of old and new public health concepts at a meeting in 1984. They addressed doubts about the raison d'être of the ÖGD, problems arising from genetic counseling, inoculations, and a new approach to the health problems of prostitutes, who were no longer controlled and supervised, but were instead informed about their health risks and invited to regular check-ups for venereal disease. Similarly, elderly citizens were contacted at local meeting-places in the local community and informed about health promotion.[82] Although nobody mentioned the Weimar notion of *Gesundheitsfürsorge* as being relevant to the newly emerging public health concept, a similarity in approach can be recognized. Thus, a 1960s critique of the German health care system pointed to the possibility of salvaging from the pre-1933 period what might be worth salvaging, and provided the basis for changes that took concrete form in the 1980s.

Notes

1. Alfons Labisch and Florian Tennstedt, "Prävention und Prophylaxe als Handlungsfelder der Gesundheitspolitik in der Frühgeschichte der Bundesrepublik (1949–ca. 1965)," in *Prävention und Prophylaxe: Theorie und Praxis eines gesundheitspolitischen Grundmotivs in zwei deutschen Staaten 1949–1990*, ed. Thomas Elkeles et al. (Berlin, 1991), 129–58.
2. Alfred Grotjahn, "Soziale Pathologie," in *Handwörterbuch der sozialen Hygiene*, 2 vols., ed. A. Grotjahn and I. Kaup (Leipzig, 1912), 2:439–43.
3. Peter Reinicke, *Tuberkulosefürsorge* (Weinheim, 1988), 48–155; Sigrid Stöckel, *Säuglingsfürsorge zwischen sozialer Hygiene und Eugenik: Das Beispiel Berlins im Kaiserreich und in der Weimarer Republik* (Berlin, 1996), 216–18.
4. Christiane Eifert, *Frauenpolitik und Wohlfahrtspflege: Zur Geschichte der sozialdemokratischen "Arbeiterwohlfahrt"* (Frankfurt am Main, 1993); Christoph Sachße, "Social Mothers: The Bourgeois Women's Movement and German Welfare-State Formation 1890–1929," in *Mothers of a New World: Maternalist Politics and the Origins of Welfare States*, ed. Seth Koven and Sonya Michel (New York and London, 1993), 136–58; Anja Schüler, *Frauenbewegung und soziale Reform: Jane Adams und Alice Salomon im transatlantischen Dialog, 1889–1933* (Stuttgart, 2004).
5. Paul Weindling, *Health, Race and German Politics between National Unification and Nazism 1870–1945* (Cambridge, 1989), 338–41; Alfons Labisch and Florian Tennstedt, *Der Weg zum Gesetz zur Vereinheitlichung des Gesundheitswesens*, 2 vols. (Düsseldorf, 1985), 1:158–59; Stöckel, *Säuglingsfürsorge*, 271–95.
6. Diane B. Paul, *The Politics of Heredity: Essays on Eugenics, Biomedicine, and the Nature-Nurture Debate* (Albany, 1998); Stefan Kühl, *Die Internationale der Rassisten: Aufstieg und Niedergang der internationalen Bewegung für Eugenik und Rassenhygiene im 20. Jahrhundert* (Frankfurt am Main, 1997).
7. Stöckel, *Säuglingsfürsorge*, 372f.
8. For details, see Labisch and Tennstedt, *Der Weg*, 1:115–16.
9. Erich Schröder, "Sinn und Praxis der Gesundheitsfürsorge," *Fortschritte der Gesundheitsfürsorge* 7 (1933): 121–29, here 121; Emilja Mitrovic, "Fürsorgerinnen im Nationalsozialismus," in *Opfer und Täterinnen*, ed. Angelika Ebbinghaus (Nördlingen, 1987), 17–20.
10. Alfred Rainer, "Zur Kommunalisierung der Gesundheitsämter," *Der öffentliche Gesundheitsdienst* 11 (1949): 128–33; Friedrich Höffken, "Das Gesundheitswesen im Staat und in der Kommunalverwaltung," *Der öffentliche Gesundheitsdienst* 14 (1952): 281–98. See also Johannes Vossen, *Gesundheitsämter im Nationalsozialismus: Rassenhygiene und offene Gesundheitsfürsorge in Westfalen 1900–1950* (Essen, 2001).

11. Hermann Redetzky, *Entwicklung, Vereinheitlichung und Demokratisierung des öffentlichen Gesundheitswesens* (Berlin, 1949), 59–78; Rainer, *Kommunalisierung*, 132.

12. See Hermann Dietrich, *Auf der Suche nach Deutschland: Probleme zur geistigen, politischen und wirtschaftlichen Erneuerung Deutschlands* (Hamburg, 1946), 20f.

13. Josef Stralau, "Die Stellung des Gesundheitsamtes in der Selbstverwaltung," *Der öffentliche Gesundheitsdienst* 14 (1953): 417–25.

14. Otto Buurman, "Vom Geiste der Arbeit in den Gesundheitsämtern," *Der öffentliche Gesundheitsdienst* 11 (1949): 17–19.

15. Labisch and Tennstedt, "Prävention und Prophylaxe," 133f.

16. Thomas Gerst, *Ärztliche Standesorganisation und Standespolitik in Deutschland 1945–1955* (Stuttgart, 1997), 65–72.

17. Rainer, *Kommunalisierung*, 128–33.

18. Franz Redeker, "Magister in Physica," *Der öffentliche Gesundheitsdienst* 11 (1949): 145–57, 185–95.

19. "In memoriam Dr. Fritz Pürckhauer," *Der öffentliche Gesundheitsdienst* 21 (1959): 359f.; Fritz Pürckhauer, "Das Gesundheitsamt im Wandel der Zeit," *Der öffentliche Gesundheitsdienst* 16 (1954): 280–82.

20. Gerst, *Standesorganisation und Standespolitik*, 99–114, 367–69.

21. For details, see ibid., 347–50.

22. Ibid., 332, 355.

23. Ibid., 334–36. For vehement protests, see *Ärztliche Mitteilungen* 39 (1954): 654ff., 731ff.

24. Josef Daniels, "Sozialreform und öffentlicher Gesundheitsdienst," *Der öffentliche Gesundheitsdienst* 18 (1956): 161–73, here 169. See also Labisch and Tennstedt, "Prävention und Prophylaxe," 144.

25. Labisch and Tennstedt, "Prävention und Prophylaxe," 155f.

26. Gerst, *Standesorganisation und Standespolitik*, 329.

27. Werner Abelshauser, *Die Weimarer Republik als Wohlfahrtsstaat* (Stuttgart, 1987), 9.

28. Wilhelm Hagen, "Die Gesundheitsfürsorge und die Neuordnung der sozialen Leistungen," *Nachrichtendienst der deutschen Vereinigung für öffentliche und private Fürsorge* (1955): 239–46.

29. Hans Achinger, Hans Muthesius, Joseph Höffner, and Ludwig Neundörfer, *Zur Neuordnung der sozialen Hilfe* (Stuttgart, 1954).

30. Hagen, "Gesundheitsfürsorge," 246.

31. *60 Jahre Gesundheitsfürsorge: Ausgewählte Aufsätze von Prof. Dr. Wilhelm Hagen* (Düsseldorf, 1978), 7–9. Ulrike Lindner, *Gesundheitspolitik in der Nachkriegszeit: Großbritannien und die Bundesrepublik Deutschland im Vergleich* (Munich, 2004), 426–28.

32. Franz Klose, "Aufgaben und Ziele vorbeugender Gesundheitsfürsorge," *Gesundheitsfürsorge* 4 (1955): 113–19, here 113f.

33. Ludwig von Manger-König, "Der öffentliche Gesundheitsdienst zwischen gestern und morgen," *Das öffentliche Gesundheitswesen* 37 (1975): 433–38, here 438.

34. Labisch and Tennstedt, "Prävention und Prophylaxe," 156.

35. "Gedanken zum Ausbau der Gesundheitsvor- und -fürsorge," *Ärztliche Mitteilungen* 36 (1951): 379–85, here 383.

36. Peter Weingart et al., eds., *Rasse, Blut und Gene* (Frankfurt am Main 1988), 161–67.

37. Carl Coerper (1886–1960), medical officer during the 1920s in Düsseldorf and *Beigeordneter* for health and welfare administration in Cologne, qualified as a university lecturer in 1931 in social hygiene, social biology, and sociology, and received a professorship in 1937. In 1950 he became leader of the Arbeitsgemeinschaft für das Gesundheitswesen, later on the Deutsche Zentrale für Volksgesundheitspflege. See *Der öffentliche Gesundheitsdienst* 21 (1960): 585f. See also *Horst Schütz, Gesundheitsfürsorge zwischen humanitärem Anspruch und eugenischer Verpflichtung: Entwicklung und Kontinuität sozialhygienischer Anschauungen zwischen 1920 und 1960 am Beispiel von Prof. Dr. Carl Coerper* (Husum, 2004).

38. Theobald Fürst, "Die konstitutionelle Diagnostik des Schularztes," *Der öffentliche Gesundheitsdienst* 11 (1949): 198–200.

39. The arguments for *Gesundheitsführung* fit well into the concept of Nazi philosopher Arnold Gehlen, though he was hardly ever cited. See Arnold Gehlen, *Der Mensch: Seine Natur und seine Stellung in der Welt* (Berlin, 1940, and numerous post-1945 reprints).

40. See Walter Schnell, *Aktuelle Probleme der Volksgesundheitspflege: Kongressbericht 1957* (Frankfurt am Main 1958), 28. Otto Buurman, "Jugend- und Eheberatung," *Mitteilungen des Niedersächsischen Landesgesundheitsrates* (1952): 7–8.

41. Fritz Pürckhauer, "Das Gesundheitsamt im Wandel der Zeit," *Der öffentliche Gesundheitsdienst* 16 (1954): 279–96.

42. Otto Buurman (1890–1967), a medical officer in 1930, qualified as a university lecturer in 1941 in Breslau. As an official of the Generalgouvernement, he was responsible for public health in the Cracow Jewish ghetto until 1943. After the war, he was a leading figure in the Lower Saxony health administration. In 1954, he became director of the department of health in the Ministry of the Interior. See *Das öffentliche Gesundheitswesen* 29 (1967): 220f. For details, see Sabine Schleiermacher, *Historische Traditionslinien öffentlicher Gesundheitspflege in Deutschland 1920–1955: Das Beispiel Niedersachsen* (unpublished research report, 1995), 23; Christopher Browning, "Genozid und Gesundheitswesen: Deutsche Ärzte und polnische Juden 1939–1945," in *Der Wert des Menschen: Medizin in Deutschland 1918–1945*, ed. Christian Pross and Götz Aly (Berlin, 1989), 322.

43. Jochen Fischer, "Stand und Zukunft der Eheberatung," *Der öffentliche Gesundheitsdienst* 14 (1952): 90–96.

44. *Kürschner Gelehrtenlexikon* (1954), 1419. Heidrun Kaupen-Haas, *Der Griff nach der Bevölkerung* (Nördlingen, 1986), 172.

45. *Informationsrundschreiben der Deutschen Arbeitsgemeinschaft für Ehe- und Jugendberatung* (1959), 19f.

46. In 1941, Kaiser-Wilhelm-Institut für Anthropologie, menschliche Erblehre und Eugenik; in 1947, Institut für Vergleichende Erbbiologie und Pathologie der Deutschen Akademie der Wissenschaften; and in 1953, the Max-Planck-Institut für Vergleichende Erbbiologie und Erbpathologie. See Kaupen-Haas, *Griff*, 173.

47. See Schleiermacher, *Historische Traditionslinien*. See also Hans-Ulrich Sons, *Das öffentliche Gesundheitswesen in Nordrhein-Westfalen nach dem Zweiten Weltkrieg bis zur Gründung der Bundesrepublik Deutschland* (Düsseldorf, 1981), 48.

48. Hans Nachtsheim, "Für und wider die Sterilisation," *Der öffentliche Gesundheitsdienst* 14 (1952): 152–56, and "Das GzVeN aus dem Jahre 1933 in heutiger Sicht," *Ärztliche Mitteilungen* 47 (1962): 1640–44; debate, 2515f.

49. Hans Nachtsheim, "Die Notwendigkeit einer aktiven Erbgesundheitspflege," *Gesundheitspolitik* 6 (1964): 321–39, here 322, 326.

50. See *Fortschritte der Medizin* 81 (1963): 711–14.

51. Jochen Fischer, "Das Problem der 'Geburtenregelung' in der ärztlichen Diskussion," *Das öffentliche Gesundheitswesen* 29 (1967): 101–4; Widukind Lenz, "Humangenetische Gesichtspunkte in der Familienplanung," *Das öffentliche Gesundheitswesen* 32 (1970): 61–67.

52. Lothar Löffler, "Gedanken des eheberatenden Arztes zur Empfängnisregelung," *Informationsrundschreiben/Deutsche Arbeitsgemeinschaft für Jugend- und Eheberatung* 86–87 (1967): 21–33.

53. Rainer Langmann, "Die Problematik der Obdachlosen aus ärztlicher Sicht," *Das öffentliche Gesundheitswesen* 29 (1967): 306–12.

54. Sabine Schleiermacher, *Sozialethik im Spannungsfeld von Sozial- und Rassenhygiene: Der Mediziner Hans Harmsen im Zentralausschuss für die innere Mission* (Husum, 1998). Furthermore, Harmsen was a founding member of the International Planned Parenthood Federation in 1948 and of the German sex counseling agency Pro Familia in 1952. See Kaupen-Haas, *Griff*, 171.

55. Hans Harmsen, "Soziale Leistungsschwäche erfordert aktive Familienplanung," *Gesundheitsfürsorge, Gesundheitsvorsorge* 17 (1967): 21–24.

56. Christian Göttsching, "Gesundheitsvorsorge—ihr Wert und ihre Problematik," *Das öffentliche Gesundheitswesen* 28 (1966): 333–45.

57. Ibid., 356.
58. H. Hufnagl, "Der ÖGD aus der Sicht eines großstädtischen Gesundheitsamtes," *Das öffentliche Gesundheitswesen* 29 (1967): 364–70; Fritz Beske, "Der ÖGD in unserer Zeit," *Das öffentliche Gesundheitswesen* 29 (1967): 353–63.
59. Ibid., 357.
60. Klaus-Peter Faerber, "Der öffentliche Gesundheitsdienst: Gestern, heute und morgen," *Das öffentliche Gesundheitswesen* 31, no. 9 (1969): 401–10.
61. W. Ciszewski, "Schweigepflicht—Schweigerecht," *Das öffentliche Gesundheitswesen* 30 (1968): 495–505; G. Terbeck, "Zur amtsärztlichen Schweigepflicht," *Das öffentliche Gesundheitswesen* 31 (1969): 390–92.
62. In 1966 the Central Committee for the Population's Health announced a prize in honor of the initiator and propagator of family welfare and comprehensive care, Marie Baum. See *Gesundheitsfürsorge* 17 (1967): 19.
63. Olga Heerdegen, "Der Einfluss des Reichsgesetzes über die Vereinheitlichung des Gesundheitswesens vom 3. Juli 1934 auf die Stellung der Fürsorgerin," *Mitteilungen des deutschen Berufsverbandes der Sozialarbeiterinnen*, May 1953. For discussion, see *Gesundheitsfürsorge* 3 (1955): 166–68.
64. Walda Rocholl, "Ländliche Familienfürsorge, ein Berufszweig der sozialen Arbeit der Gegenwart," *Nachrichtendienst der deutschen Vereinigung für öffentliche und private Fürsorge* (1964): 468–69.
65. H. Arnold, "Familienfürsorge," *Der öffentliche Gesundheitsdienst* 26 (1964): 621–28
66. H. Reuter, "Sozialarbeiterin oder Gesundheitspflegerin für das öffentliche Gesundheitswesen?" *Das öffentliche Gesundheitswesen* 30 (1968): 254–66.
67. "Stellungnahme zu dem Artikel von Ltd. Min.-Rat Dr. H. Reuter—Düsseldorf," *Der Sozialarbeiter* 9 (1968): 12f.
68. Ibid.
69. Herbert Viefhues, "Was ist Sozialarbeit?" *Das öffentliche Gesundheitswesen* 31 (1969): 411–18.
70. Herbert Viefhues, "Sozialarbeit im Gesundheitswesen," *Nachrichtendienst der deutschen Vereinigung für öffentliche und private Fürsorge* 46 (1966): 67–72.
71. Wolfgang Bäuerle, "Zur Entwicklung der Sozialarbeit," *Gesundheitsfürsorge* 16 (1966): 172–74, here 173.
72. Ilse Tägert, "Anpassung oder Emanzipation des Klienten?" *Der Sozialarbeiter* 10 (1969): 3–8.
73. Paul Kreutzer, "Sozialarbeit und Bürokratie," *Der Sozialarbeiter* 10 (1969): 13–15. See also Tilmann Moser, "Gleiche Chancen für alle? Sozialarbeit zwischen Beharrung und Kampf um Veränderung," *Der Sozialarbeiter* 11 (1970): 2–13.
74. Rainer Langmann, "Die Problematik der Obdachlosen aus ärztlicher Sicht," *Das öffentliche Gesundheitswesen* 29 (1967): 306–12.
75. Hans-Ulrich Deppe, "Zum 'Objekt' der Medizin," *Das Argument* 50 (1969): 284–98, here 287, 289, 298.
76. Udo Schagen, "Warum kritisches Jahrbuch?" *Jahrbuch für kritische Medizin* 1 (1970): 1–6.
77. Horst Krähe and Gisela Schöning, "Funktionen der Medizin und ihre Manifestation in der medizinischen Ausbildung," *Das Argument* 60 (1970): 2–16; Hans Kilian, "Kritische Theorie der Medizin," *Das Argument* 60 (1970): 87–104.
78. See the reprint of Max Mosse and Gustav Tugendreich, *Krankheit und soziale Lage* (Göttingen, 1977; orig. Munich, 1913), and the preface by Jürgen Cromm.
79. Alf Trojan and Heiko Waller, "Sozialarbeit und Medizin," *Jahrbuch für kritische Medizin* 3 (1978): 192–203.
80. Ludwig von Manger-König, "Aktuelle Probleme des öffentlichen Gesundheitswesens," *Das öffentliche Gesundheitswesen* 31 (1969): 525–29.
81. Manger-König, "Der öffentliche Gesundheitsdienst," 433.
82. *50 Jahre Gesetz über die Vereinheitlichung des Gesundheitswesens. Tagung zur Geschichte und Zukunft des Gesundheitsdienstes: 18.–19. Mai 1984 in Bremen* (Düsseldorf, 1985).

Chapter 9

DON'T LOOK BACK IN ANGER
Youth, Pop Culture, and the Nazi Past

Detlef Siegfried

❧

"Angry Young Men," the famous label applied to a group of young British writers, might well have applied to their West German counterparts. Left-wing authors like Günter Grass, Hans Magnus Enzensberger, and Martin Walser were widely seen as "angry young men" preoccupied with critical reflection on the German past and present. Anger was attributed to an entire generation during the 1960s, to those born between roughly 1938 and 1948 who became the protagonists of 1968.[1] The Nazi past, it is claimed, played a particularly important part in sparking a generational conflict that, in turn, gave a crucial impulse to West German society as a whole to come to terms with that past. As evidence, the testimony of student activists is often quoted, statements such as "you can't talk with the people who made Auschwitz."[2] The radical position of the innocent young with regard to the Nazi past appears, from this perspective, to have been a fundamental element in the generational conflict that set them at odds with their incriminated parents. But there is also evidence that conflicts within families focusing on the personal pasts of the parents might have occurred much less frequently than is commonly assumed.[3]

If the international youth movement was shaped by the common Western experience of postwar political change, growing prosperity, and exploding consumerism, its particular national form in West Germany was shaped by the Nazi past.[4] Because older Germans unquestionably bore responsibility for the two world wars and the Holocaust, the conflict between generations seemed to be more important in West Germany than in other countries. West Germans born during the Third Reich's final years or in the immediate postwar years dissociated themselves from their elders' generations. Whereas some welcomed this as a clean break with the unpleasant past, others saw it as a presumption or an undeserved benefit, or even as an inverted continuation of their parents' attachment to the past. Closer consideration of the topic reveals, however, that we actually know very little about the ways in which young West Germans dealt with the National Socialist past, or about how their attitudes toward the past influenced the development of a generational identity. I will approach this problem by examining the treatment of the Nazi past in magazines and television programs produced for young people. During the 1960s, these media became a new agent of socialization. They both reflected and shaped the outlook of the young. Moreover, the ascent of these media ran parallel to an enormous increase in self-critical public debate in West Germany about the Nazi past and a process of politicization that encompassed young people in particular.[5]

Sociological Findings

As more details of the Nazis' genocidal policies became known from the late 1950s onward, the West German public began for the first time to discuss continuities from the era of National Socialism. It became increasingly obvious that those continuities were substantial, and that they could be observed among the country's elites as well as in the thought patterns of considerable portions of the population. Even young people who were only infants when the Third Reich collapsed seemed to be influenced. The sociologist Walter Jaide, after gathering information on the political opinions of 15- to 20-year-olds in the summer of 1961, came to the conclusion that "quite a large number of young people by no means *avoid*, qualify or brush aside this period of our recent past. It is the dominant historical—although perhaps not political—problem of their consciousness."[6] The public debate that followed from the wave of anti-Semitic graffiti in 1959–60 had made it unmistakably clear to young people that National Socialism was a problem, that the problem concerned them, and that they had to dissociate themselves from it. This awareness was reflected in the responses to Jaide's survey. Of those surveyed, 16 percent refused to answer, 74 percent voiced explicit disapproval of National Socialism, and 10 percent said they saw more positive than negative elements in it. Among the latter 10 percent, only 1 to 2 percent were identified as anti-Semites, and 3 percent were classified as "followers of Hitler."

Compared to the results of surveys conduced in previous years, these findings reflected a devastating loss of support for attributes and practices connected to Nazism.[7] Jaide underscored that the respondents did not condemn their parents, but rather had a carefully differentiated view. As one respondent explained, "We cannot dissociate from the persecution of the Jews, although we had nothing to do with it. If we had lived in those days, we too would probably have succumbed to Hitler's propaganda. Also, the contemporary circumstances are relevant. We don't have any right to condemn our parents for their attitude."[8] Summarizing the attitudes of the young toward their parents and the past, Jaide noted, "Surprisingly often, youths use the expression 'we' and not 'our parents,' 'the adults,' 'the politicians,' 'the Nazis'—no, they say 'we,' 'we as Germans.'"[9]

Many young West Germans, despite their detachment from the Nazis' crimes, did feel that they belonged to an intergenerationally connected national collective. At the same time, they were very unsure of their opinions about the Third Reich.[10] While their parents, who were also unsure, could base their judgments at least in part on personal experience, young people did not have that foundation. Instead, they received often contradictory information at home, in school, and from the press. Because of the resulting uncertainty, younger Germans generally did not attempt to make judgments about the past but rather asked careful questions—if they were willing to deal with it at all.

Young people's negative views of National Socialism, it was to become clear, rested on a rather unstable foundation and were not necessarily linked to a strong willingness to come to terms with the Nazi past. After the wave of anti-Semitic graffiti, the Federal Ministry for Family and Youth reported that it perceived a growing desire among young people for reliable information about the Third Reich.[11] At the end of the critical year 1960, the Institut für Meinungsforschung in Allensbach found that 42 percent of young people believed that the information provided by schools about the recent past was poor; 22 percent thought it was sufficient; and no less than 35 percent opted for the diplomatic answer "don't know."[12] These figures differed scarcely from the findings about the opinions of older West Germans. This suggests that the younger generation had not given a strong accelerating impetus to the process of coming to terms with the past; rather, the polling results point to intergenerational common interests. In 1963, sociologist Ludwig von Friedeburg pointed out young people had "at best a relation by the schoolbook." "For most youth," he wrote, "the past does not contain anything disconcerting; they feel neither affected (*betroffen*) nor challenged to learn from it."[13] A wide-ranging study undertaken by the EMNID Institute in 1964 came to the similar conclusion that rejection of Nazism was based more on emotion than on analysis.[14] Moreover, some studies found that young people were critical of the increasingly conspicuous public discourse about the past. Many voiced disapproval, some aggressively, of the extensive attention given to the Eichmann trial even if few questioned the legitimacy of the trial itself.[15]

The public information campaigns that followed the wave of anti-Semitic vandalism along with the scandals and trials of the early 1960s succeeded in encouraging a certain sensitivity to the Nazi past. Particularly among the young, a gradual decline in anti-Semitic opinions became evident.[16] Young people were also becoming increasingly aware of politics. According to an EMNID study, young West Germans generally were more actively aware of politics than they had been a decade earlier; Gymnasium and university students in particular showed interest in politics.[17] This group was well-informed about the Third Reich and also wanted to learn more.[18] But rejection of Nazism and political awareness did not automatically go hand in hand with a willingness to examine the reality of Nazi rule in detail. Although there seems to have been a generational consensus against Nazism, it was primarily middle class university students who thought that the Nazi past bore relevance for contemporary political issues.

In subsequent surveys, the generational disparity in outlook emerged more sharply. In late 1963, for example, the institute in Allensbach found that only 3 percent of respondents in the youngest age group believed that things had gone for the best for Germans in the prewar years 1933–39, whereas no fewer than 21 percent of adults between 45 and 59 agreed with that statement.[19] A 1964 survey of the impact of the Auschwitz trial undertaken by the DIVO Institute found that West Germans between 20 and 24 were the age group best informed about the trial and that those between 16 and 19 voiced less support than any other group for a *Schlußstrich*, for bringing the debate on the Nazi past to a close. More members of these two cohorts than of any other also agreed that the trial was justified "to open the public's eyes to the horror and suffering the Germans had caused."[20] After the extreme right-wing National Democratic Party (Nationaldemokratische Partei Deutschlands, NPD) made strong showing in a series of state elections beginning in 1966, a number of surveys determined that 16 to 20 year olds were underrepresented among the party's supporters by about a third.[21]

The generations seem to have reconciled somewhat during the final third of the decade, a period of political and cultural confrontation. Opposition among the young to a *Schlußstrich* began to wane after about 1967, particularly among less educated young people. A 1968 survey found that young people outside *Gymnasien* and universities were only a little less likely than adults to support the call for a *Schlußstrich* but much more likely to do so than their better educated contemporaries.[22] The same held true when young people were asked if they considered National Socialism to be a "good idea" that had "just been badly realized." Although fundamental opposition to Nazism was most marked among university students, a survey undertaken in July 1966 found that 44 percent of them thought the Third Reich had its strong points, above all in economic matters, and more than half of them thought there should be less discussion of German misdeeds and more of foreign "war criminals" instead.[23]

These trends prompted some observers at the end of the 1960s to suggest that not only was the confrontation between the extreme left and extreme right becoming sharper within the younger generation itself, but also that a broad shift in outlook was underway. In 1969, for example, the daily *Die Welt* painted a bleak picture of the future and speculated whether "Youth 1970" was "reactionary, protofascist, [or] extreme right?"[24] It is true that the success of the NPD, the debate over *Ostpolitik*, and the cultural clashes of the late 1960s did in fact weaken the widespread opposition to the extreme right. But *Die Welt's* generalization was nonetheless wrong. Support for democracy was much more stable than it had been in the 1950s. As a survey covering the period 1962 to 1983 demonstrates, the number of young people in favor of a *Schlußstrich* declined in the long run, as did the number who could see positive aspects of Nazism.[25] The strong dissociation of the young from the symbols and values of the past is illustrated by the results of a 1968 opinion poll. Asked whether someone who had fought at Stalingrad or who had been awarded the *Ritterkreuz* commanded their respect, respondents aged 16 to 29 were strikingly less likely to reply affirmatively than those in all other age groups.[26] Changes in views of Nazism could, however, only be identified through comparatively indirect indicators, a factor which, in turn, led professional social observers to attach less and less importance to such issues. Whereas they focused on young people's attitudes about the past in the early 1960s, they shifted attention increasingly to the younger generation's views on contemporary political problems over the course of the decade.[27]

The Nazi Past in *Twen*, 1959–1965

One of the most influential media products aimed at young people during the 1960s was the magazine *Twen*. It aimed for an audience that fell between readers of *Bravo*, a teen pop-culture magazine, and *Konkret*, which was devoted to politics. A number of prominent writers contributed to *Twen*, including, for example, the jazz expert Joachim Ernst Berendt (born 1922) and the political journalists Klaus Bresser (1936) and Kai Hermannn (1938). The magazine's readers were primarily high school and university students between the ages of 16 and 25.[28] Not only in social background but also in their interests *Twen* readers exemplified the politically interested and critical, but also hedonistic, younger generation.[29]

Twen was conceived by Willy Fleckhaus, who had been involved with the union-owned youth magazine *Aufwärts*. His partner, Adolf Theobald, had previously edited *Die Entscheidung*, the magazine of the Christian Democratic Union's youth organization, and *Student im Bild*. Fleckhaus and Theobald wanted to create a modern magazine that was both entertaining and informative. From the outset, *Twen* shook up the media landscape. Its challenging articles set it apart from magazines like *Bravo*, but, at the same time, it had no reservations with regard to consumer culture. As the "dandy among the glossies," as a proponent of "consumer ideologies," as the vanguard of the "sex cult," and, not least, as a vehicle of "paralyzing criticism," *Twen* came under attack from youth organizations, public officials, and the Catholic Church.[30] But it was nonetheless successful, as its mix of music and fashion, sexuality and politics, proved to be strongly appealing.

The Nazi past did not figure as prominently in *Twen* as it did, for example, in *Konkret*. It is clear, however, that the subject did become an important element in the self-image of young people whose interests were not focused solely on politics. From the outset, *Twen* adapted the general public debate on the consequences of the Nazi past to its target readership. The first issue acknowledged the common interest of its target readers in rejecting Nazism. They were "hard to convince because their predecessors had been easy to convince."[31] This implied contrast between the generations became a basic theme in *Twen*'s efforts to come to terms with the past. In the second issue (August 1959), the editors asked bluntly, "Why don't our parents tell the truth?" Members of the older generations, the editors insisted, had no right on account of their past to pass judgment on the young for their alleged disenchantment with politics. Such criticism, linked with denunciations of the violence of rock-n-roll fans and teenagers' apolitical hedonism, could not, in the opinion of *Twen*, be taken seriously. "The same people who [in the 1930s] cheered the conceited, medal-jingling, brown-shirted lads and their bigwigs, whose world a few years later collapsed in ruins, complain today that young people have no ideals."[32] On later occasions as well, the subject of the Nazi past underscored the distance between the generations. "What has Eichmann got to do with us?" Thomas Wölfer asked in 1961. He came to the conclusion that young people in particular should learn about the past and do what they could. This way, he claimed, "what once—in the name of our country, in the name of our parents—had happened" would never be repeated.[33]

In the wake of the wave of anti-Semitic vandalism and the ensuing public debate, *Twen* set out to bring hidden anti-Semitism to the surface and counteract it. Its December 1961 issue featured the article "A Jew Looks at Germany" by the American Mary Lee Meyersohn. Describing her unpleasant experiences with contemporary Germans, Meyersohn drew a sharp distinction between the generations. She and her husband had developed "an almost physical aversion" to older Germans, she reported, but had positive expectations of the "young Germans" whom—"thank God"—they found "more sensitive." "Let us hope for the young people," she wrote.[34] That hope was called into question, however, by the flood of letters *Twen* received in response to Meyersohn's article. The editors divided the letters into three groups: "sensible" letters that demonstrated "natural humanity," "furious and anti-Semitic" letters, and "gray letters" characterized by a mix of "superficial judgment, national sensitiveness, ignorance, goodwill, stupidity, and arrogance."

These gray letters preoccupied *Twen*'s editors. In their view, the authors of these letters were truly dangerous because their anti-Semitism was not openly articulated, but rather lay dormant under a surface of seemingly innocuous attitudes. "The gray letter people worry us. Shall we leave them to their indistinct unease, their prejudices, their dangerously scanty knowledge? They solemnly vow not to think like anti-Semites, but they want Mary Lee Meyersohn to vanish from Germany. That is, on a closer view, potential anti-Semitism."[35] Sociologists had already pointed to the phenomenon of hidden anti-Semitism. Very few people openly espoused anti-Semitic views immediately following the vandalism wave of 1959–60, but studies suggested that between 14 and 23 percent of young people held at least latently anti-Semitic opinions.[36] The editors of *Twen* ran nineteen of the gray letters in the March 1962 issue and responded to them. Firmly and combatively, they criticized all forms of intolerance, all ethnic and national stereotypes, and all varieties of prejudice.

The controversy over the gray letters was taken up at a conference at the Evangelische Akademie in Tutzing in February 1962.[37] Nearly one hundred young West Germans, including many of the writers of the gray letters, were in attendance along with the editors of *Twen*, Jewish observers, and journalists. During the gathering, *Twen*'s editors declared that they had published Meyersohn's article "on purpose, with the intention to provoke." The most positive result of running the article, they argued, was that it had "uncovered young people's prejudices." A contentious debate ensued, and in the end the proponents of tolerance and antinationalism carried the day. Young participants in the debate repeated the accusation, which had run through the gray letters, that young West Germans were subject to vigorous instruction about the German past and anti-Semitism, whereas the generation of those offering that instruction entirely avoided any sort of self-criticism. As a result of this imbalance, many young people reflexively resisted the lessons about the German past that they thought their parents' generation was trying to instill.

The attempts by *Twen*'s editors at provocation bear resemblance to what was later a characteristic tactic of the New Left elite. Because contemporary "fascists" did not come out into the open, they had to be provoked into revealing themselves.[38] The group Subversive Aktion in West Germany and the Provos in the Netherlands formulated this principle theoretically and put it into practice in a variety of activities. The *Twen* campaign exemplified an educational project that eschewed conventional methods of political education in favor of open conflict. The public impact was considerable.

Following the gray letters controversy, in the years 1963–65 *Twen*'s political tone was set by the journalist Gerhard Zwerenz (born 1925). A follower of the unorthodox Marxist philosopher Ernst Bloch, Zwerenz had left East Germany after being expelled from the governing Socialist Unity Party in 1957. As a "homeless leftist," he used his column in *Twen* to comment critically on politics and culture in the Federal Republic.

Again and again, Zwerenz devoted himself to what he called the "miasma of the past."[39] He wanted to sensitize *Twen*'s readers to the contemporary relevance of National Socialism, and he wanted them to recognize that a tradition of education *zur Untertanerie* (in subjugation) had left traces in the minds of members of the young generation.[40] When the presence of the past became more obvious as a result of the Auschwitz trial and the founding of the NPD in 1964, Zwerenz explained to his readers that the "spirit" of National Socialism posed a constant threat to society. "Why does Auschwitz concern those who were not responsible for Auschwitz because they were born during the war or in the years after?" he asked. "This is why it concerns them: if the spirit of the [Auschwitz trial defendants] were to spread again, someone might imprison you because of the color of your skin or your hair, because of your ideas, because of real or supposed offenses, strap you onto an instrument of torture, and beat you with relish [until] the blood runs out of your pants."[41] And comparing the Auschwitz trial in Frankfurt with a concurrent trial in the town of Calw, where West German army officers were accused of having mistreated recruits, Zwerenz was struck by certain similarities. In both instances, he noted, nobody could remember anything. Nobody had been present, nobody had done anything, nobody had seen anything.[42] Zwerenz did not identify West Germany with the Third Reich, but, drawing attention to problematic continuities in ways of thinking, he had no doubt that a repeat of the past could occur.

In addition to condemning anti-Semitism and terror, *Twen*'s contributors also called attention to authoritarian patterns of behavior that they saw as legacies of the Nazi system. In 1963, the editors associated the term *Obrigkeit* with "death sentence, orders to kill, tax, military drill, and servitude."[43] The Nazi past as a historical phenomenon was not the main focus of their attention. They were, instead, interested primarily in contemporary society and the question of possible continuities from the Third Reich. The editors' most important message to their readers was that they should not repeat their parents' mistakes but instead fight authoritarian structures and anti-Semitic tendencies in the present.

Looking at the policy of *Twen*'s editors and the results of surveys of young West Germans, it is clear that *Twen* tried to steer the emerging sensibilities of its readers in three directions. The magazine sought to help them understand the contemporary relevance of the Nazi past, and in so doing it put greater emphasis on the generation gap than young people themselves did in connection with the discussion of the past. With the topic of Nazism, *Twen* stressed fundamental conflict between the older and younger generations in order to gain advantage for the latter in the competition for power and position. Second, *Twen* fought hidden anti-Semitism among its readers to make sure that the continuity in attitudes from the era of the Third Reich was broken once and for all at the generational line. Finally, *Twen*'s editors tried to use the subject of Nazism to politicize young West Germans and to spur them to political engagement.

National Socialism as Negative Utopia: The Apolitical *Beat Club*, 1965–1972

Many of those who gave decisive impulse to the emerging youth pop culture belonged to the so-called Forty-Five generation. They often explained their efforts to create a liberal and Western-orientated youth culture by explicitly invoking their experiences as children and teenagers in the Third Reich.[44] *Twen* founder Adolf Theobald (born 1930) belonged to this cohort, as did Manfred Weissleder (1928), founder of the Hamburg Star Club, and Fritz Rau (1930), the head of the most famous concert agency in West Germany. Theobald provided a description of the self-image of these older intermediaries in pop culture. *Twen*'s early editors, he reported, "felt cheated out of their youth by the Nazis. That's where their commitment came from."[45] For Rau, liberation from Nazi education came via Western radio broadcasters; swing music, he believed, had brought about a "denazification of body and soul."[46] Against the twofold backdrop of the Nazi past and the turn to the West, popular culture in West Germany became a melting pot not only of commercial, but also of prepolitical, often decidedly political ambitions.

Much like their colleagues in the Forty-Five generation, Nazi-era émigrés involved in postwar popular culture saw a liberating potential in commercial culture. One of them was Ernest Borneman, who developed the concept for West Germany's first youth music television program, Radio Bremen's *Beat Club*.

First aired on 25 September 1965, *Beat Club* became the world's most successful music show.[47] Borneman (born 1915) was a jazz expert and, later in his career, a prominent sexologist, but he also had extensive media experience. In the late 1920s, he had been active in the Sozialistischer Schülerbund (Union of Socialist Students) and the Kommunistischer Jugendverband (Communist Youth Association) in Berlin, and he was a follower of prominent left-wing theorists such as Karl Korsch, Wilhelm Reich, and Siegfried Bernfeld.[48] Borneman emigrated in 1933 to Great Britain, where he made a name for himself as a writer, director, and manager at the BBC. He was later associated with the Canadian National Film Board and the film department of UNESCO in Paris. After returning to Germany in the early 1960s, Borneman wrote several project proposals for Radio Bremen aimed at establishing a place for Western youth culture on West German television. Drawing on his work in Britain, in particular on the successful jazz program *Six-Five Special*, Borneman presented a decidedly emancipatory proposal for bringing popular music to television.

Traditional programs, he contended, were "built on a false logic" because they "all tried to convert, educate, or entertain the audience." But young people wanted above all to be autonomous and were, his own observations suggested, interested in only one thing, a hard beat. In this assessment, Borneman was in complete agreement with those social scientists and educators who pleaded for the acceptance of the new "private" style of West German youth as a perfectly justified defense against pressure for politicization such as had existed in the Third Reich and could now be seen in East Germany.[49] Borneman took the call for recognition of the autonomy of the young even further. He wanted to avoid both control from above as well as didacticism. He also offered a definition of privacy that implied anything but an abandonment of society. It had become obvious, he argued, that "social initiative and activity" no longer began with official organizations and institutions but rather with private actions.[50] New clubs, bands, magazines, and radio stations were springing up everywhere. Borneman wanted to bring one of these clubs to television in as unfiltered a manner as possible. By showing young people dancing to modern music, he sought to encourage young Germans' antiauthoritarianism and autonomy and to make those capacities the defining features of a new generational self-confidence. Borneman also wanted to spur the development of a distinctively German music scene that could stand comparison with its British and American counterparts. "We are looking for a new German sound, a Bremen Beat-Club-sound, just like the British Liverpool sound and the American Motown sound."[51]

The ambition of creating a German sound was gradually abandoned as *Beat Club* director Michael Leckebusch, who was nearly twenty years Borneman's junior, succeeded in pushing though his idea of an "authentic English beat program" in the second half of 1966.[52] The idea of providing the German audience exclusively with Western pop music turned out to be a recipe for success. By 1968, roughly 75 percent of all West Germans between the ages of 12 and 20 regularly watched *Beat Club*, and the show reached a worldwide audience of seventy-five million viewers. Taking stock of television music programs, the British magazine *New Musical Express* suggested in 1968 that *Beat Club* might become "the best of the bunch" and might even surpass its British competitors. The Federal Republic had thus become an international trailblazer in a field dominated by the United States a decade earlier.

Beat Club's exclusive concentration on Western pop music caused serious problems in the Federal Republic itself. Right from the start, those responsible for the show were subject to familiar nationalistic complaints about English-language pop music. A debate about national representations first arose in the fall of 1966 and lasted into the spring of 1967. A report in the *Bild-Zeitung* touched off debate again in early 1968. The increasing attention to prominent British and American groups on *Beat Club* stemmed not least from Leckebusch's extremely negative assessment of the talents of German bands. He regarded the vast majority of them as pure epigones and condensed this picture into reversed national stereotypes. German bands produced, so Leckebusch declared repeatedly, "at best second-rate titles or imitations of songs by well-known foreign bands."[53] They lacked talent, and their "crass opportunism" smothered all chance of achievement.[54] Because the West German beat scene was content to copy Anglo-Saxon models, Leckebusch contended, it continued to be "provincial."[55]

In contrast to *Twen*, *Beat Club* did not make political statements. Whereas Fleckhaus and Theobald sought to mix entertainment and instruction, Borneman and Leckebuch focused entirely on entertainment. That focus nonetheless set a political tone as a result of *Beat Club*'s Western orientation. Its success rested entirely on abandoning specifically "German" content and looking to the US and, in particular, Britain. Analysis of Nazism had no part in this move toward the West; Borneman thought any attempt to instruct or enlighten the audience should be avoided. There was rather a tacit understanding that the young should dissociate themselves from the past. Off camera, Leckebusch repeatedly expressed his view of the historically determined lines of confrontation in popular culture. He did not think much of German *Schlager* (mainstream pop songs) because they often were written by "people who in the past supported the 'Horst-Wessel-Lied' and similar songs, and who have now decided to move with the times but can't in the end bring themselves to get out of their brown shoes [i.e., abandon Nazi habits of thought]."[56] There was a general suspicion that older Germans involved in popular music had made an opportunistic acculturation that barely concealed continuity with the fascist past.

From the outset, *Beat Club* assumed that its audience had renounced German tradition, and it provocatively called attention to this assumption. After its premiere, it showed not only applauding spectators but also gave air time to disapproving and nationalist responses to the show such as, for example, "I have always confessed with pride to be a German. Today I have to say again and again: 'Poor Germany.'"[57] Wondering how to attract young viewers (and tolerant adults), Borneman had suggested early on that indignant diehards should be a regular feature of *Beat Club*.[58]

In line with the general politicization of the popular media in the wake of the "youth revolt" of 1967–68, *Beat Club* began to touch upon political issues in 1968. As Leckebusch explained the following year, the program had to serve "the critical, committed" portion of the younger generation "that doesn't accept the pure consumption of beat music." He also wanted to "teach" his audience the wisdom of "reflection, critical thinking, and not consuming everything (nicht alles fressen)"—precisely the antiauthoritarian "turn to the subject" Theodor W. Adorno had argued a decade earlier was at the core of coming to terms with the past.[59] But politicized pop fans remained a marginal audience, and *Beat Club* soon dropped the features that had been created with them in mind. The show took up politics again in 1971, but that did not help bring new viewers to its by then shrinking audience. In 1972, *Beat Club* went off the air.

The Past as an Issue in Generational Conflict

West German public discussion of the Nazi past and the interest of the young in the topic shifted focus in the mid-1960s. In the early part of the decade, the history of National Socialism and the Holocaust were the dominant subjects.[60] The Nazi past became a less frequent topic in the realm of popular culture after about 1964, although it continued to serve as the essential negative foil. Around the same time, members of the student movement took up theoretical analysis of the structural elements of fascism. The main lines of an interpretation of Nazism were in place by mid-decade. It rested on four fundamental premises. First, because of either active complicity or passive compliance, the large majority of older Germans had been entangled with Nazism and could therefore not lay claim to leadership in the present. Secondly, the mental habits of National Socialism continued to exist in hidden anti-Semitism, anticommunism, and authoritarianism. Thirdly, many in West German society and the country's political class were allowing the curtailment of democracy and thereby permitting the rise of a "new fascism." Finally, the social force capable of neutralizing and overcoming the legacy of the Nazi past was the younger generation, in particular young intellectuals. This line of argument was repeated time and again in the cultural clashes subsumed under the rubric "1968." In debates on sexuality, life style, and politics, the young took it as an almost unquestioned assumption that continuities with the Nazi past had to be severed. But while this interpretation significantly heightened the confrontation between young and old, the public debate on the Nazi past did not continue with the same intensity as in the early part of the 1960s.

A change of editors in July 1965 brought with it a change in orientation for *Twen*. The magazine would henceforth focus entirely on nonpolitical topics: relationships, fashion, and life style. The Nazi past was no longer an issue for *Twen*. This uncompromising commercialism was initially very successful, as *Twen*'s circulation rose from 100,000 in 1965 to 250,000 in 1969. With the general politicization of West German culture in the late 1960s, the magazine shifted back to its earlier policy of mixing political and nonpolitical subjects. That change served, however, only to scare away more readers than it attracted. *Twen* finally had to cease publication in May 1971.[61] Some publications aimed at least in part at students also gave less attention to Nazism after about 1966. The Auschwitz trial figured prominently, for example, in the first issue of *Kursbuch* (June 1965), which included Martin Walser's essay "Unser Auschwitz" and extracts from Peter Weiss's record of the trial. Later issues focused on a number of other subjects: the German question, structuralism, mathematics, the Vietnam War, liberation movements in Latin America, student movements in Western Europe, utopianism, anarchism, and aesthetics. Nazism continued to be an occasional subject in *Kursbuch*, but it was of interest primarily for its bearing on current political affairs. Even the political magazine *Konkret*, the most widely read of the magazines left of the SPD, paid less attention to what had been its favorite subject. *Konkret* had never been primarily interested in National Socialism as a historical phenomenon. From the outset, *Konkret* took the Third Reich as its starting point in commenting on contemporary issues, such as French policy in Algeria. In the second half of the decade, *Konkret* interpreted US involvement in Vietnam, West Germany's Emergency Laws, and Israel's conduct in the Six Day War as examples of Nazi methods.[62] It also criticized conservative attacks on the new youth culture in West Germany as a continuation of National Socialist attitudes.[63]

Popular youth magazines proliferated in the wake of the student movement, but that did not lead to increased attention to the Nazi past. *Underground*, for example, was launched in November 1968 by the publishing firm Bärmeier and Nikel. Cast as the rebellious voice of the young generation, *Underground* was targeted at high school students in particular and was intended to fill the market gap between the depoliticized *Twen* and *Konkret*, which did not take pop culture seriously. *Underground* covered popular culture as well as politics, and it thereby addressed much of what was of interest to the "progressives" among young West Germans, such as beat music and its commercialization, "revolution" as idea and practice, local underground scenes, left-wing student organizations, conscientious objection to military service, and, above all, the liberalization of sexual mores. Nazism and possible continuities from the Third Reich, by contrast, hardly figured in the pages of *Underground*.

The magazine did sometimes put forward arguments or interpretations that alluded to the past. The editors displayed an inclination, for instance, to label developments they disliked as "fascist" or "protofascist."[64] On the rare occasions when *Underground* reported directly on topics related to the past, it focused on young Germans rather than on the older generation. A report on the NPD published in the September 1969 issue dismissed the "reactionaries from yesterday" and concentrated instead on their youthful supporters. They seemed to be ordinary young people, *Underground* reported, and did not resemble their fanatic elders. Although committed to fighting the westernization of German youth culture,[65] the NPD's young supporters hardly differed from their more mainstream contemporaries. "At most, they are just a little bit more tidy, their hair is cut just a little shorter. They have girl friends, appreciate a good soccer game and a great party, and when their parents are out, they have trouble-free digs and get a little excessive." *Underground* insisted that it was important to try to engage young NPD supporters in debate on account of their generational advantage; "They are not the inveterate fathers, they are just the tempted sons." Whether we like it or not," the magazine advised, "we should start talking to them while it is still possible."

Time Is on My Side

The example of *Twen* clearly shows that the idea of a generation gap centered on the issue of Nazism was first put forward not by members of the younger generation but by older mediators in popular culture in the late 1950s. *Twen*'s founders wanted both to entertain and to instruct their audience, and toward the goal of instruction they focused, in the magazine's early years, less on the history of National Socialism than on the contemporary relevance of continuities with the Third Reich. *Beat Club*, geared to presenting pop music, did not aim at political education per se but rather encouraged democratization through individualism and a Western orientation in lifestyle. *Beat Club* did not take up the subject of the Nazi past explicitly, but it clearly defined itself and its audience with reference to the "moral negative-capital" of the older generation's attachment to the past.[66]

In its abstract form, this argument was irrefutable. It addressed the problem of West German society's "deficits of modernity" (*Modernitätsrückstände*)[67] and answered attacks on young people's cultural styles. The reproach "you with your Ami howling" (i.e., rock music) could be countered with the reply "and you with your Hitler." With a simple phrase, those born too late to be implicated in the Third Reich derived an advantage in the debate with their elders: "We just had to say 'Dachau' [to] make them feel unsure."[68]

In 1968, educator Dieter Baacke noted in his study of the West German Beat scene, "in our innumerable discussions in Beat clubs [we] met no young person who was right wing or even consciously nationalistic. Just the opposite: Beat makes them cosmopolitans."[69] As this assessment suggests, private behavior was often interpreted politically in the late 1960s—and it did not take much to be considered "progressive." Youth culture dissociated itself from the Nazi past without discussing it directly.

It had become a firmly established commonplace by the mid-1960s that National Socialism lay behind the generation gap in West Germany. This explanation was used in the clash of political opinions and cultural tastes at the end of the decade as both the range of issues at stake and the spheres of protest action expanded explosively. At the same time, the rhetoric of generational conflict was also part of a trend toward discussing Nazism in increasingly theoretical and abstract terms. As surveys found, young people dissociated from the Nazi past as a matter of course, but they were generally not very interested in coming to terms with it. Even more engaged young intellectuals primarily addressed current political problems. Their sense of time was directed toward the present and the future. Young West Germans in the early 1960s looked ahead optimistically, and they, unlike their elders, were not worried by the brief economic downturn of 1966–67.[70] Similarly, the student movement's radicalism rested not so much on a particular view of the past as on a tremendously utopian vision of the future. The optimism of the young was certainly influenced by the critical consideration of the past that had taken place in the early 1960s, but most young West Germans nonetheless did not like looking back—either in euphoria or in anger.

Notes

1. Heinz Bude, *Das Altern einer Generation: Die Jahrgänge 1938–1948* (Frankfurt am Main: 1995). My analysis, instead, covers younger cohorts, born up to the early 1950s.

2. Quoted in Klaus Briegleb, "Vergangenheit in der Gegenwart," in *Gegenwartsliteratur seit 1968*, ed. Klaus Briegleb and Sigrid Weigel (Munich, 1992), 73–115, here 91.

3. See Axel Schildt, "Die Eltern auf der Anklagebank? Zur Thematisierung der NS-Vergangenheit im Generationenkonflikt der bundesrepublikanischen 60er Jahre," in *Erinnerungskulturen: Deutschland, Italien und Japan seit 1945*, ed. Christoph Cornelißen, Lutz Klinkhammer, and Wolfgang Schwendtker (Frankfurt am Main, 2003), 317–32; Harald Welzer, "Krieg der Generationen: Zur Tradierung von NS-Vergangenheit und Krieg in deutschen Familien," in *Nachkrieg in Deutschland*, ed. Klaus Naumann (Hamburg, 2001), 552–71. At an early stage, Klaus Allerbeck pointed out that "conflict with the parents mostly was not the cause, but the result of radical commitment." Klaus Allerbeck, *Soziale Bedingungen für studentischen Radikalismus: Eine vergleichende Untersuchung in der Bundesrepublik Deutschland und den Vereinigten Staaten* (Cologne, 1971), 158.

4. Eric Hobsbawm, *Das Zeitalter der Extreme: Weltgeschichte des 20. Jahrhunderts* (Munich, 1997), 402ff.; Arthur Marwick, *The Sixties: Cultural Revolution in Britain, France, Italy, and the United States* (Oxford, 1998). See also Carole Fink, Philipp Gassert, and Detlef Junker, eds., *1968: The World Transformed* (Cambridge, 1998), and the survey by Ingrid Gilcher-Holtey, *Die 68er Bewegung: Deutschland—Westeuropa—USA* (Munich, 2001). For conceptional reflections, see Norbert Elias, *Studien über die Deutschen: Machtkämpfe und Habitusentwicklungen im 19. und 20. Jahrhundert*, ed. by Michael Schröter (Frankfurt am Main, 1994), 300ff.

5. For the change of discourse on the Nazi past, see Habbo Knoch, *Die Tat als Bild: Fotografien in der deutschen Erinnerungskultur* (Hamburg, 2001). On politicization, see Detlef Siegfried, "Vom Teenager zur Pop-Revolution, Politisierungstendenzen in der westdeutschen Jugendkultur 1959 bis 1968," in *Dynamische Zeiten: Die 60er Jahre in den beiden deutschen Gesellschaften*, ed. Axel Schildt, Detlef Siegfried, and Karl Christian Lammers (Hamburg, 2000), 582–623.

6. Walter Jaide, *Das Verhältnis der Jugend zur Politik: Empirische Untersuchungen zur politischen Anteilnahme und Meinungsbildung junger Menschen der Geburtsjahrgänge 1940–1946* (Darmstadt, 1963), 94.

7. See *EMNID-Informationen*, no. 40 (1960), and ibid., no. 8–9 (1968): A 18.

8. Jaide, *Verhältnis*, 100.

9. Ibid., 109f.

10. *Allensbach-Pressedienst*, no. 10 (1961). Indications for this can already be found in a survey, carried out in 1957, Hermann Bertlein, *Das Selbstverständnis der Jugend heute: Eine empirische Untersuchung über ihre geistigen Probleme, ihre Leitbilder und ihr Verhältnis zu den Erwachsenen* (Berlin, 1960), 76, and in *EMNID-Informationen*, no. 40 (1960).

11. Freie politische Bildungsarbeit an der Jugend der Bundesrepublik, 1 February 1960, Bundesarchiv Koblenz (BAK), B 153/1781.

12. Elisabeth Noelle and Erich Peter Neumann, eds., *Jahrbuch der öffentlichen Meinung, 1958–1964* (Allensbach, 1965), 354.

13. Ludwig von Friedeburg, "Zum Verhältnis von Jugend und Gesellschaft," in *Jugend in der modernen Gesellschaft*, ed. Ludwig von Friedeburg (Cologne, 1976), 176–90, here 184. The article was published first in 1963.

14. Viggo Graf Blücher, *Die Generation der Unbefangenen: Zur Soziologie der jungen Menschen heute* (Düsseldorf, 1966), 345.

15. Ibid.; Elisabeth Pfeil, *Die 23jährigen: Eine Generationsuntersuchung am Geburtsjahrgang 1941* (Tübingen, 1968), 323.

16. See Werner Bergmann and Rainer Erb, *Antisemitismus in der Bundesrepublik Deutschland: Ergebnisse der empirischen Forschung von 1946–1989* (Opladen, 1991), 73. On effects in the education system, see Peter Dudek, *"Der Rückblick auf die Vergangenheit wird sich nicht vermeiden lassen": Zur pädagogischen Verarbeitung des Nationalsozialismus in Deutschland, 1945–1990* (Opladen, 1995).

17. EMNID-Institut, *Junge Intelligenzschicht 1968/69: Politische Meinungen, Einstellungen und Verhaltensbereitschaften* (Bielefeld, 1969), 15.

18. Pfeil, *Die 23jährigen*, 321–23; DIVO-Pressedienst, March II, 1965, 22.

19. Noelle/Neumann, *Jahrbuch, 1958–64*, 230.

20. *DIVO-Pressedienst*, July 1964.

21. Viggo Graf Blücher, "Die Rechtsradikalen und die Bevölkerung," in *EMNID-Informationen*, no. 8–9 (1968): A16.

22. Rudolf Wildenmann and Max Kaase, *"Die unruhige Generation": Eine Untersuchung zu Politik und Demokratie in der Bundesrepublik* (Mannheim, 1968), 102f.; Günter C. Behrmann, "Politische Einstellungen und Verhaltensweisen Jugendlicher," in *Jugend zwischen Auflehnung und Anpassung: Einstellungen, Verhaltensweisen, Lebenschancen*, ed. Hans-Georg Wehling (Stuttgart, 1973), 73. Similar were the results of Jaide's survey of 15- to 19-year-old students of 1968: Walter Jaide, *Jugend und Demokratie: Politische Einstellungen der westdeutschen Jugend* (Munich, 1970), 41ff.

23. Institut für Demoskopie, Allensbach, Der deutsche Student, July 1966, BAK, Zsg. 132/1363.

24. Quoted in *EMNID-Informationen*, no. 1 (1970). Also exaggeratedly pessimistic was Karl H. Bönner, *Deutschlands Jugend und das Erbe der Väter: Wie skeptisch ist die junge Generation?* (Bergisch-Gladbach, 1967).

25. Klaus Allerbeck and Wendy J. Hoag, *16- bis 18jährige: 1962 und 1983. Projekt: Integrationsbereitschaft der Jugend im sozialen Wandel* (Frankfurt am Main, 1985), 18, 21.

26. *Allensbach-Pressedienst*, no. 1 (1968).

27. See, for example, the foreword in the second edition of Ludwig von Friedeburg and Peter Hübner, *Das Geschichtsbild der Jugend* (Munich, 1970), first published in 1964.

28. Twen-Leser. Ergebnisse einer marktsoziologischen Studie, 22 May 1967, BAK, Zsg. 132/1428; Twen 68. Redaktioneller Copy-Test, June 1968, BAK, Zsg. 132/1570; Twen-Leser: Meinungsführer in einem neuen Lebensstil, 21 August 1969, BAK, Zsg. 132/1621. On the magazine's history and profile, see Michael Koetzle, ed., *Die Zeitschrift Twen: Revision einer Legende* (Munich, 1995).

29. Compared with this, the readers of the major teenage rag *Bravo* came from younger age groups with lower levels of education. In contrast to *Twen*, political subjects were almost "systematically avoided." See Horst Holzer and Reinhard Kreckel, "Jugend und Massenmedien: Eine inhaltsanalytische Betrachtung der Jugendzeitschriften BRAVO und TWEN," *Soziale Welt* 18 (1967): 199–215, here 206.

30. dipa-Informationen zu Jugendarbeit und Erziehungswesen, 21 April 1961, BAK, B 117/54; Evangelischer Arbeitskreis für Jugendschutz NRW, Zeitschriftenbeobachtung. Bericht über die Zeitschrift Twen, [1963], Staatsarchiv Hamburg, Jugendbehörde II, Abl. v. 24.10.1986, 356-21.04-1, vol. 2.

31. Quoted in Michael Koetzle, "Die Zeitschrift Twen: Revision einer Legende," in Koetzle, *Twen*, 12–73, here 23.

32. *Twen*, Special Issue, no. 2 (1959).

33. *Twen*, no. 4 (1961): 84.

34. Mary Lee Meyersohn, "Kann man in Deutschland leben?" *Twen*, no. 7 (1961): 34–36.

35. Ibid.

36. For the results in detail, see Werner Bergmann, *Antisemitismus in öffentlichen Konflikten: Kollektives Lernen in der politischen Kultur der Bundesrepublik, 1949–1989* (Frankfurt am Main, 1997), 275.

37. See all this in *Twen*, no. 7 (1961), and ibid., no. 4 (1962).

38. See, e.g., *Twen*, no. 1 (1963): 67–70.

39. *Twen*, no. 6 (1963): 86.

40. *Twen*, no. 3 (1964): 25.

41. *Twen*, no. 5 (1964): 96.

42. *Twen*, no. 3 (1964): 25.

43. Editorial in *Twen*, no. 2 (1963).

44. On this generation's profile, see Dirk Moses, "The Forty-Fivers: A Generation between Fascism and Democracy," in *German Politics and Society* 17, no. 1 (1999): 94–126; Heinz Bude, *Deutsche Karrieren: Lebenskonstruktionen sozialer Aufsteiger aus der Flakhelfer-Generation* (Frankfurt am Main, 1987); additionally, see the case study by Jörg Lau, "Auf der Suche nach der verlorenen Normalität: Helmut Kohl und Hans Magnus Enzensberger als Generationsgenossen," in Naumann, *Nachkrieg*, 498–520.

45. Interview by Michael Koetzle, in Koetzle, *Twen*, 55.

46. Kathrin Brigl and Siegfried Schmidt-Joos, *Fritz Rau: Buchhalter der Träume* (Severin, 1985), 68.

47. Further examples include the Jewish emigrant Billy Graham, who was a prominent concert agent in the US and one of Rau's closest partners, as well as the Jewish emigrant Gustav Metzger, who as a London art school professor strongly influenced the style of rock bands such as The Who. See Wolfgang Kraushaar, "Gitarrenzertrümmerung: Gustav Metzger, die Idee des autodestruktiven Kunstwerks und deren Folgen in der Rockmusik," *Mittelweg 36*, no. 1 (2001): 2–28.

48. Curriculum Vitae Ernest Borneman, [1962], Radio Bremen (RB), Beat-Club (BC) 1; *Underground*, no. 3 (1970): 23ff.; Ernest Borneman, *Die Ur-Szene: Das prägende Kindheitserlebnis und seine Folgen* (Frankfurt am Main, 1980), 16ff.

49. Uta G. Poiger, *Jazz, Rock, and Rebels: Cold War Politics and American Culture in a Divided Germany* (Berkeley, 2000).

50. Helmut Kentler, "'Subkulturen' von Jugendlichen," *deutsche jugend* 12 (1964): 403–12, here 409.

51. Script Beat-Club 1 [September 1965], RB, BC 1.

52. Leckebusch to C.N., 30 November 1966, RB, BC 13. Leckebusch was born in 1937.

53. *Aachener Nachrichten*, 4 May 1968.

54. *Musik-Informationen*, 16 January 1967. See also Michael Leckebusch, "Warum der Beat-Club kein deutsches Programm ist—und wie es dazu kam," 7 February 1968, RB, BC Pressemappe.

55. *Höllenspiegel*, January 1970.

56. Ibid.

57. Show of 30 October 1965.

58. Jazz Club: Ein Programmvorschlag von Ernest Borneman, 8 June 1964, RB, BC 1.

59. Michael Leckebusch, Gedanken zum Beat-Club, November 1969, RB, BC Pressemappe. Adorno's statement in Theodor W. Adorno, "Was bedeutet: Aufarbeitung der Vergangenheit," in *Erziehung zur Mündigkeit: Vorträge und Gespräche mit Hellmut Becker, 1959–1969*, ed. Gerd Kadelbach (Frankfurt am Main, 1970), 10–29, here 28.

60. This becomes evident also in the main topics of school magazines. See, for example, Ulrike Heider, *Schülerprotest in der Bundesrepublik Deutschland* (Frankfurt am Main, 1984), 92ff. For the "shock" effects in the confrontation with the Nazi past, there is evidence mainly for the first

half of the 1960s. This can be seen, for instance, in the reactions to Erwin Leiser's documentary *Mein Kampf* of 1960, which, particularly in big cities, attracted "many young persons." Dieter Geldschläger, "Bericht über die Probleme und Versuche der politischen Bildung unter jungen Menschen in der Bundesrepublik Deutschland," Summer/Fall 1960, BAK, B 153/1781. See detailed information in Knoch, *Tat*, 627ff.

61. Koetzle, *Twen*, 64.

62. For this, see Helle Klausen, *"Was geht uns Eichmann an?" Et indblik i unge vesttyskeres omgang med nationalsocialismen i 1958–1968 ud fra ungdomsmedierne konkret og twen* (Copenhagen, 2002).

63. So, for example, Robert Neumann's attacks on the *Volkswartbund*, which intended to preserve the ethics of young people, published under the headline "The Cardinal's Blockwarte," or Klaus Rainer Röhl's historical classification of the *Aktion saubere Leinwand*, founded in 1964: "Not films, books, and magazines destroyed the Weimar Republic and led the youth to the mass graves of World War II, but rather the youth protector and moralizer Adolf Hitler." *Konkret*, no. 4 (1968): 43, and ibid., no. 6 (1965): 7.

64. "The radical left begins to display protofascist characteristics." *Underground*, no. 2 (1969): 45.

65. *Underground*, no. 9 (1969): 52.

66. This term comes from Gerd Koenen, *Das rote Jahrzehnt: Unsere kleine deutsche Kulturrevolution, 1967–1977* (Cologne, 2001), 97.

67. Klaus R. Allerbeck and Leopold Rosenmayr, "Neue Theorien und Materialien zur Soziologie der Jugend. Ergebnisse eines internationalen Symposiums," in *Aufstand der Jugend? Neue Aspekte der Jugendsoziologie*, ed. Klaus R. Allerbeck and Leopold Rosenmayr (Munich, 1971), 11.

68. So a contemporary witness, quoted in Kaspar Maase, *BRAVO Amerika: Erkundungen zur Jugendkultur der Bundesrepublik in den fünfziger Jahren* (Hamburg, 1992), 82.

69. Dieter Baacke, *Beat: Die sprachlose Opposition* (Munich, 1968), 118.

70. See Pfeil, *Die 23jährigen*, 275ff. and 350; Institut für Demoskopie, Allensbach, "Der Verbraucher und die Konjunktur," Frühjahr 1967, BAK, Zsg. 132. In general, see Ronald Inglehart, *Kultureller Umbruch: Wertewandel in der westlichen Welt* (Frankfurt am Main, 1989).

Chapter 10

THE SEXUAL REVOLUTION AND THE
LEGACIES OF THE NAZI PAST

Dagmar Herzog

❧

We cannot make sense of the West German New Left's conflicted relationship to the Nazi past and the Holocaust without understanding the New Left's involvement in the sexual revolution of the 1960s to 1970s. Most recent publications about 1968 as a historical watershed have ignored or downplayed the New Left's sexual politics, but in so doing they have missed the opportunity to gain a deeper understanding of the original motive forces of the student upheaval and the sources of its very particular pathos and fury in West Germany. They have also missed a chance to understand the ways the student movement, while styling itself as anti-fascist, might more usefully be understood as an anti*post*fascist movement. Many of the transformations in personal politics in which the 68ers engaged—experiments in communal living, antiauthoritarian parenting, and renegotiated sexual mores and gender relations—were elaborated against the background of the perceived legacies of the fascist past. But what the 68ers were most directly rebelling against was the postfascist settlement in West Germany—and their own experiences coming of age in the claustrophobic and conservative mid- to late 1950s. The 68ers believed that the sexual conservatism in which they were raised was a watered-down continuation of Nazism's sexual politics, and they built their own activism on behalf of sexual liberation on an interpretation of Nazism as fundamentally sex-hostile and pro-family. As it turns out, however, the 68ers based their convictions on misreadings both of the Third Reich and of the immediate post–Third Reich years.

The relationship between the sexual revolution in West Germany and the New Left student movement is not reducible to a simple equation, even though in popular parlance "1968" is often used as a shorthand reference to both. Although there was considerable voyeuristic public fascination with such flamboyantly

---

Notes for this chapter begin on page 172.

provocative experiments on the left as the (for a short time) dedicatedly promiscuous left-anarcho Kommune 1, the sexual revolution was manifestly a broader phenomenon than the New Left. From the increasing popularity of the Pill to the explosion of pornography and peepshows to the ever-growing success of entrepreneur Beate Uhse's sex aids shops and mainstream sex apostle Oswalt Kolle's advice columns and sex-enlightenment movies, the later 1960s and early 1970s saw the transformation of the sexual landscape in West Germany. Most retrospective accounts tend to give the students credit for either igniting or furthering the broader changes. Twenty years after 1968, for example, psychoanalyst and former New Left leader Reimut Reiche remembered: "We shouted 'Destroy the bourgeois nuclear family!'—and became the avant-garde of a democratic modernization in the realm of childrearing, living arrangements, gender relations, marital forms, dress and table manners—and sexual mores. I am not saying all that would not have happened without us. But without a doubt the student movement set this push for modernization in motion."[1] And sexologist Gunter Schmidt observed in 1998 that "[t]hirty years ago, the students, or rather the student movement, had the sense for the socially possible, necessary, indeed overdue transformations of sexual relationships," and that "they were the main actors of the liberal discourse."[2]

Sexual Rebellion and Postwar Culture

An examination of the New Left writings on sex from the late 1960s and early 1970s reveals a somewhat more complicated story. Although the student movement was indeed strongly motivated by sexual rebellion against the conformist culture of postwar West Germany, fueled by an intense desire for personal liberation and self-transformation, those within the student movement who thought seriously about sexual issues were also quickly repulsed by the mainstream sexualization of the culture booming all around them. (As cultural critic and former 68er Klaus Theweleit recently remembered it: "With repugnance, we took cognizance of the partner-swapping tales of bourgeois couples," as "the sex-wave spread in the so-called populace.")[3] Discomfort with the mainstream sexual revolution was strongly evident already in the earliest corpus of New Left publications on sex and family life: the texts produced by the *Kinderladen* movement for antiauthoritarian childrearing.[4] The writings of this movement thematized adults' sexuality as much as children's. The texts repeatedly include scathing and anguished attempts to explain why the bourgeois sexual revolution was most definitely not the bodily and psychic liberation for which the students were yearning. A classic sample of the typical tone—snatches of "materialist" analysis pasted together with inexpressible utopian longings—is provided by the 1970 anthology *Berliner Kinderläden*: "As long as the nuclear family survives—ultimately, for economic reasons—sexual freedom serves as a sad little palliative for daily surfeit and disgust." And: "Even if people humped around ten times more than ever before, it would not add up to real sexual liberation. For merely to amass orgasms, even if man and woman arrive at them simultaneously, can not yet be seen as a satisfying form of sexuality."[5] As these remarks suggest, it was no coincidence that sex rights activists in the New Left would within a few years turn away from the early, and often quite melodramatic, Wilhelm Reich-inspired calls for complete sexual liberation as an antifascist imperative toward more Herbert Marcuse-influenced analyses of the mainstream sexual revolution as just another aspect of repressive desublimation, while continuing to demand a form of sexual freedom linked to social criticism and social justice struggles.

Yet despite the shift away from innocent faith in sexual liberation as already in itself politically important and morally redemptive, it is worth dwelling a bit more on that early phase, which—depending on which texts and events one uses to periodize it—might be said to run from around 1966 to 1970. Although the first, so-called subjective or antiauthoritarian phase of the student movement was already over by 1968, when one looks at the student movement's involvement in *sexual* politics, the periodization is different. The first—one might call it strenuously emancipatory—phase ran a bit longer, only to be followed by more than a decade of melancholic introspection and mutual recrimination. What made the activist students' perspective on sex unique, in short, was not their advocacy of greater liberality, but rather their insistence on connecting liberated sex with progressive politics.

What we gain by focusing on the early years of the New Left is a greater sense of what drew young people into the student movement in the first place. It is important not to be reductionist here; the aim is not to suggest that political commitments were only derivative of or secondary to personal concerns, and it is certainly not to dispute either the sincerity or the significance of the political critiques and activist engagements of the New Left. What we need to acknowledge are the entanglements and reciprocal reinforcements, as well as mutual conflictedness, of political commitments and personal motivations, without ever assuming that personal motives were similarly important to everyone.[6] Keeping these caveats in mind, however, it does remain striking how many reminiscences about the early years remark that the personal was the spark for the political. In 1984, in an essay analyzing the sexual debates of the 1960s, Sabine Weissler (not a 68er but someone who had read many 68er materials) summarized it this way: "The flood of articles, lectures, discussion events, and reading circles on the question of sexual enlightenment as a part of political emancipation was incredible. There was no school or student newspaper in which this was not—long before Vietnam, emergency laws, university reform etc.—topic number one, usually intensively combated and censured by parents and authorities."[7] The 68ers' own retrospective observations confirm this sense and elaborate on it. Writer Peter Schneider, for example, confessed in 1977 that "it was a new feeling for the body, a new way of moving, of speaking, and only then a new consciousness, that attracted me."[8] Journalist Götz Eisenberg put it like this in 1979: "The anti-authoritarian movement was also a revolt of identity, a mutiny against the more or less awful consequences of authoritarian education in parental home and school, a detonation of the drilled bodies, senses, and wishes.... That which had been pushed aside and repressed by school and parental home, broke open, exploded as it were, and combined itself with the protest against external coercions and inherited authorities into an amalgam that constituted the specific dynamite and radicality of the anti-authoritarian movement."[9] Filmmaker Edgar Reitz formulated it like this: "We spoke in intellectual terms, but we felt something different.... The Left had an unending yearning for warmth."[10] And Theweleit in 1990 went so far as to suggest that a "special sort of sexual tension was the 'driving force' of 1968" in West Germany.[11]

To lend authority to its antiauthoritarianism, the New Left frequently invoked the Frankfurt School. In line with the present tendency to marginalize the New Left's "private sphere" activism, one thing that appears to be missing in the recent spate of publications on the New Left's relationship to the Frankfurt School is the ways in which student activists read Frankfurt School writings on the connections between the potential for fascism and childhood socialization within the family. Most of the recent analyses focus on the students' disgust with the Critical Theorists' refusal to turn theory into praxis and the professors' anger and repugnance at the students' "mindless" (and, especially in Jürgen Habermas's and Theodor Adorno's view, potentially fascistic) actionism.[12] Engaging with former mentors on the tensions between theory and praxis was certainly crucial to New Left activism across a range of political issues, from antiwar protest to the redefinition of the purpose and structure of the university to the analysis of the media and of aesthetics.[13] But this engagement was no less crucial in the realm of personal politics. Rereading early New Left texts now, and reading them against the writings on authority and the family by Adorno and Max Horkheimer that students cited most frequently, it becomes apparent that 68ers read the Frankfurt School's writings on sex, the family, and fascism above all through the lens of Wilhelm Reich.

Horkheimer and Adorno's essays on authority and the family contain quite nuanced assessments of the Third Reich's contradictory sexual and familial politics, and of the connections between sexual conservatism and political conservatism. But what is evident in the New Left writings on sex and the family in the late 1960s and early 1970s is a rather selective appropriation of Frankfurt School ideas. While Horkheimer, for instance, stressed that the Third Reich had tried to dispense with the family as the mediating link between the individual and the state, and argued that the appeal of fascism lay in part in the growing weakness of fathers, New Leftists tended to invoke only his notions about the psychological power of parents, the ways the very structure of the nuclear family inculcated submissiveness, and the ways in which hatred of overpowering parents, which could not be expressed directly, got repressed but then also aggressively turned onto those more vulnerable.[14] And while *The Authoritarian Personality* explicitly noted that there is such a phenomenon as the politically reactionary but also sexually active person, 68ers drew exclusively on the study's findings about the links between the potential for fascism and sexual repressedness.[15] "Fascist developments are facilitated by authoritarian character structures," opined the authors of *Berliner Kinderläden* in summarizing *The Authoritarian Personality*, after having just explained that those character structures had their roots in strict toilet-training, the suppression of child sexuality, and "strong emotional ties to parents as the only relevant objects of identification." And in their own eagerness to "smash the bourgeois nuclear family!" as the sixties slogan went, the authors of the book ignored Horkheimer's premises about the Nazis' family-smashing aims and instead, in their concern to expose the damage done by liberal as well as conservative parents, quoted his remark from the 1930s that "whether parents are lenient or strict with the child is not important, for the child's character is influenced far more by family structure than by the father's conscious aims and methods."[16] Another typical New Left childrearing text, *Kinderläden: Revolution der Erziehung oder Erziehung zur Revolution?* invoked Adorno as it summarily asserted that "the authoritarian personality" was characterized by "hostility to sex" and cited Horkheimer to explain how insecure people could become both brutal and overly submissive to authority. The same text then quoted Erich Fromm's 1936 observations about parental authority being the mirror image of, rather than the model for, societal authority, only to conclude directly from there that "in the family the child is crushed, trained to be a subordinate, a faithful Christian, a sex-hostile future 'Mr. and Mrs. Clean,' an obedient worker."[17] The point is not that Adorno, Horkheimer, or Fromm did not say what they were quoted or summarized as saying; they did. The point is that the pieces of their work that got invoked sound a great deal like Wilhelm Reich.

Wilhelm Reich's influence on the early New Left in West Germany was unparalleled. No other intellectual so moved the student movement in its early days, and to a degree unmatched either in the US or other Western European nations. This had everything to do with Reich's central argument that sexual satisfaction and sadism were mutually exclusive, and that (as he put it) "cruel character traits" were evident among those "in a condition of chronic sexual dissatisfaction," while "genitally satisfiable people" were notable for their "gentleness and goodness."[18] And it had a great deal to do with his insistence that child sexuality in particular needed to be not just tolerated, but actively celebrated, if fascism and neurosis alike were to be averted—an idea that is repeated like a mantra in dozens of early New Left writings. Reprints of Reich's work from the 1920s through the 1940s, first in bootleg form, then formally published, circulated widely in the late 1960s. No book display table on a campus was complete without Reich's *The Sexual Revolution* or *The Function of the Orgasm*, and *The Mass Psychology of Fascism* was, in the words of one former 68er, read just as "breathlessly."[19] It is indicative, too, that for a time in 1968 the outside wall of the cafeteria at the University of Frankfurt carried a graffiti slogan exhorting all passersby to "read Wilhelm Reich and act accordingly."[20] While this was obviously a humorously and seriously meant incitement to engage in more "free love," the issue that needs to be emphasized is the *moral* force of Reich's arguments. In rediscovering Reich, activists saw themselves as rescuing an aspect of the anticapitalist and sex-radical tradition of Weimar that the Nazis had wiped out or driven into exile. But what they revered most about Reich was the way he helped them rewrite conventional wisdom about the relationship between pleasure and evil. Reich's concepts seemed to lend additional legitimacy to that ubiquitous sixties slogan, "Make Love Not War." For this slogan was not just a recommendation for a more decent, and pleasurable, activity than slaughtering other human beings while risking one's own life; it was also a theory of human nature, a deeply held conviction that those who made a lot of love simply would not be interested in hurting or killing others.

The reasons for Reich's tremendous appeal at the end of the 1960s lie in the complex interrelationships between the 1940s and 1950s, between the decade of mass murder and the decade in which the future 68ers began to come of age. Reich's contention that the sexual repression of children within the family lay at the root of almost all human cruelty showed up in countless ways in the left-leaning literature of the late 1960s. For in the 1960s and 1970s, leftists and liberals alike believed that both fascism in general and the Holocaust in particular were the perverted products of sexual repression. The Marxist theoretician Wolfgang Fritz Haug declared already in 1965 that in order to understand the Third Reich it was "essential" to use the insights of psychology to identify the connection "between the suppression of sexual drives on the one hand and the anti-Jewish persecution mania and its raging in manifest cruelty on the other."[21] The sociologist Friedhelm Neidhardt in 1966 presumed as self-evident that "concentration camp murderers were in the rule 'good family men.'"[22] Philosophy PhD Arno Plack, in his magnum opus of 1967, *Die Gesellschaft und das Böse*, asserted matter-of-factly that "it would be wrong to hold the view that all of what happened in Auschwitz was typically German. It was typical for a society that suppresses sexuality."[23] And the journalist Hannes Schwenger, in his 1969 critique of "antisexual propaganda" in the postwar churches, identified the churches' attacks on "free love, premarital intercourse, adultery and divorce" as exemplifying "the language of fascism."[24]

But really it was the postwar period, especially the mid- to late 1950s and early 1960s, that the 68ers had personally experienced as sexually repressive. This was an era of intensive rhetorical overvaluation of the family; of anxieties about the damage done to women by premarital sex; of worry about what the neighbors might say if a fiancé spent the night; and of constant warnings about the deleterious effects of masturbation. You will never win the battle against your own body, one prominent Protestant physician informed young men, if you lie around in a warm bed in the morning or listen to "steamy Negro music" at night. You may succumb occasionally to temptation, a leading pedagogue warned, but "afterwards the revulsion at yourself returns in intensified form."[25] *This* is what the 68ers were rebelling against. There is a noticeable sense of a compensatory fervor at work in the ferocity of New Left activists' projects on behalf of children. The antiauthoritarian *Kinderläden* do not just permit the children to run naked and freely touch their own and each other's bodies; they vociferously celebrate this and publish elaborate reports on the most intimate details of the children's touchings. Declaring the nuclear family to be "rotten to the core," they not only rotate care giving at the centers, but actively work to rupture what they call parent-child "fixations."[26] And strikingly, they comment repeatedly on their sense of unhappiness with their own bodies: "None of the adults in our fundamentally antisexual and pleasure-hostile society was able to develop an untroubled relationship to sexuality," the Frankfurt *Kinderladen* collective complains in a typical passage, and "among adults compulsive personalities are the rule and not the exception."[27] The Stuttgarters concur: adults are all "socially crippled" beings.[28]

Indicatively, furthermore, the activists also invoke Nazism and the Holocaust. In its rage, for example, at the tendency even of liberal sex education guides to downplay pleasure and emphasize the dangers of venereal disease, the Berlin-Charlottenburg collective stingingly announced that "it is well known that the National Socialists combined their fascist racial theory with the irrational warning against the decadent Jews because they were supposedly responsible for sexually transmitted diseases."[29] Moreover, the Charlottenburgers observed at another point, anyone who insisted on the "hallowed" importance of the mother-child bond was "simply confirming what clerics, National Socialists, and Christian Democrats have already for a long time been preaching from their moral pulpits about 'the smallest cell of the state—the family.'"[30] A father working in the Berlin-Neukölln center with coy insolence informed a reporter from *Stern* not only that the parents allowed the children to masturbate and play sex-games "in peace," but that "[m]any of the children were already toilet-trained. Now they shit in their pants again. They're repeating the anal phase. That's good. Did you know that most concentration camp guards had anal difficulties in their childhood?"[31] Members of the Berlin-Lankwitz collective, meanwhile, put the anal phase at the very center of political theory: Punitive toilet-training, they contended, led to authoritarian personalities with sadistic fantasies who oppressed minorities; preoccupation with cleanliness was part and parcel of a mindset that sent people "into the oven."[32]

The New Left and the Fascist Past

The relationship of the New Left to the fascist past is a problem that is being only unevenly engaged in the recent scholarship on 1968. There is an acute imbalance between the generalizations circulating in the 1990s and early 2000s about 1968 as the occasion for a reckoning with the elders compromised by Nazism, and the more nuanced assessment of the 68ers' actually rather ambiguous relationship to the Holocaust which was more well established in the 1980s.[33] From Henryk Broder's signal piece in *Die Zeit* in 1981 to the articulate and thoughtful critiques and autocritiques produced in the course of the 1980s by Anson Rabinbach and Jessica Benjamin, Marion Kaplan, Andrei Markovits, Atina Grossmann, Michael Schneider, Peter Schneider, Klaus Hartung, and Claus Leggewie, among others, it was clear that there had been a problem with non-Jewish New Leftists' overly eager criticisms of Israel, glib generalizations about Jews, simplistic labeling of various postwar phenomena as "fascistic," and repeated marginalization of the Holocaust in a narrowly economistic reading of Nazism.[34] At the very least, this more differentiated knowledge should be consistently integrated into the current retrospective assessments of 1968. But we can also move a step further toward explaining what otherwise seems rather inexplicable—that is, the 68ers' coexisting tendencies to profound identification with and manifest insensitivity toward the murdered Jews—by paying attention to the ways the 68ers' antifascism was enmeshed in their antipostfascism because of the sexual politics of the postwar period and the particular sexual interpretations of Nazism prevalent in the 1960s.

Explaining the 68ers' contradictory relationship to the fascist past and the Holocaust thus requires a reconsideration not just of the sexual politics of the post–Third Reich era but also of the Third Reich itself. The standard view among scholars at present, so pervasive that no one seems to feel the need to document it more fully but which instead serves as a sort of foundational backdrop to other inquiries, is that the Third Reich was at its core antisex. And indisputably, there were in the Third Reich countless profoundly repressive tendencies. The Nazi Party came to power in part on a family values platform, and some of the regime's earliest moves involved the destruction of Germany's main sexological institute and numerous pornographic and risqué establishments. The regime brutally tortured and murdered homosexuals. It sterilized proletarian women on the grounds that their (purported) promiscuity was a sign of mental deficiency. It incarcerated prostitutes as asocials. And one need only think of the race defilement laws and the grotesque reproductive experiments and sexual sadism in the concentration and death camps to understand the centrality of sexual repressiveness and the most intimate of bodily invasions to the Holocaust itself. But none of these points justifies the conclusion that the Third Reich was experienced as sex-hostile by everyone. What has routinely been downplayed since the 1960s is the evidence that, for regime-loyal or regime-indifferent heterosexual "Aryans," the Third Reich was anything but repressive.[35]

The regime's brutality and the pleasures it promised to those it did not persecute were inextricably connected. The stepped-up persecution of homosexuals provided a crucial context for the injunction to heterosexual activity; the abuse and murder of those deemed unworthy of reproduction and life because of their supposed behavioral or "racial" characteristics constituted the background against which those classed as superior were enjoined to enjoy their entitlements. Sexually conservative values were preserved for the duration of the Third Reich, especially in the bourgeois middle strata and among church-affiliated individuals and groups of all strata, and Nazi spokespeople on many occasions appropriated and actively disseminated sexually conservative values. But these more conservative values were also intensively combated by the regime.

Even a cursory glance at the early years of the SS newspaper, *Das schwarze Korps*, for instance, testifies amply to the opportunistic attitude of the regime with respect to sexuality. Always carefully contradictory, the journal placed defenses of marriage and critiques of "Jewish" free love side by side with amused diatribes against bourgeois prudery. With brazen self-confidence, Nazi theorizers deliberately challenged the Catholic Church's antisexual attitude in particular, while elaborating in great detail on their own *pro*-sex position. Christian campaigns to turn the populace away from Nazism by documenting the Nazis' incitements to premarital intercourse were a running joke for the paper, which reprinted—and repudiated—the Christian complaints only then, with slight twists emphasizing the grandeur of the Nazis' racial aims, to confirm precisely the point that the party was in synch with the populace, especially its youth, on the matter of the benefits and pleasures of premarital encounters. The overwhelming message was that although romantic activity needed to take racial concerns into account, heterosexuality was fun, and parents or religious authorities who doubted that were simply out of step with the new age.[36]

One of the most peculiar phenomena of the postwar decades, then, is the sea change evident by the 1960s in interpretations of Nazism's sexual politics. For in the literature of the late 1940s and the 1950s, Nazi incitements to heterosexual activity outside of marriage were well remembered, and one is hard pressed to find anyone articulating the notion (which from the 1960s to the early twenty-first century has come to seem like a largely uncontested truth) that the Third Reich represented some sort of sexually reactionary backlash against the experimentation and openness of the Weimar years. On the contrary, the most diverse observers in the early post-1945 period expressly remarked on what they saw as a steady liberalization of heterosexual sexual mores in the first half of the twentieth century or even articulated directly the view that it was the Nazis who had spurred this liberalization. (This too constitutes a disavowal of the ways Nazi sexual incitements were imbricated with racism and genocide; nonetheless, the point stands that no one represented Nazis as particularly uptight.) Furthermore, liberal attitudes about premarital heterosexual activity continued for seven or eight years into the postwar period as well; the shift in mores that thus requires explanation is the move toward greater sexual conservatism that took place in the mid-1950s.[37]

Sociologist Ludwig von Friedeburg, for instance, in his 1953 analysis of a survey conducted in 1949 (which found fully 71 percent of West Germans questioned approved of premarital sex while only 16 percent disapproved), saw these results as confirmation that sexual mores had gradually loosened in the first half of the twentieth century.[38] Similarly, in 1950, the jurist Karl Siegfried Bader stressed the consistent trajectory toward sexual liberalization, emphasizing that the countryside had become just as liberal as the big cities, and that "the morals code of the bourgeois era is now strongly defended by an ever smaller residual group ... the old strict order has acquired the taint of the obsolete, the ridiculous." He also stressed that "the transformations of the sexual order were primarily caused by the [increasing] recognition of the woman's entitlement to the acknowledgment of *her* needs. What distinguishes today's sexual order from that of the beginning of the century is the greater assertion of female sexual rights."[39] It was not just that women were claiming their share of sexual pleasure; men no longer valued female virginity as much as they once had. In 1950, for instance, the leading sexologist Hans Giese remarked on "the ever increasing disappearance in the last two or three decades of the significance of female virginity in the erotic imagination of male consciousness."[40]

In the later 1940s and early 1950s, Catholic commentators in particular frequently reminded their readers and listeners of what they saw as a pervasive Nazi incitement to sexual activity. Postwar Catholics criticized the Nazi regime for having encouraged unmarried women into "libertinage" and raged against popular denigration of virginity as just so much "hackneyed Goebbels-claptrap."[41] The Catholic physician Anton Hofmann, in his sex advice book of 1951, criticized the way "NS-schools and the like" had forced "premature sexual contact" on young people under the guise of "'natural-free experiencing of the erotic event."[42] And the Catholic theologian Franz Arnold lamented what he saw as the Nazi-fostered stereotype that the churches were hostile to desire and worried that this "widely held notion"—that Christianity constituted "a negation of nature … the defamation of eros and sex"—"had survived the downfall of the Third Reich and its blood-mythos."[43]

In secular quarters there was also open acknowledgment that the Nazi leadership had not exactly been antisex. The semipornographic advice magazine *Liebe und Ehe* in 1951 noted as an uncontroversial fact that the Nazi state was "morally degenerate" and had "specifically in the realm of family life championed principles that were utterly at variance with the custom and law of the centuries-old Western Christian culture."[44] In the much-discussed memoirs of Himmler's personal doctor, Felix Kersten, published in 1952, Hitler and Himmler were hardly the inhibited "sex critics" that they would come to be depicted as in the 1960s and 1970s; rather, both men were portrayed as enthusiastic advocates of extramarital and bigamous heterosexuality.[45] And in his memoir published in 1958, the successful Nazi-era film director Arthur Maria Rabenalt emphasized that encouraging reproduction was not the Nazis' only aim: "The National Socialist will to eroticism, the matter-of-fact embrace of sex manifested itself far beyond these functionalist necessities, in a very free-spirited, generous, unbourgeois way." As long as sexual representations and practices stayed within the official racial guidelines, "the erotic" faced "no limit." Rabenalt added that "marriage was encouraged and propagated as the cell of state formation, but it was anything but sacrosanct." Official morality was "anything but prudish." Adultery and free love—including promiscuity among youth—were openly tolerated. Repeatedly contrasting Nazi attitudes to the (in his view) far more puritanical Stalinist ones, Rabenalt characterized the Nazis as vigorous defenders of the "all-powerful sexual drive."[46]

Meanwhile, although the 68ers could not have known this, it is noteworthy that Frankfurt School theorists too were well aware of Nazi attitudes. As has recently become clear, for example, due to the publication of Herbert Marcuse's war-era writings (from the time he worked for the American Office of Strategic Services), Marcuse's sense in the 1940s was that Nazi culture rested not on sexual repression but rather precisely on the abolition of taboos. In Marcuse's view, the Nazis encouraged sexual release and license and worked to link that release and license to racism.[47] And it is similarly relevant to note that when historian Martin Jay interviewed Erich Fromm in New York in 1968, Fromm gave the Third Reich as an example of a society that combined political unfreedom with sexual freedom.[48] Moreover, in an essay "On the Problem of the Family," which was available to 68ers but which they did not cite, Theodor Adorno in 1955 made the case that Nazism was in fact not (despite the popularity of this view in the US) the result of patriarchal German family structures, but rather, if anything, of the breakdown of such structures. And he went on to make remarks which, although elusive and iconoclastic in some ways, nonetheless provide insight into the confusing continuities between the Weimar and Nazi eras in sexual terms, despite the obviously stark political rupture of 1933. Adorno elaborated that "precisely in Germany taboos concerning such matters as virginity, legalization of cohabitation, monogamy were presumably shaken far more thoroughly after 1918 than in the Catholic-Romanist and the Puritanism- and Irish Jansenism-saturated Anglo-Saxon countries, perhaps"—he speculated with a flourish—"because in Germany the memory of an archaic promiscuity survived more stubbornly than in the through-and-through bourgeois Western world."[49]

Misunderstanding and Invented Tradition

How, we might ask, did the 68ers get so misled? Because the parents were sexually conservative in the 1950s, the 68ers assumed they had been sexually conservative in the 1930s and 1940s as well.[50] But the point is that the repressiveness of the 1950s appears not to have been inherited tradition, but rather a new invention. Indeed, it is notable that when a major survey on sexual attitudes was conducted again, in 1963, the views expressed had become considerably more conservative than they had been in 1949.[51] By the mid-1960s, when the sexual revolution began, young people had no idea that there were any pro-sex elements within Nazism, or that also the early post–World War II years had been considered an era of "erotic freedom."[52] When Oswalt Kolle, the most famous sex reformer of the 1960s, expressed the opinion in 1969 that the "broad mass" of people had "for centuries been kept from the most basic factual information," no one challenged him.[53]

What was the parents' generation's investment in fostering what appears to be a significant misunderstanding between the generations about Nazism and sex? An anecdote that former 68er Michael Schneider told in the 1980s usefully captures some of this misunderstanding. Schneider recounted: "One day an acquaintance of mine, who had suffered profoundly because of the bigotry in his Catholic home and who had grown up with many sexual taboos, discovered in his parents' attic a dust-covered photo album." One picture showed the acquaintance's—purportedly apolitical—father dressed in an SS uniform. And another "showed his father and mother sunbathing on an 'FKK' beach [i.e., a nude beach] …, a beach decorated with brown Nazi banners."[54] Few things could have been as shocking and incomprehensible to the 68er mentality than this evidence of Nazism and ordinary sensual pleasure as fully compatible; few things, obviously, in this sexually strict postwar home, had been so carefully kept from the children. Not all pleasure is about sexual pleasure, of course; the inability to acknowledge to one's children that there had been good times during the Third Reich was a broader phenomenon. The majority of those who had been adults during the Third Reich worked on many fronts to present themselves to the world and to their children as victims of Nazism, rather than as beneficiaries, bystanders, and/or participants. But to stress the broader miscommunication between the generations about all kinds of pleasures is to miss the intensity—and hence also the significance—of the 1950s elaboration of sex-hostile attitudes. What a close reading of the sex advice literature of the immediate postwar years—from Christian marriage manuals to semitrashy journals to mainstream magazines and newspapers—makes clear is that the redomestication of sex in the course of the 1950s was bound up with a complex reaction *against* Nazism—and against its defeat.[55]

The greater explicitness in sexual discourse and liberality in behavior in Germany in the "roaring twenties" in comparison with, say, Britain, is not the only peculiarity of German sexual history.[56] The fact of the fascist past and the Holocaust made the intergenerational conflict of the 1960s more intense in West Germany than elsewhere in the Western world. In 1950s West Germany, a sexually conservative stance got aggressively and insistently represented as the essence of proper morality, even as the Nazi past was still palpably present (with perpetrator trials resoundingly unpopular and former Nazi Party members pursuing successful postwar careers).[57] All Western countries had sexually conservative 1950s, but in no country but West Germany could such a narrow focus on sexual morality to the exclusion of other concerns come to seem so profoundly hypocritical. This displacement of the discourse of morality from murder to sex was clear to the 68ers. What they were not, could not have been, aware of, was how very recent the shift to sexual conservatism had been.

Notes

1. Reimut Reiche, "Sexuelle Revolution—Erinnerung an einen Mythos," in *Die Früchte der Revolte: Über die Veränderung der politischen Kultur durch die Studentenbewegung*, ed. Lothar Baier et al. (Berlin, 1988), 58.

2. Gunter Schmidt, *Sexuelle Verhältnisse: Über das Verschwinden der Sexualmoral* (Reinbek, 1998), 8. Or as Schmidt et al. put it in another essay: "Students of both sexes proved to be the *avant garde* of sexual changes in the sixties and seventies." Gunter Schmidt et al., "Changes in Students' Sexual Behaviour: 1966–1981–1996," *Scandinavian Journal of Sexology* 1, no. 3 (1998): 158.

3. Klaus Theweleit, *Ghosts: Drei leicht inkorrekte Vorträge* (Frankfurt am Main, 1998), 129. Theweleit suggests that the spread of the sexual revolution to all social strata came in the wake of the student rebellions, but the evidence from the era indicates that the changes in popular sexual attitudes and behavior were already well underway *before* the student movement even emerged as a social force. See, for example, the cover story on "Sex in Deutschland" in *Der Spiegel*, 2 May 1966, 50–69.

4. For a more detailed analysis of the *Kinderladen* movement, see Dagmar Herzog, "Antifaschistische Körper: Studentenbewegung, sexuelle Revolution und antiautoritäre Kindererziehung," in *Nachkrieg in Deutschland*, ed. Klaus Naumann (Hamburg, 2001), 521–51.

5. *Berliner Kinderläden: Antiautoritäre Erziehung und sozialistischer Kampf* (Cologne, 1970), 108–9.

6. On these matters more generally, see Peter Schneider, "'Nicht der Egoismus verfälscht das politische Engagement, sondern der Versuch, ihn zu verheimlichen,'" *Frankfurter Rundschau*, 25 June 1977, iii.

7. Sabine Weissler, "Sexy Sixties," in *CheSchahShit: Die sechziger Jahre zwischen Cocktail und Molotov*, ed. Eckhard Siepmann et al. (Berlin, 1984), 99.

8. Schneider, "'Nicht der Egoismus.'" Note also his remark that in 1968, "the personal and political needs, that later were split into mutually hostile camps, were not separated from each other, and therein lay the power of this eruption."

9. Götz Eisenberg, "Auf der Suche nach Identität," *Frankfurter Hefte* 34, no. 4 (1979): 88.

10. Klaus Eder, "Edgar Reitz im Gespräch," in Eder, *Die Zweite Heimat: Chronik einer Jugend von Edgar Reitz* (Cologne, 1993), 21.

11. Klaus Theweleit, … *ein Aspirin von der Grösse der Sonne* (Freiburg, 1990), 49. Note also Theweleit's observation in 1998: The interest in the political was manifest among many young people as an interest in the sexual. The bodies of young people in the early 1960s were sexually charged in a wholly unusual way. Theweleit, *Ghosts*, 106–7.

12. See Ingrid Gilcher-Holtey, "Kritische Theorie und Neue Linke," in *1968—Vom Ereignis zum Gegenstand der Geschichtswissenschaft*, ed. Ingrid Gilcher-Holtey (Göttingen, 1998); and Esther Leslie, "Introduction to Adorno/Marcuse Correspondence on the German Student Movement," in *New Left Review* 233 (1999): 118–23; as well as the works of Sabine von Dirke, Klaus Milich, and Wolfgang Kraushaar. On Habermas's initial support for the students but then concern about the possibility of "left fascism" (a term he coined in June 1967), see Ingrid Gilcher-Holtey, "Krach in der Familie: Die Proteste von 1967/68 lösten Streit unter ihren eigenen Vordenkern aus," *Die Zeit*, 20 June 1997, 38. On Adorno's explicit comparison between his own students' behavior and the Nazis, see his 1969 letters to Marcuse republished in the *New Left Review* 233 (1999): 128 and 131–32.

13. See Sabine von Dirke, *"All Power to the Imagination!" The West German Counterculture from the Student Movement to the Greens* (Lincoln, 1997).

14. For example, see Max Horkheimer, "Theoretische Entwürfe über Autorität und Familie: Allgemeiner Teil," in Horkheimer, *Studien über Autorität und Familie* (Paris, 1936); and Max Horkheimer, "Authoritarianism and the Family," in *The Family: Its Function and Destiny*, ed. Ruth Nanda Anshen (New York, 1949; rev. ed. 1959).

15. Adorno et al. were concerned to show that while it did appear that racially prejudiced and "potentially fascistic" personalities tended also to manifest a "moralistic rejection of instinctual tendencies," and that "it seems likely that this moral condemnation serves the purpose of externalization of, and defense against, temptation toward immoral and unconventional behavior," "crude promiscuity" was also one of the frequent characteristics of prejudiced individuals. See Theodor Adorno et al., *The Authoritarian Personality* (New York, 1950), 1, 393, 395, 420.

16. See *Berliner Kinderläden*, 13–14 and 90–91.

17. See Hille Jan Breiteneicher et al., *Kinderläden: Revolution der Erziehung oder Erziehung zur Revolution?* (Reinbek, 1971), 13, 16–17.

18. Wilhelm Reich, *Die Funktion des Orgasmus: Sexualökonomische Grundprobleme der biologischen Energie* (1st ed., 1927; repr. Cologne, 1969), 139.

19. Gunter Schmidt, "Weshalb Sex alle (Un)schuld verloren hat," *taz-magazin*, 24–25 April 1999, v. On Reich's extraordinary impact, see also Reiche, "Sexuelle Revolution," 55–57; and Eckhard Siepmann, "Genital versus Prägenital: Die Grossväter der sexuellen Revolution," in Eckhard Siepmann et al., *CheSchahShit*, 101.

20. See Peter Mosler, *Was wir wollten, was wir wurden: Studentenrevolte—zehn Jahre danach* (Reinbek, 1977), 159.

21. Wolfgang Fritz Haug, "Vorbemerkung," *Das Argument* 32 (1965): 30–31.

22. Friedhelm Neidhardt, *Die Familie in Deutschland* (Opladen, 1966), 71.

23. Arno Plack, *Die Gesellschaft und das Böse: Eine Kritik der herrschenden Moral* (Munich, 1967), 309.

24. Hannes Schwenger, *Antisexuelle Propaganda: Sexualpolitik in der Kirche* (Reinbek, 1969), 34–36. Along related lines, in his caustic evaluation of the Christian Democratic family politics of the Federal Republic, Dietrich Haensch in 1969—drawing extensively on Reich—asserted not only that "genital weakness" was the source of both fascism and brutality in wartime, but also that Hitler had only needed to intensify already existing bourgeois practices, and that these, in turn, had outlived Hitler. "The tendency to sadism is maintained by diverting the libidinal energies away from the sexual drive and towards the drive for destruction and aggression." And: "With the end of fascism the extreme intensification of sexual repression ended, but not the sexual repression itself." Dietrich Haensch, *Repressive Familienpolitik: Sexualunterdrückung als Mittel der Politik* (Reinbek, 1969), 66–67.

25. Theodor Bovet, *Von Mann zu Mann: Eine Einführung ins Reifealter für junge Männer* (Tübingen, 1954), 23; Eduard Spranger, *Psychologie des Jugendalters* (23 editions with over 100,000 copies sold by 1970), quoted in Ernst Busche, "Sexualpädagogik als Disziplinierungsmittel: Eine negative Dokumentation über Richtlinien, Methodik und Lehrerverhalten," *Das Argument* 56 (1970): 28. It is indicative of the profundity of activists' rage not only that *Das Argument*, a serious Marxist journal, in 1970 devoted an entire essay to the antimasturbation tendency of most sex education materials, but that the author could not resist taking a direct slap at Spranger: "Spranger too must have been an assiduous onanist."

26. *Für die Befreiung der kindlichen Sexualität! Kampf den falschen Erziehern!* ed. Zentralrat der sozialistischen Kinderläden West-Berlins (Berlin, 1969), 88; "Kinderschule Frankfurt, Eschersheimer Landstrasse," in *Erziehung zum Ungehorsam*, ed. Gerhard Bott (Frankfurt am Main, 1970), 55–56.

27. "Kinderschule Frankfurt," in Bott, *Erziehung zum Ungehorsam*, 51, 54.

28. "Kinderladen Stuttgart: Bericht über einen Prozess," in ibid., 21.

29. *Für die Befreiung*, 35.

30. *Kinder im Kollektiv*, ed. Zentralrat der sozialistischen Kinderläden West-Berlins (Berlin, 1969), 79.

31. Jim Kruse, quoted in Heiko Gebhart, "Kleine Linke mit grossen Rechten: Berliner APO-Mitglieder experimentieren mit ihren Kindern," *Stern*, 22 February 1969.

32. See Breiteneicher et al., *Kinderläden: Revolution*, 9–16.

33. An important exception is the work of Wilfried Mausbach. See, for example, Wilfried Mausbach, "Student Opposition and the Vietnam War in West Germany," in *Between Marx and Coca-Cola: Youth Cultures in Changing European Societies, 1960–1980*, ed. Axel Schildt and Detlef Siegfried (New York, 2005).

34. See Dagmar Herzog, "'Pleasure, Sex, and Politics Belong Together': Post-Holocaust Memory and the Sexual Revolution in West Germany," *Critical Inquiry* 24 (1998): 393–444.

35. For a fuller discussion, see Dagmar Herzog, "Hubris and Hypocrisy, Incitement and Disavowal: Sexuality and German Fascism," *Journal of the History of Sexuality* 11, no. 1–2 (2002): 3–21.

36. See, for example, "Offene Antwort auf eine katholische Kritik," *Das schwarze Korps*, 17 April 1935, 1–2; "Ist das Nacktkultur? Herr Stapel entrüstet sich!" *Das schwarze Korps*, 24 April 1935, 12; "'… Unzucht in der Soldatenzeit,'" *Das schwarze Korps*, 5 March 1936, 6; "Das uneheliche Kind," *Das schwarze Korps*, 9 April 1936, 6; "Anstössig?" *Das schwarze Korps*, 16 April 1936, 13.

37. See Dagmar Herzog, "Desperately Seeking Normality: Sex and Marriage in the Wake of War," in *Life after Death: Approaches to a Cultural and Social History of Europe during the 1940s and 1950s*, ed. Richard Bessel and Dirk Schumann (Cambridge, 2002), 161–92.

38. See Ludwig von Friedeburg, *Umfrage in der Intimsphäre* (Stuttgart, 1953), 23–24. Note as well that the numbers endorsing—and admitting having engaged in—premarital sex in West Germany at this time, especially among the women, are considerably higher than the comparable figures from England or the US. See L. R. England, "Little Kinsey: An Outline of Sex Attitudes

in Britain," *Public Opinion Quarterly* 13, no. 4 (1949): 587–600. For a concise summary of Kinsey's findings for the US, see John D'Emilio and Estelle B. Freedman, *Intimate Matters: A History of Sexuality in America* (New York, 1988), 286.

39. Karl Siegfried Bader, "Die Veränderung der Sexualordnung und die Konstanz der Sittlichkeitsdelikte," *Zeitschrift für Sexualforschung* 1, no. 3–4 (1950): 217.

40. Hans Giese, review of an essay by Max Marcuse ("Zur Psychologie der Eifersucht und der Psychopathologie ihres Fehlens," *Psyche* 3 [1950]), in *Zeitschrift für Sexualforschung* 1 (1950): 307.

41. Maria Jochum, "Frauenfrage 1946," *Frankfurter Hefte* 1 (1946): 25; Johannes Leppich, "Thema 1," in *Pater Leppich Spricht*, ed. Günther Mees and Günter Graf (Düsseldorf, 1952), 44.

42. Anton Christian Hofmann, *Die Natürlichkeit der christlichen Ehe* (Munich, 1951), 5, 38–39.

43. Franz Arnold, "Sinnlichkeit und Sexualität im Lichte von Theologie und Seelsorge," *Über das Wesen der Sexualität* (Stuttgart: 1952), 1.

44. H. Meissner, "Dreiecksehe sanktioniert," *Liebe und Ehe* 3 (1951): 413.

45. Felix Kersten, *The Kersten Memoirs, 1940–1945* (New York, 1957; German orig. 1952). Contrast the later images of "sex critic Hitler" in "Die gefallene Natur," *Der Spiegel*, 2 May 1966, 58, and of the sexually shy and uptight Himmler in Dieter Duhm, *Angst im Kapitalismus* (Lampertheim, 1972), 102.

46. Arthur Maria Rabenalt, *Film im Zwielicht* (Munich, 1958), 26–29.

47. See *Technology, War and Fascism: Collected Papers of Herbert Marcuse*, vol. 1, ed. Douglas Kellner (London, 1998). As Jeffrey Herf has recently summarized it in a review of these writings, "These are provocative ideas that deserve to be pursued further. Perhaps because the connection between Nazism and sexual repression seems so intuitively obvious, historians of German society and culture under the Nazis … have not yet taken up these bold notions proposed by Marcuse." Jeffrey Herf, "One-Dimensional Man," *The New Republic*, 1 February 1999, 39.

48. See Martin Jay, *The Dialectical Imagination: A History of the Frankfurt School and the Institute of Social Research 1923–1950* (Boston, 1973), 93, 318.

49. Theodor W. Adorno, "Zum Problem der Familie," *Gesammelte Schriften* 20, no. 1 (Frankfurt am Main, 1986), 305–6.

50. For a particularly direct articulation of this widely held view, see Ulrike Heider, "Freie Liebe und Liebesreligion: Zum Sexualitätsbegriff der 60er und 80er Jahre," in *Sadomasochisten, Keusche, Romantiker: Vom Mythos neuer Sinnlichkeit*, ed. Ulrike Heider (Reinbek, 1986), 93.

51. See "Erst die Liebe, dann die Moral? Alles über die Deutschen (15)," *Stern* 48 (1963): 43–52; and Elisabeth Noelle and Erich Peter Neumann, eds., *Jahrbuch der öffentlichen Meinung 1958–1964* (Allensbach, 1965), 589–90.

52. Walter Dittmann, "Die Krise der Ehe," *Nordwestdeutsche Hefte* 2, no. 10 (1947): 34.

53. Oswalt Kolle quoted in Knorr, "Schwierigkeiten bei der Sexualaufklärung," *Pardon* 8, no. 12 (1969): 65.

54. Michael Schneider, "Fathers and Sons, Retrospectively: The Damaged Relationship between Two Generations," *New German Critique* 31 (1984): 9–10.

55. For the full argument, see Herzog, "Desperately Seeking Normality."

56. To take just one example, compare the "unspeakability" of female pleasure in 1920s Britain with the prolix discussion of techniques for alleviating female frigidity in 1920s Germany. See Susan Pedersen, "National Bodies, Unspeakable Acts: The Sexual Politics of Colonial Policy-Making," *Journal of Modern History* 63 (1991): 647–80; Sally Alexander, "The Mysteries and Secrets of Women's Bodies: Sexual Knowledge in the First Half of the Twentieth Century," in *Modern Times: Reflections on a Century of English Modernity*, ed. Mica Nava and Alan O'Shea (London, 1996), 161–76; and Atina Grossman, "The New Woman and the Rationalization of Sexuality in Weimar Germany," in *Powers of Desire: The Politics of Sexuality*, ed. Ann Snitow et al. (New York, 1983), 153–71.

57. On this point, see also Martin Dannecker, "Die verspätete Empirie," *Zeitschrift für Sexualforschung* 14, no. 2 (2001): 173–74.

Chapter 11

THE GERMAN NEW LEFT AND
NATIONAL SOCIALISM

Michael Schmidtke

❧

The generation that came of age in West Germany in the 1960s "was probably in fact the first in Germany that did not shy away from demanding explanations face to face—from their parents, from adults in general, within the family, [and] while watching television," Jürgen Habermas observed in 1990. Student protest in West Germany, he went on to suggest, was an attempt to take account of "the collective avoidance of German responsibility [for] National Socialism and its horrors."[1] The student protesters' engagement with the Nazi past, political scientist Ekkehart Krippendorff has argued, should be seen as an attempt—possibly a successful one—to give democratic legitimacy to the Federal Republic, a product of military defeat and Allied occupation.[2] Indeed, for political scientist Claus Leggewie, 1968 marked the "antifascist reestablishment of the Federal Republic of Germany" after the missed opportunity of 1945.[3]

Some historians, by contrast, emphasize that there had already been numerous efforts to deal critically with the Nazi past before 1968. The student movement, according to one assessment, merely intensified this engagement with the past, in part employing "problematic methods" in the process.[4] Some scholars doubt that concern with the Holocaust had any part in shaping the protest movement of the late 1960s. The leaders of this movement have been accused of using the Holocaust to delegitimize the existing political system.[5] The argument that student movement was "a response to the unwillingness of the fathers' generation to face its National Socialist past," Hermann Lübbe contends, stands as one of the "myths" of the 68er generation.[6]

To determine whether—or how—the student New Left and its avant-garde, the Sozialistischer Deutscher Studentenbund (SDS), contributed toward coming to terms with Germany's Nazi past, this essay will consider three topics: the debate over the concept of fascism; the New Left critiques of alleged fascist tendencies in West German society and culture, which encompassed themes as diverse as the emergency-law, the Springer Press, and the war in Vietnam; and political education.

The Transformation of the Concept of Fascism

The New Left's theoretical confrontation with National Socialism took place first and foremost in the pages of the magazine *Das Argument*. Founded in 1959, *Das Argument* was an intellectual forum for old leftists interested in updating Marxist theory and social analysis.[7] An important spur to its reanalysis of Nazism was the publication of Ernst Nolte's *Der Faschismus in seiner Epoche* in 1963.[8] Nolte described fascism as a specific response by several European states to the challenges posed by communism. In the view of the reviewers whom *Das Argument* had asked to comment on the book, Nolte's perspective was too narrow because it focused primarily on the ideological roots of fascism and gave little attention to the economic factors that gave rise to it.[9] The reviewers likewise criticized advocates of so-called totalitarianism theory, which regarded both fascism and communism as similar forms of totalitarian power and as similarly threatening to parliamentary democracy.[10] They were accused of interpreting National Socialism as only a deviation from the "good model of civil democracy" and of not examining the structural connections between "bourgeois" democracy and fascist dictatorship. Totalitarianism theory, *Das Argument*'s reviewers contended, served to obscure bourgeois democracy's jump to fascism and to defame working class aspirations that were expressed in Bolshevism.[11]

Intellectuals associated with *Das Argument* were also critical of the Marxist-Leninist interpretation of fascism prevalent in the German Democratic Republic (GDR), which attributed the success of fascism primarily to economic factors.[12] They insisted that the social psychology of mass-mobilization also had to be taken into account. In pursuing their analyses of fascism, they discovered two writings that had fallen into oblivion since the 1930s: Walter Benjamin's examination of the war and Wilhelm Reich's investigation of the mass psychology of fascism.[13] Drawing on these texts and the work of the Frankfurt School theorists, the contributors to *Das Argument* sought to develop a new theory of fascism that was based not solely on economic models. They wanted to take social and cultural factors into account as well, but without limiting their analysis to examination of Nazi ideology. Taking a stand against the old Marxist-Leninist left as well as against "bourgeois" theories of totalitarianism, the contributors to *Das Argument* had by the mid-1960s developed a new theory of fascism that was later to play a central role in the outlook of New Left students and their understanding of the Nazi past.[14]

The intellectuals affiliated with *Das Argument* were not alone in trying to encourage a confrontation with fascism at West German universities. In the spring of 1964, the Tübingen student magazine *Notizen* included a call for an inquiry into the role of the universities in the Third Reich. As a result, a group of Tübingen professors offered a series of lectures during the 1964–65 winter semester on "German Intellectual Life and National Socialism" in which they considered the relationship of the various academic disciplines to Nazism.[15] This lecture series was covered extensively by student newspapers as well as by some mainstream papers.[16] Similar lecture programs took place in Munich, Bonn, Heidelberg, Marburg, Frankfurt, and Berlin in the course of 1965.[17]

In the opinion of *Das Argument* editor Wolfgang Fritz Haug, these lecture series did not constitute an adequate effort to deal with the Nazi past on the part of the universities. Haug examined forty-one of the lectures and argued that the professors' understanding of the past hardly differed from that of the average German citizen. The professors, he noted, used many of the same topoi and stereotypes as other West Germans in their explication of the past. According to Haug, some professors even echoed the Nazis' political arguments in their lectures by stressing Hitler's "unquestionable successes." Pointing to this "language-relationship" and the "ideological-structural continuities" between the professors' "impotent antifascism" and fascism itself, Haug concluded that scholarship had lost its independent position vis-à-vis public opinion.[18] "Those who can recognize that fascism signals the unstoppable socioeconomic decline of the bourgeoisie are also capable of appreciating what it means to pursue scholarship in this position of dependency," he wrote.[19] "If it does not want to become irrelevant, scholarship must redefine its position in society."

This provocative thesis prompted ever more groups within academia to examine their own past critically. At the 1966 *Germanistentag*, for example, the assembled specialists in German literature discussed their discipline's recent past and the lack of theoretical and scholarly engagement with it.[20] In general, though, these attempts to come to terms with the past were limited to scholarly disciplines whose members could not easily be accused of cooperation with the National Socialist regime.[21] In the view of the SDS, the hesitant attitude in other disciplines could be explained by the presence of many members who had been active in their fields during the Third Reich.[22] From the time of its founding, the SDS had undertaken a number of actions to point out the continuities in university staffing from the Third Reich to the Federal Republic. The 1959 exhibition "Ungesühnte Nazi-Justiz" caused a sensation by demonstrating continuities in personnel in the judicial system from the Third Reich to the Federal Republic.[23] The SDS also tried to find professors who had exercised unbroken influence since the Third Reich and who seemed to block the way to a scholarly confrontation with fascism.[24] In the early 1960s, the students made revelations about professors' pasts primarily in the press; from 1967 on, they also attempted direct confrontations in the lecture hall.[25] In Hamburg, for example, the SDS enacted "Go-ins" to disrupt lectures and call for the early retirement of "guilty" professors. The goal of the student troublemakers, in theory, was not to disrupt the learning process, but rather to expose "the professor who hinders the mediation of the correct consciousness."[26]

The SDS's actions were initially intended to prepare the way for scholarly and theoretical engagement with the Nazi past. But that would be possible, the SDS believed, only if the old professors were sent off. After the media reported on the first face-to-face confrontation during a lecture hall "Go-in" in November 1967, direct confrontations became more a symbolic struggle and an end in themselves. The confrontations also became increasingly personalized, in keeping with media logic. The most publicized example of this development was the series of actions directed against President Heinrich Lübke during an "anti-Lübke week" in February 1968. The SDS accused the president of having been involved in planning the construction of the Peenemünde concentration camp. The students' actions developed a dynamic of their own, and their original objective—to prepare the way for a scholarly and theoretical consideration of the Nazi past—was lost along the way.

The direct actions were in some cases launched against not only individuals with Nazi pasts but also against individuals who, although free of direct connections to Nazism, were accused of "fascist" behavior. The SDS accused Mayor Klaus Schütz of West Berlin, for example, of having used fascist methods when police shot a student demonstrator on 2 June 1967. To deliver this reproach, SDS demonstrators greeted the mayor at public functions with posters bearing messages such as "Today Pogrom and Propaganda, Tomorrow the Final Solution, Mr. Schütz." "Dachau Greets Hitler's Successors," SDS posters declared when Schütz participated in the dedication of a new memorial at the Dachau concentration camp.[27] The former camp prisoners and foreign guests on hand for the event did not understand the posters and responded with outrage. The result was a confrontation between the onetime anti-Nazis and the self-styled student antifascists.

The method of a coming to terms with the past through action increasingly developed a dynamic of its own. Even individuals who had been among the victims of National Socialism became SDS targets. After Hans Joachim Schoeps, a religion scholar of Jewish background who had to emigrate in 1938, described the radical students in the newspaper *Die Welt* as an "active terror minority" that constituted a threat to the young Federal Republic, the SDS retorted by calling Schoeps a representative of "fascist thought." The two sides met at a panel discussion in Nuremberg and traded insults, each accusing the other of fascist thought and methods.[28]

The student movement's actions prompted accusations of "left fascism." "We need neither a brown nor a red SA," the tabloid *Bild-Zeitung* wrote on 3 June 1967, following a demonstration in West Berlin that had turned violent.[29] The most prominent figure to level the reproach was, however, Jürgen Habermas.[30] In October 1967, an SDS group disrupted a meeting of the literary group Gruppe 47 and burned copies of the *Bild-Zeitung* in an effort to gain support for its protest against the paper's publisher, the Springer-Verlag. Many writers, likening the action to the Nazis' book burnings, accused the students of fascist methods.[31] By 1968, the charge of left fascism was a firmly established motif in criticism of the student movement and the SDS—and it was not only conservative critics who employed it.[32]

Some student groups responded ironically. In July 1967, for example, Kommune 1 unfurled a poster declaring "Berlin's Left Fascists Greet Teddy the Classicist" as Theodore Adorno lectured on Goethe's *Iphigenie auf Tauris* in Berlin.[33] The SDS itself argued that the accusation of left fascism created a pogrom-like atmosphere directed against critical minorities. It was eventually to liken its position to that of the German Jews in the 1930s. Rudi Dutschke tried to explain this idea in 1968; drawing on Adorno's concept of the authoritarian character, he argued that the "mental basis of fascism" had not been overcome by the defeat of the Third Reich but rather had been transmuted into anticommunism.[34] From this perspective, anticommunism had thus replaced anti-Semitism. Because authoritarian character structures still existed, the students viewed themselves as the Jews' functional equivalent, as the "Jews" of anticommunism and "long-haired substitute Jews."[35]

Individual elements of the theoretical analysis of fascism that had appeared in the pages of *Das Argument* were selectively adopted and used as weapons in public debates. Subject at once to inflationary use and simplification, the concept of fascism was transformed into a "collective symbol" that various actors—students, intellectuals, the press—competed to use. The concept of fascism no longer served primarily to explain a historical phenomenon, and the more widely the concept was used, the more common it became for antagonists to see fascist tendencies in one another's behavior.[36] A good example of this endless conflict was the notion of "fascist" sexual behavior, whatever that accusation was supposed to mean.[37]

Similar mechanisms in the diffusion of ideas could be observed in the United States as well. With the Vietnam War, the image of the United States as protector of the free world came under question.[38] Some intellectuals began to criticize American actions in Vietnam as quasi-fascist. This line of criticism had its intellectual roots in the studies that members of the Frankfurt School had undertaken during the years of exile in the US. It had become clear to them then that the Americans were not quite free of "authoritarian character structures."[39] Of the proponents of this analysis, Herbert Marcuse had the greatest influence on the American student movement. Also influential was the German intellectual Reinhard Lettau, who, like Marcuse, held a chair at the University of California, San Diego, and who had been in close contact with the SDS in Berlin. In 1968, Lettau published a study of American newspapers in which he called attention to the linguistic mechanisms of what he called "daily fascism."[40]

Given this background, it is not surprising to find elements of the German New Left's fascism analysis adopted by the American student movement. Students referred to dormitory officials as *Gauleiter*,[41] for example, and police were often greeted with cries of "Sieg Heil" at student demonstrations.[42] Another example attesting to the conspicuous presence of the German past in the US was the substitution of *Amerika* for "America," which became increasingly common in radical polemics during 1968: "This Germanic spelling was intended to convey the similarity between contemporary America and Nazi Germany."[43] These and similar allusions to "Hitler-Germany" were frequently used by the militant Weathermen, who justified their violent resistance with the slogan "We refuse to be good Germans."[44] In the US, as in the Federal Republic, the student movement was subject to accusations of left fascism: "Fascism returns to the United States not as a right-wing ideology, but almost as a quasi-leftist ideology,"[45] Irving Louis Horowitz, for example, wrote in a contemporary analysis of the student movement. Many American students did not understand why they were being called "Nazi storm troopers,[46] and, again much as in Germany, a dynamic of reciprocal accusation developed.

The American example suggests that the discursive mechanisms used by the West German student movement in dealing with the Nazi past were not entirely unique. Individual aspects of theories of fascism were taken up selectively in both countries and used as collective symbols. And in both countries students and their critics competed in making use of those symbols. Given the similar patterns of usage in the Federal Republic and the United States, it is open to question to what extent the 1960s debate about fascism and left fascism should be considered as a distinctive aspect of the West German confrontation with the Nazi past.

The Protest against "Political Cleanliness Mania"

Recent historical research has challenged the contention of the SDS that West German universities and society in general had avoided giving serious thought to the Nazi past until the late 1960s.[47] From the late 1950s on, there were in fact many attempts to deal critically with the past in the form of trials of Nazi offenders, television documentaries, plays, and political education initiatives. Thus, the way was open for the student movement when it sought to confront the West Germans with their Nazi past. But trials, documentaries, new text books, and the like were not enough, or at least not yet, for the New Left.

According to prominent New Left intellectual Hans Magnus Enzensberger, political action was needed to demonstrate that the Federal Republic was serious about the process of coming to terms with the past.[48] Enzensberger argued that participation in protest movements, such as the movement for nuclear disarmament, was crucial because only through protest could the Germans overcome their long-internalized authoritarian thinking. All protest movements, in Enzenberger's view, served as a preventative that protected against the return of authoritarian thinking.[49] The events of 2 June 1967, he contended, demonstrated that the police and much of the West German public were still gripped by a "political cleanliness mania" (*politischer Reinheitswahn*); anything that did not fit within the system was declared taboo.[50] Protest thus had a "therapeutic" function. Those who participated in protest overcame authoritarian behavior and contributed to the young republic's progress toward social democracy. Without protest, according to the SDS, political cleanliness mania could lead to the return of an "authoritarian state" as well as to a "new fascism."[51]

Against this background, every political event was taken as an indicator of how far the Federal Republic had moved toward or away from fascism. The Nazi past was taken as the standard of measurement. In the view of the SDS, the shooting of student protestor Benno Ohnesorg on 2 June 1967, was "only one link in a long chain in the process of the erosion of democracy and the return of fascist tendencies in our society."[52] The emergency laws (*Notstandsgesetze*), dubbed "Nazi Laws" (*NS-Gesetze*) by opponents, were likewise considered by the New Left to be evidence of a widespread political outlook that accepted fascism as a "political power system."[53] On 27 May 1968, students protesting the emergency laws affixed a poster with the slogan "No Second 1933" on Munich's *Siegestor* (triumphal arch). The fear of a new fascism also shaped the protest against the Axel Springer publishing house, which students accused of promoting a "pogrom mood" against them. The anti-Springer protest was believed to have "clarified the totalitarian character of the postfascist prefascist Federal Republic, which had become visible in Berlin through open police terror."[54] The Nazi past was thus present in many of the actions and campaigns of the protest movement in 1968. This presence was not simply an instrumentalization of the past to dramatize the current political situation. The students used the concept of a "new fascism" to condemn not only the institutions of the Federal Republic but also a political consciousness that, they maintained, accepted a pogrom-like atmosphere as well as fascism as a power system.

This consciousness, as Enzensberger emphasized again and again, did not exist solely in the Federal Republic; there was fertile soil for a new fascism in other countries as well. "Fascism isn't horrible because the Germans have perpetrated it, but because it is possible everywhere."[55] The student movement described the US military engagement in Vietnam, for example, as fascist, and drew comparisons between the US and the Third Reich on posters containing slogans such as "USA = SA = SS" and "Vietnam is the Auschwitz of America."[56] The SDS even assumed that the US would in the foreseeable future no longer limit its fascist tendencies to the Third World periphery, but expand them to the industrialized West as well.[57]

The Federal Republic had not yet turned into a "fascist power-system," but to many student activists the outlook of many West Germans seemed to offer fertile soil for a new fascism. From the students' perspective, it was clear that addressing the past by marking anniversaries or broadcasting documentaries about the Third Reich was not sufficient to counteract a new fascism. Political action was also needed in the form of protest movements that would overcome political cleanliness mania. Thus, for student leaders, conflict and provocation were not only means for putting their political goals before the public but also for instructing the public in the methods of democratic confrontation.

For many student activists, political action as therapy was not limited to participation in protest movements but also extended into family life. Confrontations with fathers who had actively participated in National Socialism were a central motif in the biographies of student activists. Many young people were spurred to activism by such confrontations, a method that set the West German student movement apart from its counterparts elsewhere.[58] Michael Schneider called this phenomenon the "Hamlet Complex" because the student generation was suddenly confronted by the thought of their fathers in Nazi uniforms.[59] The sixties generation, as Heinz Bude observed, was paralyzed by its fixation on its parents' pasts.[60]

The most prominent example of the archetypical 68er is Bernhard Vesper. His father, Will Vesper, had been a noted poet during the Third Reich. Vesper himself was an early participant in the student movement and was a close friend of Gudrun Ensslin, who later became a RAF terrorist. Vesper's autobiographical novel *Die Reise* (1977) was widely seen as the collective biography of an entire generation. In a review of the novel entitled "The Children of Hitler, Marx, and LSD," Armin Ayren suggested that it made no difference in the end whether Vesper's death was caused by his separation from Gudrun Ensslin or, like Kafka, by his overbearing father, because "Hitler could be considered as the ultimate cause."[61] Ayren's review gave currency to the tag "Hitler's children" that is still used in referring to the student movement.[62]

A look at the biographies of many onetime SDS activists suggests, however, that it is open to question how often young West Germans were spurred to participate in protests by confrontations with fathers. Very few had backgrounds like Vesper's. Indeed, most SDS members came from left-liberal or socialist households.[63] That was true even of the first generation of RAF members. Direct confrontation with "Nazi fathers" was, in short, the exception rather than the rule. As Jörg Schröder, Vesper's publisher, has argued, the phrase "Hitler's children" needs to be reconsidered. "Gudrun Ensslin came from a pietistic household, like Ulrike Meinhof, who had already been indoctrinated in antifascist or socialist fashion. No, the parents of the first-generation RAF [members] were antifascist, anti-imperialist, antiracist. Only their children took them too literally."[64]

It does not come as a surprise that sociological surveys conducted in the late 1960s and early 1970s came to the conclusion that conflict with parents played a crucial role for only a minority of radical students.[65] Generational conflict centered on the Nazi past cannot be considered a central cause of the student movement. The 68ers' battle against the shadows of the past was directed less against their own parents than against the representatives of the young republic, such as Kiesinger and Lübke, who had loyally served the Third Reich. The students not only accused these figures of opportunism but also held them up as representatives of the political outlook that student activism was trying to overcome. "The 'New Left' of 1967 was an answer to the cowardice and corruption of the older generation," Klaus Wagenbach wrote in 1977, adding "this political disinterest and lack of civil courage stare at us from the whole of German history, particularly from the 1930s."[66] Accordingly, the students did not retreat when intellectuals like Adorno broke with the SDS in 1968 but were more strongly motivated than ever to redress the historic lack of civil courage in Germany. They not only confronted the older generation with its Nazi past but also tried to demonstrate their own civil courage through political action.

Thus, the contribution of the New Left to West Germany's efforts to come to terms with the Nazi past lies less in the controversies over the nature of fascism and left fascism than in the political actions intended as expressions of civil courage. In the students' view, civil courage had long been lacking in Germany. The West German generational conflict of the 1960s, accordingly, was less a protest by the young against their own parents than an attempt to overcome the political cleanliness mania that the young saw as a specifically German mental structure.

Education after Auschwitz: *Kinderläden* and Communes

Education provided another area of action for the New Left. They experimented with new methods of teaching and sought to develop a new political pedagogy. In this pursuit, they were strongly influenced by the theoretical and empirical work of the Frankfurt-based Institute for Social Research (Institut für Sozialforschung, IfS), especially the writings of Theodor Adorno. Following Adorno, the New Left intellectuals saw the greatest threat to democracy not in the fascist tendencies of groups like the far-right National Democratic Party (Nationaldemokratische Partei Deutschland, NPD) but in the democratic order's own fascist tendencies. The intellectual and psychological structures of the Federal Republic's citizens, they believed, provided a potential base for a rebirth of fascism because they seemed similar to those that had led to the Third Reich.

The IfS had long focused on the interaction between society and structures of character. In its early years, it had undertaken a series of studies on authority and the family. IfS members exiled in the US during the Nazi era continued this work with the project "Studies in Prejudice," which sought to uncover the causes behind anti-Semitic prejudice in order to develop educational methods to counter it.[67] Interviews were conducted with individuals to determine their potential for authoritarian behavior. Although the research methods employed and conclusions put forward were controversial,[68] this study was an important base for that work on political education that Adorno and Max Horkheimer would later undertake in the Federal Republic.

The new political pedagogy promoted by Adorno was to have a tremendous influence on the student movement. In his the talk "Education after Auschwitz," broadcast by Westdeutscher Rundfunk on 18 April 1966, Adorno explained that "authoritarian character structures" were not identical with the "authority-worshiping German spirit" that Americans had held responsible for National Socialism.[69] Moreover, he went on to argue, a social phenomenon should not be reduced solely to a psychological question. Rather, to prevent a repetition of the past it is essential to recognize the mechanisms that "make people capable of such actions."[70] Among the mechanisms produced by authoritarian character structures Adorno included the acquired willingness of individuals to fit blindly into collectives, even to convert themselves to "material" and thus treat others like an amorphous mass.[71] To overcome this "materialized consciousness" (*verdinglichtes*

Bewusstsein), Adorno considered it essential that people be made conscious of the mechanisms producing these structure as early as possible. According to Adorno it was important to struggle against "folkways, traditions, and rites of initiation of every sort that cause physical pain to people [as] a price to be paid for belonging, for being able to feel as a part of the collective."[72] Adorno thus concluded that a new political pedagogy aimed at making young people aware of the mechanisms of subordination would be an important contribution toward coming to terms with the Nazi past.

The crucial psychological quality of an authoritarian character was its own "self-weakness." Adorno elaborated on this idea in his essay "Was bedeutet: Aufarbeitung der Vergangenheit?" (What Does 'Coming to Terms with the Past' Mean?). Authoritarian characters, he wrote, "have only a weak ego (Ich) and need, as compensation, to identify with and take cover in large collectives."[73] The Nazis had systematically instrumentalized this "self-weakness" and fulfilled the collective power fantasies of those who were powerless as individuals. For this reason, coming to terms with the past meant to "turn on the subject," i.e., to reinforce the self.[74]

Adorno's argument guided the students' experiments in counter-institutions such as communes and alternative kindergartens, the so-called *Kinderläden* (literally, child shops; many were set up in empty storefronts, hence the name). The "Studies in Prejudice" were known within the SDS since the early 1960s.[75] In one of his contributions to the widely read book *Rebellion der Studenten* (1968), Rudi Dutschke popularized Adorno's profile of the authoritarian character. The main attributes of the authoritarian character were identified as conventionalism in matters such as morality; subservience to idealized authority; animosity toward those who contravene conventional values; rejection of more subjective, imaginative, and compassionate individuals; superstition and reliance on stereotypes; and interest in the power aspects of interpersonal relations.[76] It was necessary to change these character traits, Dutschke argued, through "antiauthoritarian" education.[77] This idea can be seen as an attempt at the "practical realization of the insights of critical social theory as formulated by the Institute for Social Research" with the goal of overcoming Germany's Nazi past.[78] "Present day fascism is no longer manifest in a party or a person," Dutschke wrote, rather "it is part of the everyday socialization of the human being to the authoritarian personality; it lies in education."[79]

The first "antiauthoritarian" *Kinderladen* was established in the fall of 1967 in Frankfurt. "It was the attempt to overcome something that was internalized over generations," cofounder Monika Seifert was to later recall.[80] While working at the IfS, she had founded the study group "Authority and Family." It took up discussion of the Institute's work on the subject from the 1930s as well as the work of Wilhelm Reich and Erich Fromm. Some of these texts first became known in the Federal Republic through English translations brought along by visiting American students. Since most of these works were theoretical, Seifert and her colleagues had to develop ways to put theory into practice. The guiding pedagogic maxim was that children should not internalize rules established by authorities. Instead, in order that their self-confidence be reinforced, they should be guided by their own experience. If it was cold outdoors, for example, the children were not simply told to wear scarves; rather, it was up to them to follow Seifert's example on their own.[81]

The *Kinderläden* were an important part of the New Left's attempt to create counter-institutions to traditional ones. They also addressed a pressing need: in 1965, West German kindergartens had places for only about 30 percent of kindergarten-aged children.[82] On 26 January 1968, two hundred mothers and fathers close to the Berlin SDS gathered at the Free University of Berlin to launch an initiative that would link child education and political commitment.[83] They met again the following month during a congress on the Vietnam War and institutionalized their meetings with the establishment of the Republican Club, which would meet every Wednesday. These initiatives led to the founding of the Aktionsrat zur Befreiung der Frau (Action Council for Women's Liberation), which backed the systematic establishment of *Kinderläden*.[84]

The methods of antiauthoritarian education developed in Berlin and Frankfurt were taken up by the student movement. In 1968, "critical universities" (*kritische Universitäten*) offered courses on antiauthoritarian education.[85] Some communes also participated in the pedagogic experiments.[86] By October 1968, a dozen *Kinderläden* had been established in West Berlin, and *Kinderläden* opened in Hamburg, Bremen, Darmstadt, Cologne, Munich, Marburg, and Freiburg in the course of the following year.[87] As in Berlin, many were supported by local Republican Clubs.[88]

The *Kinderläden* model was presented to a mass audience in December 1969 when the broadcaster ARD aired the documentary *Education for Disobedience*. Featuring footage of children engaged in activities such as jumping on an old piano, the program was a sensation and provoked vehement controversy. In the days following the broadcast, ARD received more than two hundred telephone calls and seven hundred letters. The letters clearly showed that the nation was split: what some saw as evidence of the "downfall of Western civilization" was seen by others as an experiment worthy of imitation.[89] Eventually, the *Kinderladen* concept was taken up by schools of education and given scholarly consideration.[90]

Like the *Kinderläden*, communes were experiments in trying to overcome authoritarian character structures. A meeting of members of the countercultural group Subversive Aktion and of the Berlin SDS in June 1966 marked the starting point of the commune movement in the Federal Republic.[91] The central issue discussed at the meeting was the tension between political commitment and bourgeois lifestyle. It took on explosive force when Rudi Dutschke missed the first two days of the meeting because his parents had been visiting. Were parents more important than planning strategy for the revolution? To free the individual from the power of bourgeois family life, the students decided to join together in a commune. In January 1967, a group of students—Dutschke was not among them—moved into the empty apartment of writer Uwe Johnson. With the name Kommune 1 (K 1), they signaled their hope that their experiment would be imitated.

Kommune 2 followed in the course of 1967. Like K 1, K 2 criticized the nuclear family as the "most significant socialization authority of the capitalistic power system" because it served to reproduce passivity and obedience through authoritarian education.[92] A series of measures was introduced to disrupt this process of reproduction. First, a new division of labor between men and women in everyday life was introduced in order to reverse the traditional assignment of political education to men and childcare and housework to women. A second means of overcoming authoritarian personality structures was the dissolution of the couple relationship and a reorientation of sexual behavior. In this area, however, many communes eventually reverted to traditional behavior models and accepted couple relationships. Commune members who did not have partners within the commune sought them outside the commune, and group sex was rejected on the ideological grounds that it reproduced the capitalistic principle of exchange.[93] Following the founding of K1 and K2, communes were established throughout the Federal Republic over the course of 1968. The commune concept, like that of the *Kinderladen*, enjoyed considerable popularity. In a 1968, for example, it ranked first among "72 ideas for the future" in a competition sponsored by the magazine *Kursbuch*.[94]

Some experiments in communal living occurred in members' minds. Commune members tried to bring about fundamental changes in their individual psychic structures through group conversations guided by the principles of psychoanalysis.[95] These were also considered an essential contribution toward coming to terms with the past because they would counteract authoritarian character structures and thereby remove the foundations for a new fascism.

The spread of the idea of a new political pedagogy aimed at overcoming authoritarian character structures by teaching individuals to be self-reflective and self-confident owed much to the efforts of Max Horkheimer. After being named provost of the University of Frankfurt in 1951, Horkheimer systematically sought out allies such as the Sigmund Freud Institute (Frankfurt) and the Max Planck Institute for Education Research (West Berlin).[96] They were helped in their efforts to promote the new political pedagogy by the print and broadcast media. Their ideas were discussed in literary and political journals (*Kursbuch*, *Frankfurter Hefte*) as well as in mainstream newspapers and magazines (*Frankfurter Allgemeine Zeitung, Frankfurter Rundschau, Süddeutsche Zeitung, Die Zeit, Der Spiegel*).[97] As the prestige of the social sciences increased, concepts such as the authoritarian character were even taken up on television programs such as the news show *Panorama*.[98]

The network that Horkheimer and his colleagues built included the state of Hessen's Ministry of Education and a number of American and Jewish organizations that shared an interest in preventing the Federal Republic from falling into the hands of the old elites.[99] The successful diffusion of the Frankfurt School's political pedagogy thus rested not least on the efforts of the new German elites to democratize not only institutions but also "society, mentalities, indeed, each individual's personality structure."[100] This endeavor resulted in the adoption of new educational goals, the preparation of new school books, and the drafting of new syllabi for schools.[101] The Frankfurt School's pedagogic ideas were taken up by the radio program *Funkkolleg Erziehungswissenschaft* (Radio College of Pedagogy); the accompanying book had a print run of four hundred thousand copies and influenced an entire generation of teachers.[102]

For this new generation of teachers, coming to terms with the past meant not only spending more classroom time on the Third Reich, as it had for educational reformers of the early 1960s, but also changing the personality structures of the students, teaching them to be self-reflective and self-confident. Coming to terms with the past was transformed from a legal and institutional process to the task of creating a new mindset: it became "the long-term task of the morally guided internalization of a consciousness."[103] In other words, the confrontation with the Nazi past was no longer restricted to a discursive level but was increasingly anchored socioculturally.

The idea of a new political pedagogy provided a model for new social models that the student New Left attempted to implement in social experiments like the *Kinderläden* and communes. Changing the institutions of everyday life, they believed, could bring about deeper changes in mentalities and character structures than could classroom instruction. Without addressing the sociocultural sphere, Adorno argued, efforts to come to terms with the past would remain incomplete. "National Socialism lives on," he wrote, not least because the "willingness to do the unspeakable persists in humans and their surroundings."[104]

Notes

1. Jürgen Habermas, *Die nachholende Revolution* (Frankfurt am Main, 1990), 22.
2. Ekkehart Krippendorff, "Die Deutschen sind nicht mehr, was sie waren," *Der Spiegel* 23 (1987): 34.
3. Claus Leggewie, "Verordnete Gründung—verfehlte Nachgründung—vertane Neugründung," *Blätter für deutsche und internationale Politik* 6 (1993): 698.
4. Christoph Kleßmann, "1968—Studentenrevolte oder Kulturrevolution?" in *Revolution in Deutschland?* ed. Manfred Hettling (Göttingen, 1991), 90–105, here 100.
5. "Prior to the summer of 1968, the use of analogies was rooted more in political instrumentalism than in a detailed knowledge of these events." Harold Marcuse, "The Revival of Holocaust Awareness in West Germany, Israel, and the United States," in *1968: The World Transformed*, ed. Carole Fink, Philipp Gassert, and Detlef Junker (Cambridge, 1998), 421–438, here 428.
6. See Hermann Lübbe, "Der Mythos der 'kritischen Generation': Ein Rückblick," *Aus Politik und Zeitgeschichte* B20 (1988): 17–25, here 18.
7. Ingrid Gilcher-Holtey, *Phantasie an die Macht: Mai 68 in Frankreich* (Frankfurt am Main, 1995), 63–66. On *Das Argument* in Berlin, see Christiane Kohser-Spohn, *Mouvement étudiant et critique du fascisme en Allemagne dans les années soixante* (Paris, 1999), 33–35.
8. Ernst Nolte, *Der Faschismus in seiner Epoche* (Munich, 1963).

9. Eberhard Czichon, "Der Primat der Industrie im Kartell der nationalsozialistischen Macht," *Das Argument* 47 (1968): 168–92; Tim Mason, "Der Primat der Politik: Politik und Wirtschaft im Nationalsozialismus," *Das Argument* 41 (1966): 473–94.

10. See, for example, Carl Joachim Friedrich, *Totalitäre Diktatur* (Stuttgart, 1957); Hannah Arendt, *Elemente und Ursprünge totaler Herrschaft* (Frankfurt am Main, 1958); and Karl Dietrich Bracher, *Die Auflösung der Weimarer Republik* (Villingen, 1960).

11. See Reimund Reiche and Bernhard Blanke, "Kapitalismus, Faschismus und Demokratie," *Das Argument* 32 (1965): 12–30, here 29.

12. Wolfgang Fritz Haug, "Ideologische Komponenten in den Theorien über den Faschismus," *Das Argument* 33 (1964): 6–8.

13. See Walter Benjamin, "Theorien des deutschen Faschismus: Zu der Sammelschrift 'Krieg und Krieger,' ed. E. Jünger," *Das Argument* 30 (1964): 129–37; Kohser-Spohn, *Mouvement étudiant et critique du fascisme*, 39; Rainer Westphal, "Psychologische Theorien über den Faschismus," *Das Argument* 32 (1965): 30–39; Ronald Wiegand, "Herrschaft und Entfremdung: Zwei Begriffe für eine Theorie über den Faschismus," *Das Argument* 30 (1964): 138–44.

14. See also Wolfgang Kraushaar, "Von der Totalitarismus- zur Faschismustheorie: Zu einem Paradigmenwechsel in der Theoriepolitik der bundesdeutschen Studentenbewegung," in *Die Nacht hat zwölf Stunden, dann kommt schon der Tag. Antifaschismus: Geschichte und Neubewertung*, ed. Claudia Keller et al. (Berlin, 1996), 234–51.

15. AStA Tübingen, *Deutsches Geistesleben und Nationalsozialismus* (Tübingen, 1965). See also Karl Christian Lammers, "Die Auseinandersetzung mit der 'braunen' Universität: Ringvorlesungen zur NS-Vergangenheit an westdeutschen Hochschulen," in *Dynamische Zeiten: Die 60er Jahre in den beiden deutschen Gesellschaften*, ed. Axel Schildt, Detlef Siegfried, and Karl Christian Lammers (Hamburg, 2000), 148–65.

16. See, for example, Haßkamp Hauser, "Ringvorlesungen," *Notizen* 12 (1964): 3–4.

17. AStA München, *Die deutsche Universität im 3. Reich* (Munich, 1966). AStA Freie Universität Berlin, *Nationalsozialismus und die deutsche Universität* (Berlin, 1966). AStA Frankfurt, *Germanistik, eine deutsche Wissenschaft* (Frankfurt am Main, 1967). See also Hans-Ulrich Thamer, "Die NS-Vergangenheit im politischen Diskurs der 68er-Bewegung," *Westfälische Forschungen* 48 (1998): 39–53, here 47.

18. Wolfgang Fritz Haug, *Der hilflose Antifaschismus: Zur Kritik der Vorlesungsreihen über Wissenschaft und Nationalsozialismus an deutschen Universitäten* (Frankfurt am Main, 1967), 6.

19. Ibid., 13–14.

20. AStA Frankfurt, *Germanistik, eine deutsche Wissenschaft*.

21. See also Thamer, "NS-Vergangenheit," 47–48; Nina Grunenberg, "Der verspätete Anti-Faschismus und die 68er: Die BRD," in *Antifaschismus—ein deutscher Mythos*, ed. Nina Grunenberg (Reinbeck, 1993), 145–70, here 145; Christel Hopf, "Das Faschismusthema in der Studentenbewegung und in der Soziologie," in *Radikalisierte Aufklärung*, ed. Heinz Bude and Martin Kohli (Munich, 1989), 71–86, here 71.

22. See Wilfried Loth and Bernd A. Rusinek eds., *Verwandlungspolitik: NS-Eliten in der westdeutschen Nachkriegsgesellschaft* (Frankfurt am Main, 1998); Ulrich Herbert, "Rückkehr in die Bürgerlichkeit? NS-Eliten in der Bundesrepublik," in *Rechtsradikalismus in der politischen Kultur der Nachkriegszeit*, ed. Bernd Weisbrod (Hanover, 1995), 157–74.

23. See Tilman Fichter, *SDS und SPD: Parteilichkeit jenseits der Partei* (Opladen, 1988), 306–9; Willi Albrecht, *Der Sozialistische Deutsche Studentenbund (SDS): Vom parteikonformen Studentenverband zum Repräsentanten der Neuen Linken* (Bonn, 1994), 356–58; Jürgen Briem, *Der SDS: Die Geschichte des bedeutendsten Studentenverbandes in der BRD seit 1945* (Frankfurt am Main, 1976), 50, 245–48.

24. See Rolf Seelinger, *Braune Universität. Deutsche Hochschullehrer gestern und heute: Eine Dokumentation*, vol. 1 (Munich, 1964).

25. See, for example, *Politikon* 1 (1965), 3.

26. "Kritische Stellungnahme zu der Kritischen Universität in Hamburg," in *Kritische Universität, Sommer 1968* (Berlin, 1968), 49–51, here 51; "Die Radikaldemokratische Hochschulpolitik in Hamburg," in *SDS-Korrespondenz*, Sonderheft (November 1968). For Heidelberg, see Dietrich Hildebrandt, *"… und die Studenten freuen sich!" Studentenbewegung in Heidelberg 1967–1973* (Heidelberg, 1991), 98–101. For Bochum, see Norbert Kozicki, *Aufbruch im Revier: 1968 und die Folgen* (Essen, 1993), 66–69.

27. See Marcuse, "Revival of Holocaust Awareness," 426–27. See also the polemical desciption of Louis Köckert, *Dachau … und das Gras wächst …: Ein Report für die Nachgeborenen* (Munich, 1980), 108.

28. Lothar Strogies, "Die Außerparlamentarische Opposition in Nürnberg und Erlangen" (PhD diss., University of Nuremberg, 1996), 120.

29. *Bild-Zeitung*, 3 June 1967, 1.

30. Bernward Vesper, ed., *Bedingungen und Organisation des Widerstandes. Der Kongreß in Hannover: Protokolle, Flugblätter, Resolutionen* (Berlin, 1967), 101.

31. Klaus Briegleb, *1968: Literatur in der antiautoritären Bewegung* (Frankfurt am Main, 1993), 128.

32. "Studententerror," *Die Zeit*, 29 December 1967; Hans-Joachim Winkler, ed., *Das Establishment antwortet der außerparlamentarische Opposition* (Opladen, 1968); Hans Julius Schoeps and Christopher Dannenmann, eds., *Die rebellischen Studenten: Elite der Demokratie oder Vorhut eines linken Faschismus?* 2nd ed. (Munich, 1968).

33. Wolfgang Kraushaar, "Notizen zu einer Chronologie der Studentenbewegung," in Peter Mosler, *Was wir wollten* (Frankfurt am Main, 1977), 249–295, here 272.

34. Rudi Dutschke, "Vom Antisemitismus zum Antikommunismus," in *Die Rebellion der Studentenbewegung oder die neue Opposition*, ed. Rudi Dutschke et al. (Reinbek, 1968), 58–93, here 58.

35. SDS-Bundesvorstand, "Erklärung des SDS-Bundesvorstandes vom 6. Juni 1967," in *Der 2. juni 1967—Studenten zwischen Notstand und Demokratie: Dokumente*, ed. Knut Nevermann, VDS (Cologne, 1967), 97–100, here 98; Gerhard Kade, "Langhaarige Ersatzjuden," *Darmstädter Studentenzeitung* 5 (1968): 3–5; See also Dutschke, "Antisemitismus," 80; Peter Brückner, "Springerpresse und Volksverhetzung," *Kritische Justiz* 4 (1969): 131–33; "Mordanschlag auf Rudi Dutschke," SDS flyer from Frankfurt am Main, in APO-ARCHIV, Bestand SDS, SDS-Frankfurt.

36. See, for example, Hans-Helmuth Knütter, *Die Faschismus-Keule: Das letzte Aufgebot der deutschen Linken* (Berlin, 1993); Bernd A. Rusinek, "Von der Entdeckung der NS-Vergangenheit zum generellen Faschismusverdacht—akademische Diskurse in der Bundesrepublik der 60er Jahre," in Schildt et al., *Dynamische Zeiten*, 114–47.

37. Dagmar Herzog, "Pleasure, Sex, and Politics Belong Together: Post-Holocaust Memory and the Sexual Revolution in West Germany," *Critical Inquiry* 24 (1998): 393–444.

38. Marcuse, "Revival of Holocaust Awareness," 437.

39. Theodor W, Adorno, *Studien zum autoritären Charakter* (Frankfurt am Main, 1973).

40. Reinhard Lettau, *Täglicher Faschismus: Amerikanische Evidenz aus 6 Monaten* (Munich, 1971); Briegleb, *1968*, 80–84.

41. Oral History Research Office, Columbia University, New York, "The Sixties Collection," Interview with Gregory Calvert, 110.

42. Malcolm S. Burnstein, "The Un-American Committee in San Francisco," *New University Thought* 3 (1960): 9–15, here 14.

43. Irvin und Debi Unger, *Turning Point 1968* (New York, 1988), 261. The prominent student leader Jerry Rubin announced: "I am a child of Amerika." Jerry Rubin, *Do it! Scenarios for the Revolution* (New York, 1970), 12.

44. See Thomas Powers, *Diana: The Making of a Terrorist* (Boston, 1971), 155.

45. Irving Louis Horowitz, *The Struggle Is the Message* (Berkeley, 1970), 101.

46. Oral History Research Office, Columbia University, New York, "The Sixties Collection," Interview with Heather Booth, 47.

47. See, for example, Axel Schildt, "Der Umgang mit der NS-Vergangenheit in der Öffentlichkeit der Nachkriegszeit," in Loth and Rusinek, *Verwandlungspolitik*, 53.

48. See Gilcher-Holtey, "Wer definiert, was erinnert werden soll?" Unpublished manuscript (Bielefeld, 2000), 17–19.

49. See Jörg Lau, *Hans Magnus Enzensberger: Ein öffentliches Leben* (Frankfurt am Main, 1999), 193.

50. "Nachbemerkung, der nichterklärte Notstand," *Kursbuch* 12 (1968): 178–81, here 178. See also Fritz Lamm, "Demokratischer Faschismus," *Neue Kritik* 3 (1962): 6–15; Rudi Dutschke and Hans-Jürgen Krahl, "Organisationsreferat auf der 22. Delegiertenkonferenz des SDS im September 1967 in Frankfurt," reprint in *Diskus* 1 (1980): 6–9.

51. See Helmut Schauer, "Soziale Demokratie oder neuer Faschismus: Zur innenpolitischen Entwicklung der Bundesrepublik," *Neue Kritik* 5 (1964): 11–17.

52. "Rede zur Trauerfeier von Ohnesorg in Köln am 7. Juni 1967 von Peter Bubenberger (SDS)," in Nevermann, *Der 2. juni 1967*.

53. SDS-Autorenkollektiv, cited after *Der Spiegel*, 10 February 1969, 32.

54. Bernd Rabehl, "Von der antiautoritären Bewegung zur sozialistischen Opposition," in Dutschke et al., *Rebellion*, 173; Kai Hermann, "Goebbels' Nachfahren: Die Berliner Springer-Zeitungen verfälschen die Wahrheit," *Die Zeit*, 26 April 1968.

55. Hans Magnus Enzensberger, *Deutschland, Deutschland unter anderem: Äußerungen zur Politik*, 3rd ed. (Frankfurt am Main, 1968), 13.

56. See, for example, "Anti-U.S. Posters at Dachau," *New York Times*, 8 November 1966, 18; Marcuse, "Revival of Holocaust Awareness," 426.

57. See SDS flyer of February 1968 in Karl A Otto, ed., *APO: Außerparlamentarische Opposition in Quellen und Dokumenten 1960–1970* (Cologne, 1989), 209. See also Wilfried Mausbach, "Auschwitz and Vietnam: West German Protest against America's War during the 1960s." Unpublished manuscript, 1998.

58. Dörte von Westernhagen, *Die Kinder der Täter: Das Dritte Reich und die Generation danach* (Munich, 1987); Detlef Hoffmann, "Erinnerungsarbeit der 'zweiten und dritten' Generation und 'Spurensuche' in der zeitgenössischen Kunst," *Kritische Berichte* 1 (1988): 31–46; Michael Geyer and Miriam Hansen, "German-Jewish Memory and National Consciousness," in *Holocaust Remembrance: The Shapes of Memory*, ed. Geoffrey Hartmann (Oxford, 1994), 175–90; Sabine Reichel, *Zwischen Trümmern und Träumen: Aufgewachsen im Schatten der Schuld* (Hamburg, 1991); Peter Sichrovsky, *Schuldig geboren: Kinder aus Nazifamilien* (Cologne, 1987).

59. Michael Schneider, "Seine geballte Faust konnte sich auch wieder zum Händedrücken öffnen," in Rudi Dutschke, *Mein langer Marsch: Reden, Schriften und Tagebücher aus zwanzig Jahren*, ed. Gretchen Dutschke-Klotz, Hellmut Gollwitzer, and Jürgen Miermeister, 4th ed. (Reinbek, 1981), 249–51, here 250.

60. Heinz Bude, *Bilanz der Nachfolge: Die Bundesrepublik und der Nationalsozialismus* (Frankfurt am Main, 1992), 89.

61. Armin Ayren, "Die Kinder von Hitler, Marx und LSD," *Badische Zeitung*, 28–29 January 1978, 37.

62. See Jillian Becker, *Hitler's Children: The Story of the Baader-Meinhof Terrorist Gang* (London, 1978); Cora Stephan, *Der Betroffenheitskult: Eine politische Sittengeschichte* (Berlin, 1993), 102.

63. See Tilman Fichter, "Vier SDS-Generationen," *Frankfurter Hefte* 9 (1987): 798–804; "Links von den Vätern, SDS-Studenten, Kinder prominenter SPD-Politiker begründen, warum sie links von der politischen Einstellung ihrer Väter stehen," *Panorama*, 11 September 1967, Norddeutscher Rundfunk, Deutsches Rundfunk Archiv-Nr. 67-2382/F.; Klaus Allerbeck, *Soziologie radikaler Studentenbewegungen: Eine vergleichende Untersuchung in der Bundesrepublik und den Vereinigten Staaten* (Munich, 1973), 129–30; Claus Leggewie, "1968: Ein Laboratorium der nachindustriellen Gesellschaft? Zur Tradition der antiautoritären Revolte seit den sechziger Jahren," *Aus Politik und Zeitgeschichte* B20 (1988): 3–15, here 7–8.

64. Jörg Schröder, *Schröder erzählt, Folge 18: Unterm Dach* (Fuchstal-Leeder, 1994), 39–40.
65. Allerbeck, *Soziologie radikaler Studentenbewegungen*, 108.
66. Klaus Wagenbach, "Die RAF und die Neue Linke," in Wagenbach, *Eintritt frei: Beiträge zur öffentlichen Meinung* (Darmstadt, 1982), 60–74, here 61; Iring Fetscher, *Terrorismus und Reaktion* (Cologne, 1977), 52.
67. Theodor W. Adorno, *The Authoritarian Personality: Studies in Prejudice*, vol. 3 (New York, 1950), vii.
68. See Bernd Estel, *Soziale Vorurteile und soziale Urteile: Kritik und wissenschaftliche Grundlegung der Vorurteilsforschung* (Opladen, 1983), 56–59.
69. Theodor W. Adorno, "Erziehung nach Auschwitz," in Adorno, *Gesammelte Schriften*, vol. 10.2, ed. Rolf Tiedemann (Frankfurt am Main, 1977), 674–90, here 677.
70. Ibid., 676.
71. Ibid., 683–84.
72. Ibid., 684.
73. See Theodor W. Adorno, "Was bedeutet: Aufarbeitung der Vergangenheit?" in Adorno, *Gesammelte Schriften*, 561–62.
74. Adorno, *Gesammelte Schriften*, 571.
75. See, for example, Reimund Reiche, "Wendepunkte," *Das Argument* 33 (1965): 21–24, here 23.
76. Dutschke et al., "Antisemitismus," 77.
77. For reflections on the concept "antiauthoritarian," see Ingrid Gilcher-Holtey, "Kritische Theorie und Neue Linke," in *1968—Vom Ereignis zum Gegenstand der* Geschichtswissenschaft, ed. Ingrid Gilcher-Holtey (Göttingen, 1998), 168–87, here 181; Günter C. Behrmann, "Zur Publikationsgeschichte der Kritischen Theorie," in *Die intellektuelle Gründung der Bundesrepublik*, ed. Clemens Albrecht et al. (Frankfurt am Main, 1999), 247–311, here 299.
78. Heide Berndt, "Zu den politischen Motiven bei der Gründung erster anti-autoritärer Kinderläden," *Jahrbuch für Pädagogik*, Special Issue (1995): 231–50, here 231; "Befreit die Kinder," *Freiburger Studentenzeitung*, 18 June 1969, 1.
79. Dutschke et al., "Antisemitismus," 77. See also Wolff Reinhart, "Nach Auschwitz: antiautoritäre Kinderladenbewegung oder die Erziehung der Erzieher," in *Berlin und pädagogische Reformen: Brennpunkte der individuellen und historischen Entwicklung*, ed. Kuno Beller (Berlin, 1992), 71–80, here 77.
80. See Interview with Monika Seifert, in Karl Heinz Heinemann and Thomas Jaitner, eds., *Ein langer Marsch. '68 und die Folgen* (Cologne, 1993), 72–82, here 77. See also Monika Seifert and Herbert Nagel, eds., *Nicht für die Schule leben: Ein alternativer Schulversuch Freie Schule Frankfurt* (Frankfurt am Main, 1977); Regine Dermitzel, "These zur antiautoritären Erziehung," *Kursbuch* 17 (1969): 179–87.
81. Interview with Monika Seifert, in Heinemann and Jaitner, *Ein langer Marsch*, 79.
82. Ibid., 80.
83. See Berndt, "Zu den politischen Motiven."
84. Ibid., 237–39.
85. See *Kritische Universität, Sommer 68: Berichte und Programm*, ed. AstA der Freien Universität (Berlin, 1968).
86. Kommune 2, "Kindererziehung in der Kommune," *Kursbuch* 17 (1969): 147–78.
87. Autorenkollektiv, *Berliner Kinderläden* (Cologne, 1970); Autorenkollektiv Lankwitz, eds., *Kinderläden: Revolution der Erziehung oder Erziehung zur Revolution?* (Hamburg, 1971).
88. See Gerd Hirschauer, ed., *Antiautoritäre Erziehung, Kinderläden* (Pfaffenhofen, 1970).
89. See Gerhard Bott, *Erziehung zum Ungehorsam* (Frankfurt am Main, 1970), 111–14.
90. See, for example, Johannes Claaßen, ed., *Antiautoritäre Erziehung in der wissenschaftlichen Diskussion* (Heidelberg, 1973).
91. Tilman Fichter and Siegward Lönnendonker, *Kleine Geschichte des SDS* (Berlin, 1977), 100.
92. Kommune 2, "Kindererziehung in der Kommune," *Kursbuch* 17 (1969): 147–78, here 147.
93. Kommune 2, *Versuch der Revolutionierung des bürgerlichen Individuums* (Berlin, 1969), 133.

94. "Konkrete Utopie: Zweiundsiebzig Gedanken für die Zukunft," *Kursbuch* 14 (1968): 110–46, here 110–12.

95. Kommune 2, *Versuch der Revolutionierung*, 156–58.

96. See Clemens Albrecht, "'Das Allerwichtigste ist, dass man die Jugend für sich gewinnt': Die kultur- und bildungspolitischen Pläne des Horkheimer-Kreises bei der Remigration," in Albrecht et al., *Die intellektuelle Gründung der Bundesrepublik*, 97–131.

97. See Clemens Albrecht, "Die Massenmedien und die Frankfurter Schule," in Albrecht et al., *Die intellektuelle Gründung der Bundesrepublik*, 203–46.

98. See Gerhard Lampe, *Das Panorama der 60er Jahre: Zur Geschichte des ersten politischen Fernsehmagazins der Bundesrepublik* (Berlin, 1999); Bernd Sösemann, "Die 68er Bewegung und die Massenmedien," in *Mediengeschichte der Bundesrepublik Deutschland*, ed. Jürgen Wilke (Cologne, 1999), 672–97, here 682.

99. Clemens Alrecht, "Vom Konsens zur Lagerbildung," in Albrecht et al., *Die intellektuelle Gründung der Bundesrepublik*, 132–89.

100. Clemens Albrecht, "Im Schatten des Nationalsozialismus: Die politische Pädagogik der Frankfurter Schule," in Albrecht et al., *Die intellektuelle Gründung der Bundesrepublik*, 387–447, here 446.

101. Ibid., 418.

102. See Günter C. Behrmann, "Die Erzieher kritischer Kritiker als neues Staatsziel," in Albrecht et al., *Die intellektuelle Gründung der Bundesrepublik*, 448–497, here 478.

103. Albrecht, "Im Schatten des Nationalsozialismus," 447.

104. Adorno, "Was bedeutet: Aufarbeitung der Vergangenheit?" 555.

Chapter 12

PUBLIC DEMONSTRATIONS OF THE 1960S
Participatory Democracy or Leftist Fascism?

Elizabeth L. B. Peifer

⚬✧⚬

One of the greatest challenges faced by the Federal Republic of Germany was creating democrats in a democracy imposed by former enemies. Indeed, the failure of the first German republic to transform the country's political culture and political values led to its collapse and ultimately to the crimes and atrocities of the Third Reich. To break the continuities of authoritarianism and militarism, the Federal Republic would have to develop a political culture that safeguarded against a repetition of the mistakes of the past. It would have to reshape the character of its people and make them productive, independent, and morally responsible citizens. The active participation of citizens in the political process defines democracy. At the same time, the zealous activities of radical groups can endanger the fundamental balance of democratic institutions.

As part of the basic democratic structure of the Federal Republic, Article 8 of the Basic Law grants the right of assembly (*Versammlungsrecht*): "All Germans have the right to assemble peacefully and unarmed without prior notification or permission," Article 8 affirms. "In the case of outdoor assemblies," it continues, "this right may be restricted by or pursuant to a law." Political demonstrations represented a special case under the right of assembly, however, and there was a troubling gap between the constitutional articulation of *Versammlungsrecht* and the way it was understood in practice during the 1950s and 1960s.[1] The Federal Republic's legal code, with its roots in the predemocratic code of 1871, seemed to infringe upon the constitutional right of assembly and to stand at odds with the Basic Law's stipulation that "in no case may the essence of a basic right be encroached upon." The West German people themselves generally felt comfortable with restricting political demonstrations. This was the setting in which leftist demonstrators, the self-styled "extra-parliamentary opposition" (*Ausserparlamentarische Opposition*, APO), took to the streets of the Federal Republic to demand a voice in the nation's political discourse.

The demonstrations of the late 1960s provided much ammunition for the discursive battles of the time. In some respects, the debates *on* the 1960s engage the issues of the National Socialist past as much as the debates *of* the 1960s. The 68ers attempted to confront the issues of the past and break free of the lingering bondage of German authoritarianism, but the demonstrators' own actions suggested continuities with the German past. To some, the demonstrations represented the very best part of the 1960s, a healthy spirit of participatory democracy. From the perspective of the antiauthoritarian protest movement, public demonstrations served as the last bastions of protection for a democratic society against the encroachment of state authority. "The street is still the one uncensored space for proclamations and demonstrations of every kind," Peter Schütt argued in 1968. "If the rulers refuse to listen to the people, the public streets and squares remain the last schools of the nation."[2] The young demonstrators and their supporters argued that the West German system under the Christian Democratic-Social Democratic "grand coalition" failed to measure up to its true multiparty claims, that free competition favoring certain interests was anything but free, and that individuals who criticized the system were being deprived of their civil liberties. For the demonstrators, protest constituted an expression of democratic liberties. They were breaking out of the complacency and blind obedience that they felt had led the German people to the Third Reich and the Holocaust.

For the generation in power and the majority of West Germans, the demonstrations called to mind images of the mass rallies of the past and totalitarianism. The demonstrations represented mob rule rather than democratic exchange and fueled their worst fears. They saw in them the resurgence of radical politics and street fighting, a seizure of power, a breakdown of law and order that placed civil liberties in jeopardy. Hitler himself had noted the power of mass demonstrations: "The public does not understand that this fight will be decided not in the salon, but on the street."[3] Scholarly literature on demonstrations likewise reflected a distrust of the masses and emphasized the irrational qualities of crowd psychology.[4] Such attitudes heavily influenced the perceptions of student demonstrations among the public and within the ranks of government.

To what extent and in what ways did West Germans confront their nation's past in and through the demonstrations of the 1960s? Was the protest movement, as Hermann Lübbe has argued, a naïve rebellion in which little progress was made in coming to terms with the past?[5] Or were the demonstrations the linchpin of the transformation of German political culture that finally brought the past out of the closet? Was conflict a "necessary medium" for transforming a postdictatorial society into a democracy?[6] Are demonstrations an indication of a healthy democracy in which citizens demand and have access to the political process? Or do they signal governmental weakness? Were the critics of the demonstrations exhibiting the authoritarian character of unreformed fascists, or were they voicing the concerns of informed citizens whose historical memories made them aware of the frailty of democracy in Germany?

Rhetoric and Imagery

Memories of the failure of the first German republic and Germany's experience with fascism resonated through contemporary observations and interpretations of leftist activism in the late 1960s. Spurred by events such as the trial of Adolf Eichmann, the debate over extending the statute of limitations for Nazi acts of murder, and outbreaks of anti-Semitic vandalism, West German discussion of the Nazi past intensified over the course of the decade. Books such as Fritz Fischer's *Griff nach der Weltmacht* (1961), Karl Jasper's *Wohin treibt die Bundesrepublik?* (1966), and Alexander and Margarete Mitscherlich's *Die Unfähigkeit zu trauern* (1967) gave currency to the question of continuities with the past and authoritarian tendencies within the German character.[7] Confrontation with the Nazi past changed over the course of the 1960s, as detailed studies of the Third Reich and personal reflections on the experience of Nazism gave way to political conflict in the second half of the decade.[8] Once a topic for small study groups and family discussions, the issue of the past exploded onto the streets. Through public demonstrations, the debates gained a broader audience and became more politicized while simultaneously becoming less theoretically sophisticated and largely ignorant of the complexities of the historical record.

By making explicit references to individuals with Nazi pasts and to Nazi tactics and abuses, the demonstrators sought to expose unacknowledged continuities between past and present in West German society and politics. Their tactics included publicizing biographical details, as in the case of Chancellor Kurt Georg Kiesinger, or drawing historical parallels, as, for example, between press baron Axel Springer and Nazi publisher Julius Streicher. These tactics sometimes threw useful light upon contemporary debates, but they often struck many people as opportunistic, particularly when the charges proved to be inaccurate. The students' appropriation of the German past for current political purposes led to misunderstandings with onetime victims of Nazism. At a dedication ceremony at Dachau in 1968, for example, students staged a protest aimed at West Berlin Mayor Klaus Schütz. Denouncing the "fascist" methods West Berlin police had used during a demonstration on 2 June 1967, the students carried banners with slogans such as "Heute Pogrom und Propaganda, morgen die Endlösung, Herr Schütz" (Today Pogrom and Propaganda, Tomorrow the Final Solution, Herr Schütz). Holocaust survivors attending the ceremony misunderstood the student protestors, and a scuffle ensued.[9]

The rhetoric and imagery the left employed focused primarily on the Nazis' suspension of civil rights. Student groups accused the governments in Bonn and West Berlin of denying them their constitutional right to demonstrate. Leftist student groups denounced the actions of the police during a 2 June 1967 demonstration against the visiting Shah of Iran in Berlin as a systematically planned and executed maneuver to justify the declaration of a state of emergency (*Notstand*). The "terror excesses of the police," they charged, were an attempt "to silence student and extra-parliamentary opposition."[10] The APO did not limit its sociopolitical critique to institutions of the state. The Springer press, for instance, was denounced as a "monopoly" and accused of both falsifying reports and willfully manipulating public opinion.[11] Calling for the "Expropriation of Springer Press," student demonstrators declared: "We refuse to allow the terrorist opinion machine the appearance of democracy."[12]

As the state and other conservative forces sought to control the growing protest movement, the students began to see themselves as persecuted victims, as the Jews of their day.[13] Pointing to the criminalization of protest and the demonization of students by authorities and the conservative press, they argued that a "pogrom" atmosphere was being created. Indeed, conservative observers invoked the same set of attributes in denouncing the student demonstrators that, according to Klaus Theweleit, the fascists had used in their "battle against human desires": effeminacy, unhealthiness, criminality, and Bolshevism.[14] The only attribute left out was Jewishness, but that the students took upon themselves as a badge of honor. After an assassination attempt upon student leader Rudi Dutschke in April 1968—which had been preceded by the shooting death of a student during the June 1967 anti-Shah protest in Berlin and an attack upon a young man who happened to resemble Dutschke—the organizers of a protest in Göttingen issued an appeal to older citizens to remember the *Mordhetze* (incitements to murder) and political assassinations that accompanied the fall of the Weimar Republic. Echoing Martin Niemöller, they warned that the attempt upon Dutschke's life concerned all citizens, not just students, and that the Emergency Laws likewise threatened everyone, not just the APO.[15] But although they identified themselves with the victims of Nazism, the students generally did not pursue a deeper understanding of the historical experience of Jews in Germany.

Members of the press sympathetic to the students echoed these historical allusions. Writing in the *Frankfurter Rundschau*, Rudolph Ganz argued that police had welcomed the isolated acts of violence by demonstrators during the June 1967 anti-Shah protest as a pretext for a brutal onslaught.[16] Kai Hermann maintained in an article entitled "Goebbels's Successors" that the Springer press was publishing lies and half-truths in articles demonizing the students. The resulting hysteria, he argued, produced an environment ripe for political assassination or vigilante justice.[17] In the magazine *Konkret*, Stefan Aust portrayed injured demonstrators as innocent victims. Whereas the protesters threw stones out of "helpless rage," police leaders encouraged the "ruthless" use of night sticks. Subtly drawing upon Holocaust imagery, Aust reported that the demonstrators did not want a confrontation with police and stood "passively … with their hands raised above their heads," but the police "clubbed [the demonstrators], herding them like cattle, as their colleagues come in from the other side of the encirclement with their billy clubs."[18] *Extradienst* reported, "Dutschke must reckon every hour with the open lynch mob justice of fascists encouraged and supported by the authorities."[19]

In the eyes of conservative members of the West German press and public, the protesters posed the greater threat to democracy. With a chronological focus on the later years of the Weimar Republic, they positioned the demonstrators as the fascists. Critics of the 68ers highlighted the contradiction between the democracy the movement professed and the "terror" tactics it employed. While many newspapers noted "increasing radicalization" among students in June 1967, the Springer newspapers adopted a much more emotional tone. *Bild-Zeitung* reported on 3 June, "we have something against SA methods. Germans want neither brown nor red SA. They don't want columns of bullies, but peace." Critics charged that the "small radical minority" of student demonstrators were not exercising their civil rights, but on the contrary, abusing those freedoms to subvert the democratic state. Reporting on the Easter unrest of 1968, the *Berliner Zeitung* ran the headline "Youth Storm Churches and Theater." Making little mention of the attack on Dutschke that had prompted the students' actions or of Dutschke's condition, the article described the "wild demonstrations" in terms that recalled the 1938 *Kristallnacht* attacks on synagogues and Jewish-owned property.[20] Likewise, photos of the students' attempted blockade of the Springer Press were suggestive of Nazi book-burnings. *Welt am Sonntag* told of the great threat posed to the republic: "The Reichstag fire consumed the Weimar state; the attempt to send the Berlin Springer building up in flames could easily become the beginning of the end of the Federal Republic."[21]

In his comparative study of student movements in France, the United States, and West Germany, Michael Kimmel notes the difficulty German students had in drawing positive connections to a revolutionary or liberal tradition in their national culture. The negative relationship with the National Socialist past offered a far more immediate and personal reference. This, according to Kimmel, explains the greater emphasis on Third World liberation movements within the German student movement than in its French and American counterparts.[22] Particularly in the period from 1966 through early 1968, West German protestors often carried posters of Che Guevara, Ho Chi Minh, and Mao Zedong and chanted "Mo-mo-mo-ssa-deq" and "Ho-Ho-Ho-Chi-Minh." Generally speaking, most of the demonstrators had only a superficial knowledge of events in China or elsewhere. Linking their protests to struggles and conflicts elsewhere gave the protestors a sense of historic importance, of being part of a worldwide revolutionary movement. For critics, however, the Third World imagery called to mind violent, illegal guerilla movements. Moreover, for many West Germans the rather unreflective use of red banners conjured up images of Nazi Party rallies or the political gatherings on the eastern side of the Berlin Wall; in their eyes, the read banners heralded not revolutionary freedom but the dawn of totalitarianism supported by a naïve and uncritical mob.

The often aggressive and hyperbolic rhetoric demonstrators used served their goal of attracting media attention. But the demonstrators' references to Nazism and sensational press accounts also heightened tensions. As the demonstrators and their critics traded accusations of Nazi conduct, the rhetoric of public debate became increasingly sharp and more polemical than historical. The language used tended on the whole to debase discussion rather than to deepen public understanding of the past. Indeed, the content of posters and chants did little to enhance the great majority of demonstrators' understanding of the past. Much more important, as 68ers' later accounts, memoirs, and novels suggest, was the experience of participating in demonstrations.

Experience

Photos of and personal reminiscences about the demonstrations attest to the diverse array of individuals, from cross-dressing communards to young men in jacket and tie, who participated. They took part for a variety of reasons. Some, perhaps trying to lay claim to a German antifascist tradition, said the writings of Theodor Adorno, Herbert Marcuse, and Max Horkheimer had inspired them to action. Others drew upon a more traditional Marxist-Leninism. But anecdotal evidence suggests that a more important influence was the element of rebellion in popular culture—that the Rolling Stones were ultimately more important than the Frankfurt School. Many young people gravitated to the demonstrations out of a fascination with the protest movement. They "wanted to be a part of things." Many went because a boyfriend or girlfriend was going. It is thus difficult to generalize about the motivations or political consciousness of the demonstrating crowds. While many individuals initially engaged in street protests for reasons not wholly political, the immediate personal experience of confrontations with police often transformed them. As they returned home, they read reports of the incident that blatantly contradicted their own memories, undermining their trust in institutions and media. Feeling simultaneously powerless and empowered, casual and detached participants emerged from their experiences with passionate commitment. The movement expanded and gained new circles of sympathizers, but the motor driving the politicization process derived not from rational reflection and careful consideration but from rage and passionate disgust.

Rudi Dutschke called demonstrations a "learning process," the preliminary stage in consciousness-building.[23] Demonstrations made abstract theory personal, real, and immediate. "We who have grown up in an authoritarian society have a chance to break through our authoritarian character structure only when we learn to move in society as beings to whom this society belongs and to whom it is denied through the existing structure of power and domination of the system," Dutschke argued.[24] By taking to the streets and claiming public spaces, the demonstrations represented a physical revolt against authority.

The organizers of public demonstrations also sought to educate a wider audience and to draw attention to particular issues. Provocation proved a fundamental part of both consciousness-raising and publicity. "Without provocation, we would not be heard," Dutschke explained. "Therefore, provocations are essential prerequisites for public opinion."[25] The demonstrations needed to attract media attention, and provocation was a calculated strategy to create news events. Through its sensationalist tendencies and its role as an intermediary, the media shaped both the demonstrations and perceptions of them. The media, even when denunciatory in perspective, reproduced and refined relationships between student actions and broader political issues such as Vietnam or Third World liberation.[26]

If provocation was to succeed in creating solidarity in attracting media attention, the response of the police had to fit the reactionary model of intolerance. While confrontations between demonstrators and police were widely publicized and discussed, demonstrations in which both sides behaved themselves rarely received much attention. For example, the controversy over a demonstration after the International Vietnam Congress in February 1968 received far more attention than the demonstration itself. Unedited radio tapes revealed a reporter anxious for something to happen. The reporter's voice expressed disappointment each time a verbal exchange between demonstrators and police or critical bystanders failed to produce a physical confrontation.[27] Likewise, the *Sternmarsch*—a demonstration against *Stern* magazine—in Bonn in May 1968 was a disappointment so far as publicity was concerned. Demonstrators stuck to the approved route for their march and did not try to force their way into restricted areas. The police presence was minimal and unobtrusive, and the 2,000 officers on hand for back-up were not called into action. Both the *Frankfurter Allgemeine* and *Die Zeit* characterized the students as lively and fun-loving but also as almost comically well-behaved.[28]

The student movement often walked a thin line between employing confrontational strategies—intended to provoke state violence and encourage sympathy—and employing violence itself and thus alienating would-be supporters. But West German police often reacted to even peaceful protests with force. Police officers' understanding of the democratic system that they were responsible for protecting, and of the demonstrations that they were supposed to control, was different than that of the students. Many of the higher ranking officers had begun their careers in the late Weimar or early Nazi years. Much like the broader West German public, they had come to accept the democratic state but saw little scope for differences of opinion on how democratic principles might be implemented in practice. Police culture in the 1960s emphasized the soldierly virtues of camaraderie and unconditional group support.[29] In contrast to the students, they saw nonconformity and opposition as dangerous rather than essential to democracy. Bavarian officers interviewed for a study of their clashes with students argued that the use of force became necessary when students failed to follow police orders; according to the study, the officers did not question the orders they received and disparaged the demonstrators by referring to them as criminals, communists, and the like.[30] Although the police gradually altered their tactics of engagement, they still held to the Weimar-era view of mass psychology that stressed the irrationality and susceptibility to incitement of crowds.[31]

Aside from attracting media coverage, confrontations with the police helped foster a sense of solidarity among demonstrators. According to an SDS publication,

> In the collective standoff against the authoritarian force of police, the insults, the mocking, the poking fun at authority no longer remains limited to the secret fantasies of individuals. In the assault on police and even in retreat, not only do fear and pangs of remorse play a role, but also presence of mind and a flexing of muscles, weapons which for the present have been more effective against the violence of internalized constraints than against state violence. Contrary to bourgeois resentments and assumptions, in the protective anonymity of the masses the subjective energy of individuals is not annihilated but rather first comes to its own. That spontaneous action, collective initiative, self-organization of the masses could be practiced not just in discussions but were achievements of the agitating masses proves what a powerful driving force the lifting of individual repression is for the autonomy of the people....
>
> The importance the periodic *Krawalle* on the Kurfürstendamm have had for the consolidation of the antiauthoritarian movement corresponds freely with the relative lack of clarity that these actions projected outwardly.[32]

The effect these clashes had in mobilizing and uniting the APO became evident during the aftermath of the anti-Shah protests in Berlin on 2 June 1967. The confrontations between police and demonstrators that night led to the tragic death of first-time demonstrator Benno Ohnesorg. Speaking at a memorial service, Knut Nevermann voiced what many young people felt about Ohnesorg's death: "He took part in the demonstration.... Like many of us. Out of conscience, like many of us, to engage against injustice and for humanity. He was killed as one of us, who wanted to express our opinions. It could have happened to any one of us."[33] The widespread sense that "it could have been any one of us" bound a generation together in overwhelming solidarity and politicized otherwise complacent young people.

The goals of solidarity and publicity made public demonstrations important to the student movement and APO but did not make them necessarily democratic in spirit. Hitler, too, had seen the value of demonstrations:

> Mass assemblies are also necessary for the reason that, in attending them, the individual who felt himself formerly only on the point of joining the new movement, now begins to feel isolated and in fear of being left alone as he acquires for the first time the picture of a great community which has a strengthening and encouraging effect on most people. Brigaded in a company or battalion, surrounded by his companions, he will march with a lighter heart to the attack than if he had to march alone. In the crowds he feels himself in some way thus sheltered, though in reality there are a thousand arguments against such a feeling.[34]

He also noted the power of mass demonstrations in the Marxist world:

> [T]here were the gigantic mass-demonstrations with processions in which a hundred thousand men took part. All this was calculated to impress on the petty-hearted individual

the proud conviction that, though a small worm, he was at the same time a cell of the great dragon before whose devastating breath the heated bourgeois world would one day be consumed in fire and flame, and the dictatorship of the proletariat would celebrate its conclusive victory.[35]

The right of peaceful demonstration is seen today as an essential part of democracy. In the 1960s, however, two distinctly different views prevailed in the Federal Republic: one saw demonstrations as a form of participatory democracy, the other as a form of mob action manipulated by antidemocratic ringleaders.

How well did the demonstrations live up to the model of participatory democracy? Dutschke acknowledged the importance of putting theory into practice when he outlined how demonstrations should be organized: "Committees bound together by common experiences and personal friendship must take over the leadership of the demonstration, not organizers or functionaries."[36] Hitler, by contrast, had maintained, "from the outset, it is important to instill in our gatherings blind discipline and to ensure the authority of its leadership."[37] For Dutschke, meaningful participation of all demonstrators was to be encouraged as a means to building consciousness; manipulation on the part of the leadership was considered exploitative and self-defeating.

Despite the demonstrators' professed antiauthoritarian goals, a hierarchy among demonstrators had developed by the late 1960s. In 1967, Dutschke acknowledged the inefficiency of informal discussion groups in preparing for action.[38] Few students, let alone young people outside the universities or workers, were willing to commit to the focused intellectual training characteristic of the early phase of the SDS (1960–64). Action and provocation created a mass movement by attracting a broader range of participants, but the majority of those participants responded more to emotion than theory.[39] While vividly revealing the tension of modern society, satirical provocation did not require great intellectual capacity. An intellectual gap thus emerged within the movement that contributed to a sense of superiority among some members.[40] A few individuals soon came to dominate discussions, giving rise to elitism and a type of internal authoritarianism.[41] The media clearly played a role in this development. It sought leaders to explain the movement and the purpose of the demonstrations, and chose them either for their theoretical sophistication, verbal radicalism, or colorful personality. In fact, when participatory democracy did prevail, the press often criticized the demonstration as lacking direction.[42]

Dutschke himself became more and more of a media celebrity in the course of 1967 and early 1968. Bernd Rabehl recalled that "as a result, a sort of charismatic or populist type of mass democracy came into being in the SDS where people simply hung on his words, agreed with them and discussed nothing." Oskar Negt also lamented that the organizational question was not addressed and that the power of the leaders over demonstrators was not kept in check.[43] Without acknowledging it, Rabehl described the kind of mass psychology that critics of the demonstrations feared would lead to a totalitarian dictatorship like that of the Third Reich or the communist Eastern bloc.

Similar thinking about mass psychology shaped police attitudes toward crowds and demonstrations. Because the emotions of the crowd cannot be controlled, the argument ran, rational discourse is futile. Thus, while the democratic ideals of the demonstrators called for the free exchange of opposing viewpoints, the police understanding of crowd behavior taught that such dialogue proved useless and only delayed the inevitable. The strategy of the police was to separate the leader or leaders from the crowd on the assumption that the crowd would thus be rendered helpless. When possible they tried to prevent large gatherings altogether.[44] Their view of the student protests was conditioned by images of the mass rallies staged by the Nazis and communists, regardless of how demonstrators conducted themselves and the actual role of protest leaders. The police saw demonstrators not as individuals but as a collective mob in which individuals lost the ability to think for themselves and acted purely on emotion at the orders of a leader.

Jürgen Habermas was the first to charge the student protest with "left fascism."[45] Habermas, not completely unsympathetic to the movement, intended his comments as a warning of what might happen if the APO failed to reflect upon its goals and methods. The press seized on the phrase immediately, and the Springer newspapers and other conservative media outlets used it as a catchword for the "blind activism" and unacknowledged elitist and authoritarian tendencies of the student movement. Critics on the left and even within the protest movement itself noted the discrepancies between the democratic goals and the conduct of demonstrators.

Nevertheless, the demonstrations seem to have encouraged participatory politics. While acknowledging the authoritarian and terrorist offshoots of the protest movement, one must also note that the vast majority of those who took to the streets did not join radical splinter groups (the so-called *K-Gruppen*) or terrorist cells of the 1970s. While some retreated to private life, many found other outlets for political activism in *Bürgerinitiativen* (citizens' initiatives) and new social movements as well as in the mainstream political parties.

Bernd Jürgen Warneken has described the demonstration as "a physical means of expression that stands between purely verbal articulation and physical bodily engagement: it is the use of the body as a political means of expression, it uses body language to a certain extent as a form of political speech."[46] To be sure, different demonstrations sent different messages. The demonstrators generally adopted either a slow, casual gait for longer and more peaceful marches or a more energetic stride, but never a military march step. Whereas fascist and official demonstrations generally were characterized by disciplined and closed ranks, the protests of the 1960s (including many of the right-wing counterdemonstrations) maintained open and fluid borders.[47] The so-called strolling demonstrations provide an extreme example. While representing a creative and pragmatic response to prohibitions on demonstrations, the overall effect was one of democratic inclusion rather than authoritarian exclusion.

The Nazis' emphasis on *aufrechte Haltung* (erect posture or upright conduct) has been taken to mean many things. Thomas Balistier has noted that the "shoulders back, head high" posture exhibited pride and can be seen as indicative of the revisionist ideology of the Nazi Party: Germany would not bow before the dictated Versailles Peace. During the Third Reich, this body language was used to represent the freedom and vitality of the nation, but it also signaled militaristic leanings.[48] While similar terminology was used during the 1960s, the meaning was clearly different. When Dutschke used the phrase "*aufrecht gehen*," for example, the moral connotations of *aufrecht* seem to have been more important than the literal physical sense.[49] The students' posture reflected a casual attitude, and protest culture ridiculed rather than affirmed the virtues—cleanliness, order, punctuality, and so forth—traditionally associated with *aufrecht* behavior. Klaus Theweleit has noted that the Nazis saw two kinds of masses: a soldierly crowd formed with strict discipline under a leader, and the despised, formless mass that flows and teems. From this perspective, the demonstrations of the 1960s stand in stark contrast to the Nazi ideal.[50]

Although foregoing any sort of formal uniform, the demonstrators of the 1960s adopted a standard attire—blue jeans and T-shirts or sweaters—that concealed both gender and class differences. This choice of clothing reflected the financial situation of many of the struggling leftist students and their desire for "functional" clothing, but it also reflected conscious political choices. The students dressed like nonacademics. Through their "jeans-culture" they separated themselves from bourgeois norms and reflected the oppositional stance of the movement.[51] The gender divide was further blurred by the inversion of traditional hairstyles.[52] This culture of rebellion borrowed styles from popular icons such as Bob Dylan, Joan Baez, Che Guevara, and Mick Jagger.[53] The brown uniforms of the SA had also broken with prevailing norms of civilian dress during the Weimar Republic and reflected aspects of their protest against the status quo. Goebbels wrote in 1932, "all serve one common ideal, and the standardized uniform is the expression of the same conviction."[54] Individuality vanished beneath the uniform.[55] While separating themselves from the public at large by the way they dressed, the demonstrators of the late 1960s presented a colorful picture of diversity as differences in style of dress came to distinguish different factions within the APO. Such variations, one could argue, reflected the heterogeneity of protest movement.

After June 1967, many regulars at demonstrations dressed defensively in anticipation of a police assault. They purchased US Army surplus parkas and boots, ignoring their military origins. The parkas reportedly served as excellent protection against water cannons, and both the parkas and the boots were deemed excellent values and consistent with an antimaterialist ideology. Leather jackets also provided good protection. Federal Minister of the Interior Friedrich Zimmermann even considered banning leather jackets in demonstrations on the grounds that they functioned as a "passive weapon."[56] While the parkas and boots did not convey an especially militaristic image, the increasing presence of hard-hats struck many observers as not particularly compatible with peaceful protest.

Conclusion

Supporters and critics, past and present, might argue that "1968" had little to do with democracy or a democratic agenda. From the beginning, the extra-parliamentary opposition represented a heterogeneous cross section of Leftist political positions, from countercultural communards to dogmatic communists. Many of the leaders and participants espoused Marxist and neo-Marxist theories and denounced bourgeois capitalism and Western democracy. As the movement fragmented, hard-core communist groups adopted practices of an elite revolutionary avant-garde that were far removed from democratic principles. Likewise, the terrorist groups spawned by the student movement could hardly be credited with advancing the democratic order in West Germany either through their own actions or through the governmental reactions they provoked.

One must nonetheless acknowledge that thousands of demonstrators did not end up joining either the *K-Gruppen* or terrorist groups. And those groups, it should be noted, abandoned mass demonstrations as a political tool. After the splintering of the student movement in 1969–70, some individuals returned to private life, leaving politics altogether. Others returned to mainstream politics and helped transform the campaign strategies of both the SPD and CDU. Still others carried the "spirit of '68" into the new social movements and a myriad of civic initiatives. Peter Mayer-Tasch has observed that although many demonstrators later experienced a sense of "powerlessness and betrayal," student activism also "stimulated an increased political sensibility and self-awareness in people of almost all walks of life."[57]

Despite the failure of some of the students' experiments in antiauthoritarian living and education, their movement's emphasis on self-determination, codetermination, and grass roots politics produced numerous positive outcomes. Statistics on West German politics during the 1970s and 1980s point to an overwhelming expansion in political activism and grass roots activity.[58] In 1970, 1,380 demonstrations took place in the Federal Republic; in 1981, 5,722.[59] A half century earlier, an SA handbook asserted that "Germans will never be significantly moved by processions enacted by disparate groups of assorted men in civilian clothes, incapable of keeping in step, smoking and jabbering amongst themselves…. They are likely to perceive them as comical or as repulsive, perhaps even nauseating."[60] The fact that Germans today are positively moved by such groups is but one indication of how thoroughly German political culture has been transformed since the collapse of the Third Reich.

Notes

1. See Alexander P. Kostaras, *Zur strafrechtlichen Problematik der Demonstrationsdelikte* (Berlin, 1982), 19–20; Sebastian Cobler, Reiner Geulen, and Wolf-Dieter Narr, eds., *Das Demonstrationsrecht* (Reinbek, 1983); Thomas Blanke and Dieter Sterzel, "Demonstrationsfreiheit—Geschichte und demokratische Funktion," *Kritische Justiz* 4 (1981): 347–69; Ulrich K. Preuss, "Nötigung durch Demonstration—Zur Dogmatik des Art. 8 GG," in *Recht Justiz Kritik*, ed. Hans-Ernst Böttcher (Baden-Baden, 1985): 419–46. For background, see also Joachim Albrecht and Bernd Jürgen Warneken, *Als die Deutschen demonstrieren lernten* (Tübingen, 1986).
2. Peter Schütt, "Kulturpolitische Aktionen und Aufgaben der demokratischen Opposition," *Blätter für deutsche und internationale Politik* (August) 1968: 10.
3. Adolf Hitler, introduction to Heinrich Hoffmann, *Das braune Heer. 100 Bilddokumente: Leben, Kampf, und Sieg der SA und SS* (Berlin, 1932): viif.
4. See Gustave Le Bon, *The Crowd: A Study of the Popular Mind* (New York, 1921).
5. Hermann Lübbe has argued strongly against the claim that the 68ers ended the silence over Germany's fascist past and made great strides toward overcoming that past. Lübbe maintains that the student movement's antifascist critique was only a means to undermine the legitimacy of the system. See Hermann Lübbe, "Der Mythos der 'kritischen Generation': Ein Rückblick," *Aus Politik und Zeitgeschichte*, 13 May 1988, 18–19.
6. See Claudia Fröhlich and Michael Kohlstruck, "Vergangenheitspolitik in kritischer Absicht," in *Engagierte Demokraten: Vergangenheitspolitik in kritischer Absicht*, ed. Claudia Fröhlich and Michael Kohlstruck (Münster, 1999), 26.
7. Fritz Fischer, *Griff nach der Weltmacht: Die Kriegszielpolitik des kaiserlichen Deutschland 1914/18* (Düsseldorf, 1961); Karl Jaspers, *Wohin treibt die Bundesrepublik?* (Munich, 1966); Alexander Mitscherlich and Margarete Mitscherlich, *Die Unfähigkeit zu trauern: Grundlagen kollektiven Verhaltens* (Munich, 1967).
8. Detlef Siegfried, "Umgang mit der NS-Vergangenheit," in *Dynamische Zeiten: Die 60er Jahre in den beiden deutschen Gesellschaften*, ed. Axel Schildt, Detlef Siegfried, and Karl Christian Lammers (Hamburg, 2000), 100. Siegfried also argues that the critical discussion of the Nazi past was opened at least a decade before the 68ers arrived on the scene. See also Harold Marcuse, "The Revival of Holocaust Awareness in West Germany, Israel and the United States," in *1968: The World Transformed*, ed. Carole Fink, Philipp Gassert, and Detlef Junker (Washington, 1998), 421–31.
9. See Michael Schmidtke's chapter in this volume.
10. Vorbereitender Untersuchungs-Ausschuß an der FU, "Geplanter Mord!" [3 June 1967], in *Freie Universität 1948–1973: Hochschule im Umbruch*, vol. 5, *Gewalt und Gegengewalt (1967–1969)*, ed. Siegward Lönnendonker, Tilman Fichter, and Jochen Staadt (Berlin, 1983), 179.
11. For example, the Springer newspapers published a photo of a young woman with a head injury. The caption gave the impression that her injury had been caused by rowdy demonstrators; according to her own testimony, her wound was the result of police brutality. See Lönnendonker, Fichter, and Stadt, *Freie Universität*, 21. As the debate over press coverage of the 2 June incident continued, a number of collections of documents supporting the opposing positions were published. See, for example, the Axel Springer Verlag's *Studenten und Presse in Berlin* (Berlin, 1967) and the volume prepared for Studentschaft des Landes Berlin, R. P. Janz and D. Fitterling, *Berlin—2. Juni 1967. Feststellungen und Fragen: Zur Arbeit des parlamentarischen Untersuchungsausschusses des Abgeordnetenhauses von Berlin* (Berlin, 1967).
12. "SDS schreibt an BILD" (flyer issued in July 1967): Freie Universität Berlin, Archiv "APO und soziale Bewegungen," SDS-Dokumente, vol. 3.
13. See Jürgen Miermeister and Jochen Staadt, eds., *Provokationen: Die Studenten- und Jugendrevolte in ihren Flugblättern 1965–1971* (Darmstadt, 1980), 111, 144. See also Ernst Aust, "Schlagt den Faschismus, wo ihr ihn trefft: Brutaler Polizeiterror zum Schutze des Druck- und Mordhauses Springer," *Roter Morgen* (KPD/ML) (April) 1968: 1–2. It should be noted that

in the early 1960s, leftist students had strongly supported Israel and established contacts with Israeli youth. This changed dramatically in June 1967, just as the APO was catapulted into a mass movement. In the aftermath of the Arab-Israeli Six Day War, the majority of young German leftists associated Israeli Jews with American capitalism and imperialism. They sided with the Palestinians, seeing the Israelis not as victims but as oppressors. Thus, while the students were the "Jews" of 1968, the Jews had become the oppressors. Support for the Palestinian cause was interpreted by APO detractors as anti-Semitic. See Carole Fink's essay in this volume.

14. Klaus Theweleit, *Male Fantasies*, vol. 2, *Male Bodies: Psychoanalyzing the White Terror*, trans. Erica Carter (Minneapolis, 1989), 12–13.

15. "Aufruf zur Demonstration, Flugblatt zur ersten Osterdemonstration in Göttingen," reprinted in Heinz Grossmann and Oskar Negt, eds., *Die Auferstehung der Gewalt: Springerblockade und politische Reaktion in der Bundesrepublik* (Frankfurt am Main, 1968), 13.

16. Rudolph Ganz, "Langjähriger Haß hat sich blutig entladen," *Frankfurter Rundschau*, 5 June 1967.

17. Kai Hermann, "Goebbels' Nachfahren: Die Berliner Springer-Zeitungen verfälschen die Wahrheit," *Die Zeit*, 26 April 1968.

18. Stefan Aust, "Bluthunde, Tränengas, Knüppel. Staat der Gewalt: Sonderbericht über das Attentat auf Rudi Dutschke," *konkret* 5 (1968): 6–11, 37–40.

19. *Extradienst*, 24 February 1968; quoted in Rudi Dutschke, *Mein langer Marsch*, ed. Gretchen Dutschke-Klotz, Helmut Gollwitzer, and Jürgen Miermeister (Reinbek, 1980), 122.

20. "Jugendliche stürmen Kirchen und Theater," *Berliner Zeitung*, 13 April 1968.

21. "Hans-Georg von Studnitz," *Welt am Sonntag*, 14 April 1968; reprinted in Hans Joachim Winkler, ed., *Das Establishment antwortet der APO: Eine Dokumentation* (Opladen, 1968), 21.

22. Michael Kimmel, *Die Studentenbewegungen der 60er Jahre. BRD, Frankreich, USA: Ein Vergleich* (Vienna, 1998), 163–64.

23. Rudi Dutschke, "Wir fordern die Enteignung Axel Springers," *Der Spiegel*, 10 July 1967; reprinted in Rudi Dutschke, *Die Revolte: Wurzeln und Spuren eines Aufbruchs*, ed. Gretchen Dutschke-Klotz, Jürgen Miermeister and Jürgen Treulieb (Reinbek, 1983), 23; Rudi Dutschke, *Aufrecht gehen: Eine fragmentarische Autobiographie* (Berlin, 1981), 10.

24. Uwe Bergmann, Rudi Dutschke, Wolfgang Lefevre, and Bernd Rabehl, *Rebellion der Studenten oder Die Neue Opposition* (Reinbek, 1968), 77.

25. Rudi Dutschke, interview on the television program *Monitor*, 3 November 1967; quoted in Dutschke, *Mein langer Marsch*, 79.

26. SDS/KU-Autorenkollektiv, *Der Untergang der Bild-Zeitung* (Berlin, n.d.), 120ff; quoted in Klaus Hartung, "Versuch, die Krise der antiautoritaren Bewegung wieder zur Sprache zu bringen," *Kursbuch* 48 (1977): 28–29.

27. Manfred Rexin, "Reportage von der Vietnamdemonstration in West-Berlin," sound recording, 18 February 1968, Deutsches Rundfunkarchiv, Frankfurt am Main.

28. Walter Henkels, "Der Marsch auf Bonn," *Frankfurter Allgemeine Zeitung*, 13 May 1968; Rolf Zundel, "Das Notstands-Happening in Bonn," *Die Zeit*, 17 May 1968.

29. Klaus Weinhauer, "'Staatsbürger mit Sehnsucht nach Harmonie'—Gesellschaftsbild und Staatsverständnis in der Polizei," in Schildt, Siegfried, and Lammers, *Dynamische Zeiten*, 456–57.

30. Klaus Weinhauer, "Innere Unruhe: Studentenproteste und die Krise der westdeutschen Schutzpolizei in den sechziger Jahren," in *Nachkriegspolizei: Sicherheit und Ordnung in Ost- und Westdeutschland 1945–1969*, ed. Gerhard Fürmetz, Herbert Reinke, and Klaus Weinhauer (Hamburg, 2001), 314.

31. Weinhauer, "Innere Unruhe," 315.

32. SDS/KU-Autorenkollektiv, *Untergang*; quoted in Hartung, "Versuch," 28–29.

33. Rede von Knut Nevermann auf der Trauerkundgebung der FU am 8. Juni"; reprinted in Miermeister and Staadt, *Provokationen*, 107.

34. Adolf Hitler, *Mein Kampf*, trans. Ralph Manheim (Boston, 1943), 535. While the historical precedents of the Weimar Republic included a broad range of demonstrations, I have chosen

to focus primarily on Nazi demonstrations, most notably the SA and the demonstrations of state communism because these seem to have shaped postwar memories the most. See Marie-Luise Ehls, *Protest und Propaganda: Demonstrationen in Berlin zur Zeit der Weimarer Republik* (Berlin, 1997).

35. Hitler, *Mein Kampf*, 529.
36. Bergmann et al., *Rebellion der Studenten*, 81–82.
37. Hitler, *Mein Kampf*, 541.
38. Bergmann et al., *Rebellion der Studenten*, 80.
39. Dutschke, *Aufrecht gehen*, 10.
40. Bernd Rabehl, "Kampf, Kritik, Auflösung-Ausstieg und Niedergang der Studentenrevolte," *Frankfurter Hefte* 30, no. 4 (1975): 119.
41. See Gretchen Dutschke-Klotz, introduction to Dutschke, *Aufrecht gehen*, 14. One should also note that this was a male hierarchy, particularly within the SDS. Women seldom appeared as key figures in the organization or leadership of marches and rarely gave speeches. Women's frustrations with the hypocritical male antiauthoritarians led to a revolt within the SDS in the fall of 1968 and eventually to the establishment of the women's movement. The decentralized organizational structure of the women's movement represented a response to women's experiences with the hierarchical structure of the student movement.
42. As it did with the *Sternmarsch* against the Emergency Laws in Bonn in May 1968. *Die Zeit* described the indecisiveness and ineffectiveness of the action as the demonstrators marched to the French embassy to declare solidarity with French students: "The demonstration had many heads, but no head."
43. Ronald Fraser, ed., *1968: A Student Generation in Revolt* (New York, 1988), 149.
44. Weinhauer, "Staatsbürger," 466–67.
45. Hanover, 9 June 1967, following the burial of Benno Ohnesorg. Habermas was responding to certain aspects of a speech given earlier by Rudi Dutschke. Dutschke had already left the auditorium by the time Habermas spoke, and Habermas limited his critique to specific goals of the movement that, he argued, needed more reflection. Even though Habermas later clarified his comment so as not to appear as a condemnation of the entire protest movement, it was too late.
46. Bernd Jürgen Warneken, "'Massentritt': Zur Körpersprache von Demonstranten im Kaiserreich," in *Transformation der Arbeiterkultur*, ed. Peter Assion (Marburg, 1986), 65; quoted in Thomas Lindenberger, *Strassenpolitik: Zur Sozialgeschichte der öffentlichen Ordnung in Berlin, 1900–1914* (Bonn, 1995): 331.
47. Thomas Balistier notes that even in the National Socialist mass demonstrations, the masses were organized by "professional demonstrators" and the size and course of the demonstration closely controlled. Thomas Balistier, *Gewalt und Ordnung: Kalkül und Faszination der SA* (Münster, 1989), 60–61.
48. Balistier, *Gewalt und Ordnung*, 85.
49. Dutschke, *Aufrecht gehen*.
50. Theweleit, *Male Fantasies*, 4.
51. Marion Grob, *Das Kleidungsverhalten jugendlicher Protestgruppen in Deutschland im 20. Jahrhundert am Beispiel des Wandervogels und der Studentenbewegung* (Münster, 1985), 251.
52. Ute Frevert, *Women in German History: From Bourgeois Emancipation to Sexual Liberation*, trans. Stuart McKinnon-Evans (New York, 1989), 287.
53. Grob, *Kleidungsverhalten*, 235, 245, 271.
54. Joseph Goebbels, quoted in Balistier, *Gewalt und Ordnung*, 101.
55. Balistier, *Gewalt und Ordnung*, 100.
56. Grob, *Kleidungsverhalten*, 274–80.
57. Peter Cornelius Mayer-Tasch, *Die Bürgerinitiative-Bewegung* (Reinbek, 1976), 10.
58. The figures vary, but the trend toward greater participation is generally upheld in each. B. Armbruster and R. Leisner, *Bürgerbeteiligung in der Bundesrepublik: Zur Freizeitaktivität verschiedener Bevölkerungsgruppen in ausgewählten Beteiligungsfeldern (Kirchen, Parteien, Bürgerinitiativen und Vereinen)* (Göttingen, 1975); G. D. Radtke, "Die Bedeutung politischer Partizipation im

Prozess der Legitimierung politischer Herrschaft," in *Material zum Problem der Legitimität im modernen Staat*, ed. Albrecht Beckel et al. (Bonn, 1975), 14–27; R. Sehringer, "Formen der politischen und sozialen Partizipation," in *Lebensbedingungen in der Bundesrepublik: Sozialer Wandel und Wohlfahrtsentwicklung*, ed. W. Zapf (Frankfurt am Main, 1977), 843–932; Samuel H. Barnes and Max Kaase et al., *Political Action: Mass Participation in Five Nations* (Beverly Hills, 1979); D. P. Conradt, "Changing Political Culture," in *The Civic Culture Revisited*, ed. G. A. Almond and S. Verba (Boston, 1978).

59. Thomas Blanke and Dieter Sterzel, "Die Entwicklung des Demonstrationsrechts von der Studentenbewegung bis heute," in Cobler, Geulen, and Narr, *Das Demonstrationsrecht*, 84.

60. Quoted in Theweleit, *Male Fantasies*, 27.

Chapter 13

NEW LEFTISTS AND WEST GERMANY
Fascism, Violence, and the Public Sphere, 1967–1974

Belinda Davis

෴

> Nonsense! The FRG was not and is not fascistic! We can even give interviews—very nice!
>
> — Fritz Teufel[1]

The '68 era remains close to the surface of public memory: it has given way to a virtual explosion of scholarly and popular treatment. Some Germans have noted cynically how '68 has now become a third modern German past that, following on the transcendence of the Nazi and communist pasts, must be overcome.[2] The melding of these three pasts, and the raising of one through the other, follows consistently on contemporary practices within '68, a shorthand for the era from about 1965 through 1977. During that period, Germans of all political stripes regularly instrumentalized the notion of "fascism" and the need to overcome it as a means to understand and/or demonize contemporary political opponents.[3] This does not mean that such discussions were completely without substance.[4] In their bid for what they conceived as a better future for Germany, adherents of the New Left actively debated the presence of the Nazi past in the Federal Republic, above all in the intensification of state-authorized physical violence throughout this era and in the perceived ongoing corruption of the public sphere.

Yet contemporary activists who cast the "charge of fascism" (*Faschismusvorwurf*) at elements of West German state and society acknowledged that through various means it was this same society that had provoked their questioning and challenging nature. Moreover, the "public sphere(s)" created by New Left protestors themselves, through public acts, demonstrations, speeches, new forms of public assembly and action, and literally thousands of newspapers and journals, provided an imposing monument to serious public speech and argument—and

---

represented their own ongoing earnest commitment to the possibility of engaging fellow West German in critical discussion.[5] At the same time, acts of violence from all sides, though limited, became both the subject of and sometimes the conduit for these debates; charges of fascism acted for some as a justification of violence. Finally, while young West Germans pointed fingers at their elders, their activism spoke too to their conviction of their own implication in the German past, though their relation to that past remained ambivalent and troublesome for them. How "New Leftists" variously conceived of and acted on "fascism," specifically with reference to the question of violence, is a central question of this essay. This question will be examined particularly following two key moments: the shooting death of student Benno Ohnesorg in June 1967 and the dual deaths of imprisoned activist Holger Meins and Judge Günther von Drenkmann in November 1974.[6] If efforts to make political hay clearly played a role, as did varying levels of ignorance concerning the past, serious, skeptical, and engaged contributions also marked the discussion. Despite serious reflection for many on fascism, its role in fostering state and vigilante violence, and the need for violent response, the overwhelming majority of activists remained committed to communicating through one means or another with fellow West Germans as the best path to engendering change, however rapid, in that time and place. The terms of this discussion bear following as a means to trace activists' broader thinking about themselves and their country's past and future.

West Germans and the Fascist Past

The Federal Republic was defined from the beginning by its intended character as a "postfascist" state—though this signified variously for West Germans a thorough working-through of the fascist past, a concerted effort to look different than that past, or a complete break with that past, including in terms of memory. However earnestly many West Germans may have desired a total break (*Schlußstrich*) with the Nazi past, public and media discussion regularly raised that past in some form or other, even throughout the relative quiet of the 1950s, and certainly by 1960. This did not however always represent serious efforts to come to grips with that past in terms of responsibility and significance for the present.[7] The "youth" of 1967—those reaching about fifteen to twenty-five in that year—were born between 1942 and 1952: in other words those who had effectively no first-hand knowledge of (or participation in) the Nazi regime, or, those with the "mercy of a late birth," as many elders caustically characterized it.[8] Contemporaries and historians alike have linked the youth fascination with the Nazi past to its unknowability for them, including precisely in terms of their parents' general refusal to talk with them about their own experiences in this period.[9] Such fascination was a result of this often hidden knowledge, particularly at the family level, and the simultaneous saturation concerning the topic at a certain level in the public realm, through the Ulm, Eichmann, and especially Auschwitz trials, corresponding media reportage, trial transcripts, documentaries and fictional accounts from inside the country and without, highly visible debates on the statute of limitations question, etc., as well as the salutary efforts to introduce the topic in the schools, including as a part of school reform, such as it took place.

Hundreds of thousands of West German youth took to heart such warnings against the dangers of the past. They tried to reconcile these warnings with the rise of former Nazis to political prominence in the Federal Republic, the development of new radical right-wing parties alongside rashes of anti-Semitic acts in the 1960s, and a "future-oriented" vision that strove to block out the ubiquitous past. Many younger people perceived their elders generally as composed of nominal democrats (*Mitläufer der Demokratie*): those whose definition of "democracy" seemed as limited as their commitment to it. These youth also absorbed the message of the ubiquitous "fascism charge." Officials of the two German states, for example, regularly charged one another with acting as the legator of the Nazi past. In other words, there should be no surprise at youth fascination with the National Socialist past and a concomitant identity as "protectors against fascism": the best and worst of the postwar era, in all its contradictions and its publicly manifested tensions, all but ensured such a concern. Joschka Fischer has suggested that if Richard von Weizsäcker had made in 1963 his 1985 speech acknowledging ordinary Germans' implication in the Nazi past, youth protest may have felt far less necessary;[10] likewise so the violent interchanges among West Germans concerning the view of the past in the present.

There were clearly powerful psychological elements at play in this fascination and in the use of the fascism charge. Young adults in the mid-1960s felt anxious over their parents' actual or imagined complicity. Wilfried Mausbach highlights evidence that younger West Germans did not care as much that Jews had been murdered as that their parents had been murderers. Many secretly feared moreover that they were like their elders, whether this meant murderous, authoritarian, or even "pompous" or "mendacious," and sought to distance themselves as much as possible.[11] At the same time, young activists regularly hurled the charge of fascist and authoritarian at one another, confirming this feared proximity among contemporaries. Further, the Six Day War (as well as the Yom Kippur war) created a sense of "schizophrenia" for some among activists in that era, seeming to blur clear lines of "victim" and "perpetrator," as some viewed it.[12] This ambivalence spread too to views of America, as the country's involvement in Vietnam grew. It was very attractive to be able to displace "the fascist" to the other side of the Atlantic, all the more to the country that asserted its moral authority to (West) Germans in having liberated them from the Nazi regime.[13] But unconscious elements were hardly the only forces at play. For a range of reasons, antifascism, specifically with reference to the Nazi past, had drawn large numbers of students into activism from early on in the postwar period, and was perceived as a central aspect of the generational division of society. It was also a significant feature distinguishing the West German student movement from parallel movements elsewhere.[14] One activist remembered, "It all started with our whole desire to grapple with the Nazi period.... When I was a school girl it was already clear how much was swept under the rug."[15]

Youth campaigns confirmed these concerns from early on. In 1960 in Berlin, under the immediate provocation of the new "anti-Semitism wave," three thousand students and others called for the resignation of several high-level government officials who were former Nazis. Younger leftist readers responded positively to *Konkret* columnist Ulrike Meinhof's piece drawing parallels between Hitler and Christian Social Union leader Franz-Josef Strauss in a column against military build-up as early as 1961. (For his part, Strauss compared Meinhof and other activists to the virulent Nazi anti-Semite Julius Streicher.) A 1966 flyer of the Socialist German Student Union (Sozialistischer Deutscher Studentenbund, SDS) condemned "concentration camp contractor Lübke," alluding to the unwholesome past of the new Bundespräsident. Young New Left activists also condemned the perceived "structural Nazis" who formed the elite of West German politics and government more generally.[16] They formed an "extraparliamentary opposition" (außerparlamentarische Opposition, APO) in response to the "fascist" absence of a parliamentary opposition they perceived to be represented by the 1966 West German "grand coalition" government. Activists also looked beyond those in leadership positions. Martin Walser's 1965 essay "Unser Auschwitz" insisted that West Germans more broadly acknowledge the worst crimes of the Nazi past as their own. Students around the country sought to explore through lecture series and other means their own universities' "brown" past. The Free University student government made at least implicit reference to this past during all its campaigns and causes in this period, including concerning faculty personnel decisions and the right to invite public speakers. More broadly, New Left activists exhorted their peers to "Organize disobedience to the Nazi generation."[17] They thus declared themselves ready to fight against "fascism under other flags" as well: that is, imperialism, exploitation, authoritarianism, and state violence around the world. In response to screening of the 1966 film *Africa Addio*, students compared South African apartheid to Hitler's "building Jews their own cities."[18]

Police and superior officials in West Germany and West Berlin generally did not see the ensuing protest in the light activists intended: as precisely both a right and responsibility of West Germans, including those born after the end of the Third Reich.[19] From the early 1960s police regularly disbanded peaceful public student and youth gatherings, whether or not explicitly political, and including by the late 1960s those taking place on university campuses. There is a long history of physical violence between arms of the state and the populace in Germany, as in many countries.[20] In the postwar era, as earlier, there is good evidence that police regularly initiated violence with groups in public places out of a fear of losing control. But the level of preemptive and violent police response came as a shock to youth demonstrators in the 1960s (despite heavy-handed police response already to youth "*Rowdies*" and "*Halbstarken*" in the 1950s), who believed they were practicing democracy, in contrast to the Nazi past. At the same time, such police responses confirmed for them continuities with that past—and confirmed also the importance of their demonstrations. This was the case in June 1962 in the Schwabing district of Munich, as a violent police response to a nonpolitical youth gathering engendered a riot against police brutality and its "fascistic" overtones. The occasion was a turning point for many, including participant and later violent activist Andreas Baader. It was the case too in July 1964 as predominantly young protestors demonstrated peacefully against the West Berlin visit of Congolese Minister President Chombé and the Federal Republic's legitimation of his dictatorial regime. The resulting skirmish provided a new fillip to the incipient youth "movement" in West Berlin and brought activists Rudi Dutschke and Bernd Rabehl to the fore. Particularly among middle-aged and older Germans, the fracas revived interest in enacting new "emergency laws" in the Federal Republic to shore up state power against perceived threats to social order. Many West Germans of all ages saw evidence in this event and its aftermath of continuities between the Third Reich and the Federal Republic. For some, that evidence lay in the police attack on the demonstrators, while others negatively associated the disorderly political protestors with militants of an earlier period.

In response to these and like encounters with police, some young West Germans and West Berliners embraced a "political theater of violence" as one tactic. They staged symbolic events that would, they hoped, raise discussion of the actual physical violence routinely deployed, they maintained, by West German officials and also expose other perceived sites of violence and oppression. Certainly, activists in such groups as Munich's Aktion Theater and Subversive Aktion managed to elicit intensifying demonstrations of state force in response to their tactics. In 1965, a few protestors pelted West Berlin's Amerika Haus with eggs as a protest against the war in Vietnam. Police violently subdued and arrested the protestors; the act's symbolism was clearly well appreciated in some sense. Taking the action up several notches, in 1967, several activists attempted to stage a "pudding assassination" of US Vice President Hubert Humphrey during a visit to West Berlin: throwing small plastic bags of flour and paint at Humphrey was intended as an antiwar message. Police responded with preemptive force, treating the students they arrested as though the "assassination" plan had been real. Again, these activists had conveyed their message effectively—and had just as effectively elicited violent force in response. Violent official response seemed to activists at this point an unfortunate but predictable occasional by-product of the goal of opening the broad West German public's eyes to reality as they saw it.

Even many West Germans who did not condone actions such as the Humphrey "assassination" joined a crowd, some members of which were armed with tomatoes and eggs, to protest the Shah of Iran's state visit to West Berlin in June 1967. Demonstrators saw it as their responsibility, above all in the symbolically charged West Berlin, to demonstrate against state legitimation of someone they viewed as a violent, authoritarian leader. In response, police preemptively rushed the gathered demonstrators with tear gas and guns, injuring hundreds and killing first-time protestor Benno Ohnesorg. This was a major turning point for the student movement and the broader extraparliamentary opposition. It brought about a sense of crisis, of an "end of utopia," and fostered prolonged discussions of violence, fascism, and the nature of the West German state (while at the same time bringing hundreds of thousands of youth into political protest). The experience engendered pitched battles between police, New Left protestors, and others, lasting throughout the year and into 1968. New low points ensued, including the assassination attempt in April 1968 on SDS leader Rudi Dutschke, resulting in protestors' "Easter Unrest," and including considerable "violence against property." The bloody conflicts in Paris and especially the brutal suppression of the Prague Spring contributed to a generalized sense of despair, and a sense that West Germany was little more likely to succeed than Paris, and was perhaps all too much like Prague. The November 1968 "Battle of the Tegeler Weg" in Berlin represented another nadir, marked after its peaceful start by police threats and assaults, leading this time to a response of "real" violence by the activists. By the end of 1968, most activists had retreated from the streets in despair and organizational disarray as well as under an official ban on public political demonstrations, itself the source of renewed charges of fascism. This was the start for many of a move toward a broad creation of alternative cultures and "living worlds," eschewing for a time substantial direct confrontation of officials and mainstream West German/West Berlin society. A tiny number sought rather to raise the stakes through acts of demonstrative violence—though maintaining the concept of violence against property only at this point, except in self-defense, as they claimed. For them, the state's violent response was not an unfortunate by-product, but rather precisely what they sought to expose to the larger West German public.

As shaken as activists were by Ohnesorg's death, they felt equally frustrated and angry (as did to be sure many of their parents' generation). Many officials and a significant segment of the West German media cast the blame back on the activists—and on their "fascist" practices. Baden-Württemberg Minister President Hans Filbinger described youth protest in this period as "a frightful reversion to fascistic methods," and warned other students against these "radical agitators, who call themselves students, but who are actually professional revolutionaries, who exploit one's actions in a way that could have lifelong consequences," by which Filbinger simultaneously invoked the communist threat. In turn Filbinger threatened activists with official consequences of an unnamed type.[21] A number of newspapers, most infamously the Springer-owned *Bild*, boasting the largest circulation in Germany, ran dramatic, baiting headlines day after day, as it continued to do through the coming years. In the months preceding June 1967, *Bild* already typically described student protestors as employing methods "like the Nazis and communists in Weimar."[22] This dual attack on protestors only intensified after Ohnesorg's death. In response to 2 June, *Bild* editors wrote, "Now the fun and the compromise and the democratic tolerance stops. We have something against SA methods."[23] From this perspective, it was the protestors who had initiated the violence at every turn—or, at the very least, their conduct had necessitated a violent response. These newspapers described the "pudding assassination" as though the students had threatened a real murder.[24] They identified protestors as dangerous traitors who threatened West German law, order, and, by the late 1960s, the now fragile prosperity. In this sense, Benno Ohnesorg got only what he deserved—or was alternately the victim of the "FU-Chinese," an anticommunist reference to the demonstrators themselves.[25] Youth activists were the inner enemy, tied to East Germany and the Soviet Union, and bent on bringing down the fledgling "Western" state, and were thus as bad as the Nazis.[26] Simultaneously, *Bild* and other papers, as well as radio, likened New Left political theater and protest more generally to Nazi actions such as *Kristallnacht*. Most critically, some of these media outlets thereby encouraged physical violence against protestors. Even after 2 June, many articles found police responses to protests inadequate and urged "lynch justice."[27] These newspapers, in other words, offered accusations of fascism as justification for practices associated with fascism.

This language hit its mark among *Bild* readers. Thousands of primarily middle-aged "counter-demonstrators" took to the streets themselves, chillingly crying "lynch [the protestors], hang them" as well as "cut off [their] hair."[28] They wrote breathtakingly violent letters, particularly to Berlin SDS leader Rudi Dutschke, threatening his life and those of his family, as well as to the Free University student government, West Berlin-based Kommune I, Frankfurt activist Daniel Cohn-Bendit, and other groups and individuals.[29] Individuals called in to a talk show on which Cohn-Bendit appeared, claiming typically to the activist of Jewish heritage that he should be thrown into a concentration camp.[30] Marking a critical difference with their own "provocative communication," in response to media entreaties, counter-demonstrators physically attacked those they perceived as youth protestors. Unemployed painter Josef Bachman would be inspired by such press to attempt to assassinate Rudi Dutschke in April 1968. Many wrote Dutschke in the hospital to express their regret that he had survived and to threaten him with future attempts.

Bild and like-minded newspapers were hardly representative of the press or the media more broadly in their portrayal of youth activism.[31] The left-liberal *Spiegel*, along with *Die Zeit* and *Stern*, covered student political activities more judiciously and frequently gave voice to student leaders by running interviews with them. Indeed, the level of mainstream media attention to university politics generally represents a notable contrast to students' sense of being silenced and ignored. But interviewers often asked leading—and misleading—questions.[32] Presumably in a ploy to win readers, *Der Spiegel* and *Stern* also regularly printed images portraying protestors as wild and demonic, often in contrast with the impression conveyed by the text.[33] *Stern's* titillating language also often served to misrepresent activists. Television journalists would begin to broadcast ever more sensationalist images in this period, creating "surreal crime dramas" out of the violent clashes, particularly after April 1968, and increasing throughout the 1970s.[34]

For their part, the broad range of New Left activists responded in stunned shock after Ohnesorg's death. Tens of thousands of hitherto nonactive students at the university and high school levels, as well as a much broader community, now joined existing activists, roused by the death and other injuries, as well as by their sense of being unjustly characterized. Many others asserted their support for the activists. Protestors still maintained hope in the usefulness of their demonstrations in calling the attention of their fellow West Germans to what they perceived as the terribly destructive aspects of both official and media activity. But the innocence and "playfulness" of the movement were now largely gone, as many protestors now took the message that contemporary fascism was a danger not only outside the country but also within. (Some leading activists have claimed retrospectively that this was largely a political ploy on their part, that they believed this represented no newly "typical" escalation of violence.[35] But most seem to have been very genuinely concerned that this represented the beginning of a new German fascism.) A flyer of the national SDS office claimed in the aftermath of the shooting, "This is the first postwar political murder in the Federal Republic, celebrating the 'strength of order.' It reminds one of the situation in [the Weimar Republic], as police and paramilitary bands attempted to use the means of political assassination, including of suspects among their own ranks to liquidate the democratic opposition."[36] Another flyer asked, "Who is it that is actually provoking street fights?" commenting on the "enormous police forces" put in place by the "police regime à la Albertz" (mayor of Berlin).[37] The Socialist Higher Education Organization of Berlin (Sozialistischer Hochschul-Bund, SHB) castigated the reckless, murderous behavior against bearers of tomatoes and eggs in the name of "democracy" and "antiauthoritarianism."[38] SDS issued a statement claiming that actions of the police plus "paramilitary forces" (such as the paid "supporters" of the Shah) served to "invite in the fascists," creating the situation of emergency (*Notstand*) that authorities sought to avoid.[39] In response to West Berlin Mayor Klaus Schütz's characterizations of student methods as "fascistic," Berlin SDS leaders retorted, "Today pogrom and propaganda, tomorrow the final solution, Herr Schütz."[40] Rudi Dutschke responded with astonishment to the column in *Bild*, asking "who is it here that is demonstrating SA methods?"[41] Gretchen Dutschke believed "'tolerance' went only toward old Nazis."[42]

Activists and Paradoxes

The wide range of activists thus implicated turned hopefully to the broader West German public. Peace activists proclaimed, "we are not provoking anyone!" while members of the Evangelical student organization, opening their flyer with the polite "Dear Ladies and Gentlemen," protested that the students were the victims, not the perpetrators.[43] Through their messages, activists exposed two paradoxes in their thinking. First, they expressed their simultaneous sense of their own power to communicate and bring about change, and that of their own helplessness and victimization. Secondly, they telegraphed their continued hope for their ability to "convince" the larger West German public of the terrible problems they perceived, while some began to despair of the possibility of this kind of change—precisely because of the BRD's "fascistic" nature. Berlin SDS flyers addressed the public at large on the charge of fascism leveled against students, clearly maintaining hope of convincing this public, while emphasizing the excesses of officials: "Do you really believe that defenseless and weak students could organize a bloodbath? Who terrorized you from 1931 to 1933, armed Nazis or unarmed Social Democrats and communists?... Why has it been kept quiet that [Ohnesorg] was *murdered by an aimed pistol shot*?"[44] But as activist Gudrun Ensslin (who was later to lead the Red Army Faction) famously remarked, directly after the shooting of Ohnesorg, "this is the Auschwitz generation and there is no arguing with them."[45] Most activists demonstrated considerable ambivalence—and one could argue this was no less the case even for Ensslin, as subsequent acts might be interpreted. SDS leaders claimed in a flyer that the shooting was "only a link ... in a long chain in the process of the demolition of democracy and the growth of neofascist tendencies in our society," suggesting both continuity and renewed fascistic tendencies—though they maintained hope in the prospect of stemming this movement, including by making fellow Germans aware of it. Reinhard Strecker, a longtime activist against Nazi continuities in the Federal Republic, bemoaned that "especially in the wake of June 2nd," "we are powerless! They can shoot one of us and nothing happens.... They speak ... exactly as in the Third Reich."[46]

There was good cause for protestors' paradoxical sense of their own position. Certainly the negative attention they received supported a sense of their importance and influence beyond their own circles. Moreover, media attention remained ambiguous in its message. The mainstream press—both more and less responsible—badgered student association (AStA) leaders for their immediate assessment of and responses to the Six Day War, indeed as though these students were government officials responsible for making a statement to lead the public. Journalists taunted students for their insistence that, in light both of the complicated nature of the war and of the simultaneous shooting of Ohnesorg, they needed more time to think through their responses. Some reporters intimated they exerted this pressure because of the necessity of representing organized students' views.[47] (*Bild* editors for their part implied the existence of anti-Semitism and other characteristics from the Nazi past among students for not jumping to support the Israeli position, part of a way in which Axel Springer and his editors tried to assert their own break with the past, tied closely also to a Cold War vision of totalitarianism.[48]) A letter by Oskar Negt, then a well-known postdoctoral student of Jürgen Habermas, appeared prominently in the *Frankfurter Rundschau,* cynically admiring the "state apparatus with its compact forms of violence" –and excoriating the mainstream press, for turning "pudding into knives," and thereby contributing to Ohnesorg's premeditated murder."[49] This attention to student opinion as a central element of public discourse, as well as students' own prodigious writing and speech-making, occurred alongside deepening incursions against civil liberties and public expression, including the April 1968 ban on public demonstration and the forced dissolution of the SDS. Notably, those officials, publishers, and others who most virulently attacked student protestors ascribed the most power and threatening potential to the latter.

Charges of fascism abounded then from both sides in the aftermath of Ohnesorg's death. What was really behind it, from the perspective of student and APO activists? Many activists took the charge very seriously, but they did not always agree on the bases. New Leftists broadly asked: Was the West German state and society "fascist"? What characteristics defined it as such? The violence of state organs? The absence of a functional public sphere? How meaningful was the argument that West Germany more closely resembled Latin America's dictatorships—or the Third Reich—than a functioning parliamentary democracy? Did it matter whether it was closer to present Latin American or Greek dictatorships or to the Nazi past? What were the defining features of fascism itself, and how seriously ought one to take Horkheimer's dictum that whoever spoke of fascism must be willing to discuss capitalism? Was the Federal Republic postfascist, prefascist, or simply still fascist, and what did one's conclusions suggest in terms of response? Particularly after the attempt on Dutschke's life, activists also began to ask: did a negative assessment of the Federal Republic's democratic potential allow for or even require a violent response, and, if so, what kind?

After June 1967, students and other critics pointed accusingly to a dismayingly easy willingness to resort to "fascistic" violence among both officials and members of the press.[50] But in the aftermath of the shooting, few seriously entertained a physically violent response, even in self-defense, as a useful reaction. Students and other New Left activists despaired of what they saw as widespread popular acceptance of official and press representations, finding in this evidence of the political complacency of their parents and others, far more committed to order and prosperity than to democracy and the defense of civil rights, and willing to accept living in a "pseudo-democracy" (*Scheindemokratie*). National SDS leader and theorist Hans-Jürgen Krahl noted ruefully that "the forms of the liberal public sphere, nonviolent struggles for power in parliament ... all those emancipating capacities of the middle class have now long decayed."[51] Free University postdoctoral student and activist Rolf Tiedemann mournfully noted in a speech to Berlin students that it took Ohnesorg's death to draw the attention of many German citizens to these abuses of official power. But even then, he claimed, there was little condemnation of "police-state methods," nor scarcely criticism of "police terror."[52] All told, he concluded, this represented a renewed "fascization (*Faschisierung*) of society." That characterization was repeatedly invoked in SDS circles in this period as both cause and effect of state repression.[53] Still, overall such activists tried to convince members of this same society of what they perceived as the dangers of their ways. This response related to activists' uncertainty over the "fascist" character of West Germany. Their implicit definition of fascist seems to have changed over time, and the epithet's meanings multiplied as it became increasingly commonplace after the events June 1967. If activists had earlier identified particular aspects of West German state and society as fascist, now they cast these charges more directly at West German officials, in light of their own domestic actions; as one SDS flyer noted, nowhere else had representatives of the state managed to kill a student.[54]

Yet following an initial period of reaction rife with reference to the Nazi period, New Leftists made increasingly few references to that past even as they increased use of the term "fascist"; they focused rather on the Federal Republic's purported similarities with other contemporary authoritarian regimes, as well as with the United States' actions in Vietnam. This shift stemmed from numerous sources. Despite charges by some, New Leftists did not have to fully or even partially support the GDR to lend credence to the role of capitalism in fostering fascism. The series of articles on fascism in *Das Argument* provides one prominent example among many of efforts to work through this understanding.[55] Student protestors were divided and conflicted over responses to Israel after this time, and, however ill-connected, many seemed to eschew evoking a past in which Jews figured as victims. Some felt all the more ambivalent as publisher Axel Springer positioned himself as a foremost defender of Israel. Age was one significant factor in determining how implicated individual activists felt with reference to Germany's genocidal past, and this was closely related to their ability to distance themselves far more easily from the Nazi past generally, and to eschew it as a frame of reference.[56] Paradoxically, in the immediate aftermath of 2 June, many student protestors compared their own fates to that of Jews under Nazi persecution, casting themselves as terrorized victims. SDS executive members proclaimed themselves "Jews of anticommunism" and "long-haired ersatz Jews." Activist Heinz Grossmann condemned the "pogrom" against West German students and other activists and even invoked the concentration camps in describing their treatment at the hands of the state.[57] Columnist Armin Mohler noted cynically that "young West Germans wrap themselves in the bodies of Jews … to gain an advantage."[58] But this did not appear to be simple political strategizing, or at least not exclusively.

Differing Views of Fascism

Differing views of fascism were related too to the political fracturing on the left that this period helped precipitate. In the wake of violent conflict with police and other West German citizens, activists on the left began to identify themselves with various political philosophies and figures: antiauthoritarianism and Soviet-leaning Marxism-Leninism, for example, and Trotsky, Mao, and Che Guevara.[59] For some on the left, especially Moscow-allied Marxist Leninists, fascism was defined precisely by its historical anticommunism. This made any anticommunist a fascist, thereby implicating most of West German society, the very prestige and position of which was based on its Cold War anticommunism. Others found this "undifferentiated defamation" a "very blunt tool," hardly the kind of complex understanding required to devise successful counterstrategies.[60] For adherents of Mao or Che Guevara, fascism was visible most clearly in its incarnations among Southeast Asian and Latin American governments. For these activists and some others, the Federal Republic was not so much fascist as "fascistoid," a term suggestive of repressive leaders anxious to squelch political expression through physical brutality. A related perspective, drawing on both the Soviet Marxist-Leninist and Trotskyite positions, saw a more or less functional equivalence between fascism and late capitalism. For others, "fascistoid" indicated that the Federal Republic had simply not yet blossomed again into full-fledged fascism.

This variety of views of fascism that shifted focus away from the Nazi past might seem to render nugatory the "continuity question." But activists still held intense debates over whether the deadly state brutality of 2 June, coupled with irresponsible yellow press campaigns that intensified in the coming year, was evidence of a persistence of fascism in Germany. Speaking at a forum to discuss Ohnesorg's death, Frankfurt professor Ludwig von Friedeburg claimed that authorities had turned what had indeed been a democratic state into a police state. Negt, Krahl, and other activist leaders agreed that West Germany had at some level achieved its proclaimed "Western" ideals in the aftermath of the war. They found however that officials demonstrated far too great a willingness to let go of those ideals in favor of raw power and control when it suited them. Ironically, the façade of democratic liberalism, the basis (along with its anti-communism) for the new country's international prestige, was dropped most unceremoniously precisely during moments of international attention: the visits of Chombé, Humphrey, and the Shah. Citing this tendency, Rolf Tiedemann feared that "fascisization" was a deeply rooted and unbroken trend that remained hidden just below the surface of West German society.[61] Certainly the parade of West German public officials with former associations with the Nazi Party did not help mitigate this continuity thesis. Nor did such bizarre *Bild* headlines as "This wouldn't be happening with Adolf" and "Political enemies to the KZ!" that intended, apparently, to demonstrate the "fascist" qualities of the protestors.[62] Berlin SDS leader Bernd Rabehl came down on both sides of the fence, claiming ironically that the "pogrom" perpetrated against the students made clear "the totalitarian character of the postfascistic/fascistic FRG." Poet Hans-Magnus Enzensberger also spoke provocatively in terms of "old-new Nazis."[63] Still others now suggested that the continuities were less specifically with the immediately preceding regime than with the longer history of German authoritarianism.[64]

One's view on the continuity question had signal practical consequences. If fascism had remained hidden in West Germany for two decades, strategies exposing this ugly underbelly were perceived by some as positive, the first step toward attacking it. If West German officials had indeed managed to some degree to build a true alternative to the fascist past, then the increasingly insistent New Left protest was a dangerous game that risked provoking fascist qualities that might otherwise not exist. Reflecting a critical Social Democratic position, emphasizing the not always visible positive impact the student movement had made, Jürgen Habermas insisted after Ohnesorg's death that it could and should reinvigorate and democratize the public sphere. He shared activists' disgust for the actions of Berlin police and the officials who supported them. At the same time, Habermas infuriated activists by warning polemically of the dangers of "left-wing fascism," by which he characterized even the "demonstrative violence" of throwing toma- toes, a foreboding "game with terror, with fascist implications."[65] Reiterating the position he had taken before Ohnesorg's death, Habermas argued that despite his own serious reservations about the ruling CDU-SPD "grand coalition," renewed commitment to developing the West German public sphere was the only appro- priate response. Conversely he warned that justifying violent action of any sort though specious comparison of the Federal Republic to the Third Reich or other dictatorial regimes would have only negative consequences and potentially pro- voke a fascist response from the state.[66]

But after 2 June, many SDS leaders and student activists found themselves unconvinced about the prospects for the West German public sphere—at least as Habermas defined it, and this sentiment only grew for some.[67] At the same time, most demonstrated an obvious continued investment in the concept of the public sphere. Their own acts went far toward creating an alternate public sphere, in a fashion that grew exponentially in the coming years, precisely in response to their concerns for the West German state and society. But student leaders rejected Habermas's characterization of their view as "voluntarist," and as not based in the material, structural, or political realities of the Federal Republic. Indeed, they claimed, they were the more sober-minded assessors of the current situation and the possibilities it offered. Dutschke observed that the limits of what students had achieved at the Free University—the "Berlin model" to which Habermas had pointed—proved the sterility of Habermas's proposed strategies.[68] Negt maintained hope in the ability of a "determined but weak democracy-conscious minority" to defend against the "creeping fascisization of the state apparatus, which threatens to asphyxiate societal life."[69] But others felt caught in the paradox that powerful acts of communication—including throwing tomatoes, and even simply peacefully marching—were viewed as fascistic and violent, while the state clearly controlled the forces of violence and had demonstrated its willingness to use them against its own citizens. Many other young West Germans, however, felt the best course of action after the initial pitched response to the events of 2 June was to retreat from active public protest for a while and to keep careful watch on events abroad.

Some activists turned a critical eye back on the APO and the student move- ment. Among the multifarious factions and fragments, young activists railed charges of fascist tendencies against one another.[70] Trying to present themselves as more antifascist than other groups, they identified the Social Democrats as "social fascists" with little concern for the significance of such rhetoric in Germa- ny's past. Sympathetic professor Peter Brückner warned students in turn against following the model of a fascist state's reduction of human beings to ideologies and abstractions.[71] Other sympathizers also chided activists. We have already mentioned Habermas's concern about "left fascism." Writers such as Peter Sch- neider, Erich Kuby, and members of Gruppe 47 called the SDS burning of cop- ies of *Bild*, "fascist," even if intended as a "theatrical" act. In an essay entitled "Das Israelpseudo der Pseudolinken," Professor Michael Landmann identified "latent fascist tendencies" in some groups' easy and ironic attacks on Israelis as "European imperialists" and on the basis of their alliance with the United States.[72] Landmann found some of the activists thereby extremely hypocritical in their characterizations; some he found frightening, such as the leftist groups that circulated anti-Israel flyers bearing slogans like "Strike the Zionists Dead, Make the Middle East Red."[73] Unsurprisingly critics of the activists responded with a sustained "anti-Semitism charge" (*Antisemitismusvorwurf*). For West German "antifascists" this was a dangerous game, even if they were committed to a different image of the fascist danger they now envisioned.

Of greatest concern to some activists and sympathizers alike was the question of whether student "violence" in the form of throwing eggs or "pudding bombs" or even calls to burn down department stores could be related to fascism—or whether it should be seen as a serious engagement with the public sphere. Students were outraged at being caricatured as violent and dangerous hooligans when they felt they had been so careful to avoid violence. Protestors expressed despair as even "sympathetic" interviewers regularly attempted to get Rudi Dutschke to claim that he preached violence.[74] In the aftermath of the Ohnesorg murder, some activists began discussing whether pudding bombs were really enough, whether their symbolic acts could possibly communicate anything positive to the broad West German public, and whether other forms of physical violence might now be necessary, as a part of the long march through the institutions, and even without a mass basis of the working class. Some now seriously debated the usefulness of violent acts as a means to make their case, as Dutschke, Herbert Marcuse, and others formulated elaborate positions on the question.[75] Without ruling out the possibility that physical violence might at some point be necessary in some places, Dutschke and other SDS leaders, following Marcuse, ultimately rejected it as an option in West Germany for the time being. For the moment at least, most student activists followed suit, though some adhered to the formula "violence against things, yes; violence against people, no."

These debates were sharpened once more by the attack on Dutschke in April of the following year. In the wake of the now eighteen months of regular violent interaction with police, the November 1968 "battle of the Tegeler Weg" was another pivotal moment in the discussion of "fascism" and violence. The AStA executive of the Free University mounted a major discussion of "the violence question" following the conflict. Many of those attending demonstrated fundamental agreement with speaker Professor Helmut Gollwitzer's claim that only fascists acted violently without very careful consideration.[76] Increasing numbers now averred the impossibility of working within the existing "pseudo-parliamentary democracy."[77] Many allied themselves more explicitly with the myriad political factions arising out of the New Left. Although they continued with leafleting campaigns and other small-scale actions, they spent considerable time talking among themselves and writing for one another in planning for future political action. Students continued active campaigns in *Hochschulen* around the country, proclaiming strikes and other actions linking demands for reforms at their own schools with issues of international concern; indeed, strikes and other small-scale actions had increased since June 1967. The "new social movements"—from feminism to environmental awareness to antiviolence campaigns to the most local citizens initiatives, as well as to the range of "K (communist)-Groups" and antidogmatic "Basis" groups, and to the concomitant proliferation of a breath-taking counterculture, bringing in new age cohorts of activists—formed a truly impressive and vibrant alternative political scene and alternate "public spheres," though arising in part out of despair (and representing as well periodic confrontations with violence and the "violence question").[78] But the sense of unified purpose and large-scale efforts that peaked in 1967 and 1968 was accompanied by growing disbelief in the possibility of achieving transformations in domestic and foreign policy under prevailing circumstances through existing means.

Activism and Violence

It was against this background that a tiny number of activists turned to terrorism in the 1970s, which was to provoke ever greater violence and an ever deeper siege mentality in West Germany. For the broader radical left, the emergence of the small groups committed to violent activism put the questions of violence, fascism, and the public sphere in a new light—and was a cause of discomfort, fear, and despair. At the same time, they saw police violence and violent official and media rhetoric as central to creating terror and terrorists in the first place.[79] The move to break Andreas Baader out of jail in May 1970, including the first "offensively" violent act against a person, is usually seen as the "birth" of the RAF, the group on which officials and the media focused the greatest attention. Activists saw a direct link between the "fascist state" that had dissolved the SDS and the rise of such groups as the RAF, as tiny as they were.[80] Should individuals or groups who moved from benign "guerrilla theater" to "urban guerrilla" tactics, who moved from provocative rhetoric about the possibility of violence to the realization of violence, be defended? If so, should the defense be on the basis of the violent activists' message, their right to pursue the means they espoused, their claim to be acting only in self-defense, or their mistreatment and victimization at the hands of the state? Was solidarity with these activists an act of moral necessity? Would solidarity display political strength or mean political suicide? Were the RAF and the 2.Juni group—named of course for the date Ohnesorg was shot—indeed even leftist, and if so, in what sense? Was their effect not to abet the right rather than the left only misleading leftist admirers? Were they not, in their violent acts, adopting the "fascism" they claimed to seek to destroy—indeed seeming to prove Habermas's point? Or were they more prominently victims of official and press manipulations, like the broader New Left?

The series of shoot-outs and other violent incidents associated with the RAF in 1972 kept these issues in active discussion. Many declared tentative support, joining hunger strikes on behalf of political prisoners, in one case naming a youth center after a slain violent activist. Many activists as well as "sympathizers" were powerfully motivated by increasingly hateful and violent headlines above all in *Bild*. Violence reached a new level in November 1974 with the starvation of imprisoned RAF member Holger Meins and the subsequent assassination of SPD judge Günther von Drenkmann. These events unleashed a new flood of communications among leftist political groupings, reflecting a still impressive sense of political engagement on the left as well as considerable interaction even among estranged philosophical camps. Such communications were ironically in part a product of the way in which these groups had been lumped together, along with violent activists, by still more violent and hateful language in some segments of the press and in other public venues. Though many on the left had, like the broader society, largely ignored the hunger strikes undertaken by Meins and before Meins's demise, the left saw his death—another form of "extreme communication"—as a terrible failure on the part of West German officials, and as a substantiation at some level of RAF charges of prisoner torture through isolation and sensory deprivation. A widely circulated photograph of Meins's starved body was an extremely potent communication indeed, raising concern and ire even beyond the left.[81] Many took to heart Dutschke's moving graveside promise, "Holger, the struggle goes on"—despite Dutschke's own lasting ambivalence toward the RAF's strategies and assessments, including those concerning the "fascism question."

The complicated question of precisely how the struggle would be continued became much more difficult after members of the group 2.Juni assassinated Judge Drenkmann in revenge for Meins's death. To be sure, Drenkmann's murder was at least as disturbing to the broader left as Meins's death, if not more so. This was the first time these violent activists had explicitly set out with the aim of killing a particular individual—and, moreover, had chosen their victim largely as a symbol rather than for his own particular perceived transgressions. Leftists bemoaned, among other things, violent activists' apparent willingness to play into official and press representations of them as murderous beasts. They rued, too, that they would always be included in the newest charges and fresh crackdowns. Present and former activists sought new ways to talk and think about this fresh crisis. Charges of fascism figured prominently in the subsequent exchanges between leftists and their critics. The charge was also taken up by those, close philosophically to the RAF, who espoused immediate action to initiate revolution. Jürgen Seiffert claimed that the Federal Republic demonstrated an authoritarian but not fascist character, and to characterize it as such would be to play the officials' own game.[82] But Leftist university professor Christian Sigrist claimed at a teach-in following Meins's and Drenkmann's deaths that the West German state had now achieved a new postwar level of fascism and that the leftist response had to reflect that fact.[83] The Trotsky League claimed in response to Meins's death that the state itself was "terrorist" and had to be destroyed.[84] Contributors to *Revolutionärer Zorn*, coming closest to the RAF position, wrote in connection with Meins's and Drenkmann's deaths that "fascism comes as the punishment when one fails to advance the revolution." They called for "armed resistance against fascism and bourgeois violence."[85] A large number, including members of various "K Groups," concurred after Meins's death with the necessity of violent revolution in response—ultimately, at least.

But for most New Leftists, "armed resistance" and revolution remained highly questionable for the present. Use of violence would potentially reproduce the worst of the state's tactics, and would most likely end catastrophically. For all their certainty of view, Trotsky League members qualified their message to say revolution would happen only at some point in the indefinite future. They claimed that the most burning question at the moment was how to draw the working-class masses away from the hypnotic public power of *Bild*. They noted that the RAF's and 2.Juni's violence only nourished *Bild*'s apocalyptic vision.[86] Editors of *links* wrote in a special edition that precisely the threat of a "seizure of power" by Strauss and Dregger made the Drenkmann assassination, as well as the kidnapping of Peter Lorenz soon thereafter, "tactically stupid."[87] Indeed, despite a general consensus among those still active in the New Left that revolution would ultimately be necessary to transform "fascist" West Germany, activists generally continued in practice to pursue transformation from within existing and societally accepted spaces of action. Members of the German Communist Party (DKP) spent their time running workshops for and meetings with factory workers and school-age youth respectively, attempting to woo them into the party. Members of the Long March group exhorted other leftists to focus on helping the working class face and overcome the fascism of the state—by looking first to themselves.[88] The Communist Student Group (Kommunistische Studenten Gruppe, KSG) of Aachen found "the response to state torture" taken by Meins and others "absolutely necessary"—"communists and democrats" must after all fight "hard against terror," the terror of the "Hitlerian state" and its "Nazi-style executions."[89] But like most leftists, the KSG drew the line at defending Drenkmann's assassination. Many radical leftists felt the most moral response lay in renouncing and condemning all violence as a hallmark of "bourgeois morality." Daniel Cohn-Bendit would make the case that New Leftists somehow needed to negotiate some kind of rapprochement between the violent activists and the state.[90] Yet for some this seemed only to take them back to square one; indeed they saw the two "sides" as playing the same very dangerous game. Many New Leftists felt paralyzed and once again powerless in the face of the Manichean drama playing out before them, and were furious with their predicament.

These debates raised still more pointedly the paradox concerning a functioning "public sphere," as well as what constituted appropriate and effective civil acts within that space. The continued commitment to words as well as symbolic actions throughout the Left reinforced the importance of multiple public spheres, which remained intact despite the new, extreme levels of control the Schmidt government attempted to assert. This was certainly the case among the great range of "new social movements." But ongoing threats to the right to public expression—from

the issuing of emergency laws in 1968 and attendant raids on a great range of perceived leftist and "sympathetic" organizations, organs, and bookstores, to the 1972
"Radical Decree," and continuing parliamentary debates on the Civil Code—were
a constant challenge to this commitment.[91] More frequently than before, officials
worked to close down certain kinds of discussion by drawing on the Nazi past,
including making use of the term "terrorist." The press too continued to draw on
the "fascist charge" to render normal means of protest all the more difficult for
activists to pursue. It was in the pages of the daily press that Alfred Grosser applied
the moniker "Hitler's children" broadly to the heirs of the "failed" student movement for the first time. The respectable *Westdeutsche Allgemeine Zeitung* published
a cartoon, which was to become infamous, of Hitler proudly wheeling the RAF
around in a pram.[92] At the same time, officials and much of the press devoted the
greatest attention to the most violent activists. They created names for them, notably the "Baader-Meinhof Gang," and obsessively drew public attention to them. By
lumping together all those to the left of the SPD, they vindicated even the most
heavy-handed acts against the left—and sold mountains of newspapers. (The CDU
continued to bait even SPD leaders as "foster brothers of terrorism," though this
became increasingly difficult as the Schmidt government demonstrated its commitment to "antiterrorism" ever more heavy-handedly.) Far from enabling peaceful
political expression, these characterizations helped propagate general public hysteria, which ultimately threatened civil war in West Germany in the 1970s.

"New Leftists" found a great proportion of their fellow West Germans willing
to accept the newest government limits on and incursions into a meaningful public
sphere, despite the vocal protests of those outside the "youth movement" labeled
as "sympathizers." What was the point of communicating with this public, and
how could it usefully be done? Following Meins's death, Bernhard Blanke of the
Marxist-Leninist *Sozialistische Arbeiter Zeitung* (*SAZ*, Socialist Workers Newspaper)
asked how the left should respond to a recent poll that revealed that 90 percent of
the German public was against the very concept of public protest.[93] Prominent
author and sympathizer Heinrich Böll suggested in a newspaper column that the
very example of the German public's response to Meins's death—relief, titillation,
and general cheerfulness rather than concern—demonstrated that the West German public sphere had become a scene of bloodlust rather than of meaningful
debate among citizens.[94] At the same time, even the RAF itself and other violent
activists who disdained the "public sphere" were clearly highly invested in some
concept of it. For these violent activists never presumed that their acts could crush
the West German government, or beat its police force or military in any literal way,
in the sense, for example, of a mass proletarian revolution. Rather their acts were
always a form of "theater," however effective one judged it, a kind of message to
the broader German people about how corrupt their government and society was.
This is not to say that these violent activists did not really kill people, nor in any
way to suggest theirs were potentially positive strategic choices. It is to say that most
of these acts were also, particularly early on, extreme measures of communication,
even if these activists themselves claimed the uselessness of such communications.

Far more generally, acts of communication on the Left clearly telegraphed a belief that fellow West Germans could in the end be encouraged to consider their system with new eyes, and to engage in critical discussions of that system. This remained the hope of great numbers of activists throughout the 1970s.

Conclusions

Clearly, endless debates among the broader left on their relation to the violent activists was largely a focus imposed on them by the officials and others who had so effectively created discourses of "the Left" and "sympathizers." Leftist activists asked themselves whether it was worthwhile to debate, much less defend, the RAF. Editors of the Göttingen Left student publication *Politikon* identified the imprisoned activists and their closest associates as "wild little sons of *Spießbürger*."[95] It was these silly and dangerous activists, *Politikon* charged, who brought the fascist state down on the whole Left and chased the public into the arms of a fascist state. Jochen Steffen wrote in the journal *das da* that the only effect of RAF and 2.Juni was to aid a fascist state and its minions and give them "the moral upper hand."[96] "[*Bild* publisher] Springer jumps up and cries murder," Steffen noted, "and RAF makes it possible." The Marxist-Leninist group Revolutionary Struggle agreed, observing that all the RAF could accomplish was to strengthen the right and get its own members "exterminated."[97] Bernhard Blanke of the *SAZ* argued that the "fascist state" had effectively forced Drenkmann's assassination but he nonetheless condemned the act itself as the "privatized justice of the right of the fist."[98] Indeed, some members of the New Left asked whether groups like the RAF and 2.Juni actually belonged to the left—were they not after all a fascist product of a fascist state?[99] Along with others, Jochen Steffen characterized RAF tactics as entirely bourgeois.[100] The New Leftists were thus once again confronted with the question of how to fight against the prevailing situation. How effective were they and could they be in putting their own perspective before the public? The contemporary sense of siege notwithstanding, in retrospect we can say probably substantially more effective than was realized at the time, and all the more ironically as a growing West German public chafed under increasing official controls to prevent such perspectives from airing.

These questions remained in intense debate through the mid-1970s, a period of exponentially growing violence of which Meins's and Drenkmann's deaths represented one seminal moment that culminated with the dramatic events of the "German autumn" of 1977. Great numbers on the left felt struck, shaken, and saddened by these events. Thousands turned out in mourning, despite ambivalence toward RAF methods and ideology, insofar as it was developed. After 1977, as officials and media organs perceived that the "terrorist threat" had largely passed, leftists broadly were released to a degree from the need to allow the violent activist groups to define the left's agenda and issues. The 1980s would become a time of substantial political ferment on the left, with the rise of the Green Party and the new peace movement, and further proliferation of New Social Movements, encompassing innumerable "citizens' initiatives" engaged in activities from anti-nuclear protest to house-squatting. Their strategies were in large part continuous with those developed in the 1960s, but then hidden or repressed in the shadow of the "threat" of the violent activists. At the same time, the police, it has been argued, had begun to reimagine their role. Although the police remained highly visible at demonstrations, some observers maintain, they generally took a less confrontational stance against public political expression even after Helmut Kohl took power.[101] Whether this was indeed the case, public political expression occurred with strength and regularity. These actions represented significant contributions to public debate and discussion. Younger participants in these actions and campaigns may have resisted reminders from the 68ers that they had paved the way for the expansive political expression of the 1980s, but the new era still seemed to provide a lens for viewing the earlier period positively. The 1980s vindicated the efforts of 1960s activists to expand political expression and thereby force certain kinds of choices on the West German public. Indeed, Martin Geyer observes that—for better or worse—the mainstream right adopted and appropriated 1960s New Left rhetorics in the 1980s, which provided one basis of its political success in that decade and which certainly can be seen as evidence of a broader shift in West German political culture.[102]

But defenders of West German official action in the 1960s and 1970s should perhaps consider themselves lucky indeed. For reasons discussed above, it would be difficult to make the case that West Germany in this era was "fascist." Relatively few of those who entertained this view at the time would uphold it today. At the same time, it was West German officials who responded with physical force to even peaceful demonstrations, fearful of the power of demonstrators' messages, and thereby ratcheted up the level of violence and conflict against a population strikingly committed to the potential within the existing system to achieve the ideals the West German state itself purported to represent. It was West German officials and segments of the media who effectively created terrorism, not only through this conflict but also through focusing attention so fixedly on a tiny group of activists whose only real power was this attention. It was the same actors who proceeded under an indefensibly broad notion of guilt by association, thereby not only creating a far larger "enemy," but also using that "enemy" in turn as an excuse for grave and unwarranted incursions on civil rights. It was thus finally officials and others in positions of substantial power who nearly provoked civil war in West Germany, with consequences that might have been catastrophic had it not been for the underlying commitment of many, including those on the left and their broader sympathizers, to the principles for which West Germany stood. In turn, Ekkehart Krippendorf has suggested ironically that the post–June 1967 period represented the first real "postfascist" Federal Republic.[103] If 1989 can be seen as a putting of the excesses of the East German state to rest, perhaps the aftermath of 1967 and the subsequent decade can likewise be seen as a moment of overcoming, at least in part, of some of the failures of the West German state.

Notes

1. F. Teufel, "Aus Teufels Küche," *Konkret* (January 1979). This interview was carried out for *Stern* magazine, which then refused to publish it.
2. Hanna Schissler, "'Coming to Terms' with 1968," unpublished ms.; cf. variously Wolfgang Kraushaar, *Neunzehnhundertachtundsechzig als Mythos, Chiffre und Zäsur* (Hamburg, 2001); Gerd Koenen, *Das Rote Jahrzehnt: Unsere kleine deutsche Kulturrevolution 1967–1977* (Cologne, 2001); and Hermann Lübbe, "Der Mythos der 'kritischen Generation': Ein Rückblick," *Aus Politik und Zeitgeschichte* 20 (1988): 17–25. See also Elizabeth L. B. Peifer, "1968 in German Political Culture, 1967–1993: From Experience to Myth" (PhD diss., University of North Carolina, Chapel Hill, 1997); and the several pieces on the "mythology" of 1968 in Ingrid Gilcher-Holtey, ed., *1968—Vom Ereignis zum Gegenstand der Geschichtswissenschaft* (Göttingen, 1998). Cf. press discussions in the *Tageszeitung* (*TAZ*), as in Christoph Quarch, "Gewaltiger Irrtum," *TAZ*, 23 June 2001; "Fortsetzung folgt," *TAZ*, 30 April 2001; and "Bilder aus der Vergangenheit," *TAZ*, 10 March 2001.
3. This instrumentalization took place between the BRD and DDR, among generations, genders, and other categories. Compare Heinz Bude, *Bilanz der Nachfolge: Die Bundesrepublik und der Nationalsozialismus* (Frankfurt am Main, 1992); Bernd-A. Rusinek, "Von der Entdeckung der NS-Vergangenheit zum generellen Faschismusverdacht—akademische Diskurse in der Bundesrepublik der 60er Jahre," in *Dynamische Zeiten: Die 60er Jahre in den beiden deutschen Gesellschaften,* ed. Axel Schildt, Detlef Siegfried, and Karl Christian Lammers (Hamburg, 2000), 114–47; Detlef Siegfried, "Zwischen Aufarbeitung und Schlußstrich: Der Umgang mit der NS-Vergangenheit in den beiden deutschen Staaten, 1958 bis 1969," in ibid., 77–113; Bernd Leineweber, "Entsetzen und Besetzen: Zur Dialektik der Aufklärung in der Studentenbewegung," in *Frankfurter Schule und Studentenbewegung: Von der Flaschenpost zum Molotowcocktail 1946 bis 1995,* 3 vols., ed. Wolfgang Kraushaar (Hamburg, 1998), 3:99–111; Jürgen Danyel, "Die beiden deutschen Staaten und ihre nationalsozialistische Vergangenheit," in *Deutsche Vergangenheiten—eine gemeinsame Herausforderung,* ed. Christoph Kleßmann et al. (Berlin, 1999), 128–38; Philipp Gassert, *Kurt Georg Kiesinger, 1904–1988* (Munich, 2006); Harold Marcuse, "The Revival of Holocaust Awareness in West Germany, Israel, and the United States," in *1968: A World Transformed,* ed. Carole Fink et al. (New York, 1998); Dagmar Herzog, "'Pleasure, Sex, and Politics Belong Together': Post-Holocaust Memory and the Sexual Revolution in West Germany," *Critical Inquiry* 24, no. 2 (1998): 393–444; also Jane Kramer, *The Europeans* (New York, 1988), 125–47; and others in this volume.
4. Compare Axel Schildt, "Der Umgang mit der NS-Vergangenheit in der Öffentlichkeit der Nachkriegszeit," in *Verwandlungspolitik: NS-Eliten in der westdeutschen Nachkriegsgesellschaft,* ed. Wilfried Loth and Bernd A. Rusinek (Frankfurt am Main, 1998), 19–54.
5. The most immediate systematic conceptualization of the public sphere was Jürgen Habermas, *Strukturwandel der Öffentlichkeit* (Frankfurt am Main, 1962); this was central to the refashionings of the concept, implicit and explicit, that went on throughout this period. Siegfried, "Zwischen Aufarbeitung und Schlußstrich," and Rusinek, "Von der Entdeckung der NS," among others, also discuss the concept of the public sphere in this context. I employ the concept of the "New Left" as a shorthand for the larger extraparliamentary left that coalesced in the mid-1960s and continued through the 1970s. I recognize the limitations of the term; one can argue among other things that the German Communist Party (Deutsche Kommunistische Partei, DKP), dominant in the 1970s, represented an old rather than a new left.
6. June 1967 has been identified by many historians and others as a central turning point for these questions. For important periodizations of the era, compare Siegfried, "Zwischen Aufarbeitung und Schlußstrich"; Norbert Frei, *Vergangenheitspolitik: Die Anfänge der Bundesrepublik und die NS-Vergangenheit* (Munich, 1996); Horst Krüger, in *Die Zeit,* 16 February 1968.

7. The literature on these questions has grown exponentially in recent years. Compare, in addition to work cited above, also Michael Jeismann, *Auf Wiedersehen Gestern: Die deutsche Vergangenheit und die Politik von Morgen* (Stuttgart, 2001), and Rebecca Wittmann, "Indicting Auschwitz? The Paradox of the Frankfurt Auschwitz Trial," *German History* 21, no. 4 (2003): 505–32; cf. Hermann Lübbe's controversial polemic, "Der Nationalsozialismus im deutschen Nachkriegsbewusstsein," *Historische Zeitschrift* 236 (1983): 579–99.

8. Gunter Gaus (and later Helmut Kohl), quoted inter alia in Aleida Assmann and Ute Frevert, *Geschichtsvergessenheit, Geschichtsversessenheit: Vom Umgang mit deutschen Vergangenheiten nach 1945* (Stuttgart, 1999), 227. My interviews suggest that the concept of "generation" must be used with great circumspection: those of a wide range of ages considered themselves and were considered by others to be 68ers, referencing a very broad range of experiences, while many born in the same years distinguished themselves carefully from this "grouping." Moreover, differences within a single age cohort were of course great and complicated. Within the literature on generation and the postwar, compare Helmut Schelsky, *Die skeptische Generation: Eine Soziologie der deutschen Jugend* (Düsseldorf, 1963); Bude, *Bilanz*; Bernd Weisbrod, "Generation und Generationalität in der Neueren Geschichte," unpublished ms.

9. For different takes on the importance of "knowability" of the Nazi past and its transgressions, compare Martin Walser, "Unser Auschwitz," *Kursbuch* 1 (1965): 189–200; Lübbe, "Der Nationalsozialismus im deutschen Nachkriegsbewusstsein"; and Assmann and Frevert, *Geschichtsvergessenheit, Geschichtsversessenheit*. My interviews suggest that many felt they "knew" National Socialism all too well in their own family lives, including many born after 1945.

10. Cf. Thomas Schmid, "Fremde im eigenen Land: Fischer erinnert sich," *FAZ*, 17 January 2001; and cf. discussion of this piece in Christopher Schwarz, "Geschichte und Identität: Der Umgang mit der nationalsozialistischen Vergangenheit in der Bundesrepublik Deutschland der sechziger Jahre" (Magisterarbeit, University of Bonn, 2003), 4.

11. Compare author's interview Silke; Annette Schwarzenau, "'Nicht diese theoretischen Dinger, etwas Praktisches unternehmen," in *Die 68erinnen*, ed. Ute Kätzel (Berlin, 2002), 41–59, here 43. The variation in how activists viewed their parents was considerable, versus the "older generation." Many female activists writing in *Die 68erinnen* suggest that their desire to break away from their parents had more to do with avoiding their boundedness to circumscribed "women's roles," for example, than with their active or passive "collaboration" with the regime on other issues.

12. Author's interview with Rüdiger.

13. See in this same sense young West Germans' characterization of American officials' treatment of African-Americans as "fascist," and, more generally, compare Richard Lettau, "Täglicher Faschismus," *Kursbuch* 22 (December 1970): 1–44; and Wilfried Mausbach, "America's Vietnam in Germany—Germany in America's Vietnam: On the Relocation of Spaces and the Appropriation of History," in *Changing the World, Changing Oneself: Political Protest and Collective Identities in the 1960s/70s West Germany and U.S.*, ed. Belinda Davis, Martin Klimke, Carla MacDougall, and Wilfried Mausbach (forthcoming).

14. Cf. Hans-Ulrich Thamer, "Die NS-Vergangenheit im politischen Diskurs der 68er Bewegung," *Westfälische Forschungen* 48 (1998): 39–53; Olaf G. Roehler, "Antifaschismus—vom Umgang mit einem Begriff," in Ulrich Herbert and Olaf G. Roehler, *Zweierlei Bewältigung: Vier Beiträge über den Umgang mit der NS-Vergangenheit in den beiden deutschen Staaten* (Hamburg, 1992); Siegfried, "Zwischen Aufarbeitung und Schlußstrich." The League of Antifascists (Bund den Antifaschisten) was only one focal point of such activity. The sense that these youth were acting out of general ignorance and naiveté, including with reference to the Nazi past, has been broadly suggested, including by Koenen, *Das Rote Jahrzehnt*. Such youth claimed the need to learn more about that past, however successful they were. On the range of issues student protestors took up, some students made impressive efforts to learn about the relevant issues: this was of course one of the ideas beyond the "kritische" or "gegen"-Universität. See, e.g., AStA FUB, "Informationen über Persien und den Schah," distributed on 1 June 1967, in Archive of

the APO and Other Movements, Freie Universität Berlin (hereaftero APO Archive), FU-Berlin Allgemeines, 1.–9.1967. Compare Adelheid von Saldern, "Und vor allen Dingen glaube ich, daß es uns allen bis heute schwerfällt, die NS-Herrschaft als Teil der deutschen Gesellschaft zu denken," in *Versäumte Fragen: Deutsche Historiker im Schatten des Nationalsozialismus,* ed. K. Jarausch and R. Hohls (Stuttgart, 2000).

15. Author's interview with Silke. Compare for the Free University alone the references among flyers from the range of organizations as well as in the *FU Spiegel.* For flyers, compare APO Archive, Berlin FU Allgemeines, 1.–9.1967. This specific association with fascism was, however, far less pronounced among successive waves of younger West German activists.

16. Ulrike Meinhof, "Against Death," *Konkret* 3 (May 1961); cf. Meinhof, "Joachim Fest oder Die Gleichschaltung," *Konkret* 8 (1966).

17. Flyer, reprinted in *Protest! Literatur um 1968* (Marbach, 2000), 43.

18. Cf. APO Archive, File FU Flugblätter 1960–66. For an overview of such activity, cf. Siegward Lönnendonker, *Gründung einer politischen Universität* (Berlin, 1988).

19. On police in this period, cf. Klaus Weinhauer, *Schutzpolizei in der Bundesrepublik. Zwischen Bürgerkrieg und innerer Sicherheit: Die turbulenten sechziger Jahre* (Paderborn, 2003). Special riot forces were built up in the late 1960s, and an enormous expansion of policing took place in the early 1970s, in response to the perceived threat. Compare Dieter Schenk, *Der Chef: Horst Herold und das BKA* (Hamburg, 1998).

20. Cf. Thomas Lindenberger and Alf Lüdtke, eds., *Physische Gewalt: Studien zur Geschichte der Neuzeit* (Frankfurt am Main, 1995); Belinda Davis, "'Everyday' Protest, Violence, and the Culture of Conflict in Berlin, 1840–1980," in *Berlin—Washington, 1800–2000: Capital Cities, Cultural Representation, and National Identities,* ed. Christof Mauch and Andreas Daum (Cambridge, 2004); Hans Boldt, "Geschichte der Polizei in Deutschland," in *Handbuch des Polizeirechts,* ed. Erhard Denninger and Hans Lisken (Munich, 1992), 1–39; Heiner Busch et al., *"Nicht dem Staate, sondern dem Bürger dienen": Für eine bürgernahe Polizei* (Berlin, 1990). There are many forms of nonphysical and indirect state violence about which scholars and others have written; the notion of "bureaucratic violence," for example, was developed within the West German New Left in the 1960s.

21. "Filbinger: Rückfall in faschistische Methoden," *Die Welt,* 17 April 1968.

22. Included in APO Archiv File (Fritz) Teufel, n.d. "Bonn is not Weimar" was a familiar refrain from the mid-1950s, and officials often seemed at greater pains to distinguish the Federal Republic from the "disorder" of Weimar than from the Third Reich. Cf. Fritz René Allemann, *Bonn ist nicht Weimar* (Cologne, 1956).

23. Cited in Gretchen Dutschke, *Rudi Dutschke: Wir hatten barbarisches, schönes Leben* (Cologne, 1996), 130.

24. Cf. as a tiny sampling "Geplant—Berlin: Bombenanschlag auf US-Vizepräsidenten," *Bild,* 6 April 1967; "Nach dem Attentatsplan der 'Mao'-Studenten," *Bild,* 7 April 1967; "Maos Botschaft in Ost-Berlin lieferte die Bomben gegen Vizepräsident Humphrey, *Der Abend,* 6 April 1967; *Frankfurter Allgemeine Zeitung,* 6 April 1967. Compare among innumerable discussions, Oskar Negt, "Benno Ohnesorg ist das Opfer eines Mordanschlags," *Frankfurter Rundschau,* 12 June 1967; Peter Brückner, "Springerpresse und Volksverhetzung," *Kritische Justiz* 10–11 (1969): 113ff.; and Bernhard Blanke, "Dutschkismus als Gerücht—Zu einigen Elementen spätkapitalistischer Öffentlichkeit," *Neue Kritik* 47 (April 1968): 35ff.; and Frank Wolff and Eberhard Windaus, eds., *Studentenbewegung 1967–69: Protokolle und Materialien* (Frankfurt am Main, 1977), 13. Cf. Gudrun Kruip, "Restricted Support: The Role of the Axel Springer Publishing House in the Process of Westernization," presentation at the conference "The American Impact on Western Europe," German Historical Institute, Washington, DC, March 1999.

25. Cf. Dutschke, *Rudi Dutschke,* 130–31; letter from one of Benno Ohnesorg's former professors to Berlin authorities insisting that Ohnesorg was serious and well-behaved, APO Archive, File Allgemeines, 1.–9.1967.

26. On the longer tradition in Germany of youth protest and youth culture and the often fearful attititudes toward it, cf. inter alia Derek Linton, *Who Has the Youth, Has the Future* (Princeton, 1991); Elizabeth Harvey, *Youth and the Welfare State in Weimar Germany* (Oxford, 1993); Detlev Peukert, *Die Edelweißpiraten: Protestbewegungen jugendlicher Arbeiter im "Dritten Reich"* (Cologne, 1980); Uta Poiger, *Jazz, Rock, and Rebels* (Berkeley, 2000); D. Baacke, *Jugend und Subkultur* (Munich, 1972); Ludwig von Friedeburg, *Jugend in der modernen Gesellschaft* (Cologne, 1965); Helmut Schelsky, *Die skeptische Generation* (Düsseldorf, 1963); W. Kalteleiter, "Eine 'gespaltene' Generation," *Die Politische Meinung* 19, no. 156 (1974).

27. On both students' "fascism" and the need for direct response, cf. as a sampling William S. Schlamm, "Sagt Meine Meinung," *Welt am Sonntag*, reprinted without date in Rudi Dutschke, *Die Revolte: Wurzeln und Spuren eines Aufbruches* (Reinbek, 1983), 48; "Sie wollen Berlin ruinieren," *Berliner Morgenpost*, 7 April 1968; "Strafanzeige gegen Rudi Dutschke," *Die Welt*, 27 December 1967; titles cited in David Caute, *Year of the Barricades* (New York, 1988), 103; and Tilman Fichter and Siegward Lönnendonker, *Kleine Geschichte des SDS* (Berlin, 1977), 122. On provocative radio commentators, cf. ibid., 106, 122, passim.

28. Cited in Caute, *Year of the Barricades*, 102. The latter threat was also intended to impugn male protestors' masculinity on the basis of their long hair.

29. Compare *Briefe an Rudi D., Voltaire Flugschrift* 19 (Berlin, 1968); Hamburger Institut für Sozialforschung (hereafter HIS), File Kommune 1 03.03, Korrespondenz, Mäzenin, Spinner, usw.

30. "Was für ein Saujud—Anrufe beim Fernsehen," *Neues Forum,* July–August 1978. Cohn-Bendit was regularly subjected to public defamation conflating his activism with his Jewishness, and commented that he sometimes felt as he imagined his father did in the 1930s. Born of a Jewish mother, Sarah Haffner noted that *Bild* newspaper reminded her of what she had seen in the viscerally anti-Semitic Nazi tabloid *Der Stürmer*. Sarah Haffner, "Die Frauen waren der revolutionärste Teil dieser etwas revolutionären Bewegung," in Kätzel, *Die 68erinnen,* 145.

31. See, e.g., in the case of the "pudding assassination," "Berliner 'Attentäter' auf freiem Fuß—Studenten planten keinen Anschlag auf Humphrey, sagt der Ermittlungsrichter," *Süddeutsche Zeitung*, 9 April 1967.

32. Cf., e.g., the interviewer's questions concerning whether Dutschke "preached violence," in an interview with Rudi Dutschke published in *Der Spiegel*, 10 July 1967, 30–32.

33. I am developing this notion elsewhere. I thank Wulf Kansteiner for his help with this distinction.

34. Cf. Tatjana Botzat et al., "Vorwort," in Botzat et al., *Ein Deutscher Herbst: Zustände 1977* (Frankfurt am Main, 1997), 13–18.

35. Author's interview with K. D. Wolff.

36. Flyer, "Politischer Mord in Berlin," 3 June 1967, APO-Archiv, File Berlin FU Allgemeine, 1.–9.67.

37. Flyer, author unidentifiable, "An die Berliner Bevölkerung!" in APO-Archiv, File FU Allgemeines, 1.–9.67.

38. Flyer, SHB Berlin, "Student erschlagen!" 3 June 1967, in APO-Archiv, File FU Allgemeines, 1.–9.67.

39. Flyer, SDS Central Committee, Frankfurt, 3 June 1967, in APO-Archiv, File FU Allgemeines, 1.–9.67.

40. Flyer, SDS Central Committee, Frankfurt, 3 June 1967, in APO-Archiv, File FU Allgemeines, 1.–9.67.

41. Quoted in Dutschke, *Rudi Dutschke,* 130

42. Ibid., 171.

43. Flyer, Kampagne für Abrüstung, 3 June 1967, in APO-Archiv, File FU Allgemeines, 1.–9.67. See also flyer, Evangelischer Studentenbund, "Über die Vorgänge der letzten Tage," 4 June 1967.

44. Flyer, "An die Berliner Bevölkerung!" See also AStA flyer, "Wir provozieren niemand!" 3 June 1967; and flyer, SHB Berlin, "Student Erschlagen!"

45. Cf. Stefan Aust, *The Baader-Meinhof Group: The Inside Story of a Phenomenon* (London, 1987), 44; Jillian Becker, *Hitler's Children: The Story of the Baader-Meinhof Terrorist Gang* (Philadelphia, 1977), 41.

46. "Die Bedeutung der Faschismusdiskussion in den 60er Jahren," Ringvorlesung, 4 May 1988, discussion with Wolfgang Lefèvre and Reinhard Strecker, reproduced at http://www.glasnost.de/hist/apo/apo882.html.

47. Cf., among many, "Studenten-Protest in Berlin verboten: Wissenschaftssenator Stein macht von Staatsaufsicht Gebrauch. Konvent erhebt Klage," *Süddeutsche Zeitung*, 3–4 June 1967; and, less sympathetically, "Senator verbietet Studenten-Protest," *Die Welt*, 2 June 1967.

48. Cf., e.g., "FU-Studenten kneifen," *Bild-Zeitung*, 2 June 1967.

49. Oskar Negt, "Benno Ohnesorg ist das Opfer eines Mordanschlags," *Frankfurter Rundschau*, 12 June 67.

50. Cited in Dutschke, *Rudi Dutschke*, 174–75.

51. Hans-Jürgen Krahl, *Konstitution und Klassenkampf* (Frankfurt am Main, 1971), 25.

52. R. Tiedemann, "Vor Berliner Studenten," comments of June 1967, reprinted in Kraushaar, *Frankfurter Schule*, 2:237–38.

53. Ibid., 2:238; Rudi Dutschke, Bernd Rabehl, Ludwig von Friedeburg, and many others also employed this expression. Cf. also Rudi Dutschke, interview with *Der Spiegel*, 1 July 1967; and repetitions throughout Knut Nevermann, VDS, ed., *der 2. juni 1967—Studenten zwischen Notstand und Demokratie: Dokumente* (Cologne, 1967); and Uwe Bergmann, ed., *Bedingungen und Organisation des Widerstandes: Der Kongreß in Hannover* (Berlin, 1967).

54. This came before the student casualties at Kent State in Ohio (in May 1970), in Rome, and elsewhere. Here once more "the student" acted as a symbol of defenselessness. It was possibly also a sign of elitism—as if this were worse than killing a file clerk or a garbage collector—but other sources do not suggest this.

55. APO writings on the "fascism question" were legion; cf. the widely read series in *Das Argument* on "Faschismus-Theorien" beginning in 1965, vols. 30, 32, 33, 41, and 65, reprinted together (Berlin 1970); *Das Argument* editor Wolfgang Fritz Haug's *Der hilflose Antifaschismus: Zur Kritik der Vorlesungsreihe über Wissenschaft und Nationalsozialismus an deutschen Universitäten* (Frankfurt am Main, 1967); Hansmartin Kuhn, "Der lange Marsch in den Faschismus," *Politik* 45 (1974); as well as "Dossier I: Täglicher Faschismus: Evidenz aus fünf Monaten," *Kursbuch* 22 (December 1970), introduced and compiled by Reinhard Lettau, on such tendencies in the United States.

56. Compare author's interview with Rüdiger; also Wolfgang Kraushaar, *Fischer in Frankfurt: Karriere eines Aussenseiters* (Hamburg, 2001), 212.

57. Rolf Tiedemann, summary speech at forum on Ohnesorg, reprinted in Kraushaar, *Frankfurter Schule*, 2:237–38; "Sorge um politisches Bewußtsein," *Frankfurter Rundschau*, 27 April 1968; Heinz Grossmann, "Der Pogrom und der Einzelne," in Heinz Grossmann and Oskar Negt, eds., *Die Auferstehung der Gewalt: Springer-Blockade und politische Reaktion in der Bundesrepublik* (Frankfurt am Main, 1968), 10. See also "Sorge um politisches Bewußtsein," *Frankfurter Rundschau*, 17 April 1968; Autorenkollektiv, *Bürgerlicher und faschistischer Antisemitismus: Faschismusanalyse, Revolutionäre Schriften III* (Berlin, 1968); K. D. Wolff and Frank Wolff, "Zu den Oster-Aktionen," *Neue Kritik* 9, no. 47 (1968): 3–6; Oskar Negt, "Politik und Gewalt," speech reprinted in ibid., 10–23; Rudi Dutschke, "Vom Antisemitismus zum Antikommunismus," in *Rebellion der Studentenbewegung oder die neue Opposition*, ed. Uwe Bergmann et al. (Reinbek, 1968), 58–93; and speech of an SDS federal council member on "Pogromhetze," cited in Fichter and Lönnendonker, *Kleine Geschichte des SDS*, 127.

58. Armin Mohler, *Die Zeit*, 10 March 1967.

59. This overview cannot do justice to the range of political groupings, by ideological persuasion, age cohort, and other cleavages, that constituted the larger "movement." For a sense of this range, compare Gerd Langguth, *Die Protestbewegung in der Bundesrepublik Deutschland 1968–1976* (Cologne, 1976); Andrei Markovits and Philip Gorski, *The German Left: Red,*

Green and Beyond (New York, 1993); also Robert Steigerwald, *Protestbewegung: Streitfragen und Gemeinsamkeiten* (Frankfurt am Main, 1982). On the SDS specifically, cf. Fichter and Lönnendonker, *Kleine Geschichte des SDS*; Willy Albrecht, *Der Sozialistische Deutsche Studentenbund (SDS)* (Bonn, 1994); Gerhard Bauß, *Die Studentenbewegung der sechziger Jahre in der Bundesrepublik und Westberlin* (Cologne, 1977); and Michael A. Schmidtke, "Reform, Revolte, oder Revolution?" in Gilcher-Holtey, *1968*, 188–206. On the larger APO, cf. Pavel Richter, "Die Außerparlamentarische Opposition in der Bundesrepublik 1966–1968," in Gilcher-Holtey, *1968*, 35–55; on the post-SDS communist fractions, Frank Karl, *Die K-Gruppen* (Bonn, 1976). As an umbrella group, the larger AStA contained major groups that did not identify as "leftist"; the simultaneous Ohnesorg shooting and Six Day War marked a definitive split between the SDS and other left-identified groupings on the one hand and the CDU-aligned Ring Christian Democratic Students (RCDS) and the German Liberal Student organization (LSD) on the other.

60. Andreas von Weiss, *Schlagwörter der neuen Linken: Die Agitation der Sozialrevolutionäre* (Munich, 1974), 130–31. Cf. also M. Horkheimer, "Anti-Amerikanismus, Antisemitismus, und Demagogie …," reprinted in Kraushaar, *Frankfurter Schule*, 2:227–28.

61. Tiedemann, "Vor Berliner Studenten," 238.

62. Cited in Fichter and Lönnendonker, *Kleine Geschichte des SDS,* 126, from early 1968 issues.

63. Enzensberger, cited in Rusinek, "Von der Entdeckung der NS," 128.

64. Cf. Fichter and Lönnendonker, *Kleine Geschichte des SDS*, 15.

65. Jürgen Habermas, spoken contribution to the forum "Bedingungen und Organisation des Widerstandes," Hanover, 9 June 1967, reprinted in Kraushaar, *Frankfurter Schule*, 2:250–51. See also "Habermas Contra Dutschke," *Oberbaumblatt*, 26 June 1967. On "left-wing fascism," cf. also Peifer, "1968 in German Political Culture."

66. Habermas's response at this same forum to Rudi Dutschke's intervention, reproduced in Kraushaar, *Frankfurter Schule*, 2:254–55; and Habermas, letter to Erich Fried, reprinted in ibid., 2:278–79.

67. See in addition to immediate spoken responses after Habermas's charge, ranging from furious to humorous, Oskar Negt, "Studentischer Protest—Liberalismus—Linksfaschismus," in *Kursbuch* 13 (June 1968); and, from a broader range of perspectives, Wolfgang Abendroth et al., eds., *Die Linke antwortet Jürgen Habermas* (Frankfurt am Main, 1968).

68. Dutschke speech, reprinted in Bergmann, *Bedingungen und Organisation*, 78–82.

69. Oskar Negt, *Frankfurter Rundschau*, 12 June 1967, reprinted in Negt, *Keine Demokratie ohne Sozialismus* (Frankfurt am Main, 1976), 56. See also Negt's effort, along with Alexander Kluge, to systematically spell out a broader notion of the concept in subsequent years. Oskar Negt and Alexander Kluge, *Public Sphere and Experience: Toward an Analysis of the Bourgeois and Proletarian Public Sphere* (Minneapolis, 1993; German orig. 1973).

70. This was the beginning of the moment too when some early feminists claimed that just as everyone over 30 was a potential Nazi, every man was a potential rapist. Karin Walser replied in turn to fellow women activists that imagining such "evil" in men was the same as Nazis imagining it in Jews. Cf. flyer, Ostpolitischer Deutscher Studentenverband (ODS) Berlin, "Auf ein Wort, Herr Mahler und Genossen," April 1968, from APO Archiv, File Attentat Dutschke; Sibylla Flügge, "Vom Weiberrat zum Frauenprojekt: Ein persönlicher Bericht über den Beginn der neuen Frauenbewegung in Frankfurt am Main," in *Was soll ich euch denn noch erklären? Ein Austausch über Frauengeschichte(n) in zwei deutschen Staaten*, ed. Kirsten Beuth and Kirsten Plötz (Gelnhausen, 1998), 133–55; Herzog, "Pleasure, Sex, and Politics Belong Together." See also flyer, September 1967, in APO Archiv, File Flugblätter 7-9/1967; flyer, Bund Gesamtdeutscher Studenten, "HOCH LEBE der Konvent," 2 June 1967, in APO Archiv File Flugblätter 1.–9.1967.

71. Peter Brückner, *Gewalt und Solidarität. Zur Ermordung Ulrich Schmückers durch Genossen: Dokumente und Analysen* (Berlin, 1974).

72. Michael Landmann, *Das Israelpseudos der Pseudolinken* (Munich 1971; repr. ed., Berlin 1982), 30; cf. also the flyer, "Israelische Aggression?" Committee of the Jewish Student Union (including

Frank Stern and Michael Wolffsohn); and Dan Diner's demand as part of the active Frankfurt "Jewish students scene" for leftist students support for Israel, cited in Heide Berndt, "Linker Antisemitismus" (unpublished ms., 2000), 2. Herbert Marcuse also condemned this stance in his 1967 speech in Berlin. Compare Henryk Broder, *Linke Tabus* (Berlin, 1976) and Martin W. Kloke, *Israel und die Deutsche Linke: Zur Geschichte eines schwierigen Verhältnisses* (Frankfurt am Main, 1990); and see Carole Fink's piece in this volume.

73. Landmann, "Das Israelpseudo," 22, 26. The phrase was a variation on a commonplace refrain, as these things often went: compare "Schlagt die Germanistik tot, macht die blauen Blumen rot," in Peter Mosler, *Was wir wollten, was wir wurden: Studentenrevolte, 10 Jahre danach* (Reinbek, 1977), 15. Of course, the two slogans differ broadly in their implications of violence.

74. Cf. Hans-Magnus Enzensberger, "Ein Gespräch über die Zukunft mit Rudi Dutschke, Bernd Rabehl und Christian Semler," *Kursbuch* 14 (1968): 146–74; Blanke, "Dutschkismus als Gerücht," 35–38.

75. Cf. Dutschke, interview in *Der Spiegel*, 10 July 1967, 30–32; Dutschke, interviewed in *Konkret* 3 (1968); Herbert Marcuse, "Das Problem der Gewalt," reprinted in *Das Ende der Utopie*, ed. H. Kumitzky and H. Kuhn (Berlin, 1967), 47–54, along with replies, ibid., 73–78; Enzensberger, "Ein Gespräch"; discussions in *Kursbuch* 12 (April 1968), issue "Der nicht erklärte Notstand" for a sense of the discussion within SDS leadership.

76. See figures in Langguth, *Die Protestbewegung*, 95, 102–3.

77. Cf., e.g., R. Dutschke, "Professor Habermas," in Kraushaar, *Frankfurter Schule und Studentenbewegung*, 2:251.

78. New alternative papers, such as *Agit 883*, regularly made humor out of their regular discussions of the fascist state and society; see the cartoon in the issue dated 20 March 1969, in which a woman and an alien sit next to each other, reading *Bild* and *BZ* (headline: "Roter Terror") with the caption "Seid braun zueinander." Periodicals such as *Langer Marsch* adopted a less jocular style, running instead lengthy treatments of "fascism" in present and past forms.

79. Compare Belinda Davis, "From Starbuck to Starbucks, or Terror: What's in a Name?" *Radical History Review* 85 (2002): 37–57, and Davis, "Zwischen Terror und Rückzug: Politischer Raum und Verhandlungsstrategien in der BRD der 70er Jahre," in *Innere Sicherheit und Terrorismus in der Bundesrepublik der 1970er Jahre*, ed. H.-G. Haupt et al. (Frankfurt am Main, 2006).

80. Author's interview with Rüdiger.

81. The image of his (second) arrest on ARD television had already aroused profound concern for the way that a man "could be treated as a pig." Author's interview with Rüdiger.

82. Cited in "Wenn von der RAF geredet wird, herrscht nur noch frei flottierende Angst," *Politikon* (December 1975).

83. Sigrist, speech at Teach-In, 26 November 1974, reprinted in *"Holger, der Kampf geht weiter!" Dokumente und Beiträge zum Konzept Stadtguerilla* (Gaiganz, 1975), 21–26. For an effort to treat seriously Meins's political thinking, see Gerd Conradt, *Starbuck—Holger Meins: Ein Porträt als Zeitbild* (Berlin, 2001).

84. Trotski Liga Deutschland, "Verteidigt die Genossen der RAF!" in *"Holger,"* 69–72.

85. *Revolutionärer Zorn* (May 1976), treating also Ulrike Meinhof's and Siegfried Buback's deaths in continuation of the discussion initiated over Meins.

86. Trotski Liga Deutschland, "Verteidigt die Genossen der RAF!" in *"Holger,"* 69–72.

87. *links sozialistische Zeitung,* Extrablatt 3/1975

88. Compare "Holger Meins, Drenkmann, und die Linke," *Langer Marsch*, January 1975.

89. KSG Aachen, *Roter Pfeil* [n.d., though probably December 1974), reprinted in *"Holger,"* 61–63.

90. Compare Wolfgang Kraushaar, *Fischer in Frankfurt: Karriere eines Außenseiters* (Hamburg, 2001), 102 passim.

91. Cf. Michael Schneider, *Demokratie in Gefahr? Der Konflikt um die Notstandsgesetze* (Bonn, 1986); Maren Krohn, *Die gesellschaftliche Auseinandersetzung um die Notstandsgesetze* (Cologne,

1981); and Jeremy P. Varon, *Bringing the War Home: The Weather Underground, the Red Army Faction, and Revolutionary Violence in the Sixties and Seventies* (Ithaca, 2004). *Konkret* (July 1976), 26–27, provides a summary of parliamentary action reducing the right of political expression in the period following Meins's and Drenkmann's deaths.

92. Cf. Erich Böhme, "Mann, o Mann," *Spiegel* 38 (1977); Alfred Grosser, cartoon from *Westdeutsche Allgemeine Zeitung*, reprinted without date in *Ein Deutscher Herbst*, 75.

93. Bernhard Blanke, "Bedingungen sozialistischer Solidarität," *Sozialistische Arbeiter Zeitung*, November 1974.

94. H. Böll, interview, *Frankfurter Rundschau*, November 1974. See also Böll's important column in *Der Spiegel*, "Will Ulrike Gnade oder freies Geleit?" January 1971. Compare RAF members' reply first in 1974, attacking "the Bölls who take the death of a desk-based murderer more seriously than the death of a revolutionary"; cf. Aust, *The Baader-Meinhof Group*, 267. See also RAF, ed., *Über den bewaffneten Kampf* (Berlin, 1971).

95. See "Wenn von der RAF." Cf. Böhme, "Mann, o Mann": "[W]hat in the world differentiates this killer quintet of the last week from the fascistoid executioner of Rosa Luxemburg, what from the 'direct action' murderer of Walther Rathenau?" See also W. Gerns et al., *Opportunismus heute* (Frankfurt am Main, 1974).

96. Jochen Steffen, "Wem nutzt Baader-Meinhof?" *das da* (November 1974).

97. Revolutionären Kampf, "Isolationshaft ist Mord," *Wir wollen Alles!* (November 1974).

98. Blanke, "Bedingungen sozialistischer Solidarität."

99. S. Stefan, "Holger Meins, Drenkmann, und die Linke," in *Langer Marsch* (November 1974); see on this also Wolfgang Kraushaar's piece, originally penned in 1977, "Die Schleyer-Entführung: 44 Tage ohne Opposition," in *Der Blinde Fleck*.

100. Steffen, "Wem nutzt Baader-Meinhof?"

101. Cf. Martin Winter, "Police Philosophy and Protest Policing in the Federal Republic of Germany, 1960–1990," in *Policing Protest: The Control of Mass Demonstrations in Western Democracies*, ed. Donatella della Porta and Herbert Reiter (Minneapolis, 1998). Klaus Weinhauer among others has taken a more cautious view of this transformation; cf. Weinhauer, *Schutzpolizei*; see also Klaus Weinhauer, "'Staatsbürger mit Sehnsucht nach Harmonie': Gesellschaftsbild und Staatsverständnis in der Polizei," in Schildt, Siegfried, and Lammers, *Dynamische Zeiten*, 444–70.

102. Martin Geyer, "The Language of the Political—the Politics of Language: West Germany after 1968," unpublished ms.

103. Cited in Claus Leggewie, "A Laboratory of Post-Industrial Society: Reassessing the 1960s in Germany," in Fink et al., *1968*, 289.

Chapter 14

CONSERVATIVE INTELLECTUALS AND THE DEBATE OVER NATIONAL SOCIALISM AND THE HOLOCAUST IN THE 1960s

Joachim Scholtyseck

❧

As the 1960s opened, a prosperous West Germany was taking its place among the community of civil societies. By the end of the decade, the country was beset by sociopolitical upheaval. Almost inevitably, the question arose whether this sudden change was in some way related to the National Socialist past. Had there been, as a growing chorus of critical voices charged, a far-reaching repression of all that concerned the Nazi regime and the Holocaust during the conservative postwar years?

Conservative Intellectuals: A Definition

Defining the term "conservative" is a hazardous task, given the veritable babel of tongues in discussion of the subject.[1] This holds true especially since the label had only very limited appeal during the second postwar era. In these years, the Federal Republic was essentially a conservative state. The Swiss historian J. R. Salis has referred to a "federal republican ideology" characterized by "staunch anticommunism, Catholic conservatism, occidental Europeanism [*abendländisches Europäertum*], strict adherence to the rule of law, a capitalist middle-class ethos, and a deep mistrust against anything coming from the East as well as against the nationalist hubris that had characterized Hitler's dictatorship."[2] Paradoxically, though, there were few voices claiming to speak on behalf of the conservative position. As one commentator pointedly noted, "Should some historian of conservatism three thousand years hence inquire into the spectrum of political parties during the early years of the FRG, his search for a professedly conservative party would very likely be futile."[3]

Notes for this chapter begin on page 252.

This state of affairs was undoubtedly a consequence of National Socialism. During a phase of moral uncertainty, many conservatives had supported the Third Reich or at least refrained from criticizing it.[4] Although they came to realize Nazism and conservatism had little in common, their wavering before 1945 later led to the situation, as Eugen Gerstenmaier noted in 1962, that "no large party in Germany could benefit from labeling itself conservative."[5] At the same time, a redefinition of conservative positions started to become evident. After the experience of the Third Reich, replacing the totalitarian state with a constitutional democracy seemed desirable, and many conservatives became supporters of the Federal Republic even while remaining rather skeptical toward many of the developments that modernization entailed. It was thus no longer possible—if it ever had been—to equate "conservative" with "reactionary" because the "conversion of the conservative portion of the population to democracy within the CDU" was a cornerstone of the Federal Republic.[6] For many conservatives, it turned out to be a stroke of luck that they could no longer draw on Prussia and its discredited military heritage. Instead, they came to see that it was imperative to develop a new conservative understanding of what this new state was about. Bernard Willms asked whether precisely such a "reappraisal of the country's achievement" might enable conservatives to forge "projective concepts" next to which the "abstract barbarism of many a middle-class revolutionary must appear as a reactionary stance."[7]

The intellectual "conservative revolution" of the Weimar era had not survived the Third Reich. Hardly anyone in the Federal Republic drew upon the ideas of its major proponents, figures such as Oswald Spengler and Ernst Jünger. Their writings seemed like the fossilized remains of some long-extinct species shrouded in mystery.[8]

For the purposes of this essay, the term "conservative" will refer not only to those who labeled themselves as such. Whether one referred to oneself as a conservative or resented that label, the representative figures of the young democratic state reflected the conservative stance of the majority of the West German population, which, particularly in view of the Soviet threat, was content with the slogan "no experiments." For that reason the Christian Democrats (CDU/CSU) and many Free Democrats (FDP) explicitly or implicitly affirmed conservative values. Conservative elites and conservative intellectuals are treated here as a single group because engagement with National Socialism was largely an intellectual pursuit. Furthermore, the purview of this essay will not be limited to politicians: all who participated in the "circulation of ideas," as Jean Francois Sirinelli has phrased it, will be considered as intellectuals.[9]

A Difficult New Beginning

The way in which West German society and its decision-makers dealt with the legacy of the Third Reich has been the subject of much debate. In a strongly polarized dispute frequently marked by gross simplifications, it has sometimes been argued that the alleged repression of the Nazi past constitutes "a second guilt."[10] Other commentators have dismissed that line of argument as the "myth of a second guilt."[11] There appears to be no middle ground in this controversy. For example, it is common to point to the "complete reintegration" of National Socialist elites within West German society and to refer to the supposed deferral of a critical debate about National Socialism as an "original sin [Erbsünde] that has not been remedied even today."[12] What precisely the concomitant "political and moral catastrophe" might have been remains anyone's guess—after all, the history of the Federal Republic during the 1950s and 1960s can just as well be read as a "paragon of noncatastrophic development."[13] Another reproach alleges that during the Adenauer era, people were "not sufficiently willing or able" to take a "morally convincing stance of unequivocal condemnation." An "official posture of detachment" is supposed to have served a compensatory function and to have left the question of guilt and responsibility unanswered.[14]

It is certainly true that at the outset, confrontation with the past had been undertaken only half-heartedly.[15] But, contrary to received opinion, there was not a concerted silence over National Socialism and the Holocaust. From the mid-1950s on, West German historians "displayed a sober, nonmoralizing approach" in their treatment of the Nazi era. It therefore seems unwarranted to talk of either "moralism" or a "complete blockage."[16] Peter Steinbach has referred to an "ambivalence" evident during the 1950s. On the one hand, prosecution of individuals for Nazi crimes remained incomplete and was in many ways unsatisfactory; on the other, the integration of the large group of politically incriminated persons constituted a "remarkable achievement of German postwar society."[17]

A real engagement with the Nazi past did take place within academic circles and, to a lesser degree, in the public realm, but nothing comparable was to be observed in the private sphere. Hermann Lübbe has tried to get to the bottom of this "communicative silence" about the crimes committed during World War II. According to Lübbe, the phenomenon of the "repression" of the National Socialist past ought to be interpreted as a "necessary sociopsychological and political medium for the transformation of the postwar citizenry" of the Federal Republic. Only by means of "a certain silence" was it possible for the German people to reform themselves and to return to the path of law and morality. The majority of Germans had followed Hitler, and the integration of many of those former supporters of National Socialism would hardly have been possible without the "communicative silence" of the 1950s, Lübbe maintains. "The new German state had to be established against the ideology and politics of National Socialism. It could hardly have been established against the majority of the people."[18]

Thus far, Lübbe's hypotheses have been met with much skepticism.[19] This is all the more peculiar as one historian, the then young Wolfgang Mommsen, defended the repression of the memories of the Third Reich as early as 1961. "The tendency to repress memories of the Hitler-era is not simply indicative of a lack of honesty," Mommsen wrote. "To some degree it is a necessary component of a natural healing process."[20]

During the 1960s, the integration of those who had come to participate in the National Socialist movement through "seduction or force" had proven to be largely successful. The time had now come to ask the critical questions that an established democracy had both the moral obligation and the capacity to put up with. In 1959, the historian of ancient history Alfred Heuss criticized the "auto-suggestive drive" of the Germans to "repress our recent past and thereby pretend that we are unhistorical beings."[21] While the nascent democracy could not have been expected to "dwell on the past of its citizenry as a permanent and harsh accusation,"[22] the Federal Republic's capacity to undertake a self-reflexive and critical review of the past had developed along with its prosperity and its integration within the West. The coming of age of a new generation[23] in the late 1950s contributed to this reappraisal, as did a substantial number of new discoveries about the character of the Third Reich.[24] The academic community also began to cast a new, self-critical light on its own role in the years between 1933 and 1945,[25] even if, as Eric Vogelin complained in 1966, this process advanced at a snail-like pace.[26]

Beginning in the late 1950s, the era of National Socialism started to make the headlines in very specific ways.[27] In 1958, the rather cumbersomely named Central Office of the State Justice Administrations for the Investigation of National Socialist Crimes (Zentrale Stelle der Landesjustizverwaltungen zur Aufklärung nationalsozialistischer Gewaltverbrechen) was established in Ludwigsburg. Simultaneously, the prosecution of onetime SS members, the so-called Einsatzgruppen trial, in Ulm marked the opening of a series of major trials under German jurisdiction. These trials raised anew the question of individual responsibility for crimes perpetrated during the Nazi era. On Christmas 1959, swastikas were scrawled on the recently consecrated Cologne synagogue; this act of vandalism spurred nervous apprehension among the West German public.[28] During the late 1950s, the willingness of conservative parties to integrate former Nazis was pushed to its limits when former high-ranking Nazi Party officials began to display political ambitions. A combination of moral and tactical considerations made it appear increasingly inopportune to assign party offices to incriminated persons, especially since the German Democratic Republic kept a watchful eye for such developments and knew how to turn them to its advantage. The conviction took hold that "beyond personal guilt, political responsibility for the National Socialist dictatorship and its crimes had to be a decisive criterion for whether a former member of the party was acceptable for an official post."[29]

The Eichmann trial in Jerusalem mesmerized the public until the execution of the defendant in June 1962, and so did the Auschwitz trial in Frankfurt. Against the backdrop of an "unmistakable growing open-mindedness," it became possible not only to address isolated issues but also to start raising fundamental questions about the causes behind the persecution of the Jews and the "final solution."[30] With regard to criminal prosecution, the public tended to be more lenient than conservative intellectuals. Whereas conservative politicians, historians, and theologians like Paul Mikat, Oswald von Nell-Breuning, Helmuth Plessner, Karl

Rahner, Josef Ratzinger, Konrad Repgen, and Otto B. Roegele called for a public debate on whether to extend the statute of limitations on Nazi crimes,[31] the majority of West Germans regarded such a debate as unnecessary. Nearly 90 percent did not consider themselves to be implicated in the Holocaust and did not believe that they ought to feel guilty in any way.[32] This attitude was one of the reasons why growing numbers of intellectuals and public officials began to demand that National Socialism figure more prominently in school curricula. The state education ministers instituted student field trips to concentration camp memorials "in order to provide forceful instruction about the criminal acts of the National Socialist regime."[33] These changes in political consciousness occurred long before the 68ers called for intensified engagement with the Nazi past.

On account of these shifts in outlook, new approaches to addressing the past became possible. The "intellectual foundation of the republic" took place in 1959, as Friedrich Tenbruck has pointed out, not in 1968.[34] The achievements of the 1950s in "coming to terms with the past" no longer seemed sufficient: the "desire to be left alone after all these bitter years, which the young ones so often misconstrue as repression"[35] now met with less and less sympathy. The achievements of the *Wirtschaftswunder* (economic miracle) were now taken for granted and broad acceptance of the maxims of the Adenauer era was on the wane. With the "*Spiegel* affair,"[36] an articulate and powerful liberal counter-elite stepped onto the national stage. Meanwhile, the satirical magazine *Pardon*, which first appeared in September 1962, began to lampoon the "spirit of the age" with ingenious irony.

These changes also heralded a phase of reorientation for West Germany's conservatives. Partly in response to external pressure and partly as a matter of choice, they began to address deep-seated conflicts of conscience and, after "the questionable normalization of German life and thought," came to accept the necessity of holding themselves accountable.[37] In a kind of summary of his own political position, Armin Mohler conceded in 1962 that National Socialism had contained a "strong conservative current" in its "ideological cauldron." After the swastika incident and the "Eichmann year," he wrote, it was going to be difficult but all the more important for conservatives to oppose a "moralization of politics."[38] Mohler had styled himself as the sole representative of German conservatism in this essay, but many conservatives defensively agreed with his argument that "German conservatism has become a victim of fascism."[39] But he was indeed alone in questioning the legitimacy of the Eichmann trial. Much as West German conservatives disapproved of the obvious breech of international law in the defendant's abduction in Argentina, most of them shared the widely held view that Israel had a "historical right" to bring Eichmann to court. Most also condoned the way the trial was conducted and its outcome.[40]

Golo Mann regarded Mohler's lament as one-sided. The question had to be considered, he argued, whether conservatives might not have brought about their defeat themselves as their "crude anti-Semitism and foolish nationalism" had paved the way for Hitler.[41] With his characteristic skepticism and anthropological pessimism, he asked how human beings, "creatures supposedly endowed with reason," could have planned and executed Auschwitz. Mann's answer was that historical events were essentially contingent and could not be understood as a process. "That man is free, that he can use his freedom to do good, but rather often uses it to do evil, that is an age-old Christian insight." This anthropological interpretation of the Holocaust immediately earned him the reproach of proponents of Critical Theory of being "covertly anti-Semitic."[42] During a time of increasing moral righteousness, Mann's cultural pessimism had less appeal than the Enlightenment belief in the perfectibility of humankind. The same applied for Arnold Gehlen, who in 1969 characterized Hitler as a "follower of Nietzsche" and the Third Reich as an example of the "paranoid dynamic" let loose by the ruthless assertion of "blind and greedy self-interest." For Gehlen, the upshot was that here, as in so many other cases, Hegel's insight held true that "man as such, by nature as well as in his self-reflection, is evil."[43]

Eugen Gerstenmaier, the Christian Democratic president (speaker) of the Bundestag, took a similar line of argument against Mohler. Known for his sober and nuanced stance on Germany's responsibility for Nazism,[44] Gerstenmaier remarked that conservatism had been done in by its "mostly uncritical adoption of the nationalist posture" and its "belated dissociation from the demon of National Socialism."[45] Klaus Harpprecht, who at that time still regarded himself as a staunch conservative, had pointed out as early as the late 1950s that hardly a day passed without some politician, scholar, newspaper columnist, or radio commentator appealing to the conscience of the German people. He mistrusted Mohler, whom he regarded as an heir to the "conservative revolution" that had supported Hitler: the Third Reich had turned against all that was truly conservative, Harpprecht insisted, and Hitler's seizure of power had been a revolution not only against democracy, liberalism, and Marxism, but "a revolution against the way of life of the *Bürgertum*."[46] Caspar von Schrenck-Notzing—who ranked with Mohler as one of the most belligerent conservative intellectuals—thought that a "normalization" of political consciousness would be possible only when "the institutions are pulled out of the emotional slush, out of the depressive myth of 'coming to terms with the past.'"[47] Hans-Georg von Studnitz, an editor of the newspaper *Christ und Welt* who stubbornly refused to be converted to the reconstructed brand of conservatism, expressed his regret that the German people had "made a mission out of the role of the vanquished." He demanded that the "criminal heritage of National Socialism be eliminated more swiftly and more silently."[48] However, von Studnitz's individualistic stance led to his dismissal from *Christ und Welt* within less than a year. In the meantime, *Die Zeit* had supplanted *Christ und Welt* as the West German weekly with the highest circulation, a development that reflected the rapidly changing intellectual climate in the Federal Republic.

Rüdiger Altmann, one of the proponents of reconstructed conservatism, remained skeptical about the viability of a "settling of accounts" with the past, since most Germans during the Weimar era had been wishing for an authoritarian government, be it from the left or the right. The "moral compulsion to deny their own past" had not only turned many academics and politicians into hypocrites but was also "casting an oppressive gloom on a large part of the older generation."[49] At the same time, Altmann expressed his dismay at "that dubious mixture of justification and discrediting of the dark past" and the "moral weakness of the generation which had been bound to the Third Reich by conviction or as a matter of convenience."[50]

In 1963, Rudolf von Thadden affirmed the "collective liability of the German people" for the actions of the Third Reich. "The murder of the Jews will be attached to Germany's name even when every personal memory of it will have faded," he noted. This liability, which he distinguished sharply from "collective guilt," ought also to be seen as an opportunity for the nation, he argued.[51]

The Catholic Church took the complacent stance during the 1950s that it had been less susceptible to National Socialism than its Protestant counterpart. This made the wave of vitriolic attacks on Pope Pius XII prompted by Rolf Hochhuth's play *Der Stellvertreter* all the more shocking. Fritz Fischer's hypotheses about German responsibility for the outbreak of World War I led to a heated controversy because it seemed to hint at a continuity in Germany's ambitions between 1914 and 1945 that would have projected Germany's guilt even further back into the past. Conservative historians in particular vehemently opposed this line of argument, which traced a peculiarly German penchant for aggressive behavior from Bethmann Hollweg to Hitler.[52] The dispute got out of hand. In his personal correspondence, Gerhard Ritter, who as an acknowledged enemy of National Socialism was in a rather comfortable position, did not shy away from denouncing Fischer as a "Nazi quickly converted to democracy."[53] Such harsh invective was merely another sign of the sea change West Germany's intellectual climate was undergoing. This transformation prompted a thorough review of the received interpretations of the Nazi regime, and conservative intellectuals played an important part in the process.[54]

National Socialism as a "Demon"

A central element of conservative explanations of the rise of National Socialism was an insistence on its "demonic" character. Starting from a pessimistic worldview that incorporated the notion of original sin as a determining factor in historical processes, West German conservatives were strongly inclined to interpret the era of the Third Reich as a "temptation" in an anthropological sense. The "demonization" of Hitler undoubtedly also functioned as a kind of safety valve as it deflected responsibility from the German people as a whole. Critics charged that such demonological interpretations were aimed more at "an exorcist disassociation than at an historical explanation."[55] That charge is, however, at best only half accurate. It does not take into account the fact that this explanatory model had gained currency while Hitler was still in power and had a measure of plausibility. As Hitler spoke of "providence," his desperate and helpless opponents frequently made reference to the "diabolical forces" he seemed to be in league with.

It is therefore quite understandable that conservative opponents of National Socialism, too, tried to explain what Friedrich Meinecke called the "German catastrophe" by diabolical irrationalism.[56] Their early attempts to explain the sheer monstrosity of National Socialism, like those of many others, dealt mostly in abstractions. Their inclination to come to terms with the past and to confront guilt and responsibility was by no means weak, but in the years immediately following the war it was often given expression "indirectly or in symbolically encrypted form."[57] The Jewish historian Hans-Joachim Schoeps, who returned from exile in 1964, was profoundly in tune with such sentiments when he tried, rather simplistically, to explain Hitler and the Holocaust as the result of "the delusions of a handful of madmen."[58] Gerhard Ritter, too, frequently referred to the "demonism of power" in his reflections on Nazism, and Hans Rothfels drew attention to the "demonism of the totalitarian."[59] There is no question that the demonization of Hitler could serve apologetic ends, as when Hjalmar Schacht described Hitler as "a demonic, diabolical genius."[60] Yet to view such causal explanations as nothing but an afterglow of the myth of the Führer and as serving first and foremost "an alleviating function," as Bernd Faulenbach does,[61] seems off the mark—especially in light of the fact that the metaphor of "Hitler the demon" came increasingly under attack from the right. As early as 1951, Gerhard Ritter warned of the "formation of new myths" representing Hitler as "an absolute Satan"[62] and thereby obscuring rather than clarifying matters. Armin Mohler criticized the tendency to dramatize the Third Reich as something absurd or completely incommensurable, which he viewed as the most comfortable to avoid a genuine engagement with the phenomenon of National Socialism. In any case, by the mid-1960s, the evocation of National Socialism's demonic character had become obsolete among West German conservatives.

National Socialism as a Secular Religion

One reason behind the appeal of the metaphor of National Socialism's demonic nature was West German conservatism's roots in Christianity. In 1950, Hans Zehrer likened a conservatism that tried to do without Christianity to "a lady with nothing below the waist."[63] The demand for a "rechristianization" as the proper response to the moral confusions of National Socialism could count on broad support, especially as it latched onto a more general critique of the secular tendencies of the day. The barbarization of much of German society and culture under the Nazis was presented as being at least partly a result of secularization, a line of argument sometimes used in a broad rejection of the ideas of the Enlightenment.[64] Since secularization was not a specifically German development but affected "the occident" as a whole, discussion specifically of those causes of National Socialism that were peculiar to Germany could thereby be avoided. During the Cold War, this explanatory scheme of the "incursion of demons into a godless world"[65] became a staple everywhere in the Western world. The

Christian interpretation continued to be characterized by confessional divisions. Because the Catholic Church had seen itself in opposition to the Prussian element in German culture ever since the time of Bismarck's *Kulturkampf*, it could lay claim to a longstanding anti-Prussian and anti-National Socialist tradition, unlike the Protestant Church with its more obvious affinity to "state power."

Against the backdrop of this "occidental dispute," Armin Mohler emphasized the necessity of a "historical understanding" of the Nazi era. Scientific doctrines of race and anti-Judaism had been an "international phenomenon" and not limited to Germany alone.[66] Drawing on the work of the Jewish historian of ideas Jacob Talmon, he characterized Hitler's regime as a new religion in a secularized world.[67] In his agreement with Talmon's theory, Mohler was on common ground with many contemporary conservatives who saw National Socialism as but one more product of the humanist progressivism that had resulted in the Jacobin Terror a century and a half earlier. Gerhard Ritter also drew on Talmon's ideas, and while he did not join in the simplistic attempt to track the origins of National Socialism back to the ideas of the French Revolution, he nonetheless held to the position that "without the breakthrough of egalitarian and totalitarian democratism [*Demokratismus*] … the totalitarian one-party states" of the twentieth century would not have been possible.[68] These conservative attempts to establish a leftist pedigree for National Socialism as well as for Italian fascism have found some resonance in recent scholarship.[69] The interpretation of National Socialism as a messianic political religion expounded by the Catholic intellectual Waldemar Gurian, among others, was picked up in an unjustly neglected paper by Hans-Joachim Gamm.[70] This approach is, however, now gaining attention, thanks in part to a new interest in the idea of an "age of extremes" (Eric Hobsbawm).[71]

National Socialism as a Phenomenon of "Mass Society"

Closely connected with the critique of secularization was the argument that the alienating effects of mass society had made possible the totalitarian temptation. It drew on an on-going dispute about politics and culture as well as on the works of Hans Freyer, Arnold Gehlen, and José Ortega y Gasset. The symbiotic relationship of "mass and power" which Elias Canetti had outlined became a key concept in conservative explanations of the Nazi era.[72] For example, Hans-Joachim Merkatz, putting forward a common conservative line of argument, located the roots of the totalitarian state in "bureaucracy and the exercise of the people's sovereignty by plebiscite." As deeper causes, he cited the "rise and impoverishment of mass man" in modern technical civilization and the "nihilism" resulting from secularization.[73]

Such interpretations were supported by contemporary theories of totalitarianism. It is too easy to disparage the models proposed by Zbigniew Brzezinski, Carl J. Friedrich, and Hannah Arendt as products of the Cold War.[74] For one, the intellectual foundations of those models were laid long before the conflict between East and West began; moreover, the interpretations built upon them are still topical.[75] In the late 1950s, conservative thinkers incorporated them in their own reflections on an "age of totalitarianism." Lending persuasive force to this explanatory scheme was a popular anti-Soviet consensus during the late 1950s and early 1960s. Casting the conflict as a confrontation between a totalitarian dictatorship of the masses and the Christian occident, conservatives could count on broad approval. National Socialism thus appeared as a "fateful result of modern alienation" that had been successfully overcome, while there was now a much greater danger lurking in the East.[76] In day-to-day politics in West Germany, the past was not necessarily repressed but it certainly was pushed to the sidelines. Communism was seen as the most important contemporary incarnation of totalitarianism, and the ideological conflict with communism rather than the crimes of National Socialism occupied center stage. With a certain self-righteousness, conservatives presented their advocacy of closer political ties with the West and their anticommunism as simultaneously a turn to Western values and a decisive turn away from National Socialism. But conservative commentators paid little heed to a fact that has become the subject of much attention today, namely, that the totalitarian ideologies of the twentieth century—Stalinism, fascism, and National Socialism—had also marked a clear turning away from liberalism and democracy. Still, most conservatives had come to the conclusion that despite the rise of the masses, the *Vermassung*, that they held responsible for the rise of National Socialism, there was in fact no viable alternative to the Western model of democracy.[77] During the 1940s and 1950s, they had still rejected the parliamentary model, but by the 1960s even sociologists like Arnold Gehlen und Helmut Schelsky had withdrawn their harsh criticism of "the masses"—with far-reaching consequences for the conservative understanding of democracy. Gerhard Ritter, who in 1945 had asked whether the danger of degenerating into a "leader's party" was not intrinsic to all "mass parties,"[78] came during the 1960s to acknowledge the achievements of democracy without reservation.

The difficulty of reconciling the conservatives' endorsement of Western values with their continuing criticism of the consequences of the Enlightenment went largely unnoticed. In any case, the Federal Republic under Adenauer, with its fusion of the "economic doctrine of neoliberalism with the Anglo-Saxon concept of parliamentary democracy," presented such a marked departure from the goals and ideals of National Socialism that the conservatives' acceptance of the new social, political, and economic order has been called a "crucial reorientation."[79] This consensus on values led to an almost complete integration of the various conservative factions, even though there was a resurgence of criticism of the Americanization of German society—a hallmark of a specifically conservative cultural pessimism—as the West German economy returned to normal during the 1950s and 1960s. The crucial difference between the old and new variants of this argument was that the proponents of a "moderate cultural anti-Americanism"[80]—thinkers as Hans Freyer, Arnold Gehlen, Giselher Wirsing, and Hans Zehrer—took as their ideal not a race-oriented National Socialism, but a culturally defined "Europe of the mind."

With the increasing dynamism and prosperity of the Federal Republic, the conservatives' cultural pessimism gave way to a new perspective that carried with it a new understanding of National Socialism. The "apocalyptic tone, the traditional antimodernism, Luddism and cranky antiurbanism, the whining about the rule of the masses"[81] all appeared increasingly anachronistic. As West German conservatives' contempt for democratic mass society dwindled, their critique of all utopian endeavors came to the fore. The points of convergence between that critique and theories of totalitarianism were obvious: with the extermination of the Jews, the Nazi regime had tried to put into practice a racist utopia. The condemnation of Hitler's ideas fit snugly with the condemnation of the class-based utopianism of socialist-communist provenance.

The Holocaust

Even though the Holocaust was at the center of public attention after the end of the Third Reich, historical research lagged behind. This was partly due to a lack of access to relevant sources, and partly to the fact that the regime had treated the "final solution" as a state secret. Research-based information about the genesis of the Holocaust became publicly available only in the course of the 1950s. Following the Adenauer government's efforts to make material restitution for the Holocaust during the 1950s, West German conservatives sought to open dialogue with Jewish intellectuals in the 1960s. On 21 November 1962, Eugen Gerstenmaier gave a speech entitled "Die Wandlung der Deutschen" (The Transformation of the German People) at the Hebrew University of Jerusalem. In it, he scathingly denounced the "hysterical nationalism" he regarded as a precondition for the rise of National Socialism. While Gerstenmaier considered the desire to "come to terms with the past" as misdirected, he pointed out the necessity of correcting the historical consciousness of the German people:

> This sense of history has been so dislocated as a result of the happenings of the past thirty years, has become so uncertain and so diffused that it seems to be an even more problematical affair than our present feeling of nationhood. It is true that we can point to a number of honorable efforts which include the complete revision of our schoolbooks, [and] the conscientious work of the Institut für Zeitgeschichte [in] Munich.... But as far as our history is concerned—our history at least from the Seven Years' War up to the Treaty of Rapallo—all this is for many Germans—perhaps indeed for most of them—still shrouded in obscurity.[82]

He also commented on the Eichmann trial, which demanded a "renewed soul-searching from the entire German nation":

> I cannot deny that all this sooner or later begins to impose an excessive strain on one's own conscience, and not only does the light of reason shine as a result of this heart-searching, but there also appear dark shadows—shadows brought into being by the

knowledge that even the most severe form of penitence will be unable to make up for this monstrous guilt. It is not unnatural therefore that there should be quite a number of people who feel that it is time to put an end to all this and to abandon any further idea of punishment. At the same time, I do not think that this latter idea will gain any permanent footing in German parliamentary proceedings, and the system of penalty and penitence will remain.[83]

Guilt, Shame, and the *Schlußstrich* Debate

The "fatigue" Gerstenmaier perceived is an indicator that claims of a "silence" about the Third Reich were certainly unfounded by the early 1960s. A common thread running through the various conservative opinions about the Nazi past voiced during the course of that decade was the idea of a "collective sense of shame," which was put forward as an alternative to the notion of "collective guilt" that Karl Jaspers had introduced after the war.[84] By acknowledging this "collective shame," the German people would assume the responsibility that large parts of the population still refused to accept. Gerhard Ritter, for example, confessed "a measure of moral responsibility" for all the crimes of Hitler's regime, the Holocaust in particular. In the face of history, Ritter wrote in 1962, a people "must be held responsible for whom it is applauding.... Certainly: the masses were blinded by the masterful demagogue, and a sober political judgment cannot be expected from the populace when even such an outstanding politician as Winston Churchill was wavering for some time." It nonetheless remained a "troubling and shameful fact" for Ritter "that so many Germans—some of my colleagues included—were not morally repelled" by Hitler. He considered this breakdown of ethical judgment to be "the fault or at least a moral failure of a large, a very large majority of the German people, with the most fateful consequences." At the same time, against the background of the Fischer controversy, Ritter opposed the contemporary tendency to move toward the opposite extreme. In West German schools and universities, he alleged, the former worship of the nation-state had been replaced by a "super-revisionism fixated on the total vilification of Germany's past."[85]

Armin Mohler, by contrast, used the notion of collective shame to advance a rather questionable argument for a complete amnesty for all Germans who had been convicted of crimes in connection with the Third Reich. An amnesty was not the same as a "not guilty" verdict, he maintained, nor would it justify the crimes that had been committed. An amnesty would, rather, stand as an admission that there were situations in which justice was simply impossible. Mohler went on to call for a temporary moratorium on all historical research on National Socialism: "[A]ll in all, after being expropriated for nonscholarly purposes for such a long time, it could only be good for the discipline of contemporary history to be put under quarantine for a while."[86] He concluded by insisting that it was time to close the books on the Nazi past—*einen Schlußstrich ziehen* (literally, to draw a line under)—in order to turn the German people back into "a normal nation."[87] Mohler's views were, however, arguably well outside of the conservative mainstream. His position within the conservative spectrum was rather like that of Hans Freyer, who had clearly "fallen off the radar" even though he continued to publish.[88]

The sweeping reproach that conservatism as a whole had "called for a 'closing of the case'" is a gross simplification.[89] Many conservatives did not, however, want to see the search for national identity limited to the troubling heritage of the twelve years of the Third Reich. Owing to his anti-Nazi past, Konrad Adenauer—who refused to accept the notions of both collective guilt and collective shame—was able to address the questions relating to the Third Reich much more freely than most of his political colleagues and opponents. As attitudes toward the resistance to Hitler changed and talk of "betrayal" gave way to praise of "heroic acts," Adenauer wryly commented that it now appeared as though there had been "more people involved in the plot of 20 July than there are living in all of Germany."[90] Although he was under no illusion as to how many of the Germans who had succumbed to National Socialism were now trying to disguise that uncomfortable truth, he also professed a dislike "for that interminable neurotic gabbling about the Nazi past."[91] He even went so far as to breach an unwritten rule in 1966 that had been rigorously observed up to that point. During a visit to Jerusalem in May of that year, 1966, Adenauer was told by Israeli Prime Minister Levi Eshkol that "the Israeli people are waiting for a renewed proof that the German people recognize the terrible burden of the past." Adenauer retorted in a manner that openly showed his annoyance at what he regarded as a calculated exploitation of the past—after all, a new treaty providing economic aid to Israel was about to be signed.[92] Such a performance was possible only for somebody whose self-esteem was bolstered by the knowledge that he had opposed Hitler.

While voicing views like Adenauer's was not unusual either in private or in public, conservatives as a rule did not do so. But it was precisely the pluralism of middle-class society—the newly opened space for dissent—that the conservative establishment could adduce as proof that West Germany had taken the lessons of the past to heart. Although Adenauer never really trusted the German people, the majority of conservatives during the 1960s regarded a revival of extreme nationalism as highly unlikely. More clearly than observers on the left, they recognized that steadily increasing automobile ownership, travel, and consumption signaled West Germany's arrival in the world of Western values. Some conservatives mourned this process as a cultural loss. But there was nonetheless an overarching consensus among conservatives that the Federal Republic and its citizens had become immune to the temptations of totalitarian rule.

Another "Helpless Antifascism"

During the 1960s, the representatives of conservatism were faced with an image of National Socialism that left them disoriented and helpless. They were quickly put on the defensive as a result, first, of media attention to former Nazi officials who continued to fill positions of authority in the Federal Republic and, later in the decade, of the resurgence of the Marxist interpretation of fascism and National Socialism. The misleading and one-sided character of this criticism, put forward with a "holier than thou" attitude,[93] is now evident. The conservative interpretations of Nazism current at the time may have been unsatisfactory because they failed to identify the root causes of the regime's crimes, but, in hindsight, they now appear much more plausible than the polemic verbiage which prevailed in the mid-1960s that characterized "fascism" as a "form of bourgeois rule" (Reinhard Kühnl).

Conservative intellectuals faced a threefold challenge. First, the neo-Marxist explanation of National Socialism, harkening back to the Comintern's official view in 1933, regarded fascism as "the open terroristic dictatorship of the most reactionary, most chauvinistic and most imperialistic elements of the monetary capital."[94] West German conservatives found themselves in the awkward position of having to defend the liberal and market-oriented Federal Republic against the radical attacks of their leftist opponents. Secondly, conservatives had to defend their own interpretation of National Socialism, which saw capitalism as only one of several factors responsible for the ascent of the Nazis. Thirdly, they had to defend themselves against allegations that the National Socialist past had been suppressed during the 1950s in order to veil the continuity of capitalist structures in Germany.[95]

This threefold challenge overtaxed the strength of conservatives, who were unexpectedly thrust into service as the defenders of the Federal Republic. And regardless of their responses, there was a strong desire among West Germans for sociopolitical change. One manifestation of change was the formation of the Christian Democratic-Social Democratic "grand coalition," which was not without consequences for conservatism. The formerly reliable mechanisms of integration were starting to wear out, and the CDU lost its ability to rein in the far right. The rise of a nationalist opposition and the founding of the far-right National Democratic Party (Nationaldemokratische Partei Deutschlands, NPD) were unsettling to conservatives, as the liberal and left public consistently pointed out the elements of racist ideology in the program of the neonationalist movement.

Because reconstructed conservatism in the Federal Republic had abandoned ideological components with a racist bent, the declining appeal of conservative ideas in the late 1960s must be seen partly as reflecting this renunciation. However, this was hardly enough to positively define what the role of conservatism should be in a world that was changing under the impact of the politics of détente. The relevant debates on National Socialism and the Holocaust were increasingly conducted elsewhere, as well. One might characterize the overall mood of the times with a variation on the title of a book that was to appear much later: "The intellectual winds were blowing from the left."[96]

Conclusion

Conservatives were intensely engaged with the problem of National Socialism during the 1960s. Naturally, their interpretations diverged from those of the left, which hinged on the "capitalist" character of "fascism." Comparing the various explanations of National Socialism with the benefit of more than thirty years' hindsight, one is tempted to concur with Friedrich Nietzsche, who once said that the truth is always "untimely" because the *Zeitgeist* has a propensity to error. The neo-Marxist analyses of the 1960s are now largely discredited, whereas the interpretations of the conservative authors discussed here—the anthropological hypothesis about man's innate capacity for evil, the attention to the seductive power of totalitarian regimes and their ability to manipulate the dynamics of "mass and power," the notion of the alienating effects of secularization and the concomitant rise of political religions—today increasingly command the attention of historians. That in itself is a clear sign of the falsity of the widely held notion that Germany started to seriously engage its troubling past only in 1968.[97] Undoubtedly, it will be objected that one should not mistake "quickly learned political rituals of condemnation" for the "real thing."[98] But this would not be doing justice to the earnest efforts of the period. An argument that ignores all efforts to come to an understanding of National Socialism prior to 1968 will serve to muffle historical research. Those who pass judgment from the comfortable position of never having been exposed to the threat of totalitarian seduction should recall Saul Friedländer's dictum: "It is not enough that accounts of the Nazi era express the belated—and more or less self-congratulatory—moral righteousness of their authors."[99]

Notes

1. Axel Schildt, *Konservatismus in Deutschland: Von den Anfängen im 18. Jahrhundert bis zur Gegenwart* (Munich, 1998), 9.
2. Jean R. von Salis, *Geschichte und Politik* (Zurich, 1971), 214.
3. Kurt Lenk, *Deutscher Konservatismus* (Frankfurt am Main, 1989), 174.
4. Ernst Nolte, "Konservativismus und Nationalsozialismus," in *Konservativismus*, ed. Hans Gerd Schumann (Cologne, 1974), 244–60.
5. Eugen Gerstenmaier, "Was heißt heute konservativ?" *Der Monat* 14 (1965): 27–30, here 27. In a variation of this theme, Johannes Gross pointed out that political conservatism came to enjoy popularity only after it had vanished. Johannes Gross, *Lauter Nachworte: Innenpolitik nach Adenauer* (Stuttgart, 1965), 222.
6. Richard Löwenthal, "Stabilität ohne Sicherheit: Vom Selbstverständnis der Bundesrepublik Deutschland," *Der Monat* 30 (October 1978): 75–84, here 80.
7. Bernard Willms, *Die Antwort des Leviathan: Thomas Hobbes' politische Theorie* (Neuwied, 1970), 130.
8. Hermann Lübbe, quoted in *Frankfurter Allgemeine Zeitung*, 26 February 1992. See Stefan Breuer, *Anatomie der Konservativen Revolution* (Darmstadt, 1993), 201.

9. Jean François Sirinelli, "Intellectuels," in *Dictionnaire historique de la vie politique française au XXe siècle* (Paris, 1995), 524–27, here 524. See generally the discussion in Gangolf Hübinger, "Die politischen Rollen europäischer Intellektueller im 20. Jahrhundert," in *Kritik und Mandat: Intellektuelle in der deutschen Politik*, ed. Thomas Hertfelder and Jean François Sirinelli (Stuttgart, 2000), 30–44.

10. Ralph Giordano, *Die zweite Schuld oder von der Last Deutscher zu sein* (Hamburg, 1987).

11. Manfred Kittel, *Die Legende von der "Zweiten Schuld": Vergangenheitsbewältigung in der Ära Adenauer* (Berlin, 1993).

12. Ulrich Herbert, "Deutsche Eliten nach Hitler," *Mittelweg 36* (1999): 66–82, here 74.

13. Hans-Peter Schwarz, "Die ausgebliebene Katastrophe: Eine Problemskizze zur Geschichte der Bundesrepublik," in *Den Staat denken: Theodor Eschenburg zum Fünfundachtzigsten*, ed. Hermann Rudolph (Berlin, 1990), 151–73, here 151.

14. Martin Broszat and Saul Friedländer, "Um die 'Historisierung des Nationalsozialismus': Ein Briefwechsel," *Vierteljahrshefte für Zeitgeschichte* 36 (1988): 339–72, here 341f.

15. Norbert Frei, *Vergangenheitspolitik: Die Anfänge der Bundesrepublik und die NS-Vergangenheit*, 2nd ed. (Munich, 1997), 16.

16. Broszat and Friedländer, "Um die 'Historisierung des Nationalsozialismus,'" 344.

17. Peter Steinbach, *Nationalsozialistische Gewaltverbrechen: Die Diskussion in der deutschen Öffentlichkeit nach 1945* (Berlin, 1981), 42f.

18. Hermann Lübbe, "Der Nationalsozialismus im deutschen Nachkriegsbewußtsein," *Historische Zeitschrift* 236 (1983): 579–99, here 585f. See Hermann Lübbe, "Deutschland nach dem Nationalsozialismus 1945–1990," in *Vertuschte Vergangenheit: Der Fall Schwerte und die NS-Vergangenheit der deutschen Hochschulen*, ed. Helmut König, Wolfgang Kuhlmann, and Klaus Schwabe (Munich, 1997), 182–206, esp. 203–6.

19. Even Frei does not reflect upon this interpretation and mentions Lübbe only in a footnote. Frei, *Vergangenheitspolitik*, 9.

20. Wolfgang J. Mommsen, "Historisches Denken der Gegenwart," in *Fischer-Lexikon Geschichte*, ed. Waldemar Besson (Frankfurt am Main, 1961), 92–102, here 100.

21. Alfred Heuss, *Verlust der Geschichte* (Göttingen, 1959), 61. On Heuss, see Stefan Rebenich, "Alfred Heuss: Ansichten seines Lebenswerkes," *Historische Zeitschrift* 271 (2000): 661–73.

22. Peter Graf Kielmansegg, *Lange Schatten: Vom Umgang der Deutschen mit der nationalsozialistischen Vergangenheit* (Berlin, 1989), 19.

23. See Dirk Moses's convincing analysis in his essay, "Die 45er: Eine Generation zwischen Faschismus und Demokratie," *Die Neue Sammlung* 40 (2000): 233–63. See also Heinz Bude, "Die Erinnerung der Generationen," in *Vergangenheitsbewältigung am Ende des zwanzigsten Jahrhunderts*, ed. Helmut König, Michael Kohlstruck, and Andreas Wöll (Opladen, 1998), 69–85.

24. Hermann Graml, "Die verdrängte Auseinandersetzung mit dem Nationalsozialismus," in *Zäsuren nach 1945*, ed. Martin Broszat (Munich, 1990), 169–80; Udo Wengst, "Geschichtswissenschaft und 'Vergangenheitsbewältigung' in Deutschland nach 1945 und nach 1989/90," *Geschichte in Wissenschaft und Unterricht* 46 (1995): 189–205. A pointed refutation of the interpretation of conservative "*Entsorgung*" of the German past can be found in Joachim Fest, "Die Vergangenheit wurde nicht verdrängt," in Rudolph, *Den Staat denken*, 118–21.

25. Andreas Flitner, ed., *Deutsches Geistesleben und Nationalsozialismus: Eine Vortragsreihe der Universität Tübingen* (Tübingen, 1965); Flitner, *Die deutsche Universität im Dritten Reich: Eine Vortragsreihe der Universität München* (Munich, 1966); Flitner, *Nationalsozialismus und die deutsche Universität. Universitätstage 1966: Veröffentlichung der Freien Universität Berlin* (Berlin, 1966); Eric Voegelin, "Die deutsche Universität und die Ordnung der deutschen Gesellschaft," in *Die deutsche Universität im Dritten Reich*, 241–82, here 280.

26. Voegelin, "Die deutsche Universität," 280.

27. For a historiographical overview, see Steinbach, *Nationalsozialistische Gewaltverbrechen*, esp. 38–53.

28. Juliane Schwibbert, "Die Kölner Synagogenschmierereien Weihnachten 1959 und die Reaktionen in Politik und Öffentlichkeit," *Geschichte in Köln* 33 (1993): 73–96. On the role of

the East German intelligence service (Staatssicherheitsdienst), see Michael Wolffsohn, *Die Deutschland-Akte: Juden und Deutsche in Ost und West. Tatsachen und Legenden* (Munich, 1995), 17–26.

29. Thomas Schlemmer, "Grenzen der Integration: Die CSU und der Umgang mit der nationalsozialistischen Vergangenheit—der Fall Dr. Max Frauendorfer," *Vierteljahrshefte für Zeitgeschichte* 48 (2000): 675–742, here 676, 708, and 720.

30. Peter Steinbach, "Nationalsozialistische Gewaltverbrechen in der deutschen Öffentlichkeit nach 1945," in *Vergangenheitsbewältigung durch Strafverfahren?* ed. Jürgen Weber and Peter Steinbach (Munich, 1984), 13–39, here 26.

31. See Simon Wiesenthal, ed., *Verjährung? 200 Persönlichkeiten des öffentlichen Lebens sagen nein* (Stuttgart, 1965).

32. Elisabeth Noelle and Erich Peter Neumann, eds., *Jahrbuch der öffentlichen Meinung 1958–1964* (Allensbach, 1965), 227 and 229; Nolle and Neumann, eds., *Jahrbuch der öffentlichen Meinung 1965–1967* (Allensbach, 1967), 204.

33. *Amtsblatt des Bayerischen Staatsministeriums für Unterricht und Kultur,* cited in Clemens Vollnhals, "Zwischen Verdrängung und Aufklärung: Die Auseinandersetzung mit dem Holocaust in der frühen Bundesrepublik," in *Die Deutschen und die Judenverfolgung im Dritten Reich,* ed. Ursula Büttner (Hamburg, 1992), 357–92, here 373. On the turn at the beginning of the 1960s, see Falk Pingel, "Nationalsozialismus und Holocaust in westdeutschen Schulbüchern," in *Der Umgang mit dem Holocaust—Europa—USA—Israel,* ed. Rolf Steininger (Vienna, 1994), 221–32.

34. Friedrich H. Tenbruck, "Von der verordneten Vergangenheitsbewältigung zur intellektuellen Gründung der Bundesrepublik," in *Die intellektuelle Gründung der Bundesrepublik: Eine Wirkungsgeschichte der Frankfurter Schule,* ed. Clemens Albrecht, Günter C. Behrmann, Michael Bock, Harald Homann, and Friedrich H. Tenbruck (Frankfurt am Main, 1999), 78–96.

35. Michael Bock, "Metamorphosen der Vergangenheitsbewältigung," in Albrecht et al., *Die intellektuelle Gründung der Bundesrepublik,* 530–66, here 547.

36. The "Spiegel affair" was triggered by an article of *Der Spiegel* magazine in 1962, which led to accusations of treason and ended in confiscations and arrests of leading journalists. The ensuing public outcry led to a political reshuffling of Adenauer's cabinet and altered the political and cultural landscape of West Germany. It is widely seen as a turning point on Germany's way toward modern democracy.

37. Helmut Krausnick, "Unser Weg in die Katastrophe von 1945: Rechenschaft und Besinnung heute," *Aus Politik und Zeitgeschichte* B 19/62 (1962): 229–40, here 229.

38. Armin Mohler, "Konservativ 1962," *Der Monat* 14 (1962): 163, 23–29.

39. Ibid.

40. See the documents in Hans Lamm, ed., *Der Eichmann-Prozeß in der deutschen öffentlichen Meinung* (Frankfurt am Main, 1961).

41. Golo Mann, "Konservative Politik und konservative Charaktere," *Der Monat* 14 (1962): 165, 49–54.

42. Clemens Albrecht, "Warum Horkheimer Golo Mann einen "heimlichen Antisemiten" nannte: Der Streit um die richtige Vergangenheitsbewältigung," in Albrecht et al., *Die intellektuelle Gründung der Bundesrepublik,* 189–202.

43. Arnold Gehlen, *Moral und Hypermoral: Eine pluralistische Ethik* (Frankfurt am Main, 1969), 119.

44. See the speech he delivered at the Hebrew University in Jerusalem on 21 November 1962 and his speech at the Hebrew University on 4 August 1966, both of which are reprinted in Rolf Vogel, ed., *Deutschlands Weg nach Israel: Eine Dokumentation* (Stuttgart, 1967), 262–66; in the English edition of the Vogel anthology, published under the title *The German Path to Israel: A Documentation* (London, 1969), the speech appears on pages 144–59. See also Eugen Gerstenmaier, *Neuer Nationalismus? Von der Wandlung der Deutschen* (Stuttgart, 1965), esp. 7–15.

45. Eugen Gerstenmaier, "Was heißt heute konservativ?" *Der Monat* 14 (1965): 166, 27–30, here 27.

46. Klaus Harpprecht, "Verteidigung des Altmodischen," *Der Monat* 14 (1962): 165, 59–63.

47. Caspar Freiherr von Schrenck-Notzing, "Wider die Gefühlspolitik," *Der Monat* 14 (1962): 165, 56–59, here 58.

48. Hans-Georg von Studnitz, *Bismarck in Bonn: Bemerkungen zur Außenpolitik* (Stuttgart, 1964), 14 and 19. See also Nils Asmussen, "Hans-Georg von Studnitz: Ein konservativer Journalist im Dritten Reich und in der Bundesrepublik," *Vierteljahrshefte für Zeitgeschichte* 45 (1997): 75–119.

49. Rüdiger Altmann, "Sehnsucht nach Selbstbewußtsein," in *Vom Geist der Zeit*, ed. Adolf Frisé (Gütersloh, 1966), 165–69, here 167.

50. Rüdiger Altmann, "Der Verdacht, ein Staat zu sein," in *Zensuren nach 20 Jahren Bundesrepublik*, ed. Rüdiger Altmann et al. (Cologne, 1969), 9–25, here 12f.

51. Rudolf von Thadden, "17. Juni: Nach zehn Jahren," *Neue Sammlung* 3 (1963): 383–87, here 387.

52. For an assessment of Fischer's work in the light of recent research, see Klaus Hildebrand, *Deutsche Außenpolitik 1871–1918*, 2nd ed. (Munich, 1994), 79–92. Still very useful is Gregor Schöllgen, "Griff nach der Weltmacht? 25 Jahre Fischer-Kontroverse," *Historisches Jahrbuch* 106 (1986): 386–406.

53. Ritter to Fritz Epstein, 15 February 1963, in *Gerhard Ritter: Ein politischer Historiker in seinen Briefen*, ed. Klaus Schwabe and Rolf Reichardt (Boppard, 1984), 576.

54. For a concise overview, see Jean Solchany, "Vom Antimodernismus zum Antitotalitarismus: Konservative Interpretationen des Nationalsozialismus in Deutschland 1945–1949," *Vierteljahrshefte für Zeitgeschichte* 44 (1996): 373–94.

55. Broszat and Friedländer, "Um die 'Historisierung des Nationalsozialismus,'" 342.

56. Friedrich Meinecke, *Die Deutsche Katastrophe: Betrachtungen und Erinnerungen* (Wiesbaden, 1946).

57. Barbro Eberan, *Wer war an Hitler schuld? Die Debatte um die Schuldfrage 1945–1949* (Munich, 1985), 205.

58. Hans-Joachim Schoeps, *Unbewältigte Geschichte: Stationen deutschen Schicksals seit 1763* (Berlin, 1964), 206f.

59. Hans Rothfels, "Die Geschichtswissenschaft in den dreißiger Jahren," in *Die deutsche Universität im Dritten Reich*, 90–107, here 99; Gerhard Ritter, *Carl Goerdeler und die deutsche Widerstandsbewegung* (Stuttgart, 1956), 12.

60. *Die Zeit*, 30 September 1948.

61. Bernd Faulenbach, "NS-Interpretationen und Zeitklima: Zum Wandel in der Aufarbeitung der jüngsten Vergangenheit," *Aus Politik und Zeitgeschichte* B 22/87 (1987): 19–30, here 22. See also Ulrich von Hehl, *Nationalsozialistische Herrschaft* (Munich, 1996), 50.

62. Ritter to Heinz Roscher, 5 September 1951, in Schwabe and Reichardt, *Gerhard Ritter*, 474.

63. Cited in Axel Schildt, "Solidarisch mit der Schuld des Volkes: Die öffentliche Schulddebatte und das Integrationsangebot der Kirchen in Niedersachsen nach dem Zweiten Weltkrieg," in *Rechtsradikalismus in der politischen Kultur der Nachkriegszeit: Die verzögerte Normalisierung in Niedersachsen*, ed. Bernd Weisbrod (Hanover, 1995), 269–96, here 269.

64. See Martin Greschat, "'Rechristianisierung' und 'Säkularisierung': Anmerkungen zu einem europäischen interkonfessionellen Interpretationsmodell," in *Christentum und politische Verantwortung: Kirchen in der Nachkriegszeit*, ed. Jochen-Christoph Kaiser and Anselm Doering-Manteuffel (Stuttgart, 1990), 1–24.

65. Schildt, *Konservatismus*, 215

66. Armin Mohler, *Was die Deutschen fürchten* (Stuttgart, 1965), 96, 98.

67. Jacob L. Talmon, *Die Ursprünge der totalitären Demokratie* (Cologne, 1961).

68. Gerhard Ritter to Andreas Dorpalen, 3 July 1962, in Schwabe and Reichardt, *Gerhard Ritter*, 572; see also Ritter to Otto Vossler, 22 April 1963, in ibid., 582.

69. On National Socialism, see, e.g., Karl Dietrich Bracher, *Zeit der Ideologien* (Stuttgart, 1982); on Italian fascism, see Zeev Sternhell, *Die Entstehung der faschistischen Ideologie: von Sorel zu Mussolini* (Hamburg, 1999).

70. Hans-Joachim Gamm, *Der braune Kult: Das Dritte Reich und seine Ersatzreligion* (Hamburg, 1962); Waldemar Gurian, "Totalitarianism as Political Religion," in *Totalitarianism*, ed. Carl J. Friedrich (New York, 1964). On "messianism," see Klaus Schreiner, "'Wann kommt der Retter Deutschlands?' Formen und Funktionen von politischem Messianismus in der Weimarer Republik," *Saeculum* 49 (1998): 107–60.

71. Michael Burleigh, *Die Zeit des Nationalsozialismus* (Frankfurt am Main, 2000), esp. 13–41; Hans Maier, ed., *Totalitarismus und politische Religionen: Konzepte des Diktaturvergleichs*, vol. 3: *Deutungsgeschichte und Theorie* (Paderborn, 2003); Eric Hobsbawm, *Age of Extremes: The Short Twentieth Century, 1914–1991* (London, 1994).

72. Elias Canetti, *Masse und Macht* (Düsseldorf, 1960); the English translation was published as *Crowds and Power* in 1962. See also Ulrich Lappenküper, Joachim Scholtyseck, and Christoph Studt, eds., *Masse und Macht im 19. und 20. Jahrhundert* (Munich, 2003).

73. Hans-Joachim von Merkatz, *Die konservative Funktion: Ein Beitrag zur Geschichte des politischen Denkens* (Munich, 1957).

74. Hannah Arendt, *The Origins of Totalitarianism* (New York, 1951); Carl J. Friedrich, "The Unique Character of Totalitarian Society," in *Totalitarianism: Proceedings of a Conference held at the American Academy of Arts and Sciences* (Cambridge, MA, 1954), 47–60.

75. The use of the term "totalitarianism" here follows Karl Dietrich Bracher, *Zeitgeschichtliche Kontroversen: Um Faschismus, Totalitarismus, Demokratie* (Munich, 1976); Bracher's approach remains valid today. For recent discussion of the concept, see Eckhard Jesse, ed., *Totalitarismus im 20. Jahrhundert: Eine Bilanz der internationalen Forschung* (Bonn, 1996); Hans Maier, ed., *"Totalitarismus" und "Politische Religionen": Konzepte des Diktaturvergleiches* (Paderborn, 1996); Wolfgang Wippermann, *Totalitarismustheorien: Die Entwicklung der Diskussion von den Anfängen bis heute* (Darmstadt, 1997).

76. Schildt, *Konservatismus*, 228.

77. Helga Grebing, *Konservative gegen die Demokratie: Konservative Kritik an der Demokratie in der Bundesrepublik* (Frankfurt am Main, 1971), 84–103.

78. Winfried Schulze, *Deutsche Geschichtswissenschaft nach 1945* (Munich, 1989), 215.

79. Hans-Jürgen Puhle, "Konservatismus und Neo-Konservatismus: Deutsche Entwicklungslinien seit 1945," in *Gegen Barbarei: Essays Robert M. W. Kempner zu Ehren*, ed. Rainer Eisfeld and Ingo Müller (Frankfurt am Main, 1989), 399–423, here 404.

80. Philipp Gassert, "Was meint Amerikanisierung? Über den Begriff des Jahrhunderts," *Merkur* 617–618 (2000): 785–96, here 793. See also Joachim Scholtyseck, "Anti-Amerikanismus in der deutschen Geschichte," *Historisch-Politische Mitteilungen* 10 (2003): 23–42.

81. Schildt, *Konservatismus*, 236.

82. Eugen Gerstenmaier, "The Change in the German Outlook," reprinted in Vogel, *The German Path to Israel*, 145–58; here, 150.

83. Ibid., 155.

84. Karl Jaspers, *Die Schuldfrage* (Heidelberg, 1946).

85. Gerhard Ritter to Pieter Geyl, 16 January 1962, in Schwabe and Reichardt, *Gerhard Ritter*, 563f.

86. Mohler, *Was die Deutschen fürchten*, 112–39.

87. Ibid., 101.

88. Jerry Z. Muller, *The Other God That Failed: Hans Freyer and the Deradicalization of German Conservatism* (Princeton, 1987), 384.

89. Schildt, *Konservatismus*, 240.

90. "Wortprotokoll der Sitzung vom 17. November 1949," *Akten zur Auswärtigen Politik der Bundesrepublik Deutschland: Adenauer und die Hohen Kommissare*, vol. 1 (Munich, 1989), 27.

91. Hans-Peter Schwarz, *Adenauer. Der Staatsmann: 1952–1967* (Stuttgart, 1991), 527.

92. See Yeshayahu A. Jelinek and Rainer Blasius, "Ben Gurion und Adenauer im Waldorf Astoria," *Vierteljahrshefte für Zeitgeschichte* 45 (1997): 309–44, here 321.

93. As, for example, in Harold Marcuse, "The Revival of Holocaust Awareness in West Germany, Israel, and the United States," in *1968: The World Transformed*, ed. Carole Fink, Philipp Gassert, and Detlev Junker (Cambridge, 1998), 421–38.

94. *Wörterbuch der Geschichte, A-K* (East Berlin, 1984), 290.

95. See, for example, Wolfgang Fritz Haug, *Der hilflose Antifaschismus: Zur Kritik der Vorlesungsreihen über Wissenschaft und NS an deutschen Universitäten*, 3rd ed. (Cologne, 1970).

96. Claus Leggewie, *Der Geist steht rechts: Ausflüge in die Denkfabriken der Wende* (Berlin, 1987).

97. The Italian path to confrontation with the fascist past has been even more twisted. See Jens Petersen's recent historiographical overview, "Der Ort Mussolinis in der Geschichte Italiens nach 1945," in *Europäische Sozialgeschichte: Festschrift für Wolfgang Schieder*, ed. Christof Dipper, Lutz Klinkhammer, and Alexander Nützenadel (Berlin, 2000), 505–24, here 523.

98. Frei, *Vergangenheitspolitik*, 11.

99. Broszat and Friedländer, "Um die 'Historisierung des Nationalsozialismus,'" 351.

Chapter 15

CATHOLIC STUDENT FRATERNITIES, THE NATIONAL SOCIALIST PAST, AND THE STUDENT MOVEMENT

Michael Hochgeschwender

❧

Probably no period, with the possible exception of the Nazi era, has had as major an impact on German academic fraternities as the late 1960s. All of the once powerful fraternity organizations lost membership[1] as well as political and social influence in the closing years of the decade. As a new reformist attitude gained ground, personal networks that had been built up over decades collapsed. Several factors were decisive in this process. The most important may have been an increasing stress on individualism. The reorganization of the West German party system must also be mentioned; one result was that Catholic fraternities lost the support of the Christian Democratic Union. Another important, if less immediate, factor must not be forgotten: all fraternities, including the Catholic ones, bore the burden of having not yet come to terms with the Nazi past.

Any attempt to tell the fraternities' story must be provisional. Although there has been considerable research done on social, political, and cultural developments in the Federal Republic of Germany during the 1960s, fraternity students have not yet received much attention from historians.[2] Aside from Marxist or neo-Marxist studies that deal with the fraternities in an extremely critical fashion and describe them as a monolithic bloc,[3] we only find scattered articles in *Festschriften* and journals. Source material is also a problem. The records of individual fraternities, for example, have generally been dispersed and are also usually confidential. We must therefore rely on the official sources of the fraternity associations, such as their magazines and the minutes of their meetings. Neither the memory of internal conflicts nor the complexity of everyday life in the fraternities is captured in full in such records. The available

Notes for this chapter begin on page 271.

sources generally address matters of great concern to those active in the fraternities—traditions, rules of conduct, and institutional history—but not the issues of interest to historians.

One further point must be mentioned. Not only were the fraternities much more multifaceted and fragmented than an outsiders' prima facie view would tend to acknowledge, but their membership fluctuated to a degree that is often underestimated. Many members, students or *Alte Herren* (alumni), were quite mobile, and especially the students tended to change universities quite freely. This factor led to changing majorities within the fraternities. "Charismatic" students and alumni have been at least as important in forming the character of a fraternity as the official policy of the nationwide associations. Their influence is not even necessarily identical with the social or political majority within a given fraternity. It has had more to do with traditional and personal concepts of *auctoritas* than with the modern notion of democratic rule. However, any historian has to be aware of these restrictions in order to avoid simplistic judgments.

I will concentrate on the Catholic fraternity associations, in particular the Cartellverband katholischer deutscher Studentenverbindungen (CV) and the Kartellverband katholischer deutscher Studentenvereine (KV). This choice is not arbitrary. The so-called dueling fraternities (Burschenschaften, Corps, Landsmannschaften, Turnerschaften, and Sängerschaften) are certainly of interest to historians. But the Catholic associations offer us some advantages. First, up into the 1970s, they were closely connected with the West German Catholic milieu,[4] i.e., with the mainstream of believers and the diverse institutions and organizations at the center of Catholic life. That connection sheds light on the Catholic milieu as a whole. Secondly, the Catholic fraternities are of special interest because of their ambiguous relationship with National Socialism. Thirdly, the experience of the fraternities offers fresh insights into the rapid decline of the Catholic milieu in West Germany that began in the 1960s.[5]

I will argue that the relative decline of the Catholic student fraternities in the 1960s and 1970s was caused by their inability to come to terms with their own past. This was compounded by the functional and legitimizing character of German Catholic *Vergangenheitspolitik* after World War II and even more so by the difficult circumstances of Catholic existence after the Second Vatican Council. In the first section of this essay, I will sketch the history of the German fraternities and their relations with National Socialism. In the second section, I will concentrate on the Catholic fraternity associations during the 1950s and 1960s. They represented the majority of the students who, in the 1960s, were unwilling to demonstrate against the social and political system of the Federal Republic. Fundamentally, they did not understand what the student protests were about; they by and large supported the existing order and viewed the student movement skeptically or with hostility. Without taking such students into consideration, it is impossible to assess accurately the potential of the reform proposals and ideologies of the era.

The German Fraternity System

The history of the German fraternity system is a history of constant change and self-reform.[6] Nearly every era before 1933 had its own particular variety of fraternity adapted to the sociopolitical circumstances of the day. For over 150 years, the dueling fraternities had dominated the social scene. As time went by, they became more and more differentiated. The most important were the Corps and the Burschenschaften, which were joined in the 1880s by the Verband der Vereine Deutscher Studenten (VVdSt), an explicitly anti-Semitic organization of young reserve officers. All these associations adhered to the principle of *Satisfaktion*, which combined elements of a feudal code of honor with militaristic rituals.[7] There was also a certain homogeneity in the social backgrounds and political attitudes of their members; by and large, they came from aristocratic and upper-middle-class families, considered themselves the representatives of the better part of German society, and, after 1871, were loyal supporters of the Prussian-dominated German empire.[8] The fraternity movement was dominated by the Corps after 1871. The Corps gloried in its tradition of camaraderie and did not try to define itself in intellectual or political terms. This contributed to the fraternities' limited appeal among more intellectual German students.[9]

Thus, in the early 1890s a new element arose within the German fraternity movement: anti-Semitism. The founding of the radically anti-Semitic VVdSt[10] was followed by growing unrest. Many fraternities that had previously accepted assimilated Jewish students began in the 1890s to exclude Jews as student anti-Semitism spread.[11] Around 1900, the Burschenschaft divided into an anti-Semitic, *völkisch*-nationalist right wing and progressive-reformist left wing.[12] Austria and Southern Germany became regional strongholds of student anti-Semitism, but anti-Semitism was strongest among Protestant and national-liberal students. Smaller, predominantly Protestant universities elsewhere in Germany also joined the anti-Semitic movement; they would later become centers of National Socialist activism.

It was thus not the shocking experience of defeat in 1918 that gave rise to anti-Semitism and ultra-nationalism within the fraternities. Even before 1914, juvenile radicalism and discontent with the alleged vacuousness of bourgeois culture had resulted in immature protests.[13] After 1918, the great majority of dueling fraternities did not accept the Weimar Republic as legitimate,[14] but neither did they adapt entirely to National Socialist ideas and values after 1933. Nazism's modernizing elements—its notion of the egalitarian *Volksgemeinschaft*, for instance, its euphoric view of technological progress, and its promotion of a party-led mass culture—never found enthusiastic support among traditionalist and reactionary fraternities. The Nazis realized, consequently, that the so-called *Waffenstudenten* were not reliable partners.[15]

The Catholic fraternities were the product of ultramontanism and the *Kulturkampf*.[16] Because this struggle between church and state served as the Catholic fraternities' founding myth, they found it difficult to take up the pan-German nationalism that began to gain ground among German Catholics in the 1890s.

Loyalty to a fatherland dominated by Protestant rulers and aristocrats could never be fully reconciled with loyalty to church and pope. The Catholic fraternities were outcasts in German academic life long after the *Kulturkampf* of the 1870s. This was intensified by the marked social differences between the Catholic and Protest fraternities. The members of the Catholic fraternities came mainly from petit bourgeois or rural families; there were few aristocrats and virtually no members of the urban middle class. Another distinctive attribute of the Catholic fraternities was their proximity to the Center Party, which was widely regarded with suspicion within the allegedly apolitical academic community. Finally, the strict ecclesiastical ban on dueling contributed to a sense of separateness that stood in competition with a desperate desire to become an integral part of the German academic community. This profound tragedy was intensified by the fact that the Catholic fraternities' very otherness allowed them to survive their social heterogeneity. This dilemma between an unwilled but functional distinctiveness and the desire for integration was never overcome. The anomalous position of the Catholic fraternities culminated in the *Akademischer Kulturkampf* of 1906–7 as the dueling associations attempted, in part through violence, to force the Catholic fraternities to abandon university life. This attack, mounted under the guise of a defense of "academic freedom," was led by the "progressive" technical universities.[17] Only when Kaiser Wilhelm II refused to order the disbanding of the CV and the KV did anti-Catholicism cease to be an important force in university life. Grateful Catholic students thereafter tried to compensate for their marginalization with hyper-nationalism, especially during World War I.

Political conflicts within the Catholic fraternities became more virulent in the wake of the war. The KV and the Unitas-Verband wissenschaftlicher katholischer Studentenvereine (UV), in effect the leftist republican wing of the Catholic fraternity movement, were superficially involved in the social reformism associated with Berlin priest Carl Sonnenschein and social Catholicism.[18] On the other hand, the CV firmly embraced a traditionalist position. The CV's right wing and the Ring katholischer deutscher Burschenschaften (RKDB) sympathized with conservative, antirepublican extremists, whereas left-wing CV-fraternities, the KV, and the UV accepted the Weimar republic.[19] Despite warnings from ecclesiastical authorities, anti-Semitism became a real problem.[20] There had certainly been a premodern anti-Judaism among German Catholics before the 1920s, but there was a distinct change during the Weimar years. Within the fraternity associations, anti-Semitism generally went hand-in-hand with rejection of the republic. While officially rejecting the anti-Semitic *Arierparagraph* adopted by the Burschenschaft at the turn of the century, elements within the CV and the RKDB turned openly anti-Semitic. The Bavarian CV, influenced by the Austrian CV and the Christian Social Party, became a stronghold of right-wing Catholic thought. Inside the KV only the few aristocratic fraternities also accepted the anti-Semitic and corporatist framework of Othmar Spann and Martin Spahn.[21] After 1925–26, the CV even sometimes abandoned the traditional all-Catholic alliance in university politics and joined nationalist coalitions with dueling fraternities.[22]

The situation was different on the left. The KV and the UV never openly questioned the republic and strictly rejected the idea of forming coalitions with the nationalists. This was not, however, normally a result of democratic impulses. The KV was afraid of losing political control in broad coalitions and therefore opposed them.[23] Like the CV, the KV and the UV remained within the confines of a Catholic perspective. They were patriotic, anticommunist, and ultramontane in outlook. They regarded liberalism, fascism, and communism as atheistic, revolutionary, and anti-Catholic. The KV and the UV maintained coalitions with Jewish fraternities in student parliaments up to 1933.

Very few Catholics joined the Nazi student organization, the Nationalsozialistischer Deutscher Studentenbund (NSDStB) before 1933. The majority of Nazi Catholic students came from the ranks of the RKDB and some from the CV; hardly any NSDStB members were affiliated with the KV or the UV. Catholic students were comparatively underrepresented among the membership of the NSDStB and were outnumbered by students affiliated with reformist and patriotic groups such as the Großdeutsche Finkenschaften and the Akademische Gildenschaften.[24] January 1933 brought a fundamental change. Until the *Reichskonkordat* between the Third Reich and the Vatican and the self-destruction of the Center Party, the Catholic fraternities maintained a critical position toward National Socialism. But when it became clear that the Church would not oppose the new regime, the fraternity associations began to vie for advantages.[25] Their central objective was the institutional survival of the fraternities. They were even willing to give up defining elements of their identity, including the uniformly Catholic background of their membership. Fraternities that held to a strict Catholic position had to leave the umbrella associations.[26] However, at least internally the fraternities tried to regain authority and to stay Catholic. But in 1935–36 most of them gave up and were disbanded. Only the alumni organizations, the *Altherrenschaften*, survived intact.[27]

Before their dissolution, the Catholic fraternities held disparate and complex attitudes toward the empire, the Weimar Republic, and the Third Reich. They were inclined to right-wing conservatism and were critical of the Weimar Republic. But they never collaborated with the Nazi regime in Germany, and their premodern or antimodern traditionalism helped them maintain some distance from an ideology far too radical for them to accept. Although they had preferred monarchy to democracy, they did not favor National Socialism over democracy. And while only a tiny minority of Catholic fraternity members was to participate in the anti-Nazi resistance, the activities of former fraternity members after World War II guided the renewal of the fraternity movement.

The Reestablishment of Fraternities World War II

The main force behind the reestablishment of the Catholic (and other) fraternities after the war was not the students but rather the *Altherrenschaften*. These alumni associations had survived the Nazi era as informal groups and were formally reestablished in 1946–47. They later wooed students willing to embrace fraternity traditions and pass them on.[28] Perhaps unintentionally, the *Alte Herren* established a structural and personal continuity that was to influence the fraternities' view of the past. The *Alte Herren* who reestablished the alumni associations in 1947 were the same ones who had led them in 1933 and who had tried to get along with the Nazis. Their actions would not be forgotten or forgiven by the ardent Catholics who had left the fraternities in 1933.[29] Consequently, the reestablished *Altherrenschaften* had no interest in critical discussion of their pasts.[30]

That does not mean, however, that the fraternities and alumni associations entirely ignored the recent past during the early postwar period. Between roughly 1947 and 1953, they engaged in a debate on their past and future. It dealt only superficially, however, with Nazism and the murder of the European Jews.[31] Many students who did not belong to fraternities were concerned about fraternity members' nationalist attitudes and unwillingness to take part in such anti-Nazi activities as, for example, the demonstrations against former Nazi film director Veit Harlan and other Third Reich figures.[32] The fraternities thus frequently found themselves in conflict with nonmember students and university officials.[33]

Catholic and non-Catholic fraternity associations tried to avoid the topic of the Nazi past in their postwar rhetoric. They were much more interested in recruiting new members from the so-called skeptical generation.[34] But the former young soldiers criticized the traditional ritualism of *Comment, Kneipe,* and *Commers.* The postwar debate within the fraternity movement thus more or less paralleled the debates of the 1920s and did not take up the contemporary discussion of National Socialism. The postwar discussion addressed the same issues and reforms that had dominated the discussions after 1918, when the Catholic fraternities defended themselves against *neustudentisch* (neostudent) movements. The *Alte Herren* were reminded of the old conflicts between the *Gruppe Bier* (beer group, i.e., traditionalists) and the *Gruppe Geist* (mind group, i.e., reformers).[35] The reformers wanted new and more attractive programs. Instead of alcohol-laden rituals and adherence to a symbolic concept of honor, they called for intellectual discussions, religious contemplation, and social activism. These ardently antitraditionalist proposals sometimes made reference to the loss of innocence after 1933 and the besmirched reputation of the fraternities,[36] but arguments for reform generally had a more presentist focus.

Some newly founded fraternities cast themselves in a neostudent,[37] reformist mode. The *Comment* was reformed. Compulsory drinking was kept to a minimum,[38] and many younger students proved averse to singing sentimental and overly patriotic songs.[39] As a result, the fraternities' customary activities became more diverse. Classes, discussions, social programs, and religious events became more important. The last were undoubtedly encouraged by contemporary discussion of the need to reevangelize Germany—a specifically Catholic approach to dealing with the Nazi past.[40]

Debate within the fraternities died down in the early 1950s as a new generation of students succeeded the war veterans in the Federal Republic's universities.

Moderate reformism became a normal and unquestioned part of the fraternities' everyday life. Further discussion seemed unnecessary or was conducted on an abstract level that did not take the fraternities' histories into consideration. This disinclination to address the Nazi past was reinforced within the Catholic fraternities by the prevailing view of the past among West German Catholics. Up to the 1970s, many German Catholics viewed National Socialism as a demonic accident. If anyone could be considered guilty, it was non-Catholic Germans.[41] As in the early 1930s, Catholic intellectuals still interpreted National Socialism as a bastard child of the French Revolution; like liberalism and communism, National Socialism was seen as a result of Protestant individualism, modernity, anarchy, materialism, and atheism.[42] These arguments shared nineteenth-century ultramontanist premises about modernity, and National Socialism was dissociated from German history as Catholic intellectuals associated it with a universal and ongoing process. And as the murder of the Jews seemed to be an incidental consequence of the chain of developments linking the Reformation, the French Revolution, and the advent of totalitarianism, it did not seem to be important to denounce it explicitly.

The Catholic fraternities tended to hold on to their traditional critique of modernity,[43] but, in contrast to the dueling societies,[44] they had no problem accepting the new political system of the Federal Republic. The West German state, especially during the Adenauer era, in many ways seemed to be *their* state.[45] While their members were less successful in business life than their counterparts from the Corps and Burschenschaften, the Catholics were very active in political and ecclesiastical networking. They held to the minority strategy of securing their social position by gaining political power.[46] Many high-ranking West German politicians and governmental officials—including presidents,[47] chancellors, Bundestag members, and state leaders—were members of the CV and the KV. Catholic politicians and officials also joined with priests and teachers in recruiting new members and placing them in positions of authority. Opportunities to bring Catholic ideas to bear on social welfare and family policy thus increased dramatically during the early years of the Federal Republic.[48] They could proudly boast that the Federal Republic was the first acceptable German state since 1866, and they shared the zealous anticommunism that was the ideological cement binding West German society as a whole.[49] The Catholic fraternities accepted the idea of Western European integration in principle along with the more conservative Catholic *Abendlandsidee* (Occidentalism). Both were integral parts of a Catholic vision of Germany's future.[50]

With their acceptance of the Federal Republic as a "Catholic" state in the 1950s, the Catholic fraternities were more willing to integrate themselves into the German social and political order than at any previous point in history.[51] They also felt more closely tied to the Catholic milieu than at any time since the *Kulturkampf*. Accordingly, they accepted the milieu's historical narrative, its *Vergangenheitspolitik*, without question.[52]

This *Vergangenheitspolitik* became even more important with each Catholic political success because, in the general perception of the milieu, it would minimize anti-Catholic pressure and, therefore, reduce the milieu's very foundation. The inner coherence of West German Catholicism gradually vanished; internal tensions grew as it became increasingly clear that only outside pressure had held Catholics of different classes and socioeconomic interests together. The milieu rapidly fragmented during the late 1950s. This led to an intensified search for new formulas to establish and legitimize Catholic identity. The *Kulturkampf* no longer provided the German Catholic community with an appealing founding myth, but historical experience seemed to be the only source capable of providing German Catholicism with a defining idea. Resistance against National Socialism thus became the new integrating foundational myth. It was supported by Pope Pius XII,[53] who took the symbolically significant step of appointing several German cardinals in 1945 and who emphatically opposed the theory of collective guilt.

These developments encouraged many West German Catholics to view themselves as heroic opponents of National Socialism.[54] The struggles over crucifixes in schools and euthanasia, the Catholic vote in 1932 and 1933, the priests and laymen killed in the concentration camps, the quarrels between the bishops and the Nazi Party leadership, and the heroic survival of some Catholic youth organizations—all served as historical reference points for this Catholic master narrative.[55] My concern here is not the historical veracity of this narrative, but rather its function in West German society during the early years of the Federal Republic, especially in relations between the Catholic milieu and the rest of society. In putting forward this narrative, Catholics did profit from the absence of serious competitors. The conservative military officers who had plotted against Hitler had yet to be cleared of the taint of high treason, while the communist opponents of Nazism were anything but popular in ardently anticommunist West Germany. It is thus not surprising that Catholic resistance to Nazism became a central element of collective identity and memory construction among West German Catholics. It was even able to replace older *Kulturkampf* memories. Certain problematic issues, like the compromises some bishops had made with the Nazi leadership, were eliminated from the discourse. Others, like the 1933 concordat between the Vatican and the Nazi government, became subjects of debate and interpretation among West German Catholics.[56]

The Catholic fraternities did not want to be left behind. It was more difficult for them, however, to reconstruct their past than it was for other Catholic organizations, such as the Kolping-Werk, Catholic workers' groups, and parochial youth groups.[57] They thus adopted what seemed to be a promising strategy: anything that could not be fitted into a heroic narrative would be omitted. No mention was made, for instance, of the tactics the fraternities used to survive institutionally in 1933–34. The years 1929–33 and the fraternities' final months of existence in 1935–36, on the other hand, were discussed intensively. Within this heroic framework, the understanding of resistance evidently had to change. For the period before 1933, the fraternities and the episcopate figured as active agents in the narrative; for the period from 1933 onward, the focus shifted to heroic individuals who acted as representatives of the whole. The fraternities per se figured as agents in the post-1933 narrative only with regard to their participation in the Corpus Christi processions.[58] With the help of this interpretative scheme, it was possible for the fraternities to fit themselves into the general Catholic narrative.

Although certain topics were passed over in silence, sensitive issues were by no means avoided entirely.[59] This critical discourse was characterized by a rhetorical self-reassurance. The fraternity members used a mixture of neoscholastic and contemporary existentialist stylistic elements. They would first emotionally question their own position, engaging in a formalized, superficial self-criticism and self-accusation. They would then ask what Catholics could and should have done differently during the Third Reich. That question led in turn to a comparison of the Catholic position to those of other groups. The usual conclusion was that the Catholic response had been the only one that was possible and justified.[60] Critical discussions did not necessarily employ all of these elements, but the outcome was always the same.[61]

At least as important as this discursive self-reassurance were the fraternities' martyrs, the heroic individuals who had opposed Nazism.[62] Many *Alte Herren* had indeed been executed for their opposition to the regime. They were later politically instrumentalized. In some cases, the very existence of such figures was used to bolster the specious argument that the fraternities as organizations had participated in the resistance movement.[63] This strategy was entirely consistent with the postwar tendency to reinterpret individual resistance as evidence of collective resistance.

Until about 1960, the Catholic fraternities were able to use this strategy without too much difficulty. Few members of West German society really wanted to know too much about the past, and the fraternities flourished. Following their modest internal reforms and adaptation to the Catholic milieu's historical narrative, the fraternities saw their membership grow over the course of the 1950s. Indeed, the Adenauer era stands alongside the 1920s as a peak period of fraternity activity. Roughly 30 percent of West German students during the 1950s belonged to fraternities, and the Catholic fraternities fully participated in this trend. Indeed, they were stronger and more powerful than ever. But they were in no way prepared to face what would happen to them in the 1960s.

The CV first entered into critical discussion of its role during the Nazi era in 1959. Writing under the pseudonym Lynkeus, an anonymous member demanded for the first time in a CV publication that the association critically review its past. Lynkeus even acknowledged that a renewed anti-Semitism and nationalism had become evident in West Germany.[64] One year later, CV member Josef Brandlmeier declared it absolutely necessary that West Germans analyze the problem of anti-Semitism. He traced anti-Semitism back to antiquity and broke with the Catholic historical narrative in explicitly denying that it had been a product of modernity and nationalism. But Brandlmeier held to the Catholic line in insisting that anti-Semitism had never been of theological relevance. [65] Despite these calls for a more critical evaluation of the Third Reich, coming to terms with the past at the close of the 1950s meant above all learning from the distant past.[66] The years between 1933 and 1945 were virtually nonexistent in this discussion.[67]

The Crisis of West German Catholicism

The crisis that Catholic fraternities subsequently experienced was paralleled and caused by the crisis of West German Catholicism. Paradoxically, success may have been the cause of that crisis; after years of social and political success, Catholic self-confidence began to slip in the late 1950s and then rapidly vanished. But not only did West German Catholics lose their sense of shared aims, they also increasingly questioned their founding myth. Before 1960, only marginalized leftist Catholic intellectuals openly cast doubt on the church's account of German Catholicism during the Nazi dictatorship. But figures such as Eugen Kogon, Walter Dirks, and Heinrich Böll never reached a majority of their fellow Catholics. Following the death of Pius XII, however, the Vatican's response to Nazism again came under criticism. At about the same time, the West German Catholic historical narrative came under attack from the Schmittian Catholic Ernst-Wolfgang Böckenförde, the nationalist Protestant Ralf Hochhuth, and the left-wing Catholic Carl Améry.[68] Their criticism undermined the legitimating function of that narrative. These disparate attacks upon the Catholic historical synthesis were influenced by the 1950s debate on the Catholic quest for moral and political leadership in West Germany. The ground for new anti-Catholic onslaughts was prepared by political scientists such as Thomas Ellwein, who argued that clericalism posed a serious threat to West German democracy, and politicians such as the Social Democrat Carlo Schmid, who feared the "hibernization" of West Germany.[69] West German Catholics became even more perplexed when their conservative ideology and self-definition was challenged by the reformist course of the new pope, John XXIII, who unexpectedly reached out to Social Democrats and communists.

The Catholic milieu found itself in an agonizing position during the discussion that followed the staging of Hochhuth's play *Der Stellvertreter* in 1964.[70] While socialists, trade unionists, and left-wing Catholics applauded Hochhuth's often superficial criticism, the normally patronizing German bishops were paralyzed and remained silent. The Catholic press, however, responded to Hochhuth with acid counterattacks. Together with the rest of the Catholic milieu, the fraternities came under attack. They were not able, though, to assume leadership or mount an intellectually sound defense of the Catholic position. Instead, they apologetically reiterated the Catholic historical narrative and made clear that they were sharply opposed to any criticism of the Catholic position during the Third Reich.

In principle, this reaction was understandable. The fraternities were still led by the *Alte Herren* who had survived the Nazi era, whether in opposition or otherwise. They honestly believed in their take on the past, and it was nearly impossible to dissuade them from it. As a result, the fraternities clung to the Catholic view of history and the cult of the martyrs—a reflex from the *Kulturkampf* era. They had no problem holding on to this stance until about 1970. There was no lack of young people who shared mainstream Catholic views, and problems of legitimization and identity were suppressed or postponed.

Moreover, West German Catholics also faced more pressing problems than the past. The Second Vatican Council had inspired much hope and much fear among

Roman Catholics all over the world.[71] For the still quite conservative Catholic fraternities, the immediate effect of the council was to give fresh impetus to their critics on the Catholic left. Thus, although the fraternities were in principle in favor of the council,[72] it indirectly undermined them ideologically.[73] Vatican II accelerated the implosion of the West German Catholic milieu and made clear the lack of cultural unity among German Catholics. That was especially disturbing to the fraternities because they, more than any other Catholic association, were based on an ideological and cultural consensus.

The Catholic fraternities' identity rested on their loyalty to their traditions: the heritage of ultramontanism, unwavering loyalty to the pope,[74] the memory of the *Kulturkampf,* and their anti-Nazi resistance. The focus on the present and the future spurred by the Vatican Council and taken up by the Catholic left indirectly undermined the essential traditionalism of the fraternities. As their cultural foundations crumbled, the fraternities gradually lost their social base, and, as a result, their base of political power. That, in turn, led to problems in recruiting new members and later placing them in positions of authority. The fraternities began to lose their dominant position among Catholic students. Increasingly, Catholic students organized themselves in student congregations (*Katholische Hochschulgemeinden*) or joined the Christian Democratic Ring christlich-demokratischer Studenten (RCDS), which was dominated by antitraditionalists. The fraternities thus found themselves trapped in a vicious circle, as declining influence on campus led to loss of influence off campus, which in turn further eroded their position among student organizations. It became less a matter of course that Catholic teachers, priests, and politicians would encourage Catholic students to join the fraternities. During the 1970s, the old networks broke down definitively.

In addition to these medium-term developments, the Catholic fraternities were also confronted with a more immediately pressing question that arose in the wake of Vatican II. The KV in particular experienced an intense internal debate over the meaning of ecumenism—over the question of whether it was permissible to take Protestants as members of Catholic fraternities. Many Catholic organizations had been admitting Protestants as members for decades; within the fraternities it had become an informally permitted practice during the 1950s. As long as the structure of the Catholic milieu was intact, this issue did not pose a serious problem. After 1965, however, some KV fraternities wanted a "progressive" solution that would allow Protestants to become regular members. According to those modernizers, the spirit of Vatican II automatically led to the conclusion that the exclusionist and traditionalist standpoint was wrong. Some fraternity activists were more taken with the idea of expanding the pool of potential new members at a time of declining enrollment. A difficult, sometimes bitter, struggle between *Aktivitates* and *Altherrenschaften* ensued. It lasted until 1971, when the KV opted to allow its fraternities to decide the issue of Protestant membership for themselves.

It is not surprising that the CV and KV, confronted with these problems, did not participate actively when the redefinition of Catholic *Vergangenheitspolitik* became an item on the agenda of the crumbling Catholic establishment. But it was impossible for the fraternities to simply ignore the questions about their past posed by the radical student movement. The fraternities' reactions varied considerably, but apologetics dominated. It took the fraternities about a decade to ponder the issue.[75] Despite questions about the activities of CV and KV fraternities during the critical years of 1933 and 1934, the traditional historical narrative was by no means abandoned. To the contrary, heroic Catholic resistance remained the central focus of the narrative, and less attractive aspects of the narrative, such as anti-Semitism, figured less prominently than they had in the late 1950s. There were, however, serious attempts to write the histories of the fraternity associations in the late 1960s and the early 1970s.[76]

A further development was of great importance. Generational change within the fraternities was inevitable. Alumni members who had been students in the 1920s and 1930s were being replaced by alumni and student members of the 1950s and 1960s. Moreover, many new student members did not fully share the traditional beliefs and values of the Catholic milieu.[77] These changes made possible a functional restructuring of the historical narratives from the inside.[78] Ultimately, however, this was not sufficient. During the "progressive" 1970s, the Catholic fraternities painfully found themselves without a vital ideological center. Anticommunism did not provide an adequate basis for a new orientation,[79] nor could an often sterile opposition to the governments of Willy Brandt and Helmut Schmidt.[80]

The Catholic fraternities demonstrated more flexibility in another discussion that was loosely linked to discussion of the Nazi past. It should not be forgotten that university reform, not *Vergangenheitspolitik*, had been the trigger for the student protest movement. On this subject, Catholic students were not hindered by conservative self-exculpation and taboos.[81] Quite the opposite: they knew that the established system, dominated by a class-conscious Protestant *Bildungsbürgertum*, discriminated against them as Catholics. They thus had some sympathy for radical students' demands, or at least those demands that were not linked to far-reaching, overtly revolutionary aims.[82] Even attacks on professors for their Nazi pasts were acceptable as long none of the targets were Catholic. This limited acceptance of the student movement among Catholics quickly gave way when the movement became increasingly radical and revolutionary,[83] and the Catholic fraternities openly scorned calls for fundamental change in West German society.[84]

The brief collaboration between the Catholic fraternities and the student movement rested on a misunderstanding. Catholics' views on university reform were in no way compatible with those of the liberals or radicals. They generally favored a more conservative approach. They stressed the values of solidarity and communitarianism, for instance, and argued for the merits of the traditional curricula and the *studium generale*. They sought reforms in matters such as subsidies for poor students, especially Catholics. Reform, in their view, was a process of evolution within traditional parameters, not the overthrow of established authorities.[85] Moreover, they tried to integrate Catholic ideas—about natural law, for example—into the university curricula. The deep divide between the Catholic fraternity members and the 68ers was perhaps most evident when the fraternity members continued to employ conservative rhetoric in criticizing mass society and the mass university.[86]

Catholic Resistance to the Student Movement

Like the West German Catholic milieu, the fraternities reacted in response to criticism from the student movement and did not take the initiative in the debates of the 1960s. Despite the efforts of post–Vatican II left-wingers within the church, German Catholics tended to react according to established patterns. They may have been aware of the necessity for social and educational reforms, and some may have had a measure of sympathy for the 68ers. But ultimately West German Catholics opposed all but the most modest reform measures, and the great majority opposed any form of cooperation with the student movement. Thus, in many ways the story of the Catholic response to the 68ers is a story of noncommunication. Catholic responses to the student movements' critical questions about the Nazi past were even more disappointing.

There are several explanations for the unsophisticated response of the Catholic fraternities to the student movement. For one, until the early 1970s the fraternities recruited their members from a Catholic milieu that, although increasingly fragmented, was still very homogeneous in outlook. West German Catholics traditionally did not accept ideas for radical social change. Revolutionary rhetoric like that of the student radicals was certain to alienate most Catholics. Moreover, the students' notions of participatory democracy had no appeal to conservative and moderate Catholics.

Catholic resistance to calls for social change was all the firmer when the past was instrumentalized in making the case for reform. West German Catholics' self-confidence was based firmly on their own historical master narrative, their own social and political myths. The resistance to Nazism supplanted the *Kulturkampf* as the main element of the Catholic interpretation of German history. In 1968, this founding myth came under pressure from two directions—from radical students as well as from the growing Catholic left that was benefiting from the post–Vatican II crisis of ecclesiastical tradition. The situation was exacerbated by the implosion of the Catholic establishment during the 1960s.

West German Catholics did not understand the practical purpose of student radicalism. The social and political order of the Federal Republic fulfilled most of their aspirations; in their eyes, it was the best and most stable state they could wish for. Catholic politicians had dominated the government since the founding of the Federal Republic, and the predominantly catholic CDU and CSU ruled the nation. The 68ers' radical critique of the Federal Republic thus struck most Catholics as senseless and counterproductive. By the interpretive scheme still accepted by the overwhelming majority of West German Catholics, the students were nothing but communists—and anticommunism was still strong among Catholics in the late 1960s.

This anticommunist tradition made it impossible for the Catholics, especially conservative fraternity members, to understand the heterodox aspects of student radicalism. The combination of the students' Marxist rhetoric and libertarian lifestyle (which was at least as reprehensible as Marxism in the view of many Catholics) did nothing to encourage communication between student radicals and Catholic fraternities. It allowed the Catholic fraternities to evade any further discussion and to entrench themselves behind their version of the Catholic historical narrative.

This evasive strategy was made easier by the behavior of the fraternities' critics. It was all but impossible for the members of traditionalist organizations like the fraternities to discuss their cherished history with long-haired, pot-smoking rebels.[87] Moreover, the critics often pressed their arguments in an offensive manner. Their criticism, often couched in radical rhetoric, was not always supported by historical fact. If the CV and the KV single-mindedly emphasized the positive aspects of their opposition to the National Socialist government, many radicals insulted the Catholic fraternities with broad, undifferentiated accusations of collaboration with the Nazis. Neither the radicals nor the fraternity members were prepared for anything else than mutual disrespect.

In sum, the Catholic fraternities were not flexible enough to deal adequately with the changing *Zeitgeist* of the late 1960s and early 1970s. In response to outside pressure, they initiated some internal reforms, including another liberalization of the *Comment*. This was meant to be a reaction to criticism from the New Left. It was, however, not very successful. In university affairs, the fraternities were linked with the Christian Democratic RCDS. This association ultimately helped the RCDS more than it did the fraternities, as the RCDS became the most important political representative of conservative students. The majority of fraternity members withdrew from politics and public affairs, which accelerated the social marginalization of the fraternities. Despite their resignation in the face of change, the fraternities were able to survive institutionally, albeit with a less homogeneous, less traditional, and less Catholic membership. The sudden decline of the CV, the KV, and the other associations was intertwined with the decline of the West German Catholic establishment. Together with the fraternities, the Catholic establishment lost its inner momentum.

Notes

1. Heribert Raisch, ed., *Festschrift für Karl-Heinz Schröder: Beiträge zur Geschichte der Burschenschaft Derendingia* (Tübingen, 1989), 109.
2. Cf. the instructive review article by Matthias Stickler, "Neuerscheinungen zur Studentengeschichte seit 1994: Ein Forschungsbericht über ein bisweilen unterschätztes Arbeitsfeld der Universitätsgeschichte," *Jahrbuch für Universitätsgeschichte* 4 (2001): 262–70.
3. Cf. Ludwig Elm, ed., *Füxe, Burschen, Alte Herren* (Cologne, 1993).

4. With regard to the milieu concept, cf. Karl-Egon Lönne, "Katholizismus-Forschung," *Geschichte und Gesellschaft* 26 (2000): 128–70; Peter Lösche and Franz Walter, "Katholiken, Konservative und Liberale: Milieus und Lebenswelten bürgerlicher Parteien in Deutschland während des 20. Jahrhunderts," *Geschichte und Gesellschaft* 26 (2000): 471–92; Christoph Köster and Antonius Liedhegener, "Historische Milieus als Forschungsaufgabe," *Westfälische Forschungen* 48 (1998): 593–601, and Karl Gabriel, "Zwischen Tradition und Moderne: Katholizismus und katholisches Milieu in den fünfziger Jahren der Bundesrepublik," in *Kirchliche Zeitgeschichte: Urteilsbildung und Methoden*, ed. Anselm Doering-Manteuffel and Kurt Nowak (Stuttgart, 1996), 248–62.

5. Karl Gabriel, "Zwischen Aufbruch und Absturz in die Moderne: Die Katholische Kirche in den 60er Jahren," in *Dynamische Zeiten: Die 60er Jahre in den beiden deutschen Gesellschaften*, ed. Axel Schildt et al. (Hamburg, 2000), 528–43; and Karl Gabriel, "Die Katholiken in den 50er Jahren: Restauration, Modernisierung und beginnende Auflösung eines konfessionellen Milieus," in *Modernisierung im Wiederaufbau: Die westdeutsche Gesellschaft der 50er Jahre*, ed. Axel Schildt and Arnold Sywottek (Bonn, 1993), 418–32.

6. Cf. Konrad H. Jarausch, *Deutsche Studenten, 1800–1970* (Frankfurt am Main, 1984); Peter Krause, *"O alte Burschenherrlichkeit": Die Studenten und ihr Brauchtum* (Graz, 1997); Thomas Nipperdey, *Deutsche Geschichte, 1866–1918*, vol. 1: *Arbeitswelt und Bürgergeist* (Munich, 1998), 581–86; Walter M. Brod, "Das Korporationswesen an der Universität Würzburg im 19. und 20. Jahrhundert," in *Studentenschaft und Korporationen an der Universität Würzburg*, ed. Ulrich Becker et al. (Würzburg, 1982), 75–79.

7. With regard to the controversy over the duel's feudal or nonfeudal character, cf. Ute Frevert, *Ehrenmänner: Das Duell in der bürgerlichen Gesellschaft* (Munich, 1991); Kevin McAleer, "What Price Glory?" *WerkstattGeschichte* 4, no. 11 (1995): 55–63; Dietmar Klenke, "War der 'deutsche Mann' im 19. Jahrhundert 'bürgerlich' oder 'feudal'?" *WerkstattGeschichte* 4, no. 12 (1995): 56–64.

8. Manfred Studier, *Der Corpsstudent als Idealbild der Wilhelminischen Ära* (Schwenfeld, 1990).

9. Cf. *150 Jahre Tübinger Burschenschaft* (Tübingen, 1966), 17–21.

10. Marc Zirlewagen, ed., *Kaisertreue—Führergedanke—Demokratie: Beiträge zur Geschichte des Verbandes der Vereine Deutscher Studenten* (Cologne, 2000).

11. Bruno Weil, *Juden in der deutschen Burschenschaft: Ein Beitrag zum Streit um die konfessionelle Studentenverbindung* (Straßburg, 1905); *Festschrift zum 75-jährigen Bestehen der Strassburger Burschenschaft Arminia zu Tübingen, 1886–1961* (Tübingen, 1961), 11–12.

12. Helmut Krassmüller and Ernst Anger, *Die Geschichte des Allgemeinen Deutschen Burschenbundes (ADB), 1883–1933 und das Schicksal der ehemaligen ADB-Burschenschaften* (Gießen, 1989), 30–66.

13. Stefan Breuer, *Ordnungen der Ungleichheit: Die deutsche Rechte im Widerstreit ihrer Ideen, 1871–1945* (Darmstadt, 2001); Uwe Puschner, *Die völkische Bewegung im wilhelminischen Kaiserreich: Sprache, Rasse, Religion* (Darmstadt, 2001).

14. *Tübinger Burschenschaft*, 23.

15. Cf. Helma Brunck, *Die Deutsche Burschenschaft in der Weimarer Republik und im Nationalsozialismus* (Munich, 1999), 359. Dieter Langewiesche, "Die Universität Tübingen in der Zeit des Nationalsozialismus: Formen der Selbstgleichschaltung und der Selbstbehauptung," *Geschichte und Gesellschaft* 23 (1997): 618–46, develops a similar thesis concerning the university of Tübingen, but without reference to the fraternities.

16. *Academia* 49, no. 1 (1956): 4; ibid., 49, no. 5 (1956): 108; ibid., 51, no. 7 (1958): 213.

17. *Studentenwörterbuch* (1987), s.v. "Akademischer Kulturkampf."

18. Josef Forderer, *Katholische Studentenverbindung Alamannia-Tübingen: Von den Anfängen bis zur Gegenwart* (Tübingen, 1962), 119–22; *Academia* 49, no. 1 (1956): 15; and ibid., 49, no. 8 (1956): 174–77.

19. Cf. Michael Hochgeschwender, "K. St.V. Rheno-Frankonia und der Nationalsozialismus," in *100 Jahre K.St.V. Rheno-Frankonia, 65 Jahre K.St.V. Tannenberg* (Würzburg, 1992), 27–72.

20. Peter Stitz, *Der CV, 1919–1938: Der hochschulpolitische Weg des Cartellverbandes der katholischen deutschen Studentenverbindungen vom 1: Weltkrieg bis zur Vernichtung durch den Nationalsozialismus* (Munich, 1970), 45–46, 95–99. Concerning the controversy over Catholic anti-Semitism, cf. Olaf Blaschke, *Katholizismus und Antisemitismus im Deutschen Kaiserreich* (Göttingen, 1997), and Uwe Mazura, *Zentrumspartei und Judenfrage, 1870/71–1933: Verfassungsstaat und Minderheitenschutz* (Mainz, 1994).

21. Cf. Gabriele Clemens, *Martin Spahn und der Rechtskatholizismus der Weimarer Republik* (Mainz, 1983).

22. Stitz, *Der CV*, 87–94.

23. Hochgeschwender, "Rheno-Frankonia," 48.

24. Peter Spitznagel, "Studentenschaft und Nationalsozialismus in Würzburg," in Becker et al., *Studentenschaft*, 89–137; Otto Kramer, *Die Katholische Studentenverbindung Frankonia, 1919–1979* (Vienna, 1980), 41–44.

25. Stitz, *Der CV*, 130–307; Forderer, *Alamannia*, 154–201.

26. Hochgeschwender, "Rheno-Frankonia," 57–58.

27. Kramer, *Frankonia*, 86; Spitznagel, "Studentenschaft," 130; cf. Siegfried Scheweck-Maul, "'Durchhalten, solange es geht': Ein katholischer Studentenverband im Dritten Reich: Der CV," *GDS-Archiv* 4 (1998): 53–67.

28. *Burschenschaft Arminia*, 60; Forderer, *Alamannia*, 202–58; Paul Warmbrunn, "Wiederbegründung von Altherrenschaft und Aktivitas nach dem Zweiten Weltkrieg (1945–1951)," in *Geschichte der Katholischen deutschen Studentenverbindung Markomannia*, ed. Thomas Sauer and Ralf Vollmuth (Cologne, 1996), 135–56.

29. Hochgeschwender, "Rheno-Frankonia," 58.

30. Cf. *Academia* 52, no. 8 (1959): 276–81.

31. One of the very few exceptions was the prayer of CV pastor Alfons Fleischmann in Plötzensee (1959), in which he indirectly mentioned the Jewish victims of National Socialism, *Academia* 52, no. 10 (1959): 338: "Gib allen Opfern des Nationalsozialismus und des vergangenen Krieges aus allen Völkern, Rassen und Sprachen die ewige Ruhe." Quite different was a sermon by Bishop Franz Hengsbach in Dachau (1960), in which he spoke of everybody's guilt, while interpreting this guilt in a universal manner by integrating it into a theology of sin and grace, *Academia* 53, no. 9 (1960): 279–81.

32. Heribert Adam, "Studentenschaft und Hochschule: Möglichkeiten und Grenzen studentischer Politik" (PhD diss., Frankfurt am Main, 1965), 83–111.

33. Cf. *Academia* 50, no. 7 (1957): 176–77, 184; ibid., 51, no. 5 (1958): 145–48. The university and the fraternities quarreled about the right to openly show the fraternities' colors. The Catholic fraternities argued that their colors were denominational symbols and had nothing to do with the Nazi past of the dueling fraternities.

34. *Academia* 52, no. 2 (1959): 46–47.

35. Kurt-Georg Kiesinger, *Dunkle und helle Jahre: Erinnerungen, 1904–1958* (Stuttgart, 1989), 86.

36. Cf. the Popp-Papers, KV-Archiv, Mönchengladbach—for instance, the letters by P. Umpfenbach, OFM, 16 January 1948.

37. For example, the K.D.St.V. Rheinfels; cf. *Academia* 50, no. 8 (1957): 216–17.

38. *Academia* 50, no. 4 (1957): 49–50.

39. *Academia* 51, no. 10 (1958): 332.

40. Wolfgang Löhr, "Rechristianisierungsvorstellungen im deutschen Katholizismus, 1945–1948," in *Christentum und politische Verantwortung im Nachkriegsdeutschland*, ed. Jochen-Christoph Kaiser and Anselm Doering-Manteuffel (Stuttgart, 1990), 25–41.

41. *Academia* 49, no. 1 (1956): 14–16.

42. *Academia* 49, no. 2 (1956): 28; ibid., 49, no. 7 (1956): 149; ibid., 52, no. 7 (1959): 230–34. The Catholic fraternity students, moreover, shared the common Catholic opinions against mass society, consumerism, and other phenomena of everyday modernity. Cf. *Academia* 50,

no. 4 (1957): 80–82; ibid., 50, no. 6 (1957): 125; ibid., 51, no. 6 (1958): 178–83; ibid., 51, no. 7 (1958): 209–10; ibid., 52, no. 2 (1959): 70–77; ibid., 53, no. 4 (1960): 112–17.

43. *Academia* 49, no. 1 (1956): 18–19; ibid., 50, no. 3 (1957): 55–60. In 1958, the Archbishop of Cologne, Joseph Cardinal Frings, wrote a pastoral letter against the dueling fraternities; cf. *Academia* 51, no. 3 (1958): 92.

44. With some qualifications, cf. *Tübinger Burschenschaft*, 27–33, and the *Bericht des Hochschulexekutivkomitees des Kongresses für die Freiheit der Kultur* vom 7.10.1951, Bundesarchiv Koblenz, NL 160 (Pechel III), Bd. 100.

45. *Academia* 49, no. 1 (1956): 18–20; ibid., 50, no. 7 (1957): 175. Cf. *Academia* 51, no. 8 (1958): 249–54, and ibid., 51, no. 9 (1958): 288–93, embracing Christian democracy.

46. *Academia* 51, no. 6 (1958): 203.

47. *Academia* 52, no. 7 (1959): 226–29, on President Heinrich Lübke (CV).

48. *Academia* 49, no. 2 (1956): 25–32.

49. *Academia* 49, no. 8 (1956): 186–88; ibid., 51, no. 1 (1958): 15–19; ibid., 51, no. 10 (1958): 322–30.

50. *Academia* 49, no. 2 (1956): 31; ibid., 49, no. 5 (1956): 111–16; ibid., 52, no. 1 (1959): 16–18; ibid., 52, no. 8 (1959): 273–76.

51. *Academia* 51, no. 2 (1958): 44; ibid., 51, no. 5 (1958): 150; ibid., 53, no. 1 (1960): 1.

52. Cf. Karen Riechert, "Der Umgang der katholischen Kirche mit historischer und juristischer Schuld anläßlich der Nürnberger Hauptkriegsverbrecherprozesse," in *Siegerin in Trümmern: Die Rolle der katholischen Kirche in der deutschen Nachkriegsgesellschaft*, ed. Joachim Köhler and Damian van Melis (Stuttgart, 1998), 18–41, and Damian van Melis, "Der katholische Episkopat und die Entnazifizierung," in Köhler and van Melis, *Siegerin*, 42–69.

53. *Academia* 51, no. 8 (1958): 241–47; ibid., 51, no. 9 (1958): 274; ibid., 52, no. 4 (1959): 107.

54. *Academia* 49, no. 6 (1956): 121–27; ibid., 49, no. 7 (1956): 133–37.

55. Cf. Johannes Neuhäusler, *Kreuz und Hakenkreuz: Der Kampf des Nationalsozialismus gegen die katholische Kirche und der katholische Widerstand* (Munich, 1946); Benedicta Maria Kempner, *Priester vor Hitlers Tribunalen* (Munich, 1966). A more elaborate version is presented by Heinz Hürten, *Verfolgung, Widerstand und Zeugnis: Kirche im Nationalsozialismus* (Mainz, 1987).

56. P. Ludwig Volk, SJ, *Das Reichskonkordat vom 20. Juli 1933* (Mainz, 1972); Klaus Gotto and Konrad Repgen, eds., *Die Katholiken in Dritten Reich* (Mainz, 1980).

57. Klaus Gotto, *Die Wochenzeitung* Junge Front/Michael: *Eine Studie zum katholischen Selbstverständnis und zum Verhalten der jungen Kirche gegenüber dem Nationalsozialismus* (Mainz, 1970); Heinz-Albert Raem, *Katholischer Gesellenverein und Deutsche Kolpingsfamilie in der Ära des Nationalsozialismus* (Mainz, 1982); Jürgen Aretz, *Katholische Arbeiterbewegung und Nationalsozialismus* (Mainz, 1978); Barbara Schellenberger, *Katholische Jugend im Dritten Reich* (Mainz, 1975).

58. Walter R. Konrad, "Markomannia vom 60. Stiftungsfest 1931 bis zum Ende des Zweiten Weltkrieges," in Sauer and Vollmuth, *Markomannia*, 17–134.

59. Cf. Forderer, *Alamannia*, 223.

60. *Academia* 52, no. 2 (1959): 41.

61. Cf. *Academia* 52, no. 6 (1959): 204–6, where influence of National Socialism on the CV before 1933 was denied.

62. Cf. P. Robert Jauch, OFM, "Hans Wölfel," in *K.St.V. Rheno-Frankonia im KV zu Würzburg, 1892–1982* (Würzburg, 1982), 121–48; Hochgeschwender, "Rheno-Frankonia," 71–72; *Academia* 49, no. 4 (1956): 89–90; ibid., 49, no. 5 (1956): 102–4; ibid., 52, no. 5 (1959): 182–85; ibid., 53, no. 10 (1960): 326–30; *Burschenschaft Arminia*, 51, with similar tendencies in the Burschenschaften.

63. Willy Popp an die Bayerische Landesentschädigungskammer vom 2.1.1953, Popp-Papers, KV-Archiv, Mönchengladbach; *Academia* 50, no. 2 (1957): 31–33, with regard to whether Catholics were persecuted as a group. The cult of the martyrs had not only sociopolitical implications; the legal implications were far more important.

64. *Academia* 52, no. 2 (1959): 37–41. This article was certainly written under the impression of swastika graffiti on synagogues in 1958–59. Cf. *Academia* 51, no. 2 (1958): 54–56, on anti-Semitism, and *Academia* 49, no. 3 (1956): 70, on nationalism. The critique of radical nationalism was a classic topos of Catholic political opinion; for example, cf. *Academia* 52, no. 5 (1959): 153–58, based on the teaching of Pope Pius XII.

65. *Academia* 53, no. 9 (1960): 282–88; ibid., 53, no. 10 (1960): 324–25. Interestingly, the author distinguished only between pagan anti-Judaism and modern Christian anti-Semitism, and not between a premodern, Christian, and nonracist, anti-Judaism and a modern racist anti-Semitism, as became common after 1968.

66. *Academia* 52, no. 4 (1959): 108–12.

67. Cf. *Academia* 51, no. 1 (1958): 11–13; ibid., 51, no. 6 (1958): 205–6; ibid., 52, no. 3 (1959): 78–81.

68. Erwin Gatz, "Alte Bundesrepublik," in *Kirche und Katholizismus seit 1945*, vol. 1: *Mittel, West- und Nordeuropa*, ed. Erwin Gatz (Paderborn, 1998), 53–131.

69. Cf. Bericht von Carlo Schmid an das Internationale Exekutivkomitee des Congress for Cultural Freedom vom 29.–30. Dezember 1952, University of Chicago, Regenstein Library, Department of Special Collections, IACF/CCF-Archiv, Serie II, Box 3, Folder 2; and Thomas Ellwein, *Klerikalismus in der deutschen Politik* (Munich, 1955).

70. Cf. Ulrike Wunderle, "Das Ende des katholischen Jahrzehnts" (MA thesis, Tübingen, 2000).

71. Peter Hünermann, ed., *Das II. Vatikanum—christlicher Glaube im Horizont globaler Modernisierung: Einleitungsfragen* (Paderborn, 1998); Franz-Xaver Kaufmann and Arnold Zingerle, eds., *Vatikanum II und Modernisierung: Historische, theologische und soziologische Perspektiven* (Paderborn, 1996); Otto Hermann Pesch, *Das Zweite Vatikanische Konzil, 1962–1965* (Würzburg, 1993).

72. *Academia* 64, no. 2 (1971): 67–77; ibid., 64, no. 5–6 (1971): 142–45.

73. *Academia* 64, no. 5–6 (1971): 149–50.

74. *Academia* 64, no. 1 (1971): 32–33.

75. Cf. *Academia* 64, no. 1 (1971): 31, 53–66; ibid., 64, no. 2 (1971): 83–86; ibid., 64, no. 5–6 (1971): 148; ibid., 65, no. 1 (1972): 1.

76. For example, Stitz, *Der CV*.

77. Christian Krause et al., eds., *Zwischen Revolution und Resignation: Alternativkultur, politische Grundströmungen und Hochschulaktivitäten in der Studentenschaft*, 2nd ed. (Bonn, 1981), 175.

78. Cf. Franz Brendle, "Alamannia und die 68er Bewegung: Über das Verhältnis einer katholischen Korporation zu den Studentenunruhen," in *Katholische Studentenverbindung Alamannia zu Tübingen: Festschrift zur 125-Jahr-Feier* (Tübingen, 1998), 21–39; Thomas Sauer, "Tradition und Neuorientierung: Markomannia in den fünfziger und sechziger Jahren," in Sauer and Vollmuth, *Markomannia*, 157–78; Harald Krenberger, "Die 'unruhigen' 68er Jahre der Markomannia," in ibid., 179–88.

79. *Academia* 64, no. 1 (1971): 56; ibid., 64, no. 2 (1971): 63; ibid., 64, no. 3 (1971): 102–2; ibid., 65, no. 1 (1972), 18.

80. *Academia* 64, no. 1 (1971): 46–48; ibid., 65, no. 1 (1972), 2–3, 9–12.

81. Helge Kleifeld, "Bildungs- und Hochschulpolitik der Verbindungen, 1945–1961," *GDS-Archiv* 4 (1998): 90–99. Furthermore, cf. *Alamannenblätter* 37 (1967): 1–3, 9–10.

82. *Academia* 64, no. 1 (1971): 1–13.

83. Ibid., 34–35.

84. *Alamannenblätter* 38 (1968): 7–10; ibid., 39 (1969): 1–4.

85. *Academia* 49, no. 3 (1956): 49–72; ibid., 49, no. 8 (1956): 178–86; ibid., 50, no. 4 (1957): 83–93; ibid., 50, no. 8 (1957): 189–201; ibid., 51, no. 3 (1958): 65–84; ibid., 51, no. 10 (1958): 313–19.

86. *Academia* 65, no. 2 (1972): 49–51, 54–55.

87. *Academia* 64, no. 5–6 (1971): 154–55.

Chapter 16

TURNING AWAY FROM THE PAST
West Germany and Israel, 1965–1967

Carole Fink

∽

The German people know the horror and terror of war.… They know that force and war are no suitable means to achieve national goals or to solve international controversies.[1]

After a period of emphasizing continuities and minimizing turning points, scholars are once more acknowledging the existence of "markers," events that signify a process of transformation. Halfway through the Cold War, between 1965 and 1967, there was a pronounced shift in West German-Israeli relations. These two states, born at almost the same time out of war and partition, had developed a special bond during the early Cold War years. When international and domestic politics changed in the mid-1960s, so, too, would relations between Bonn and Tel Aviv along with the attitudes toward the past that underlay these ties.

The "Special Relationship," 1952–1964

For sixteen years after the founding of the Federal Republic, there existed no official diplomatic relations between West Germany and Israel. Instead, there was an unofficial bond that began with the Luxembourg restitution agreement of 1952 and was expanded by the secret arms deals concluded four years later and by the economic arrangements of 1960.[2]

West Germany and Israel had no shared history. The past that linked them was dominated by the Holocaust and only minimally by the many centuries of German-Jewish history. Their rapprochement in 1952, although laced with historical

---

Notes for this chapter begin on page 286.

and moralistic rhetoric, was forged out of the political necessities of the present. In that turbulent Cold War year, Konrad Adenauer required moral credibility to establish his government firmly in the Western camp, and David Ben Gurion desperately needed financial resources to settle immigrants from Arab lands and expand Israel's security and economic base.

On 10 September 1952, after hectic and arduous negotiations, a treaty was signed in the Luxembourg City Hall without handshakes or public display. West Germany agreed to compensate Jewish survivors and also to pay Israel reparations-in-kind (*Shilumim*) over a period of fourteen years in the amount of DM 3.5 billion. Israel, for its part, reluctantly acquiesced in Bonn's figures, in its insistence on giving formal precedence to its own refugees and deportees, and, significantly, in its characterization of the tiny state not as the sole representative of the entire Jewish people,[3] but as the refuge of Holocaust survivors.[4]

There was considerable opposition in West Germany.[5] A public opinion poll in September 1952 revealed that only 11 percent of the population unqualifiedly endorsed the agreement, 44 percent considered it "superfluous," 24 percent agreed, but considered the amount "too high," and 21 percent were undecided.[6] By December 1952, only 26 percent favored and 49 percent opposed ratification.[7] Faced with the Arab League's threats, only 12 percent of the West German population considered the Luxembourg agreement more important than the threatened sanctions.[8] Nevertheless, in the spring of 1953, the two tough, aged political leaders, Konrad Adenauer and David Ben Gurion, each forced to draw on opposition parties for crucial support, achieved ratification of the first tie between the Third Reich's successor and the remnants of Hitler's victims collected on territory some thousand miles away.[9]

Earlier writers have termed the ensuing twelve years a "golden age" of reconciliation and cooperation between two widely different, distant entities; but in truth the years of the unofficial German-Israel bond were grayer than gold.[10] The Bonn-Tel Aviv tie, never the primary one for either country, developed within a larger international framework. The United States remained their principal benefactor as well as their adviser, intermediary, and arbiter in almost every aspect of their relationship, especially in the area of arms supplies. The Soviet Union remained each country's adversary, the overlord of seventeen million East Germans and almost three million Soviet Jews. In dealing with the US, the Soviet Union, or the emerging Third World, Bonn and Tel Aviv often sacrificed the other's interests. In 1953, the FRG placated the Arab League by providing generous economic grants to Tel Aviv's sworn enemies,[11] and Israel wooed Bonn's communist neighbors in order to ease the plight of the remaining Jews of Eastern Europe.

Both states reaped substantial rewards from their initial agreement. Germany received economic benefits, regained its sovereignty, and entered NATO.[12] Israel built its infrastructure and expanded its military. Not surprisingly, by 1956 the strains of the special relationship became manifest. The vast majority of the German public condemned Israel's attack on Egypt, which it had secretly coordinated with the Anglo-French strike at Suez.[13] The Bonn government, alarmed over the rift between the US and its NATO allies and refusing to choose between Israel and Egypt, declared its neutrality.[14]

In the aftermath, the FRG agreed reluctantly to replace the US as an arms supplier to Israel;[15] but it also became "astonishingly active" in the Arab world, greatly expanding its economic and political ties with Egypt and the oil-producing states.[16] Moreover, in order to thwart East Germany's inroads into the nonaligned world, Bonn issued the Hallstein Doctrine, threatening to break relations with any regime that recognized the German Democratic Republic. Based on the Arabs' noisy protests over the Luxembourg agreement, West Germany had handed them a new form of blackmail and foreclosed the establishment of diplomatic relations with Israel.[17]

The reluctant partners continued to follow separate paths. By 1960, West Germany, which helped found the new Common Market, had achieved economic success, political stability, and a growing international reputation. Israel, on the other hand, was beset with political infighting, border threats, and a mounting trade imbalance with Europe as well as a costly, uphill struggle to gain friends in the nonaligned world. On the surface, the relationship appeared smooth.[18] Under Aktion Sühnezeichen, Bonn sent its youth to Israel to work on social projects; in December 1959, the first delegation from the Max Planck Institute visited the Weizmann Institute; and in October 1961, the first German volunteers arrived at Kibbutz Urim and the first German students traveled to Israel.[19] At their first face-to-face meeting in March 1960 at the Waldorf Astoria Hotel in New York, Adenauer offered Ben Gurion unrestricted, low-interest loans for Israeli development projects.[20]

Israel continued to raise the specter of the past. It protested the eruption of neo-Nazism and anti-Semitic incidents, the ubiquity of former Nazi officials in West German public life, and, above all, the presence of German rocket scientists in Egypt producing "weapons of mass destruction."[21] Israel's capture of Adolf Eichmann created enormous tension between the two states. The trial of the manager of mass murder between April and December 1961, aimed at educating young Israelis in the crimes of the Third Reich and asserting the indispensability of the state of Israel, also reproved the Federal Republic for its laxness in prosecuting war criminals.[22]

Despite Adenauer and Ben Gurion's efforts to quell the furor, the result was to widen the distance between West Germans and Israelis.[23] During the Eichmann trial, the Berlin Wall was erected. For Bonn's critics, it symbolized not only a punishment for the Nazis' crimes but also the failure of Adenauer's cold warriorism. A new generation of West Germans rallied increasingly to the opposition Social Democrats, who advocated realism and conciliation toward the world beyond the Wall. The Israeli population, on the other hand, linking the revelations of the Eichmann trial with the perilous present, remained unified in its nationalist militancy toward Germany and the rest of the world. In response to popular outrage, the Ben Gurion government reluctantly placed new barriers on Israeli citizens' travel to West Germany.[24]

From Bonn's perspective, the "special," unofficial relationship was inherently asymmetric, volatile, and shallow.[25] Although the SPD and certain labor and religious leaders expressed sympathy toward Israel, German diplomats and businessmen disliked Israel's exactions. Many older Germans still despised Jews, grumbled over the "blood payments" to Israel,[26] and were unconcerned about the Nazis' crimes.[27] Moreover, a growing number of youths resented the burden of their parents' generation.[28] Nevertheless, any move by Bonn to "normalize" its ties with Tel Aviv risked opening the wounds of the past.

Crisis and Redefinition: 1965–1966

By the beginning of 1965, West Germany had become the world's third largest economy, exporting two-thirds of its products outside of Europe to Asia, Africa, and the Western hemisphere.[29] That same year, it underwent its first solo international crisis. With Adenauer gone and new leaders in Washington and Moscow, Bonn faced a challenge to the core of its Cold War policy, its stance toward the German Democratic Republic, which would also affect its relationship with Israel.

Beginning in October 1964, Bonn received two major blows to its efforts to court the Israelis and the Arabs.[30] First was the exposure of its quasi secret arms shipments to Israel that triggered uproar in the Arab world and in the Bundestag.[31] Next came the announcement of Egyptian president Gamal Abdel Nasser's invitation to Walter Ulbricht to pay an official visit to Egypt in February 1965, the first ever extended by a noncommunist state to the GDR chief.[32] Caught between an onerous obligation and a grave threat to its claim to represent the entire German people—with the German public in an uproar,[33] its Western allies deaf to its complaints,[34] and its enemies mocking its dilemma[35]—Bonn wavered, but ultimately assumed a new stance in the Middle East.

West Germany's new chancellor, Ludwig Erhard, proceeded to carve out a path that exceeded Adenauer's and Washington's directions and defied his Foreign Ministry as well.[36] After a disastrous effort to mollify Egypt, he announced the cessation of all arms sales to "areas of tension" but also his decision to establish full diplomatic relations with Israel. Ignoring the domestic clamor to enforce the Hallstein Doctrine, Erhard coolly awaited the Arabs' response. After a hastily assembled foreign ministers' conference in Cairo, ten Arab governments (Egypt, Algeria, Syria, Jordan, Iraq, Lebanon, Saudi Arabia, Kuwait, Sudan, and Yemen) withdrew their ambassadors from Bonn; three (Libya, Morocco, and Tunisia) refused to do so; but no Arab state recognized the GDR.[37]

Israel, largely ignored by Erhard, preferred arms to diplomatic formalities but ultimately accepted the latter. It nevertheless placed powerful pressure on Bonn, largely through US sources, to relent on the promised tanks.[38] During the strained negotiations in the spring of 1965, Germany refused further arms shipments and terminated Adenauer's unrestricted loans, but offered to conclude a new economic agreement.[39] In the May 1966 accord, Israel again acquiesced in all West Germany's conditions, and Bonn immediately assured the Arabs that "no arms were involved."[40]

Despite the Arabs' retaliation, many Germans welcomed the decision to recognize Israel.[41] Bonn, freed from an awkward status, was now determined to normalize the special relationship with Israel. But the Israelis resisted. The Tel Aviv government led the international chorus that forced a reluctant Bundestag to extend the statute of limitations against Nazi war criminals until 1969.[42]

The exchange of ambassadors produced more prickly episodes. The arrival in Tel Aviv of Dr. Rolf Pauls, a blunt former Wehrmacht major who had lost an arm in the service of his Führer and had served as deputy military attaché under Franz von Papen in Nazi Germany's embassy in Turkey, was accompanied by violent protests by the Israeli right.[43] The first Israeli ambassador to West Germany, Asher Ben Natan, who spent part of his first day in Germany attending a Holocaust memorial ceremony in Cologne, throughout his four-year term insisted that the content of German-Israeli relations would never be "normal."[44] Ben Natan found the old guard of the Auswärtiges Amt "cold, reserved, pro-Arab" and generally hostile to the establishment of bilateral relations; noting so many former Nazi Party members in positions of power, Israelis referred to Bonn as a "Republic of Restoration."[45]

In obtaining recognition, Israel had won a substantial moral victory. Bonn's decision to become the eighty-eighth state to send an emissary to Tel Aviv seemed once and for all to refute Nasser's claim of the "irregularity" of its existence.[46] Yet there were no Israeli expressions of gratitude.[47] Terming the establishment of formal relations an "oppressive necessity,"[48] Foreign Minister Abba Eban insisted that Bonn "had a special responsibility to strengthen Israel."[49] Neither he nor Eshkol shared Ben Gurion's warmth toward the FRG, and both were prepared to risk Germany's interests to advance Israel's.[50] They were backed by the mainstream Israeli public which viewed the division of Germany as "too mild a punishment" for the crimes of the Third Reich and the *Wirtschaftswunder* as a "perversity."[51]

Tensions rose in May 1966 during Adenauer's emotional, eight-day visit to Israel, which provoked widespread student demonstrations and an aggressive police response. At a public reception, *der Alte* rebuked Eshkol's statement that Germany "still had a long way to go" by insisting that the events referred to were "past."[52] Two months later, Helmut Schmidt, the leader of the SPD's parliamentary group, warned his Israeli hosts against "sacrificing all of West Germany's … interests without regard to the consequences."[53]

Things came to a boil over Israel's *Ostpolitik*. In 1965, Eshkol, hoping for closer relations with the new Soviet leaders, had endorsed the Kremlin's formula for global coexistence: respect for existing boundaries and peaceful settlement of territorial conflicts. He urged Moscow to liberalize conditions for Soviet Jewry and increase Jewish emigration, and also to apply its Tashkent-mediator role to the Middle East. Israel, for its part, advertised its independence from Washington and Bonn by withholding support for America's crusade in Vietnam and advocating a denuclearized Germany.[54] Visiting Warsaw in May 1966, Eban flattered his hosts and infuriated Bonn by announcing his recognition of the Oder-Neisse line.[55]

Germany responded on 30 June 1966. In a scalding speech at the International Fair in Tel Aviv, Ambassador Pauls scored the "schizophrenic" wave of Germanophobia in the Israel press and in public utterances—"the worst in twenty years."[56] Pauls cautioned the Israelis against "portray[ing] the Germany of 1966 on Nazi lines," insisting that Israel respect the Federal Republic's national interests.[57] Answering Eban's admonition that the Jewish people "awaited deeds" from Germany to admit it back into the family of nations, Pauls stated that the FRG already occupied a respected place in the world and required no "special authorization." Bilateral ties between Germany and Israel would improve, he insisted, only when their relations were governed "not by the past but by the future."[58]

Tensions soon evaporated. Nahum Goldmann, one of the negotiators of the Luxembourg Agreement, used the occasion of the World Jewish Congress meeting in Brussels on 4–5 August 1966 to laud Germany's generosity and score the "viperous" Israeli press. Israel finally approved student and cultural exchanges with Germany and ended its censorship of German music and films.[59] And after the Soviet Union had rebuffed all its entreaties,[60] Israel had to turn back to the West and to West Germany.

Still hoping to capitalize on their new relationship, Israel pressed Bonn to promote its associate membership in the Common Market. Eshkol counted on Erhard's support against the "Arabists in the Auswärtiges Amt" but also enlisted the media magnate Axel Springer in his campaign to make Bonn Israel's faithful intercessor.[61] Until Erhard's last days in office, Israel hectored Bonn against sustaining "the policies of the Third Reich."[62]

In West Germany, the events of 1965–66 had created a serious backlash. The state had been battered by its first solo international crisis. Despite all their achievements, the FRG and its people had been treated with anger and scorn and made to feel eternally vulnerable for the Nazi past.[63] Not unexpectedly, there was an outburst of anti-Semitism.[64] In November 1966, the ultra-right National Democratic Party (Nationaldemokratische Partei Deutschlands, NPD) received 8 percent of the popular vote in the state elections in Hessen and Bavaria, provoking alarm in Israel and the United States.[65] And on the night of 27–28 November, the Jewish monument at Dachau was covered with swastikas and anti-Semitic slogans.[66]

Erhard's fall in late 1966 was due largely to West Germany's first economic crisis, but the prolonged crisis over Israel also contributed. The strains of 1965–66, the loss of close personal ties between leaders, and the hyperbolic language in the press and public utterances cast their shadow over German political life as well.

The Six Day War

In November 1966, a new political era began in Bonn and Europe with the formation of a "grand coalition" government led by the Christian Democrat Kurt Georg Kiesinger as chancellor and the Social Democrat Willy Brandt as foreign minister.[67] This opening to the SPD, which within three years would become the leading partner in a Left-Center government, signaled a more self-assured, less penitent West Germany prepared to revise its Cold War shibboleths and build bridges between Western and Eastern Europe.[68] Within two months, the FRG established diplomatic ties with Romania, breaching not only the Soviet bloc but the Hallstein Doctrine as well.[69]

There were immediate implications for the Middle East. In order to launch its detente policy in Europe, Bonn had to mend its fences with the Arab oil producers on whom its economic and political fortunes depended.[70] Bonn's aim was not only to curb Soviet penetration of NATO's southern flank but also to restore its own prestige in the region. At once, Kiesinger and Brandt began courting moderate Arab governments.[71] But the Arab League, imitating Israel's rhetoric, insisted that the new Bonn government had to "merit reconciliation." In meetings with the league's director in April 1967, Brandt and Kiesinger offered a DM 2.5 million aid package for the Palestinian refugees in return for resuming diplomatic relations; but Bonn refused to sacrifice its ties with Israel.[72]

Israel watched these developments warily. In December 1966, it had led the protests over the NPD's electoral gains and criticized Kiesinger's Nazi past.[73] Ignoring the changes in Bonn, Tel Aviv applied its old peremptory tone, countering Germany's "groveling toward the Arabs" with renewed demands for its support in the Common Market.[74] Israel found a new ally in Günter Grass, a sharp critic of the Grand Coalition, who implored Brandt to provide "help urgently needed."[75] To emphasize the old bond, Ben Gurion and Eban attended Adenauer's funeral, but they returned sorely disappointed over Kiesinger's evasiveness.[76]

The outbreak of the Six Day War on 5 June 1967 created a shock in West Germany. Despite Nasser's belligerence and Soviet threats against Israel, Bonn was unprepared for Israel's lightning attacks on Gaza and Suez and for its decisive military victories in less than a week over Egypt, Syria, and Jordan. The FRG immediately declared a "neutral policy of nonintervention."

Ignored by all parties, Bonn reverted to a classic Cold War perspective, viewing the Six Day War as a calamity that increased its vulnerability and isolation.[77] West Germany's reputation was tarnished by Arab and communist charges that its arms had enabled Israel to launch its aggression.[78] The GDR insisted that Israel's blitzkrieg was modeled on Bonn's strategic plans to conquer East-Central Europe.[79] Moreover, the pillars of Bonn's security were shaken. Not only had Washington failed to restrain Israel,[80] but its European partners had taken no unified stance against a grave threat to NATO's southern flank. How would the West respond to a threat against West Berlin?[81] Once the war ended, cooler minds prevailed. Bonn acknowledged that the Soviet Union had neither intervened militarily nor was likely to retaliate in Europe and that only East Germany had zealously followed Moscow's lead.[82] Faced with an oil boycott and other economic burdens,[83] the FRG launched a major moral offensive, assuring the world that it had ceased all arms sales to the Middle East, offering generous aid to the new Palestinian refugees, and renouncing the use of force to achieve national goals.[84] Kiesinger vowed to replace "obsolescent antagonisms" with a policy of cooperation and of bridging the "gulf between ... North and South ... rich and poor ... white and colored."[85]

Behind Bonn's high-minded pronouncements was an aroused German public. There was a huge outpouring of popular support for an endangered Israel.[86] Spurred by a long, elaborate Israeli media campaign, led by the energetic Ben Natan and the ardent Grass, Israel was portrayed as David facing Goliath, as a liberal democracy menaced by aggressive, corrupt Arab regimes and as a Western bulwark against Soviet expansion.[87]

Israel's old image as the refuge of Holocaust survivors made an even more powerful impression.[88] Although prohibiting military-age citizens to volunteer for service in Israel, Bonn dispatched twenty thousand gas masks to guard against an attack similar to the one Nasser had launched in Yemen.[89] On 7 June, Brandt told the Bundestag that nonintervention did not mean "moral indifference" or "neutrality of the heart."[90] Schmidt went further: "Much as we value the traditional friendship of our people with the Arab peoples, we must protest the intention of their leaders to destroy Israel [die Absicht ihrer Führer, Israel zu vernichten]."[91] Referring to the *Vernichtungsparole* of Israel's enemies, Rainer Barzel, the leader of the CDU/CSU parliamentary group, evoked the UN convention on genocide.[92]

Among the middle generation of thirty-five to fifty-year-old West Germans, there were strong expressions of responsibility for the Israelis. In his passionate editorial "Israel Must Live!" Rudolf Augstein expressed this group's unease that the survivors of Nazi genocide had faced annihilation for the second time.[93] There was nevertheless a limit to these protective sentiments. Although 55 percent of West Germans favored Israel over Egypt in June and 59 percent by mid-summer, 77 percent of West Germans approved their government's policy of nonintervention.[94]

The Six Day War also evoked a new picture, of warrior Israel, and of a kinship in arms.[95] In *Die Welt* on 10 June 1967, Mathias Walden described the "heart-stirring" sentiments kindled by Israel's military victory. Like a "purifying thunderstorm" it had dispersed West Germany's "ignorance" and complacency along with the "unclean thoughts" recently advanced by the NPD.[96]

After twelve years of the repression of German militarism, the Six Day War appeared to make the use of arms respectable.[97] The Springer press barely concealed its admiration for the new Prussians of the Middle East and for the latter-day Rommels, Dayan and Rabin. *Bild am Sonntag* exulted: "There are no more borders in the Berlin of the Middle East," and *Welt am Sonntag* warned "The Israelis did not win their freedom cheaply; neither will the Germans get theirs."[98] From the ultra-right came this complaint: "Imagine a German general vowing never to give up [our Mandelbaum Gates] Breslau, Königsberg, Eger, and Weimar. He wouldn't dare!"[99]

Not all Germans supported Israel's cause.[100] The champions of strict neutrality included the FDP opposition representing business interests, and veteran Foreign Ministry officials who feared the consequences in the Arab world.[101] *Die Zeit* chided Israel for risking a "Third World War,"[102] and the *Frankfurter Allgemeine Zeitung* disputed the notion of a purifying thunderstorm: "No Gordian knot had been smashed," no peace was in sight.[103]

Others openly expressed an anti-Israel stance.[104] From the neo-Nazi press came a wave of attacks on the Zionists' Nazi-like war crimes[105] and ridicule of Israel's "underdog" status.[106] The *Deutsche Wochen-Zeitung*, alluding to the foreign minister's illegitimate birth, accused "Frahm-Brandt" of placing the "whole responsibility for World War II on West Germany's shoulders" and called it a "strange world" that applauded Israel's crushing "preventative war."[107]

At the opposite end of the political spectrum was Germany's New Left. Struck by the elder generation's mixed messages of atonement and forgetfulness and lacking experience of World War II and Hitler's concentration camps, they identified with their own day's oppressed people in Greece, Cuba, Vietnam, Iran, and Palestine, and they placed Israel in the camp of the imperialists.[108] On 9 June, a student delegation accosted Ben Natan with the demand for Israel's withdrawal from the occupied territories.[109] Paralleling the neo-Nazis, the New Left's theoreticians attacked Israel's "manipulation" of German public opinion.[110]

The graphic images of Arab suffering split West Germany's liberal community. Some, but not all, German Jews, who had gravitated toward the Left, grieved over the humiliation of the Arabs.[111] Some, but not all, middle-aged intellectuals echoed the leftist critique of a militarist Israel and expressed solidarity with the Palestinians.[112] One noteworthy exception was the "Joint Declaration by Twenty Representatives of the German Left Concerning the Middle East Conflict" that strongly supported Israel.[113]

Although Israel suffered heavy casualties in the Six Day War, its overwhelming victory diminished its image in West Germany as a victim and dependent.[114] When Israel appeared to be in danger, more than half the German public had poured out its sympathy; but when neither its military victory nor the superpowers' negotiations brought peace to the Middle East, these same West Germans, facing their own dangerous borders, explicitly rejected Israel's path. According to the emerging new consensus of Bonn's leaders and its population, the way to peaceful change in Central Europe lay in disarming Germany's enemies through conciliation, not confrontation.[115] And the strength to promote this peaceful change would require more realism, and more balance, in the Middle East.[116]

Turning Away from the Past?

Although the Six Day War provided the catalyst for the transformation of German-Israeli relations, the ground had already been prepared. During the preceding tumultuous fifteen-year period, along with tokens of cooperation and reconciliation there had been accusations and frayed tempers, secrecy and betrayal, top-level negotiation and public disinterest.

After 1961, the year of the Wall and of Eichmann's trial, Germany's path diverged from Israel's. From a loyal follower of Washington, Bonn became a more independent international actor; from the conservative Adenauer regime it moved toward a left-centrist politics; from a *Wirtschaftswunder* dependent on the West's domination of energy resources, it became a vulnerable economy buffeted by crises in the Third World; and from a penitent toward Israel, it insisted on more normal relations.

The emergence of the vocal New Left in the 1960s, reinforcing Adenauer's old critics, intensified the process of change. These young Germans, scarred by their parents' equivocations over Nazism and by the moral morass of the Vietnam war, were less terrified of communism, less reverent toward the United States, less yearning to demand the reunification of Germany as the precondition for peace in Europe, and also less automatically sympathetic to Israel.

Israel's overwhelming victory in 1967, its occupation of vast areas of Arab territory, and its growing dependence on the United States recast the increasingly fractious relationship between Bonn and Tel Aviv. Although Israel retained the support of West German churches and trade unions, local community and youth groups as well as the influential German-Israeli society, no German political party since 1967 has automatically supported its policies.[117] Since the Six Day War, every German government has publicly insisted on a normal, not a special, relationship. And after the political and oil shocks of 1967, Bonn placed itself firmly within the European framework in dealing with the Israeli-Arab struggle.

The unofficial ties remained, and the Holocaust remained its moral base;[118] even the most ardent *Ostpolitiker* never renounced Bonn's "special moral obligation emanating from our past."[119] More importantly, the military, intelligence, and economic bonds, formed between 1952 and 1964, have survived until the present, outlasting the Cold War and several Middle Eastern conflicts.[120] For both countries, this "pragmatic" connection has also remained a secondary policy, infused with a volatile blend of morality and *Realpolitik*, personal bonds and popular criticism, and burdened by pressures from the United States and the Arab countries.[121]

Nonetheless, in a real as well as symbolic sense, the period between 1965 and 1967 marked a transition in German-Israeli relations, when West Germany's sense of its past and its future diverged from Israel's. For at least another generation, mainstream Israelis continued to link their national identity and destiny with the crimes of the Third Reich. Mainstream West Germans, on the other hand, in pursuit of a peaceful, European solution to their national problem, viewed the Nazi past through a more distant lens; and the Berlin Republic, working toward an expanded European future, has continued in this direction.

Notes

I should like to thank the Mershon and Melton Centers of the Ohio State University for research support, and Prof. Detlef Junker for his helpful comments.

1. Letter from Ambassador Baron Sigismund von Braun, Permanent Observer of the Federal Republic of Germany to the United Nations, 29 June 1967, in United Nations, "Fifth Emergency Special Session, 17 June–18 Sept. 1967," *Proceedings of the General Assembly* (New York, 1968), A/6737.
2. The most useful studies of German-Israeli relations include Jekutiel Deligdisch, *Die Einstellung der Bundesrepublik Deutschland zum Staat Israel: Eine Zusammenfassung der Entwicklung seit 1949* (Bonn-Bad Godesberg, 1974); Lily Gardner Feldman, *The Special Relationship between West Germany and Israel* (Boston, 1984); Michael Wolffsohn, *Ewige Schuld? 40 Jahre deutsch-jüdisch-israelische Beziehungen*, 2nd ed. (Munich, 1988); Inge Deutschkron, *Israel und die Deutschen: Das schwierige Verhältnis*, new ed. (Cologne, 1991); Ralph Giordano, ed., *Deutschland und Israel: Solidarität und Bewährung* (Gerlingen, 1991); George Lavy, *Germany and Israel: Moral Debt and National Interest* (London, 1996), and Markus A. Weingardt, *Deutsch-israelische Beziehungen: Zur Genese bilateraler Verträge 1949–1996* (Konstanz, 1997). None, however, uses archival materials.
3. As Bonn officially claimed was its own position on behalf of the Germans of Central Europe.
4. Yeshayau A. Jelinek, "Political Acumen, Altruism, Foreign Pressure or Moral Debt—Konrad Adenauer and the 'Shilumim,'" *Tel Aviver Jahrbuch für deutsche Geschichte* 19 (1990): 77–102. On Germany's adroit use of the divisions between Israelis and representatives of the larger Jewish world, see Ronald Zweig, "German Reparations and Israeli-Diaspora Relations," *Zionism* 14 (1989): 232–39. On Adenauer's assumption of the burdens of the past, without a deep alteration of Germany's political consciousness, see Mary Fulbrook, *German National Identity after the Holocaust* (Cambridge, 1999), 66–67.
5. And in Israel as well, where critics derided the paucity of the sums or challenged the whole idea of collecting money and establishing ties with Germany.
6. E. Noelle and E. P. Neumann, eds., *Jahrbuch der öffentlichen Meinung, 1947–1955* (Bonn, 1956), 130.
7. A. J. Merritt and R. L. Merritt, eds., *Public Opinion in Semisovereign Germany: The HICOG Surveys, 1949–1955* (Urbana-Champaign, 1980), 198. Eleven percent of the opponents stated that Israel itself was "not a war victim."
8. Michael Wolffsohn, "German Opinions on Israel, 1949–1986," *The Jerusalem Journal of International Relations* 19, no. 4 (1988): 81–82.
9. Michael Wolffsohn, "Das deutsch-israelische Wiedergutmachungsabkommen von 1952 im internationalen Zusammenhang," *Vierteljahrshefte für Zeitgeschichte* 36, no. 4 (1988): 691–732.
10. Yeshayahu A. Jelinek, ed., *Zwischen Moral und Realpolitik. Deutsch-israelische Beziehungen 1945–1965: Eine Dokumentensammlung* (Tel Aviv, 1997).
11. Peter Hünseler, *Die aussenpolitischen Beziehungen der Bundesrepublik Deutschland zu den arabischen Staaten von 1949–1980* (Frankfurt am Main, 1980).
12. Karl W. Deutsch and Lewis J. Edinger, *Germany Rejoins the Powers: Mass Opinion, Interest Groups, and Elites in Contemporary German Foreign Policy* (Stanford, 1959).
13. An Allensbach poll conducted during the Sinai campaign revealed that 10 percent of West Germans sided with Israel, 56 percent with Egypt, 6 percent neither, and 28 percent were undecided. A subsequent poll by EMNID revealed that 60 percent of the West German population opposed Israel's behavior and 31 percent were undecided. Figures quoted in Werner Bergmann and Rainer Erb, *Anti-Semitism in Germany: The Post Nazi Epoch Since 1945*, trans. Belinda Cooper and Allison Brown (New Brunswick, 1997), 172–73.
14. Konrad Adenauer, *Erinnerungen, 1955–1959* (Frankfurt am Main, 1969), 3:226, describes Bonn's difficult decision.

15. Details in Shimon Peres interview with *Der Spiegel*, 24 February 1965, and with "Lui," *Deutsche Ausgabe*, parts 1 and 2 (August–September 1979): 74–84.

16. Sven Olaf Berggötz, *Nahostpolitik in der Ära Adenauer: Möglichkeiten und Grenzen, 1949–1963* (Düsseldorf, 1988), 459–61.

17. Rüdiger Marco Booz, *"Hallsteinzeit": Deutsche Aussenpolitik, 1955–1972* (Bonn, 1995), 78–80.

18. When Volkswagen entered the Israeli market, the first Beetles elicited more stares than protests. At least one radio announcer, a native-born Sabra, refused to read this commercial: "Volkswagen— ein Auto ohne Probleme." Avi Primor, *"… mit Ausnahme Deutschlands"* (Berlin, 1997), 84–87.

19. Franz von Hammerstein, "The Germans' Work for Peace: 'Operation Atonement,'" *Patterns of Prejudice* 7, no. 3 (1973): 7–10.

20. Lavy, *Germany and Israel*, 53–55.

21. *Der Spiegel*, no. 13 (1963): 70, quoting the Israeli press.

22. Lavy, *Germany and Israel*, 77.

23. Along with the two leaders' reassurances on the solidity of the special relationship (quoted in Deligdisch, *Die Einstellung der Bundesrepublik Deutschland*, 66, 69), Ben Gurion agreed not to embarrass Bonn by calling several leading West German figures (including Adenauer's former state secretary, Hans Globke, the author of the official commentary on the Nuremberg race laws) to give evidence at the trial in return for the delivery of "certain weapons." Interview with Franz Josef Strauss in *International Herald Tribune*, 9 March 1965.

24. *New York Times*, 14 January 1962; *Israel Digest* 5, no. 2 (19 January 1962).

25. At the time there was a comparable shallowness in the Franco-German bond, also steeped in historical symbolism, based largely on pragmatic goals, and shaped by the personal ties between two aged leaders. The 1963 Franco-German treaty kindled opposition across the political spectrum of both countries.

26. Frank Stern, *The Whitewashing of the Yellow Badge: Antisemitism and Philosemitism in Postwar Germany*, trans William Templer (Oxford, 1992), 429.

27. According to the Israelis, neo-Nazis still flung the epithet, "Man hat wohl vergessen, sie zu vergasen" at those known or suspected to be Jews. Primor, *"… mit Ausnahme Deutschlands,"* 72–75, 79.

28. "Their fathers had left them a bad mortgage, and they can't understand why they're being asked to pay it off." Günter Grass, "Ben and Dieter," in Grass, *Speak Out! Speeches, Open Letters, Commentaries*, trans. Ralph Mannheim (New York, 1968), 90–91.

29. See A. W. Rhodes to Foreign Office [FO] Bonn, 23 January 1965, GB [Great Britain, Public Record Office], FO [Records] 371/183006.

30. Hans-Herbert Gaebel, "Unangenehme Möglichkeiten," *Frankfurter Rundschau*, 31 October 1964, 3, also blamed Bonn for its futile efforts to seek US favor.

31. *Die Welt*, 27 October 1964; *New York Times*, 31 October 1964. Although the sources remain mysterious, some have alleged that Israel attempted to pressure Bonn on formal recognition. Nasser's outrage was disingenuous; he not only knew for two years of these arms sales but was receiving ten times more weapons from the Soviet Union. Only West Germany's parliamentarians and public had been left ignorant of the government's expanded arms trade with Israel.

32. *Neues Deutschland*, 4 February 1966. It is likely that Moscow urged this invitation in order to capitalize on Bonn's embarrassment and promote its ally's interests in the Third World.

33. The SPD opposition announced a "Diplomatic Stalingrad," Aumale to MAE [France, Ministry of Foreign Affairs] Bonn, 13 February 1965, FMAE [Archives of the French Ministry of Foreign Affairs] Z206. The *Abendpost*, 16 February, wrote that Bonn's diplomacy had sunk to "absolute zero"; the *Handelsblatt*, 16 February, declared, "We have as good as lost the Middle Eastern game on both sides"; the independent *Stuttgarter Zeitung*, 16 February, announced that "German dignity and German reputation have sunk in the waters of the Nile"; *Die Zeit*, 19 February, lamented being "caught between the pipers of Cairo and Jerusalem"; and *Der Spiegel*, 24 February, complained that "the world laughs at Bonn." Only the *Frankfurter Allgemeine Zeitung*, 8 March, sided with the government but criticized its errors and vacillation.

34. The London *Observer*, 14 February 1965, chided Bonn for its blundering and for raising tensions in the Middle East. Aumale to MAE, Bonn, 13 February 1965, Seydoux to MAE, Bonn, 10, 21 February and 8, 10, 12 March 1965, FMAE Z206 describe Bonn's bitter plight as do British envoys in Bonn, Paris, Cairo, Washington, Tel Aviv, and Moscow, January–February 1965, GB FO 371/183009. On 20 March 1965, W. W. Rostow described a "lonely, unfairly treated" Germany, resentful that "everything we try to do fails, because others exploit our war guilt." Memorandum in NSF [National Security Files] Country File, Germany, Box 189, LBJ [Lyndon B. Johnson Presidential Library, Austin, Texas).

35. Yuri Primakov, "Bonn's Big Bluff," *Pravda*, 18 February 1966. Also, Alexander to FO, Moscow, 1 April 1965, GB FO 371/183016.

36. Hans Spier, *Crisis and Catharsis in the Middle East, 1965: A Chapter in German Foreign Policy* (New York, 1967). On the Auswärtiges Amt's coolness toward Israel, see Carstens to missions, 3 November 1964, *Akten zur auswärtigen Politik der Bundesrepublik Deutschland* 1964, vol. 2 (Munich, 1995), 308–9.

37. Taylor to FO, Bonn, 6 April 1965, GB FO 371/183006; Palmer to Rusk, Tel Aviv, 13 April 1965, NSF, Komer Files, Box 29, LBJ.

38. Tank arrangements detailed in NSF, "Israel Security: Tanks (1965), Komer Files, Box 33, LBJ; also Komer memo for the President (Secret), Washington, 23 April 1965, LBJ Presidential: 1963–1969. Confidential Name Files (R. W. Komer), Box 145, LBJ.

39. G. H. Middleton, "The Federal Republic's Middle East Crisis," Bonn, 27 August 1965, GB FO 371/183010. Details in Deutschkron, *Israel und die Deutschen*, 180–311.

40. Seydoux to MAE, Bonn, 14 May 1966, FMAE Z207.

41. E.g., *Frankfurter Rundschau*, 9 March 1965; *Süddeutsche Zeitung*, 9 and 10 March 1965; and Jörg Seelbach, *Die Aufnahme der diplomatischen Beziehungen zu Israel als Problem der deutschen Politik seit 1955* (Meisenheim a. Glan, 1970), 115–16. *Die Welt*, ardently pro-Israel, on 7 March, scored the "abrupt sacrifice" of the undertaking to Israel "on the altar of German-Arab relations," and on 16 March welcomed the "politically long overdue … readjustment of our relationship with Israel." On the other hand, the *Frankfurter Allgemeine Zeitung*, 11 and 12 March 1965, fretted over the consequences and warned Israel against posing too many "conditions"; *Die Zeit*, 19 March 1965, also deplored the consequences.

42. Details in Jeffrey Herf, *Divided Memory: The Nazi Past in the Two Germanys* (Cambridge, 1997), 337–42.

43. See reports by H. B. Walker, British Embassy in Damascus, 13 May 1966, and N. Aspin, British Embassy Tel Aviv, 16 June 1966, GB FO 371/186428. Also Rolf Pauls, "… In the Sense of the Interest of Both Partners," in *Thirty Years of Diplomatic Relations Between the Federal Republic of Germany and Israel* (Frankfurt am Main, 1995), 50–54.

44. Asher Ben Natan, "Die Chancen der Normalisierung—Interview," *Diskussion* 7, no. 18 (1966): 3–4. Also author's interview with Ben Natan, 10 August 1997. The appointment of Ben Natan, formerly an arms negotiator for Israel, had stirred adverse reactions in West Germany.

45. Primor, "… *mit Ausnahme Deutschlands,"* 157. Yohanan Meroz, for a short time member of the Israeli mission in Cologne and Israel's third ambassador to Bonn, expressed amazement that the head of the Auswärtiges Amt's Near East Division, Voigt, had been the last consul of the Third Reich in Jerusalem. Yohanan Meroz, *In schwieriger Mission* (Berlin, 1986).

46. Eliezar Livne, "Collapse of a Policy," *New Outlook* 8, no. 2 (1965).

47. The Israel election campaign during the summer of 1965, pitting Ben Gurion against Eshkol, included a fierce debate over the new settlement with Germany.

48. Quoted in Friedrich W. Husemann, "The German Israeli Relationship," in *Thirty Years*, 124–25.

49. Pauls to AA [Auswärtiges Amt], Tel Aviv, 12 April 1966, PA AA [Germany, Auswärtiges Amt, Politisches Archiv] B36/238.

50. Pauls to AA, Tel Aviv, 6 April 1966, PA AA B36/241, 24 April 1966, ibid., B36/238; Gehlhoff to Pauls, Bonn, 24 June 1966, ibid.

51. Pauls to AA, Tel Aviv, 29 June 1966, PA AA B36/238.

52. Aspin to Goodison, Tel Aviv, 19 May 1966, GB FO 371/186810.

53. Despite Schmidt's bluntness and his war service on the Eastern front, the visit, which included calls on Golda Meir, Abba Eban, and military officials as well as a trip to a kibbutz, was deemed a success by both sides. According to Pauls, Schmidt assured his hosts that a socialist victory in Germany would "change less than Israel expects." PA AA B36/239; cf. WED [West European Division of the Israeli foreign ministry] to Bonn, Tel Aviv, 27 July 1966, ISA [Israel State Archive, Jerusalem] PM [Prime Minister's Files] Ger. [Germany] 7229/10.

54. Negative evaluations from the perspective of German-Israeli relations in Pauls to AA, Tel Aviv, 21 January 1966, PA AA B36/237, 12 April 1966, 18 May 1966, ibid., B36/238; and of Israel's informal relations with NATO, Morris to FO, Tel Aviv, 10 January 1966; Hadow Reports, Tel Aviv, 17, 25 January 1966, GB FO 371/186803. Cf. Avigor Dagan, *Moscow and Jerusalem: Twenty Years of Relations between Israel and the Soviet Union* (London, 1970).

55. Blumenfeld to AA, Warsaw, 16 May 1966, PA AA B36/242; Pauls to AA, Tel Aviv, 18 May 1966, ibid., B36/238, 20 May 1966, ibid., B36/241. Two right-wing Bundestag deputies mocked the Erhard government on 26 May for lavishly supporting a foe of the FRG's most venerable border claims, ibid., B36/240.

56. Included were protests over performances of Wagner, Orff, and Strauss.

57. Pauls's text, cleared with the Auswärtiges Amt but not with Erhard, PA AA B36/240. See also Aspin to FO, Tel Aviv, 7 July 1966, GB FO 371/186810; Israeli Mission to FM, Cologne, 6 July 1966, ISA 4011/5.

58. Privately, Pauls had already chided his hosts on their lack of gratitude toward Bonn, the hectoring tone of the Knesset, and the government's German-baiting to woo Moscow. WED memoranda, 22 October 1965, 4 February 1966, ISA, PM Ger. 7229/10.

59. Török to AA, Tel Aviv, 15 August 1966, PA AA B36/238; also, Aufzeichnung, Bonn, 8 February 1967, ibid., B36/275. For details of the new agreements, see ibid., B36/240.

60. Reported, with *Schadenfreude*, in Pauls to AA, Tel Aviv, 15 August 1966, PA AA B36/238, 26, 29 September 1966, 5 December 1966, ibid., B36/241.

61. Between 7 and 15 November 1966, Springer spent eight days in Israel at the invitation of Israeli Foreign Ministry. Accompanied by Pauls, he met Eshkol and Eban and placed a cornerstone for the National Library (to which the Hamburg Foundation had contributed DM 3.6 million). Jeudy to MAE, Hamburg, 18 November, FMAE Z207. Springer to Brandt, 23 January 1967, Willy Brandt papers, Aussenminister/9 SPD Archives Bonn, urged the new government to support Israel's associate membership. Although Israel had numerous press representatives in West Germany, in 1966 *Die Welt* was the only German newspaper with a full-time correspondent in Israel.

62. Pauls to AA, Tel Aviv, 13 October 1966, PA AA B36/240. Gehlhoff, Vermerk, Bonn, 19 October 1966, ibid. Cf. *Die Welt*, 23 January 1967. The Israeli press commented bitterly over the release of Albert Speer in September 1966, Pauls to AA, Tel Aviv, 4 October 1966, PA AA B36/237.

63. *Die Zeit*, 19 March 1965.

64. Herley to MAE, Düsseldorf, 6 January 1966, FMAE Z110, reported that 60 percent of the members of Germany's National Trade Union (DBG) had refused to sign a petition in favor of closer relations with Israel. Also see reports of Jewish cemetery desecrations in the Rhineland, Württemberg, and Bavaria, in Herley to MAE, Düsseldorf, 4 January and 30 June 1966, Favre to MAE, Stuttgart, 28 February, Mleux to MAE, Munich, 4 March, 1966, FMAE Z110.

65. Lucet to MAE, Washington, 23 November 1966, FMAE Z110; Pauls to AA, Tel Aviv, 2 December 1966, PA AA B36/238. Harold C. Relyea, "The Continuing Watch on the Rhine," *Journal of International and Comparative Studies* 3, no. 2 (1970): 1–2, discusses the connection between Israeli pressure over war crimes and the rise of the NPD.

66. Mleux to MAE, Munich, 1 December 1966, FMAE Z110.

67. McGee to State Dept., Bonn, 2 November 1966, NSF Country File, Germany, Box 187, Memos, Vol. XI, LBJ.

68. See Brandt's statement, *Frankfurter Allgemeine Zeitung*, 26 January 1966, and his speech before the Council of Europe in Strasbourg, 24 January 1967, reported in FMAE Z174.

69. Seydoux to MAE, Bonn, 31 May 1967, reported in FMAE Z169.

70. Theodor Hanf, "Die Bedeutung der arabischen Staaten für die Bundesrepublik," in *Handbuch der deutschen Aussenpolitik*, ed. Hans-Peter Schwarz (Munich, 1975), 319–25. In 1966, the FRG imported 75.6 tons of oil (one-fourth of the total 319.1 tons for all of Western Europe); its main suppliers were Kuwait, Libya, Iraq, Saudi Arabia, Iran, and Algeria. Peter Lieser, *Die Bedeutung der Ölimportabhängigkeit für die Nahost-Politik der Bundesrepublik Deutschland von 1964 bis 1972* (Hamburg, 1976); Earl Fry and Raymond A. Gregory, "The International Implications of West Germany's Energy Policy," *German Studies Review* 1, no. 2 (1978): 173–99.

71. "Stand unserer Überlegungen zum deutsch-arabischen Verhältnis," [early 1967], PA AA B36/274. "Perspectives de reprise des relations diplomatiques entre l'Allemagne Fédérale et les pays arabes," Paris, 17 March 1967, FMAE Z207. Bonn reestablished diplomatic ties with Jordan in February 1967.

72. Cabinet decision, 26 January 1967 on aiding refugees, PA AA B36/271; Brandt-Hassuna talks, 19–21 April 1967, ibid.; also Aufzeichnung, Bonn, 25 April 1967, ibid., B36/274; Seydoux to MAE, Bonn, 8 April 1966, FMAE Z207.

73. That month, however, Israel's own stature sank after its massive retaliatory raid on Palestinian bases in Jordan brought forth a unanimous vote of condemnation by the Security Council. The three-thousand-man operation, the largest since the 1956 Suez attack, demolished a town, caused at least thirty civilian deaths, smashed the Jordanian Army, and elicited a sharp condemnation from the US. W. W. Rostow for the President, Washington, 16 November 1966, LBJ Presidential, 1963–1969, Israel Memos, Vol. 6, LBJ. Pauls to AA, Tel Aviv, 14 November 1966, PA AA B36/241, termed the raids a "massive political mistake."

74. WED memorandum, 23 December 1966, ISA 4011/8, and Shek note, 11 April 1967, ibid., 4011/7.

75. Grass to Brandt, Berlin, 5 April 1967, PA AA B36/297. During Grass's call at the Foreign Ministry, the WED's director warned of the "price" of appeasing the Arabs and asked: "Is Willy Brandt still a socialist?"

76. Pauls to AA, Tel Aviv, 27 April 1967, PA AA B36/298; also La Sablière to MAE, Tel Aviv, 27, 28 April 1967, FMAE Z207; Ben Natan to Foreign Ministry, Bonn, 18 April 1967, ISA FM 4011/7. Because the funeral fell on the first day of the Jewish Passover, both walked the five miles from the ambassador's residence to the Bundestag but declined to attend the interment.

77. *Rheinischer Merkur* [CDU], *Vorwärts* [SPD], and *Die Zeit* [Independent], 9 June 1967. On 23 June, the *Rheinischer Merkur* deplored the appearance of a heavily armed Soviet fleet in the Eastern Mediterranean and on 7 July complained of Europe's inability to oppose limited wars of aggression; *Christ und Welt* [CDU], on 23 June, lamented the "disintegration of the Atlantic alliance." See also, unsigned Aufzeichnung, 23 June 1967, PA AA B36/284.

78. *Neues Deutschland*, 9 June 1967; Walther to AA, Moscow, 10 June 1967, PA AA B36/283, quoting the Soviet press's mockery of Bonn's "alleged neutrality." See also the officially inspired pamphlet by Tadeusz Walichnowski, *Israel and the German Federal Republic* [sic], trans. Aleksander Trop-Kryski (Warsaw, 1968).

79. Aufzeichnung betr. die Haltung der Regierung in Ostberlin während des Nahostkonfliktes im Zeitraum von 24. Mai bis 7. Juli 1967, PA AA DDR II A1/82.00 Bd. 687.

80. See strong critiques of Washington for its distraction over Vietnam in *Vorwärts* and *Die Zeit*, 1 June 1967.

81. Gehlhoff, "Die Lage im Nahen Osten," Bonn, 16 June 1967, PA AA B36/284.

82. "Nahost Konflikt und Deutschland-Politik, Bonn, 21 June 1967, Germ. PA AA B36/258; Walther to AA, Moscow, 21 August 1967, ibid., B32/252; Angelika Timm, *Hammer, Zirkel, Davidstern: Das gestörte Verhältnis der DDR zu Zionismus und Staat Israel* (Bonn, 1997), 230–66.

83. The immediate economic shocks included the closing of the Suez Canal (catching the FRG short of supertankers) and the two-month Arab oil embargo against the US, Great Britain, and

West Germany, which reduced Arab oil supplies to Western Europe by 30 percent in June and July and 10–15 percent in August; Montfort to AA, Kuwait, 19 June 1967 (two messages), PA AA B36/274; Manfred Horn, *Die Energiepolitik der Bundesregierung von 1958 bis 1972* (Berlin, 1977), 146–47; and the "gold shock," beginning with the Soviet Union's withdrawal from the market a year earlier and exacerbated by the war (Edward Fried Files, Box 2, NSF, LBJ).

84. Braun letter to the President of the General Assembly, 29 June 1967, footnote 1.

85. Speech to the annual meeting of the Deutsche Gesellschaft für Auswärtige Politik, 23 June 1967, quoted in Rolf Vogel, ed., *The German Path to Israel* (London, 1969), 301–2.

86. *Der Spiegel*, 12 June 1967, published a full-page appeal for government and popular support for the "people of Israel threatened with extermination." Inspired by Günter Grass, three hundred Berlin youths volunteered for civilian service in Israel. In Bonn, some one thousand doctors, nurses, workers, soldiers, and youths offered their services to the Israeli Embassy, which also received several thousand letters containing financial donations. In Frankfurt, an artists' auction yielded DM 21,000, the Bank für Gemeinwirtschaft purchased Israeli bonds to the value of 3 million marks, and the city donated an additional DM 30,000. Hamburg doctors donated DM 35,000 worth of medical supplies, and Stuttgart contributed DM 30,000 worth of bandages. During the first two weeks of June 1967, in scores of German cities in towns, there were massive pro-Israel demonstrations and fund-raising campaigns by church, municipal, and private organizations. On 6 June, the national German labor organization announced its intention to purchase 3 million marks worth of Israeli bonds. "Erklärung des deutschen Gewerkschaftsbundes zum Krieg in Nahost," Willy Brandt papers, Aussenminister/9 SDP Archive, Bonn.

87. Lila Orbach, *The Role of the Media in International Affairs: An Analysis of the Media's Role in Relations between West Germany and Israel* (MA thesis, University of Massachusetts at Amherst, 1988). Hermann Meier-Cronemeyer, "Israel-zwischen Legende und Wirklichkeit," *Gewerkschaftliche Monatsschriften* 18 (1967): 225–34. There were no comparable media programs by the Arabs. See Friedmann Buttner, "German Perceptions of the Middle East Conflict: Images and Identifications during the 1967 War," *Journal of Palestine Studies* [Lebanon] 6, no. 2 (1977): 68, 70–72; Sami Musallam, *Zum Araberbild in der bundesrepublikanischen Presse* (Bonn, 1976); Daniel Glass, *Die Dritte Welt in der Presse der Bundesrepublik Deutschland* (Frankfurt am Main, 1979).

88. Before the fighting erupted, the public appeal launched by SPD deputy, Dr. Adolf Arndt, read: "We cannot be silent when the Israeli people is threatened with genocide. The state of Israel is the last home of many who hail from our country and who escaped from the genocide committed against European Jewry and engineered by Germans." Quoted in Deligdisch, *Die Einstellung der Bundesrepublik Deutschland*, 184

89. Bowing to Defense Minister Schröder's objections, the gas masks were taken from civilian stores. *Frankfurter Allgemeine Zeitung*, 2 and 8 June 1967. Returned, unused, in July, they nevertheless represented a major propaganda coup.

90. "… unsere Nichteinmischung und damit Neutralität im völkerrechtlichen Sinne des Wortes keine moralische Indifferenz und keine Trägheit des Herzens bedeuten kann." Deutscher Bundestag, 5. Wahlperiode, 111. Sitzung, Bonn, 7 June 1967, *Verhandlungen*, 5304.

91. Ibid., 5270

92. Ibid., 5276–77.

93. "Israel soll leben!" *Der Spiegel*, 12 June 1967; Hans-Werner Kögel, *Das Israel-Bild in Deutschland* (Frankfurt am Main, 1985).

94. Institut für Demoskopie, *Jahrbuch der öffentlichen Meinung, 1965–1967* (Allensbach, 1967), 475. In July 1967, 59 percent of West Germans favored Israel's holding of all of Jerusalem, but only 19 percent favored its retaining the other conquered territories, 36 percent favored partial return, 16 percent favored the return of all the conquered territories, and 29 percent had no opinion. Institut für Demoskopie, *The Germans: Public Opinion Polls, 1967–1980*, ed. Elisabeth Noelle-Neumann (Westport, 1981), 467. Israel received copies of these polls (ISA

FM 4013/2). On Bonn's divisions over a "united Jerusalem," see Aufzeichnung, 6 June 1967, PA AA B36/298.

95. It may also have evoked the feeling that the successes of the "survivors" had mitigated the horrors of the Nazi past. Lavy, *Germany and Israel*, 156.

96. "Our people … suspected of self-satisfied ignorance and … of succumbing to the egomania of affluence gave evidence of spontaneous participation [and] vivid concern for the small, courageous Jewish people … a committed satisfaction with the … miracles of Israel's achievements. The Israeli troops' advance was felt by most people I spoke with … as 'heart stirring' as a struggle of a brother people that had been won here…. A sultry murkiness of unclean sentiments had caused anxiety among us and among observers abroad. Into this oppressive atmosphere … the war in the Near East struck like a purifying thunderstorm."

97. *Die Zeit*, 7 July 1967. Some Germans saw in Israel's military success a "drama of German history reenacted and this time brought to a successful conclusion." Friedmann Büttner, "German Perceptions of the Middle Eastern Conflict," *Journal of Palestine Studies* 6, no. 2 (1977): 66.

98. *Der Spiegel*, 26 June 1967. The adulatory language recalled the virtually untranslatable metaphors of Wehrmacht communiqués during World War II. Shortly before the war's outbreak, *Die Welt* referred to the "*Einsatzbereitschaft*" of the Israelis; at the end, the *Neue Revue* celebrated the "desert foxes." The terms *Blitzkrieg* and *Blitzsieg* were also back in fashion.

99. *Deutsche Wochen-Zeitung*, 30 June 1967.

100. Basdevant to MAE, Düsseldorf, 8 June 1967, FMAE Z207; also Seydoux to MAE, Bonn, 7 and 8 June, ibid.

101. The FDP, which had opposed restitution, recognition, and the extension of the statute of limitations, protested the sending of "war materiel"—gas masks and lorries—and demanded a stronger declaration of neutrality. *Frankfurter Allgemeine Zeitung*, 7 June 1967.

102. Theo Sommer, "Nach dem Blitzkrieg-welcher Friede?" *Die Zeit*, 9 June 1967.

103. *Frankfurter Allgemeine Zeitung*, 10 June 1967.

104. One letter writer volunteered to aid Nasser in eliminating the "world's most ancient disturber of the peace," Klaus Seibel in *Der Spiegel*, 12 June 1967, 9; another saw parallels between 1967 and the Nazi aggression in 1939. Joachim Doss, ibid., 26 June 1967, 18. See also Institute of Jewish Affairs, *The Middle East Crisis and the Reaction of the Radical Right: New Themes in the Hate Propaganda* (London, 1967).

105. *Deutsche National und Soldaten-Zeitung*, 9, 16, 23, 30 June and 7 July. The 20 July article, "Auschwitz in the Desert," accusing the Israelis of mass murder, copied charges in *Izvestia*, 16 June 1967.

106. According to the *Deutsche Wochen-Zeitung*, 23 June 1967, this was scarcely a David-and-Goliath situation, since the Israeli Army numbered 250,000, the Egyptians only 50,000 and Jordan no more than 30,000.

107. *Deutsche Wochen-Zeitung*, 16 and 23 June 1967.

108. Horst Stemmler and Walmot Falkenberg, "Der Konflikt im Nahen Osten," *Neue Kritik* 42–43 (August 1967): 68; see also Redaktion *Arbeiterkampf*, *Deutsche Linke zwischen Israel und Palästina* (Hamburg, 1988), and DIAK (Deutsch-Israelischer Arbeitskreis für Frieden im Nahen Osten), *Solidarität und deutsche Geschichte: Die Linke zwischen Antisemitismus und Israelkritik* (Berlin, 1987).

109. Interview with Ben Natan, Tel Aviv, 10 August 1997. Protests disrupted his speeches in a dozen universities. Asher Ben Natan, "Bridges over Many Chasms," in *Thirty Years*, 41–42.

110. Kurt Bachmann, "Model psychologischer Kriegsvorbereitung: Zur Manipulierung der öffentlichen Meinung zur Nahostkrise," *Marxistische Blätter: Zeitschrift für Wissenschaftlichen Sozialismus* (Frankfurt) 5, no. 4 (1967): 22–25. See also François Bondy, "Die Europäische Linke und der Nahostkrieg 1967," *Zeitschrift für Politik* 16, no. 1 (1969): 72–92.

111. Dan Diner, "Jewish Socialization and Political Identity in West Germany," in *Germans and Jews since the Holocaust: The Changing Situation in West Germany*, ed. Anson Rabinbach and Jack Zipes (New York, 1986), 133. Misgivings toward Israel were voiced by the poet Erich Fried,

who had fled Austria in 1938 and declared his solidarity with the new victims of 1967: "Your longing was to become/Like the European nations/who murdered you/Now you've become like them./.../The impression of the naked feet/in the desert sand/will last longer than the marks/of your bombs and your tanks." Fried, *Höre, Israel* (Frankfurt am Main, 1983), 61.

112. Martin W. Klocke, *Israel und die deutsche Linke: Zur Geschichte eines schwierigen Verhältnisses* (Frankfurt am Main, 1990), 106–132. Significantly, the once radical Gruppe 47 dissolved in 1967, split between supporters of the extraparliamentary opposition and gradualists such as Grass.

113. The declaration, drafted by Ernst Erdös and Michael Landmann, was signed by eighteen Jewish and non-Jewish notables, including Ernst Bloch, Iring Fetscher, Helmut Gollwitzer, Walter Jens, Alexander Mitscherlich, Uwe Johnson, Martin Walser, Günter Grass, and Ludwig von Friedeburg. Anson Rabinbach, "Introduction," in Rabinbach and Zipes, *Germans and Jews Since the Holocaust*, 23. See also the passionate defense of Israel by Heinz-Joachim Heydorn, "Nahost-Konflikt und jüdische Existenz," *Gewerkschaftliche Monatshefte* 18, no. 4 (1967): 461–64.

114. Meron Medzini, "Israel's Changing Image in the German Mass Media," in *Wiener Library Bulletin* 26, nos. 3–4 (1972–73): 8, 11; Werner Bergmann, *Antisemitismus in öffentlichen Konflikten: Kollektives Lernen in der politischen Kultur der Bundesrepublik, 1949–1989* (Frankfurt am Main and New York, 1997), 302–3.

115. Three days after the war erupted, Brandt drew links between the Six Day War and the renunciation of force in Europe. Speech to the Eighth Europäische Gemeindetag in Berlin, 8 June 1967, in Willy Brandt, *Aussenpolitik, Deutschlandpolitik, Europapolitik: Grundsätzliche Erklärungen während des ersten Jahres im Auswärtigen Amt* (Berlin, 1968), 72–76.

116. See Bahr to Brandt, Bonn, 4 July 1967, Egon Bahr papers, 442, SPD Archive, Bonn.

117. Willi Eichler, "Moralischer Bankrott der Verantwortlichen," *Geist und Tag: Zeitschrift für Politik und Kultur* 22, no. 3 (1967): 129–32, raising the issue of human-rights abuses and Palestinian rights, called for Israel's evacuation of the conquered territories.

118. Hermann-Josef Rupieper, ed., *Der Holocaust in der deutschen und der israelischen Erinnerungskultur* (Halle, 2000); Moshe Zimmerman and Oded Heilbronner, eds., *'Normal' Relations: Israeli-German Relations* [in Hebrew] (Jerusalem, 1993).

119. Statement by Willy Brandt, *Davar*, 26 November 1982.

120. "Despite Pain, Germany Quietly Forges Strong, Fruitful Links to Israel," *New York Times*, 4 March 2001.

121. Shlomo Shafir, *Ambiguous Relations: The American Jewish Community and Germany since 1945* (Detroit, 1999), 240–41.

Chapter 17

GERMANY'S PR MAN
Julius Klein and the Making of Transatlantic Memory

S. Jonathan Wiesen

❦

In 1962, a group of advertisers met with members of West Germany's Federal Press Office to discuss strategies for improving the country's international reputation.[1] Disturbed by the negative publicity accompanying the recent trial of Adolf Eichmann, these "image-persuasion" (*Image-Beeinflussung*) experts studied the results of a survey that had recently been conducted in dozens of countries.[2] Participants from around the world had been asked to discuss their impressions of Germany and its people. From Europe and Asia, to Africa, Latin America, and the South Pacific, a plethora of negative stereotypes abounded. In Italy, Germans were seen as having "a weakened sense of individuality" and a "blind obedience to authority"; in Yugoslavia, Germans were seen as "warlike," "imperialistic," "aggressive," and "dangerous." In the countries of the British Commonwealth, respondents linked images from World War II to a pathological German character: Germans were portrayed as "authoritarian," "inflexible," "disinclined toward self-criticism," and "brutal."

No less fascinating were Germany's positive connotations, which almost always had to do with hard work and ingenuity. In India, Germans were seen as technically advanced and industrious. In the countries of the Middle East, Germany was portrayed as scientifically, culturally, and economically progressive. In Thailand, Malaya, and the Philippines, Germans were seen as "diligent," if also "warlike." Strikingly, in almost every country, the economic prowess of Germany was juxtaposed with a longstanding view of Germans as products of a Prussian, militarist tradition and with more recent memories of war and mass murder.

Notes for this chapter begin on page 305.

While most of the stereotypes about Germany were not particularly new, they came at a uniquely inopportune time, when Germans were reeling from the Berlin Wall crisis and the widely publicized trial of Adolf Eichmann. Yet the Federal Press Office's survey was a boon of sorts for publicity experts. While it revealed the persistence of old clichés, now reinforced by the very real horrors of World War II, it also offered the strategies for counteracting negative perceptions of Germany. The solution to the country's publicity woes, the survey appeared to indicate, lay in its economy. The country could alter the association of Germany with military aggression and brutality by promoting images of resourcefulness and industrial ingenuity, and thereby forge healthy international relations.

This essay places the West German economy within broader discussions of memory in the long 1960s.[3] By looking specifically at the work of Julius Klein, a Chicago public relations executive who represented West German corporate and political interests in the United States, it will examine the 1960s as the decade in which Nazi crimes became an increasingly public concern, one that was intertwined with Germany's economic success, Cold War anxieties, and the reputation of its political and business leaders. As recent historians have argued, the 1960s witnessed the emergence of a "populist approach to the past" (*vergangenheitspolitischer Populismus*)[4] in which the West German people, through the media of television, books, newspaper articles, and public debates, "internalized"[5] the Nazi past and began to see it as a permanent component of West Germany's own self-understanding.

But what were the features of this self-understanding? I will argue that during the Cold War, West German national identity was very much predicated on the idea that the country's economy was one of its greatest assets and, just like products themselves, had to be aggressively marketed to the international public. In the struggle against Soviet communism, the economy was promoted as a bastion of freedom and democracy. Yet ironically, with the emerging discussion of Nazi crimes, West Germans also identified the economy as the force behind some of the very crimes they were grappling with in the 1960s. The persistent discussion of business immorality—whether in the form of rearmament under Hitler, the use of compulsory labor, or the presence of "Nazi industrialists" in the Federal Republic—reveals that West Germany's reliance on its economy as a source of national regeneration was risky.[6] This paradoxical understanding of the economy as both the locus of Nazi crimes and the key to overcoming this past was not new to the 1960s. Indeed in the decade prior, companies and publicity agents fended off accusations of corporate criminality in order to bolster international trade or defend the system of free enterprise. But during the 1960s, historical memory played a more complex and more public role than in the 1950s. As the focus of discussions about "the past" shifted from the abstract crimes of Hitler or "totalitarianism" to the destruction of European Jewry as a singular historical event, public relations advisers in the FRG and the United States were forced to promote the German economy under the gaze of an increasingly scrutinizing and vocal public.

Industry and Memory in the 1950s

Cultivating positive images of the economy has long been a special concern of German policy makers and business leaders. Since the nineteenth century, Germany has been seen as the land of precise craftsmanship, high quality, and ingenuity, whether in the smallest shop or in the large steel factories of the Ruhr. After World War II, fostering a positive image of the West German economy and its representatives became a crucial endeavor, as material and political reconstruction relied on both the aid of foreigners (most notably the United States) and their willingness to purchase German products. During the years of reconstruction in the 1950s and continuing through the boom years of the 1960s, the Federal Republic depended on a healthy trade relationship with foreign countries. In particular, industrialists and politicians identified the United States, a former enemy and current ally, as the most pressing site for aggressive public relations. It was one of the largest markets for German goods, and major firms were establishing subsidiaries and factories throughout the United States to accompany America's own corporate expansion within the Federal Republic.[7]

The Achilles' heel in this otherwise healthy relationship between the two countries was the lingering memory of the Nazi past, particularly industry's compromised behavior during the Third Reich. In the immediate wake of the war, industrialists and politicians expressed concern that German industry would face a major crisis of legitimacy as it tried to rebuild. As the public at home and abroad debated the legacies of forced and slave labor, "Aryanized" property, and corporate profiteering, companies like Siemens and Krupp hired publicity experts to disseminate images of industry as the target of unfounded accusations. In the rubble of their factories in 1945, businessmen began mapping out strategies of self-presentation that would persist until this very day. Industrialists portrayed themselves as victims of a totalitarian state that had forced them to use compulsory labor and accommodate themselves to a criminal regime. The Nazis, publicists argued, had stripped companies of their freedom to maneuver and the ability make their own business decisions.[8] German PR advisers spent much energy appealing to the public to ignore claims of industrial complicity and to embrace the industrialist as the bearer of German entrepreneurial traditions and as the protagonist in the story of the country's "miraculous" comeback.[9]

By the end of the 1950s, West German industry was less on the defensive than a decade prior, when factories were dismantled and business leaders had been convicted in Nuremberg. The booming economy of the late 1950s and early 1960s appeared to provide West German industry with more breathing room. As the fruits of prosperity reached the average German, and as unions and the political left came to a modus vivendi with corporate owners and managers, businessmen felt more confident about their abilities to fend off lingering memories of the past. Nonetheless, there were still reminders in the early 1960s of German industry's behavior under National Socialist rule. The German Democratic Republic was the chief purveyor of attacks on ex-Nazis and industrialists active in West German public life.[10] But also in the United States, a flood of polemical books like Tete Tetens's *The New Germany and the Old Nazis* promulgated the already popular view that Adenauer's government harbored Nazi criminals and placated industrialists, who found salvation in the land of the "Economic Miracle."[11] In short, while corporate profits soared and most of the world eagerly conducted business with Germany, images of forced and slave labor and industrialized mass murder persisted. This legacy of industrial crimes so preoccupied West German political and economic elites that they felt compelled to pursue and refine their international public relations strategies well into the 1960s.

Julius Klein and German-American PR

One of the central figures in this attempt to rebuild the public face of Germany's economy was General Julius Klein, one of the more significant, if underresearched, figures in postwar German-American relations. In the 1950s and 1960s, West German companies and the government in Bonn relied on Klein to foster positive perceptions of the Federal Republic and its economic institutions, and to steer the American public away from negative images lingering from World War II. Through his contacts with German firms and, in particular, representatives in the German government, Julius Klein personifies the extent to which publicity in the 1960s remained an often desperate, transatlantic effort to both reckon with and repress the past. As a figure whose career straddled the 1950s and 1960s, Klein also came to embody the tension between Germany's growing economic power, on the one hand, and the emergence of a national discourse about Nazi crimes on the other.

Klein's central role in German-American public relations can be traced back to the founding of the Federal Republic in 1949, when individual firms began to develop aggressive publicity programs both at home and abroad. In 1951, for example, Bayer and IG Farben in dissolution cast about for a PR representative in the United States who would cultivate ties with American businessmen. They settled upon an eccentric Christian activist named Frary von Blomberg. When it was discovered that Blomberg had a somewhat mysterious past that included pro-Nazi speeches in 1942, his services were terminated. Bayer eventually hired Julius Klein. Klein was a retired Jewish army general, a former national commander of the Jewish War Veterans of America, and the director of a successful public relations firm with offices in Chicago, Washington, DC, and Frankfurt am Main.[12] In addition, Klein was an active Republican lobbyist who was in the good graces of both political parties in Washington.[13] Finally, Klein worked behind the scenes during reparations negotiations in the early 1950s and could rightfully boast of enjoying the confidence of Israeli Prime Minister David Ben-Gurion as well as West German Chancellor Konrad Adenauer, two leaders who conferred with Klein throughout the 1950s and 1960s regarding West German-Israeli relations.[14] It is not accidental that a company like Bayer traded a controversial Christian missionary for a pro-business Jewish general with close contacts in Washington and Jerusalem. Given its association with crimes against the Jews, most notably at IG Farben's synthetic rubber factory at Auschwitz-Monowitz, Bayer distanced itself from any suggestion of anti-Semitism and was careful not to invite any more bad publicity by remaining with Blomberg.[15]

Bayer instead pinned its hopes on Julius Klein, who became the most important spokesman for West German business and foreign policy interests in the United States.[16] His chief funding source was the Wiesbaden-based Society for German-American Cooperation (Förderkreis für Deutsch-Amerikanische Zusammenarbeit), essentially a financial cover organization made up of politicians and industrialists who were devoted to fostering German-friendly sentiments in the United States.[17] Throughout the 1950s and 1960s, Klein was paid $150,000 a year[18] to counter accusations of industrial complicity in Nazi crimes and to generate positive stories about West Germany and its economy in the American press. He represented a number of clients besides Bayer, including Mannesmann, Rheinmetall, Daimler Benz, and the Flick concern, as well as the West German state of Hessen. His firm also received fees from property owners seeking to recover assets seized by the United States.[19] His most notable and controversial client in this area was Deutsche Bank head Hermann Josef Abs, whom Klein had met through Israeli Prime Minister Ben-Gurion. Portrayed by critics as "Hitler's banker," Abs was seeking from the Eisenhower administration the return of $600 million of assets seized by the United States during the war.[20]

In the late 1950s and 1960s, Klein undertook his most controversial public relations task when he faced off against the Conference on Jewish Material Claims against Germany, which represented former wartime forced laborers seeking compensation from some of the largest West German firms.[21] Klein represented both IG Farben in 1957 and Rheinmetall in 1966 during their respective mediations with the Claims Conference.[22] When IG Farben agreed to a financial settlement, Klein issued a statement denying the company's legal and moral liability stemming from the employment of Jewish labor in Auschwitz. In press releases and in speeches by friends in the United States Congress, Klein portrayed the payments not as confessions of guilt or responsibility, but as magnanimous gestures on the part of West German firms, which themselves had been "manipulated" by Hitler and the SS.[23]

In addition to his rather notorious work on behalf of German firms, Klein also worked with members of the West German government, including Chancellors Konrad Adenauer and Ludwig Erhard, Foreign Minister Heinrich von Brentano, and Adenauer's chief of staff, State Secretary Hans Globke. Klein's closest confidant in Bonn, Globke was undoubtedly the most controversial figure in West German public life. He had written one of the official commentaries on the Nuremberg racial laws of 1935, which defined and categorized Jews, stripped them of their citizenship, and banned sexual relations and marriage between "Aryans" and "non-Aryans."[24] While the postwar revival of Globke's career has remained the source of discussion for fifty years,[25] the state secretary's private papers have only recently been made available, and we can now develop a clearer picture of how actively

Globke worked with PR agencies in America to better the reputation of Germany.[26] For his part, Klein, over the course of the late 1950s and 1960s, maintained confidential contact with Globke regarding the Federal Republic's public image in the United States and Germany. Together, they successfully orchestrated the crafting of pro-German speeches by American politicians, for example, and the placing of German-friendly blurbs in newspapers and political publications.

In the spring of 1960, Klein was at the peak of his career, responsible for publicity for Konrad Adenauer's visit to the United States. With a recent wave of anti-Semitic actions around Germany and Europe in the news, Klein and Globke worried that the vocal response to these events could tarnish this visit by one of America's closest allied leaders and leave a scar on German-American relations.[27] In conjunction with Globke, Klein encouraged one of his political friends, former Nuremberg prosecutor Senator Thomas Dodd of Connecticut, to address the problems in Germany, namely, the defacement of Cologne's synagogue in 1959 and the subsequent appearance of swastikas and the desecration of Jewish cemeteries throughout West Germany. In his long speech on the Senate floor, entitled "Anti-Semitism, the Swastika Epidemic, and Communism," Dodd attempted to place these anti-Semitic acts in a Cold War context. After paying lengthy reference to the murder of six million Jews and the reawakened memories of "the most terrifying acts of Nazi bestiality," the senator argued that anti-Semitism was not a specific German problem but, more than anything, "a tool of the communist conspiracy." Dodd launched into a vociferous attack on communism and the treatment of Jews in the Eastern bloc, while referring to the thirty thousand Jews in Germany "who enjoy complete freedom of religion, complete equality before the law, complete acceptance." He also spoke of the origins of Nazi anti-Semitism, which could be attributed essentially to one individual, Hitler, and his "psychopathic hatred of Jews." After praising the Germans' postwar embrace of democracy and economic freedom, he addressed at length the issue of ex-Nazis in Adenauer's government. While not denying that some "house-cleaning" had to be done, he downplayed the influence of ex-Nazi Party members and defended the innocence of Refugee Minister Theodor Oberländer, Interior Minister Gerhard Schröder, and, at great length, Hans Globke.[28] The state secretary, he argued, had written his Nuremberg commentaries only in a "torment of conscience" and had purposely put loopholes into the laws so that Jews could take advantage of them and save themselves from Nazi persecution.[29] With this speech, Dodd had laid out clearly the position of Bonn and its spokespeople: the Federal Republic, because of its booming economy and its devotion to the democratic Western alliance, was a necessary ally in the fight against communism. It was rife with neither anti-Semites nor ex-Nazis, and the American public should put to rest any lingering resentment toward their former enemy.

Thomas Dodd's speech represents a significant moment in the West German and American publics' confrontation with the Holocaust.[30] Dodd's interpretation of Nazi crimes as emanating from a single, demonic figure in Hitler was not new. Nor was his attempt to link the reputation of the Federal Republic to Cold War struggles.

What *was* new was his direct and lengthy reference to Jewish victimization in a public forum, his defense of ex-Nazis notwithstanding. Gone was the vague language of "past misdeeds" and "totalitarian crimes." Senator Dodd had inaugurated the decade with a remarkably open reference to the persecution of Jews, even if his ultimate and ironic aim was to protect the very country and people who had perpetrated the crimes he outlined. With its focus on anticommunism and its defense of West Germany, Dodd's speech satisfied policy makers in Bonn and Washington. The speech was printed in the Congressional Record of 1960, and Julius Klein immediately sent fifty copies to Globke, to be distributed around Germany.[31]

The Dodd speech was only one example of how German-American PR, as personified at the time by Julius Klein, was a transatlantic enterprise that entailed the sometimes-puzzling combination of promoting the West German economy, confronting past crimes, and openly defending ex-Nazis who exercised political power. Indeed, for Julius Klein, this concern for the reputation of West Germany's public figures took on an exaggerated importance disproportionate to any real or perceived threat that personal attacks represented. Whenever Hans Globke was criticized for his past during the 1960s, Klein came to his defense, spreading the word that the state secretary had been a devout Catholic and a great friend to the Jews during the Third Reich and afterwards in his support of reparations to Israel and Holocaust survivors. Klein also came to the defense of President Heinrich Lübke and, later, Chancellor Kurt Georg Kiesinger, both of whom were assailed in the international press for their association with the Nazi Party.[32] Not surprisingly, in response to his vigorous defense of former Nazis and West German companies, Klein incurred the wrath of the Jewish War Veterans Association, which distanced itself from its former commander. Even his close associates were dismayed. Wrote one friend with respect to Globke (a man who, he argued "had Jewish blood on his hands"): "How much more proof is needed before definite action—even at the risk of losing some German business—is undertaken by Julius to eliminate this monster from his influential position? For that matter, stop the reawakened NAZIS."[33]

As these condemnations of Klein illustrate, the easy flow of West German political and business money across the Atlantic did not go unnoticed or uncriticized in America. In May 1963, the Senate Foreign Relations Committee, under the chairmanship of William Fulbright, heard testimony from Klein, who was under suspicion for having received at least $400,000 from the German government and a "mysterious group of West German industrialists."[34] Klein was under investigation as a registered agent of the West German government. He had raised the funds to promote the cause of the Federal Republic during the 1960 Eisenhower-Khrushchev summit, an act that was not as such illegal but which, according to American law, had to be accompanied by complete disclosure of financial backers.[35] The hearing did not lead to any charges, but when Klein's industrial clients learned that their connection in America had been cross-examined for his lobbying activities, they withdrew their contracts with him, and Klein suffered a serious loss of business and prestige in Germany. To control the damage, Klein asked Senator Dodd to fly to Germany and lobby on his behalf. Dodd did so during a trip in 1964, but his willingness to help a friend and fellow cold warrior, as well as other accusations of graft, eventually led to a public scandal and Dodd's own censure in the Senate in 1967.[36]

Further controversy came in 1966, when Klein lobbied on behalf of Rheinmetall during its slave labor negotiations with the Claims Conference. The company and Klein insisted on the firm's lack of responsibility for its use of forced labor under Hitler.[37] But by now the American public was much more wary of such overt campaigns to assert the innocence of German industry, and Jewish organizations pressured the US government (unsuccessfully) to cancel a $75 million weapons contract with the arms manufacturer. In the aftermath of a settlement, Klein was again queried in the House of Representatives about his relationship to West German industry, and his testimony, in turn, provoked the anger of the Senate Foreign Relations committee, which was investigating the activities of foreign lobbyists.[38]

By that time Klein had already begun to fade out of transatlantic politics, having angered the Kennedy administration by criticizing its overtures to the Soviet Union.[39] His German clients severed almost all of their ties with him after the Dodd controversy and the Rheinmetall protests, and, by the end of the decade, Klein no longer was a key player in German-American public relations. But he maintained his close international connections, and he lobbied German companies like Volkswagen and philanthropies like the Thyssen Foundation to support a variety of causes on behalf of American Jews and German-American relations, most notably the building of a national shrine to the Jewish war dead in Washington.[40] He also kept up his correspondence with Hans Globke and penned a memoir, never to be published, that included a chapter bearing the title "My Friendship with Dr. Globke."[41] In one of his last letters to Globke, Klein bemoaned the demonstrations against the Vietnam War playing out in the streets of Chicago in 1968.[42]

Memory, the Economy, and the Cold War

The story of Julius Klein provokes a host of questions. How does one account for Klein's publicity activities on behalf of West German industry and the West German government? How would somebody so identified with both the American Jewish community and the state of Israel come to the defense of ex-Nazis? Why did West German interests need such a spokesperson in the United States? Certainly, questions about Klein's personal motivations demand a social-psychological explanation, one that addresses the desire of Jews (particularly those of German heritage) to fit into American culture by proving their anticommunist credentials while maintaining some support of their country of origin.[43]

Shlomo Shafir has argued that while West German foreign policy makers paid careful attention to (and often exaggerated) Jewish influences in American public life, Jewish Americans also worked with West Germany, often ambivalently, in order to promote Jews' social position in the United States, the well-being of Israel, and, indirectly, "the evolution of a better Germany."[44] Klein certainly fits this model of the American Jew of German descent who was able, through participating in the fight against communism and the support of Atlantic unity, to promote a form of assimilation previously denied to Jews. But with his rabid hatred of communism and his direct financial links to German companies, Klein was rather unrepresentative of American Jewry. Unlike the majority of Jews, he was a hard-core Republican, and his attempts to defend democracy translated into a deep-seated devotion to a country that many American Jews associated with genocide. While Jewish perceptions of West Germany were ambivalent and often tortured, Klein's transition from supporter of reparations to seeming lackey of West German interests increasingly indicated a Germanophilia that few of his colleagues could comprehend and many came to condemn.

Regardless of his anomalous position within the Jewish community, it is important to place Klein's pro-German activities in its broader Cold War context, when the Berlin Wall and the Cuban Missile Crisis preoccupied the world in the early 1960s. Julius Klein did embody the eagerness of many prominent Americans—whether politicians or businessmen, whether Jewish or not—to promote the stability of West Germany as a bulwark against communism. In his own words, Klein referred to his work as "'political' public relations"[45]—"for the Germans—for the free world."[46] For Klein and his backers, "political" PR was inevitably "economic" PR. West Germany's success and reputation were grounded in its ability to produce and export high quality manufactured goods. As long as the world identified the Federal Republic's economy as its greatest asset, a company's fate, in a sense, mirrored that of the entire nation. Conversely, from the perspective of an individual company, portraying the Federal Republic and its leaders in a benevolent light would have a salutary effect on the reputation of German industry and thus increase international business and corporate profits. The government in Bonn and business leaders throughout the Federal Republic knew how closely the American public was watching the trials of former Nazi perpetrators. With slave labor negotiations and news stories about potential boycotts of German companies, like Rheinmetall in 1966, PR for the West German economy became a key aspect of the Federal Republic's foreign policy.

Klein's own reflections on his work shed further light on the relationship between Nazi crimes, business complicity, and transatlantic public relations during the Cold War. In a confidential report from the early 1960s entitled "Public Relations für Deutschland," Klein repeatedly insisted that the legacy of corporate complicity with Nazism (which he falsely argued had been totally disproved in Nuremberg) represented a danger to the success of West German industry, which was so essential to defending the "free world." Since those companies suspected of past crimes "represent a considerable portion of [Germany's] total industrial potential ... the West German government should pay close attention to the efforts of these companies and introduce any public relations measures that can correct false impressions."[47] In short, Klein saw West Germans' and Americans' mounting attention to the recent past as potentially damaging to both countries' economic interests. This aversion to a wider discussion of Nazi crimes is ironic, given that Klein always remained a self-identified Jew and a supporter, at least in the abstract, of German *Wiedergutmachung*. Klein felt that there should be discussion of Nazi crimes, but that it had to be kept to a minimum lest it compromise the good faith efforts that he felt Germany had already demonstrated through its reparations agreement with Israel in 1952.[48] Klein and his coworkers in the United States and West Germany saw memory as the first link in a chain of developments that could hurt both countries. Public trials and published critiques of German industry, suggested Klein, promoted Soviet attacks on politicians like Globke and businessmen like Friedrich Flick, thereby damaging the reputation of Germany and the Western fight against communism. Klein surely understood that German industrialists had not emerged from the Nazi years untainted. But he did subscribe to a view prevalent among American and West German conservatives that private institutions had had very little room to maneuver in a totalitarian state and thus could not ultimately be held accountable for the use of forced labor.[49] Whatever his true understanding of corporate criminality, to Klein, historical memory simply came with too high a price tag—namely, the potential for lost business with West Germany, damaged reputations, and the weakening of a Cold War ally.

Julius Klein's story begs the question of why West Germans felt the need to promote their economy so aggressively to the American public in the first place. Why, when their country's economy was expanding at a record pace, did political and business elites still rely on shopworn arguments about German industry's "innocence" under National Socialism? This particular attention to German industry and the reputation of capitalism was not just a pragmatic reflection of international tensions and the need to sell products in the United States. Rather, these Cold War exigencies converged with the increasing public attention to the Holocaust and the role of memory in West German society itself during the 1960s. With each new moment of public memory—whether it was the Eichmann and Auschwitz trials or the parliamentary debates on extending the statute of limitations for prosecuting Nazis—came more precise attacks on German industry's contribution to Nazi crimes and the power of big business in the Federal Republic. Writers such as Kurt Pritzkoleit and Bernt Engelmann published books that specifically pointed to the continuities between the Nazi economy, its leaders, and the wealthy business moguls in the Federal Republic.[50] Continuing a discussion that had already begun with the founding of West Germany, these writers argued that Bonn granted inordinate political and economic power to individual bankers and industrialists, like Friedrich Flick, Alfried Krupp von Bohlen und Halbach, and Hermann Josef Abs, who had played key roles in the Nazi economy and who presided over a vast network of corporate holdings. Moreover, these discourses on industrial guilt dovetailed with more scholarly attempts in West Germany to question the nature of late capitalism and its relationship to systems of domination.[51]

In short, the legacy of corporate crimes had multiple components and symbols, manifested in the GDR's ideological attacks on West German "fascism," the domestic debate over the power of industry, the Old and New Left's varied analyses of capitalism, and the student movement's own critique of free enterprise.[52] Moreover, the Federal Press Office's study from 1962 suggests the extent to which the rest of the world simultaneously marveled at the West German economy and feared that it could lead to new forms of "imperialism" and global domination. German-American PR was therefore a direct expression of elite fears that the link between capitalism and criminality would somehow undermine the Federal Republic's position in the world economy. In this regard, we can see how, during the prosperous years of the 1960s, economic success at once alleviated and reinforced the anxieties associated with both the Cold War and growing public awareness of the Holocaust.

In discussing memory and the economy in the 1960s, one should not underestimate West Germans' and Americans' engagement with Nazi crimes during the 1950s or publicists' attempts to divert attention from corporate misconduct. As I have indicated, during the early "Miracle Years,"[53] company and government leaders were already promoting the rapidly growing economy as the source of Germany's salvation.[54] The legacies of Auschwitz, forced and slave labor, and mechanized murder were never far from the minds of these policy makers. But these damning images manifested themselves more indirectly and abstractly than in the 1960s. Nazi crimes informed discussions about totalitarianism, mass society, and the nature of Hitler's particular evil rather than public discourses about the extermination of Europe's Jews.[55] The Nazi past was seen more as a "mystical riddle"[56] than as a problem of individual guilt and national self-understanding.

Axel Schildt has portrayed 1958 as the inaugural year of the "long 1960s," a decade that saw "the return of the past."[57] While the past, arguably, had never gone away, events like the Ulm Einsatzgruppen trial and the wave of anti-Semitism in the late 1950s did spark a new historical consciousness that would remain present through the following decade and beyond. Ironically—or perhaps quite plausibly—it was at the very moment when economic prosperity reached the average West German[58] that discussions of Auschwitz and mass crimes moved squarely into the open. The years of reconstruction were over, and West Germans felt more comfortable examining their compromised past and, by extension, the role of the economy in the Holocaust. If, in the 1950s and 1960s, the economy provided for everyday comforts and international respect, it was also the site of harsh and incriminating memories.

Transatlantic public relations reflected this tension embodied in the economy—at once the site of crimes during the Third Reich and the motor of prosperity and national regeneration. PR in the 1960s was a Janus-faced enterprise, partly pragmatic and partly a genuine effort to grapple with Germany's past. It reflected both a calculating desire to defend the free market, sometimes at the cost of historical distortion, and an emerging willingness to confront Nazi crimes in the name of a "new," more responsible Germany. Memory, as manifested in

PR, was an active process of selection and creation. It necessarily played out in the open, during a decade in which, according to Detlef Siegfried, "the public … served as the catalyst for a self-conscious debate about the norms and values of a post–National Socialist West German society."[59] Julius Klein—as representative of Jewish-American interests, fair-weather champion of reparations, passionate spokesman of big business, and public defender of ex-Nazis—embodied the complex and ambivalent nature of memory that defined the long 1960s.

Notes

1. Secretary of Peter Gilow to Herr Diehl of the Presse-und Informationsamt der Bundesregierung, 19 October 1962, in Peter Gilow Papers, Box 7 (Clients), file "1962 July to 1969 Dec. (Bundespresseamt)," J. Walter Thompson Company Archives, Frankfurt Office Records, Hartman Center for Sales, Advertising, & Marketing History in the Rare Book, Manuscript, and Special Collections Library, Duke University, Durham, North Carolina (hereafter, J. Walter Thompson/Duke).

2. See packet of surveys attached to letter from Reg. Dir. Dr. H. Zühlsdorff im Bundespresseamt to Peter Gilow of JWT Frankfurt, 11 July 1962, Gilow Papers, Box 7 (Clients), file "1962 July to 1969 Dec. (Bundespresseamt)," J. Walter Thompson/Duke.

3. For some recent publications that deal with *Vergangenheitsbewältigung* in the 1950s and 1960s, see the review article by Alf Lüdtke, "'Coming to Terms with the Past': Illusions of Remembering, Ways of Forgetting Nazism in West Germany," *Journal of Modern History* 65 (September 1993): 542–72; Norbert Frei, *Vergangenheitspolitik: Die Anfänge der Bundesrepublik und die NS-Vergangenheit* (Munich, 1996); Gary S. Schaal and Andreas Wöll, eds., *Vergangenheitsbewältigung: Modelle der politischen und sozialen Integration in der bundesdeutschen Nachkriegsgeschichte* (Baden-Baden, 1997); Ulrich Brochhagen, *Nach Nürnberg: Vergangenheitsbewältigung und Westintegration in der Ära Adenauer* (Hamburg, 1994).

4. Quote by Norbert Frei in Detlef Siegfried, "Zwischen Aufarbeitung und Schlußstrich: Der Umgang mit der NS-Vergangenheit in den beiden deutschen Staaten 1958 bis 1969," in *Dynamische Zeiten: Die 60er Jahre in den beiden deutschen Gesellschaften*, ed. Axel Schildt, Detlef Siegfried, and Karl Christian Lammers (Hamburg, 2000), 77–113.

5. "Internalization" is Siegfried's phrase in ibid., 109.

6. For two strong collections of recent research on business and National Socialism, see Lothar Gall and Manfred Pohl, eds., *Unternehmen im Nationalsozialismus* (Munich, 1998), and Irmtrud Wojak and Peter Hayes, *"Arisierung" im Nationalsozialismus: Volksgemeinschaft, Raub und Gedächtnis* (Frankfurt am Main, 2000). See also Paul Erker, *Industrie-Eliten in der NS Zeit: Anpassungsbereitschaft und Eigeninteresse von Unternehmern in der Rüstung-und Kriegswirtschaft, 1936–1945* (Passau, 1994); Peter Hayes, *Industry and Ideology: IG Farben in the Nazi Era* (Cambridge, 1987); Neil Gregor, *Daimler-Benz in the Third Reich* (New Haven, 1998); Hans Mommsen and Manfred Grieger, *Das Volkswagenwerk und seine Arbeiter im Dritten Reich* (Düsseldorf, 1996). For excellent introductions to the theme of compulsory labor, see Ulrich Herbert, *Hitler's Foreign Workers: Enforced Foreign Labor in Germany under the Third Reich* (Cambridge, 1997); and Norbert Frei, Sybille Steinbacher, and Bernd C. Wagner, eds., *Ausbeutung, Vernichtung, Öffentlichkeit: Neue Studien zur nationalsozialistischen Lagerpolitik* (Munich, 2000).

7. Heinz Hartmann, *Amerikanische Firmen in Deutschland* (Cologne and Opladen, 1963).

8. This view of industrial impotence during World War II has been challenged by a number of recent books. See, e.g., Piotr Setkiewicz, "Häftlingserbeit im KZ Auschwitz III-Monowitz: Die

Frage nach der Wirtschaftlichkeit der Arbeit," in *Die nationalsozialistischen Konzentrationslager: Entwicklung und Struktur*, 2 vols., ed. Ulrich Herbert et al. (Göttingen, 1998), 2:558–83.

9. On industrialists' postwar portrayal of the Nazi years, see S. Jonathan Wiesen, *West German Industry and the Challenge of the Nazi Past, 1945–1955* (Chapel Hill, 2001).

10. See, e.g., Nationale Front des Demokratischen Deutschlands, *Brown Book: War and Nazi Criminals in West Germany* (East Berlin, 1965).

11. Tete Tetens, *The New Germany and the Old Nazis* (New York, 1961); an earlier book dealing with this same theme is Alistair Horne, *Return to Power: A Report on the New Germany* (New York, 1956). The most notorious example of an "ex-Nazi" in public life was Adenauer's state secretary, Hans Globke. On Globke and other compromised figures in power, see John P. Teschke, *Hitler's Legacy: West Germany Confronts the Aftermath of the Third Reich* (New York, 1999); Klaus Gotto, ed., *Der Staatssekretär Adenauers: Persönlichkeit und politisches Wirken Hans Globkes* (Stuttgart, 1980), and Brochhagen, *Nach Nürnberg*.

12. For introductions to Klein's career, see Benjamin Ferencz, *Less than Slaves: Jewish Forced Labor and the Quest for Compensation* (Cambridge, 1979), 134–36; Shlomo Shafir, *Ambiguous Relations: The American Jewish Community and Germany Since 1945* (Detroit, 1999), 186–88; *The Investigation of Senator Thomas J. Dodd* [Hearings before the Senate Select Committee on Standards and Conduct, June–July 1966] (Part 1, Relationship with Julius Klein); and James Boyd, *Above the Law* (New York, 1968), 206.

13. In 1954, Klein unsuccessfully sought the Republican senatorial nomination in Illinois.

14. On Klein's early involvement in West German–Israeli relations, see Constantin Goschler, *Wiedergutmachung: Westdeutschland und die Verfolgten des Nationalsozialismus (1945–1954)* (Munich, 1992), 275ff.; see also the transcripts of the *Monitor* interview with Julius Klein (15 July 1966), 6, in NL Hans Globke (I-070), File 033/1, Archiv für Christlich-Demokratische Politik an der Adenauer Stiftung, Sankt Augustin (ACDP). "You may be proud of your important contribution to normalize the relations between Israel and Western Germany." David Ben-Gurion to Klein, 4 August 1965, NL Globke, I-070-033/2, ACDP. On Klein's tendency to exaggerate his importance during reparations negotiations, see Shafir, *Ambiguous Relations*, 419n19.

15. On the sometimes bizarre correspondences between Blomberg and Bayer, see NL Ulrich Haberland, 271/1.1.4, Bayer Achive, Leverkusen (BAL). For the correspondences between the company and Julius Klein, see NL Haberland, 271/1.1.5, BAL.

16. Klein was not the only PR firm to represent German interests. There was also the Roy Bernard agency in New York City, as well as the work of the various German consulates throughout the United States.

17. On this organization, see Klein's speech to the Wirtschaftspolitische Gesellschaft in Bonn, 1956, NL Otto A.H. Vogel, Box 148, Industrie- und Handelskammer für Augsburg und Schwaben, Augsburg. See also *The Investigation of Senator Thomas J. Dodd*, 10. The organization published a newsletter called *Überseebericht* in Germany and *Overseas Report* in America.

18. Drew Pearson, "Dodd and the Ex-Nazi," *New York Post*, 9 February 1966.

19. See Fritz Berg to Ulrich Haberland, regarding Klein's activities to protect German property abroad, 7 January 1960, NL Haberland, 271/1.1.5., BAL.

20. *Monitor* interview with Klein (15 July 1966), 3, in NL Globke (I-070/033/1), ACDP.

21. On the activities of the Claims Conference, see Ferencz, *Less than Slaves*; Ernst Katzenstein, "Jewish Claims Conference und die Wiedergutmachung nationalsozialistischen Unrechts," in *Die Freiheit des Anderen: Festschrift für Martin Hirsch*, ed. Hans Jochen Vogel, Helmut Simon, and Adalbert Podlech (Baden-Baden, 1981), 219–41; and Shafir, *Ambiguous Relations*.

22. Ferencz, *Less than Slaves*, 136.

23. "That such a private settlement can be made without government pressure is a sign of the new spirit in Germany which seeks to make redress for the wrongs of the Nazi era." Quoted from "Cartel with a Conscience," *Chicago Daily Sun-Times*, 7 February 1957, 35. See also Ferencz, *Less than Slaves*, 49. On the portrayal of IG Farben as a company "forced to use the concentration camp labor by the SS," see the speech of New York Congressman Herbert Zelenko in

the *U.S. Congressional Record—House of Representatives*, 14 February 1957, 2064. On the IG settlement, see Constantin Goschler, "Streit um Almosen: Die Entschädigung der KZ-Zwangsarbeiter durch die deutsche Nachkriegsindustrie," in *Sklavenarbeit im KZ* (*Dachauer Hefte 2*) (Munich, 1993), 175–94.

24. Globke, in fact, had never been a member of the Nazi Party. See Hans-Peter Schwarz, *Konrad Adenauer: A German Politician and Statesman in a Period of War, Revolution and Reconstruction* (Oxford, 1995), 466.

25. See Brochhagen, *Nach Nürnberg*, passim; and Teschke, *Hitler's Legacy*, 173–220.

26. This essay relies primarily on the recently opened Julius Klein correspondences in the Globke files (NL Globke, I-070), ACDP. Some of Klein's private papers can also be found in the Jewish War Veterans Archives in Washington, DC. Studies that have drawn on this archive include Shafir, *Ambiguous Relations*; and Goschler, *Wiedergutmachung*.

27. On this wave of anti-Semitism in 1959–60, see Siegfried, "Zwischen Aufarbeitung und Schlußstrich," 79.

28. Oberländer had taken part in the Hitler putsch of 1923 and risen in the ranks of the Nazi Party. Schröder had been a member of the SA.

29. Speech by Senator Dodd in the *Proceedings and Debates of the 86th Congress, 2nd Session*, 15 March 1960, 5561–70.

30. According to Peter Novick, the term "Holocaust" was not in common parlance before the late 1960s. I will therefore be using the term as a useful anachronism to represent the Nazis' genocide of Europe's Jews. See Peter Novick, *The Holocaust in American Life* (Boston, 1999), chap. 9.

31. Major General Kenneth Buchanan, VP and General Manager of Julius Klein Public Relations Inc. to Globke, 5 April 1950, NL Globke, I-070-031/2, ACDP.

32. On the public discourse about Lübke and Kiesinger, see Bernd-A. Rusinek, "Von der Entdeckung der NS-Vergangenheit zum generellen Faschismusverdacht—akademische Diskurse in der Bundesrepublik der 60er Jahre," in Schildt, Siegfried, and Lammers, *Dynamische Zeiten*, 114–47.

33. Fred Schiller to [undecipherable name], 24 October 1961, NL Globke, I-070-031/2, ACDP.

34. "Ex-General, Lobbyist for Bonn, Testifies at Closed Hearing," *Washington Post*, 15 May 1963.

35. Ibid.

36. See Steven Schada, "The Dodd Censure: A Case Study in Senatorial Ethics" (MA thesis, Western Illinois University, 1972).

37. "Ex-Nazi Magnates Won't Pay Debts," *Denver Post*, 4 March 1966. On the details of the Claims Conference negotiations, see Ferencz, *Less than Slaves*, 130–54.

38. See, respectively, *Proceedings and Debates of the 89th Congress, 2nd Session*, 22 June 1966, 13909, and 14 July 1966, 15658.

39. Shafir, *Ambiguous Relations*, 188.

40. Aktennotiz für das Archiv des National Shrine to the Jewish War Dead, Washington, DC, 30 December 1968, NL Globke, I-070-033/2, ACDP. Neither organization supported Klein. Volkswagen cited its "policy of not contributing to religious groups." See Arthur R. Railton of Volkswagen of America, Inc. to Klein, 21 January 1969, in ibid.

41. Klein to Globke, 13 January 1969, NL Globke, I-070-033/2, ACDP.

42. Klein to Globke, 29 August 1968, NL Globke, I-070-033/2, ACDP.

43. Klein's grandfather had come from Germany in 1848. On the relationship of American Jews to West Germany, see Shafir, *Ambiguous Relations*, and Novick, *The Holocaust in American Life*.

44. Shafir, *Ambiguous Relations*, 360.

45. Klein to Globke, 6 April 1960, NL Globke, I-070-031/2, ACDP.

46. *Monitor* interview with Klein, 15 July 1966, 3.

47. "Public Relations für Deutschland" (confidential report by Julius Klein's Frankfurt a.M office), undated, ca. 1960, NL Globke, I-070-031/2, ACDP.

48. Klein to Globke, 13 January 1969, NL Globke, I-070-032/2, ACDP.

49. For a representative expression of this view, see Hans Eckhardt Kannapin, *Wirtschaft unter Zwang* (Cologne, 1966).

50. Bernt Engelmann, *Meine Freunde, die Manager* (Darmstadt, 1963); Engelmann, *Unternehmen ohne Unternehmer* (Berlin, 1966); and Kurt Pritzkoleit, *Gott erhält die Mächtigen: Rück- und Rundblick auf den deutschen Wohlstand* (Düsseldorf, 1963).

51. See, e.g., the post-1960s work by Jürgen Habermas, *Legitimationsprobleme im Spätkapitalismus* (Frankfurt am Main, 1973).

52. On the political left, critiques of capitalism, and generational conflicts, see, as an introduction, Anselm Doering-Manteuffel, "Eine neue Stufe der Verwestlichung? Kultur und Öffentlichkeit in den 60er Jahren," in Schildt, Siegfried, and Lammers, *Dynamische Zeiten*, 661–72. On protests against capitalism, see Carole Fink, Philipp Gassert, and Detlef Junker, eds., *1968: The World Transformed* (Cambridge, 1998), 17.

53. Hanna Schissler, ed., *The Miracle Years: A Cultural History of West Germany, 1949–1968* (Princeton, 2001).

54. On publicity on behalf of the West German economy, see A. J. Nicholls, *Freedom with Responsibility: The Social Market Economy in Germany, 1918–1963* (Oxford, 1994).

55. On these multiple discourses in the 1950s, see Axel Schildt, *Moderne Zeiten: Freizeit, Massenmedien und "Zeitgeist" in der Bundesrepublik der 50er Jahre* (Hamburg, 1995).

56. Siegfried, "Zwischen Aufarbeitung und Schlußstrich," 87.

57. Ibid., 78.

58. On the transformation of West Germany into a consumer society by the end of the 1950s, see Michael Wildt, "Privater Konsum in Westdeutschland in den 50er Jahren," in *Modernisierung im Wiederaufbau: Die westdeutsche Gesellschaft der 50er Jahre*, ed. Axel Schildt and Arnold Sywottek (Bonn, 1993), 275–89.

59. Siegfried, "Zwischen Aufarbeitung und Schlußstrich," 109.

Chapter 18

AUSCHWITZ AND THE NUCLEAR *SONDERWEG*
Nuclear Weapons and the Shadow of the Nazi Past

Susanna Schrafstetter

൙

In 1954, the West German Chancellor Konrad Adenauer forswore the development of nuclear weapons by the Federal Republic as a precondition for West Germany's admission into NATO.[1] The Federal Republic's renunciation of nuclear
weapons can be seen both as a beginning and an endpoint. It was the last of the
Allied restrictions on a defeated aggressor, it marked the integration of the newly
established country into the military alliance of the West, and it indicated a
step toward West Germany's gradual assumption of sovereignty.[2] Gaining sovereignty and equality with other European states was a primary goal of Adenauer's
Westpolitik, which relied for its success on close integration with the West. The
Western Allies, however, still fearful of a future resurgent Germany, demanded a
German renunciation of all weapons of mass destruction in return for their assent
to German rearmament. Adenauer agreed to the terms but was at pains to stress
that Bonn's renunciation was regarded *rebus sic stantibus*, and would therefore be
subject to future reconsideration.

Indeed, almost immediately after signing the 1954 declaration, Bonn signaled
that it was unwilling to preclude the nuclear option forever, and began to press for
revision of the treaty obligations. Three main reasons for this are apparent. First,
the nuclear option was seen as a powerful diplomatic lever in negotiations with the
Soviets, especially in relation to German unification, and it augmented Adenauer's
"position of strength" approach toward the Soviet Union. Second, the ascent of
Britain and France into the "nuclear club" in 1952 and 1960, respectively, underscored the Federal Republic's second class status within the Western alliance.
Finally, the lack of influence over NATO nuclear strategy worried the Germans, as
it was becoming clear to many in Bonn that should the Cold War turn into a hot

war, Germany would be transformed into a nuclear battlefield over which the Germans themselves would have no control.[3] The latter concern was compounded by the launch of the Soviet satellite Sputnik in 1957, which was seen to have ended the nuclear invulnerability of the United States. The Germans—in common with other European nations—harbored increasing doubts over the credibility of the American security guarantee for Western Europe. To reassure the Germans, the Eisenhower administration deployed American nuclear weapons in the Federal Republic. The nuclear delivery systems were administered through a dual key system in which the actual warheads remained under American control.

NATO plans for a "nuclearization" of the newly established West German Army, the Bundeswehr, provoked a heated debate within West Germany. Politicians and pundits, nuclear scientists and novelists, Christian leaders, and the German Campaign against Nuclear Death (GCND)—all voiced their fears of nuclear extinction. The antinuclear campaign of 1958 to 1960 was closely intertwined with the memory of Germany's recent past. The decision to provide nuclear weapons to the Bundeswehr reignited fears of a powerful and reactionary German military and of the devastation it wrought in two world wars.[4] Despite initial success, by the early 1960s the antinuclear movement had lost momentum. A government campaign focusing on the Soviet threat and communist infiltration of the GCND had a powerful impact on the population, which felt safer under the American nuclear umbrella than outside of it. Disagreements among the antinuclear activists also contributed to the decline of the movement. When, for example, an antinuclear platform led to a disappointing result in a July 1958 election in North Rhine-Westphalia, the Trade Union Federation (Deutscher Gewerkschaftsbund, DGB) and the Social Democratic Party (SPD) withdrew their support from the antinuclear movement.[5]

While domestic protest had abated by the early 1960s, the international debate on the Federal Republic's nuclear status was only heating up. Two issues dominated the agenda: the Multilateral Nuclear Force (MLF)[6] and the Nuclear Non-Proliferation Treaty (NPT).[7] First introduced by the Eisenhower administration and again proposed by that of John F. Kennedy, the MLF—a multinational nuclear surface fleet under NATO command—was designed to give Bonn a limited role in the nuclear defense of the Western Alliance. It was hoped that the scheme would satisfy West German national nuclear aspirations. Supporters of the MLF in Washington also sought to curtail Britain's independent nuclear role and to constrain the French nuclear arsenal within a NATO command structure. Various plans for a multilateral force were discussed between 1960 and 1967 but little progress was made. The idea of the fleet eventually sank as the United States gave priority to a nuclear nondissemination agreement, which was signed in August 1968. Progress in the negotiations for the NPT had been blocked by the Soviet Union's objection that the MLF constituted a form of nuclear proliferation to West Germany. In short, the Kremlin would only sign a nondissemination agreement if the MLF were dropped. West Germany finally acceded to the NPT in November 1969. By that time, the country had intensively debated its nuclear status for well over a decade. While that debate was going on, the trauma of Germany's past had come to the surface in the Federal Republic. The process of *Vergangenheitsbewältigung*, of coming to terms with the past, painfully reminded the Germans that the end of the prewar era had not yet arrived, contrary to Chancellor Ludwig Erhard's proclamation in 1965.[8]

Two decades after Auschwitz, West German society as well as the Federal Republic's external allies and opponents were compelled to face two interrelated questions: should a German state be allowed the option of possessing weapons of mass destruction, and how should Germans deal with the legacy of mass murder? West German *Geschichtspolitik*, exemplified by the decision to provide financial compensation to victims of Nazism, was part of an effort to erase the stigma of Germany's past, a stigma that manifested itself in the externally imposed renunciation of nuclear weapons. Although West German nuclear policy and allied restrictions upon it were in large measure consequences of Germany's past, this topic has been examined primarily in the context of Cold War bipolarity and NATO policy. Not enough effort has been made to analyze how the process of *Vergangenheitsbewältigung* influenced the debate over West German nuclear weapons.[9] This essay, then, will investigate how the Nazi past was deployed as an argument in discussions about the Federal Republic's nuclear status in the 1960s.

A Nuclear Role within an Alliance Structure?

During the Kennedy administration, the United States regarded the prevention of Franco-German nuclear collaboration under the 1963 Franco-German Friendship Treaty as one of the most immediate benefits of a NATO nuclear force.[10] In the long run, American fears focused on a Federal Republic that, frustrated over its second-class status within NATO, might begin to explore a path toward unification and neutrality.[11] The fear of resurgent German military power, unconstrained by an alliance structure, was a major motivation behind plans to grant the Federal Republic some limited control over nuclear weapons. The prospect of a neutral Germany not only raised concerns about Soviet influence, it also brought to mind the historical example of Imperial Germany, which was seen as having been a dangerous, loose cannon in the heart of Europe. This argument was used by supporters of the MLF both in the US State Department and in the Federal Republic. Opponents of the MLF also drew from the well of German history to justify their rejection of the scheme. In *Der Spiegel*, publisher Rudolf Augstein likened enthusiasm for the MLF to "the Germans' worship of the military, which has led them into two catastrophic defeats."[12] He argued that the MLF would be a first step to a German national nuclear capability, comparing the situation to the military restrictions of the Weimar years. Augstein asked, "Didn't the Reichswehr's cardboard tanks soon have iron treads?"[13]

In December 1964, the Johnson administration gradually withdrew its support for the MLF for a number of reasons. French and British reluctance to give up their national capabilities as well as their opposition to German participation played an important role. Soviet hostility and concern over global proliferation after the first Chinese nuclear test in October 1964 also contributed to the decision.[14] Officials in Bonn suspected, however, that other reasons contributed to this development. In the West German foreign ministry it was assumed that blunders in West German *Geschichtspolitik* had had a direct influence on the failure of the MLF. Freiherr von Braun, the West German observer at the United Nations, explained to US NATO Ambassador Thomas Finletter that the West German government believed that the US had opted out of the MLF because of the outcry inside the United States over the German reluctance to extend the statute of limitations for Nazi crimes.[15] Facing a wave of anti-German public opinion, von Braun reasoned, the Johnson administration found it hard domestically to sell a plan that would place the Germans within reach of nuclear weapons.

In 1969 the West German ambassador in Washington, Rolf Pauls, speculated that the rise of the far right-wing National Democratic Party (Nationaldemokratische Partei Deutschlands, NPD) in Germany was an additional reason for the reluctance of West Germany's allies to share control over nuclear weapons with the Germans, and thus for the demise of the NATO nuclear force.[16] Pauls argued that the Federal Republic's allies feared that, sooner or later, extreme German nationalism would raise its ugly head again in the form of a West German government that included a neo-Nazi party. Therefore, despite the fact that the Germans were seen as reliable allies for now, they would nonetheless never be allowed to have control over nuclear weapons.

The German concerns do show that the foreign ministry was sensitive to the repercussions that an ill-fated *Geschichtspolitik* and the rise of neo-Nazism might have on US (and British) nuclear policy, and specifically on the ultimate decision about whether the Germans should have a share of control over weapons of mass destruction. In this context, the West German ambassador to NATO, Wilhelm Grewe, made an interesting suggestion concerning West Germany's adherence to the Nuclear Non-Proliferation Treaty. He argued that the Federal Republic should not sign the treaty in the foreseeable future. Bonn would likely continue to be pressured for its signature, he argued, but could afford to resist signing—unless electoral support for the neo-Nazi NPD increased. Only then, Grewe reasoned, could the German government no longer resist pressure to sign the treaty.[17]

The NPT and the Resonance of German History

At the end of 1966, the US announced an official agreement with the Soviet Union for a global nondissemination treaty. The decision caused an outcry in the Federal Republic. Initial reactions from the CDU/CSU were completely negative. The NPT was described as "worse than the Morgenthau plan," "another Versailles," or "nuclear complicity with the Soviets."[18] The comparisons employed by Bonn's NPT opponents reflected an attempt to establish a pattern of anti-German actions from the end of World War I to the Cold War. They alleged a continuity of excessively harsh treatment of Germany by the Western powers—and *not* a continuity of German power-seeking from the *Kaiserreich* to the Third Reich, as a new generation of historians was beginning to suggest.[19] In the Weimar years the restrictions placed on the Reichswehr did not allow Germany to have an air force; now it was nuclear weapons. Germany, so the argument went, had to renounce great power status and reconcile itself to military and technological inferiority. Moreover, the discriminatory controls the NPT imposed on states without nuclear weapons would bar the Federal Republic from technological progress even in the realm of civil nuclear technology. In this respect the NPT seemed to embody a realization of Morgenthau's plans to turn Germany into a pastoral country; the NPT would mean not only nuclear renunciation, but economic impotence as well.

Chancellor Kiesinger trumpeted his resolve that "nobody will get me to sign this surrender"—a formulation characterized by one newspaper as "an unfortunate choice of words, if you keep in mind that not that long ago [Germans] said, 'there will never be a surrender.'"[20] Franz Josef Strauss, the head of the CSU and a former defense minister, was keen to point out that such discrimination against the Federal Republic could lead in the end to a neutralized Germany caught defenselessly between the two blocs. In such a situation, Strauss continued, it might not take long before "a new Führer would promise and also acquire nuclear weapons for Germany."[21] Strauss went a step beyond the argument that the Western powers were continuing to treat Germany unfairly; if this policy were to continue, he warned, the allies should not be surprised if another Hitler were to appear. In effect, he turned the argument that Germany should not have weapons of mass destruction on account of its recent past completely on its head. He exploited the Nazi past as an argument *in favor* of West German shared control over nuclear weapons.

The dangers of a reemergence of the extreme right had become a convenient pretext for conservatives to justify highly questionable demands, such as the release of the so-called *Kriegsverurteilte* (war convicts, that is, individuals tried and sentenced for war crimes).[22] The feeling that Germany was indeed singled out by the nonproliferation treaty was manifested in the shrill language used by its German opponents. Other governments opposed to the treaty, such as those in Italy or India, did not react as strongly and emotionally as did the German government and, for that matter, many German newspapers. When it came to the NPT, the rhetoric of the *Bayernkurier*, the newspaper of the Christian Social Union, was probably only matched in its vociferousness by Beijing's *People's Daily*.

This is all the more interesting inasmuch as the Federal Republic, like other nonnuclear weapon states, had some reasonable and legitimate concerns about the NPT. These included the implications of the treaty for the use of civil nuclear energy and the planned 25-year duration of the treaty, which exceeded the duration of the NATO treaty itself. But negotiations with the allies began to focus on these issues only after the first emotional (over)reactions had provoked comments from abroad that were unenthusiastic at best and scathing at worst. In a sharp critique of what he perceived as an orchestrated anti-NPT campaign that he feared might damage the Federal Republic's international image, the journalist Sebastian Haffner compared the rhetorical outbursts of the treaty's critics to the "propaganda campaigns under Goebbels."[23]

For their part, supporters of the NPT also used analogies to the German past. Writing in the weekly *Die Zeit,* the journalist Helmut Külz drew on the comparison between the Versailles treaty and the NPT, pointing out that the right's attacks on the *Verzichtspolitiker* (politicians of [nuclear] renunciation) was reminiscent of the Weimar-ear vilification of the so-called *Novemberverbrecher* (November criminals), the term used by Nazis and others on the right to derogate the leaders of the 1918 revolution. He argued that a nationalist, antidemocratic political right considered it "fashionable again" to stigmatize as criminals those who took responsibility for Germany's past.[24] Külz argued that signing the NPT and recognizing the Oder-Neisse border were preconditions for reconciliation and better relations with Poland and the Soviet Union. Provisions for German disarmament and realigned borders had been laid down in the Potsdam agreement, and, in this respect, nuclear renunciation represented nothing more than the delayed implementation of the Potsdam agreement. Külz pointed out that if there had been a peace treaty with Germany shortly after the war, Germany would have had little choice but to accept the eastern border and the renunciation of nuclear weapons.[25] *Der Spiegel* also argued that the NPT was simply the last of the victorious Allies' restrictions on Germany, and accused the CDU of attempting to win World War II retroactively through clever alliance policies and a strategy of playing the United States off against the Soviet Union.[26] Implicit in such a policy was a refusal to accept Germany's defeat and a line of continuity from the Third Reich to the Federal Republic, in which German nuclear diplomacy and Adenauer's policy of strength replaced the tanks of the *Wehrmacht.*

Internationally, West Germany was also in the spotlight of the NPT negotiations. The Federal Republic was one of the countries whose signature was considered crucial for the success of the treaty. Many reasons were given—West Germany's geo-strategic position, its technological and economic capabilities—but foreigners, unlike the West Germans themselves, rarely mentioned the Nazi past directly in urging the Federal Republic to sign the treaty. In fact, West Germany's allies were at pains to point out that Bonn's signature—like those of Italy, India, and Israel—was in the interest of global nonproliferation. Nonetheless, there were occasional allusions to the German past. A major objective of British nonproliferation policy, as Prime Minister Harold Wilson liked to say, was to avoid a "German finger on the nuclear trigger."[27] Bonn reacted very strongly to comments of this sort, which hinted at German militarism or suggested that German sovereignty should be limited. Wilson's phrase triggered an official complaint and the request that Wilson not use it, as it damaged an ally's international reputation.[28] Similarly, the West German government was furious to learn that during Soviet premier Aleksey Kosygin's visit to Britain, the Wilson government did not rebut Kosygin's statement that "Germany must sign NPT whether she likes it or not."[29]

Although diplomats did not admit to it *publicly*, there were clear indicators that the Federal Republic was regarded as a special case during the NPT negotiations. The intensive bilateral talks on the treaty between Washington and Bonn from 1967 to 1969 were one indication. In Britain, the phrase "to keep Germany non-nuclear" became almost a mantra, akin to Cato's famous "Carthage ought to be destroyed." The Americans noted, somewhat bemused, that during bilateral talks on the MLF, British Minister of Defense Denis Healey "deliver[ed] a dissertation on the dangers of whetting of German [nuclear] appetites."[30] While Britain's concern to protect its own status as a nuclear member of the Western alliance undoubtedly played a role, concerns stemming from the recent history of the new German ally could not be suppressed. With respect to the latter, confidential allied consultations reveal a refreshing amount of bluntness: French Foreign Minister Maurice Couve de Murville told his Italian colleague Giuseppe Saragat that "the French would not mind Italian nuclear weapons but that they were categorically opposed to a German nuclear capability as one could never be sure whether the Germans might not try to solve territorial disputes by force again. One had to be careful."[31] In 1963 Prime Minister Macmillan explained to John F. Kennedy that he, like the Kremlin leadership, objected to German control over nuclear weapons for historical reasons. In private, Macmillan expressed his fears about the rise of a future nationalist German leader renouncing the 1954 accords and seeking national control over nuclear weapons—a danger, Macmillan argued, that could be avoided by the immediate conclusion of a global nonproliferation treaty.[32] Ironically, President Lyndon Johnson, at a time when he still supported the scheme, tried to impress the benefits of the MLF on Macmillan's successor, Harold Wilson, arguing that a German share in the MLF might prevent the rise of a another Hitler: "The President told the Prime Minister that a stitch in time saves nine, and that if we couldn't solve this problem and tie the Germans in there was some 17-year-old right now in Germany who would be a 20-year-old little Hitler in another three years.... He had just won an election by preaching against discrimination in the United States, and he could not now preach in favor of discrimination in international affairs."[33] Apparently, at least for a while, Johnson bought Strauss's argument according to which continued discrimination against West Germany in the Western Alliance might facilitate the rise of a new führer.

There is, then, clear evidence that the legacy of the German past had some influence on NATO nuclear policy. Internationally, German diplomats were rarely confronted with blunt reminders of German militarism or allied lack of trust in the stability of the Federal Republic. But it is evident that lessons learned from historical experience shaped allied nuclear policy toward West Germany to some degree. Doubts about the sturdiness of Germany's democratic structures were at the core of allied concern. But even though the Nazi past informed the opinions of Germany's allies, it did not arise directly as a factor in negotiations with West Germany over nuclear policy. In the Federal Republic itself, references to the German past served mainly to justify opinions with regard to the country's nuclear status. In addition, there was some tangible concern over the impact of the rise of neo-Nazism and the debate about the statute of limitations on allied nuclear policy toward Germany. But within the Federal Republic, little explicit connection was made between the nuclear debate and prominent issues of *Geschichtspolitik*, such as compensation for victims of Nazi persecution or the Frankfurt Auschwitz trial.[34] References to the past were exploited to underscore discrimination against the Federal Republic, but what did not take place was a frank, thorough discussion about the wisdom of asserting the right to any kind of German nuclear option in the wake of German's recent past of mass murder.

Even in the late 1950s, at the height of public interest in nuclear issues, the nuclear debate had not been dominated by considerations of the Nazi past. To be sure, many voices had openly linked a renunciation of nuclear weapons to Germany's role in two world wars and the Holocaust.[35] They had understood their protest not just as one against nuclear weapons but as one in favor of democracy and a conscious break with the German past. This attitude was reflected in the chant, "You German people, you have nearly always marched for wrong aims. At the end, there was only rubble."[36] But just as many protesters refrained from referring directly to the Nazi past. They called for global disarmament, an end to nuclear testing, "peace and social security," and "bread for the world, not bombs."[37] While the oft-expressed fear of "nuclear death" and global annihilation was partly rooted in experiences of devastation during World War II,[38] it stemmed from the perspective of the German victims of Allied bombing and not from an abhorrence of Germany's own war crimes. The "Göttingen manifesto," issued by a group of German physicists, cited Germany's size and geography in arguing in favor of nuclear renunciation. Many in the Protestant Church argued that Christian belief did not allow a positive or neutral position toward weapons of mass destruction. To be sure, the vehemence of Christian antinuclear protests may have been linked with a desire to compensate for the churches' depressing record during the Nazi era.[39] But it should be emphasized that in his sermons against nuclear armament, Pastor Martin Niemöller did not recognize a *specifically* German responsibility to reject nuclear weapons.[40] As Alice Holmes Cooper has pointed out, "arguments against nuclear weapons were directed against nuclear weapons per se"[41] rather than against German-controlled nuclear weapons in particular.

By the mid-1960s the public had lost much of its interest in nuclear matters. People had been concerned about nuclear weapons in general, and in particular against nuclear weapons on German soil, weapons of mass destruction close to their homes—no matter who controlled them. Abstract schemes about nuclear sharing did not generate as much interest. The few Easter Marchers of the mid-1960s carried familiar slogans but little reference to the MLF was made. One group of protesters in southern Germany brought along a donkey bearing a sign that read, "Hurray to the MLF! I am a donkey and I'm for atomic weapons."[42] All parties recognized that the MLF or the NPT did not constitute central election issues. The domestic debate, though heated, was limited to a small circle of politicians, scientists, journalists, and civil servants. Later in the 1960s, the extra-parliamentary opposition (APO) was far more interested in other issues, such as the Vietnam War, than in the question of Germany's renunciation of nuclear weapons.[43] The 1968 Easter March was dominated by Vietnam, with nuclear disarmament being relegated to the sidelines.[44]

Through the 1970s and into the early 1980s, when the peace movement was fighting the NATO "double track decision" for the deployment of Pershing and cruise missiles in Germany, the expression "nuclear Holocaust" almost became a cliché. Peace activists now openly linked German renunciation of nuclear weapons to the prevention of another Auschwitz.[45] Yet this position did not primarily imply a special German responsibility for the renunciation of weapons of mass destruction—what it really expressed was a comparison between the American strategy of nuclear deterrence and the Nazi-German policy of calculated mass murder.[46] These comparisons between the US and the Third Reich had in fact originated during student protests against the Vietnam War.[47]

Coming to Terms with the Past in a Cold War Context

Matthias Küntzel has argued that Bonn was unwilling to give up the nuclear option because the Federal Republic had never genuinely come to terms with the past.[48] Referring to a proposal put forward by Thomas Schelling, a Harvard professor and expert in military strategy, in 1966,[49] Küntzel contends that renunciation of nuclear weapons and unconditional support of the NPT would have earned Bonn international respect and would have been the logical thing to do for a country that had started two world wars. Perhaps this position does not sufficiently take into account the legitimate concerns not only the Federal Republic but many other nonnuclear weapons states voiced about the NPT at the time, but it was also clear that sooner or later West Germany would have to sign the treaty as it was written. Küntzel is right to point out that the Germans were reluctant to face their past during the early 1950s,[50] although this argument is less persuasive with regard to the late 1950s and the 1960s. Still, it is interesting to ask why this option was not even discussed, especially as the US State Department also saw the advantages of such a course. In April 1966, presidential adviser Francis Bator wrote to Johnson, "[I]f they [the Germans] could only see it, there is a role which would not only enhance German prestige but could even advance unification and would engage German energies in a constructive way for the first time in a century. The hardest but crucial step would be for the Germans unilaterally to renounce collective as well as national ownership of nuclear weapons and to justify this as an essential step toward nonproliferation, world-wide arms control, a European settlement and unification. By making a virtue out of nonnuclear status, by resisting, in spite of their economic capacity, the temptation to imitate France's narrow nationalism, the Germans could really put themselves in a position to play a major role in the world at large."[51] Three and a half years after Bator had pondered these ideas, West Germany had indeed renounced collective as well as national ownership of nuclear weapons—without gaining anything in return—and the international impression created was one of German reluctance and resentment, rather than one of German contrition and high-mindedness.

The West Germans had clung to a strategy for overcoming nuclear abstention by means of integration into a European body, in the expectation that co-ownership of nuclear weapons would be acceptable to Bonn's allies. The first attempt toward nuclear integration, the FIG agreement to produce nuclear warheads in a joint Franco-German-Italian effort,[52] had been put to a halt by General de Gaulle in 1958. Chancellors Konrad Adenauer, Ludwig Erhard, and Kurt-Georg Kiesinger, as well as Minister of Defense Franz Josef Strauss, saw a future European nuclear force under NATO aegis as a means eventually to gain (nuclear) equality for the FRG.[53] This strategy lay in shambles once the MLF had been abandoned. Instead, in 1968 the Germans were expected to sign a treaty that would foreclose any "European option," which for some was tantamount to the prospect of never achieving full political rehabilitation, and of having to carry the stigma of Germany's past forever.

Two subtle issues of perception should also be taken into account that promoted a separation of the nuclear debate from Germany's past. Firstly, there was a gradual change in how nuclear weapons were perceived. By the 1960s, as the horrors of World War II's destruction were fading into the past, atomic weapons were increasingly seen as status levers and diplomatic tools rather than as weapons of mass destruction. The principle of Mutual Assured Destruction (MAD), it was believed, would ensure that they would not be used as weapons, and that people, especially the Germans, could learn to live with the bomb. At the same time, Britain had demonstrated how nuclear diplomacy could guarantee a significant amount of international influence to an imperial power in decline.[54] If Britain regarded nuclear diplomacy as a tool to influence US foreign policy, why should Germany not be able to use nuclear diplomacy to extract concessions from the Soviet Union?

The second issue of perception, which was especially pertinent in the international context, was that the Cold War facilitated "the normalization of the German past." In the West, Germany's past was seen through the prism of totalitarianism. West Germans were not alone in seeing the Federal Republic as the antipode to both the German Democratic Republic and the Third Reich, nor were they the only members of the Western alliance to maintain a *Beschweigen der Vergangenheit*—a silence about the past—for the sake of the Bonn Republic's stability. This was especially relevant because propaganda from Moscow constantly pointed to the danger of West German militarism. The communist threat similarly influenced perceptions of the Bundeswehr, particularly among Americans. West German officers were increasingly seen as comrades-in-arms in the fight against communism, and the legend of German military strength revived and spread in the US.[55] Indeed, despite the Nuremberg trials, the myth of the *saubere Truppe* (untarnished forces) persevered not only within Germany.[56] More generally, West Germany's allies had more pressing issues than Germany's past. This is illustrated by the decision for West German rearmament and the London Debt Agreement of 1953—which effectively deferred all claims against Germany resulting from

World War II. By the late 1950s, President Eisenhower may even have been willing to grant the Germans control over nuclear weapons.[57] At that time the Holocaust did not play an important role in the public consciousness of the US; it only began to do so in the late 1960s and 1970s.[58] The Johnson administration pressed hard for a German signature on the NPT, but the treaty was but one issue on a list of US demands ranging from support for the Vietnam War to the off-set agreement. President Nixon, who succeeded Johnson in 1969, had little interest in the NPT. Despite the qualms officials in London had about the prospect of a "German finger on the nuclear trigger," the British government was willing to reduce its pressure on the Germans to sign the NPT in order to obtain German support for Britain's second application to the European Economic Community.[59]

Yet what Bonn failed to understand was that despite the apparent "normalization of the German past," and despite Cold War politics and anticommunism, the NATO allies ultimately drew the line at the prospect of German nuclear weapons—shared or otherwise—*because* of Germany's past, even if there were no *explicit* statements to that effect, and even if Eisenhower, Johnson, and de Gaulle occasionally dangled a "nuclear carrot" in front of Bonn.[60] The extent of delusion revealed itself most starkly when the Kiesinger government attempted to include in the NPT treaty a clause that would keep open a "European nuclear option."[61] Rationally, some of the NPT's opponents in West Germany understood the link between the Nazi past and the nuclear question, but for a long time they resisted accepting the inevitable political and diplomatic consequences of that link. Chancellor Kiesinger, for his part, could only talk about the burden of history in a very repressed manner. To colleagues of the CDU/CSU *Fraktion*, he confided, "[W]e all know what we undergo, what we feel [about having to sign the NPT]. But we also know that what we are being asked to do [amounts to] the reaffirmation of a most unfortunate heritage from a most unfortunate past (*unseligen Vergangenheit*).[62]

There were some long-term ironies embedded in these developments, as the Gulf War and the breakup of Yugoslavia would later show. West Germany's limitation to checkbook diplomacy in the Gulf War stemmed from German antimilitarism and unspoken German fears about international abhorrence of Germans in combat rather than from the actual concerns of their NATO allies. Awareness of international sensitivity toward German military action had been growing since the 1950s, yet, at the time of the Gulf War, Germany was expected to take a more active role in international relations. In fact, the single squadron of jets dispatched to Turkey caused raised eyebrows in Washington because of the perceived lack of German support. By contrast, Bonn's unilateral push for the recognition of Slovenia and Croatia in the course of the war in Yugoslavia prompted resentment from its allies. As Konrad Jarausch has noted, "if the Germans asserted themselves, they were attacked for resorting to Nazi tactics, if Bonn held back, it was accused of lacking leadership."[63]

Since 1990, conservative German historians have celebrated German reunification as the end of the imposed *Sonderweg* of national division, and have revived claims for a great power role for Germany, sometimes including vague hints that Germany might now be in a position to end its nuclear *Sonderweg* as well.[64] Arnulf Baring, for example, has suggested that the united Germany might now reopen the discussion about a German nuclear capability.[65] Forced to take responsibility for its past and renounce the development of nuclear weapons, Germany, so it seemed, had again deviated from the historical development of the US, Britain, and France. But the notion of a German nuclear *Sonderweg* is off the point given that the policy of nuclear nonproliferation is older than the bomb itself, that British and particularly French arsenals were developed against American wishes, and that the majority of nations sooner or later foreswore the development of nuclear weapons. Nuclear abstention may have made some feel less secure (or inferior), but it certainly did not hinder West German social or political development or prevent economic prosperity.

The notion of a nuclear *Sonderweg* raises yet another issue: the relationship between historians, nuclear history, and the German past. Two examples must suffice here to show how even in scholarly accounts of German nuclear history we encounter the tendency to avoid discussing nuclear policy within the context of Germany's Nazi past. Both examples refer to Adenauer's 1954 renunciation of nuclear weapons. In 1995 Karl Heinz Kamp wrote that "the categorical plea to adhere to a nonnuclear status was a logical consequence of Germany's postwar position as a destroyed and occupied country."[66] Was it not first and foremost a consequence of German aggression and war crimes, and not one of defeat? Hans Peter Schwarz obscured the historical links more subtly in 1989 by asking whether Adenauer would have liked to turn the Federal Republic into a nuclear power on the model of Great Britain. "If he could have done so, probably," Schwarz replies. "But he was well aware that the crown was out of reach for West Germany. He had understood ... the peculiarities of the West German situation so clearly that—given the circumstances—to him only those complicated and contradictory models of nuclear sharing appeared realistic and therefore rationally desirable."[67] Compare this to a quote from Alfred Mierzejewski's biography of Ludwig Erhard: "Like Adenauer before them, [Erhard and Foreign Minister Gerhard Schröder] failed to recognize that because of Germany's commission of war crimes and crimes against humanity during World War II, West German access to nuclear weapons was unacceptable to any of its allies, to say nothing of the Soviet Union and the people of Eastern Europe."[68]

Conclusion

We have seen that there were obvious links between Germany's Nazi past and nuclear policy during the 1960s. In the debate over the MLF and the NPT, both supporters and opponents of the treaty cited the Nazi past in arguing their positions. Many West Germans regarded the nuclear abstention imposed by the *Ausland* as a manifestation of the stigma that still separated the Bonn republic from its European partners and rivals alike. In 1954 the Adenauer government had no choice but to accept renunciation, but in the years following Bonn worked steadily to water it down. Nuclear renunciation, later formalized by the Federal Republic's accession to the NPT, was thus a reminder of the past—a past the increasingly successful republic hoped to overcome through integration in the West.[69] Fighting tenaciously for the European option, Bonn failed to realize that ultimately none of Germany's allies wanted to see German control over nuclear weapons, not even in the form of joint ownership. The allies were partly to blame for this but one can empathize with John McCloy, US High Commissioner for Germany, who had noted in 1952 that the Germans seemed strangely unaware of "what kind of difficulties stemmed from the past in granting West Germany the right to resume nuclear research at all."[70]

Post-1990 fantasies about a possible change in Germany's nuclear status may reflect both the stigma of inequality that some Germans still feel vis-à-vis Britain and France as well as the tenacious hope that in a post–Cold War environment a European nuclear force could eventually be realized. Sluggish progress toward the implementation of the European Union's "European Security and Defense Policy" (exemplified by the lack of success with respect to the establishment of the European Rapid Reaction Force) has suggested that any future integration of European nuclear capabilities will remain confined to the realm of the imagination. In today's world, debates about a German nuclear capability seem strangely out of place, as German efforts to achieve "equality" with Britain and France focus on gaining a permanent seat on the UN Security Council.

Notes

I would like to thank Stefan Berger and Winfried Süss for their comments on earlier versions of this essay.

1. For details, see Catherine Kelleher, *Germany and the Politics of Nuclear Weapons* (New York, 1975), 26–28; Peter Fischer, *Atomenergie und staatliches Interesse: Die Anfänge der Atompolitik in der Bundesrepublik Deutschland 1949–1955* (Baden-Baden, 1994), 141–44; Matthias Küntzel, *Bonn und die Bombe: Deutsche Atomwaffenpolitik von Adenauer bis Brandt* (Frankfurt am Main, 1993), 19–22.
2. Kelleher, *Germany*, 11.
3. Exercise Carte Blanche, a NATO war game conducted in 1955, clearly demonstrated that nuclear conflict with the Red Army would wipe Germany off the map. See Kelleher, *Germany*, 35–43; Fischer, *Atomenergie*, 193–97.
4. See Marc Cioc, *Pax Atomica: The Nuclear Defence Debate in West Germany during the Adenauer Era* (New York, 1988), 70. For German opposition to rearmament and nuclear weapons, see Michael Geyer, "Cold War Angst: The Case of West German Opposition to Rearmament and Nuclear Weapons," in *The Miracle Years: A Cultural History of West Germany 1949–1968*, ed. Hanna Schissler (Princeton, 2001), 376–408.
5. Karl Otto, *Vom Ostermarsch zur APO* (Frankfurt am Main, 1977), 62; Christoph Klessmann, *Zwei Staaten eine Nation: Deutsche Geschichte 1955–1970* (Bonn, 1988), 160–61.

6. Much research has been done on the ill-fated MLF proposal. Recent studies include Christoph Bluth, *Britain, Germany and Western Nuclear Strategy* (Oxford, 1995); Stephen Twigge and Len Scott, *Planning Armageddon: Britain, the US and the Command of Western Nuclear Forces 1945–64* (Amsterdam, 2000); Ronald Granieri, *The Ambivalent Alliance: Konrad Adenauer, the CDU/CSU, and the West, 1949–1966* (New York, 2003); Beatrice Heuser, *NATO, Britain, France and the FRG: Strategies and Forces for Europe, 1949–2000* (Basingstoke, 1998); Christoph Hoppe, *Zwischen Teilhabe und Mitsprache: Die Nuklearfrage in der Allianzpolitik Deutschlands 1959–66* (Baden-Baden, 1993); Colette Barbier, "La force multilatérale dans le débat atomique français," *Revue d'Histoire Diplomatique* 107 (1993): 55–89; Pascaline Winand, *Eisenhower, Kennedy and the United States of Europe* (New York, 1993).

7. On the NPT, see Glenn Seaborg, *Stemming the Tide: Arms Control in the Johnson Years* (Lexington, 1987). On the West German signature, see Helga Haftendorn, *Kernwaffen und die Glaubwürdigkeit der Allianz: Die NATO Krise von 1966/67* (Baden-Baden, 1994), 148–66; Susanna Schrafstetter, *Die dritte Atommacht: Britische Nichtverbreitungspolitik im Dienst von Statussicherung und Deutschlandpolitik 1952–68* (Munich, 1999), 173–78; Küntzel, *Bonn*, 119–205; Susanna Schrafstetter and Stephen Twigge, *Avoiding Armageddon: Europe, the United States, and the Struggle for Nuclear Nonproliferation, 1945–1970* (Westport, 2004), 182–94.

8. Helmut Dubiel, *Niemand ist frei von der Geschichte: Die nationalsozialistische Herrschaft in den Debatten des Deutschen Bundestages* (Cologne, 2000), 98.

9. Beatrice Heuser has examined historical and cultural influences on nuclear strategy. See Beatrice Heuser, *Nuclear Mentalities? Strategies and Beliefs in Britain, France and the FRG* (London, 1998), and Heuser, "Historical Lessons and Discourse on Defence in France and Germany 1945–1990," *Rethinking History* 2 (1998): 199–237.

10. Hoppe, *Teilhabe*, 100.

11. Lyndon Baines Johnson Library, Austin (hereafter, LBJL), NSF, Spurgeon Keeny file, box 7, "Dangers from a Psychotic Germany," undated 1965.

12. *Der Spiegel*, 16 December 1964.

13. Ibid.

14. On the demise of the MLF, see Susanna Schrafstetter and Stephen Twigge, "Trick or Truth? The British ANF Proposal, West Germany and US Non-proliferation Policy," *Diplomacy and Statecraft* 11 (2000): 161–84.

15. *Akten zur Auswärtigen Politik der Bundesrepublik Deutschland 1965*, Doc. Nr. 411, von Braun an Krapf, 10 November 1965.

16. *Akten zur Auswärtigen Politik der Bundesrepublik Deutschland 1969*, Doc. Nr. 66, Pauls an Auswärtiges Amt, 17 February 1969.

17. *Akten zur Auswärtigen Politik der Bundesrepublik Deutschland 1968*, Doc. Nr. 283, Grewe an Ruete, 5 September 1968.

18. *Welt am Sonntag*, 12 February 1967; *Die Welt*, 20 February 1967; *Bild*, 21 February 1967. Küntzel, *Bonn*, 157–60; Adrian Schertz, *Die Deutschlandpolitik Kennedys und Johnsons* (Cologne, 1992), 421; Bluth, *Britain*, 167.

19. The "Fischer Controversy" was unleashed by the publication of Fritz Fischer, *Griff nach der Weltmacht* (Darmstadt, 1961).

20. *Neue Rhein (Ruhr) Zeitung*, 15 July 1968.

21. *Rheinischer Merkur*, 27 August 1965.

22. Norbert Frei, *Vergangenheitspolitik: Die Anfänge der Bundesrepublik und die NS-Vergangenheit* (Munich, 1996), 212, 230–31. Note the terminology: *Verbrecher* (criminals) is replaced by *Verurteilte* (convicts). On the tactic of raising the specter of "another Hitler," see also Heuser, "Historical Lessons," 224–25.

23. *Stern*, 5 March 1967.

24. *Die Zeit*, 23 June 1967.

25. Ibid.

26. *Der Spiegel*, 15 July 1968.

27. Schrafstetter, *Atommacht*, 138.
28. Politisches Archiv des Auwärtigen Amtes, Ref. II B1 Bd. 972, Aufzeichnung von MD Werz, 16 May 1966.
29. *The Times*, 5 February 1967.
30. LBJL, NSF, Country File: UK, box 214, Memorandum of Conversation, 7 December 1964.
31. Quoted in Matthias Schulz, "Integration durch eine europäische Atomstreitmacht?" *Vierteljahrshefte für Zeitgeschichte* 53 (2005): 275–313, here 308. It seems that these remarks were passed on to the German ambassador in Italy, Herbert Blankenhorn. See *Akten zur Auswärtigen Politik der Bundesrepublik Deutschland 1964*, Doc. 375, Anm. 9.
32. National Archives, Kew (formerly Public Record Office), FO 371/171235, Macmillan to Kennedy, 12 March 1963.
33. LBJL, NSF, Files of McGeorge Bundy box 18, Memorandum for the Record, 7 December 1964.
34. On West German compensation policy, see Hans Günter Hockerts, Claudia Moisel, and Tobias Winstel, eds., *Grenzen der Wiedergutmachung: Die Entschädigung für NS-Verfolgte in West- und Osteuropa, 1945–2000* (Göttingen, 2006). On the Frankfurt Auschwitz trial, see Rebecca Wittmann, *Beyond Justice: The Auschwitz Trial* (Cambridge, MA, 2005), and Devin O. Pendas, *The Frankfurt Auschwitz Trial 1963–65* (New York, 2006).
35. For several examples, see Heuser, *Mentalities*, 181. Heuser points out that the slogan "Lieber rot als Massenmörder" (Better Red than mass murderer), which contained a direct reference to the Nazi past, was changed to "Lieber rot als tot" (Better Red than dead).
36. Song from an Easter March in the Ruhrgebiet, quoted in Holger Nehring, "National Internationalists: British and West German Protest against Nuclear Weapons, the Politics of Transnational Communications and the Social History of the Cold War 1957–1964," *Contemporary European History* 14 (2005): 559–82, here 569. The article contains an excellent comparison of the British and German protest movements and their aims.
37. Bundesarchiv, Militärarchiv Freiburg, BW2/20203, Ostermarsch 1961, Dokumentation und Photos. Bundesarchiv Koblenz, B106/16053, Kampf dem Atomtod (1956–59).
38. Geyer, "Angst," 398. Geyer argued that "in the single-minded emphasis on collective death, German angst differed significantly from the 'nuclear fear' of the Americans but showed some remarkable similarities with the 'writing ground zero' of the Japanese." Ibid.
39. Alice Holmes Cooper, *Paradoxes of Peace: German Peace Movements since 1945* (Ann Arbor, 1996), 34; Heuser, *Mentalities*, 192.
40. Martin Niemöller, *Zur atomaren Rüstung* (Darmstadt, 1959), 30.
41. Cooper, *Paradoxes*, 41. On the Protestant Church and antinuclear protest, see also Cioc, *Pax Atomica*, 92–115.
42. Bundesarchiv, Militärarchiv Freiburg, BW2/20258 Ostermarsch 1964, photographs.
43. See Küntzel, *Bonn*, 131–32. On the student movement, see the chapters by Belinda Davis and Elizabeth Peifer in this volume.
44. Bundesarchiv, Militärarchiv Freiburg, BW2/20358, Ostermarsch 1968.
45. Dubiel, *Geschichte*, 193–98, and Jeffrey Herf, *War by Other Means: Soviet Power, West German Resistance, and the Battle of the Euromissiles* (New York, 1991), 185–92.
46. Herf, *War*, 186.
47. See Wilfried Mausbach, "Auschwitz and Vietnam: West German Protest against America's War during the 1960s," in *America, the Vietnam War and the World*, ed. Andreas Daum, Lloyd Gardner, and Wilfried Mausbach (New York, 2003), 279–98.
48. Küntzel, *Bonn*, 273–76.
49. Thomas Schelling, "Kontinuität und Neubeginn in der NATO," *Europa Archiv* 21, no. 13 (1966): 461–73.
50. On the 1950s, see, for example, Frei, *Vergangenheitspolitik*; Jeffrey Herf, *Divided Memory: The Nazi Past in the Two Germanys* (Cambridge, MA, 1997); Aleida Assmann and Ute Frevert, *Geschichtsvergessenheit, Geschichtsversessenheit: Vom Umgang mit deutschen Vergangenheiten nach*

1945 (Stuttgart, 1999); Peter Reichel, *Vergangenheitsbewältigung in Deutschland: Die politisch-justitielle Auseinandersetzung mit der NS-Diktatur nach 1945* (Bonn, 2003); Antonia Grunenberg, *Die Lust an der Schuld* (Berlin, 2001).

51. LBJL, NSF Country File, box 185, Memorandum for the President, 4 April 1966.

52. On the FIG project, see Colette Barbier, "Les négations franco-germano-italiennes en vue de l'établissement d'une coopération militaire nucléaire au cours des années 1956–1958," *Revue d'Histoire Diplomatique* 104 (1990): 81–114; Eckart Conze, "La coopération franco-germano-italienne dans le domaine nucléaire dans les années 1957–58: Un point de vue allemande," in ibid., 115–32.

53. See Schulz, "Integration," 303–8; Beatrice Heuser, "The European Dream of Franz Josef Strauss," *Journal of European Integration History* 4 (1998): 75–103, here 91–99.

54. The Anglo-American special relationship, the Nassau agreement of 1962, Britain's role in the negotiations for the Partial Test Ban Treaty (1963), and the MLF serve as examples.

55. David Clay Large, *Germans to the Front: West German Rearmament in the Adenauer Era* (Chapel Hill, 1996), 198–99; Hew Strachan, "Die Vorstellungen der Anglo-Amerikaner von der Wehrmacht," in *Die Wehrmacht: Mythos und Realität*, ed. Rolf Dieter Müller and Hans-Erich Volkmann (Munich, 1999), 92–104.

56. Questioning this view is Alaric Searle, *Wehrmacht Generals, West German Society and the Debate on Rearmament, 1949–1959* (Westport, 2004), 285.

57. Marc Trachtenberg, *A Constructed Peace: The Making of the European Settlement, 1945–1963* (Princeton, 1999), 209–10.

58. Detlef Junker, "Das adoptierte Leiden," *Tagblatt*, 9 February 2001.

59. Schrafstetter, *Atommacht*, 198–99.

60. A lot has been written on General de Gaulle's vague references to German participation in the *force de frappe* to win West German support for his European design and to prevent the realization of the MLF. See, for example, Horst Osterheld, *Aussenpolitik unter Bundeskanzler Ludwig Erhard 1963–1966* (Düsseldorf, 1992), 100; Heuser, "Dream," 93–97; Heuser, *NATO*, 151–56; Schulz, "Integration," 300–303; Trachtenberg, *Peace*, 372–74; Schrafstetter, *Atommacht*, 121.

61. Heuser, "Dream," 99; Schrafstetter and Twigge, *Armageddon*, 184.

62. Archiv für Christlich Demokratische Politik, St. Augustin, Protokolle der Sitzungen der CDU/CSU Fraktion im Bundestag VIII-001, 1013/1, 21 February 1967.

63. Konrad Jarausch, *The Rush to German Unity* (Oxford, 1994), 206.

64. See Stefan Berger, *The Search for Normality: National Identity and Historical Consciousness in Germany since 1800* (Oxford, 1997), 186–87.

65. Arnulf Baring, *Deutschland, was nun?* (Berlin, 1991), 209–10.

66. Karl Heinz Kamp, "Germany and the Future of Nuclear Weapons in Germany," *Security Dialogue* 26 (1995): 280.

67. Hans Peter Schwarz, "Adenauer und die Kernwaffen," *Vierteljahrshefte für Zeitgeschichte* 37 (1989): 577. In this case, the original German is worth noting: "Heißt das, daß Adenauer die Bundesrepublik gerne zur Kernwaffenmacht nach dem Modell Großbritanniens … gemacht hätte? Hätte er gekonnt, wahrscheinlich. Doch ihm war bewusst, daß die Trauben für den deutschen Fuchs zu hoch hingen. Er hatte … die Bedingtheiten der bundesdeutschen Lage so klar begriffen, daß ihm nach Lage der Dinge immer nur jene bekannterweise komplizierten und widersprüchlichen Formen der nuklearen Teilhabe realisierbar und damit auch vernünftigerweise erstrebenswert erschienen."

68. Alfred Mierzejewski, *Ludwig Erhard: A Biography* (Chapel Hill, 2004), 189.

69. On the importance of Europe as a new source of identity for the Germans, see Heuser, *Mentalities*, 225–29.

70. John McCloy, quoted in Fischer, *Atomenergie*, 49.

Contributors

Bernhard Brunner received his PhD from the University of Freiburg and is the author of *Der Frankreich-Komplex: Die nationalsozialistischen Verbrechen in Frankreich und die Justiz der Bundesrepublik Deutschland* (Göttingen, 2002).

Belinda Davis teaches modern German and European history at Rutgers, the State University of New Jersey. She is the author of *Home Fires Burning: Food, Politics, and Everyday Life in World War I Berlin* (Chapel Hill, 2000).

Carole Fink teaches modern European history at The Ohio State University. Her books include *The Genoa Conference: European Diplomacy, 1921–1922* (Chapel Hill, 1984); *Marc Bloch: A Life in History* (Cambridge, 1989); *1968: The World Transformed*, co-edited with Philipp Gassert and Detlef Junker (Cambridge, 1998); and *Defending the Rights of Others: The Great Powers, the Jews, and International Minority Protection, 1878–1938* (Cambridge, 2004).

Philipp Gassert teaches recent and contemporary history at the University of Heidelberg and the Heidelberg Center for American Studies. He is the author of *Amerika im Dritten Reich: Ideologie, Propaganda und Volksmeinung 1933–1945* (Stuttgart, 1997), and *Kurt Georg Kiesinger 1904–1988: Kanzler zwischen den Zeiten* (Munich, 2006). With Carole Fink and Detlef Junker, he co-edited *1968: The World Transformed* (Cambridge, 1998).

Dagmar Herzog teaches modern German history and the history of sexuality at the Graduate Center, City University of New York. She is the author of *Intimacy and Exclusion: Religious Politics in Pre-Revolutionary Baden* (Princeton, 1996), and *Sex after Fascism: Memory and Morality in Twentieth-Century Germany* (Princeton, 2005). She is also the editor of *Sexuality and German Fascism* (New York, 2004).

Michael Hochgeschwender teaches American studies at the University of Munich. He is the author of *Freiheit in der Offensive? Der Kongreß für Kulturelle Freiheit und die Deutschen* (Munich, 1998), and *Wahrheit, Einheit, Ordnung: Der amerikanische Katholizismus und die Sklavenfrage 1835–1870* (Paderborn, 2005).

Konrad H. Jarausch teaches modern German and European history at the University of North Carolina, Chapel Hill, and has also served as co-director of the Zentrum für Zeithistorische Forschung in Potsdam. Among his many books are *The Enigmatic Chancellor: Bethmann Hollweg and the Hubris of Imperial Germany, 1856–1921* (New Haven, 1973); *Students, Society and Politics in Imperial Germany: The Rise of Academic Illiberalism* (Princeton, 1982); *Deutsche Studenten 1800–1970* (Frankfurt am Main, 1984); *The Unfree Professions: German Lawyers, Teachers and Engineers, 1900–1959* (New York, 1990); *The Rush to German Unity* (New York, 1994); *Versäumte Fragen: Deutsche Historiker im Schatten des Nationalsozialismus*, co-edited with Rüdiger Hohls (Stuttgart, 2000); *Shattered Past: Reconstructing German Histories*, co-authored with Michael Geyer (Princeton, 2003); and *After Hitler: Recivilizing Germans, 1945–1995* (Oxford, 2006).

Habbo Knoch teaches modern and contemporary history at the University of Göttingen. He is the author of *Die Tat als Bild: Fotografien des Holocaust in der deutschen Erinnerungskultur* (Hamburg, 2001).

Jürgen Lillteicher is a historian at the Dubnow Institute for Jewish History and Culture, University of Leipzig. He is the author of *Die Rückerstattung jüdischen Eigentums in Westdeutschland nach dem Zweiten Weltkrieg: Eine Studie über Verfolgungserfahrung, Rechtsstaatlichkeit und Vergangenheitspolitik 1945–1971* (Freiburg, 2003), and co-editor, with Constantin Goschler, of *"Arisierung" und Restitution: Die Rückerstattung jüdischen Eigentums in Deutschland und Österreich nach 1945 und 1989* (Göttingen, 2002).

Marc von Miquel is a historian at the Villa ten Hompel Historical Site, Münster. He is the author of *Ahnden oder amnestieren? Westdeutsche Justiz und Vergangenheitspolitik in den sechziger Jahren* (Göttingen, 2004).

Elizabeth L. B. Peifer teaches modern European and German history at Auburn University, in Montgomery, Alabama. She is the author of numerous articles on Germany in the 1960s.

Michael Schmidtke received his PhD from the University of Bielefeld and is the author of *Der Aufbruch der jungen Intelligenz: Die 68er Jahre in der Bundesrepublik und den USA* (Frankfurt am Main, 2003).

Joachim Scholtyseck teaches recent and contemporary history at the University of Bonn. He is the author of *Alliierter oder Vasall? Italien und Deutschland in der Zeit des Kulturkampfes und der "Krieg-in-Sicht"-Krise 1875* (Cologne, 1994), and *Robert Bosch und der liberale Widerstand gegen Hitler 1933 bis 1945* (Munich, 1999).

Karen Schönwälder is a scholar at the Social Science Research Center in Berlin. She is the author of *Historiker und Politik: Geschichtswissenschaft im Nationalsozialismus*

(Frankfurt am Main, 1992), and *Einwanderung und ethnische Pluralität: Politische Entscheidungen und öffentliche Debatten in Großbritannien und der Bundesrepublik von den 1950er bis zu den 1970er Jahren* (Essen, 2001).

Susanna Schrafstetter teaches modern German and recent European history at the University of Nebraska-Lincoln. She is the author of *Die dritte Atommacht: Britische Nichtverbreitungspolitik im Dienst von Statussicherung und Deutschlandpolitik 1952–1968* (Munich, 1999), and the co-author, with Stephen Twigge, of *Avoiding Armageddon: Europe, the United States, and the Struggle for Nuclear Nonproliferation, 1945–1970* (Westport, 2004).

Detlef Siegfried teaches modern European history at the University of Copenhagen. He is the author of *Zwischen Einheitspartei und "Bruderkampf": SPD und KPD in Schleswig-Holstein 1945/46* (Kiel, 1992), and *Der Fliegerblick: Intellektuelle, Radikalismus und Flugzeugproduktion bei Junkers 1914 bis 1934* (Bonn, 2001). He has co-edited, with Axel Schildt and Karl Christian Lammers, *Dynamische Zeiten: Die 60er Jahre in den beiden deutschen Gesellschaften* (Hamburg, 2000), and, with Axel Schildt, *Between Marx and Coca-Cola: Youth Cultures in Changing European Societies, 1960–1980* (New York, 2005).

Alan E. Steinweis teaches modern European history and Judaic Studies at the University of Nebraska-Lincoln. He is the author of *Art, Ideology and Economics in Nazi Germany: The Reich Chambers of Music, Theater, and the Visual Arts* (Chapel Hill, 1993), and *Studying the Jew: Scholarly Antisemitism in Nazi Germany* (Cambridge, MA, 2006). He is the co-editor, with Daniel E. Rogers, of *The Impact of Nazism: New Perspectives on the Third Reich and Its Legacy* (Lincoln, 2003).

Sigrid Stöckel teaches history at the Medizinische Hochschule Hannover. She is the author of *Säuglingsfürsorge zwischen sozialer Hygiene und Eugenik: Das Beispiel Berlins im Kaiserreich und in der Weimarer Republik* (Berlin, 1996), editor of *Die "rechte Nation" und ihr Verleger: Politik und Popularisierung im J.-F.-Lehmanns-Verlag 1890–1979* (Berlin, 2002), and co-editor, with Ulla Walter, of *Prävention im 20. Jahrhundert: Historische Grundlagen und aktuelle Entwicklungen in Deutschland* (Weinheim, 2002).

Klaus Weinhauer teaches contemporary German history at the University of Bielefeld. He is the author of *Alltag und Arbeitskampf im Hamburger Hafen: Sozialgeschichte der Hamburger Hafenarbeiter 1914–1933* (Paderborn, 1994), and *Schutzpolizei in der Bundesrepublik. Zwischen Bürgerkrieg und innerer Sicherheit: Die turbulenten sechziger Jahre* (Paderborn, 2003).

S. Jonathan Wiesen teaches German and European history at Southern Illinois University, Carbondale. He is the author of *West German Industry and the Challenge of the Nazi Past, 1945–1955* (Chapel Hill, 2001).

SELECT BIBLIOGRAPHY

Albrecht, Clemens, et al., eds. *Die intellektuelle Gründung der Bundesrepublik: Eine Wirkungsgeschichte der Frankfurter Schule.* Frankfurt am Main, 1999.

Albrecht, Willy. *Der Sozialistische Deutsche Studentenbund (SDS): Vom parteikonformen Studentenverband zum Repräsentanten der Neuen Linken.* Bonn, 1994.

Aretz, Jürgen, Günter Buchstab, and Jörg Dieter Gauger, eds. *Geschichtsbilder: Weichenstellungen deutscher Geschichte nach 1945.* Freiburg, 2003.

Assmann, Aleida, and Ute Frevert. *Geschichtsvergessenheit, Geschichtsversessenheit: Vom Umgang mit deutschen Vergangenheiten nach 1945.* Stuttgart, 1999.

Baier, Lothar, ed. *Die Früchte der Revolte: Über die Veränderung der politischen Kultur durch die Studentenbewegung.* Berlin, 1988.

Barnouw, Dagmar. *Germany 1945: Views of War and Violence.* Bloomington, 1996.

Berg, Nicolas. *Der Holocaust und die westdeutschen Historiker: Erforschung und Erinnerung.* Göttingen, 2003.

Bergmann, Werner. *Antisemitismus in öffentlichen Konflikten: Kollektives Lernen in der politischen Kultur der Bundesrepublik, 1949–1989.* Frankfurt am Main, 1997.

Bergmann, Werner, and Rainer Erb. *Anti-Semitism in Germany: The Post-Nazi Epoch Since 1945.* Trans. Belinda Cooper and Allison Brown. New Brunswick, 1997.

Brink, Cornelia. *Auschwitz in der Paulskirche: Erinnerungspolitik in Fotoausstellungen der 60erJahre.* Frankfurt am Main, 2001.

_____. *Ikonen der Vernichtung: Öffentlicher Gebrauch von Fotografien aus nationalsozialistischen Konzentrationslagern nach 1945.* Berlin, 1998.

Brochhagen, Ulrich. *Nach Nürnberg: Vergangenheitsbewältigung und Westintegration in der Ära Adenauer.* New ed. Berlin, 1999.

Brunner, Bernhard. *Der Frankreich-Komplex: Die nationalsozialistischen Verbrechen in Frankreich und die Justiz der Bundesrepublik Deutschland.* Göttingen, 2004.

Bude, Heinz. *Bilanz der Nachfolge: Die Bundesrepublik und der Nationalsozialismus.* Frankfurt am Main, 1992.

_____. *Das Altern einer Generation: Die Jahrgänge 1938–1948.* Frankfurt am Main, 1995.

_____. *Deutsche Karrieren: Lebenskonstruktionen sozialer Aufsteiger aus der Flakhelfer-Generation.* Frankfurt am Main, 1987.

Bude, Heinz, and Martin Kohli, eds. *Radikalisierte Aufklärung.* Munich, 1989.

Buruma, Ian. *The Wages of Guilt: Memories of War in Germany and Japan.* New York, 1994.

Cioc, Marc. *Pax Atomica: The Nuclear Defence Debate in West Germany during the Adenauer Era.* New York, 1988.

Classen, Christoph. *Bilder der Vergangenheit: Die Zeit des Nationalsozialismus im Fernsehen der Bundesrepublik Deutschland 1955–1965.* Cologne, 1999.

Confino, Alon, and Peter Fritzsche, eds. *The Work of Memory: New Directions in the Study of German Society and Culture.* Urbana, 2002.

Conrad, Sebastian. *Auf der Suche nach der verlorenen Nation: Geschichtsschreibung in Westdeutschland und Japan 1945–1960.* Göttingen, 1999.

Cornelissen, Christoph, Lutz Klinkhammer, and Wolfgang Schwendtker, eds. *Erinnerungskulturen: Deutschland, Italien und Japan seit 1945.* Frankfurt am Main, 2003.

Danyel, Jürgen, ed. *Die geteilte Vergangenheit: Zum Umgang mit Nationalsozialismus und Widerstand in beiden deutschen Staaten.* Berlin, 1995.

Deutschkron, Inge. *Israel und die Deutschen: Das schwierige Verhältnis.* New ed. Cologne, 1991.

Dirke, Sabine von. *"All Power to the Imagination!" The West German Counterculture from the Student Movement to the Greens.* Lincoln, 1997.

Dudek, Peter. *„Der Rückblick auf die Vergangenheit wird sich nicht vermeiden lassen": Zur pädagogischen Verarbeitung des Nationalsozialismus in Deutschland, 1945–1990.* Opladen, 1995.

Elkeles, Thomas, ed. *Prävention und Prophylaxe: Theorie und Praxis eines gesundheitspolitischen Grundmotivs in zwei deutschen Staaten 1949–1990.* Berlin, 1991.

Fairchild, Erika S. *German Police: Ideals and Reality in the Post-War Years.* Springfield, 1988.

Feldman, Lily Gardner. *The Special Relationship between West Germany and Israel.* Boston, 1984.

Fichter, Tilman. *SDS und SPD: Parteilichkeit jenseits der Partei.* Opladen, 1988.

Fink, Carole, Philipp Gassert, and Detlev Junker, eds. *1968: The World Transformed.* Cambridge, 1998.

Frei, Norbert. *1945 und wir: Das Dritte Reich im Bewußtsein der Deutschen.* Munich, 2005.

_____. *Vergangenheitspolitik: Die Anfänge der Bundesrepublik Deutschland und die NS-Vergangenheit.* Munich, 1996.

_____, ed. *Karrieren im Zwielicht: Hitlers Eliten nach 1945.* Frankfurt, 2001.

Frei, Norbert, Dirk van Laak, and Michael Stolleis, eds. *Geschichte vor Gericht: Historiker, Richter und die Suche nach Gerechtigkeit.* Munich, 2000.

Frese, Matthias, ed. *Demokratisierung und gesellschaftlicher Aufbruch: Die sechziger Jahre als Wendezeit der Bundesrepublik.* Paderborn, 2003.

Friedrich, Jörg. *Die kalte Amnestie: NS-Täter in der Bundesrepublik.* Munich, 1994.

Fulbrook, Mary. *German National Identity after the Holocaust.* Cambridge, 1999.

Fürmetz, Gerhard, Herbert Reinke, and Klaus Weinhauer, eds. *Nachkriegspolizei: Sicherheit und Ordnung in Ost- und Westdeutschland 1945–1969.* Hamburg, 2001.

Gassert, Philipp. *Kurt Georg Kiesinger, 1904–1988: Kanzler zwischen den Zeiten.* Munich, 2006.

Gassert, Philipp, and Pavel A. Richter, eds. *1968 in West Germany: A Guide to Sources and Literature of the Extra-Parliamentarian Opposition.* Washington, 1998.

Gilcher-Holtey, Ingrid. *Die 68er Bewegung: Deutschland—Westeuropa—USA.* Munich, 2001.

_____, ed. *1968: Vom Ereignis zum Gegenstand der Geschichtswissenschaft.* Göttingen, 1998.

Giordano, Ralph. *Die zweite Schuld oder von der Last Deutscher zu sein.* Cologne, 2000.

Glaser, Hermann. *Deutsche Kultur 1945–2000.* Munich, 1997.

Goschler, Constantin. *Schuld und Schulden: Die Politik der Wiedergutmachung für NS-Verfolgte seit 1945.* Göttingen, 2005.

Goschler, Constantin, and Jürgen Lillteicher, eds. *„Arisierung" und Restitution: Die Rückerstattung jüdischen Eigentums in Deutschland und Österreich.* Göttingen, 2002.

Habermas, Jürgen. *Die Normalität einer Berliner Republik.* Frankfurt am Main, 1995.

Heider, Ulrike. *Schülerprotest in der Bundesrepublik Deutschland*. Frankfurt am Main, 1984.
Heimann, Thomas. *Bilder von Buchenwald: Die Visualisierung des Antifaschismus in der DDR (1945–1990)*. Cologne, 2005.
Heineman, Elisabeth D. *What Difference Does a Husband Make? Women and Marital Status in Nazi and Postwar Germany*. Berkeley, 1999.
Heinemann, Karl Heinz, and Thomas Jaitner, eds. *Ein langer Marsch: '68 und die Folgen*. Cologne, 1993.
Henkys, Reinhard, ed. *Die nationalsozialistischen Gewaltverbrechen: Geschichte und Gericht*. Stuttgart, 1964.
Herbert, Ulrich. *Best: Biographische Studien über Radikalismus, Weltanschauung und Vernunft 1903–1989*. Bonn, 1996.
———, ed. *Wandlungsprozesse in Westdeutschland: Belastung, Integration, Liberalisierung 1945–1980*. Göttingen, 2002.
Herbert, Ulrich, and Olaf Groehler. *Zweierlei Bewältigung: Vier Beiträge über den Umgang mit der NS-Vergangenheit in den beiden deutschen Staaten*. Hamburg, 1992.
Herbst, Ludolf, and Constantin Goschler, eds. *Wiedergutmachung in der Bundesrepublik Deutschland*. Munich, 1989.
Herf, Jeffrey. *Divided Memory: The Nazi Past in the Two Germanys*. Cambridge, MA, 1997.
Herzog, Dagmar. *Sex after Fascism: Memory and Morality in Twentieth-Century Germany*. Princeton, 2005.
Hettling, Manfred, ed. *Revolution in Deutschland?* Göttingen, 1991.
Heuser, Beatrice. *Nuclear Mentalities? Strategies and Beliefs in Britain, France and the FRG*. London, 1998.
Hildebrandt, Dietrich. „… *und die Studenten freuen sich!" Studentenbewegung in Heidelberg 1967–1973*. Heidelberg, 1991.
Hockerts, Hans Günter, Claudia Moisel, and Tobias Winstel, eds. *Grenzen der Wiedergutmachung: Die Entschädigung für NS-Verfolgte in West- und Osteuropa, 1945–2000*. Göttingen, 2006.
Hoffmann, Detlef, ed. *Das Gedächtnis der Dinge: KZ-Relikte und KZ-Denkmäler 1945–1995*. Frankfurt am Main, 1998.
Hoffmann, Uwe. *Die NPD: Entwicklung, Ideologie und Struktur*. Frankfurt am Main, 1999.
Hürter, Johannes, and Hans Woller, eds. *Hans Rothfels und die deutsche Zeitgeschichte*. Munich, 2005.
Jarausch, Konrad H. *After Hitler: Recivilizing Germans, 1945–1995*. Oxford, 2006.
Jarausch, Konrad H., and Michael Geyer. *Shattered Past: Reconstructing German Histories*. Princeton, 2003.
Jarausch, Konrad H., and Martin Sabrow, eds. *Verletztes Gedächtnis: Zeitgeschichte und Erinnerung im Konflikt*. Frankfurt am Main, 2002.
Jeismann, Michael. *Auf Wiedersehen Gestern: Die deutsche Vergangenheit und die Politik von morgen*. Munich, 2001
Jelinek, Yeshayahu. *Deutschland und Israel, 1945–1965: Ein neurotisches Verhältnis*. Munich, 2004.
Kaiser, Jochen-Christoph, and Anselm Doering-Manteuffel, eds. *Christentum und politische Verantwortung im Nachkriegsdeutschland*. Stuttgart, 1990.
Kielmansegg, Peter Graf. *Lange Schatten: Vom Umgang der Deutschen mit der nationalsozialistischen Vergangenheit*. Berlin, 1989.
Kittel, Manfred. *Die Legende von der „Zweiten Schuld": Vergangenheitsbewältigung in der Ära Adenauer*. Berlin, 1993.
Knoch, Habbo. *Die Tat als Bild: Fotografien des Holocaust in der deutschen Erinnerungskultur*. Hamburg, 2001.

Koenen, Gerd. *Das Rote Jahrzehnt: Unsere kleine deutsche Kulturrevolution 1967–1977.* Cologne, 2001.

Koetzle, Michael, ed. *Die Zeitschrift Twen: Revision einer Legende.* Munich, 1995.

Köhler, Joachim, and Damian van Melis, eds. *Siegerin in Trümmern: Die Rolle der katholischen Kirche in der deutschen Nachkriegsgesellschaft.* Stuttgart, 1998.

König, Helmut, Michael Kohlstruck, and Andreas Wöll, eds. *Vergangenheitsbewältigung am Ende des zwanzigsten Jahrhunderts.* Opladen, 1998.

Kozicki, Norbert. *Aufbruch im Revier: 1968 und die Folgen.* Essen, 1993.

Kraushaar, Wolfgang. *1968 als Mythos, Chiffre und Zäsur.* Hamburg, 2000.

_____. *Fischer in Frankfurt.* Hamburg, 2001.

_____, ed. *Frankfurter Schule und Studentenbewegung: Von der Flaschenpost zum Molotow-cocktail 1946 bis 1995.* Hamburg, 1998.

Lampe, Gerhard. *Das Panorama der 60er Jahre: Zur Geschichte des ersten politischen Fernseh-magazins der Bundesrepublik.* Berlin, 1999.

Lavy, George. *Germany and Israel: Moral Debt and National Interest.* London, 1996.

Lillteicher, Jürgen. *Die Rückerstattung jüdischen Eigentums in Westdeutschland nach dem Zweiten Weltkrieg: Eine Studie über Verfolgungserfahrung, Rechtsstaatlichkeit und Vergangen-heitspolitik 1945–1971.* Freiburg, 2003.

Loth, Wilfried, and Bernd A. Rusinek, eds. *Verwandlungspolitik: NS-Eliten in der west-deutschen Nachkriegsgesellschaft.* Frankfurt am Main, 1998.

Marcuse, Harold. *Legacies of Dachau: The Uses and Abuses of a Concentration Camp, 1933–2001.* Cambridge, 2001.

Matz, Reinhard. *Die unsichtbaren Lager: Das Verschwinden der Vergangenheit im Gedenken.* Reinbek, 1993.

Miquel, Marc von. *Ahnden oder amnestieren? Westdeutsche Justiz und Vergangsheitspolitik in den sechziger Jahren.* Göttingen, 2004.

Moeller, Robert G. *War Stories: The Search for a Usable Past in the Federal Republic of Germany.* Berkeley, 2001.

Moller, Sabine. *Die Entkonkretisierung der NS-Herrschaft in der Ära Kohl.* Hanover, 1998.

Moses, Dirk. "The Forty-Fivers: A Generation Between Fascism and Democracy." *German Politics and Society* 17, no. 1 (1999): 195–227.

Müller, Ingo. *Furchtbare Juristen: Die unbewältigte Vergangenheit unserer Justiz.* Munich, 1987.

Naumann, Klaus, ed. *Nachkrieg in Deutschland.* Hamburg, 2001.

Otto, Karl A., ed. *APO: Außerparlamentarische Opposition in Quellen und Dokumenten 1960–1970.* Cologne, 1989.

Pendas, Devin O. *The Frankfurt Auschwitz Trial 1963–1965: Genocide, History, and the Limits of the Law.* Cambridge, 2006.

Poiger, Uta G. *Jazz, Rock, and Rebels: Cold War Politics and American Culture in a Divided Germany.* Berkeley, 2000.

Rabe, Karl-Klaus. *Umkehr in die Zukunft: Die Arbeit der Aktion Sühnezeichen/Friedensdienste.* Bornheim-Merten, 1983.

Reichel, Peter. *Politik mit der Erinnerung: Gedächtnisorte im Streit um die nationalsozialistische Vergangenheit.* Munich, 1995.

_____. *Vergangenheitsbewältigung in Deutschland: Die politisch-justitielle Auseinandersetzung mit der NS-Diktatur nach 1945.* Bonn, 2003.

Rückerl, Adalbert. *NS-Verbrechen vor Gericht.* Heidelberg, 1982.

Rupieper, Hermann-Josef, ed. *Der Holocaust in der deutschen und der israelischen Erinne-rungskultur.* Halle, 2000.

Santner, Eric L. *Stranded Objects: Mourning, Memory, and Film in Postwar Germany*. Ithaca, 1990.

Schaal, Gary S., and Andreas Wöll, eds. *Vergangenheitsbewältigung: Modelle der politischen und sozialen Integration in der bundesdeutschen Nachkriegsgeschichte*. Baden-Baden, 1997.

Schildt, Axel. *Ankunft im Westen: Ein Essay zur Erfolgsgeschichte der Bundesrepublik*. Frankfurt am Main, 1999.

Schildt, Axel, and Detlef Siegfried, eds. *Between Marx and Coca-Cola: Youth Cultures in Changing European Societies, 1960–1980*. New York, 2005.

Schildt, Axel, Detlef Siegfried, and Karl Christian Lammers, eds. *Dynamische Zeiten: Die 60er Jahre in den beiden deutschen Gesellschaften*. Hamburg, 2000.

Schildt, Axel, and Arnold Sywottek, eds. *Modernisierung im Wiederaufbau: Die westdeutsche Gesellschaft der 50er Jahre*. Bonn, 1993.

Schissler, Hanna, ed. *The Miracle Years: A Cultural History of West Germany, 1949–1968*. Princeton, 2001.

Schmidtke, Michael. *Der Aufbruch der jungen Intelligenz: Die 68er Jahre in der Bundesrepublik und den USA*. Frankfurt am Main, 2003.

Schönwälder, Karen. *Einwanderung und ethnische Pluralität: Politische Entscheidungen und öffentliche Debatten in Grossbritannien und der Bundesrepublik Deutschland von den 1950er bis zu den 1970er Jahren*. Essen, 2001.

Schrafstetter, Susanna, and Stephen Twigge. *Avoiding Armageddon: Europe, the United States, and the Struggle for Nuclear Nonproliferation, 1945–1970*. Westport, 2004.

Schwan, Gesine. *Politik und Schuld: Die zerstörerische Macht des Schweigens*. Frankfurt am Main, 1997.

Shafir, Shlomo. *Ambiguous Relations: The American Jewish Community and Germany since 1945*. Detroit, 1999.

Steinbach, Peter. *Nationalsozialistische Gewaltverbrechen: Die Diskussion in der deutschen Öffentlichkeit nach 1945*. Berlin, 1981.

Steinweis, Alan E., and Daniel E. Rogers. *The Impact of Nazism: New Perspectives on the Third Reich and Its Legacy*. Lincoln, 2003.

Stern, Frank. *The Whitewashing of the Yellow Badge: Antisemitism and Philosemitism in Postwar Germany*. Trans. William Templer. Oxford, 1992.

Teschke, John P. *Hitler's Legacy: West Germany Confronts the Aftermath of the Third Reich*. New York, 1999.

Thamer, Hans-Ulrich. "Die NS-Vergangenheit im politischen Diskurs der 68er-Bewegung." *Westfälische Forschungen* 48 (1998): 39–53.

Varon, Jeremey. *Bringing the War Home: The Weather Underground, the Red Army Faction, and Revolutionary Violence in the Sixties and Seventies*. Berkeley, 2005.

Weber, Jürgen, and Peter Steinbach, eds. *Vergangenheitsbewältigung durch Strafverfahren? NS-Prozesse in der Bundesrepublik Deutschland*. Munich, 1984.

Weingardt, Markus A. *Deutsch-israelische Beziehungen: Zur Genese bilateraler Verträge 1949–1996*. Konstanz, 1997.

Weinhauer, Klaus. *Schutzpolizei in der Bundesrepublik. Zwischen Bürgerkrieg und Innerer Sicherheit: Die turbulenten sechziger Jahre*. Paderborn, 2003.

Weinke, Annette. *Die Verfolgung von NS-Tätern im geteilten Deutschland: Vergangenheitsbewältigung 1949–1969*. Paderborn, 2002.

Weisbrod, Bernd, ed. *Akademische Vergangenheitspolitik: Beiträge zur Wissenschaftskultur der Nachkriegszeit*. Göttingen, 2002.

_____, ed. *Rechtsradikalismus in der politischen Kultur der Nachkriegszeit*. Hanover, 1995.

Werkentin, Falco. *Die Restauration der deutschen Polizei: Innere Rüstung von 1945 bis zur Notstandsgesetzgebung*. Frankfurt am Main, 1984.

Werz, Michael, ed. *Antisemitismus und Gesellschaft: Zur Diskussion um Auschwitz, Kulturindustrie und Gewalt.* Frankfurt am Main, 1995.

Wiesen, S. Jonathan. *West German Industry and the Challenge of the Nazi Past, 1945–1955.* Chapel Hill, 2001.

Wittmann, Rebecca. *Beyond Justice: The Auschwitz Trial.* Cambridge, MA, 2005.

Wolfrum, Edgar. *Geschichtspolitik in der Bundesrepublik Deutschland: Der Weg zur bundesrepublikanischen Erinnerung 1948–1990.* Darmstadt, 1999.

Zweig, Ronald W. *German Reparations and the Jewish World: A History of the Claims Conference.* Boulder, 1987.

INDEX